Clinical Handbook of Complex and Atypical Eating Disorders

Clinical Handbook of Complex and Atypical Eating Disorders

EDITED BY

LESLIE K. ANDERSON

STUART B. MURRAY

AND

WALTER H. KAYE

OXFORD
UNIVERSITY PRESS

Oxford University Press is a department of the University of Oxford. It furthers
the University's objective of excellence in research, scholarship, and education
by publishing worldwide. Oxford is a registered trade mark of Oxford University
Press in the UK and certain other countries.

Published in the United States of America by Oxford University Press
198 Madison Avenue, New York, NY 10016, United States of America.

Library of Congress Cataloging-in-Publication Data
Names: Anderson, Leslie, 1976– editor. | Murray, Stuart, 1982– editor. |
Kaye, Walter H., 1943– editor.
Title: Clinical handbook of complex and atypical eating disorders /
edited by Leslie K. Anderson, Stuart B. Murray, Walter H. Kaye.
Description: New York, NY : Oxford University Press, [2018] |
Includes bibliographical references and index.
Identifiers: LCCN 2017022822 (print) | LCCN 2017024925 (ebook) |
ISBN 9780190630416 (updf) | ISBN 9780190671778 (epub) |
ISBN 9780190630409 (paperback)
Subjects: | MESH: Feeding and Eating Disorders—complications |
Feeding and Eating Disorders—therapy Classification: LCC RC552.E18 (ebook) |
LCC RC552.E18 (print) | NLM WM 175 |
DDC 362.196/8526—dc23
LC record available at https://lccn.loc.gov/2017022822

9 8 7 6 5 4 3 2 1

Printed by WebCom, Inc., Canada

CONTENTS

PART II Atypical Symptom Presentations

PART III Atypical Populations

This is a tremendous book that all clinicians and researchers in the eating disorders field should have. As the editors rightly point out, the epithet "atypical" is a misnomer when applied to eating disorders, given that it applies to at least one-third of the clinical population being described. If we add the term "complex" as used here to cover issues of comorbidity, unusual eating disorder presentations, and subpopulation differences, then perhaps the title of the book should have been the *Handbook of Typically Complex Eating Disorders* because what the book addresses are the daily conundrums that we face all the time when working with our patients. The authors, of course, fully recognize the value of the main eating disorder diagnostic groupings and the great progress that has been made in some areas in developing effective evidence-based treatments for eating disorders. What they have set out to do is to map systematically the areas in which the broad brushstrokes of current evidence do not provide a very clear picture and need to be supplemented by smaller scale research findings, evidence from outside of our field, or more theoretically driven suppositions.

Discussions about evidence-based practice sometimes get reduced to the narrower concept of evidence-based or validated treatments. However, most experts would agree with Kazdin's (2008) definition of evidence-based practice as "clinical practice that is informed by evidence about interventions, clinical expertise, and patient needs, values, and preferences and their integration in decision making about individual care" and that the term *evidence* should be understood broadly as not just findings from randomized controlled trials but, rather, as all relevant, up-to-date research findings. The problem is that for the individual clinician, the most readily available evidence derives from findings from randomized controlled trials, meta-analyses, and systematic reviews that focus primarily on the main diagnostic groups. There is, of course, a wealth of other research that can and should inform the clinician's decisions relating to individual patients. This may include general psychotherapy research including, for instance, studies of the therapeutic alliance or processes that promote motivation to change, the impact of attachment relationships on the development of trust within the therapeutic relationship, or general research on the differential impact of particular types of therapeutic styles (e.g., collaborative, open-ended therapeutic styles in comparison with more directive, structured approaches), dependent on the type of family style or cultural-determined predispositions. There is moderator and mediator research relevant to the specific disorder, research on treatment fidelity, and much more. Although treatment trials offer the most robust template to provide the basic direction for treatment, clinicians must use their clinical judgment to integrate other relevant research evidence as well as their own clinical expertise to best effect. The more a particular patient differs in his or her clinical or demographic profile from the patient population of the relevant treatment trials, the more the clinician has to rely on "other research" findings and clinical judgment to be able to deliver good, evidence-based practice. The difficulty, of course, is to identify the relevant "other research." Well, for atypical and complex eating disorders, this hurdle has just been significantly reduced—this book provides the perfect resource.

There is a great deal more I could say about this book. It is well researched, pretty comprehensive, and thought-provoking, but actually the quality of the book speaks for itself. Go read the book.

Ivan Eisler

Leslie K. Anderson, PhD, is a Clinical Associate Professor of Psychiatry at the University of California, San Diego, and Training Director at the UC San Diego Eating Disorders Center for Treatment and Research. Her research interests are in eating disorder treatment development and evaluation, especially with regards to complex, comorbid eating disorders and adaptations of DBT and family based treatment. She has published multiple peer-reviewed articles and two books in this area, and is the co-editor of the journal Eating Disorders: The Journal of Treatment and Prevention.

Stuart B. Murray, DClinPsych, PhD, is an Assistant Professor of Psychiatry at the University of California, San Francisco, and Director of the National Association for Males with Eating Disorders. His research interests relate to eating disorders in males, and the development of precision treatments for anorexia nervosa. He has presented his work internationally, and has published more than 75 scientific manuscripts to date, in addition to 3 edited books relating to eating disorders.

Walter H. Kaye, MD, FAED, is a Professor of Psychiatry at the University of California, San Diego and Director of the UC San Diego Eating Disorders Research and Treatment Program. His current research is focused on exploring the relationship between brain and behavior using brain imaging and investigating new treatments in anorexia and bulimia nervosa. Dr. Kaye has an international reputation in the field of eating disorders and is the author of more than 400 articles and publications.

CONTRIBUTORS

Liana Abascal, PhD, MPH
Assistant Professor
California School of Professional
    Psychology at Alliant
    International University
Clinical Psychologist
Behavioral Diabetes Institute
San Diego, CA, USA

Kelly C. Allison, PhD, FAED
Associate Professor of Psychology
    in Psychiatry
Perelman School of Medicine
University of Pennsylvania
Philadelphia, PA, USA

Leslie K. Anderson, PhD
Clinical Associate Professor
    and Training Director
UCSD Eating Disorders Center
    for Treatment and Research
San Diego, CA, USA

**Jon Arcelus, MD, MSc,
FRCPsych, PhD**
Professor in Mental Health
    and in Transgender Health
Institute of Mental Health
The University of Nottingham
Nottingham, UK

Jessica H. Baker, PhD
Associate Research Director
UNC Center of Excellence
    for Eating Disorders
Assistant Professor
Department of Psychiatry
University of North Carolina
    at Chapel Hill
Chapel Hill, NC, USA

Amy Baker Dennis, PhD
Clinical Associate Professor
Department of Psychiatry
University of South Florida
Tampa, FL, USA
Dennis & Moye & Associates
Bloomfield Hills, MI, USA

Laura A. Berner, PhD
Postdoctoral Scholar
Department of Psychiatry
University of California, San Diego
San Diego, CA, USA

**Walter Pierre Bouman, MD, MA,
MSc, FRCPsych, UKCPreg**
Consultant Psychiatrist–Sexologist/
    Head of Service
Nottingham National Centre
    for Transgender Health
Nottingham, UK

Timothy D. Brewerton, MD, DFAPA, FAED, DFAACAP, HCEDS
Clinical Professor
Psychiatry and Behavioral Sciences
Medical University of South Carolina
Charleston, SC, USA

Tiffany A. Brown, PhD
Postdoctoral Research Fellow
Department of Psychiatry
University of California, San Diego
San Diego, CA, USA

Cynthia M. Bulik, PhD, FAED
Department of Psychiatry
Gillings School of Global
    Public Health
University of North Carolina
    at Chapel Hill
Chapel Hill, NC USA;
Medical Epidemiology and
    Biostatistics
Karolinska Institutet
Stockholm, Sweden

Scott Crow, MD
Professor
Psychiatry
University of Minnesota
Minneapolis, MN, USA

Gina Dimitropoulos, PhD, RSW, AAMFT Approved Supervisor
Assistant Professor
Faculty of Social Work
University of Calgary
Calgary, Alberta, Canada

Kamryn T. Eddy, PhD
Co-Director
Eating Disorders Clinical and
    Research Program
Massachusetts General Hospital
Associate Professor of Psychology
Department of Psychiatry
Harvard Medical School
Boston, MA, USA

Ivan Eisler
Professor of Family Psychology and
    Family Therapy
Institute of Psychiatry
Kings College London
London, UK

Fernando Fernández-Aranda, PhD, FAED
Professor
Psychiatry and CIBERobn
    Research Unit
University Hospital of
    Bellvitge-IDIBELL
Barcelona, Spain

Jamie D. Feusner, MD
Professor
Department of Psychiatry
    and Biobehavioral Sciences
Semel Institute for Neuroscience
    and Human Behavior
David Geffen School of Medicine at the
    University of California, Los Angeles
Los Angeles, CA, USA

K. Jean Forney, MS
Doctoral Candidate
Department of Psychology
Florida State University
Tallahassee, FL, USA

Tara E. Galovski, PhD
Director
Women's Health Sciences Division,
    National Center for PTSD
VA Boston Healthcare System
Associate Professor of Psychiatry
Boston University School of Medicine
Boston, MA, USA

Ann Goebel-Fabbri, PhD
Clinical Psychologist
Private Practice
Brookline, MA, USA

Emily K. Gray, MD
Medical Director
Pediatric and Adolescent Eating
  Disorder Program
Assistant Clinical Professor
Department of Psychiatry
University of California, San Diego
La Jolla, CA, USA

Scott Griffiths, PhD
NHMRC Early Career Research Fellow
Melbourne School of Psychological
  Sciences
University of Melbourne
Melbourne, Victoria, Australia

Walter H. Kaye, MD, FAED
Professor
Department of Psychiatry
Director
UCSD Eating Disorder Research
  and Treatment Program
San Diego, CA, USA

Pamela K. Keel, PhD, FAED
Professor
Department of Psychology
Florida State University
Tallahassee, FL, USA

Grace Kennedy, BA
Graduate Student
Department of Psychology
Florida State University
Tallahassee, FL, USA

Alexandra Keyes, BSc, MSc
Trainee Clinical Psychologist
Department of Psychology
King's College London
London, UK

Stephanie Knatz Peck, PhD
Assistant Clinical Professor
Department of Psychiatry
University of California, San Diego
La Jolla, CA, USA

Daniel Le Grange, PhD
Benioff UCSF Professor in Children's
  Health and Eating Disorders
Director
Department of Psychiatry
UCSF Weill Institute for
  Neurosciences
University of California, San Francisco
San Francisco, CA, USA

Jocelyn Lebow, PhD
Assistant Professor
Department of Psychiatry and
  Behavioral Sciences
University of Miami
Miami, FL, USA

Katharine L. Loeb, PhD
Professor
School of Psychology, Ph.D. Program
  in Clinical Psychology
Fairleigh Dickinson University
Teaneck, NJ, USA

Danyale McCurdy-McKinnon, PhD
Clinical Psychology Director
UCLA Fit for Healthy Weight
  Program, Department of Pediatrics
Mattel Children's Hospital at the
  University of California, Los
  Angeles
Los Angeles, CA, USA

Jessie Menzel, PhD
Psychologist
Department of Psychiatry
University of California, San Diego
San Diego, CA, USA

Helen B. Murray, BA
Department of Psychology
Drexel University
Philadelphia, PA, USA

Stuart B. Murray, DClinPsych, PhD
Assistant Professor
Eating Disorder Program
Department of Psychiatry
University of California,
    San Francisco
San Francisco, CA, USA

Marisol Perez, PhD
Associate Professor and
    Associate Chair
Department of Psychology
Arizona State University
Tempe, AZ, USA

Carolyn R. Plateau, PhD
Lecturer in Psychology
National Centre for Sport
    and Exercise Medicine
Loughborough University
Loughborough, Leicestershire, UK

Valentina Postorino, PhD
Postdoctoral Psychology Fellow
Department of Pediatrics
Emory University School of Medicine,
    Marcus Autism Center
Atlanta, GA, USA

Tamara Pryor, PhD, FAED
Adjunct Associate Professor
Department of Psychiatry
University of Kansas
Wichita, KS, USA
Chief Clinical Director
Director of Clinical Research
Eating Disorder Center of Denver
Denver, CO, USA

Ana L. Ramirez, PhD
Clinical Psychologist
Department of Psychiatry
University of California, San Diego
San Diego, CA, USA

Cristin D. Runfola, PhD
Clinical Instructor
Department of Psychiatry and
    Behavioral Sciences
Stanford University School of
    Medicine
Stanford, CA, USA

Jenna L. Schleien, BA
Doctoral Student
School of Psychology, PhD Program
    in Clinical Psychology
Fairleigh Dickinson University
Teaneck, NJ, USA

William G. Sharp, PhD
Assistant Professor & Director
Department of Pediatrics Feeding
    Disorders Program
Marcus Autism Center
Emory University
Atlanta, GA, USA

Leslie Sim, PhD, ABPP
Associate Professor of Psychology
Department of Psychiatry
    and Psychology
Mayo Clinic
Rochester, MN, USA

April Smith, PhD
Assistant Professor
Department of Psychology
Miami University
Oxford, OH, USA

Jennifer J. Thomas, PhD
Co-Director
Eating Disorders Clinical
    and Research Program
Massachusetts General Hospital
Associate Professor
Department of Psychiatry
Harvard Medical School
Boston, MA, USA

Julie G. Trim, PhD
Assistant Clinical Professor
Department of Psychiatry
University of California, San Diego
San Diego, CA, USA

Eva Trujillo-ChiVacuán, MD
Medical Director/Clinical Professor
Eating Disorders Center/Pediatrics
  and Adolescent Medicine
Comenzar de Nuevo/Tecnológico
  de Monterrey
Monterrey, NL, México

David Veale, MD, FRCPsych, FBPsS, MD
Professor
Department of Psychology
King's College London
London, UK

Amy Wagner, PhD
Staff Psychologist
PTSD Clinical Team
VA Portland Health Care System
Associate Professor
Department of Psychiatry
Oregon Health & Science University
Portland, OR, USA

Lucene Wisniewski, PhD, FAED
Chief Clinical Integrity Officer
The Emily Program
Adjunct Assistant Professor of
  Psychological Sciences
Case Western Reserve University
Cleveland, OH, USA

INTRODUCTION

Treating patients with eating disorders is a notoriously challenging undertaking. Patients tend to have a deep ambivalence toward their symptoms and can be medically compromised. Treatment outcomes lag behind those of other psychiatric ailments, and relapse and treatment dropout remain unacceptably high. As evidence-based treatment for eating disorders continues to evolve, however, we now have access to rigorously tested treatment protocols, such as cognitive–behavioral therapy (CBT), family-based treatment (FBT), and dialectical behavior therapy, that can be useful in treating a wide variety of eating disorders. However, most clinicians treating eating disorders discover early in their career that a sizable number of patients present with additional comorbidities or characteristics that set them apart from the patients for whom these treatments were developed. Currently, even when taking account the recently modified diagnostic framework of DSM-5, 30–50% of all eating disorder presentations in clinical practice remain in the undifferentiated other specified feeding or eating disorder (OSFED) category. Within this OSFED spectrum, and in keeping with the rapidly evolving nature of eating disorder psychopathology, an incredibly diverse array of illness presentations is beginning to emerge, for which no controlled treatment trials have been conducted.

Further still, few eating disorders present without comorbidity, and the range and extent of co-occurring psychopathology can present profound challenges to the application of evidence-based treatment. Despite this, strictly controlled treatment development trials often exclude those with severe comorbidity, leaving a void in our understanding of the treatment of our most complex patients. Underscoring this void, the extent of comorbidity is associated with poorer treatment outcome and relapse.

Further compounding the clinical challenges in keeping pace with this evolving eating disorder psychopathology, the affected demographic is increasingly diverse. Eating disorders can no longer be thought of as disorders that exclusively affect Caucasian, affluent female teenagers. In addition, by virtue of many controlled treatment trials having focused on this specific population, a gap in our treatment understanding applies as to how best to treat these disorders in a broader range of demographic populations who have been absent from controlled trials, such as males, ethnic minorities, and transgender populations.

For example, most experienced eating disorder clinicians know that a teenager with recent-onset anorexia nervosa is most likely best treated with FBT, but less is known about the treatment of a teenager with anorexia nervosa who is also transgender and suicidal. Similarly, available evidence suggests that the first line of treatment for an adult woman with bulimia should be enhanced CBT, but what if her trauma history and diabetes seem to be factoring strongly into her clinical presentation?

In cases such as these, good clinicians consult: They talk to expert colleagues, obtain additional training and supervision, or search the extant literature. The purpose of this book is to collate what is known about an array of complicating factors for patients with eating disorders, serving as an accessible introduction to each of the comorbidities and symptom presentations highlighted in the volume. The *Clinical Handbook of Complex and Atypical Eating Disorders* presents the available data about atypical and complex eating disorders, in addition to what is known about treatment approaches. Each chapter is written by a leading expert in the field. The first section contains chapters on the treatment of eating disorders with various psychiatric comorbidities, including trauma, borderline personality disorder, substance use, suicidality, anxiety disorders, and autism spectrum disorders, which may greatly complicate the application of standard treatment approaches. The second section contains chapters exploring treatment of eating disorders with atypical symptom presentations that (1) are not located as a specific diagnostic category in diagnostic criteria for eating disorders; (2) centrally feature eating disorder pathology; and (3) have emerging data suggesting the distinct nature of the syndrome, including purging disorder, muscle dysmorphia, night eating syndrome, and anorexia nervosa with a history of obesity. The final section includes chapters that focus on how to adapt eating disorder treatment for atypical populations typically neglected in controlled treatment trials: LGBT, pediatric, male, ethnically diverse, and older adult populations.

Cutting edge and practical, this volume is designed to be an accessible resource for clinicians and researchers involved in the treatment of eating disorders. Each chapter includes a review of clinical presentation, prevalence, treatment approaches, resources, and conclusions and future directions.

Clinical Handbook of Complex

and Atypical Eating Disorders

Evidence-Based Treatments and the Atypical/Complex Conundrum

JENNA L. SCHLEIEN, GINA DIMITROPOULOS,
KATHARINE L. LOEB, AND DANIEL LE GRANGE ■

"Real-world" eating disorder presentations rarely fit neatly into the diagnostic categories defined in the *Diagnostic and Statistical Manual of Mental Disorders* (DSM). It is generally understood by those involved in the diagnosis, study, or treatment of eating disorders that these are heterogeneous entities because great variation is found in symptom presentations and affected populations. Disordered eating presentations that are comorbid with other mental disorders, that do not map directly onto current diagnostic criteria, and that occur in atypical populations are more frequently seen in clinical practice than they are attended to in the literature. This chapter provides an overview of the evolution of the diagnostic and treatment approach of atypical and complex eating disorders and illuminates the mismatch between clinical presentations and evidence-based interventions. First, this chapter introduces the conundrum of applying controlled treatment studies to atypical and complex comorbid eating disorder presentations. Then, it examines atypical eating disorder presentations, followed by complex comorbid eating disorder presentations. It also reviews proposed solutions to the atypical/complex eating disorder "problem." Last, it discusses future directions relevant to atypical and complex eating disorder presentations and current challenges surrounding the development and implementation of targeted interventions.

THE CONUNDRUM OF APPLYING CONTROLLED TREATMENT STUDIES TO ATYPICAL AND COMPLEX PRESENTATIONS

The most robust approach for assessing treatment effectiveness includes the random allocation of individuals to conditions; adequate sample sizes to ensure sufficient statistical power; a clearly defined intervention with monitoring of fidelity of implementation; and outcome measures that are theoretically and clinically relevant, ecologically valid, and carried out blind to treatment group (Maughan, 2013). One method of meeting these stringent criteria is the use of randomized controlled trials (RCTs), considered the gold standard for intervention studies (Maughan, 2013; Salmond, 2008; Wiebe & Hill, 2011). In an RCT, each participant has the same random or near-random chance of being assigned to each condition as the next participant (Wiebe & Hill, 2011). Furthermore, RCTs are controlled, which isolates the effect of the intervention by ruling out confounding variables (Salmond, 2008). In this way, RCTs are more precise and accurate assessments of treatment modalities than anecdotal reports or uncontrolled case series (Correll, Kishimoto, & Kane, 2011). As rigorous evaluations of cause and effect, RCTs are critical in illuminating the effectiveness of different treatment modalities.

Although RCTs are widely considered the highest quality research design for intervention studies, their integrity and success are not guaranteed (Salmond, 2008; Wiebe & Hill, 2011). Good RCTs are tightly controlled, which includes a thorough identification of potential confounding factors (Salmond, 2008) and randomizing whenever possible to ensure the equivalence of the comparison groups on all factors but the intervention (Kerlinger & Lee, 2000). In addition, tightly controlled RCTs include clear but simple eligibility criteria that promote a narrow focus on groups with specific characteristics (e.g., symptoms) in common (Wiebe & Hill, 2011). In RCTs designed to test various forms of eating disorder treatment, participants commonly meet criteria for the same DSM-defined disorder or spectrum thereof and may fall within a defined range for age or body mass index. In addition, participants are typically excluded if they have other psychiatric conditions requiring immediate treatment (e.g., major depression with suicidality, schizophrenia, and acute medical complications) and if they have already been treated with the form of psychotherapy being tested. Restricted inclusion criteria provide an RCT with high internal validity, but these stringent criteria are also associated with limited external validity, making the results much less generalizable to the heterogeneous populations seeking treatment (Correll et al., 2011), including atypical eating disorders. Furthermore, RCTs tend to be conducted on majority samples (i.e., White, middle-class women), further limiting external validity. In addition, there is a scarcity of knowledge about the response to treatment in patients with complex presentations, such as comorbid emergent disorders (Correll et al., 2011). Stringent inclusion criteria, considered paramount to a good RCT, have created challenges because limited research has been conducted with the atypical and complex eating disorder populations that make up a sizeable portion of treatment-seeking, clinical samples. Furthermore, the degree to which treatments based on RCTs can be applied or will be effective with atypical and complex populations is questionable. This renders evidence-based clinicians much less well equipped in devising treatment approaches for these individuals. There is no simple solution. However, as discussed later in this chapter, the body of literature on evidence-based interventions for atypical populations is growing.

Just as RCTs are critical in demonstrating the effectiveness of treatment modalities for atypical disordered eating presentations, they are equally important for complex comorbid presentations. Although challenging, these RCTs are possible to conduct. For instance, individuals with suicidality are typically excluded from RCTs, but research has shown that suicidality is a feasible target for RCTs with proper clinical attention, safeguards, and intervention (Linehan et al., 2015; March et al., 2007; Meltzer, 2002). This suggests that complex presentations such as comorbid eating disorders and suicidality, or other acute issues previously excluded from RCTs, can be included in well-designed RCTs with a multimodal intervention. Other presentations that are frequently comorbid with eating disorders and that do not necessarily constitute acute risk (e.g., depression, obsessive–compulsive disorder, and mild substance use) pose fewer problems and typically permit a primary focus on the eating domain. Another way to study atypical and/or complex populations is by examining moderators within the context of RCTs. Specifically, severity and complexity of eating disorder presentations may moderate treatment outcomes. In an RCT comparing family-based treatment (FBT) and adolescent-focused therapy (AFT) for anorexia nervosa (AN), Le Grange and colleagues (2012) found that eating-related obsessionality and eating disorder-specific psychopathology moderated end-of-treatment outcomes such that individuals with higher baseline scores on these indices benefitted more from FBT than from AFT. An RCT comparing dosage of family therapy for adolescent AN concluded that individuals with more severe and persistent eating-related obsessive–compulsive thinking, as well as individuals from non-intact families, received greater benefit from long-term therapy (Lock, Agras, Bryson, & Kraemer, 2005). Based on these results, it is possible that complex eating disorder presentations may benefit more from a higher dose of FBT or a combination of different treatment modalities such as FBT and dialectical behavior therapy (DBT).

ATYPICAL EATING DISORDER PRESENTATIONS

Diagnostic criteria for eating disorders have evolved over iterations of the DSM, reflecting shifting notions of what constitutes an eating disorder. The third edition of the DSM (DSM-III; American Psychiatric Association [APA], 1980) formally recognized two categories of eating disorders: AN and bulimia nervosa (BN). DSM-III eating disorders could also be classified as "atypical," which was intended to "indicate a category within a class of disorders that is residual to the specific categories in that class" (APA, 1980, p. 32). This served as an acknowledgment that not all disordered eating presentations seen in clinical practice could be covered by DSM-III diagnostic criteria. The revision of DSM-III (DSM-III-R; APA, 1987) further refined the diagnostic criteria for eating disorders, for example, by including a minimum frequency of binge-eating episodes for BN. In the fourth edition of the DSM (DSM-IV; APA, 1994), the "atypical" classification advanced into an *eating disorder not otherwise specified* (EDNOS) category, which was added to capture all other clinically significant disordered eating that did not meet criteria for AN or BN. In addition, the subclassification into restricting and binge-eating/purging types was added to criteria for AN. Criteria for binge-eating disorder (BED) were also provided in the appendix of DSM-IV as an example of EDNOS and a category in need of further study (APA, 1994). BED was officially added as its own diagnostic category in DSM-5 (APA, 2013). In addition to AN, BN, and BED, the DSM-5 feeding and eating disorders category currently includes pica, rumination disorder, and avoidant/restrictive food intake disorder (ARFID; APA, 2013).

Across iterations of the DSM, subsets of atypical eating disorders, such as BED, have ultimately found "homes" as primary diagnostic categories. This reflects an evolution in our increasing recognition that atypical presentations are, in fact, increasingly typical. Nonetheless, many eating disorder presentations continue to be classified in catch-all categories such as EDNOS. DSM-IV to DSM-5 reflected a shift in the name of this category from EDNOS to *other specified feeding or eating disorder* (OSFED; APA, 1994, 2013).

According to DSM-5, OSFED applies to presentations in which symptoms characteristic of a feeding and eating disorder that cause clinically significant distress or impairment in social, occupational, or other important areas of functioning predominate (APA, 2013). At the same time, these symptoms do not meet the full criteria for any of the disorders in the feeding and eating disorders diagnostic class (APA, 2013). It is important to note that the name of this category recently changed from EDNOS to OSFED, and most of the research to date has been done on EDNOS according to DSM-IV criteria (APA, 1994). Therefore, research using OSFED criteria will capture fewer cases now that more have presumably been absorbed into newer AN and BN categories, as well as ARFID. For the purposes of this chapter, the term EDNOS is used when DSM-IV criteria were utilized in the research, and the term OSFED is used when DSM-5 criteria were utilized (APA, 1994, 2013).

Research suggests that EDNOS represents a majority of patients presenting for treatment (Striegel-Moore, Wonderlich, Walsh, & Mitchell, 2011). DSM-5 has been demonstrated to decrease the prevalence of OSFED in treatment-seeking (Birgegard, Norring, & Clinton, 2012; Fairburn & Cooper, 2011) and community samples (Keel, Brown, Holm-Denoma, & Bodell, 2011; Machado, Gonçalves, & Hoek, 2013; Stice, Marti, & Rohde, 2013), but OSFED prevalence rates remain at 15–30% of cases (Allen, Byrne, Oddy, & Crosby, 2013).

Atypical presentations do, in fact, share some common features. The majority of these cases have clinical features that resemble AN and BN but at different levels or in various combinations (Crow, Agras, Halmi, Mitchell, & Kraemer, 2002;

Fairburn et al., 2007; Waller, 1993). Furthermore, most disordered eating presentations include an overvaluation of shape and weight (including its manifestation, such as body checking and extreme feelings of fatness), persistent attempts to follow stringent dietary rules, weight-control behavior (e.g., self-induced vomiting, excessive exercise, and laxative misuse; Fairburn & Cooper, 2011), low self-esteem, and mood intolerance in the presence of binge eating (Lampard, Tasca, Balfour, & Bissada, 2013). In other words, individuals with atypical presentations tend to exhibit disabling concern over eating, shape, and weight (Turner & Bryant-Waugh, 2004). Despite shared features, these presentations are naturally heterogeneous. Presentations differ in demographics (e.g., ethnicity and educational level), eating disorder symptoms (e.g., the presence and frequency of binge eating, self-induced vomiting, laxative use, diuretic use, and fasting), and comorbid psychopathology (Binford & Le Grange, 2005; Crow et al., 2002). It has also been suggested that they differ in the extent to which affected individuals succeed in undereating, which consequently leads to variation in weight (Fairburn & Cooper, 2011).

It is apparent that there are some similarities and differences among atypical presentations. As Walsh and Kahn (1997) wisely highlighted, "we study what we define" (p. 369). Therefore, little is known about the course, outcome, or treatment of atypical presentations because they are, by definition, not demarcated in distinct DSM categories. Consequently, individuals with EDNOS/OSFED are typically excluded from research (Fairburn & Bohn, 2005). Even studies that include atypical presentations tend to vary in their definitions of what constitutes EDNOS/OSFED (Keel, Brown, Holland, & Bodell, 2012). The research that has been conducted suggests that atypical eating disorder cases are no different than typical cases in terms of severity of pathology, degree of secondary psychosocial impairment, and outcomes (Castellini et al., 2011; Fairburn et al., 2007; Grilo et al., 2007; Keel, Gravener, Joiner, & Haedt, 2010; Ricca et al., 2001; Turner & Bryant-Waugh, 2004). In addition, despite the relative stability of the overarching categorization of eating disorders, there is a great deal of cross-diagnostic flux because many patients with OSFED go on to meet full eating disorder criteria (Castellini et al., 2011; Herzog, Hopkins, & Burns, 1993; Milos, Spindler, Schnyder, & Fairburn, 2005). High diagnostic crossover may suggest that current classification schemes distinguish between various phases of a single disorder rather than between different disorders. DSM utilizes a categorical approach to describe psychopathology, in which eating disorders are classified into discrete categories. Some researchers and theorists have also proposed incorporating dimensional models into eating disorder classification, in which one or more dimensions underlie a continuum of eating disorders (Wildes & Marcus, 2013; Williamson, Gleaves, & Stewart, 2005). For instance, research suggests that the cognitive correlates of disordered eating (e.g., body dissatisfaction and drive for thinness) are dimensional, in that they are continuous with normality and thus represent varying degrees of impairment or severity (Holm-Denoma, Richey, & Joiner, 2010). Discussion about categorical versus dimensional approaches to eating disorder taxonomy continues to exist (Williamson et al., 2005).

ATYPICAL DEMOGRAPHIC PRESENTATIONS

There are limited specific data indicating whether current treatments adequately address any potential unique needs of diverse populations such as individuals with eating pathology beginning in midlife, males, people with different sexual orientations, children, individuals from diverse cultural backgrounds, and athletes. Disordered eating presentations in these populations are complicated by person-level factors such as gender, aging, and sexual orientation. These factors may generate additional issues in therapy relevant to formulation, the understanding of maintaining variables, and consequent levels of intricacy to treatment.

The erroneous perception that AN and BN predominantly affect Caucasian, adolescent females from privileged economic backgrounds contributes to community-based clinicians overlooking those who do not fit this stereotype and not providing appropriate referrals and needed treatment in a timely manner. RCTs commonly include adolescent or young adult Caucasian females and neglect patients of different ages, ethnic backgrounds, or sexual orientations. For example, despite increasing numbers of RCTs in adolescent populations, few RCTs have been devoted specifically to diverse populations, with the exceptions of samples of gay men at high risk of developing eating disorders recruited from the community (Brown & Keel, 2015), ethnic minorities presenting with bulimia nervosa (Chui, Safer, Bryson, Agras, & Wilson, 2007), ethnic minorities presenting with BED (Thompson-Brenner et al., 2013), and ethnic minorities recruited from the community (Stice, Marti, & Cheng, 2014). It is important to not only increase mental health literacy about atypical eating disorders but also educate health and mental health care professionals that a diversity of individuals including males, older individuals, and those from diverse ethnic, racial, and economic backgrounds are vulnerable to OSFED, purging disorders, and muscle dysmorphia (Cohn, Murray, Walen, & Wooldridge, 2016; Murray & Anderson, 2015).

COMPLEX EATING DISORDER PRESENTATIONS

Complex presentations include eating disorders occurring with other significant psychiatric issues and comorbidities, such as trauma, substance use, self-harm and suicidality, personality disorders, body dysmorphic disorder, autism spectrum disorder, and anxiety. Between 20% to 95% of patients with eating disorders are also afflicted with comorbid psychiatric disorders, the most common being mood, anxiety, obsessive–compulsive, and substance use disorders (Blinder, Cumella, & Sanathara, 2006; Bühren et al., 2014; Herzog, Keller, Sacks, Yeh, & Lavori, 1992; Hudson, Hiripi, Pope, & Kessler, 2007; Kaye, Bulik, Thornton, Barbarich, & Masters, 2004; Milos, Spindler, & Schnyder, 2004; Spindler & Milos, 2004; Ulfvebrand, Birgegård, Norring, Högdahl, & von Hausswolff-Juhlin, 2015; Zaider, Johnson, & Cockell, 2000). The application of a protocol designed only for an eating disorder to a case with complex comorbidities is often completely inadequate. Thus, clinicians need guidance on how to select, sequence, and implement treatment for psychiatric comorbidities. Unfortunately, very few RCTs exist that are designed to examine treatments of eating disorders with psychiatric comorbidities. There are a few notable exceptions in substance use (Courbasson, Nishikawa, & Dixon, 2012; Courbasson, Nishikawa, & Shapira, 2011) and borderline personality disorder (Thompson-Brenner et al., 2016).

Clinical decision algorithms are an important tool for clinicians in the treatment of patients with eating disorders. A crucial question germane to the treatment of these patients is whether to address both disorders simultaneously or, if not, which disorder to treat first. These questions are important because sequential treatment may lead to worsening or relapse of symptoms in one disorder as the other improves (Courbasson, Smith, & Cleland, 2005), and symptoms from the untreated disorder may interfere with recovery from the disorder being treated first (Sutherland, Weaver, McPeake, & Quimby, 1993). For example, although many suggestions have been made for concurrent treatment of eating and substance use disorders with cognitive–behavior therapy (CBT; Grilo, Sinha, & O'Malley, 2002; Sinha & O'Malley, 2000; Sysko & Hildebrandt, 2009) and DBT (Grilo et al., 2002), empirically validated clinical decision algorithms do not exist. However, the research that does exist suggests that both disorders can be treated successfully and simultaneously with DBT (Courbasson et al., 2012) and mindfulness-action based CBT (Courbasson et al., 2011). Similarly, for comorbid eating disorders and obsessive–compulsive disorder, one study showed that they can be treated simultaneously and effectively with a cognitive–behavioral approach emphasizing exposure and response prevention (Simpson et al., 2013).

A stepped care approach is one way to think about how, and in what order, to best treat comorbid conditions. In a stepped care approach, treatments are provided in sequential order according to patient need and available treatment resources (Wilson, Vitousek, & Loeb, 2000). This approach has been proposed as an effective way to treat BN and BED, particularly because treatments can be costly in terms of time and money, in addition to unnecessarily invasive (Fairburn, Agras, & Wilson, 1992; Gamer & Needleman, 1997; Wilson et al., 2000). The starting point is the simplest, least intrusive, and least costly treatment (e.g., guided self-help), and more complex or intensive interventions are provided if the patient does not respond (e.g., fluoxetine and then individual therapy) (Mitchell et al., 2011; Wilson et al., 2000). Stepped care models have been shown to be efficacious for BN (Davis, McVey, Heinmaa, Rockert, & Kennedy, 1999; Mitchell et al., 2011; Palmer, Birchall, McGrain, & Sullivan, 2002; Treasure, Schmidt, Troop, & Todd, 1996). Importantly, this approach appears to be cost-effective compared to individual CBT (Crow et al., 2013). A stepped care model validated by research could guide clinicians in how to best treat eating disorders with psychiatric comorbidities in a way that is both cost-effective and individually tailored.

PROPOSED SOLUTIONS TO THE ATYPICAL/COMPLEX EATING DISORDER "PROBLEM"

Notwithstanding some knowledge about the course, outcome, and treatment of atypical and complex eating disorder presentations, considerable gaps in the literature remain regarding their similarities and differences. With the current framework, an abundance of unspecified, atypical presentations is unaccounted for, rendering the controlled study of heterogeneous presentations difficult and evidence-based practice with these populations challenging. Although none of them solve this "problem" completely, diverse solutions have been proposed to the issue of how to parse out atypical presentations. Some suggest small alterations to existing DSM criteria under the premise that criteria are too strict (Watson & Andersen, 2003; Wilson & Sysko, 2009). This solution would entail reclassifying some cases of OSFED into existing DSM categories. DSM-5 was responsive to some of these previously proposed, research-supported alterations, including removing amenorrhea from the AN diagnostic criteria, raising the weight threshold for AN (Watson & Andersen, 2003), and lowering the frequency threshold for binge eating and purging for BN (Wilson & Sysko, 2009). A second proposed solution is selecting some atypical cases and placing them in new diagnostic groups, as has historically occurred with BED and ARFID (as described previously). Presentations that have been proposed and are currently under study include night eating syndrome, purging disorder, AN with a history of obesity, muscle dysmorphia, and specific phobia of vomiting, which are discussed in detail in other chapters in this book.

A third potential solution is to invent and validate new diagnostic schemes. For example, Walsh and Sysko (2009) introduced a scheme called "broad categories for the diagnosis of eating disorders," which consists of the hierarchical categories of AN and behaviorally similar disorders, BN and behaviorally similar disorders, BED and behaviorally similar disorders, and EDNOS. The authors state that this classification system would substantially reduce the size of the EDNOS category while providing other advantages, such as accurate diagnosis in settings in which a comprehensive psychiatric assessment is not feasible. Alternatively, Fairburn and Cooper (2011) offer the option of subdividing eating disorder cases based on their dominant clinical feature, which would produce two groups: one characterized by recurrent weight control methods (i.e., self-induced vomiting and laxative misuse), often accompanied by subjective binge eating, and another that includes attempts to follow extreme dietary rules. The authors note that the former has been termed "purging disorder" and that the latter may be best labeled "restrained eating disorder." Some have even queried if the field should move away from diagnosis altogether or, less radically, migrate to a "scientist–practitioner" model of eating disorders (Waller, 1993). The goal of the scientist–practitioner model (Barlow, 1981) is to bridge the gap between research and clinical work. An eating disorder conceptualization would include the variance in symptoms common to all individuals afflicted (e.g., general concern with control over food, weight, and body shape), the variance unique to the individual (e.g., history of low weight), and the variance that applies to some clusters of sufferers (e.g., body image distortion). Fourth, statistical methods such as cluster analysis, latent profile analysis, taxometric analysis, and Q-analysis of clinicians' opinions have also been used to yield clinically relevant groupings (Keel, Crosby, Hildebrandt, Haedt-Matt, & Gravener, 2013; Mitchell et al., 2007; Turner, Bryant-Waugh, & Peveler, 2009; Westen & Harnden-Fischer, 2001). Accordingly, some argue that eating disorder classification may be improved by including dimensional assessments in the current categorical scheme because evidence suggests that eating disorders vary in severity along a continuum in addition to type (Wildes & Marcus, 2013; Williamson et al., 2005). This idea resonates with the recent initiative of the National Institute of Mental Health, the Research Domain Criteria (RDoC), which is a call to investigate the phenotypic dimensional structure of psychopathology. In this way, RDoC is an attempt to understand the full range of human behavior by considering both psychology and biology in the understanding and classification of mental disorders (Insel et al., 2010).

In addition to the RDoC, the transdiagnostic framework may be employed to help with the goal of understanding the maintaining factors that connect or distinguish disorders. In 2003, Fairburn, Cooper, and Shafran introduced a transdiagnostic theory of disordered eating intended to supplement the cognitive–behavioral theory of BN and expand it to broad disordered eating. Fairburn and colleagues argue that in addition to a dysfunctional system for evaluating self-worth, a combination of clinical perfectionism, core low self-esteem, mood intolerance, and interpersonal difficulties maintains eating pathology in certain patients. Derived from this newly proposed transdiagnostic theory is a unified treatment plan that targets the core psychopathology of eating disorders called enhanced cognitive–behavior therapy (CBT-E; Fairburn, 2008). Hence, the transdiagnostic approach allows for the development and use of treatment protocols that can assist individuals with a range of eating disorder presentations that are all functionally impairing or causing clinically significant distress.

In some ways, the transdiagnostic approach has effectively addressed the former gaps in the literature (Fairburn, 2008; Fairburn et al., 2003). Most important, a transdiagnostic approach better reflects clinical realities, given the sheer number of patients with atypical eating disorders presenting for treatment (Fairburn, 2008). A transdiagnostic theory and treatment approach also allows for the effective treatment of all eating disorders with an emphasis on understanding and addressing common maintaining factors (Fairburn, 2008; Fairburn et al., 2003). Clinicians thus have an evidenced-based intervention at their disposal that matches the range of clinical presentations, and they are not left questioning how best to treat their patients who do not fit primary DSM diagnostic categories. The transdiagnostic approach is also sensitive to a developmental perspective. It removes the necessity of awkwardly applying DSM criteria to children and adolescents (Loeb et al., 2011), who often present atypically as eating disorders emerge (Workgroup for Classification of Eating Disorders in Children and Adolescents [WCEDCA], 2007). Children and adolescents regularly fail to meet diagnostic criteria for reasons both similar to and different from those of adults, including developing abstract thinking skills necessary to self-recognize and endorse aspects of psychological criteria for eating disorders (WCEDCA, 2007).

On the other hand, the transdiagnostic approach is imperfect. For example, in reference to his "trans-transdiagnostic" model, Waller (2008) argues that eating disorders should be relocated in the broader category of anxiety disorders for reasons including the high degree of comorbidity between anxiety and eating disorders, the frequent antecedence of anxiety to eating concerns (Bulik, Sullivan, Fear, & Joyce, 1997; Swinbourne et al., 2012), and the fact that actions frequently characteristic of eating disorders (e.g., food restriction, binging, purging, and body checking) can be viewed as safety behaviors that reduce anxiety in the short term (Pallister & Waller, 2008). In addition, the transdiagnostic approach assumes a common set of maintaining factors, but differences have been shown, particularly between AN and BN, in factors such as disease course (e.g., diagnostic crossover), prognostic indicators, outcome (e.g., remission and mortality rates) (Keel & Brown, 2010), and neurobiological and neurocognitive factors (Van den Eynde et al., 2011; von Hausswolff-Juhlin, Brooks, & Larsson, 2015; Zucker, Moskvich, & Soo, 2011; Zucker et al., 2007). The transdiagnostic approach has also been criticized for having the potential to de-emphasize the seriousness of AN and consequently shrink funding for treatment (Birmingham, Touyz, & Harbottle, 2009). In essence, however, although a multitude of solutions have been proposed in attempting to accommodate the challenges presented in the recognition and treatment of atypical and complex presentations, no one has, as yet, clearly informed treatment guidelines in these populations.

CONCLUSION AND FUTURE DIRECTIONS

It is important to continue to clarify our conceptualization of eating disorders in terms of psychological, sociocultural, and neurobiological factors that may be shared or distinct between different presentations. The eating disorder field is in pressing need of more unification in its evidence-based applications and treatment decision algorithms so that clinicians can best serve individuals with both atypical and complex presentations. Research should strive to be clinically relevant, which will depend on posing appropriate questions and answering them in a way that is both interesting and easily digestible (Waller, 1993). As described previously, RCTs should be conducted to provide information about treatment moderators and outcomes for individuals with atypical presentations, atypical demographics, or complex comorbid presentations. Although RCTs remain the gold standard of empirical cause-and-effect treatment research, meaningful and scientifically rigorous information can also be derived from clinically oriented research methods such as single-case designs, patient series designs, qualitative methods, and quasi-experimental designs (Waller, 1993). Consistent with a scientist–practitioner model (Barlow, 1981), a primary goal of the eating disorders field should be to bridge the gap between research and clinical work.

The body of literature on evidence-based interventions for atypical and complex populations is growing. For example, two RCTs have been conducted in outpatient transdiagnostic samples of adult patients who had an eating disorder but were not markedly underweight (Fairburn et al., 2009) and with adult patients with any form of eating disorder (Fairburn et al., 2015). In addition, two non-controlled studies have shown that CBT-E for adults with a full range of eating disorders (Byrne, Fursland, Allen, & Watson, 2011) and for adults with bulimia and atypical eating disorders (Knott, Woodward, Hoefkens, & Limbert, 2015) is generalizable to treatment in a clinical context.

In addition to conducting research with broad transdiagnostic samples, it may also be beneficial to delineate between atypical presentations so that targeted research protocols can be developed and tested. Some research has endeavored accordingly. RCTs have shown varying degrees of success with treatment for night eating syndrome (Pawlow, O'Neil, & Malcolm, 2003; Wal, Maraldo, Vercellone, & Gagne, 2015). However, there is a dearth of research on other presentations such as specific phobia of vomiting or purging disorder, or even ARFID and rumination disorder, both of which are primary diagnoses in DSM-5. It may be helpful to further divide atypical presentations into new diagnostic groups, as is being done with night eating syndrome, purging disorder, AN with a history of obesity, muscle dysmorphia, and specific phobia of vomiting.

Evidence-based treatment research for atypical and complex eating disorders is challenging to conduct and interpret. For one, inclusion/exclusion criteria for atypical and complex presentations vary, making it difficult to generalize to a truly transdiagnostic sample. The heterogeneity inherent in a transdiagnostic sample is good for ecological validity and generalizability of results, but there will be many individuals to whom the results may not be applicable. Another significant hurdle is that outcome variables in these studies will be less uniform than those in studies focusing on a single type of disorder because definitions of success vary across presentations. That is, quantifying recovery across presentations is imprecise. This has been resolved in transdiagnostic treatment studies with measures that equalize pathology among multiple presentations, such as by using a global Eating Disorder Examination interview score (EDE, 16th edition; Fairburn, Cooper, & O'Connor, 2008) as a measure of severity of eating disorder features or using a score less than one standard deviation above the community mean to define remission (Fairburn et al., 2015). In this way, it is crucial to compare the normalization of eating pathology to community, as opposed to clinical, samples. Normative comparisons such as this have been commonly used to quantify and classify clinically significant change (Kazdin, 2003; Kendall, Marrs-Garcia, Nath, & Sheldrick, 1999).

There are myriad challenges for clinicians and patients alike in terms of adherence to evidence-based treatment in the context of complex and atypical presentations and populations. A lack of diagnostic clarity in atypical cases may make it more tempting for clinicians to attend to broader concerns and lose sight of eating disorder treatment protocol. In addition, adherence is difficult in cases with competing, clinically significant comorbidities. This may be especially challenging for clinicians who are not as practiced with manual-based treatments. Particularly without validated clinical decision algorithms, addressing comorbid disorders is an added challenge to remaining focused on the treatment protocol. Without evidenced-based manuals or guidelines to follow, therapists may feel lost, ineffective, or anxious, which may negatively affect the therapeutic relationship in a way that is detrimental to therapeutic outcomes. At the same time, patients with atypical presentations may not feel as connected to supportive communities, given that these are often based on specific diagnoses. In addition, if not assigned an official DSM diagnosis, patients and insurers alike may perceive the patients' disorders as less severe (often unrealistically). Such factors may contribute to decreased treatment seeking and access.

In summary, the field of eating disorders has historically been plagued by a mismatch between patients seeking treatment with real-life eating disorder presentations and the dearth of evidence-based interventions and algorithms to best meet these patients' needs. Newer models conceptualizing eating disorders in novel ways have been introduced to address this conundrum. Research is increasingly shifting to include populations of individuals with atypical and complex eating disorder presentations. As further findings emerge, clinicians will be able to more effectively serve all individuals with eating disorders.

REFERENCES

Allen, K. L., Byrne, S. M., Oddy, W. H., & Crosby, R. D. (2013). DSM-IV-TR and DSM-5 eating disorders in adolescents: Prevalence, stability, and psychosocial correlates in a population-based sample of male and female adolescents. *Journal of Abnormal Psychology, 122,* 720–732.

American Psychiatric Association. (1980). *Diagnostic and statistical manual of mental disorders* (3rd ed.). Washington, DC: Author.

American Psychiatric Association. (1987). *Diagnostic and statistical manual of mental disorders* (3rd ed., rev.). Washington, DC: Author.

American Psychiatric Association. (1994). *Diagnostic and statistical manual of mental disorders* (4th ed.). Washington, DC: Author.

American Psychiatric Association. (2013). *Diagnostic and statistical manual of mental disorders* (5th ed.). Arlington, VA: American Psychiatric Publishing.

Barlow, D. H. (1981). On the relation of clinical research to clinical practice: Current issues, new directions. *Journal of Consulting and Clinical Psychology, 49,* 147–155.

Binford, R. B., & Le Grange, D. (2005). Adolescents with BN and eating disorder not otherwise specified–purging only. *International Journal of Eating Disorders, 38,* 157–161.

Birgegard, A., Norring, C., & Clinton, D. (2012). DSM-IV versus DSM-5: Implementation of proposed DSM-5 criteria in a large naturalistic database. *International Journal of Eating Disorders, 45,* 353–361.

Birmingham, C. L., Touyz, S., & Harbottle, J. (2009). Are AN and BN separate disorders? Challenging the "transdiagnostic" theory of eating disorders. *European Eating Disorders Review, 17,* 2–13.

Blinder, B. J., Cumella, E. J., & Sanathara, V. A. (2006). Psychiatric comorbidities of female inpatients with eating disorders. *Psychosomatic Medicine, 68*, 454–462.

Brown, T. A., & Keel, P. K. (2015). A randomized controlled trial of a peer co-led dissonance-based eating disorder prevention program for gay men. *Behaviour Research and Therapy, 74*, 1–10.

Bühren, K., Schwarte, R., Fluck, F., Timmesfeld, N., Krei, M., Egberts, K., ... Herpertz-Dahlmann, B. (2014). Comorbid psychiatric disorders in female adolescents with first-onset AN. *European Eating Disorders Review, 22*, 39–44.

Bulik, C. M., Sullivan, P. F., Fear, J. L., & Joyce, P. R. (1997). Eating disorders and antecedent anxiety disorders: A controlled study. *Acta Psychiatrica Scandinavica, 96*, 101–107.

Byrne, S. M., Fursland, A., Allen, K. L., & Watson, H. (2011). The effectiveness of enhanced cognitive behavioural therapy for eating disorders: An open trial. *Behaviour Research and Therapy, 49*, 219–226.

Castellini, G., Sauro, C. L., Mannucci, E., Ravaldi, C., Rotella, C. M., Faravelli, C., & Ricca, V. (2011). Diagnostic crossover and outcome predictors in eating disorders according to DSM-IV and DSM-5 proposed criteria: A 6-year follow-up study. *Psychosomatic Medicine, 73*, 270–279.

Chui, W., Safer, D. L., Bryson, S. W., Agras, W. S., & Wilson, G. T. (2007). A comparison of ethnic groups in the treatment of BN. *Eating Behaviors, 8*, 458–491.

Cohn, L., Murray, S. B., Walen, A., & Wooldridge, T. (2016). Including the excluded: Males and gender minorities in eating disorder prevention. *Eating Disorders, 24*, 114–120.

Correll, C. U., Kishimoto, T., & Kane, J. M. (2011). Randomized controlled trials in schizophrenia: Opportunities, limitations, and trial design alternatives. *Dialogues in Clinical Neuroscience, 13*, 155–172.

Courbasson, C., Nishikawa, Y., & Dixon, L. (2012). Outcome of dialectical behaviour therapy for concurrent eating and substance use disorders. *Clinical Psychology & Psychotherapy, 19*, 434–449.

Courbasson, C. M., Nishikawa, Y., & Shapira, L. B. (2011). Mindfulness-action based cognitive behavioral therapy for concurrent binge eating disorder and substance use disorders. *Eating Disorders, 19*, 17–33.

Courbasson, C. M. A., Smith, P. D., & Cleland, P. A. (2005). Substance use disorders, anorexia, bulimia, and concurrent disorders. *Canadian Journal of Public Health, 96*, 102–106.

Crow, S. J., Agras, W. S., Halmi, K. A., Fairburn, C. G., Mitchell, J. E., & Nyman, J. A. (2013). A cost effectiveness analysis of stepped care treatment for BN. *International Journal of Eating Disorders, 46*, 302–307.

Crow, S. J., Agras, W. S., Halmi, K., Mitchell, J. E., & Kraemer, H. C. (2002). Full syndromal versus subthreshold AN, BN, and binge eating disorder: A multicenter study. *International Journal of Eating Disorders, 32*, 309–318.

Davis, R., McVey, G., Heinmaa, M., Rockert, W., & Kennedy, S. (1999). Sequencing of cognitive–behavioral treatments for BN. *International Journal of Eating Disorders, 25*, 361–374.

Fairburn, C. G. (2008). *Cognitive behavior therapy and eating disorders*. New York, NY: Guilford.

Fairburn, C. G., Agras, W. S., & Wilson, G. T. (1992). The research on the treatment of BN: Practical and theoretical implications. In G. H. Anderson & S. H. Kennedy (Eds.), *The biology of feast and famine: Relevance to eating disorders* (pp. 317–340). New York, NY: Academic Press.

Fairburn, C. G., Bailey-Straebler, S., Basden, S., Doll, H. A., Jones, R., Murphy, R., . . . Cooper, Z. (2015). A transdiagnostic comparison of enhanced cognitive behaviour therapy (CBT-E) and interpersonal psychotherapy in the treatment of eating disorders. *Behaviour Research and Therapy, 70,* 64–71.

Fairburn, C. G., & Bohn, K. (2005). Eating disorder NOS (EDNOS): An example of the troublesome "not otherwise specified" (NOS) category in DSM-IV. *Behaviour Research and Therapy, 43,* 691–701.

Fairburn, C. G., & Cooper, Z. (2011). Eating disorders, DSM-5 and clinical reality. *British Journal of Psychiatry, 198,* 8–10.

Fairburn, C. G., Cooper, Z., Bohn, K., O'Connor, M. E., Doll, H. A., & Palmer, R. L. (2007). The severity and status of eating disorder NOS: Implications for DSM-V. *Behaviour Research and Therapy, 45,* 1705–1715.

Fairburn, C. G., Cooper, Z., Doll, H. A., O'Connor, M. E., Bohn, K., Hawker, D. M., . . . Palmer, R. L. (2009). Transdiagnostic cognitive–behavioral therapy for patients with eating disorders: A two-site trial with 60-week follow-up. *American Journal of Psychiatry, 166,* 311–319.

Fairburn, C. G., Cooper, Z., & O'Connor, M. (2008). Eating disorder examination (Edition 16.0D). In C. Fairburn (Ed.), *Cognitive behavior therapy and eating disorders* (pp. 265–308). New York, NY: Guilford.

Fairburn, C. G., Cooper, Z., & Shafran, R. (2003). Cognitive behaviour therapy for eating disorders: A "transdiagnostic" theory and treatment. *Behaviour Research and Therapy, 41,* 509–528.

Gamer, D. M., & Needleman, L. D. (1997). Sequencing and integration of treatments. In D. M. Garner & P. E. Garfinkel (Eds.), *Handbook of treatment for eating disorders* (2nd ed., pp. 50–66). New York, NY: Guilford.

Grilo, C. M., Pagano, M. E., Skodol, A. E., Sanislow, C. A., McGlashan, T. H., Gunderson, J. G., & Stout, R. L. (2007). Natural course of BN and of eating disorder not otherwise specified: 5-year prospective study of remissions, relapses, and the effects of personality disorder psychopathology. *Journal of Clinical Psychiatry, 68,* 738–746.

Grilo, C. M., Sinha, R., & O'Malley, S. S. (2002). Eating disorders and alcohol use disorders. *Alcohol Research & Health, 26,* 151–160.

Herzog, D. B., Hopkins, J. D., & Burns, C. D. (1993). A follow-up study of 33 subdiagnostic eating disordered women. *International Journal of Eating Disorders, 14,* 261–267.

Herzog, D. B., Keller, M. B., Sacks, N. R., Yeh, C. J., & Lavori, P. W. (1992). Psychiatric comorbidity in treatment-seeking anorexics and bulimics. *Journal of the American Academy of Child & Adolescent Psychiatry, 31,* 810–818.

Holm-Denoma, J. M., Richey, J. A., & Joiner, T. J. (2010). The latent structure of dietary restraint, body dissatisfaction, and drive for thinness: A series of taxometric analyses. *Psychological Assessment, 22,* 788–797.

Hudson, J. I., Hiripi, E., Pope, H. J., & Kessler, R. C. (2007). The prevalence and correlates of eating disorders in the National Comorbidity Survey Replication. *Biological Psychiatry, 61,* 348–358.

Insel, T., Cuthbert, B., Garvey, M., Heinssen, R., Pine, D. S., Quinn, K., . . . Wang, P. (2010). Research domain criteria (RDoC): Toward a new classification framework for research on mental disorders. *American Journal of Psychiatry, 167,* 748–751.

Kaye, W. H., Bulik, C. M., Thornton, L., Barbarich, N., & Masters, K. (2004). Comorbidity of anxiety disorders with anorexia and BN. *American Journal of Psychiatry, 161,* 2215–2221.

Kazdin, A. (2003). Clinical significance: Measuring whether interventions make a difference. In A. Kazdin (Ed.), *Methodological issues and strategies in clinical research* (3rd
ed., pp. 691–710). Washington, DC: American Psychological Association.

Kazdin, A.E. (2008). Evidence-based treatment and practice: New opportunities to
bridge clinical research and practice, enhance the knowledge base, and improve
patient care. *American Psychologist, 63* (3), 146–159. P. 147.

Keel, P. K., & Brown, T. T. (2010). Update on course and outcome in eating disorders.
International Journal of Eating Disorders, 3, 195–204.

Keel, P. K., Brown, T. A., Holland, L. A., & Bodell, L. P. (2012). Empirical classification of
eating disorders. *Annual Review of Clinical Psychology, 8*, 381–404.

Keel, P. K., Brown, T. A., Holm-Denoma, J., & Bodell, L. P. (2011). Comparison of DSM-
IV versus proposed DSM-5 diagnostic criteria for eating disorders: Reduction of
eating disorder not otherwise specified and validity. *International Journal of Eating
Disorders, 44*, 553–560.

Keel, P. K., Crosby, R. D., Hildebrandt, T. B., Haedt-Matt, A. A., & Gravener, J. A. (2013).
Evaluating new severity dimensions in the DSM-5 for bulimic syndromes using mix-
ture modeling. *International Journal of Eating Disorders, 46*, 108–118.

Keel, P. K., Gravener, J. A., Joiner, T. E., Jr., & Haedt, A. A. (2010). Twenty-year follow-up
of BN and related eating disorders not otherwise specified. *Internal Journal of Eating
Disorders, 43*, 492–497.

Kendall, P., Marrs-Garcia, A., Nath, S., & Sheldrick, R. (1999). Normative comparisons for the evaluation of clinical significance. *Journal of Consulting and Clinical
Psychology, 67*, 285–299.

Kerlinger, F. N., & Lee, H. B. (2000). *Foundations of behavioral research*. Belmont,
CA: Wadsworth.

Knott, S., Woodward, D., Hoefkens, A., & Limbert, C. (2015). Cognitive behaviour therapy for BN and eating disorders not otherwise specified: Translation from randomized controlled trial to a clinical setting. *Behavioural and Cognitive Psychotherapy, 43*,
641–654.

Lampard, A. M., Tasca, G. A., Balfour, L., & Bissada, H. (2013). An evaluation of the
transdiagnostic cognitive–behavioural model of eating disorders. *European Eating
Disorders Review, 21*, 99–107.

Le Grange, D., Lock, J., Agras, W. S., Moye, A., Bryson, S. W., Jo, B., & Kraemer, H. C.
(2012). Moderators and mediators of remission in family-based treatment and adolescent focused therapy for AN. *Behaviour Research and Therapy, 50*, 85–92.

Linehan, M. M., Korslund, K. E., Harned, M. S., Gallop, R. J., Lungu, A., Neacsiu, A. D.,
. . . Murray-Gregory, A. M. (2015). Dialectical behavior therapy for high suicide risk
in individuals with borderline personality disorder: A randomized clinical trial and
component analysis. *JAMA Psychiatry, 72*, 475–482.

Lock, J., Agras, W. S., Bryson, S., & Kraemer, H. C. (2005). A comparison of short- and
long-term family therapy for adolescent AN. *Journal of the American Academy of
Child & Adolescent Psychiatry, 44*, 632–639.

Loeb, K. L., Le Grange, D., Hildebrandt, T., Greif, R., Lock, J., & Alfano, L. (2011). Eating
disorders in youth: Diagnostic variability and predictive validity. *International Journal
of Eating Disorders, 44*, 692–702.

Machado, P. P. P., Gonçalves, S., & Hoek, H. W. (2013). DSM-5 reduces the proportion
of EDNOS cases: Evidence from community samples. *International Journal of Eating
Disorders, 46*, 60–65.

March, J. S., Silva, S., Petrycki, S., Curry, J., Wells, K., Fairbank, J., . . . Severe, J. (2007). The Treatment for Adolescents with Depression Study (TADS): Long-term effectiveness and safety outcomes. *Archives of General Psychiatry, 64*, 1132–1144.

Maughan, B. (2013). Editorial: "Better by design"—Why randomized controlled trials are the building blocks of evidence-based practice. *Journal of Child Psychology and Psychiatry, 54*, 225–226.

Meltzer, H. Y. (2002). Suicidality in schizophrenia: A review of the evidence for risk factors and treatment options. *Current Psychiatry Reports, 4*, 279–283.

Milos, G., Spindler, A., & Schnyder, U. (2004). Psychiatric comorbidity and Eating Disorder Inventory (EDI) profiles in eating disorder patients. *Canadian Journal of Psychiatry, 49*, 179–184.

Milos, G., Spindler, A., Schnyder, U., & Fairburn, C. G. (2005). Instability of eating disorder diagnoses: Prospective study. *British Journal of Psychiatry, 187*, 573–578.

Mitchell, J. E., Agras, S., Crow, S., Halmi, K., Fairburn, C. G., Bryson, S., & Kraemer, H. (2011). Stepped care and cognitive–behavioural therapy for BN: Randomised trial. *British Journal of Psychiatry, 198*, 391–397.

Mitchell, J. E., Crosby, R. D., Wonderlich, S. A., Hill, L., Le Grange, D., Powers, P., & Eddy, K. (2007). Latent profile analysis of a cohort of patients with eating disorders not otherwise specified. *International Journal of Eating Disorders, 40*, S95–S98.

Murray, S. B., & Anderson, L. K. (2015). Deconstructing "atypical" eating disorders: An overview of emerging eating disorder phenotypes. *Current Psychiatry Reports, 17*, 86.

Pallister, E., & Waller, G. (2008). Anxiety in the eating disorders: Understanding the overlap. *Clinical Psychology Review, 28*, 366–386.

Palmer, R. L., Birchall, H., McGrain, L., & Sullivan, V. (2002). Self-help for bulimic disorders: A randomised controlled trial comparing minimal guidance with face-to-face or telephone guidance. *British Journal of Psychiatry, 181*, 230–235.

Pawlow, L. A., O'Neil, P. M., & Malcolm, R. J. (2003). Night eating syndrome: Effects of brief relaxation training on stress, mood, hunger, and eating patterns. *International Journal of Obesity, 27*, 970–978.

Ricca, V., Mannucci, E., Mezzani, B., Di Bernardo, M., Zucchi, T., Paionni, A., . . . Faravelli, C. (2001). Psychopathological and clinical features of outpatients with an eating disorder not otherwise specified. *Eating and Weight Disorders, 6*, 157–165.

Salmond, S. S. (2008). Randomized controlled trials: Methodological concepts and critique. *Orthopaedic Nursing, 27*, 116–124.

Simpson, H. B., Wetterneck, C. T., Cahill, S. P., Steinglass, J. E., Franklin, M. E., Leonard, R. C., . . . Riemann, B. C. (2013). Treatment of obsessive–compulsive disorder complicated by comorbid eating disorders. *Cognitive Behaviour Therapy, 42*, 64–76.

Sinha, R., & O'Malley, S. S. (2000). Alcohol and eating disorders: Implications for alcohol treatment and health services research. *Alcoholism: Clinical and Experimental Research, 24*, 1312–1319.

Spindler, A., & Milos, G. (2004). Psychiatric comorbidity and inpatient treatment history in bulimic subjects. *General Hospital Psychiatry, 26*, 18–23.

Stice, E., Marti, C. N., & Cheng, Z. H. (2014). Effectiveness of a dissonance-based eating disorder prevention program for ethnic groups in two randomized controlled trials. *Behaviour Research and Therapy, 55*, 54–64.

Stice, E., Marti, C. N., & Rohde, P. (2013). Prevalence, incidence, impairment, and course of the proposed DSM-5 eating disorder diagnoses in an 8-year prospective community study of young women. *Journal of Abnormal Psychology, 122*, 445–457.

Striegel-Moore, R. H., Wonderlich, S. A., Walsh, B. T., & Mitchell, J. E. (2011). *Developing an evidence-based classification of eating disorders: Scientific findings for DSM-5.* Arlington, VA: American Psychiatric Association.

Sutherland, L. A., Weaver, S. N., McPeake, J. D., & Quimby, C. D. (1993). The Beech Hill Hospital eating disorders treatment program for drug dependent females: Program description and case analysis. *Journal of Substance Abuse Treatment, 10*, 473–481.

Swinbourne, J., Hunt, C., Abbott, M., Russell, J., St. Clare, T., & Touyz, S. (2012). The comorbidity between eating disorders and anxiety disorders: Prevalence in an eating disorder sample and anxiety disorder sample. *Australian and New Zealand Journal of Psychiatry, 46*, 118–131.

Sysko, R., & Hildebrandt, T. (2009). Cognitive–behavioural therapy for individuals with BN and a co-occurring substance use disorder. *European Eating Disorders Review, 17*, 89–100.

Thompson-Brenner, H., Franko, D. L., Thompson, D. R., Grilo, C. M., Boisseau, C. L., Roehrig, J. P., . . . Wilson, G. T. (2013). Race/ethnicity, education, and treatment parameters as moderators and predictors of outcome in binge eating disorder. *Journal of Consulting and Clinical Psychology, 81*, 710–721.

Thompson-Brenner, H., Shingleton, R. M., Thompson, D. R., Satir, D. A., Richards, L. K., Pratt, E. M., & Barlow, D. H. (2016). Focused vs. broad enhanced cognitive behavioral therapy for BN with comorbid borderline personality: A randomized controlled trial. *International Journal of Eating Disorders, 49*, 36–49.

Treasure, J., Schmidt, U., Troop, N., & Todd, G. (1996). Sequential treatment for bulimia nervosa incorporating a self-care manual. *British Journal of Psychiatry, 168*, 94–98.

Turner, H., & Bryant-Waugh, R. (2004). Eating disorder not otherwise specified (EDNOS): Profiles of clients presenting at a community eating disorder service. *European Eating Disorders Review, 12*, 18–26.

Turner, H., Bryant-Waugh, R., & Peveler, R. (2009). An approach to sub-grouping the eating disorder population: Adding attachment and coping style. *European Eating Disorders Review, 17*, 269–280.

Ulfvebrand, S., Birgegård, A., Norring, C., Högdahl, L., & von Hausswolff-Juhlin, Y. (2015). Psychiatric comorbidity in women and men with eating disorders: Results from a large clinical database. *Psychiatry Research, 230*, 294–299.

Van den Eynde, F., Guillaume, S., Broadbent, H., Stahl, D., Campbell, I. C., Schmidt, U., & Tchanturia, K. (2011). Neurocognition in bulimic eating disorders: A systematic review. *Acta Psychiatrica Scandinavica, 124*, 120–140.

von Hausswolff-Juhlin, Y., Brooks, S. J., & Larsson, M. (2015). The neurobiology of eating disorders—A clinical perspective. *Acta Psychiatrica Scandinavica, 131*, 244–255.

Wal, J. V., Maraldo, T. M., Vercellone, A. C., & Gagne, D. A. (2015). Education, progressive muscle relaxation therapy, and exercise for the treatment of night eating syndrome: A pilot study. *Appetite, 89*, 136–144.

Waller, G. (1993). Why do we diagnose different types of eating disorder? Arguments for a change in research and clinical practice. *European Eating Disorders Review, 1*, 74–89.

Waller, G. (2008). A "trans-transdiagnostic" model of the eating disorders: A new way to open the egg? *European Eating Disorders Review, 16*, 165–172.

Walsh, B. T., & Kahn, C. B. (1997). Diagnostic criteria for eating disorders: Current concerns and future directions. *Psychopharmacology Bulletin, 33,* 369–372.

Watson, T. L., & Andersen, A. E. (2003). A critical examination of the amenorrhea and weight criteria for diagnosing AN. *Acta Psychiatrica Scandinavica, 108,* 175–182.

Westen, D., & Harnden-Fischer, J. (2001). Personality profiles in eating disorders: Rethinking the distinction between axis I and axis II. *American Journal of Psychiatry, 158,* 547–562.

Wiebe, S., & Hill, M. D. (2011). On the urgent need for successful randomized controlled trials in neurosciences. *Canadian Journal of Neurological Sciences, 38,* 383–384.

Wildes, J. E., & Marcus, M. D. (2013). Incorporating dimensions into the classification of eating disorders: Three models and their implications for research and clinical practice. *International Journal of Eating Disorders, 46,* 396–403.

Williamson, D. A., Gleaves, D. H., & Stewart, T. M. (2005). Categorical versus dimensional models of eating disorders: An examination of the evidence. *International Journal of Eating Disorders, 37,* 1–10.

Wilson, G. T., & Sysko, R. (2009). Frequency of binge eating episodes in BN and binge eating disorder: Diagnostic considerations. *International Journal of Eating Disorders, 42,* 603–610.

Wilson, G. T., Vitousek, K. M., & Loeb, K. L. (2000). Stepped care treatment for eating disorders. *Journal of Consulting and Clinical Psychology, 68,* 564–572.

Workgroup for Classification of Eating Disorders in Children and Adolescents. (2007). Classification of child and adolescent eating disturbances. *International Journal of Eating Disorders, 40,* S117–S122.

Zaider, T. I., Johnson, J. G., & Cockell, S. J. (2000). Psychiatric comorbidity associated with eating disorder symptomatology among adolescents in the community. *International Journal of Eating Disorders, 28,* 58–67.

Zucker, N. L., Losh, M., Bulik, C. M., LaBar, K. S., Piven, J., & Pelphrey, K. A. (2007). AN and autism spectrum disorders: Guided investigation of social cognitive endophenotypes. *Psychological Bulletin, 133,* 976–1006.

Zucker, N., Moskvich, A., & Soo, A. (2011). Neuropsychological aspects of eating disorders. *Psychiatric Annals, 41,* 539–546.

PART I

Psychiatric Comorbidities

2

Clinical Guidelines for the Treatment of Anxiety in Eating Disorders

STEPHANIE KNATZ PECK, STUART B. MURRAY, AND WALTER H. KAYE ■

INTRODUCTION

Eating disorders (EDs) such as anorexia nervosa (AN) and bulimia nervosa (BN) are serious and complex psychological disorders characterized by aberrant eating behaviors in response to a relentless pursuit for thinness and a desire to change weight and shape. Specifically, AN is characterized by an inability to maintain an appropriate body weight accomplished primarily by the restriction of food intake. BN involves binge-eating behaviors and excessive compensatory behaviors used to purge caloric intake (American Psychiatric Association, 2013). Prevalence estimates of these illnesses are 0.3% and 1%, respectively (Smink, Van Hoeken, & Hoek, 2012). Despite the relative rarity of these illnesses, they are important psychiatric problems due to their high mortality and morbidity rates and associated physical and psychological sequelae (Birmingham, Su, Hlynsky, Goldner, & Gao, 2005; Papadopoulos, Ekbom, Brandt, & Ekselius, 2009). Although the onset of EDs usually occurs during adolescence or early adulthood, with the course and outcome varying in length and prognosis (Keel & Brown, 2010), a substantial portion of individuals with AN and BN remit after 5–10 years (Keel, Mitchell, Miller, Davis, & Crow, 1999; Steinhausen, 2002). However, a notable portion of individuals remain ill with a chronic protracted course of illness that can be deadly. Indeed, mortality rates of EDs remain among the highest of any psychiatric illness, estimated to be greater than 5% (Crow et al., 2009; Sullivan, 1995).

In terms of etiology, EDs have a complex pathogenesis that is poorly under-stood. A contemporary understanding of these illnesses points to a diathesis–stress model, whereby genetic and biological vulnerabilities necessary for the development of these illnesses are triggered by an immediate environmental stressor, leading to alterations in eating habits that eventually cross the threshold into illness. In recent decades, substantial brain imaging research has emerged elucidating the contribution of biological factors to these illnesses. Studies point to premorbid, genetically determined temperament and personality traits that render an individual vulnerable to AN and BN (Kaye, Fudge, & Paulus, 2009; Lilenfeld, Wonderlich, Riso, Crosby, & Mitchell, 2006). Interestingly, many of these traits are not unique to EDs but also underlie other psychiatric illnesses, including anxiety disorders (ADs) such as obsessive–compulsive disorder (OCD), obsessive–compulsive personality disorder (OCPD), generalized anxiety disorder (GAD), social phobia, and specific phobias (Degnan & Fox, 2007).

Certainly, among EDs, the highest degree of comorbidity lies with ADs (Bulik, Sullivan, Fear, & Joyce, 1997; Kaye, Bulik, Thornton, Barbarich, & Masters, 2004). For instance, clinical and epidemiological studies indicate that a significant number of individuals diagnosed with an ED report a life-time comorbid AD. The lifetime prevalence of a diagnosis of one or more ADs among individuals with AN and BN has been estimated to be between 23% and 71% (Godart, Flament, Perdereau, & Jeammet, 2002; Kaye et al., 2004). The most commonly reported ADs are OCD, simple phobias, and social phobia, with rates of these disorders being the same across AN and BN diagnoses (Kaye et al., 2004). Studies estimate prevalence rates of comorbid OCD ranging from 24.1% to 41%, whereas the prevalence rate of social phobia has been estimated to be 20% (Godart et al., 2002; Kaye et al., 2004). Other ADs, such as GAD and posttraumatic stress disorder (PTSD), are reported to be less common but still significantly more prevalent relative to healthy controls (Godart et al., 2002; Kaye et al., 2004). Although most anxiety disorders have been shown to be equally prevalent across ED diagnoses, some studies suggest that OCD is more prevalent in AN than in BN (Godart et al., 2002; Lilenfeld et al., 1998). Furthermore, PTSD has been shown to be three times more frequent in those with BN compared to AN (Kaye et al., 2004).

Phenomenology of Anxiety in Eating Disorder Presentations

In terms of temporal onset, ADs generally appear to precede the onset of an ED (Kaye et al., 2004), although mixed findings emerge when delineating between diagnostic subtypes of AD. In a seminal study examining prevalence rates of ADs in a large sample of individuals with EDs, Kaye et al. found that the onset of OCD, social phobia, specific phobia, and GAD preceded the onset of the ED. In contrast, PTSD, panic disorder, and agoraphobia tend to develop later in life and after the onset of an ED. Conversely, other studies have found an ED diagnosis to precede the onset of both OCD and GAD (Godart et al., 2002), and therefore temporal relationships between specific AD diagnoses and EDs continue to be inconclusive. Nevertheless, there is substantial evidence indicating that the onset of an AD precedes the onset of EDs in a large proportion of cases (between 50% and 60%) (Godart et al., 2002; Kaye et al., 2004). A substantial portion of individuals with EDs report the onset of an AD occurring in childhood, indicating that etiological factors influencing the development of these disorders are likely trait based and appear early in the course of life. Furthermore, Kaye and colleagues found that lifetime ADs among family members of those with EDs are also significantly more common, suggesting that ADs and EDs may share traits belonging to a common phenotype. Indeed, the temporal relationship between pathological anxiety and disordered eating suggests that clinical and subclinical anxiety may play an etiological role in the development of a future ED, which renders the co-presentation of anxiety and eating disorders both likely and complex.

However, in addition to the shared phenotypic traits and shared genetic predispositions, the phenomenology of EDs may give rise to both profound and sustained anxiety. That is, when considering AN, for instance, and the characteristic intense fear of weight gain, the principal treatment target to normalize patient weight may inherently trigger symptomatic anxiety and fear (Murray, Loeb, & Le Grange, 2016). Similarly, BN may also be characterized by an overvaluation of the thin body ideal, with concomitant compensatory efforts designed to counterbalance caloric intake. With treatment principally focusing on the removal of compensatory measures, this too may result in profound anxiety. As such, the issue of anxiety within the EDs is complex and multifaceted.

ANXIETY IN EATING DISORDERS

Prognostic Implications

The presence of an AD has a significant negative impact on both ED symptom severity and prognosis, which, as alluded to previously, is particularly profound in early onset presentations. The presence of comorbid anxiety has been shown to predict poor outcome, showing relationships to unremitting ED symptoms and higher mortality rates (Button, Chadalavada, & Palmer, 2010; Hjern, Lindberg, & Lindblad, 2006; Milos, Spindler, Ruggiero, Klaghofer, & Schnyder, 2002). In the context of AN in particular, food consumption typically triggers sustained anxiety, with a greater degree of premeal anxiety, for instance, being related to reduced caloric consumption at meals (Steinglass et al., 2010), suggesting a functional impact of anxiety in EDs. Furthermore, the degree to which anxiety is reported in EDs is actually comparable to the severity of anxiety reported in clinical ADs, and ecological momentary analyses demonstrate how temporally distributed peaks in ED symptomatic behaviors co-occur with spikes in self-reported anxiety (Lavender et al., 2013). Moreover, Weltzin et al. (1995) suggest that significant anxiety not only reduces compliance with therapy but also often leads to premature termination of treatment. In adolescent EDs, eating-related obsessionality, a factor underlying ADs such as OCD and OCPD, influenced the degree of success with family-based treatment (FBT) (Le Grange et al., 2012). Cumulatively, these data suggest that when treating EDs, anxiety is an important factor to consider due to its potential impact on ongoing symptomatology, recovery, treatment delivery, and the uptake of treatment.

The Relationship Between Anxiety Disorders and Eating Disorders: A Shared Behavioral Profile

The prevalence of anxiety and related disorders among EDs is both striking and noteworthy. The significant proportion of co-occurring ADs among those with EDs raises important questions about the nature of the relationship. Specifically, what are the common factors that predispose an individual to the development of both illnesses? To date, the emerging evidence relating to this question indicates that the frequent co-occurrence of these two illness types suggests a shared genetic transmission expressed as common underlying vulnerabilities. Both descriptive, qualitative reports and personality assessments indicate that individuals with both AN and BN EDs tend to possess general trait anxiety (Kaye, 2008; Kaye et al., 2004; Wagner et al., 2006). Historically, trait anxiety was most commonly associated with only ADs; however, research examining the role of anxiety in eating disorders has found premorbid trait anxiety to be an underlying personality factor related to the development and maintenance of EDs (Kaye et al., 2004). Furthermore, ED individuals possess personality features that are commonly associated with ADs, including a tendency toward being overcontrolled, harm avoidant, and elevated levels of obsessionality (Kaye, 2008; Wagner et al., 2006; Wonderlich, Lilenfeld, Riso, Engel, & Mitchell, 2005). These traits are also commonly known to characterize a variety of ADs, including OCD, GAD, and social phobia (Degnan & Fox, 2007; Handley, Egan, Kane, & Rees, 2014; Hettema, Neale, & Kendler, 2001).

These behavioral traits, which tend to be stable over time, are significantly associated with a range of ADs, as well as both AN and BN, thus implicating these factors as the common link. The overarching commonality between ADs and EDs is a critical consideration because it suggests that the relationship between these illnesses is best understood and explained as underlying traits that predispose an individual to the development of both diagnostic subsets. This trait-driven framework is in line with more contemporary conceptualizations, which call for psychiatric illnesses to be conceptualized based on underlying behavioral domains (Insel et al., 2010). Furthermore, neurobiological research studying the underlying mechanisms of ED behavior suggests that similar neuronal pathways are being engaged in ED behaviors and AD behaviors alike and points to the experience of anxiety as a common driver of behaviors in both illness types. It is common for clinicians to refer to specific diagnostic overlap, such as a reference to the comorbidity rates between AN and OCD or between BN and social phobia. Although categorically accurate, a more descriptive conceptualization of this overlap is one that explains the link in terms of shared underlying traits and neurobiological mechanisms. (For an example of the description of ED–AD overlap, see Example 2.1.)

The Functional Role of Anxiety in Eating Disorders

Trait anxiety can be characterized as the tendency to attend to, experience, and report anxiety across contexts. Individuals with EDs are prone to experiencing anxiety surrounding food-related stimuli but also in other general contexts. Importantly, the experience of anxiety is considered to be a key fundamental process driving ED behaviors. Those with EDs report experiencing fear and anxiety in response to food and other ED-related stimuli and/or the perceived threat of weight gain (Steinglass et al., 2010). These factors remain cardinal symptoms of these illnesses. Eating disorder behaviors, such as restriction, binging, and purging, have been conceptualized as a method to control, modify, or avoid anxious experiences (Crosby et al., 2009; Haedt-Matt & Keel, 2011; Kaye, Strober, & Klump, 2003; Vitousek & Manke, 1994). Specifically, in both AN and BN, ED behaviors can be used as a method to avoid perceived threat and/or stimuli that provoke anxiety, including food.

The Role of Anxiety in Anorexia Nervosa

Individuals with AN commonly experience anxiety in response to food-related stimuli. Descriptive reports and testimonials from individuals suggest that the anxiety experienced in response to food results from both the perceived threat of weight gain and feared expectation of a deterioration in mood and physical state. This conditioned response comes about from past experiences and is then "expected" in response to food. This then results in individuals experiencing anticipatory anxiety in response to food about the consequences of engaging in eating (i.e., fear of weight gain). Restriction is then used as a way to avoid these expected outcomes. This process of fear conditioning, in which food—a perceived threat—is evaded in response to an anticipated negative or feared outcome/consequence (weight gain), is the same basic process that underlies ADs and is a primary driver of abnormal eating behaviors (Murray, Loeb, et al., 2016; Murray, Treanor, et al., 2016; Strober, 2004).

The Role of Anxiety in Bulimia Nervosa

Bulimia nervosa behaviors such as binging and purging serve as methods to control and subvert negative emotions, including anxiety. Studies show that experiences of anxiety are altered in response to engaging in bulimic behaviors, suggesting that these behaviors are used as a method to control anxious feelings. Studies measuring momentary anxiety in BN demonstrate that anxiety may precede the onset of a bulimic behavior and then subsequently decrease following a bulimic action (Lavender et al., 2013). The effect of this is that BN behaviors are negatively reinforced by successful avoidance of anxious experiences, thereby perpetuating a continuation of BN behaviors. Similarly, avoidance as a negative reinforcement mechanism is a fundamental process theorized to underlie fears in ADs.

Example 2.1: Clinician Example for Explaining Eating Disorder–Anxiety Disorder Diagnostic Overlap

Providing clients with psychoeducation can be a powerful intervention because it lends credibility to a clinician and can motivate clients to receive related interventions. Psychoeducation on the underlying neurobiology can be particularly compelling because it explains EDs from a biological framework, implicitly sending a message of non-blame. Such an approach can be enormously therapeutic in allowing individuals to change their relationship to their symptoms. In the specific case of anxiety and EDs, explaining common vulnerability factors can improve awareness of common reasons for engaging in ED and AD behaviors alike, opening the door for clinicians to both target common mechanisms and assist clients (and relevant family members) in upholding a nonjudgmental attitude toward their symptoms. The following is an example of a way in which this overlap can be explained to a client with an AD–ED comorbidity or one who exhibits anxious traits:

> Eating disorders and anxiety disorders commonly occur together. In fact, almost two-thirds of people with eating disorders have been diagnosed with an anxiety disorder! This overlap is not a coincidence. It turns out that people with EDs and those with ADs share very similar personality traits. Both groups of people have high trait anxiety, which means that by nature, they tend to worry more than others [without these illnesses]. Most often, this worry is in anticipation of something, or worrying about consequences. We call this "anticipatory anxiety." This worry can lead to avoiding certain things or situations [use examples relevant to the person]. This applies to disordered eating too—anticipatory anxiety about what will happen if you eat leads to avoiding eating [restriction] or another ED behavior like purging. Other personality traits that predispose someone to both EDs and ADs are obsessionality, perfectionism, and harm avoidance. How do you think this applies to you?

Summary

Anxiety is a fundamental process underlying ED behaviors. The shared underlying mechanisms in EDs and ADs explain the commonalities in personality trait profiles and the significant comorbidity rates among these two diagnoses. Furthermore, even in the absence of a comorbid anxiety disorder, it is critical to understand that anxiety plays a fundamental role in driving disordered eating. Understanding the functional role of anxiety in ED behaviors is important and implicates anxiety as a primary treatment target in reducing ED behaviors. In the following section, treatment considerations are discussed based on the previously presented information. Specifically, information on the current knowledge base related to this comorbidity is reviewed, followed by general clinical recommenda-tions for integrated assessment and treatment for this concurrent presentation. Novel treatment methods are also discussed, including targeting common under-lying mechanisms and personality and behavioral traits.

CLINICAL GUIDELINES FOR TREATING CONCURRENT EATING AND ANXIETY PROBLEMS

Despite the wealth of research confirming the overlap between ADs and EDs and the functional role of anxiety to disordered eating, there is a paucity of knowledge concerning treatment considerations for this common comorbidity. Evidence-based treatments exist for both sets of illnesses but have not been discussed in an integra-tive manner. Furthermore, there are no proven treatments specifically focused on targeting anxious traits or common underlying mechanisms that tend to be more stable over time and persist even upon remission from EDs. Given the informa-tion that has been substantiated through the study of AD–ED overlap, important questions arise concerning concurrent and integrative treatment that urgently need addressing. Despite the lack of evidence surrounded integrative treatment methods for EDs and ADs, this section serves as a guide to clinical treatment based on expert knowledge about the role of anxiety in eating disorders. Here, recommendations are formulated that specifically pertain to the unique presentation of anxiety within EDs in an effort to elucidate areas in need of continued study and to provide prelim-inary guidelines based on clinical knowledge and experience.

Assessment and Diagnosis

As mentioned previously, anxiety that meets the threshold for diagnosis is relatively common among ED individuals, with lifetime prevalence estimates ranging from 23% to 71% (Godart et al., 2002; Kaye et al., 2004). Given the substantial prevalence, when working with ED individuals, it is important to conduct a thorough diagnostic evaluation assessing for past and present ADs. Furthermore, given that treatment of EDs necessarily brings about the most feared outcome within these disorders (i.e., weight gain), treatment in and of itself may cultivate sustained and profound anxiety, and upon assessment it is important to delineate between symptoms of anxiety relating to treatment of one's eating disorder and clinical anxiety in and of itself. Keeping in mind that ADs most commonly precede the onset of the ED and can occur in childhood, it is important to ascertain historical data to assess for childhood anxiety. It is important to be aware of the presence of a childhood AD, irrespective of a cur-rent AD, because it may have prognostic implications. Such a diagnosis may indicate the presence of strong premorbid traits (outlined previously), which in turn may influence treatment outcome. Table 2.1 provides a list of standard assessments for common comorbid ADs and personality traits. The majority of

Table 2.1 CLINICAL ASSESSMENT DEVICES FOR ANXIETY

Construct	Assessment Device	Assessment Type
Anxiety disorder	Structured Clinical Interview for DSM-5	Structured clinical interview
Trait anxiety	State–Trait Anxiety Inventory	Self-report
Perfectionism	Frost Multidimensional Perfectionism Scale	Self-report
Obsessive–compulsive symptomatology	Yale–Brown Obsessive Compulsive Scale II	Semistructured interview/self-report
Harm avoidance	Temperament and Character Inventory	Self-report
Reward/punishment sensitivity	Sensitivity to Punishment and Sensitivity to Reward Scale	Self-report
Behavioral inhibition	Behavioral Inhibition Scale	Self-report
Uncertainty intolerance	Intolerance of Uncertainty Scale	Self-report

the assessments included in the table are self-report assessments that are easy to administer and may inform treatment.

Given the robust evidence base that points to the ubiquity of premorbid traits in EDs (harm avoidance, obsessionality, perfectionism, and trait anxiety), a global evaluation that assesses for the presence of these traits may also be clinically relevant. Assessments capturing the degree of severity of these constructs may provide more specific information about particular traits of relevance. For example, a clinician administers the Yale–Brown Obsessive Compulsive Scale (Goodman et al., 1989) to a client with AN and determines that the client has moderate to severe symptoms of obsessionality despite not meeting criteria for an OCD diagnosis. Upon further questioning, the clinician discovers an extreme drive for order and symmetry and a tendency to be highly rule-bound. This information is then used to tailor an appropriate structure for the client's meal plan based on these tendencies. Because the clinician knows that the client thrives within the bounds of high levels of structure and predictability, specific rules are assigned with regard to the client's meal plan, such as precise times of meals and snacks and one or two specific food choices to be eaten at each meal. This example illustrates the ways in which trait assessment can assist clinicians with choosing therapeutic strategies that appeal to specific personality styles to maximize effectiveness.

Current Treatment Approaches

Treatments for EDs and ADs differ despite possessing shared underlying vulnerabilities and functional mechanisms. Here, a brief overview of treatment approaches for both classes of illnesses is provided.

ANXIETY DISORDERS

Cognitive–behavioral therapy (CBT) is the most widely accepted and efficacious treatment for ADs. Research has shown CBT to be effective for panic disorder, phobias, social anxiety disorder, OCD, and GAD (Otte, 2011). CBT treatment includes cognitive interventions aimed at modifying maladaptive cognitions and beliefs and also behavioral experiments emphasizing new learning, habituation and desensitization to central fears, and extinguishing avoidance and other safety behaviors. With respect to OCD, behavioral experiments also include improving response prevention of compulsive behaviors.

EATING DISORDERS

Cognitive–behavioral therapy is also used for treatment of EDs. CBT-E is an enhanced version of CBT developed specifically for EDs and modified to target maladaptive cognitions specifically related to eating, shape, and weight concerns. CBT-E is considered the gold-standard treatment for BN, demonstrating efficacy in reducing bulimic behaviors (Fairburn, Cooper, & Shafran, 2003; Fairburn et al., 2009). Interpersonal therapy is another treatment that has been shown to be efficacious with BN, with comparable effects to CBT (Agras, Walsh, Fairburn, Wilson, & Kraemer, 2000). CBT-E has also been used for AN; however, it has not demonstrated primacy over other available treatments, and reported effects are generally minor. To date, no treatments have emerged as efficacious for adults with AN (Watson & Bulik, 2013). With respect to adolescent EDs, FBT is a robust and efficacious treatment for adolescent AN (Lock et al., 2010). For adolescent BN, both CBT and FBT have been shown to be efficacious (Le Grange, Crosby, Rathouz, & Leventhal, 2007; Schmidt et al., 2007). Although treatment research allows clinicians to delineate specific, recommended treatments for both EDs and ADs, the presence of a comorbidity complicates the picture because clinicians must make decisions about how and whether to treat two distinctive disorders and, if so, whether to use an integrated theoretical approach.

COMORBID EATING DISORDERS AND ANXIETY DISORDERS

To date, there are no unified protocols for EDs comorbid with ADs, with the exception of comorbid ED–OCD (discussed later). In the presence of both illnesses, a clinician must make important decisions concerning the optimal way to treat this comorbidity. Ideally, an integrated treatment approach that identifies treatment targets for both ED and AD problems should be constructed to ensure that both problems are sufficiently addressed. Constructing a comprehensive treatment plan requires careful consideration of various factors, including the appropriate prioritization of treatment targets and the selection of appropriate treatment types. The following section discusses methods for selecting appropriate treatments and prioritizing treatment targets. Following this, multiple methods for treating concurrent EDs–ADs are reviewed, including separate treatment delivered concurrently and a unified treatment in which targets are established from both illness types and treatment is delivered in an integrated manner. Last,

novel methods for treating this comorbidity are proposed, including a transdiagnostic cognitive–behavioral model targeting fear extinction and neurobiologically informed treatments targeting shared underlying personality traits. A case
example is presented next and referred to throughout the following sections for
the purposes of illustration.

Case Example

Sofia is a 23-year-old female diagnosed with BN and social phobia. Upon beginning
treatment, her ED symptoms included binging and purging approximately 10 times
per week and an ED cycle characterized by days of food restriction, during which
she ate less than 300 kcal/day, followed by days of continuous binging and purging.
Her weight was within the normal range for her height, but recent labs showed electrolyte imbalances, likely due to excessive purging. Due to her social phobia, Sofia
avoided all social situations besides attending work on a daily basis. She reported
suffering from anxiety characterized by physical symptoms in social situations, with
occasional panic attacks. The clinician treating Sofia determined that binging, purging, and restriction behaviors should be targeted first due to their potential medical
consequences. Furthermore, she determined that Sofia's eating pathology is having
negative impacts on her social functioning. First, time spent binging and purging
is taking away from time she could be spending socializing and is also being used
as an avoidance behavior. Second, binging and purging result in negative emotions,
including guilt and shame, that further discourage her from pursuing social contact.
The clinician uses the 20-session CBT-E protocol to target Sofia's BN symptoms.
By session 16, Sofia has reduced binge/purge behaviors to three times per week
and is no longer engaging in restriction. She continues to endorse body dissatisfaction and anxiety around eating. At this point, the clinician reassesses presenting
symptomatology and its impact on functioning. Despite not being abstinent from
ED symptoms, because the social phobia is severely impacting her social functioning, symptoms and behaviors related to social concerns are interwoven into treatment. Treatment targets are rank-ordered based on their impact on functioning and
include (1) social avoidance, (2) reduction of binge/purge behaviors, and (3) body
image dissatisfaction. To target social avoidance, the clinician utilizes a CBT protocol for social anxiety in which cognitive restructuring is used to modify beliefs
about the perceived threat from others, and exposure experiments are used to vio-
late expectancies and to allow the client's situational anxiety to habituate.

Treatment Selection and Behavioral Target Identification

SELECTING TREATMENT FOR A COMORBID ANXIETY AND EATING DISORDER
Despite the fact that a comprehensive treatment package is unavailable for most
comorbid ED–AD presentations, effective treatments do exist for many eating

and anxiety disorder subtypes. Evidence-based treatment should be used for those illness subtypes for which an efficacious treatment exists. Thus, for someone presenting with an AD, primary consideration should be given to utilizing a targeted CBT protocol. Similarly, an evidence-based treatment should be selected for the treatment of ED subtypes. In the case example, Sofia has a diagnosis of both BN and social phobia. As such, the clinician selected CBT-E for BN symptoms and a CBT protocol for social anxiety.

Prioritizing Treatment Targets

When considering how to deliver combined treatment, behaviors that are life-threatening or have the potential to impact physical health should be prioritized. Most often, these will fall under the umbrella of the ED diagnosis. Thus, due to their effect on physical health, ED symptoms often take precedence relative to other psychological illnesses.

It can be difficult to separate out which symptoms of anxiety predated the onset of the ED versus which are a result of the starvation state induced by the ED. Keys' seminal Minnesota Starvation Study demonstrated that semistarvation can result in psychiatric and cognitive impairments including significant obsessionality around food, ritualistic behavior, and perseveration (Keys, Brožek, Henschel, Mickelsen, & Taylor, 1950). This suggests that the acute state of illness may cause or amplify anxious traits. In further support of this, studies comparing differences in traits during acute phases of illness and after recovery have shown that traits are exaggerated by illness state (Harrison, Tchanturia, & Treasure, 2010; Kaye & Strober, 1999; Lilenfeld et al., 2000). This is an important consideration because it indicates that disordered eating causes physiological processes that lead to symptoms of anxiety. As such, targeting irregular eating patterns should be prioritized and occur first or, at a minimum, simultaneously with targeting of anxiety symptoms. Indeed, it is not uncommon for clinicians to see a clinically meaningful change in anxiety symptoms following the resumption of regular meals and snacks or upon restoration of weight.

Once life-threatening behaviors and physiological issues have been addressed, other treatment targets surrounding both the eating and the anxiety problem can be established. Behavioral targets should be prioritized based on the degree to which they are impeding functioning. For example, if a client presents with concurrent OCD and AN, ideally, a clinician would first ensure that treatment is focused on restoring the client to an appropriate weight. This is particularly important because OCD symptoms could be exacerbated or be an artifact of a client's compromised weight status. Accordingly, at this stage of treatment, targeting OCD symptoms directly may be unproductive. Ideally, treatment should focus on supporting return to a healthy weight status due to the relative severity of this symptom. Once medical conditions are ruled out, secondary treatment targets can be established. With this in mind, upon remission from symptoms causing physiological changes, treatment may alternate between targeting ED symptoms and anxiety symptoms. In practice, however, this may be difficult due to the limitations in effective treatment options for EDs. EDs can be treatment-resistant, and currently available treatments have limited efficacy. As such, clinicians should re-evaluate the treatment plan if lack of progress in eating symptoms results in a delay in targeting meaningful AD symptoms, and a combined, multimodal approach (described later) can be considered.

In the case example, the clinician began targeting Sofia's social phobia after she established a regular eating pattern (no restriction) and binging and purging behaviors were reduced but stable. Upon regulating her intake patterns and reducing binging and purging behaviors, her social avoidance was more prominently impeding her functioning compared to her ED behaviors. Furthermore, her ED behaviors remained stable at three times per week and did not appear to be further decreasing.

Once appropriate treatments are selected for each diagnosis and behavioral targets are identified, decisions about how to prioritize treatment targets and deliver dual treatment must be made. Options for an eating disorder clinician to consider in delivering ED–AD treatments include a referral to an anxiety disorder specialist for separate but concurrent specialist treatment, a unified treatment protocol that concomitantly targets both symptom clusters, or an approach that targets shared underlying personality and temperament traits.

Separated, Concurrent Treatment

In the presence of an AD that is severely impacting functioning, affected individuals can receive concurrent treatment from a separate provider who specializes in evidence-based treatments for ADs. This is recommended if the AD is causing severe impairment but cannot be addressed immediately due to the prioritization of ED-related goals. For example, if a client has a concurrent diagnosis of AN and OCD, an ED provider may need all treatment resources to focus on weight restoration and ED behaviors. However, if the OCD spans beyond eating issues and compulsive rituals are severely impacting functioning, a clinician may decide to refer the client to see an OCD specialist. Treatment coordination should involve providing psychoeducation to the AD provider regarding the potential impacts of the ED on anxiety status (e.g., low weight exacerbating OCD rituals). After rank ordering treatment targets related to both the diagnoses of BN and the diagnoses of social phobia, Sofia's clinician decided not to refer to an outside specialist because the ED symptoms were (1) more imminent, (2) impeding her ability to engage in any social activities or experiments due to the amount of time that they were consuming, and (3) exacerbating her social anxiety due to the negative emotions experienced following ED behaviors.

Integrated Treatment Approaches

Integrated treatment approaches involve a multimodal treatment plan targeting both eating pathology and symptoms of anxiety. Multidiagnostic treatments are complex and require careful consideration of the order in which the targeted symptoms are addressed (see Prioritizing Treatment Targets). A unified protocol may also be appropriate when treatment is focused on targeting a shared underlying mechanism such as avoidance, conditioned fear, or a shared personality trait. In these instances, both anxiety and eating pathology can be targeted with interventions aimed at a common mechanism. Given the broader shift toward a more mechanistic understanding of psychopathology (Insel et al., 2010), a number of novel approaches are emerging that focus on treating mechanisms underlying eating pathology that are also known to drive anxiety (Hill, Peck, Wierenga, & Kaye, 2016). Integrated treatments that have been proposed primarily borrow from cognitive–behavioral models of treatment established for ADs, which are based on a mechanistic understanding of how symptoms are maintained (Pallister & Waller, 2008; Simpson et al., 2013). These treatment approaches are discussed next.

EATING DISORDERS AND OBSESSIVE–COMPULSIVE DISORDER

Integrated, multimodal treatment has been proposed for comorbid OCD and EDs, with a protocol that is designed to address eating-, weight-, and shape-related obsessions and compulsions using exposure and response prevention (ERP) methods, in addition to more traditional OCD behaviors (Simpson et al., 2013). According to this model and provided that one is trained in ERP methods, a multimodal protocol addressing both traditional OCD and eating-related pathology can be delivered in conjunction with more standard treatment targeting the ED, including meal planning. Even in the absence of an OCD diagnosis, if an ED individual exhibits obsessive or rule-bound thoughts and ritualistic behaviors around eating, an ERP approach focused on extinguishing ritualistic behaviors may also be considered. Preliminary data collected from ED individuals enrolled in a residential program suggest that such an approach is effective in reducing both OCD and ED severity (Simpson et al., 2013).

INTEGRATED COGNITIVE–BEHAVIORAL THERAPY APPROACHES

Because a cognitive–behavioral framework has been used for both conceptualization and treatment in EDs and ADs, some experts suggest targeting ADs and EDs concurrently (Pallister & Waller, 2008). This can be done by targeting shared underlying factors and maladaptive coping strategies using a cognitive–behavioral framework. Under this framework, avoidance behaviors pertinent to both disordered eating and anxiety are considered and targeted simultaneously. Avoidance behaviors that serve to mitigate the experience of anxiety and act as maintenance factors in both disorders are targeted directly using CBT methods. Such a treatment includes a range of behavioral experiments aimed at reducing safety behaviors involved with both eating and anxiety. In addition, cognitive interventions include modifying and restructuring threat-related cognitions (Pallister & Waller, 2008). Given the relative success of CBT with ADs and BN, it is possible that an integrated CBT framework focused on (1) targeting maladaptive thoughts related to both worry and eating, shape, and weight and (2) imposing behavioral experiments focused on exposure to noxious stimuli (e.g., binge food and relevant anxiety-related stimuli) and preventing a response that serves to diffuse feelings (binge eating) may prove effective. For AN, it is less likely that such a method would be potent given the lack of evidence supporting CBT for AN. The lack of support for CBT in AN may suggest that mechanisms driving restrictions are unique and thus require a different treatment approach.

EXPOSURE AND RESPONSE PREVENTION

Exposure and response prevention, a CBT method, has been used to effectively treat a wide array of ADs, including OCD and simple phobias. ERP methods for bulimia were carried out and written on extensively in the 1980s and 1990s until a large-scale randomized controlled trial determined that the method did not impart any additional significant benefits to standard CBT (Bulik, Sullivan, Carter, McIntosh, & Joyce, 1998).

Recently, ERP methods have been proposed for AN based on data supporting the overlap of EDs with anxiety. The model is based on the premise that anxiety in response to eating-related stimuli and the feared outcome of weight gain yields eating-related fears, avoidance behaviors, and ritualistic ED behaviors used as safety behaviors. According to this theoretical framework, targeting underlying anxiety, or fear of food, via ERP reduces ED behaviors (Murray, Loeb, et al., 2016; Murray, Treanor, et al., 2016; Steinglass et al., 2011, 2014). Preliminary pilot data showed a reduction in premeal anxiety and an increase in caloric intake following the intervention; however, effect sizes were small, and larger scale trials are needed to determine the efficacy of the approach.

Targeting Shared Underlying Personality Traits

In addition to targeting shared underlying mechanisms, shared temperament and personality traits can also be targeted as a way to improve both ED- and AD-related behaviors, given the shared commonalities. Temperament and personality traits associated with both illnesses include trait anxiety, perfectionism, harm avoidance, and obsessionality. As predisposing factors, these traits may be important treatment targets, particularly because of their enduring nature. Indeed, studies suggest that the presence and severity of certain anxiety-related traits predict poor outcome, implicating these traits as critical treatment targets. Despite established data affirming the potency of these characteristics in determining eating pathology, there are no proven treatments that directly target them. Research is currently underway to establish a temperament-based treatment for adult EDs (Kaye et al., 2015; Knatz, Wierenga, Murray, Hill, & Kaye, 2015) that focuses on improving clients' understanding of these traits and their relationship to eating pathology. Importantly, this treatment assumes that traits are premorbid and biologically driven and thus are persistent rather than transient. As such, rather than attempting to change them, clients learn to use them in constructive (vs. destructive) ways and learn tools to cope with deficits resulting from these traits. For example, for a client with low tolerance for uncertainty and high levels of obsessionality, a highly structured meal plan that allows for consistency and sameness in food choices but ensures caloric sufficiency may enable weight progress and meal regularity by reducing the anxiety associated with the unknown. For a client who is highly sensitive to punishment, outcomes may be improved by using an established system of accountability with a family member or provider whereby certain goals must be attained and met in order to continue participating in college or a sport. Although a unified protocol for targeting this underlying temperament is not currently available, possessing a working knowledge of the role of anxiety and related traits will assist providers in delivering more focused interventions that could potentially improve outcomes.

CONCLUSION AND FUTURE DIRECTIONS

Eating disorders and anxiety disorders are highly comorbid, and the presence of anxiety within EDs has important prognostic and treatment implications. The co-occurrence of these illnesses is likely related to shared vulnerability factors including a common temperament profile and shared functional mechanisms driving both ED and AD behaviors. Given the substantial degree of co-occurrence and the overlap in underlying vulnerabilities, clinical guidelines for the assessment and treatment for an ED–AD diagnosis are critical. Recommendations for multidiagnostic clients could improve treatment outcomes and assist providers with organizing treatment targets for complex cases. Treatment providers should be aware of the impact that the presence of an AD has on treatment and prognosis and, furthermore, be aware of resources for unified protocols. In addition, understanding shared vulnerability factors allows clinicians to make informed decisions about treatment and to construct an integrated treatment approach that considers underlying mechanisms and thus will improve the likelihood of having a successful impact.

REFERENCES

Agras, W. S., Walsh, B. T., Fairburn, C. G., Wilson, G. T., & Kraemer, H. C. (2000). A multicenter comparison of cognitive–behavioral therapy and interpersonal psychotherapy for bulimia nervosa. *Archives of General Psychiatry, 57*(5), 459–466.

American Psychiatric Association. (2013). *Diagnostic and statistical manual of mental disorders* (5th ed.). Arlington, VA: American Psychiatric Publishing.

Birmingham, C. L., Su, J., Hlynsky, J. A., Goldner, E. M., & Gao, M. (2005). The mortality rate from anorexia nervosa. *International Journal of Eating Disorders, 38*(2), 143–146.

Bulik, C. M., Sullivan, P. F., Carter, F. A., McIntosh, V. V., & Joyce, P. R. (1998). The role of exposure with response prevention in the cognitive–behavioural therapy for bulimia nervosa. *Psychological Medicine, 28*(3), 611–623.

Bulik, C. M., Sullivan, P. F., Fear, J. I., & Joyce, P. R. (1997). Eating disorders and antecedent anxiety disorders: A controlled study. *Acta Psychiatrica Scandinavica, 96*(2), 101–107.

Button, E. J., Chadalavada, B., & Palmer, R. L. (2010). Mortality and predictors of death in a cohort of patients presenting to an eating disorders service. *International Journal of Eating Disorders, 43*(5), 387–392.

Crosby, R., Wonderlich, S., Engel, S., Simonich, H., Smyth, J., & Mitchell, J. (2009). Daily mood patterns and bulimic behaviors in the natural environment. *Behaviour Research and Therapy, 47*, 181–188.

Crow, S. J., Peterson, C. B., Swanson, S. A., Raymond, N. C., Specker, S., Eckert, E. D., & Mitchell, J. E. (2009). Increased mortality in bulimia nervosa and other eating disorders. *American Journal of Psychiatry, 166*(12), 1342–1346.

Degnan, K. A., & Fox, N. A. (2007). Behavioral inhibition and anxiety disorders: Multiple levels of a resilience process. *Development and Psychopathology, 19*(3), 729–746.

Fairburn, C. G., Cooper, Z., Doll, H. A., O'Connor, M. E., Bohn, K., Hawker, D. M., . . . Palmer, R. L. (2009). Transdiagnostic cognitive–behavioral therapy for patients with eating disorders: A two-site trial with 60-week follow-up. *American Journal of Psychiatry, 166*(3), 311–319.

Fairburn, C. G., Cooper, Z., & Shafran, R. (2003). Cognitive behaviour therapy for eating disorders: A "transdiagnostic" theory and treatment. *Behaviour Research and Therapy, 41*(5), 509–528.

Godart, N. T., Flament, M. F., Perdereau, F., & Jeammet, P. (2002). Comorbidity between eating disorders and anxiety disorders: A review. *International Journal of Eating Disorders, 32*(3), 253–270.

Goodman, W. K., Price, L. H., Rasmussen, S. A., Mazure, C., Fleischmann, R. L., Hill, C. L., . . . Charney, D. S. (1989). The Yale–Brown obsessive compulsive scale: I. Development, use, and reliability. *Archives of General Psychiatry, 46*(11), 1006–1011.

Haedt-Matt, A., & Keel, P. (2011). Revisiting the affect regulation model of binge eating: A meta-analysis of studies using ecological momentary assessment. *Psychological Bulletin, 137*, 660–681.

Handley, A. K., Egan, S. J., Kane, R. T., & Rees, C. S. (2014). The relationships between perfectionism, pathological worry and generalised anxiety disorder. *BMC Psychiatry, 14*(1), 1.

Harrison, A., Tchanturia, K., & Treasure, J. (2010). Attentional bias, emotion recognition, and emotion regulation in anorexia: State or trait? *Biological Psychiatry, 68*(8), 755–761.

Hettema, J. M., Neale, M. C., & Kendler, K. S. (2001). A review and meta-analysis of the genetic epidemiology of anxiety disorders. *American Journal of Psychiatry, 158*(10), 1568–1578.

Hill, L., Peck, S. K., Wierenga, C. E., & Kaye, W. H. (2016). Applying neurobiology to the treatment of adults with anorexia nervosa. *Journal of Eating Disorders, 4*(1), 31.

Hjern, A., Lindberg, L., & Lindblad, F. (2006). Outcome and prognostic factors for adolescent female in-patients with anorexia nervosa: 9- to 14-year follow-up. *British Journal of Psychiatry, 189*(5), 428–432.

Insel, T., Cuthbert, B., Garvey, M., Heinssen, R., Pine, D. S., Quinn, K., . . . Wang, P. (2010). Research domain criteria (RDoC): Toward a new classification framework for research on mental disorders. *American Journal of Psychiatry, 167*(7), 748–751.

Kaye, W. (2008). Neurobiology of anorexia and bulimia nervosa. *Physiology & Behavior,* *94*(1), 121–135.

Kaye, W. H., Bulik, C. M., Thornton, L., Barbarich, N., & Masters, K. (2004). Comorbidity of anxiety disorders with anorexia and bulimia nervosa. *American Journal of Psychiatry, 161*(12), 2215–2221.

Kaye, W. H., Fudge, J. L., & Paulus, M. (2009). New insights into symptoms and neurocircuit function of anorexia nervosa. *Nature Reviews Neuroscience, 10*(8), 573–584.

Kaye, W. H., & Strober, M. (1999). Neurobiology of eating disorders. In D. E. Charney, E. J. Nestler, & B. S. Bunney (Eds.), *Neurobiological foundations of mental illness* (pp. 891–906). New York, NY: Oxford University Press.

Kaye, W. H., Strober, M., & Klump, K. L. (2003). Neurobiology of eating disorders. In A. Martin, L. Scahill, D. S. Charney, & J. F. Leckman (Eds.), *Pediatric psychopharmacology: Principles & practice* (pp. 224–237). New York, NY: Oxford University Press.

Kaye, W. H., Wierenga, C. E., Knatz, S., Liang, J., Boutelle, K., Hill, L., & Eisler, I. (2015). Temperament-based treatment for anorexia nervosa. *European Eating Disorders Review, 23*(1), 12–18.

Keel, P. K., & Brown, T. A. (2010). Update on course and outcome in eating disorders. *International Journal of Eating Disorders, 43*(3), 195–204.

Keel, P. K., Mitchell, J. E., Miller, K. B., Davis, T. L., & Crow, S. J. (1999). Long-term outcome of bulimia nervosa. *Archives of General Psychiatry, 56*(1), 63–69.

Keys, A., Brožek, J., Henschel, A., Mickelsen, O., & Taylor, H. L. (1950). *The biology of human starvation* (2 vols.). St. Paul, MN: University of Minnesota.

Knatz, S., Wierenga, C. E., Murray, S. B., Hill, L., & Kaye, W. H. (2015). Neurobiologically informed treatment for adults with anorexia nervosa: A novel approach to a chronic disorder. *Dialogues in Clinical Neuroscience, 17*(2), 229.

Lavender, J. M., De Young, K. P., Wonderlich, S. A., Crosby, R. D., Engel, S. G., Mitchell, J. E., . . . Le Grange, D. (2013). Daily patterns of anxiety in anorexia nervosa: Associations with eating disorder behaviors in the natural environment. *Journal of Abnormal Psychology, 122*(3), 672.

Le Grange, D., Crosby, R. D., Rathouz, P. J., & Leventhal, B. L. (2007). A randomized controlled comparison of family-based treatment and supportive psychotherapy for adolescent bulimia nervosa. *Archives of General Psychiatry, 64*(9), 1049–1056.

Le Grange, D., Lock, J., Agras, W. S., Moye, A., Bryson, S. W., Jo, B., & Kraemer, H. C. (2012). Moderators and mediators of remission in family-based treatment and adolescent focused therapy for anorexia nervosa. *Behaviour Research and Therapy, 50*(2), 85–92.

Lilenfeld, L. R., Kaye, W. H., Greeno, C. G., Merikangas, K. R., Plotnicov, K., Pollice, C., . . . Nagy, L. (1998). A controlled family study of anorexia nervosa and bulimia nervosa: Psychiatric disorders in first-degree relatives and effects of proband comorbidity. *Archives of General Psychiatry, 55*(7), 603–610.

Lilenfeld, L. R., Stein, D., Bulik, C. M., Strober, M., Plotnicov, K., Pollice, C., . . . Kaye, W. H. (2000). Personality traits among currently eating disordered, recovered and never ill first-degree female relatives of bulimic and control women. *Psychological Medicine, 30*(6), 1399–1410.

Lilenfeld, L. R., Wonderlich, S., Riso, L. P., Crosby, R., & Mitchell, J. (2006). Eating disorders and personality: A methodological and empirical review. *Clinical Psychology Review, 26*(3), 299–320.

Lock, J., Le Grange, D., Agras, W. S., Moye, A., Bryson, S. W., & Jo, B. (2010). Randomized clinical trial comparing family-based treatment with adolescent-focused individual therapy for adolescents with anorexia nervosa. *Archives of General Psychiatry, 67*(10), 1025–1032.

Milos, G., Spindler, A., Ruggiero, G., Klaghofer, R., & Schnyder, U. (2002). Comorbidity of obsessive–compulsive disorders and duration of eating disorders. *International Journal of Eating Disorders, 31*(3), 284–289.

Murray, S. B., Loeb, K. L., & Le Grange, D. (2016). Dissecting the core fear in anorexia nervosa: Can we optimize treatment mechanisms? *JAMA Psychiatry, 73*(9), 891–892.

Murray, S. B., Treanor, M., Liao, B., Loeb, K. L., Griffiths, S., & Le Grange, D. (2016). Extinction theory and anorexia nervosa: Deepening therapeutic mechanisms. *Behaviour Research and Therapy, 87*, 1–10.

Otte, C. (2011). Cognitive behavioral therapy in anxiety disorders: Current state of the evidence. *Dialogues in Clinical Neuroscience, 13*(4), 413–421.

Pallister, E., & Waller, G. (2008). Anxiety in the eating disorders: Understanding the overlap. *Clinical Psychology Review, 28*(3), 366–386.

Papadopoulos, F. C., Ekbom, A., Brandt, L., & Ekselius, L. (2009). Excess mortality, causes of death and prognostic factors in anorexia nervosa. *British Journal of Psychiatry, 194*(1), 10–17.

Schmidt, U., Lee, S., Beecham, J., Perkins, S., Treasure, J., Yi, I., . . . Johnson-Sabine, E. (2007). A randomized controlled trial of family therapy and cognitive behavior therapy guided self-care for adolescents with bulimia nervosa and related disorders. *American Journal of Psychiatry, 164*(4), 591–598.

Simpson, H. B., Wetterneck, C. T., Cahill, S. P., Steinglass, J. E., Franklin, M. E., Leonard, R. C., . . . Riemann, B. C. (2013). Treatment of obsessive–compulsive disorder complicated by comorbid eating disorders. *Cognitive Behaviour Therapy, 42*(1), 64–76.

Smink, F. R., Van Hoeken, D., & Hoek, H. W. (2012). Epidemiology of eating disorders: Incidence, prevalence and mortality rates. *Current Psychiatry Reports, 14*(4), 406–414.

Steinglass, J. E., Albano, A. M., Simpson, H. B., Wang, Y., Zou, J., Attia, E., & Walsh, B. T. (2014). Confronting fear using exposure and response prevention for anorexia nervosa: a randomized controlled pilot study. *International Journal of Eating Disorders, 47*(2), 174–180.

Steinglass, J. E., Sysko, R., Glasofer, D., Albano, A. M., Simpson, H. B., & Walsh, B. T. (2011). Rationale for the application of exposure and response prevention to the treatment of anorexia nervosa. *International Journal of Eating Disorders, 44*(2), 134–141.

Steinglass, J. E., Sysko, R., Mayer, L., Berner, L., Schebendach, J., Wang, Y., . . . Walsh, B. T. (2010). Pre-meal anxiety and food intake in anorexia nervosa. *Appetite, 55*, 214–218.

Steinhausen, H. C. (2002). The outcome of anorexia nervosa in the 20th century. *American Journal of Psychiatry, 159*(8), 1284–1293.

Strober, M. (2004). Pathologic fear conditioning and anorexia nervosa: On the search for novel paradigms. *International Journal of Eating Disorders, 35*(4), 504–508.

Sullivan, P. F. (1995). Mortality in anorexia nervosa. *American Journal of Psychiatry, 152*(7):1073–1074.

Vitousek, K., & Manke, F. (1994). Personality variables and disorders in anorexia nervosa and bulimia nervosa. *Journal of Abnormal Psychology, 103*, 137–147.

Wagner, A., Barbarich-Marsteller, N. C., Frank, G. K., Bailer, U. F., Wonderlich, S. A., Crosby, R. D., . . . Kaye, W. H. (2006). Personality traits after recovery from eating disorders: Do subtypes differ? *International Journal of Eating Disorders, 39*(4), 276–284.

Watson, H. J., & Bulik, C. M. (2013). Update on the treatment of anorexia nervosa: Review of clinical trials, practice guidelines and emerging interventions. *Psychological Medicine, 43*(12), 2477–2500.

Wonderlich, S. A., Lilenfeld, L. R., Riso, L. P., Engel, S., & Mitchell, J. E. (2005). Personality and anorexia nervosa. *International Journal of Eating Disorders, 37*(Suppl. 1), S68–S71.

3

Treating Eating Disorder–Posttraumatic Stress Disorder Patients

A Synthesis of the Literature and New Treatment Directions

JULIE G. TRIM, TARA E. GALOVSKI, AMY WAGNER, AND TIMOTHY D. BREWERTON ∎

Eating disorder (ED) patients who report a history of trauma—or furthermore, those who meet full criteria for posttraumatic stress disorder (PTSD)—pose several challenges to the practitioner wishing to deliver evidence-based treatment (EBT). ED practitioners may have expertise in eating disorders, but few ED practitioners have strong training or experience with PTSD and associated comorbidities (Trottier, Monson, Wonderlich, McDonald, & Olmstead, 2016). Working with this subgroup requires specialized training in PTSD assessment and, of course, treatment. Diagnosing PTSD can be difficult in ED individuals because ED symptoms can "mask" or suppress PTSD symptoms, and PTSD symptoms can overlap with other psychiatric disorders such as major depressive disorder (Brady, Killeen, Brewerton, & Lucerini, 2000; Gros, Price, Magruder, & Frueh, 2012). ED practitioners and their patients are faced with complex questions: When to start PTSD treatment? What type of PTSD treatment to use? When to pause or stop PTSD treatment (if a problem arises)? Although research on EDs and PTSD is abundant, clear guidelines for treating this population are lacking.

TRAUMA EXPOSURE

Traumatic events are common in the general population, with the majority of the US population experiencing at least one traumatic event during the course of their lives (e.g., natural disasters, motor vehicle accidents, combat, sexual and/ or physical assaults, and domestic violence episodes) (Kessler, Sonnega, Bromet, Hughes, & Nelson, 1995). A host of factors influence risk for trauma exposure, including age, gender, race and ethnicity, culture, socioeconomic status, geographical locale, and other individual factors (for review, see Lowe, Blachman-Forshay, & Koenen, 2015). Following a traumatic event, many people exhibit behaviors or symptoms of PTSD, but typically these symptoms decrease over time. Risk for the development of PTSD varies by several factors, including the type of trauma (sexual assaults and rape are associated with the highest rates of PTSD) (Bronner et al., 2009), the number of traumas experienced (Finkelhor, Ormrod, & Turner, 2007), prior history of anxiety and depression (Dickstein, Suvak, Litz, & Adler, 2010), stress reactivity/sensitivity, poor social support, and genetic predisposition (Brewerton, 2015; Lowe, Galea, Uddin, & Koenen, 2014).

PREVALENCE RATES OF TRAUMA WITHIN THE EATING DISORDER POPULATION

Prevalence rates of trauma among individuals with EDs have varied considerably due to methodological differences across studies (e.g., differences in recruitment and assessment), but they have ranged from 37% (Dalle Grave, Rigamonti, Todisco, & Oliosi, 1996) to 100% (Mitchell, Mazzeo, Schlesinger, Brewerton, & Smith, 2012). For example, the studies by Dalle Grave and colleagues and Mitchell and colleagues were conducted in different countries (Italy vs. the United States, respectively), were conducted during different time periods, and, perhaps most important, used considerably different definitions of trauma. Nonetheless, the majority of studies in this area have found significantly higher prevalence rates of trauma exposure in ED individuals compared to the general population (Dansky, Brewerton, Kilpatrick, & O'Neil, 1997). Mitchell and colleagues, for example, analyzed data from 2,980 participants in the National Comorbidity Study–Replication who were assessed for ED symptoms. They found that 100% of men and women with bulimia nervosa (BN) or anorexia nervosa (AN) endorsed some form of trauma during their lives, as did 90% of women and 98% of men with binge-eating disorder (BED). In all diagnostic and gender groups, the rates of an interpersonal trauma ranged from 64% in women with BED to 100% in men and women with BN or AN (Table 3.1).

Of the various types of trauma, ED pathology has been repeatedly linked with abuse, particularly childhood sexual abuse (CSA) (Brewerton, 2007; Wonderlich, 2001). Reyes-Rodriguez and colleagues (2011) found that the most common traumatic events reported by participants with PTSD were sexual-related traumas during childhood (40.8%) and during adulthood (35.0%). Other studies have also demonstrated that individuals with childhood physical and sexual abuse were at elevated risk for EDs (Johnson, Cohen, Kasen, & Brook, 2002; Léonard, Steiger, & Kao, 2003). Virtually all studies that have examined the chronology of trauma exposure and ED onset have shown that the traumatic event typically preceded the ED (Brewerton, 2007; Dansky et al., 1997). This has led several investigators

Table 3.1 TYPES OF TRAUMA BY EATING DISORDER IN WOMEN
AND MEN— NATIONAL COMORBIDITY STUDY REPLICATION

Women	BN ($n = 45$)	BED ($n = 75$)	AN ($n = 18$)
Any type of trauma	100%	90%	100%
Any interpersonal trauma	78%	64%	71%
Men	**BN ($n = 7$)**	**BED ($n = 30$)**	**AN ($n = 3$)**
Any type of trauma	100%	98%	100%
Any interpersonal trauma	100%	74%	68%

AN, anorexia nervosa; BED, binge-eating disorder; BN, bulimia nervosa.

SOURCE: Adapted from Mitchell, K., Mazzeo, S. E., Schlesinger, M. R., Brewerton, T. D., & Smith, B. R. (2012). Comorbidity of partial and subthreshold PTSD among men and women with eating disorders in the National Comorbidity Survey–Replication study. *International Journal of Eating Disorders, 45*(3), 307–315.

to conclude that trauma exposure (and most notably CSA) is a nonspecific risk factor for ED development (Brewerton, 2004, 2005, 2006, 2007; Smolak & Murnen, 2002).

Although trauma exposure appears to be more common among individuals with bulimic symptoms (e.g., BN and AN-purge or AN-binge/purge), some data suggest that there are also higher rates in individuals with AN compared with the general population. For example, Woodside and Staab (2006) estimated that approximately 50% of patients with AN–restrictive type (AN-R) and 80% of those with AN–binge/purge type (AN-BP) who admitted to their inpatient ED unit endorsed a history of physical and sexual abuse. Carter, Bewell, Blackmore, and Woodside (2006) found similar results in their examination of ED symptoms, general psychopathology, and CSA in 77 consecutive inpatients diagnosed with AN: 48% reported CSA that preceded the development of their ED, and significantly higher rates of CSA were found in patients with AN-BP compared to those with AN-R.

HISTORY OF MULTIPLE TRAUMATIC EVENTS

ED–PTSD individuals who report a history of several types of sexual abuse (or abuse perpetrated by different individuals) seem to be at risk for a myriad of psychological problems. Ackard and Neumark-Sztainer (2003) reported that girls with a history of multiple forms of sexual abuse were more likely than their nonabused peers to binge, vomit, abuse laxatives and diet pills, fast, and contemplate suicide. Likewise, boys with multiple forms of abuse had statistically significant odds ratios for laxative abuse, vomiting, diet pill abuse, thinking about/attempting suicide, binge eating, and fasting. In addition, using an adult population-based sample (N = 1,987), Schoemaker, Smit, Bijl, and Vollebergh (2002) observed that a history of multiple abuses appeared to be a specific risk factor for BN as well as a dual diagnosis disorder (comorbid psychiatric + substance use disorder).

PREVALENCE RATES OF PTSD WITHIN THE EATING DISORDER POPULATION

Several investigators have posited that individuals with an ED may be more susceptible to developing PTSD than non-ED individuals. As is widely known, many individuals with an ED have one or more comorbid anxiety disorders that often predate the ED (Bulik, Sullivan, Fear, & Joyce, 1997; Kaye, Bulik, Thornton, Barbarich, & Masters, 2004). This predisposition to anxiety has been shown to result in a "heightened perception of a reaction to threat, as well as increased sensitivity to stress, trauma, and adversity" (Brewerton, 2015, p. 452). For example, Strober (2004) posited that ED individuals exhibit more extreme fear conditioning and are more resistant to fear extinction compared to people without EDs. Thus, the experience of threat or danger is subjective, and people with EDs may be more prone to perceive a situation as threatening or traumatic (Brewerton, 2015).

In US adults (general population), the lifetime prevalence of PTSD is estimated to be 6.4% (Breslau, Troost, Bohnert, & Luo, 2013). Prevalence rates of PTSD in the ED population are less clear, in part because few studies have examined PTSD rates, specifically, in this population (Brewerton, 2007). There are also important methodological differences between studies (e.g., use of different PTSD measures and examining lifetime vs. current PTSD rates) that make comparisons and generalizations difficult. The studies that do exist seem to indicate a slightly higher rate of PTSD among ED populations.

For example, the National Women's Study (NWS), the most comprehensive study to date on trauma, PTSD, EDs, and associated comorbidities, examined PTSD rates among women with EDs (N = 3,006) (Dansky et al., 1997). Participants with BN or BED had significantly higher lifetime PTSD rates than the non-ED participants. Specifically, 37% of women with BN met criteria for lifetime PTSD compared to 21% in BED and approximately 12% in non-ED participants. Current PTSD rates followed a different pattern: 21.4% of those with BN met criteria, whereas those with BED had comparable (and, in fact, slightly lower) rates of current PTSD compared to non-ED participants (1.7% in BED and 4.2% in non-ED participants). Importantly, the prevalence of BN was significantly higher among participants who were raped and met PTSD criteria (10.4%) compared to participants who had been raped and did not have PTSD (2%) or those who did not report a rape history (2%). This demonstrates that having a trauma or abuse history *in and of itself* is not associated with having an ED; instead, having PTSD is associated with having an ED (Dansky et al., 1997). This is consistent with Brewerton's (2007) finding that PTSD mediated the effect of trauma on ED development.

Prevalence rates were also higher in the Genetics of Anorexia Nervosa Collaborative Study, a 12-site study consisting of 400 families in which 2 or more relatives met criteria for AN. Reyes-Rodriguez and colleagues (2011) found that 13.7% of women with AN ($n = 753$) in this study met criteria for lifetime PTSD (compared to 11.7% in the general population). Importantly, women with AN-P were much more likely to meet PTSD criteria than those who solely restricted (i.e., AN-R). Although many studies on AN and PTSD unfortunately have not examined differences across AN subtypes, data from this study demonstrate that PTSD is more common in "bulimic EDs" than in nonbulimic/pure restricting EDs.

CHARACTERISTICS OF EATING DISORDER PATHOLOGY IN ED–PTSD INDIVIDUALS

Individuals with PTSD and EDs present with a range of ED diagnoses and behaviors. However, as noted previously, studies have repeatedly shown that binging and purging behaviors are core ED features in this population (Brewerton, 2004; Wonderlich, Brewerton, Jocic, Dansky, & Abbott, 1997). Binging or overeating may be a self-soothing strategy in ED-PTSD. Some investigators have argued that ED-PTSD individuals may experience "food addiction," which is based on the notion that highly palatable foods act like substances of abuse in the brain (Gearhardt et al., 2011). Eating foods in excess may therefore serve to numb a traumatized individual from unpleasant feelings and memories and to decrease emotional arousal, which are core features of PTSD (Brewerton, 2014; Hirth, Rahman, & Berenson, 2011).

Research indicates that purging behaviors likely have a similar function. In an ecological momentary assessment study of 119 women with BN, including 20 with PTSD and 99 without, Karr and colleagues (2013) showed that those in the PTSD group had greater mean daily levels of negative affect and a greater frequency of bulimia behaviors compared to those without PTSD. In addition, results indicated that the PTSD group had a faster acceleration in positive affect after purging. This suggests that purging may function as a powerful emotion regulation strategy in individuals with PTSD, possibly even more "effective" in the short term than in people without PTSD. It is not surprising, then, that ED–PTSD individuals are more likely to engage in multiple forms of purging compared to ED individuals without PTSD (Brewerton, Dansky, Kilpatrick, & O'Neil, 1999; Dansky et al., 1997).

Binging and purging appear to be more associated with trauma and PTSD than food restriction. However, as noted previously, the prevalence of trauma exposure and PTSD also seems to be greater in restricting-type AN than in the general population (Reyes-Rodriguez et al., 2011). Individuals with AN tend to be highly anxious, harm avoidant, cognitively rigid, and less able to tolerate uncertainty (Brewerton & Dennis, 2016). If someone with these traits experiences a traumatic event that disrupts his or her worldview, restriction can provide a sense of structure, predictability, and control (Serpell, Treasure, Teasdale, & Sullivan,

1999). In addition, if restriction results in AN, the individual may reach a place of emotional numbness and may feel powerful or invincible, which may be welcome experiences for a traumatized individual (Kyriacou, Easter, & Tchanturia, 2009).

GREATER PSYCHIATRIC COMORBIDITY IN ED–PTSD POPULATIONS

ED–PTSD individuals tend to have significantly greater psychiatric comorbidity compared to ED individuals without PTSD (Brewerton, 2007; Carter et al., 2006; Danksy et al., 1997). Common comorbid disorders include substance use disorders (Brewerton & Brady, 2014; Dansky, Brewerton, & Kilpatrick, 2000; Killeen et al., 2015), mood disorders (Dansky et al., 2000), impulse control disorders (Fernandez-Aranda et al., 2008), and borderline personality disorder (BPD) (Brewerton, 2007; Hoerster et al., 2015; Wonderlich et al., 1997; Wonderlich, Joiner, Keel, Williamson, & Crosby, 2007). Using data from the NWS, Brewerton and colleagues (2015) found significant relationships between the number of purging behaviors used and lifetime rates of victimization, PTSD, major depressive disorder, alcohol abuse, and total comorbid disorders. These comorbidities may impart greater ED psychopathology as well as a more complicated course of recovery. In fact, the presence of a diagnosis of PTSD is a significant predictor of poor prognosis in EDs (Herpertz-Dahlmann et al., 2001; Keel & Brown, 2010). Therefore, it has been suggested that PTSD must be addressed in order for the individual to fully recover from the ED (Brewerton, 2004, 2007, 2015).

THE IMPACT OF PTSD ON EATING DISORDER TREATMENT

Psychiatric comorbidity may complicate treatment for any psychiatric disorder, and this can certainly be true with PTSD. In general, studies differ to the extent that non-ED comorbid disorders (e.g., anxiety disorders) are found to contribute to poorer outcomes in PTSD, with some citing no negative impact on treatment outcome and others suggesting it may impede progress (Rauch, Eftekhari, & Ruzek, 2012; Steenkamp, Litz, Hoge, & Marmar, 2015; van Minnen, Zoellner, Harned, & Mills, 2015). EBTs for PTSD have generally shown success with treatment gains generalizing to other psychiatric conditions, but the extent of improvements in comorbid conditions ranges across studies (Steenkamp et al., 2015; van Minnen et al., 2015; Watts et al., 2013).

From the authors' experience, when an ED patient has PTSD, there are certain areas of sensitivity or conflict that arise in ED treatment and present additional barriers to success. The experience of a traumatic event can cause significant shifts in survivors' views of the world, self, and others. Disruptions in one's sense of safety, trust, power/control, intimacy, and esteem have been shown to be particularly salient in trauma survivors, with implications for the development and maintenance of more long-term consequences such as PTSD (Janoff-Bulman,

1989). Anecdotally, it is often these areas that pose additional challenges to the clinician treating ED–PTSD patients. This can happen in several ways:

Safety: Safety may, for example, be associated with weight in some ED–PTSD individuals who experienced trauma when they were a particular size or weight. Size/weight may be intentionally manipulated to provide a sense of protection against being re-traumatized (e.g., "Since I was sexually assaulted when I was at an appropriate weight, staying underweight will keep me safe."). This shift in worldview (in this case, concerning body weight) suggests that the survivor is considering his or her weight to be the factor that caused the assault (e.g., "If I hadn't looked a certain way, I wouldn't have been raped."). It is precisely these types of self-blaming beliefs that may maintain PTSD for a trauma survivor.

Trust: It is generally difficult for ED individuals to trust their treatment providers with regard to food, weight, and exercise recommendations. With an ED–PTSD patient, there are often additional barriers to trust given that interpersonal traumas (e.g., abuse or assault) often lead to a general distrust of others.

Power/control: ED–PTSD patients often report feeling "in control" if they are able to make choices about their food and weight, and treatment typically involves letting go and allowing others (e.g., a dietitian) to influence these decisions. For ED–PTSD patients, this seems to trigger a strong pull to regain control and may lead these patients to "dig their heels in" and refuse to follow their team's recommendations. Power/control issues may also emerge in intensive ED treatment settings, which are highly structured and supervised. The rules of the treatment center may lead ED–PTSD patients to feel extremely safe (i.e., one of the only safe places they have) or could be perceived as an unnecessary restriction of their rights, power, and control.

All of these sensitivities (i.e., safety, trust, and power/control) make sense given the patient's history. However, they can lead to a "bumpy road" in treatment and, in some cases, may result in dropout or premature termination from treatment.

EMPIRICALLY SUPPORTED PTSD TREATMENTS

During the past three decades, research on PTSD and trauma-related disorders has proliferated. A host of evidence-based psychological and pharmacological interventions for the treatment of posttraumatic distress continue to gain empirical support, with several being identified as front-line therapies. These front-line therapies include prolonged exposure (PE; Foa et al., 1999), cognitive processing therapy (CPT; Resick, Monson, & Chard, 2014), stress inoculation training (Meichenbaum & Cameron, 1989), trauma-focused cognitive–behavioral therapy (for children and adolescents; Cohen, Mannarino, Perel, & Staron, 2007), and eye movement desensitization reprocessing (EMDR; Shapiro, 2001). These therapies have consistently demonstrated large effect sizes across clinical trials for primary outcomes, and they have shown similar efficacy across a host of secondary outcomes, clinical correlates, and in important areas of patient functioning.

THE STATE OF THE LITERATURE ON PTSD TREATMENT IN EATING DISORDER INDIVIDUALS

Although there is now a sizable evidence base for these PTSD treatments, there are few guidelines or "best practices" for treating PTSD in ED–PTSD individuals. Trottier and colleagues' (2016) article on "front-line" ED clinicians' perceptions and utilization of trauma-focused therapy highlights clinicians' eagerness for such guidelines. Clinicians surveyed in that study viewed trauma-related symptoms as a major obstacle to ED recovery, and the majority anticipated that PTSD treatment for their patients would reduce self-harm and suicidality and improve eating disorder symptoms, long-term outcomes, the therapeutic alliance and treatment retention. Despite these anticipated benefits, clinicians reported considerable barriers to delivering PTSD treatment to their patients. Potential barriers listed in the survey included (1) uncertainty about how to integrate trauma work with ED treatment, (2) lack of training in trauma-focused treatment, (3) institutional financial constraints, (4) not an institutional priority, (5) belief that trauma-focused treatment is a "long-term" endeavor, (6) preference for individualized treatment, (7) perceived readiness of the patient for trauma-focused work, and (8) concerns about psychiatric decompensation. Approximately half of participating clinicians anticipated at least four of these barriers, and 12% anticipated all eight. Furthermore, clinicians' comfort level in delivering EBT for PTSD was low (Trottier et al., 2016).

It is understandable that ED clinicians may feel uneasy. The ED clinician must make several decisions in formulating a plan for PTSD treatment, and some of these decisions may be fairly arbitrary given the dearth of research in this area. Possibly the least arbitrary (although still complex) of these decisions is determining when the patient is ready for PTSD treatment. In some cases, other problems should be addressed prior to starting PTSD treatment (e.g., danger to self/others, safety concerns, and psychological conditions that interfere with the patient's ability to receive or benefit from PTSD treatment), but PTSD treatment can be started as soon as these issues are resolved (Resick et al., 2014). Brewerton (2004) argued that within the ED population, PTSD treatment should not begin until (1) the patient indicates a readiness to begin trauma work, (2) the patient is adequately nourished and able to process information emotionally and cognitively, (3) the patient's eating disorder symptoms are relatively under control, and (4) the patient has demonstrated an adequate level of distress tolerance. Clinicians who work primarily with PTSD may be cautious about delaying treatment because delays may "collude" with or perpetuate avoidance. ED clinicians may be less concerned with trauma-related avoidance and more focused on ED symptom abatement. Although PTSD clinicians and ED clinicians agree on the need for stabilization of severe eating disorder symptoms prior to commencing trauma work, there is no consensus on exact readiness criteria, and to date, there is a lack of conclusive research on the best approach.

A related issue is sequencing of ED and PTSD treatment, which has been the subject of much debate and is a critical consideration in treatment planning. Treatment can be sequential (i.e., with ED treatment first or PTSD treatment first) or concurrent/integrated (i.e., provided at the same time). There are some well-founded arguments for sequential treatment. First, treating one condition first might be important for safety reasons. If the patient is medically compromised due to the ED (or if the patient is stable but malnourished enough to affect cognitive functioning), the ED should be treated first—at least until these issues have resolved. Second, treating one condition first may be important for reducing barriers to effectiveness of the other treatment. If the patient is reliant on ED behaviors (or substance use, etc.) to manage difficult emotions, PTSD treatment may not be as effective. Alternatively, if the clinician conceptualizes the ED behaviors as trauma-related avoidance and is able to convince the patient that avoidance perpetuates PTSD, the patient may be sufficiently motivated to decrease ED behaviors so that PTSD treatment can be more effective.

One of the problems with sequential treatment, however, is that treating one disorder can often lead to a worsening of the other, resulting in a self-perpetuating cycle that can prevent recovery from both disorders (Ackard & Brewerton, 2010; Levitt, 2007). PTSD treatment involves confronting painful memories and emotions, so the ED patient may have increased behaviors in order to cope. These behaviors, in turn, serve to aid the patient in avoiding unpleasant trauma-related memories and emotions, and this avoidance maintains PTSD. Concurrent treatment can be effective at minimizing this "whack-a-mole" phenomenon of replacing one set of symptoms with another. Consequently, during the past 30 years, there has been a growing recognition of the value of *concurrent* or *integrated* treatment across several comorbidities, and this approach has been advocated for ED–PTSD treatment (Brewerton, 2004; Levitt, 2007; Trottier et al., 2016).

In the absence of clear data on how to prioritize treatment targets, a case formulation approach is recommended (Brewerton, 2004; Persons, 2005). This is a case-by-case approach in which functional links between behaviors are hypothesized, tested, and continually refined, and appropriate interventions are delivered based on these links (for a detailed description, see Persons, 2005). For example, a clinician may hypothesize that a patient began exercising 3 hours a day because it facilitated avoidance of trauma-related emotions and memories and gave her a sense of safety because she was becoming strong and "tough." Once these functional links are understood, the clinician can prioritize treatment and deliver an appropriate EBT for the primary treatment target.

Another decision in treatment planning is determining which PTSD treatment will be used. As noted previously, four EBTs for PTSD are considered the "gold standard"—PE, CPT, EMDR, and trauma-focused CBT (TF-CBT)—and outcomes have been very similar across these treatments. To date, there have not been any large-scale randomized clinical trials (RCTs) comparing PTSD treatments "head-to-head." The Veterans Administration (VA) is currently conducting the first PTSD study of this scope—a 17-site RCT of PE and CPT called CERV-PTSD (Comparative Effectiveness Research for Veterans with PTSD). This study will yield important data on the relative effectiveness of CPT and PE, as well as moderators of treatment outcome (i.e., which treatment works best for which kinds of clients).

Given the paucity of comparative research on PTSD treatments in general, it is not surprising that there are no data that clearly indicate which treatment(s) is most effective for individuals with EDs. Moreover, ED clinicians may not be utilizing EBTs for PTSD in their work with these patients. The study by Trottier and colleagues (2016) suggests that ED clinicians as a whole are not very comfortable (or even familiar) with EBTs for PTSD. On a Likert scale of 1 (not at all) to 5 (extremely), the mean level of clinician comfort and familiarity with EBTs for PTSD was a 2. Of those who delivered PTSD treatment, 31% reported using TF-CBT for children and adolescents, 25% used CPT, 7% used PE, 4% used EMDR, and 20% used a treatment that was not evidence-based. It is unclear how ED clinicians decide which PTSD EBT to use (if they are trained in more than one EBT). Patient preference has been shown to contribute to treatment outcome, so it is generally advised to discuss this collaboratively with the patient (Schumm, Walter, Bartone, & Chard, 2015).

To the authors' knowledge, only two outcome studies have been published on the use of an evidence-based PTSD treatment in an ED–PTSD sample. Mott, Menefee, and Leopolous (2012) reported a case study of a woman in a residential treatment center who received daily CPT sessions and imaginal exposure twice weekly. Mitchell, Wells, Mendes, and Resick (2012) studied 65 women with PTSD who completed the Eating Disorder Inventory-2 (EDI-2; Garner, 1991) at the start and end of CPT. Both studies showed pre–post improvements in PTSD scores, and the latter study also documented improvements on several subscales of the EDI-2.

Mott and colleagues (2012) noted that because CBT is a first-line treatment for both EDs and PTSD, teaching patients how to challenge cognitive distortions may target a shared vulnerability and thus be a logical treatment choice. Therefore, CPT or PE may be an effective treatment for many patients with EDs. However, ED–PTSD individuals with more pronounced emotion dysregulation may require a treatment approach that takes into account all of their problem behaviors. These patients may engage in high-risk behaviors (e.g., self-injury and active suicidal ideation) and have significant therapy-interfering behaviors (e.g., using substances before coming to therapy), which can undermine the effectiveness of PTSD treatment.

AN EMERGING TREATMENT APPROACH TO MULTIPROBLEM INDIVIDUALS WITH PTSD: THE DIALECTICAL BEHAVIOR THERAPY PROLONGED EXPOSURE PROTOCOL

Dialectical behavior therapy (DBT; Linehan, 1993) has strong empirical support for the treatment of behaviors related to BPD, and it has also been shown to be effective with a range of other problems and diagnoses (Miller, 2015). Stage I targets indices of behavioral dyscontrol, with the overall goals of safety and behavioral control. Consistent with other stage-oriented approaches for PTSD, PTSD is a primary target for stage II DBT, addressed after behavioral control is established in stage I. However, in Linehan's original treatment manual, readiness criteria were not specifically defined, nor was a particular approach for the treatment of PTSD articulated (although Linehan has always promoted the utilization of exposure for PTSD and empirically supported protocols for different disorders within DBT as treatment-indicated). Harned, Linehan, and colleagues (Harned, Korslund, Foa, & Linehan, 2012; Harned, Korslund, & Linehan, 2014) have developed a protocol for treating PTSD within DBT, integrating PE with standard DBT (referred to as "DBT PE"). PE was chosen over other trauma processing therapies because exposure-based interventions are most compatible with DBT and have strong empirical support (Harned, 2013; Linehan, 1993). Individuals in DBT PE receive standard DBT, including individual DBT, skills groups, and telephone coaching, as well as PE as outlined by Foa, Hembree, and Rothbaum (2007). As in standard PE, DBT PE sessions include a pre-exposure phase, exposure sessions (both in vivo and imaginal exposure), and a consolidation/termination phase.

A key component of DBT PE is a behaviorally specific and theoretically based set of readiness criteria (Box 3.1) that prioritize the reduction of high-risk behavior and the acquisition of emotion regulation strategies prior to starting PTSD treatment. Because avoidance is a central feature of PTSD, some degree of avoidance about starting trauma processing is to be expected; otherwise, the patient might not meet criteria for PTSD. However, when the avoidance takes the form of a high-risk behavior (e.g., self-mutilation) or a significant therapy-interfering behavior (frequent purging used to suppress emotions), PTSD treatment may not be effective. Therefore, prior to starting DBT PE, the therapist uses motivation and commitment strategies to "sell" the patient on PE for trauma and explains that maladaptive behaviors need to be dramatically reduced or eliminated for the treatment to be effective.

Pre-exposure sessions orient the patient to the treatment, link PTSD treatment to the patient's main treatment goals, obtain a detailed trauma history, and determine the traumatic event(s) that will be the focus of the imaginal exposure. A primary goal of the pre-exposure phase is to increase motivation and willingness to engage in the treatment. In addition to obtaining the patient's commitment to complete homework assignments, the patient must also commit to refraining from self-harm and other problematic behaviors that could interfere with the treatment. To this end, the therapist and patient develop a Post-Exposure Skills

Box 3.1

GUIDELINES FOR STARTING TRAUMA TREATMENT

ED Guidelines[1]

1. Establish chronology/sequence of events and educate about all disorders.
2. Identify functional links between disorders—for example, binge eating, purging, and starvation may serve as possible strategies to facilitate avoidance/numbing, decrease hyperarousal, and regulate trauma-related states ("self-medication hypothesis").
3. Address first the current level of danger, risk, and/or brain/body impairment.
4. Establish the patient's readiness to begin trauma work.
5. Establish that the patient is nourished and able to process information emotionally and cognitively.
6. Patient's ED symptoms are relatively under control.
7. Patient demonstrates an adequate level of distress tolerance.

DBT PE Guidelines[2]

1. Patient is not at imminent risk of suicide.
2. Patient has not had any recent (past 2 months) life-threatening behavior.
3. Patient has the ability to control life-threatening behaviors in the presence of cues for those behaviors.
4. There is no serious therapy-interfering behavior.
5. PTSD is the highest priority target for the client and the client wants PTSD treatment *now*.
6. Patient has the ability and willingness to experience intense emotions without escaping.

---

[1] Adapted from Brewerton, T. D. (2004). Eating disorders, victimization and PTSD: Principles of treatment. In T. D. Brewerton (Ed.), *Clinical handbook of eating disorders: An integrated approach* (pp. 509–545). New York, NY: Dekker.

[2] Adapted from Harned, M. S. (2013). Treatment of posttraumatic stress disorder with comorbid borderline personality disorder. In D. McKay & E. Storch (Eds.), *Handbook of treating variants and complications in anxiety disorders* (pp. 203–221). New York, NY: Springer.

Plan, which includes DBT skills to improve coping and prevent dysfunctional behaviors.

The DBT PE protocol includes procedures for addressing higher target behaviors if they arise during the course of PE. In most cases, PE is temporarily stopped until the higher target behavior is sufficiently addressed (no longer occurring). Harned (2013) outlines specific considerations regarding whether to stop the protocol and when to resume exposure, taking into account the riskiness of the behavior, the degree to which the behavior interferes with the treatment, and the potential rein-forcing and punishing effects of stopping exposure. When the protocol is on hold, sessions focus on addressing the higher target behaviors with standard DBT proce-dures (e.g., conducting a behavioral chain analysis on the behavior).

The data on DBT PE are compelling. In both an open trial and an RCT, individuals who received DBT PE showed significant reductions in PTSD symptoms as well as reductions in suicidal ideation, depression, dissocia-tion, shame, trauma-related guilt cognitions, and anxiety (Harned et al., 2012, 2014). Importantly, those who received DBT PE did not evidence worsening of suicidal behavior, suggesting that even among highly disordered individuals, a trauma-processing treatment for PTSD is well tolerated and effective when embedded within DBT.

APPLYING THE DBT PE PROTOCOL TO ED–PTSD PATIENTS

DBT PE is a relatively new protocol, and there have not yet been any published studies on the implementation of it in the ED–PTSD population. It appears to be a promising approach to treating PTSD in ED–PTSD patients—particularly those with severe or complex presentations—and it fits in well with the treat-ment recommendations that have been made for ED–PTSD patients. A close look at Brewerton's and Harned's readiness criteria will show considerable theo-retical overlap (see Box 3.1). Both emphasize that the patient needs to be willing to reduce avoidance behaviors and to have adequate distress tolerance skills to facilitate the experiencing of intense or difficult emotions. This is because PTSD treatment may not be effective if trauma-related thoughts and emotions are sup-pressed through maladaptive behaviors. Brewerton's criterion of being adequately nourished seems consistent with Harned and colleagues' criterion of "no major therapy-interfering behaviors" because being inadequately nourished is a unique (and important) therapy-interfering behavior seen in ED patients. Currently, it is little data on whether the use of a different EBT for PTSD (e.g., CPT) would be equally effective if the DBT PE principles were followed (i.e., readiness criteria and review of higher treatment targets). As mentioned previously, there is evidence that CPT may be an effective treatment for individuals with ED– PTSD. Trim and colleagues at the University of California-San Diego are applying PE principles to PTSD-ED patients and have found promising results. Data were collected on 15 female patients age 18–40 (M_{age} = 25.16, SD = 5.67) completed 12 group sessions of CPT while enrolled in UCSD's ED partial hospitalization or intensive outpa-tient program. They completed self-report measures of PTSD symptoms (PCL-5; Blevins, Weathers, Davis, Witte, & Domino, 2015), depressive symptoms (BDI-II; Beck, Steer, & Brown, 1996), and eating pathology (EDEQ; Mond, Hay, Rodgers, & Owen, 2006) pre- and post-treatment. Paired samples t-tests indicated that there were statistically significant improvements in PTSD symptoms (M = 11.47, SD = 11.73) post-treatment, $t(14)$, 3.79, $p < .01$. Furthermore, decreases in ED pathology and depressive symptoms trended towards being statistically significant,

$t(7) = 2.23$, $p = .06$, and $t(7) = 2.21$, $p = .06$, respectively. These preliminary data suggest that integrating CPT into ED treatment may be effective in concurrently treating ED and PTSD symptoms in this population (unpublished data, 2017).

CONCLUSION

This chapter reviewed the state of the literature on treating PTSD in individuals with a co-occurring ED. Although there is considerable research on prevalence and comorbidity rates in ED–PTSD individuals, there is a dearth of studies on PTSD treatment for ED patients. Important "who, what, where, when, and why" questions have not been adequately answered (and in some cases have not been asked):

Who: ED–PTSD patients who meet readiness criteria are appropriate for PTSD treatment. However, it has been suggested that ED individuals with subthreshold PTSD can also greatly benefit from PTSD treatment (Brewerton, 2007; Mitchell, Mazzeo, et al., 2012). What is the cut-off point or threshold that determines appropriateness for PTSD treatment?

What: The most robust literature on ED–PTSD patients seems to be with CPT. However, no empirical studies have compared EBTs for PTSD in ED–PTSD individuals. Because there are not any evidence-based recommendations supporting the use of one EBT over another, clinicians seem to be using the PTSD treatment(s) that they were trained in or with which they are most familiar.

When: Although the DBT PE protocol provides a helpful framework for determining PTSD treatment readiness, it does not explicitly address ED-related targets such as weight loss/gain, binge or purge episodes, and so on. If the patient loses 3 pounds or has a dramatic increase in compensatory behaviors during trauma treatment, what should the clinician do? How much does the clinician "allow" for a temporary increase in those behaviors at the beginning of trauma treatment, as is often the pattern?

Why: This has been a neglected area within the ED field for some time, despite an accumulating literature indicating that these patients are at significantly higher risk for higher severity, more psychiatric comorbidity, and worse outcomes. ED clinicians believe that PTSD treatment can be very important for their patients, but many have concerns about delivery of PTSD treatment.

These are extremely important questions—questions that need to be answered through rigorous research. Thus far, treating these patients has involved pulling bits of information from various literatures (e.g., PTSD research and research on self-injurious patients with trauma) with little empirical guidance. People with EDs have characteristics that may prove important and distinct from those without EDs, and these characteristics may impact the acceptability and effectiveness of standard PTSD treatments. During the past decade, functional magnetic resonance imaging studies have substantiated that there are significant neurobiological alterations in individuals with EDs (Kaye, 2008), and these differences could have important implications for the development as well as the treatment of PTSD in ED individuals.

RECOMMENDATIONS FOR THERAPISTS

For the ED practitioner wanting to deliver evidence-based PTSD treatment, the authors have several recommendations. First, it is imperative to receive training from a reputable source on PTSD assessment and treatment and, ideally, to consult regularly with an expert in PTSD treatment. As a starting point, free online courses on CPT and TF-CBT are available on the MUSC.edu website (https://cpt.musc.edu and https://tfcbt.musc.edu), but more intensive training is often required in order to begin delivering PTSD treatment. Some VA hospitals offer 2-day and 3-day trainings, which are often followed by 6 months of weekly consultation calls to improve adherence to the protocol. The National Center for PTSD (www.ptsd.va.gov) can also be a helpful resource for practitioners to obtain consultation and access information related to PTSD.

Once trained in an evidence-based PTSD treatment, the authors recommend that practitioners utilize the DBT hierarchy with complex, comorbid patients to prioritize treatment targets and structure treatment. The DBT hierarchy monitors patient safety, minimizes behaviors that undermine or interfere with therapy, and provides a framework or "road map" for treatment. DBT PE principles may not only enhance treatment effectiveness but also allow ED practitioners to feel less trepidatious delivering PTSD treatment to their patients. Furthermore, because many PTSD patients would like to be free of their symptoms, making PTSD treatment contingent on elimination of higher treatment targets (i.e., life-threatening behavior and therapy-interfering behavior) can be a highly effective strategy for reducing both PTSD and higher treatment targets.

Finally, the authors encourage ED practitioners to use DBT PE principles (on treatment readiness, etc.) to pilot new treatments that integrate DBT with other evidence-based PTSD treatments, such as CPT, and to publish outcome data. One of the most important conclusions of the study by Trottier and colleagues (2016) is that more research is needed on the treatment of ED–PTSD patients. ED clinicians may perceive PTSD treatment as highly beneficial for some of their patients, but without dissemination of effective and safe treatments, practitioners will continue to struggle with how to best help this high-risk, difficult-to-treat population.

REFERENCES

Ackard, D. M., & Brewerton, T. D. (2010). Co-morbid trauma and eating disorders: Treatment considerations and recommendations for a vulnerable population. In

M. Maine, B. H. McGilley, & D. W. Bunnell (Eds.), *Treatment of eating disorders* (pp. 251–268). London, England: Elsevier.

Ackard, D. M., & Neumark-Sztainer, D. (2003). Multiple sexual victimizations among adolescent boys and girls: Prevalence and associations with eating behaviors and psychological health. *Journal of Child Sexual Abuse, 12*, 17–37.

Beck, A. T., Steer, R. A., & Brown, G. K. (1996). Beck depression inventory-II. *San Antonio, 78*(2), 490–498.

Blevins, C. A., Weathers, F. W., Davis, M. T., Witte, T. K., & Domino, J. L. (2015). The posttraumatic stress disorder checklist for DSM-5 (PCL-5): Development and initial psychometric evaluation. *Journal of Traumatic Stress, 28*(6), 489–498.

Brady, K. T., Killeen, T. K., Brewerton, T., & Lucerini, S. (2000). Comorbidity of psychiatric disorders and posttraumatic stress disorder. *Journal of Clinical Psychology, 61*, 22–32.

Breslau, N., Troost, J. P., Bohnert, K., & Luo, Z. (2013). Influence of predispositions on post-traumatic stress disorder: Does it vary by trauma severity? *Psychological medicine, 43*(2), 381–390.

Brewerton, T. D. (2004). Eating disorders, victimization and PTSD: Principles of treatment. In T. D. Brewerton (Ed.), *Clinical handbook of eating disorders: An integrated approach* (pp. 509–545). New York, NY: Dekker.

Brewerton, T. D. (2005). Psychological trauma and eating disorders. *Review of Eating Disorders, 1*, 137–154.

Brewerton, T. D. (2006). Comorbid anxiety and depression and the role of trauma in children and adolescents with eating disorders. In T. Jaffa & B. McDermott (Eds.), *Eating disorders in children and adolescents* (pp. 158–168). Cambridge, England: Cambridge University Press.

Brewerton, T. D. (2007). Eating disorders, trauma and comorbidity: Focus on PTSD. *Eating Disorders, 15*, 285–304.

Brewerton, T. D. (2015). Stress, trauma and adversity as risk factors in the development of eating disorders. In M. Levine & L. Smolak (Eds.), *Wiley handbook of eating disorders* (pp. 445–460). New York, NY: Guilford.

Brewerton, T. D. (2016). *Trauma, posttraumatic stress disorder, and eating disorders.* Retrieved from https://www.nationaleatingdisorders.org/trauma-posttraumatic-stress-disorder-and-eating-disorders

Brewerton, T. D., & Brady, K. T. (2014). The role of stress, trauma and PTSD in eating disorders, substance use disorders, and addictions. In T. D. Brewerton & A. B. Dennis (Eds.), *Eating disorders, addictions, and substance use disorders: Research, clinical and treatment aspects* (pp. 379–404). Berlin, Germany: Springer.

Brewerton, T. D., & Dennis, A. B. (2016). 3 Perpetuating Factors in Severe and Enduring Anorexia Nervosa. Managing Severe and Enduring Anorexia Nervosa: A Clinician's Guide, 28.

Bronner, M. B., Peek, N., Vries, M. D., Bronner, A. E., Last, B. F., & Grootenhuis, M. A. (2009). A community-based survey of posttraumatic stress disorder in the Netherlands. *Journal of Traumatic Stress, 22*(1), 74–78.

Bulik, C. M., Sullivan, P. F., Fear, J. L., & Joyce, P. R. (1997). Eating disorders and antecedent anxiety disorders: A controlled study. *Acta Psychiatrica Scandinavica, 96*, 101–107.

Carter, J. C., Bewell, C., Blackmore, E., & Woodside, D. B. (2006). The impact of childhood sexual abuse in anorexia nervosa. *Child Abuse & Neglect, 30*(3), 257–269.

Cohen, J. A., Mannarino, A. P., Perel, J. M., & Staron, V. (2007). A pilot randomized controlled trial of combined trauma-focused CBT and sertraline for childhood PTSD symptoms. *Journal of the American Academy of Child & Adolescent Psychiatry, 46*(7), 811–819.

Dalle Grave, R., Rigamonti, R., Todisco, P., & Oliosi, P. (1996). Dissociation and traumatic experiences and eating disorders. *European Eating Disorders Review, 4*(4), 232–240.

Dansky, B. S., Brewerton, T. D., & Kilpatrick, D. G. (2000). Comorbidity of bulimia nervosa and alcohol use disorders: Results from the National Women's Study. *International Journal of Eating Disorders, 27*(2), 180–190.

Dansky, B. S., Brewerton, T. D., Kilpatrick, D. G., & O'Neil, P. M. (1997). The National Women's Study: Relationship of victimization and posttraumatic stress disorder to bulimia nervosa. *International Journal of Eating Disorders, 21*(3), 213–228.

Dickstein, B. D., Suvak, M., Litz, B. T., & Adler, A. B. (2010). Heterogeneity in the course of posttraumatic stress disorder: Trajectories of symptomatology. *Journal of Traumatic Stress, 23*(3), 331–339.

Fernández-Aranda, F., Pinheiro, A. P., Thornton, L. M., Berrettini, W. H., Crow, S., Fichter, M. M., . . . & Rotondo, A. (2008). Impulse control disorders in women with eating disorders. *Psychiatry Research, 157*(1), 147–157.

Finkelhor, D., Ormrod, R. K., & Turner, H. A. (2007). Poly-victimization: A neglected component in child victimization. *Child Abuse & Neglect, 31*(1), 7–26.

Foa, E. B., Dancu, C. V., Hembree, E. A., Jaycox, L. H., Meadows, E. A., & Street, G. P. (1999). A comparison of exposure therapy, stress inoculation training, and their combination for reducing posttraumatic stress disorder in female assault victims. *Journal of Consulting and Clinical Psychology, 67*(2), 194.

Foa, E. B., Hembree, E. A., & Rothbaum, B. O. (2007). *Prolonged exposure therapy for PTSD: Emotional processing of traumatic experiences.* New York, NY: Oxford University Press.

Garner, D. M. (1991). *Eating Disorder Inventory-2: Professional manual.* Odessa, FL: Psychological Assessment Resources.

Gearhardt, A. N., Yokum, S., Orr, P. T., Stice, E., Corbin, W. R., & Brownell, K. D. (2011). Neural correlates of food addiction. *Archives of General Psychiatry, 68*(8), 808–816.

Gros, D., Price, K., Magruder, A., & Frueh, C. (2012). Symptom overlap in posttraumatic stress disorder and major depression. *Psychiatry Research, 126,* 267–270.

Harned, M. S. (2013). Treatment of posttraumatic stress disorder with comorbid borderline personality disorder. In D. McKay & E. Storch (Eds.), *Handbook of treating variants and complications in anxiety disorders* (pp. 203–221). New York, NY: Springer.

Harned, M. S., Korslund, K. E., Foa, E. B., & Linehan, M. M. (2012). Treating PTSD in suicidal and self-injuring women with borderline personality disorder: Development and preliminary evaluation of a dialectical behavior therapy prolonged exposure protocol. *Behaviour Research and Therapy, 50,* 381–386.

Harned, M. S., Korslund, K. E., & Linehan, M. M. (2014). A pilot randomized controlled trial of dialectical behavior therapy with and without the dialectical behavior therapy prolonged exposure protocol for suicidal and self-injuring women with borderline personality disorder and PTSD. *Behavior Research and Therapy, 55,* 7–17.

Herpertz-Dahlmann, B., Müller, B., Herpertz, S., Heussen, N., Hebebrand, J., & Remschmidt, H. (2001). Prospective 10-year follow-up in adolescent anorexia nervosa—course, outcome, psychiatric comorbidity, and psychosocial adaptation. *Journal of Child Psychology and Psychiatry, 42*(5), 603–612.

Hirth, J. M., Rahman, M., & Berenson, A. B. (2011). The association of posttraumatic stress disorder with fast food and soda consumption and unhealthy weight loss behaviors among young women. *Journal of Women's Health, 20*(8), 1141–1149.

Hoerster, K. D., Jakupcak, M., Hanson, R., McFall, M., Reiber, G., Hall, K., & Nelson, K. M. (2015). PTSD and depression symptoms are associated with binge eating among US Iraq and Afghanistan veterans. *Eating Behaviors, 17*, 115–118.

Janoff-Bulman, R. (1989). Assumptive worlds and the stress of traumatic events: Applications of the schema construct. *Social Cognition, 7*(2), 113–136.

Johnson, J. G., Cohen, P., Kasen, S., & Brook, J. S. (2002). Childhood adversities associated with risk for eating disorders or weight problems during adolescence or early adulthood. *American Journal of Psychiatry, 159*(3), 394–400.

Kaye, W. H. (2008). Neurobiology of anorexia and bulimia nervosa. *Physiology and Behavior, 94*(1), 121–135.

Kaye, W. H., Bulik, C. M., Thornton, L., Barbarich, N., & Masters, K. (2004). Comorbidity of anxiety disorders with anorexia and bulimia nervosa. *American Journal of Psychiatry, 161*, 2215–2221.

Keel, P. K., & Brown, T. A. (2010). Update on course and outcome in eating disorders. *International Journal of Eating Disorders, 43*(3), 195–204.

Kessler, R. C., Sonnega, A., Bromet, E., Hughes, M., & Nelson, C. B. (1995). Posttraumatic stress disorder in the National Comorbidity Study. *Archives of General Psychiatry, 52*, 1048–1060.

Killeen, T. K., Back, S. E., & Brady, K. T. (2015). Implementation of integrated therapies for comorbid post-traumatic stress disorder and substance use disorders in community substance abuse treatment programs. *Drug and Alcohol Review, 34*(3), 234–241.

Kyriacou, O., Easter, A., & Tchanturia, K. (2009). Comparing views of patients, parents, and clinicians on emotions in anorexia. *Journal of Health Psychology, 14*(7), 843–854.

Léonard, S., Steiger, H., & Kao, A. (2003). Childhood and adulthood abuse in bulimic and nonbulimic women: Prevalences and psychological correlates. *International Journal of Eating Disorders, 33*(4), 397–405.

Levitt, J. L. (2007). Treating eating disorder patients who have had traumatic experiences: A self-regulatory approach. *Eating Disorders, 15*, 359–372.

Linehan, M. (1993). *Cognitive–behavioral treatment of borderline personality disorder.* New York, NY: Guilford.

Lowe, S. R., Blachman-Forshay, J., & Koenen, K. C. (2015). Trauma as a public health issue: Epidemiology of trauma and trauma-related disorders. In U. Schnyder & M. Cloitre (Eds.), *Evidence based treatments for trauma-related psychological disorders* (pp. 11–40). New York, NY: Springer.

Lowe, S. R., Galea, S., Uddin, M., & Koenen, K. C. (2014). Trajectories of posttraumatic stress among urban residents. *American Journal of Community Psychology, 53*(1-2), 159–172.

Meichenbaum, D., & Cameron, R. (1989). Stress inoculation training. In D. Meichenbaum & M. Jaremko (Eds.), *Stress reduction and prevention* (pp. 115–154). New York, NY: Springer.

Miller, A. L. (2015). Introduction to a special issue dialectical behavior therapy: Evolution and adaptations in the 21st century. *American Journal of Psychotherapy, 69*(2), 91–95.

Mitchell, K. S., Mazzeo, S. E., Schlesinger, M. R., Brewerton, T. D., & Smith, B. R. (2012). Comorbidity of partial and subthreshold PTSD among men and women with eating disorders in the National Comorbidity Survey–Replication study. *International Journal of Eating Disorders, 45,* 307–315.

Mitchell, K. S., Wells, S. Y., Mendes, S. A., & Resick, P. A. (2012). Treatment improves symptoms shared by PTSD and disordered eating. *Journal of Traumatic Stress, 25*(5), 535–542.

Mond, J. M., Hay, P. J., Rodgers, B., & Owen, C. (2006). Eating Disorder Examination Questionnaire (EDE-Q): norms for young adult women. *Behaviour Research and Therapy, 44*(1), 53–62.

Mott, J. M., Menefee, J. S., & Leopolous, W. S. (2012). Treating PTSD and disordered eating in the wake of military sexual trauma. *Clinical Case Studies, 11*(2), 104–118.

Persons, J. B. (2005). Empiricism, mechanism, and the practice of cognitive–behavior therapy. *Behavior Therapy, 36*(2), 107–118.

Rauch, S. A., Eftekhari, A., & Ruzek, J. I. (2012). Review of exposure therapy: A gold standard for PTSD treatment. *Journal of Rehabilitation Research and Development, 49*(5), 679–688.

Resick, P. A., Monson, C. M., & Chard, K. M. (2014). *Cognitive processing therapy: Veteran/military version: Therapist's manual.* Washington, DC: US Department of Veterans Affairs.

Reyes-Rodriguez, M. L., Von Holle, A., Ulman, F., Thornton, L. M., Klump, K. L., Brandt, H., . . . Bulik, C. M. (2011). Post traumatic stress disorder in anorexia nervosa. *Psychomatic Medicine, 73*(6), 419–497.

Schoemaker, C., Smit, F., Bijl, R. V., & Vollebergh, W. A. (2002). Bulimia nervosa following psychological and multiple child abuse: Support for the self-medication hypothesis in a population-based cohort study. *International Journal of Eating Disorders, 32,* 381–388.

Schumm, J. A., Walter, K. H., Bartone, A. S., & Chard, K. M. (2015). Veteran satisfaction and treatment preferences in response to a posttraumatic stress disorder specialty clinic orientation group. *Behaviour Research and Therapy, 69,* 75–82.

Serpell, L., Treasure, J., Teasdale, J., & Sullivan, V. (1999). Anorexia nervosa: Friend or foe? *International Journal of Eating Disorders, 25*(2), 177–186.

Smolak, L., & Murnen, S. K. (2002). A meta-analytic examination of the relationship between child sexual abuse and eating disorders. *International Journal of Eating Disorders, 31,* 136–150.

Steenkamp, M. M., Litz, B. T., Hoge, C. W., & Marmar, C. R. (2015). Psychotherapy for military-related PTSD: A review of randomized clinical trials. *Journal of the American Medical Association, 314*(5), 489–500.

Strober, M. (2004). Pathologic fear conditioning and anorexia nervosa: On the search for novel paradigms. *International Journal of Eating Disorders, 35,* 504–508.

Trottier, K., Monson, C. M., Wonderlich, S. A., McDonald, D. E., & Olmstead, M. P. (2016). Frontline clinicians' perspective on and utilization of trauma-focused therapy with individuals with eating disorders. *Eating Disorders, 24,* 1–15.

van Minnen, A., Zoellner, L. A., Harned, M. S., & Mills, K. (2015). Changes in comorbid conditions after prolonged exposure for PTSD: A literature review. *Current Psychiatry Reports, 17,* 1–16.

Watts, B. V., Schnurr, P. P., Mayo, L., Young-Xu, Y., Weeks, W. B., & Friedman, M. J. (2013). Meta-analysis of the efficacy of treatments for posttraumatic stress disorder. *Journal of Clinical Psychiatry, 74*(6), 541–550.

Wonderlich, S. A., Brewerton, T. D., Jocic, Z., Dansky, B. S., & Abbott, D. W. (1997). Relationship of childhood sexual abuse and eating disorders. *Journal of the American Academy of Child and Adolescent Psychiatry, 36*, 1107–1115.

Wonderlich, S. A., Crosby, R. D., Mitchell, J. E., Thompson, K. M., Redlin, J., Demuth, G., Smyth, J., & Haseltine, B. (2001). Eating disturbance and sexual trauma in childhood and adulthood. *International Journal of Eating Disorders, 30*(4), 401–412.

Wonderlich, S. A., Joiner, T. E., Keel, P. K., Williamson, D. A., & Crosby, R. D. (2007). Eating disorder diagnoses: Empirical approaches to classification. *American Psychologist, 62*(3), 167–180.

Woodside, B. D., & Staab, R. (2006). Management of psychiatric comorbidity of anorexia nervosa and bulimia nervosa. *Therapy in Practice, 20*(8), 655–663.

4

The Complex Relationship Between Eating Disorders and Substance Use Disorders

Clinical Implications

AMY BAKER DENNIS AND TAMARA PRYOR ■

INTRODUCTION

Eating disorders (ED) and substance use disorders (SUD) frequently co-occur but are rarely treated in a comprehensive integrated manner. Substance abuse programs often do not admit patients with active eating disorders. Likewise, ED programs usually admit patients with over-the-counter diet pill, laxative, or diuretic abuse but exclude patients addicted to alcohol, benzodiazepines, cannabis, stimulants, or opiates. Unfortunately, this practice leads to consumer confusion, extends time in treatment, increases treatment costs, and can compromise continuity of care as patients travel through different levels of care (Dennis, Pryor, & Brewerton, 2014). In addition, studies suggest that patients who receive nonintegrated services have poorer treatment outcomes (Drake et al., 2001; Weisner, Mertens, Tam, & Moore, 2001).

The primary goal of this chapter is to elucidate the complex relationship between ED and SUD to help the treating professional create an integrated treatment plan that addresses both disorders and any other co-occurring conditions. To date, there are no randomized controlled treatment trials (RCTs) to guide the clinician in the treatment of this population. Our goal is to help the clinician create a flexible, individualized treatment plan that addresses both the ED and the SUD. This chapter content is based on our understanding of the research on evidence-based treatments (EBTs) in both fields and more than seven decades of combined clinical expertise in treating ED patients with comorbid conditions.

The chapter begins with a brief review of the prevalence of these comorbid disorders, followed by a discussion of how these disorders are similar and different from each other. Evidence-based treatments for each disorder are discussed, and recommendations on how to take "best practices" from both fields to formulate a treatment plan that addresses the specific needs of the patient are presented. The chapter concludes with case examples of different combinations of ED and SUD and demonstrates the importance of understanding the adaptive function of both disorders when developing an effective intervention.

PREVALENCE AND COMORBIDITY

According to The National Center on Addiction and Substance Abuse (CASA, 2003), approximately 50% of individuals with ED abuse alcohol or other illicit substances compared to 9% of the general public. Likewise, approximately 35% of individuals with SUD report having an ED (CASA, 2003). During the past three decades, meta-analyses have reported on rates of alcohol use disorder (AUD) and SUD in ED (Calero-Elvira et al., 2007). These studies report a strong association between SUD and anorexia nervosa–binge/purge subtype (AN-BP) and bulimia nervosa (BN) with no association between AUD/SUD and anorexia nervosa–restricting subtype (AN-R).

A multicenter study (Fouladi et al., 2015) explored the prevalence of alcohol and substance use in 2,633 participants with ED. The sample was divided into six ED subgroups (AN-R, AN-BP, BN, binge-eating disorder [BED], purging disorder [PD] and eating disorder not otherwise specified [EDNOS]). They found the highest prevalence of alcohol use (80%) and substance use (50.3%) in the BN subgroup compared to the AN-R group, which reported the lowest use (29.5% and 2.6%, respectively). In this study, the most prevalent drugs used were sedatives (19.4%), cannabis (11.9%), and caffeine pills (10%).

In addition to the substances reviewed in the previously mentioned studies, it is important to remember that individuals with ED also use and abuse a variety of other substances. "Over-the-counter" (OTC) products are substances that can be purchased in a pharmacy without a prescription, but they also include substances that can be bought in a health food store, grocery store, or on the Internet. Laxatives are the most common OTC substances utilized by individuals with ED, with prevalence rates ranging from 26% to 67% (Steffen, Mitchell, Roerig, & Lancaster, 2007). Approximately 31% of individuals with BN report using diuretics, and 64% use diet pills for weight loss purposes (Roerig et al., 2003).

Individuals with ED also use caffeine, nicotine, and artificial sweeteners to suppress appetite. In a large study of female twins, researchers reported that 26% of AN subjects and 23% of BN subjects met the criteria for caffeine disorder, and 52% of AN subjects and 45% of BN subjects were regular smokers (Baker, Mitchell, Neale, & Kendler, 2010). Finally, Klein, Boudreau, Devlin, and Walsh (2006) explored the weekly use of sorbitol (i.e., sugar-free gum), diet beverages, and artificial sweeteners in female ED patients. They found that women with

AN-BP and BN (the two groups that endorsed purging) reported higher use of chewing gum and diet beverages compared to women with AN-R. However, the weekly consumption of packets of artificial sweetener was significantly higher in the AN-R group.

Individuals with SUD rarely enter treatment without other psychiatric comorbidities. Approximately 23% of individuals with SUD have at least two additional comorbid disorders, and researchers have found that 28% of those seeking treatment for SUD will have five or more comorbid disorders (Compton, Thomas, Stinson, & Grant, 2007). Disorders that are commonly comorbid with SUD include mood disorders, anxiety disorders, posttraumatic stress disorder (PTSD), and borderline personality disorder.

THE COMPLEX RELATIONSHIP BETWEEN EATING DISORDERS AND SUBSTANCE USE DISORDERS

Eating disorders and substance use disorders are complex psychopathologies. It appears that alcohol and other substance abuse is more prevalent in ED subgroups that engage in binge eating/purging or just purging, with lower rates of SUD in individuals with AN-R. Clinically, the assumption is that individuals with AN-R have high levels of avoidance and obsessional thinking and will limit alcohol consumption due to the "caloric content" or avoid psychoactive drugs because they fear intoxication might lead to "loss of control." However, there is a significant body of research that elucidates the relationship between food restriction/starvation and the use of psychoactive substances (Carroll, France, & Meisch, 1979; Specker, Lac, & Carroll, 1994). This research has found that food deprivation leads to increased self-administration of virtually any psychoactive drug, including alcohol, nicotine, cocaine, amphetamines, barbiturates, phencyclidine, and opioids.

It is important for the clinician to be aware that substance abuse can begin before, occur concurrently with, or begin after the onset of an ED. Franko and colleagues (2008) conducted a prospective study of 246 patients with either AN or BN and explored the relationship between ED and AUD. Approximately 17% of the participants reported a history of AUD at intake. Franko et al. found that over the course of the study, 11 women experienced a new episode of AUD, and by 9 years' follow-up, an additional 24 individuals with no history of AUD had developed one. Kessler and colleagues (2005) found that rates of SUD increase in older patients, with one study reporting 50% of BN patients abusing alcohol by age 35 years (Beary, Lacey, & Merry, 1986). A 10-year prospective follow-up study of 95 non-substance using, adolescent patients hospitalized for AN found that 50% of the AN-BP patients and 12% of the AN-R patients developed a new SUD after discharge (Strober, Freeman, Bower, & Rigali, 1996). The study found that AN patients who engaged in binge eating had a higher chance for the development of SUD during the 10-year follow-up period and that there was a greater likelihood of SUD in a first-degree relative.

A review of the literature suggests that ED patients with co-occurring SUD have more severe ED and SUD symptomatology, higher relapse rates, more severe medical complications, and are more functionally impaired than individuals with ED alone (Courbasson, Smith, & Cleland, 2005; Garcia-Gomez, Gonzalez, del Barrio, & Garcia, 2009). Personality traits, specifically impulsivity (which is common in both ED and SUD), predict poorer outcome in the treatment of BN (Keel & Mitchell, 1997).

Based on the previously reviewed information, there are several important issues to keep in mind when treating this comorbid group. First, it is recommended that a thorough assessment at intake be made for the presence of substance use/abuse in all patients with ED, regardless of their initial ED diagnosis. A good assessment should include not only alcohol intake, prescription medications (e.g., attention deficit disorder medications, thyroid medications, and insulin), illicit substances, and over-the-counter and Internet supplements but also caffeine (pills, soft drinks, and coffee), tobacco, and the use of artificial sweeteners. Second, because SUD can develop at any time during the course of ED treatment, frequent monitoring and inquiry into substance use should occur throughout the treatment process.

SHARED CHARACTERISTICS AND DIFFERENCES

ED and SUD are both serious, life-threatening conditions. The presence of either disorder increases the risk of suicide, and when they are left untreated, they have high mortality rates (Bulik et al., 2008). They are both long-term, relapsing illnesses associated with significant medical complications and cognitive impairment that interferes with social, occupational, and interpersonal functioning.

Denial is another hallmark of both disorders. Individuals with AN often deny restricting, overexercising, purging, or low weight, even in the face of emaciation and serious medical complications. Underreporting substance use and/or quantities consumed is common in individuals with AUD/SUD. Individuals with AN, like substance abusers, rarely seek psychological treatment voluntarily. Most patients are referred by a concerned school counselor, coach, or physician, or they are coerced into treatment by a friend or family member.

Behaviorally, these two disorders appear quite similar. As alcohol/drug use continues and tolerance builds, patients describe intense cravings and uncontrollable consumption, despite negative consequences. Similarly, ED patients (particularly individuals with BN and BED) report powerful food cravings and a sensation of "loss of control" that leads to overconsuming. Food, drugs, and alcohol are often used for their mood-altering effects; to escape, avoid, or numb; or to manage negative emotional states.

As mentioned previously, there are high rates of mood, anxiety, PTSD, impulse control, and personality disorders in both ED and SUD. Trauma, including childhood sexual or physical abuse, rape, neglect, or witnessing violence, increases the risk for the development of both ED and SUD (Brewerton & Brady, 2014).

Finally, both disorders "run in families" and are heritable conditions. Studies report that 50–80% of the phenotypic variance found in AUD/SUD is due to genetic factors (Hicks, Krueger, Iaconco, & Patrick, 2004). Adolescents of parents who abuse illicit drugs are 45–79% more likely than the general population to abuse drugs (Agrawal & Lynskey, 2006). Likewise, twin studies in AN and BN, designed to distinguish environmental from genetic effects, reported that 50–80% of the contribution to liability is genetic (Bulik et al., 2006). Eating disorders are more prevalent in families in which another relative has an ED (Strober, Freeman, Lampert, Diamond, & Kaye, 2000).

A body of animal research is exploring the relationship between eating disorders and addictions (Murray, Gordillo, & Avena, 2014). Some researchers speculate that "highly palatable" foods (sugar, fats, salt, and caffeine) are potentially addictive and act much like licit and illicit substances of abuse in the brain (Avena, Gold, Kroll, & Gold, 2012). To date, however, there is a lack of human research evidence that individuals with ED are "allergic" or "addicted" to certain food substances or experience tolerance, physical dependence, or withdrawal.

From a psychological and pharmacological perspective, ED and SUD are unique disorders that are conceptualized and treated quite differently. Although both ED and SUD are classified as psychiatric illnesses and listed in the fifth edition of the *Diagnostic and Statistical Manual of Mental Disorders* (DSM-5; American Psychiatric Association, 2013), during the past several decades, there has been a strong movement by employee assistance programs and the medical community to view AUD and SUD as chronic *medical* illnesses that can be arrested but not cured. Treatment for SUD is designed to help patients increase restraint, and abstinence is considered the path to sustain remission. Most addiction treatment facilities focus solely on the elimination of the AUD/SUD because attempting to treat additional comorbid conditions (e.g., trauma, obsessive–compulsive disorder, and personality disorders) would be cost prohibitive. Although several pharmacological agents have been identified to assist in the treatment of AUD/SUD (i.e., medication-assisted therapy), there is still stigma attached to utilizing medications to treat substance abusers, and this treatment option remains underutilized (Kissin, McLeod, Sonnefeld, & Stanton, 2006). Individuals with SUD are strongly encouraged to continue participation in self-help programs (Alcoholics Anonymous [AA] and Narcotics Anonymous [NA]) during remission because this has been found to improve outcome and decrease relapse (Donovan et al., 2008).

Eating disorders are conceptualized as complex, curable *psychiatric* illnesses that require aggressive psychological intervention, medical management, and, in some instances, psychopharmacological intervention to treat target symptoms and/or other comorbid conditions. One of the primary goals of treatment is to moderate overcontrol (i.e., eliminate dieting, food restriction, and compensatory behaviors) and normalize eating patterns. Most ED treatment facilities attempt to treat the "whole person," which includes any other comorbid conditions. Self-help programs are not considered an essential component of ED treatment or recovery, and lifelong participation is not required to prevent relapse.

INTEGRATED TREATMENT

Defining Integrated Treatment

Integrated treatment for co-occurring psychiatric disorders has been detailed at length elsewhere (Kelly, Daley, & Douaihy, 2012; National Institute on Drug Abuse, 2012). Based on these sources, Dennis et al. (2014) developed a working definition of integrated treatment for patients with ED and SUD that includes the following elements: (1) a comprehensive screening utilizing evidence-based screening and assessment instruments to determine the presence of ED, SUD, and any other psychiatric disorders; (2) a complete medical evaluation that includes a medical history, review of systems, physical examination, and laboratory testing; (3) an individualized comprehensive treatment plan utilizing empirically supported treatment processes (McLellan, 2010), developed by the treatment team; (4) services are provided by individual therapists and treatment teams that are highly skilled in the delivery of EBT for ED/SUD and other comorbid psychiatric disorders; (5) services are provided in the same location by the same treatment providers utilizing a stepwise integrated approach; (6) development of a specific plan for patient movement through different levels of care to other integrated treatment programs to ensure continuity of care; and (7) development of a plan or contract with outside services that will be utilized during treatment but not available "onsite" (i.e., methadone maintenance and AA/NA meetings).

Rationale for Integrated Treatment

During the past two decades, there has been a significant movement in the mental health field toward integrated treatment for patients with co-occurring psychiatric disorders. Compared to patients who receive nonintegrated treatment, individuals who receive integrated treatments have reduced substance use; show significant improvement in psychiatric symptoms and functioning; and have decreased hospitalizations, fewer arrests, increased housing stability, and improved quality of life (Drake et al., 2001). To date, there are no studies that compare sequential or parallel treatment for ED/SUD patients to integrated treatment for this population. However, Dennis et al. (2014) hypothesize that integrated treatment for this population would improve treatment delivery, reduce time in treatment, lessen consumer confusion, reduce overall treatment costs, and improve treatment outcome.

Currently, a majority of the treatments provided for this comorbid population in the ED and SUD fields are being provided in a *sequential* or *parallel* manner, and the availability of fully integrated treatment is seriously lacking. There are very few addiction treatment centers that screen, admit, or treat SUD patients with active eating disorders (Gordon et al., 2008; Killeen et al., 2011). Similarly, very few ED programs provide integrated screening, assessment, and treatment of

SUD on site, and even fewer employ specialized professionals who are certified or licensed to treat SUD and addictions (Dennis & Helfman, 2010a).

Lack of access to integrated programing leaves the dually diagnosed patient vacillating between his or her ED and SUD (Dennis & Helfman, 2010b). It is not uncommon for patients who enter treatment for their SUD to experience an increase in ED symptoms as they are working on recovery. Likewise, patients being treated for an ED often increase their substance use when attempting to normalize their eating patterns and eliminate compensatory behaviors. As a result, even programs that do not admit patients with these co-occurring disorders may see the emergence or reemergence of the ED or SUD during the treatment process.

EVIDENCE-BASED TREATMENTS

This section focuses on a brief review of EBT SUD. The authors strongly believe that clinicians who work with eating disorders should be skilled in the treatment of complex psychopathology and well trained in EBT for all comorbidities that are common in ED. A more comprehensive discussion of EBT for both ED and SUD can be found elsewhere (Dennis & Pryor, 2014a, 2014b).

There has been a considerable amount of research exploring the efficacy of both psychological and pharmacologic interventions for the treatment of AUD and SUD. Similar to the treatment of ED, cognitive–behavioral therapy (CBT) has been found to be effective in the treatment of AUD (Miller & Wilbourne, 2002), cocaine use disorder (Carroll, Rounsaville, Nich, & Gordon, 1994), cannabis use disorder (Copeland, Swift, Roffman, & Stephans, 2001), opiate use disorders (Linehan et al., 2002), and polysubstance abuse (Pollack et al., 2002). Other EBTs for AUD/ SUD include motivational interviewing, an evidence-based, client-centered approach aimed at facilitating behavior change; dialectical behavior therapy (DBT; Linehan et al., 2002), a form of CBT that incorporates mindfulness strategies and focuses on affect regulation; contingency management, an intervention that applies operant conditioning principles of rewards and consequences; and 12-step facilitation, a structured, evidence-based, manual-driven approach designed to promote abstinence and active participation in a 12-step program. There are also several EBTs for adolescent SUD, including multidimensional family therapy, brief strategic family therapy, functional family therapy, and multisystemic therapy (for review, see Murray, Labuschagne, & Le Grange, 2014).

US Food and Drug Administration (FDA)-approved medications are currently available to assist in the treatment of AUD and opioid use disorder. Disulfiram (Antabuse) is an oral medication that is used to decrease the likelihood of alcohol consumption due to its highly unpleasant side effects when combined with alcohol. Naltrexone (Revia, orally administered; Vivitrol, injectable) is an opioid receptor antagonist that blocks the reinforcing effects of alcohol and has been found to be effective in reducing relapse (Williams, 2005). The most recently FDA-approved medication for AUD is acamprosate (Campral), which was found to reduce relapse rates when combined with psychosocial treatments (Rosenthal, 2011). There are also five FDA-approved medications for the treatment of opioid use disorders: methadone, buprenorphine (Subutex), buprenorphine/naloxone (Suboxone and Zubsolv), and naltrexone (Vivitrol) (for review, see Ruiz & Strain, 2011).

TREATMENT PLANNING

This section discusses the necessary components for developing a working treatment plan for patients with co-occurring ED/SUD. Good case formulation requires a comprehensive understanding of predisposing, precipitating, and perpetuating factors as well as the adaptive function of the patient's symptoms and behaviors. It also requires a detailed timeline that outlines the sequence of symptom onset and an understanding of how symptoms are functionally linked and affect each other.

Case Formulation

Treating the individual with both ED and SUD can often be a daunting process, and with multiple behaviors to target, it can be difficult to know where to begin. To date, there are no EBTs specifically for this dual-diagnosed population. Most EBTs target single disorders and do not incorporate strategies to address multiple diagnoses. With few exceptions, RCTs in the ED field have excluded patients with co-occurring SUD (Gadalla & Piran, 2007). As a result, the treatment team must create an individualized case formulation and treatment plan that incorporates evidence-based practices from both fields.

Case formulation is a clinically useful tool that helps the therapist (treatment team) conceptualize all the "moving parts" of a patient's problems and understand how they logically fit together (Persons, 2008). It explores the central underlying mechanisms that predispose, precipitate, and perpetuate their current symptom constellation. Precipitating factors are events or circumstances that contribute to the onset of the disorder. Biological (medical conditions), social, psychological, or environmental factors can be the catalyst for or trigger the onset of symptoms. Perpetuating factors are circumstances that maintain dysfunctional behaviors or debilitating symptoms. Understanding what maintains the individual's symptoms can inform the development of more effective treatment interventions. (For further information on perpetuating factors, see Brewerton & Dennis, 2016.)

Another important task in a case formulation is assessing for the presence and scope of comorbid conditions. This can be particularly difficult in patients with ED/SUD. For example, depression can be present prior to the onset of an ED, concurrent with an ED, or the result of engaging in ED behaviors (i.e., dietary restraint, significant weight loss, and use of compensatory behaviors). Some symptoms of ED resemble features of anxiety disorders, including an intense fear of gaining weight (phobic fears), a relentless drive for thinness (obsessional thinking), and calorie counting and excessive exercising (compulsive behaviors designed to reduce anxiety). Likewise, depression commonly occurs with chronic use or withdrawal from many substances, and stimulant abuse can resemble severe anxiety or even mania. Therefore, it is essential to conduct a thorough assessment that includes a history and chronology (timeline) of symptoms in order to determine their functional relationship.

Initial Case Formulation for Louise

Leslie has been an extremely anxious person since childhood (**Predispose**). Her parents were both highly success professionals who traveled for their jobs. The youngest of four siblings, Leslie often felt abandoned and fearful when her parents were not readily available (**Precipitant**). She began binge eating at age 11 years and gained a significant amount of weight (**Symptoms/problem**). She was teased and humiliated by classmates, which led to preoccupation with weight loss and body image (**Precipitant**). At age 14 years, she started smoking cigarettes (**Symptom/problem**). At age 15 years, she was diagnosed with attention deficit disorder/attention deficit hyperactivity disorder (ADD/ADHD) and placed on stimulant medications, which led to significant weight loss but also sleeping problems (**Symptoms/problem**). She attributes attracting her first boyfriend to the weight loss (**Perpetuating factor**). In college, she became overwhelmed with the pace and amount of work required to get good grades. She began using more stimulants than prescribed, as well as cannabis (before bed each night), benzodiazepines, alcohol, and opiates to help her manage her escalating anxiety and sleep disturbances (**Symptoms/problem**). Opiate use led to chronic constipation and the abuse of 50–60 laxatives a day (**Symptom/problem** and **Perpetuating factor**). She presented for treatment with a 15 body mass index (BMI), AN-BP (laxative abuse), generalized anxiety disorder, and polysubstance abuse.

Adaptive Function of Eating Disorders

Another component of case formulation is the exploration of the adaptive function of the patient's symptoms and behaviors. Uncovering the physical, psychological, social, or interpersonal problems that the ED/SUD manages or solves and identifying the secondary gains that result from engaging in these behaviors can provide the clinician with insight into predisposing, precipitating, and perpetuating factors. These symptoms/behaviors serve a purpose (e.g., answer a question, solve a problem, fulfill an unmet need, and alter the environment in a positive way—despite negative consequences).

Eating disorder symptoms and behaviors can be viewed as methods of managing underlying psychological, social, interpersonal, familial, or physical problems. Taking charge of one's body—managing food intake, weight, and shape—can be viewed as a method to generate a subjective sense of mastery over a world that feels "out of control." Patients may perceive that engaging in rigid control of the body improves their life (e.g., improve athletic prowess and attract a romantic partner), offsets or prevents a life event (e.g., delay attendance to college and prevent parental divorce), or changes a mood state (e.g., reduce depression or anxiety and enhance self-esteem). The most common adaptive functions in ED patients include the following: (1) to control appetite, manage hunger, and/or promote weight loss; (2) to manage maturity fears; (3) to provide structure, predictability, and control; (4) to consolidate a self-identity; (5) to get attention or help; (6) to change the current environment; (7) to manage other comorbid disorders, such as anxiety or mood disorders; (8) to escape, avoid, or numb; (9) to manage sexual conflicts; and (10) to punish the negative self. (For further information on adaptive function in ED, see Brewerton & Dennis, 2016; Dennis et al., 2014.)

Adaptive Function of Substance Use in Eating Disorder Patients

For the purpose of this chapter, the adaptive function of substance use in individuals with ED is explored. Each of the following sections begins with a brief overview of a category of drugs, their effects on the brain and body, and a chart that outlines possible adaptive functions.

CANNABIS

Cannabis is sold and administered in preparations that vary in potency. The most common preparation is the dried plant form, which is smoked and ranges from 3% to 27% THC concentration. Cannabis is also dissolved and ingested in the form of drinks, candy, and baked goods ("edibles") (Dennis & Pryor, 2014b). The cannabis "high" typically occurs within 1 minute, reaches a peak in 15–30 minutes, and persists for up to 4 hours (Budney, Vandrey, & Fearer, 2011). The sensations of euphoria, relaxation, and increased auditory and visual perceptions produced by psychoactive strains of cannabis are due almost entirely to its effect on the cannabinoid receptors in the brain.

There are three primary strains of cannabis: sativa, indica, and hybrids. Sativa is an activating strain of cannabis that tends to energize the user and produces a cerebral high. It can relieve the symptoms of depression, attention deficit disorder, fatigue, and mood disorders. Indica is a more sedating strain that produces relaxation and full-body effects and has been identified as preferred by the majority of our ED patients. Hybrids are varying combinations of these two strains that are thought to balance the positive effects of both.

Figure 4.1 is a diagram of possible adaptive functions for cannabis use. We argue that cannabis may serve as a perceived coping tool and an adaptive response to the physical, psychological, familial, and social problems that may precipitate and/or maintain an ED. Little has been written about the adaptive function of

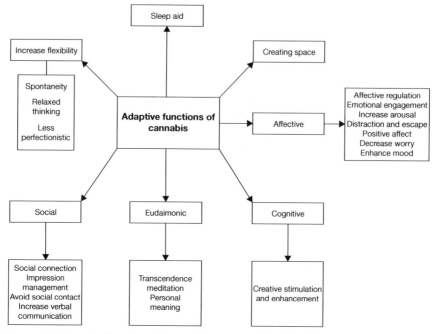

Figure 4.1 Adaptive functions of cannabis.

cannabis use in individuals with ED; however, anecdotal reports from our comorbid patients are very consistent.

Katie, a 32-year-old woman with a history of chronic relapsing AN, reports that she has recently discovered that cannabis helps her slow her mind and observe her disordered thoughts. She states,

> I'm finally able to feel hungry instead of nauseous and uncomfortable. I'm able to step back and see my irrational thoughts for what they are—irrational. It gives me the space to look at the thought and go, wow that fear is ridiculous; nothing bad is going to happen if I eat this. It also makes food taste better and eating more enjoyable. Anorexia is a control thing for me—excessive perfectionism—so it's a relief to have something that allows me to let go and be more flexible.

For some, cannabis has been an alternative to the psychotropic drugs prescribed to them for co-occurring conditions such as obsessive–compulsive disorder, depression, and other anxiety disorders. Katie states,

> Prozac and Lexapro decreased my anxiety, but they made me feel numb, apathetic, and flat, just like my eating disorder. Cannabis does the opposite. It heightens my senses and makes me feel more connected with my emotions and the world around me.

CENTRAL NERVOUS SYSTEM DEPRESSANTS

Different classes of central nervous system (CNS) depressants work in different ways; however, they all increase the efficiency of synaptic transmission of the neurotransmitter gamma-aminobutyric acid (GABA) and thereby inhibit brain activity. All CNS depressants produce a calming or drowsy effect beneficial to those suffering from anxiety or sleep disorders, as often reported by individuals with eating disorders. They are prescribed for a wide range of problems and provide relief from muscle tension, pain, insomnia, panic attacks, and seizure disorders and are also used as general anesthetics. This class includes alcohol, sedative hypnotics (benzodiazepines, barbiturates, and nonbenzodiazepine or "Z drugs"), and narcotics (heroin as well as the licit prescription pain relievers oxycodone, hydrocodone, codeine, morphine, fentanyl, and others).

Brittany, a 22-year-old college senior, presents with a 6-year history of BN that began after a break-up with her first boyfriend. Upon starting college, Brittany became part of a group of friends whose activities all involved drugs and alcohol. Brittany reports prescription drug abuse, specifically hydrocodone; alcohol binges; and experimentation with MDMA, cocaine, and LSD. At age 20 years, she began using heroin, and she reports that she has been injecting "at least" one or two points per day with friends. Brittany expresses concern about the steady increase in her binging and purging (8–10 times per day), but she claims the heroin use is "just to hang with friends and to feel accepted and not so worried about fitting in." She claims that using heroin gives her "a feeling of comfortable numbness and a warm feeling all over [her] body." Brittany states, "If I don't go on the nod, I feel light and airy and as if I am in a place where only good seems to exist." Brittany recognizes that the binging and purging "just stopped working" as a way to feel better and the heroin "stepped in to take its place" (Figure 4.2).

CENTRAL NERVOUS SYSTEM STIMULANTS

Central nervous system stimulants "speed up" mental and physical processes in the body. Stimulants are a class of drugs that are prescribed for the treatment of narcolepsy, ADD/ADHD, treatment-resistant depression, HIV-related neuropsychiatric symptoms, and obesity (Hill & Weiss, 2011). Central nervous system stimulants activate the psychological reward system in the brain and increase the release of dopamine, resulting in pleasurable effects. Prescription stimulants include amphetamines (e.g., Dexedrine and Adderall), methamphetamine (e.g., Desoxyn) and methylphenidate (e.g., Ritalin and Concerta), and lisdexamfetamine dimesylate (e.g., Vyvanse); illegal derivatives include cocaine, crack cocaine, powder or crystal methamphetamine, and synthetic cathinones/mephedrone (also known as bath salts). They are frequently used and abused recreationally by individuals who are not being treated for the previously mentioned conditions.

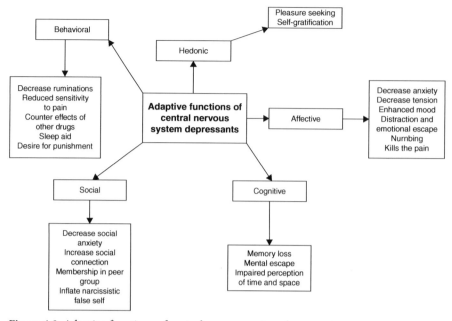

Figure 4.2 Adaptive functions of central nervous system depressants.

Mandy, a 26-year-old woman, reports that her binging began during the time she was being sexually molested by a family member. In the seventh grade, she began playing volleyball and comparing herself to her teammates. She soon began a cycle of restricting, binging, and purging. By age 16 years, she was dating someone who introduced her to "meth." Mandy claims she stopped binging and purging, had no appetite, and lost 60 pounds. She was pleased to be given the nickname "Skeletor." As described in Figure 4.3, Mandy reports that the "meth" helped her feel more

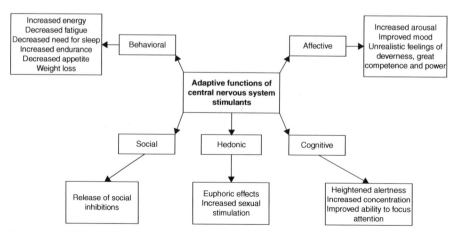

Figure 4.3 Adaptive functions of central nervous system stimulants.

motivated, more energetic, and more social and talkative. She felt smarter and more powerful. However, she eventually started skipping school, stealing money from her mother, and drinking alcohol to try to come down from the high. Mandy was court ordered to drug treatment following a conviction for driving while intoxicated. It was during the SUD treatment that her eating disorder "kicked back in again."

Adaptive Functions of Leslie's Substance Abuse

Several adaptive functions can be identified in Leslie's case. First, the binge eating at age 11 years served as a **method of coping with premorbid anxiety and provided self-soothing** in the absence of her parents. The initiation of smoking not only **reduced her appetite** but also **provided her with a group of peers** who were all engaging in the same behavior. Although the medication for her ADHD significantly **improved her ability to study** and complete assignments, it also **curbed appetite**, which resulted in dieting, skipping meals, and significant **weight loss**. She attributed her weight loss to her rigid control over her food intake. Because she "paired" weight loss with attracting a boyfriend, her automatic thought was "I am only acceptable to others if I am thin." In college, the increase in her stimulant use was associated with the automatic thought of "College is ten times harder and requires far more focus than high school. I also want to avoid the freshman 15." Her significant dieting led to a significant increase in substance consumption. Her polysubstance abuse was partly **to fit in with her peer group** but also served as a method to **manage hunger and anxiety, counteract the effects of stimulant abuse, and medicate her sleep disturbance.** Leslie's initial use of laxatives had nothing to do with her ED, and she did not perceive it as a form of purging. Rather, it was designed **to counteract the side effects of constipation from opiate abuse**.

Treatment Plan for Leslie

Leslie's treatment team consisted of an outpatient therapist, a dietitian, an internal medicine physician, and a psychiatrist. It was determined that Leslie's substance dependence on benzodiazepines and narcotics required detox with medical supervision. In addition, her laboratory work revealed some electrolyte abnormalities, dehydration, an iron deficiency, and the presence of cannabis. With a BMI of 15, she would be required to normalize her eating patterns and gain a significant amount of weight. She was referred to a residential treatment facility that provided integrated treatment for both disorders. Treatment was ordered as follows:

1. Medical detox for benzodiazepines and narcotics and cessation of stimulant laxatives with an increase in fiber supplements and fluids were initiated. Food exposure began with five small meals per day

(dependent on nausea and/or vomiting from detox). She began journaling a chronology of ED/SUD with the support of a therapist to help her begin to understand the functional links between her disorders.

2. CBT was selected as the foundation for intervention because much of Leslie's ED and SUD symptoms and behaviors were to manage premorbid anxiety and dysfunctional automatic thoughts around weight, shape, and appearance.

3. Once she was completely detoxed and rebound edema was managed, the treatment focused specifically on weight gain and normalization of eating patterns.

4. She was started on an antidepressant to help manage her anxiety around weight gain and eating.

5. She attended all group sessions with other patients who had both ED and SUD.

6. She took part in all milieu experiences, including DBT skills building, cooking classes, psychoeducational presentations, expressive therapies, and NA meetings.

7. Individual therapy was a key element in her recovery and helped her to explore the adaptive function of her ED/SUD and to develop a stronger sense of self-directedness.

8. Monitoring of her medical status, weight gain, food intake, bathroom, and exercise took place daily.

9. She achieved a BMI of 18 and was discharged back to her treatment team for aftercare in an outpatient setting. She maintained her weight on an outpatient basis and is now at a BMI of 19 with no restricting or purging behavior. She continues on daily fiber supplements but is no longer preoccupied with "being regular" and has completely abstained from using stimulant laxatives. She is alcohol and drug free except for a "nightly bowl" of indica to help her relax and sleep.

CONCLUSION

Clinical evidence indicates that outcomes are enhanced when a combination of EBT modalities is offered in a comprehensive, integrated treatment plan that addresses both ED and SUD. Although both ED and SUD are clearly disorders highlighted by dysfunction, they also represent adaptive attempts to meet a broad range of biopsychosocial problems, skills deficits, and co-occurring psychiatric problems. The integrated treatment model presented in this chapter proposes that this adaptive context warrants acknowledgment and may serve as a helpful guide for clinicians until further research can contribute to its refinement.

REFERENCES

Agrawal, A., & Lynskey, M. (2006). The genetic epidemiology of cannabis use, abuse and dependence. *Addiction, 101*, 801–812.

American Psychiatric Association. (2013). *Diagnostic and statistical manual of mental disorders* (5th ed.). Arlington, VA: American Psychiatric Publishing.

Avena, N. M., Gold, J. A., Kroll, C., & Gold, M. S. (2012). Further developments in the neurobiology of food and addiction: Update on the state of the science. *Nutrition, 28*, 341–343.

Baker, J. S., Mitchell, K. S., Neale, M. C., & Kendler, K. S. (2010). Eating disorder symptomatology and substance use disorders: Prevalence and shared risk in a population based twin sample. *International Journal of Eating Disorders, 43*(7), 648–658.

Beary, M. L., Lacey, J. H., & Merry, J. (1986). Alcoholism and eating disorders in women of fertile age. *British Journal of Addictions, 81*(5), 685–689.

Brewerton, T. D., & Brady, K. (2014). The role of stress, trauma and PTSD in the etiology and treatment of eating disorders, addictions and substance use disorders. In T. D. Brewerton & A. B. Dennis (Eds.), *Eating disorders, addictions and substance use disorders: Research, clinical and treatment perspectives* (pp. 379–404). Berlin, Germany: Springer.

Brewerton, T. D., & Dennis, A. B. (2016). Perpetuating factors in severe and enduring anorexia nervosa: A clinician's guide. In S. Touyz, D. Le Grange, P. Hay, & H. Lacey (Eds.), *Managing severe and enduring anorexia nervosa*. New York, NY: Taylor & Francis/Routledge.

Budney, A. V., Vandrey, R. L., & Fearer, S. (2011). Cannabis. In P. Ruiz & E. Strain (Eds.), *Lowinson and Ruiz's substance abuse: A comprehensive textbook* (5th ed., pp. 214–237). Philadelphia, PA: Lippincott Williams & Wilkins.

Bulik, C. M., Sullivan, P. F., Tozzi, F., Furberg, H., Lichtenstein, P., & Pedersen, N. L. (2006). Prevalence, heritability and prospective risk factors for anorexia nervosa. *Archives of General Psychiatry, 63*, 305–312.

Bulik, C. M., Thornton, L., Pinheiro, K., Klump, K. L., Brandt, H., Crawford, S., . . . Kaye, W. H. (2008). Suicide attempts in anorexia nervosa. *Journal of Psychosomatic Medicine, 70*(3), 378–383.

Calero-Elvira, A., Krug, I., Davis, K., Lopez, C., Fernandez-Aranda, F., & & Treasure, J. (2009). Meta-analysis on drugs in people with eating disorders. *European Eating Disorders Review, 17*(4), 243–259.

Carroll, K., Rounsaville, B., Nich, C., & Gordon, L. (1994). One-year follow-up of psychotherapy and pharmacotherapy for cocaine dependence: Delayed emergence of psychotherapy effects. *Archives of General Psychiatry, 51*, 177–197.

Carroll, M., France, C., & Meisch, R. (1979). Food deprivation increases oral and intravenous drug intake in rats. *Science, 205*, 319–321.

Compton, W. M., Thomas, Y. F., Stinson, F. S., & Grant, B. F. (2007). Prevalence, correlates, disability and comorbidity of DSM-IV drug abuse and dependence in the United States. *Archives of General Psychiatry, 64*, 566–576.

Copeland, J., Swift, W., Roffman, R., & Stephans, R. (2001). A randomized controlled trial of brief cognitive–behavioral interventions of cannabis use disorder. *Journal of Substance Abuse Treatment, 21*, 55–64.

Courbasson, C. M., Smith, P. D., & Cleland, P. A. (2005). Substance use disorders, anorexia, bulimia, and concurrent disorders. *Canadian Journal of Public Health, 96*, 102–106.

Dennis, A. B., & Helfman, B. (2010a). *Availability of treatment for substance use disorders in established eating disorder facilities: A pilot study.* Unpublished data.

Dennis, A. B., & Helfman, B. (2010b). Managing the eating disorder patient with a comorbid substance use disorder. In M. Maine, B. H. McGilley, & D. W. Bunnell (Eds.), *Treatment of eating disorders: Bridging the research–practice gap* (pp. 233–249). London, England: Elsevier.

Dennis, A. B., & Pryor, T. (2014a). Introduction to eating disorders for substance abuse specialists. In T. D. Brewerton & A. B. Dennis (Eds.), *Eating disorders, addictions and substance use disorders: Research, clinical and treatment perspectives* (pp. 199–226). Berlin, Germany: Springer.

Dennis, A. B., & Pryor, T. (2014b). Introduction to substance use disorders for eating disorder specialists. In T. D. Brewerton & A. B. Dennis (Eds.), *Eating disorders, addictions and substance use disorders: Research, clinical and treatment perspectives* (pp. 227–266). Berlin, Germany: Springer.

Dennis, A. B., Pryor, T., & Brewerton, T. D. (2014). Integrated treatment principles and strategies for patients with eating disorders, substance use disorders, and addictions. In T. D. Brewerton & A. B. Dennis (Eds.), *Eating disorders, addictions and substance use disorders: Research, clinical and treatment perspectives* (pp. 461–490). Berlin, Germany: Springer.

Donovan, D. M., Anton, R. F., Miller, W. R., Longabaugh, R., Hosking, J. D., & Youngblood, M.; COMBINE Study Research Group. (2008). Combined pharmacotherapies and behavioral interventions for alcohol dependence: Examination of posttreatment drinking outcomes. *Journal of Studies on Alcohol and Drugs, 69,* 5–13.

Drake, R., Essock, S., Shaner, A., Carey, K., Minkoff, K., Kola, L., . . . Rickards, L. (2001). Implementing dual diagnosis services for clients with severe mental illness. *Psychiatric Services, 52,* 469–476.

Fouladi, F., Mitchell, J. E., Crosby, R. D., Engel, S. G., Crow, S., Hill, L., . . . Steffen, K. J. (2015). Prevalence of alcohol and other substance use in patients with eating disorders. *European Eating Disorders Review, 23*(6), 531–536.

Franko, D. L., Dorer, D. J., Keel, P., Jackson, S., Manzo, M., & Herzog, D. (2008). Interaction between eating disorders and drug abuse. *Journal of Nervous and Mental Disorders, 196,* 556–561.

Gadalla, T., & Piran, N. (2007). Co-occurring eating disorders and alcohol use disorders in women: A meta-analysis. *Archives of Women's Mental Health, 10,* 133–140.

Garcia-Gomez, M., Gonzalez, J. O., del Barrio, A. G., & Garcia, N. A. (2009). Rhabdomyolysis and drug abuse in a patient with bulimia nervosa. *International Journal of Eating Disorders, 42,* 93–95.

Gordon, S. M., Johnson, J. A., Greenfield, S. F., Cohen, L., Killeen, T., & Roman, P. M. (2008). Assessment and treatment of co-occurring eating disorders in publicly funded addiction treatment programs. *Psychiatric Services, 59*(9), 1056–1059.

Hicks, B., Krueger, R., Iaconco, W., & Patrick, C. (2004). Family transmission and heritability of externalizing disorders. *Archives of General Psychiatry, 61,* 922–928.

Hill, K., & Weiss, R. D. (2011). Amphetamines and other stimulants. In P. Ruiz & E. Strain (Eds.), *Lowinson and Ruiz's substance abuse: A comprehensive textbook* (5th ed., pp. 238–254). Philadelphia, PA: Lippincott Williams & Wilkins.

Keel, P. K., & Mitchell, J. E. (1997). Outcome in bulimia nervosa. *American Journal of Psychiatry, 154,* 313–321.

Kelly, T., Daley, D., & Douaihy, A. (2012). Treatment of substance abusing patients with comorbid psychiatric disorders. *Addictive Behavior, 37*, 11–24.

Kessler, R. C., Berglund, P., Demler, O., Jin, R., Merklangas, K. R., & Walters, E. (2005). Lifetime prevalence and age of onset distributions of DSM-IV disorders in the National Comorbidity Survey Replication. *Archives of General Psychiatry, 62*, 593–602.

Killeen, T. K., Greenfield, S. F., Bride, B. E., Cohen, L., Gordon, S. M., & Roman, P. M. (2011). Assessment and treatment of co-occurring eating disorders in privately funded addiction treatment programs. *American Journal of Addictions, 20*(3), 205–211.

Kissin, W., McLeod, C., Sonnefeld, L., & Stanton, A. (2006). Experience of a national sample of qualified addiction specialists who have and have not prescribed buprenorphine for opioid dependence. *Journal of Addictive Diseases, 25*, 91–103.

Klein, D. A., Boudreau, G. S., Devlin, M. J., & Walsh, B. T. (2006). Artificial sweetener use among individuals with eating disorders. *International Journal of Eating Disorders, 39*(4), 341–345.

Linehan, M., Dimeff, L., Reynolds, S., Comtois, K., Welch, S., Heagerty, P., & Kivlahan, D. (2002). Dialectical behavior therapy versus comprehensive validation therapy plus 12-step for the treatment of opioid dependent women meeting criteria for borderline personality disorder. *Drug and Alcohol Dependence, 67*, 13–26.

Miller, W., & Wilbourne, P. (2002). Mesa Grande: A methodological analysis of clinical trials of treatments for alcohol use disorders. *Addictions, 97*, 265–277.

McLellan, A. T. (2010). *Address to steering committee.* National Institute on Drug Abuse Clinical Trials Network. Bethesda, MD.

Murray, S., Gordillo, M., & Avena, N. (2014). Animal models of eating disorders, substance use disorders, and addictions. In T. D. Brewerton & A. B. Dennis (Eds.), *Eating disorders, addictions, and substance use disorders: Research, clinical and treatment perspectives* (pp. 3–21). Berlin, Germany: Springer.

Murray, S. B., Labuschagne, Z., & Le Grange, D. (2014). Family and couples therapy for eating disorders, substance use disorders and addictions. In T. D. Brewerton & A. B. Dennis (Eds.), *Eating disorders, addictions and substance use disorders: Research, clinical and treatment perspectives* (pp. 563–586). Berlin, Germany: Springer.

National Institute on Drug Abuse. (2012). *Principles of drug addiction treatment: A research-based guide* (3rd ed.). Bethesda, MD: National Institutes of Health, National Institute of Drug Abuse.

Persons, J. B. (2008). *The case formulation approach to cognitive–behavior therapy.* New York, NY: Guilford.

Pollack, M., Penava, S., Bolton, E., Worthington, S., Allen, G., Farach, F., & Otto, M. (2002). A novel cognitive–behavioral approach for treatment-resistant drug dependence. *Journal of Substance Abuse Treatment, 23*, 335–342.

Roerig, J., Mitchell, J., de Zwaan, M., Wonderlich, S., Kamran, S., Engbloom, S., . . . Lancaster, K. (2003). The eating disorders medicine cabinet revisited: A clinician's guide to appetite suppressants and diuretics. *International Journal of Eating Disorders, 33*(4), 445–457.

Rosenthal, R. (2011). Alcohol abstinence management. In P. Ruiz & E. Strain (Eds.), *Lowinson and Ruiz's substance abuse: A comprehensive textbook* (5th ed., pp. 477–493). Philadelphia, PA: Lippincott Williams & Wilkins.

Ruiz, P., & Strain, E. (2011). *Lowinson and Ruiz's substance abuse: A comprehensive textbook* (5th ed.). Philadelphia, PA: Lippincott Williams & Wilkins.

Specker, S. M., Lac, S. T., & Carroll, M. E. (1994). Food deprivation history and cocaine self-administration: An animal model of binge eating. *Pharmacology Biochemistry and Behavior, 48*, 1025–1029.

Steffen, K., Mitchell, J., Roerig, J., & Lancaster, K. (2007). The eating disorder medicine cabinet revisited: A clinician's guide to ipecac and laxatives. *International Journal of Eating Disorders, 40*, 360–368.

Strober, M., Freeman, R., Bower, S., & Rigali, J. (1996). Binge eating in anorexia nervosa predicts later onset of substance use disorder: A ten-year prospective, longitudinal follow-up of 95 adolescents. *Journal of Youth and Adolescence, 25*, 519–532.

Strober, M., Freeman, R., Lampert, C., Diamond, J., & Kaye, W. (2000). Controlled family study of anorexia nervosa and bulimia nervosa: Evidence of shared liability and transmission of partial syndromes. *American Journal of Psychiatry, 157*, 393–401.

The National Center on Addiction and Substance Abuse. (2003). *Food for thought: Substance abuse and eating disorders.* New York, NY: Author.

Weisner, C., Mertens, J., Tam, T., & Moore, C. (2001). Factors affecting the initiation of substance abuse treatment in managed care. *Addiction, 96*(5), 705–716.

Williams, S. (2005). Medications for treating alcohol dependence. *American Family Physician, 72*, 1775–1780.

5

Suicidality, Self-Injurious Behavior, and Eating Disorders

LESLIE K. ANDERSON, APRIL SMITH, AND SCOTT CROW ■

Self-injurious behaviors, including both suicidal and nonsuicidal forms of self-injury, and eating disordered behavior co-occur at remarkably high rates (25–50%; Svirko & Hawton, 2007), are often treated with similar therapeutic approaches, and there is evidence that both types of behaviors may function to regulate emotion. Given these similarities, this chapter explores the assessment and treatment of self-injurious behavior—with a specific focus on suicidal ideation and behaviors—within eating disorder patients.

Suicidal ideation and behavior encompasses a wide range of thoughts and behaviors, ranging from passive ideation (e.g., fleeting thoughts of not wanting to be around) to lethal or near lethal suicide attempts. Different terms are used to describe these behaviors; Table 5.1 provides a list of terms and definitions. Whereas suicidal behavior falls into a larger category of self-injurious behavior, self-injurious behavior (SIB) can be engaged in with or without suicidal intent. Nonsuicidal self-injury typically refers to acts of self-harm such as cutting, burning, scratching, picking, or otherwise damaging the skin. However, many researchers have begun to advocate that eating disorder behaviors, which can result in pain and significant physical damage, be considered self-injurious behaviors as well (for review, see Brausch & Muehlenkamp, 2014).

Unfortunately, many people die due to their inability to desist from engaging in life-threatening eating disorder behaviors. Although we would characterize these eating disorder behaviors as self-injurious, in the absence of engaging in the behavior with the clear intent of dying, we would not characterize eating disorder behaviors as suicidal or as a form of "slow suicide." Although some individuals with an eating disorder may wish to die from their disorder, this is not always the case. As Joiner (2010) notes, typically people with anorexia

are not getting thin to die, they are "dying to be thin." Thinness is the goal, and people with the syndrome crave it as much as people crave a substance

Table 5.1 TERMS DESCRIBING SUICIDAL BEHAVIOR

Term	Definition
Self-injurious behavior	Broad category referring to self-inflicted injury that can be engaged in with or without suicidal intent.
Nonsuicidal self-injury	Self-inflicted injury that is engaged in without suicidal intent.
Suicide	Self-inflicted injury resulting in death for which there is evidence that the decedent intended to kill him- or herself.
Suicide attempt	A potentially self-injurious behavior with a nonfatal outcome for which there is evidence that the person intended at some level to kill him- or herself. A suicide attempt may or may not result in injuries.
Suicidal act	A potentially self-injurious behavior for which there is evidence that the person intended at some level (nonzero) to kill him- or herself. A suicidal act may result in death (completed suicide), injury, or no injury.
Suicide plan	A proposed method of carrying out a course of action that will lead to a potentially self-injurious outcome.
Suicide threat	A verbal or nonverbal interpersonal action that stops short of a self-harmful act which communicates or suggests that a suicide-related behavior might occur in the near future.
Suicidal ideation	Thoughts of suicide, death, and/or engaging in suicide-related behavior. Ideation can range from passive ("I wish I was dead") to active ("I want to kill myself").

SOURCE: Adapted from Silverman, M. M., Berman, A. L., Sanddal, N. D., O'Carroll, P. W., & Joiner, T. E. (2007). Rebuilding the Tower of Babel: A revised nomenclature for the study of suicide and suicidal behaviors: Part II. Suicide-related ideations, communications and behaviors. *Suicide and Life-Threatening Behavior, 37*(3), 264–277.

> to which they are addicted. . . . In the minds of these individuals, the goal is not death, but the goal, whether of thinness or of drug use, is, to them, worth the danger of death. (pp. 198–199)

Anorexia nervosa (AN) is one of, if not the most, lethal psychological disorders (Arcelus, Mitchell, Wales, & Nielsen, 2011), and it is estimated that up to 10% of individuals with the disorder will die (American Psychiatric Association, 2013). Although medical complications resulting from starvation-related health issues are the leading cause of death, suicide is believed to be the second leading cause of death. In fact, meta-analyses suggest that individuals with AN are 18–31 times more likely to die by suicide than age- and gender-matched individuals in the general population (Keshaviah et al., 2014; Preti, Rocchi, Sisti, Camboni, & Miotto, 2011). Although death by suicide is less common in bulimia nervosa (BN) compared to AN, rates of suicide attempts are elevated. In fact, research suggests that individuals with BN may attempt suicide at even greater rates than those with AN (i.e., 3–20% for AN and 25–35% for BN; Franko & Keel, 2006). Fewer studies have examined suicide and attempts in binge-eating disorder (BED), but the handful of studies that have done so suggest that individuals with BED have similar levels of ideation and attempts as those with BN (Pisetsky, Thornton, Lichtenstein, Pedersen, & Bulik, 2013). Overall, approximately one-third of individuals with AN, BN, and BED report suicidal ideation (Carano et al., 2012; Milos, Spindler, Hepp, & Schnyder, 2004; Swanson, Crow, Le Grange, Swendsen, & Merikangas, 2011).

Although suicidal behavior can co-occur with any type of disordered eating, research suggests it may be more common among certain clinical presentations. For instance, in their thorough review, Franko and Keel (2006) found that suicide attempts were correlated with purging behaviors (both laxative use and self-induced vomiting), depression, substance use, and a history of childhood maltreatment (i.e., physical and/or sexual abuse). These correlates were supported by a more recent narrative review that noted additional risk factors that should be considered in eating disorder patients, including "illness severity, co-occurring psychiatric illnesses including borderline personality disorder and substance abuse, excessive exercise, and alexithymia" (Kostro, Lerman, & Attia, 2014, p. 7). This review also reported that adolescents with eating disorders may be particularly vulnerable to suicidal behavior, and this vulnerability was recently demonstrated in adolescents with BED as well (Forrest, Zuromski, Dodd, & Smith, 2017).

However, it should be noted that the longitudinal literature examining prospective predictors of suicidality in eating disorder samples is extremely limited. A recent meta-analysis (Smith, Velkoff, Ribeiro, & Franklin, 2017) revealed that the presence of either eating disorder symptoms or eating disorder diagnosis increased risk for suicide attempts by twofold. However, eating disorder diagnosis was not found to predict death by suicide. There were too few longitudinal studies to examine more specific predictors (e.g., symptom type or diagnosis) or whether eating disorders longitudinally predicted suicidal ideation.

EATING DISORDERS AND THE INTERPERSONAL PSYCHOLOGICAL THEORY OF SUICIDE

The interpersonal psychological theory of suicide (IPTS; Joiner, 2005) is a leading theory of suicide that has garnered strong empirical support (Bryan, Morrow, Anestis, & Joiner, 2010; Joiner, Van Orden, Witte, Selby, et al., 2009; Monteith, Menefee, Pettit, Leopoulos, & Vincent, 2013; Van Orden, Witte, Gordon, Bender, & Joiner, 2008). The IPTS proposes that interactions among three constructs— that is, perceived burdensomeness, thwarted belongingness, and acquired capability for suicide—lead to suicide ideation, plans, attempts, and death (Joiner, 2005).

These three constructs were described in detail by Joiner in 2005. Perceived burdensomeness refers to the mental miscalculation that one's death is worth more than one's life and is characterized by self-hate and a sense of ineffectiveness. Thwarted belongingness results when one of the fundamental human needs—to belong—is not met. Thwarted belongingness is characterized by a perceived absence of reciprocally caring relationships and loneliness. Finally, according to the IPTS, evolution has seen to it that humans have a strong self-preservation instinct and inherently fear death. Thus, in order to make a suicide attempt, the IPTS asserts that one must override this self-preservation instinct by developing a *capability* for suicide—in other words, one must become fearless about death and tolerant of the pain involved in making the attempt. The capability for suicide is in part genetically determined (Smith et al., 2012), but it can also develop over the course of one's life through exposure to fearsome and painful experiences. Notably, recent research has found that eating disorder behaviors are related to all three of the IPTS constructs (Dodd, Smith, & Bodell, 2014; Forrest et al., 2016; Smith et al., 2013; Witte et al., 2016). Specifically, in a collegiate sample, Dodd and colleagues (2014) found that people who engaged in dietary restraint had increased negative life events at a later time point. These increased negative life events in turn predicted increased thwarted belongingness and perceived burdensomeness. Furthermore, Forrest and colleagues (2016) found that body dissatisfaction, fasting, binging, and laxative abuse were related to burdensomeness in a mixed residential eating disorder sample. In a sample of people with BN, Smith and colleagues (2013) found that overexercise predicted suicidal behavior, and in an independent collegiate sample, this relationship was found to flow through acquired capability. Witte and colleagues (2016) found that when eating disorder behaviors were considered together, self-induced vomiting predicted pain tolerance, and vomiting and laxative use predicted fearlessness about death. Thus, people with eating disorders (EDs) may be predisposed toward all three IPTS constructs.

EMPIRICALLY BASED RISK ASSESSMENT

The first step in treating self-injurious behavior is assessment. Note that many clinicians are often reluctant to assess for suicide (Gould et al., 2005). This reluctance can stem from multiple sources, including taboos about suicide, feeling like one does not have the proper training to assess and deal with suicidality should it be endorsed, and believing that talking about suicide may "prime" or "prompt" an individual into thinking more about suicide. Regarding the latter, research has found that assessing for suicide does not increase suicidality (Gould et al., 2005); in fact, when assessment is done warmly, competently, and with a rationale provided, it can increase rapport and lead to better clinical outcomes (Jobes, 2012). Suicide risk assessment may be particularly important for ethnic minorities, as Morrison and Downey (2000) found that ethnic minorities were less likely to spontaneously discuss suicidal thoughts at intake compared to Caucasians, and these thoughts were uncovered only with suicide risk assessment.

There are a number of suicide risk assessment frameworks. This chapter focuses on two frameworks that are empirically based and available to the public: Joiner's Suicide Risk Assessment (JSRA) and the Linehan Risk Assessment and Management Protocol (LRAMP). Joiner's assessment model, based on the interpersonal theory of suicide, is a semistructured interview that results in an individual being classified into one of four risk categories: low, moderate, severe, and extreme (Chu et al., 2015). This assessment was designed and developed for outpatient use. Note that these categories are flexible, and individuals can fall in between categories (e.g., low–moderate and moderate–severe). Although Joiner's model incorporates many standard elements, there are some novel aspects, including the emphasis placed on multiple attempter status, perceived burdensomeness, thwarted belongingness, and the capability for suicide. The standard elements of the JSRA include assessment of previous suicidal behavior; current suicidal symptoms; plans, methods, and means for suicide; suicidal desire; and suicidal intent.

As noted previously, when assessing for previous suicidal behavior, the JSRA focuses on determining how many previous attempts there have been and the timing of these attempts. This emphasis stems from research that finds that individuals who are multiple attempters (i.e., have attempted two or more times) are at greater risk for a future attempt than are single attempters (Forman, Berk, Henriques, Brown, & Beck, 2004; Miranda et al., 2008). Furthermore, although a previous attempt elevates risk throughout the lifetime (Suominen et al., 2004), previous attempters are most at risk approximately 6 months to 2 years after their attempt. In addition, the JSRA includes an assessment of "other significant risk factors," which include perceived burdensomeness, thwarted belongingness, and the capability for suicide. The JSRA also incorporates empirically based risk factors, such as nonsuicidal self-injury, hopelessness, precipitating and current stressors, psychopathology, impulsivity, and acute risk factors for suicide. These acute risk factors include agitation, irritability, social withdrawal, severe weight loss, severe affective states, and sleep disturbances (e.g., insomnia, nightmares, and nighttime panic attacks) (Chu et al., 2015).

After conducting the JSRA, the clinician should have enough information to assign the patient to a risk category. The JSRA then has suggested actions for each associated risk category (Table 5.2). Once the risk assessment is concluded, the clinician should make sure to document the assessment. For more information about the JSRA, see Chu and colleagues' (2015) summary article, which includes a risk assessment decision tree and provides suggested wording for documentation. Proper documentation should include both the level of client suicide risk and the actions that were taken; notably, documentation is crucial for minimizing legal risks. According to the Joiner model, part of the management of suicidality includes routine assessment; thus, it is recommended that at the beginning of each session clinicians check in with patients who are categorized as higher than low risk for suicide about any increases in suicidality. If an increase is reported, then the clinician should complete the full risk assessment to determine appropriate

Table 5.2 JOINER SEVERITY RATINGS AND RECOMMENDED ACTIONS
IN SUICIDE ASSESSMENT

Rating	Description	Actions
Low risk	• No symptoms of suicidal ideation. • Non-multiple attempter with ideation that is limited in intensity and duration, no/mild plans or preparations for an attempt, and no/few risk factors. • Multiple attempter with no other risk factors.	• Evaluate social supports and enlist help from family and/or friends. • Give emergency numbers (e.g., 1-800-273-TALK, 911, or Crisis Text Line [741-741]). • Create a safety plan (see Stanley & Brown, 2012). • Monitor risk regularly and document.
Moderate risk	• Non-multiple attempter with moderate–severe suicidal desire/ideation, no/mild plans and preparations for an attempt, and two or more risk factors. • Non-multiple attempter with moderate–severe plans and preparations. • Multiple attempter plus one other risk factor.	In addition to actions listed for low risk, add: • Midweek phone check-in. • Means safety. • Inform patient about additional treatment options. • Try to enlist family or friends to also check-in on patient.
Severe risk	• Non-multiple attempter plus moderate–severe plans and preparations for an attempt and one or more risk factors. • Multiple attempter plus two or more risk factors.	In addition to steps for low and moderat9.5e risk, add: • Consult supervisor or colleague before patient leaves. • Patient should be monitored continuously. • Consider hospitalization or other emergency mental health options.
Extreme risk	• Non-multiple attempter plus severe plans and preparations for an attempt and two or more risk factors. • Multiple attempter plus severe plans and preparations for an attempt.	• Work with a supervisor or colleague to get patient safe, likely through hospitalization or other emergency mental health options.

SOURCE: Adapted from Chu, C., Klein, K. M., Buchman-Schmitt, J. M., Hom, M. A., Hagan, C. R., & Joiner, T. E. (2015). Routinized assessment of suicide risk in clinical practice: An empirically informed update. *Journal of Clinical Psychology, 71*(12), 1186–1200.

actions and whether a reclassification of risk is necessary. For low-risk patients, clinicians may wish to check in about changes in suicidality on a biweekly basis. Although some may worry that checking in about suicide so frequently will upset patients, typically when adequate rationale is provided, patients are amenable to these check-ins, which generally take only a few minutes. Joiner has likened these check-ins to having one's blood pressure and temperature taken every time one visits the doctor—these measures are the standard of care and are taken to ensure the patient's safety (Joiner, personal communication).

The second risk assessment to consider is the LRAMP (Linehan, Comtois, & Ward-Ciesielski, 2012). There are two versions of the LRAMP—one to be used by assessors, such as those conducting research trials, and one to be used by treatment providers. Here, the version for outpatient treatment providers is reviewed. Whereas the Joiner model advocates for routine risk assessment check-ins, the LRAMP differs in that risk assessment is recommended only under certain conditions: (1) when treatment starts, (2) any time a patient makes a suicide attempt, (3) any time a patient engages in self-injurious behaviors, (4) when a patient makes a suicidal threat, or (5) when a patient reports an increase in his or her desire to die by suicide (Linehan et al., 2012).

If one of the previously mentioned conditions is met, the clinician should then begin the LRAMP. Given the high priority placed on not reinforcing suicidality, clinicians are asked to first thoroughly evaluate whether there may be a significant reason not to proceed with the assessment (e.g., suicidality appears to be an operant behavior that could be reinforced through assessment or suicidality appears to be an escape behavior that can be targeted via identification of precipitating and vulnerability factors in session). Provided there is no reason not to continue, the clinician proceeds with the semistructured risk assessment. This risk assessment includes an evaluation of both empirically based risk and protective factors. Specifically, the LRAMP includes documentation of any suicidality or SIB since the last session. A comprehensive checklist of imminent risk factors and imminent suicide protective factors is included to assist the clinician in assessing and documenting all relevant factors.

In addition, the LRAMP guides the clinician to provide appropriate clinical intervention. The assessment concludes with recommendations for clinical treatment actions aimed at the suicidal/self-injurious behaviors and when the patient will next be evaluated for suicide risk.

EMPIRICALLY BASED TREATMENT

No psychotherapy is effective with a dead patient (Mintz, 1968, as cited in Linehan, 1993). Thus, when a patient indicates that he or she is suicidal or engages in suicidal behavior, such as suicide planning or preparations or obtaining lethal means, the focus of therapy must shift to preventing suicide. As therapists, we must always be on the side of life and do our best to both keep our patients alive and help them obtain a life worth living (Linehan, 1993).

Most guidelines for managing suicidal risk contain common elements (Wasserman et al., 2012). Careful assessment and evaluation, as outlined in the previous section, is a critical first step regardless of how the suicidal thoughts or behaviors are communicated. Second, psychiatric hospitalization can be considered depending on the severity of the risk of suicide. Although hospitalization provides some level of increased security for the patient, it certainly is not a foolproof method of ensuring safety (Hunt et al., 2010). Third, any acute suicidal crises must be managed in the short term, and this might involve increased monitoring and social support; removal of lethal means; and the reduction of acute psychiatric symptoms such as anxiety, insomnia, depression, and psychotic symptoms. Fourth, long-term treatment plans must prioritize suicide prevention, perhaps actively involving family members so that they are aware of signs of increased risk.

Dialectical behavior therapy (DBT; Linehan, 1993) is a well-validated treatment that was developed specifically for patients with suicidality and self-harm (Panos, Jackson, Hasan, & Panos, 2014). Perhaps more than any other treatment for suicidality, DBT has thoroughly articulated a series of treatment strategies for interacting with suicidal patients in a way to minimize risk of immediate suicide, as well as risk of recurrence of suicidality in the future. In addition, DBT describes how to prioritize the targeting of suicidal behaviors in a context of multiple, comorbid high-risk behaviors. The remainder of this chapter discusses how to adapt and use these strategies with suicidal eating disorder patients. Suicidal behaviors or communications are unfortunately, but understandably, sometimes reinforced by the patient's environment. For example, communicating to a loved one that you are so distressed that you are considering suicide may result in that person reassuring you that he or she loves you, taking your pain more seriously, spending extra time with you to make you feel better, or other similarly reinforcing actions. Thus, in the face of suicidal communication, the therapist must have prevention of suicide as the number one goal but must also do so in a way that minimizes the risk of reinforcing the suicidal behavior and thus making it more likely to occur again.

EMPIRICALLY BASED TREATMENT STRATEGIES

Eating disorder patients may be chronically suicidal, with long-standing thoughts that they would be better off dead, rumination about planning suicide, and so on. Alternatively, they may be intermittently acutely suicidal, with an imminent idea, plan, and/or intent to attempt suicide. Of course, some patients have both chronic thoughts of suicide and intermittent, acute episodes of suicidality. The interventions for both situations—chronic suicidality and acute suicidality—are different, but there is some overlap. The strategies in this section may be used in either case, although it is clearly important to reserve certain interventions, such as hospitalization, for acute intense bouts of suicidality.

Prioritizing Suicidal Behaviors

In DBT, behaviors are targeted in order according to a hierarchy. Suicidal behaviors are considered Target 1 and are accorded the highest priority in session if and when they occur. Therapy interfering behaviors are Target 2, and quality-of-life (QOL) interfering behaviors are Target 3. QOL interfering behaviors include behaviors and symptoms that interfere with having a life worth living but are not immediately life-threatening, such as substance use, interpersonal problems, and impulsive sexual behaviors.

Eating disorders are generally considered Target 3 behaviors because although they may eventually lead to serious medical problems, they are typically not immediately life-threatening. However, under certain circumstances, eating disorder behaviors are considered Target 1. It has been suggested that eating disorder behaviors be considered Target 1 when the patient has been evaluated as medically unstable (e.g., meets criteria for bradycardia, arrhythmia, or electrolyte abnormalities) and therefore requires immediate medical attention because this increases the risk for sudden death (Wisniewski, Safer, & Chen, 2007). Thus, when a clinician deems ED behaviors serious enough that they are immediately life-threatening, those behaviors may be addressed very similarly to suicidal ideation or behavior.

Suicidal Behaviors as Maladaptive Problem Solving

In DBT, the clinician views all suicidal behaviors as maladaptive problem-solving behaviors, whereas the patient often views suicide as a solution to the problems in his or her life. While the solution of suicide is on the table, it is difficult to find motivation to solve actual problems in life. For instance, one can imagine a patient who is very depressed and suicidal and who might state, "Why should I brush my teeth today since I am planning on killing myself?" The idea of killing himself would actually prevent him from doing anything, major or minor, that would improve his life.

Therapist Stance

In DBT, the therapist maintains a characteristic, overarching stance of nonapproval of suicidality. The therapist never agrees that suicide is an effective solution or in any way gives permission for suicide. Certainly, the therapist would never employ some sort of paradoxical strategy and instruct the patient to kill him- or herself or express disbelief that the patient would actually carry out the suicidal behavior. It can be very useful to simply and emphatically instruct the patient not to do it. Furthermore, the therapist generates hopeful statements and solutions. If a solution is not immediately available, the therapist should remind the patient that together they are a team and that they will continue to focus on solving the problem together.

Validation of Pain

When a patient is expressing suicidality, therapists must strike a delicate balance between validating the patient's pain and invalidating the idea of suicide as a solution to that pain. It is important to attend to and express understanding of the feelings of intense psychological pain that led the patient to engage in suicidal behavior.

Removal of Means

If the patient has lethal means that he or she plans to use, such as pills, knives, or a gun, the therapist must instruct the patient to dispose of them. These items could be turned over to the therapist if in session, or the patient could go home and retrieve the items and bring them to the therapist. Alternatively, the patient and the therapist could together ask someone in the patient's social network to hold the items, or the patient could dispose of the means while on the phone with the therapist. It is important that the therapist ask the patient to dispose of the means and follow up to ensure this has actually happened.

Behavioral Chain Analysis

Behavioral chain analysis (BCA) is a key skill in DBT, and it is designed to assess the problem, what is causing it, what the barriers are to solving it, and what skills the patient can use to solve it. Importantly, BCA can uncover the function of the behavior, which in the case of suicidal behavior might be that it seems like a solution to problems, feelings of relief, attention from loved ones, and so on (for a detailed description of BCAs, see Linehan [1993] and Rizvi & Ritschel [2014]). In-depth BCAs should be done after instances of suicidal behaviors or eating disorder behaviors when health is compromised, especially if those behaviors were recent, to clarify the environmental factors, emotional and cognitive responses, and actions that led to the suicidal behavior, as well as the behavior's consequences. The therapist should ask questions that highlight the idea that suicidal responses are not necessary or inevitable responses to the circumstances (e.g., "At what point did the thought of suicide cross your mind?" and "Did you consider the consequences of purging on your heart?").

Social Support

When a patient reports suicidal ideation, intent, and/or a plan, mobilizing the social network can be a crucial part of the treatment plan. A therapist could personally stay in contact with the patient or could solicit help from the patient's significant others, family members, or other members of the treatment team.

Phone Coaching

In DBT, the therapist is available between sessions to provide coaching by phone and/or text. Phone coaching is offered to help patients learn to ask for help effectively, generalize skills usage to outside of session, offer a venue for repairing ruptures in the therapeutic relationship, and provide more therapeutic support outside of regular session. A major function of phone coaching is for the patient to ask for help before acting on urges for suicide or self-harm. Importantly, the therapist and patient agree at the outset that they will not engage in phone coaching for 24 hours after the patient has self-harmed or attempted suicide. The purpose of the 24-hour rule is to ensure that suicidal behavior is not reinforced by increased therapist contact but, instead, the patient is rewarded for reaching out before acting on urges.

Skills-Based Crisis Plan

The therapist should help the patient develop a behavioral plan for avoiding suicide. This likely involves identifying alternative behaviors, skills to use, and/or asking the patient to call for help before engaging in suicidal behaviors. This type of crisis plan focuses on what the patient *will* do, in terms of using skills and enlisting social support, as opposed to simply focusing on avoiding suicidal behavior. If possible, this plan should include removal of means.

Commitment and Contracts

Regardless of the plan developed, the therapist must obtain the patient's commitment to acting in accordance with the plan and avoiding suicidal behavior. Although it is fairly common for clinicians to use written no-suicide contracts, there is no evidence that these contracts prevent suicidal behavior (Joiner, Van Orden, Witte, & Rudd, 2009), and they might actually create a false sense of security for clinicians (Simon, 2002).

Differential Reinforcement

The therapist should keep behavioral principles in mind when deciding how to handle patients' suicidality. This involves helping the patient understand the negative effects of suicidality, being careful not to reinforce the suicidality, and reinforcing nonsuicidal coping responses. The therapist should help the patient understand the emotional impact of suicidality on others and how suicidality can burn people out. Suicidality does not solve the patient's problems, and it actually can prevent the patient from focusing on problem solving. For instance, in the example described previously, the patient was so focused on suicide that he could not engage in daily maintenance behaviors such as brushing his teeth. In addition, over time, suicidality can erode the patient's self-esteem.

It is natural for people, including mental health providers, to pay more attention when a patient is suicidal. People may be tempted to make more encouraging, validating statements, such as "Please don't hurt yourself. We all care about you so much and we couldn't stand it if we lost you." Unfortunately, this uptick in warmth and attention may actually reinforce suicidality and make it more likely to occur in the future. Thus, the therapist should carefully balance the need for providing increased support when a patient is suicidal with the need to remain mindful of not having this increased attention and warmth occur only in response to suicidality. In practice, this balance might involve provision of a great deal of attention and warmth in response to nonsuicidal, healthy coping responses and responding to intermittent suicidal behavior with a matter-of-fact tone that ensures safety but does not provide prolonged extra contact. Similarly, the therapist may intervene in the patient's environment if others are responding in such a way that differentially rewards suicidal behavior or communication over problem solving or coping.

Higher Level of Care

When a therapist has attempted everything that can reasonably be tried to get a patient to commit to following a crisis plan and the patient continues to refuse or does not believe that he or she can keep him- or herself safe, voluntary or involuntary hospitalization may be considered. Hospitalization provides a more intensive period of observation and care, but it also runs the risk of reinforcing suicidality or disrupting the course of outpatient care. However, when the suicide risk appears very high and/or the individual appears incapable of acting in his or her best interest, hospitalization must be seriously considered. For eating disorder patients who appear to be at chronically higher risk of life-threatening behaviors (but not necessarily acutely suicidal), a higher level of eating disorder treatment might also be considered, such as partial hospital or residential.

Summary of Empirically Based Treatment Strategies

Although the previously discussed strategies may seem deceptively straight-forward on paper, they are very rarely so simple in clinical practice. In DBT, a consultation team composed of other clinicians is a required component of the treatment. At a minimum, in these high-risk situations, it is essential that any clinician treating a patient with an eating disorder and suicidality have access to peer consultation as needed. One of the factors that makes treating patients with suicidality and eating disorders so difficult is that sometimes reducing one behavior appears to lead to an increase in another type of behavior. For example, sometimes patients will say that the process of weight restoration is so distressing to them that it leads them to feel suicidal. Applying the DBT target hierarchy with the assistance of a consultation team can be very helpful in these situations.

CONCLUSION

Working with eating disorder patients is a high-risk endeavor in and of itself, given the associated medical complications. In addition, those with eating disorders have elevated rates of self-injurious behaviors and suicidality; thus, a clinician treating eating disorders should expect to encounter these behaviors. Clinicians treating patients with eating disorders and suicidality must continually assess for and be competent in treating suicidality. Although use of evidence-based interventions and a multidisciplinary treatment team can help prevent suicide, our field has yet to determine how to detect and eliminate all risk of suicide. Our field must continue to refine and improve methods of assessment and treatment for those with SIB and suicidality.

RESOURCES

American Foundation for Suicide Prevention: https://afsp.org
Joiner's Suicide Risk Assessment (JRSA): https://psy.fsu.edu/~joinerlab/
    measures/Joiner%20Lab--Risk%20Assessment.pdf
Linehan Risk Assessment and Management Protocol (LRAMP): http://depts.
    washington.edu/uwbrtc/wp-content/uploads/LSSN-LRAMP-v1.0.pdf
National Suicide Prevention Lifeline: http://www.suicidepreventionlifeline.
    org/gethelp.aspx

REFERENCES

American Psychiatric Association. (2013). *Diagnostic and statistical manual of mental disorders* (5th ed.). Arlington, VA: American Psychiatric Publishing.
Arcelus, J., Mitchell, A. J., Wales, J., & Nielsen, S. (2011). Mortality rates in patients with anorexia nervosa and other eating disorders: A meta-analysis of 36 studies. *Archives of General Psychiatry, 68*(7), 724–731.
Brausch, A. M., & Muehlenkamp, J. J. (2014). Experience of the body. In L. Claes & J. J. Muehlenkamp (Eds.), *Non-suicidal self-injury in eating disorders* (pp. 237–253). Berlin, Germany: Springer.
Bryan, C. J., Morrow, C. E., Anestis, M. D., & Joiner, T. E. (2010). A preliminary test of the interpersonal–psychological theory of suicidal behavior in a military sample. *Personality and Individual Differences, 48*, 347–350.

Carano, A., De Berardis, D., Campanella, D., Serroni, N., Ferri, F., Di Iorio, G., . . . Di Giannantonio, M. (2012). Alexithymia and suicide ideation in a sample of patients with binge eating disorder. *Journal of Psychiatric Practice, 18*(1), 5–11.

Chu, C., Klein, K. M., Buchman-Schmitt, J. M., Hom, M. A., Hagan, C. R., & Joiner, T. E. (2015). Routinized assessment of suicide risk in clinical practice: An empirically informed update. *Journal of Clinical Psychology, 71*(12), 1186–1200.

Dodd, D. R., Smith, A. R., & Bodell, L. P. (2014). Restraint feeds stress: The relationship between eating disorder symptoms, stress generation, and the interpersonal theory of suicide. *Eating Behaviors, 15*, 567–573.

Forman, E. M., Berk, M. S., Henriques, G. R., Brown, G. K., & Beck, A. T. (2004). History of multiple suicide attempts as a behavioral marker of severe psychopathology. *American Journal of Psychiatry, 161*, 437–443.

Forrest, L. N., Bodell, L. P., Witte, T. K., Siegfried, N., Bartlett, M. L., Goodwin, N., . . . Smith, A. R. (2016). Associations between eating disorder symptoms and suicidal ideation through thwarted belongingness and perceived burdensomeness among eating disorder patients. *Journal of Affective Disorders, 195*, 127–135.

Forrest, L. N., Zuromski, K. L., Dodd, D. R., & Smith, A. R. (2017). Suicidality in adults and adolescents with binge-eating disorder: Results from the National Comorbidity Survey Replication and Adolescent Supplement. *International Journal of Eating Disorders, 50*, 40–49.

Franko, D. L., & Keel, P. K. (2006). Suicidality in eating disorders: Occurrence, correlates, and clinical implications. *Clinical Psychology Review, 26*(6), 769–782.

Gould, M. S., Marrocco, F. A., Kleinman, M., Thomas, J. G., Mostkoff, K., Cote, J., & Davies, M. (2005). Evaluating iatrogenic risk of youth suicide screening programs: A randomized controlled trial. *Journal of the American Medical Association, 293*(13), 1635–1643.

Hunt, I. M., Windfuhr, K., Swinson, N., Shaw, J., Appleby, L., & Kapur, N. (2010). Suicide amongst psychiatric in-patients who abscond from the ward: A national clinical survey. *BMC Psychiatry, 10*, 14.

Jobes, D. A. (2012). The Collaborative Assessment and Management of Suicidality (CAMS): An evolving evidence-based clinical approach to suicidal risk. *Suicide & Life-Threatening Behavior, 42*(6), 640–653.

Joiner, T. E. (2005). *Why people die by suicide.* Cambridge, MA: Harvard University Press.

Joiner, T. E. (2010). *Myths about suicide.* Cambridge, MA: Harvard University Press.

Joiner, T. E., Van Orden, K. A., Witte, T. K., & Rudd, M. D. (2009). *The interpersonal theory of suicide: Guidance for working with suicidal clients.* Washington, DC: American Psychological Association.

Joiner, T. E., Van Orden, K. A., Witte, T. K., Selby, E. A., Ribeiro, J. D., Lewis, R., & Rudd, M. D. (2009). Main predictions of the Interpersonal–psychological theory of suicidal behavior: Empirical tests in two samples of young adults. *Journal of Abnormal Psychology, 118*, 634–646.

Keshaviah, A., Edkins, K., Hastings, E. R., Krishna, M., Franko, D. L., Herzog, D. B., . . . Eddy, K. T. (2014). Re-examining premature mortality in anorexia nervosa: A meta-analysis redux. *Comprehensive Psychiatry, 55*, 1773–1784.

Kostro, K., Lerman, J. B., & Attia, E. (2014). The current status of suicide and self-injury in eating disorders: A narrative review. *Journal of Eating Disorders, 2*(1), 19.

Linehan, M. M. (1993). *Cognitive–behavioral treatment of borderline personality disorder.* New York, NY: Guilford.

Linehan, M. M., Comtois, K. A., & Ward-Ciesielski, E. (2012). Assessing and managing risk with suicidal individuals. *Cognitive and Behavioral Practice, 19*(2), 218–232.

Milos, G., Spindler, A., Hepp, U., & Schnyder, U. (2004). Suicide attempts and suicidal ideation: Links with psychiatric comorbidity in eating disorder subjects. *General Hospital Psychiatry, 26*(2), 129–135.

Mintz, R. S. (1968). Psychotherapy of the suicidal patient. In H. L. P. Resnik (Ed.), *Suicidal behaviors: Diagnosis and management* (pp. 271–296). Boston: Little, Brown.

Miranda, R., Scott, M., Hicks, R., Wilcox, H. C., Munfakh, J. L. H., & Shaffer, D. (2008). Suicide attempt characteristics, diagnoses, and future attempts: Comparing multiple attempters to single attempters and ideators. *Journal of the American Academy of Child & Adolescent Psychiatry, 47*(1), 32–40. doi:http://dx.doi.org/10.1097/chi.0b013e31815a56cb

Monteith, L. L., Menefee, D. S., Pettit, J. W., Leopoulos, W. L., & Vincent, J. P. (2013). Examining the interpersonal–psychological theory of suicide in an inpatient veteran sample. *Suicide and Life-Threatening Behavior, 43*, 418–428.

Morrison, L. L., & Downey, D. L. (2000). Racial differences in self-disclosure of suicidal ideation and reasons for living: Implications for training. *Cultural Diversity and Ethnic Minority Psychology, 6*(4), 374.

Panos, P. T., Jackson, J. W., Hasan, O., & Panos, A. (2014). Meta-analysis and systematic review assessing the efficacy of dialectical behavior therapy (DBT). *Research on Social Work Practice, 24*(2), 213–223.

Pisetsky, E. M., Thornton, L. M., Lichtenstein, P., Pedersen, N. L., & Bulik, C. M. (2013). Suicide attempts in women with eating disorders. *Journal of Abnormal Psychology, 122*(4), 1042–1056.

Preti, A., Rocchi, M. B. L., Sisti, D., Camboni, M. V., & Miotto, P. (2011). A comprehensive meta-analysis of the risk of suicide in eating disorders. *Acta Psychiatrica Scandinavica, 124*(1), 6–17.

Rizvi, S. L., & Ritschel, L. A. (2014). Mastering the art of chain analysis in dialectical behavior therapy. *Cognitive and Behavioral Practice, 21*, 335–349.

Simon, R. I. (2002). Suicide risk assessment: What is the standard of care? *Journal of the American Academy of Psychiatry and the Law, 30*, 340–344.

Smith, A. R., Fink, E. L., Anestis, M. D., Ribeiro, J., Gordon, K. H., Davis, H., . . . Joiner, T. E. (2013). Exercise caution: Over-exercise is associated with suicidality in bulimia nervosa. *Psychiatry Research, 26*, 246–255.

Smith, A. R., Ribeiro, J. D., Mikolajewski, A., Taylor, J., Joiner, T. E., & Iacono, W. G. (2012). An examination of environmental and genetic contributions to the determinants of suicidal behavior among male twins. *Psychiatry Research, 197*, 60–65.

Smith, A. R., Velkoff, E. A., Ribeiro, J. D., & Franklin, J. (2017). ED symptoms and diagnosis in the longitudinal prediction of suicidal behavior: A meta-analysis. Submitted for publication.

Stanley, B., & Brown, G. K. (2012). Safety planning intervention: A brief intervention to mitigate suicide risk. *Cognitive and Behavioral Practice, 19*(2), 256–264. doi:http://dx.doi.org/10.1016/j.cbpra.2011.01.001

Suominen, K., Isometsa, E., Suokas, J., Haukka, J., Achte, K., & Lonnqvist, J. (2004). Completed suicide after a suicide attempt: A 37-year follow-up study. *American Journal of Psychiatry, 161*, 562–563.

Svirko, E., & Hawton, K. (2007). Self-injurious behavior and eating disorders: The extent and nature of the association. *Suicide and Life-Threatening Behavior, 37*(4), 409–421.

Swanson, S. A., Crow, S. J., Le Grange, D., Swendsen, J., & Merikangas, K. R. (2011). Prevalence and correlates of eating disorders in adolescents: Results from the National Comorbidity Survey Replication Adolescent Supplement. *Archives of General Psychiatry, 68*(7), 714–723.

Van Orden, K. A., Witte T. K., Gordon, K. H., Bender, T. W., & Joiner, T. E. (2008). Suicidal desire and the capability for suicide: Tests of the interpersonal–psychological theory of suicidal behavior among adults. *Journal of Consulting and Clinical Psychology, 76*, 72–83.

Wasserman, D., Rihmer, Z., Rujescu, D., Sarchiapone, M., Sokolowski, M., Titelman, D., . . . Carli, V. (2012). The European Psychiatric Association (EPA) guidance on suicide treatment and prevention. *European Psychiatry, 27*(2), 129–141.

Wisniewski, L., Safer, D., & Chen, E. (2007). Dialectical behavior therapy and eating disorders. In L. A. Dimeff, & K. Koerner (Eds.), *Dialectical behavior therapy in clinical practice: Applications across disorders and settings; dialectical behavior therapy in clinical practice: Applications across disorders and settings* (pp. 174–221, Chapter xx, 363 Pages) Guilford Press, New York, NY. Retrieved from https://search.proquest.com/docview/621880860?accountid=14524

Witte, T. K., Zuromski, K. L., Gauthier, J. M., Smith, A. R., Bartlett, M., Siegfried, N., . . . Goodwin, N. (2016). Restrictive eating: Associated with suicide attempts, but not acquired capability in residential patients with eating disorders. *Psychiatry Research, 235*, 90–96.

6

Eating Disorders and Borderline Personality Disorder

Strategies for Managing Life-Threatening and Therapy-Interfering Behaviors

LUCENE WISNIEWSKI AND LESLIE K. ANDERSON ■

Borderline personality disorder (BPD) is one of the most common personality disorder diagnoses observed in patients with eating disorders (EDs) (Cassin & von Ranson, 2005). The diagnostic criteria for BPD (American Psychiatric Association, 2013) can be organized according to five categories of behavioral, emotional, and cognitive dysregulation (Linehan, 1993). First, individuals with BPD have emotional dysregulation, including emotional instability and reactivity, and problems with anger. Second, they experience interpersonal dysregulation, including unstable relationships and efforts to avoid loss. Third, they tend to have behavioral dysregulation, including suicide threats, parasuicide, and self-damaging, impulsive behaviors including substance use. Fourth, they experience cognitive dysregulation and disturbances, such as depersonalization, dissociation, and even delusions. Fifth, they have self-dysfunction in the form of unstable self-image and chronic feelings of emptiness.

This chapter briefly reviews the prevalence and presentation of co-occurring ED and BPD and the treatment approaches for working with this population. The chapter focuses on dialectical behavior therapy (DBT), the most widely studied evidence-based treatment for BPD, which is also the only treatment that has been adapted specifically for an ED–BPD population. Because ED–BPD patients tend to have multiple, challenging treatment targets, this chapter explores in depth how to use treatment strategies from DBT to effectively target life-threatening and therapy-interfering behaviors.

PREVALENCE OF EATING DISORDERS AND COMORBID BORDERLINE PERSONALITY DISORDER

There is debate in the literature about whether BPD can be accurately diagnosed in an individual with an active ED due to the difficulty distinguishing between chronic traits that are attributed to a PD and transient states that may improve when the ED is in remission (Vitousek & Stumpf, 2005). However, it appears that individuals with ED are likely to also suffer from BPD, with studies showing that approximately 25–30% of patients with anorexia nervosa (AN) and bulimia nervosa (BN) meet criteria for BPD, whereas up to 12% of those with binge-eating disorder meet criteria for BPD (Cassin & von Ranson, 2005; Sansone, Levitt, & Sansone, 2005). BPD is particularly common among individuals who, regardless of diagnosis, engage in binge eating, which makes sense considering that impulsivity, sensation seeking, and novelty seeking are typical of binge-eating syndromes (Cassin & von Ranson, 2005). Likewise, in studies of patients with BPD, up to 54% meet criteria for a lifetime ED (Zanarini, Frankenburg, Hennen, Reich, & Silk, 2004).

COMPLEXITIES OF COMORBID PRESENTATIONS

The hallmark feature of BPD is intensely experienced emotions and a marked difficulty regulating them. Eating disorder treatment involves exposure to an array of intensely feared weight- and food-based cues, which additionally elevates emotion dysregulation in patients with both an ED and BPD. A number of studies have found that individuals with both ED and BPD present with a more complicated clinical picture compared to individuals with ED alone, in terms of both eating pathology and more severe problems with depression, anxiety, impulse control, and affect dysregulation (Zeeck, Birindelli, Sandholz, Joos, Herzog, & Hartmann, 2007). Risk of suicide is elevated among those with eating disorders, with studies showing that those with AN and BN are 7–31 times more likely to have a fatal suicide attempt than those without eating disorders (Preti, Rocchi, Sisti, Camboni, & Miotto, 2011). In addition, it is estimated that almost 10% of those with BPD will eventually commit suicide (Pompili, Girardi, Ruberto, & Tatarelli, 2005), meaning that individuals with both ED and BPD are likely an extremely high-risk group in terms of suicidality.

When BPD traits are present, ED treatment can be more complicated, with patients being less likely to respond to treatment and more likely to be perceived negatively by treatment providers (Woollaston & Hixenbaugh, 2008). Individuals with ED and BPD also tend to engage in a myriad of behaviors that have the potential to impede therapy, which can cause challenges for therapists, who may be faced with clinical dilemmas with regard to limiting these behaviors, attending to health-threatening or self-destructive behaviors without reinforcing them, in addition to ensuring that these behaviors do not supersede the therapeutic focus on ED symptoms.

TREATMENT APPROACHES

A subset of patients fail to respond to traditional evidence-based approaches to eating disorders, and some research has suggested that comorbid BPD is associated with treatment nonresponse (Johnson, Tobin, & Dennis, 1990). Regarding the literature on treating BPD, researchers have suggested that effective treatment for ED–BPD must include an integrated and comprehensive approach that focuses not only on the ED symptoms but also on interpersonal skills, affect regulation, and impulse control (Zeeck et al., 2007). Whereas there is a robust literature on the treatment of BPD alone, there is very little on treating the co-occurrence of ED and BPD. Medication, including antidepressants, second-generation antipsychotics, and mood stabilizers, has been shown to be somewhat effective in treating core symptoms and associated psychopathology in BPD (Lieb, Völlm, Rücker, Timmer, & Stoffers, 2010). Currently, a number of promising psychological treatments are available for BPD, including mentalization-based treatment (Bateman & Fonagy, 2010), transference-focused psychotherapy (Yeomans, Levy, & Caligor, 2013), DBT (Linehan, 1993), and various psychodynamic approaches (for review, see Haskayne, Hirschfeld, & Larkin, 2014).

In terms of psychological approaches, DBT is considered the gold standard treatment for BPD, with more than 12 randomized controlled trials showing its efficacy for this population (Kliem, Kröger, & Kosfelder, 2010). DBT is intended for patients with multiple diagnoses and includes strategies for targeting problem behaviors using a model of emotion dysregulation and according to a hierarchy of severity. Although DBT was originally developed for BPD and suicidality, it has been adapted specifically for patients with a primary ED (Anderson, Murray, Rockwell, Le Grange, & Kaye, 2015; Safer, Robinson, & Jo, 2010). Furthermore, DBT is the only treatment approach that has been adapted and tested specifically for patients with both ED and BPD, thus making it the likely treatment of choice for this population (Ben-Porath, Wisniewski, & Warren, 2009; Chen, Matthews, Allen, Kuo, & Linehan, 2008; Federici & Wisniewski, 2013). DBT appears to play a critical role in increasing ED–BPD patients' sense of efficacy regarding their ability to regulate affect (Ben-Porath et al., 2009). Perhaps most important, DBT provides a framework for conceptualizing and treating behaviors that may be life-threatening as well as therapy-interfering behaviors.

Certainly, therapists working with ED–BPD patients need to be prepared to clinically address self-harm, suicidality, impulsive behaviors, and/or difficulties in the therapeutic relationship because these behaviors are common characteristics of the BPD diagnosis. Part of what makes this so difficult is that when patients have multiple different behaviors, it is difficult to prioritize which ones to target, and making progress toward one goal is often derailed by the emergence of another behavior or crisis. The next section describes the DBT approach to targeting the multiple, complex behaviors that are characteristic of those diagnosed with both ED and BPD, and it provides specifics on how to manage behaviors that interfere with making progress in treatment.

DIALECTICAL BEHAVIOR THERAPY: PHILOSOPHY
AND STRATEGIES

DBT is an outpatient, cognitive–behavioral treatment that includes four components: skills training groups, individual sessions, telephone coaching, and a therapist consultation team. In skills training groups, patients learn skills for regulating
their emotions, including mindfulness, distress tolerance, emotion regulation,
and interpersonal effectiveness. Individual sessions are designed to help patients
stay motivated and use skills instead of engaging in impulsive or self-destructive
behaviors. Telephone coaching is available outside of regularly scheduled sessions
and provides assistance to patients in generalizing the skills they are learning to
situations and urges that occur outside of sessions. The therapist consultation team
meets weekly with the purpose of increasing adherence to the model and providing support to the therapists treating this difficult population (Linehan, 1993).

In working with patients with a variety of impulsive and life-threatening behaviors, as well as crises that frequently threaten to derail therapy, it is important to
have a plan for setting an agenda and staying on track. In DBT, behaviors are
approached in order depending on their importance within the target hierarchy
(for a detailed explanation of the target hierarchy, see Linehan, 1993). The first set
of behaviors, Target 1 behaviors, includes any behavior that could be imminently
life-threatening. If Target 1 behaviors occur, they are always accorded top priority; these are discussed later in the form of a detailed behavioral chain analysis. In
BPD, these behaviors commonly include self-harm by cutting or burning, suicidal
ideation, or suicide attempts and can also include suicide threats or planning and
urges to engage in these behaviors. Eating disorders can also be lethal; in fact, they
have the highest rates of morbidity and mortality of any psychiatric condition
(Arcelus, Mitchell, Wales, & Nielsen, 2011). Thus, under certain circumstances,
such as when a patient has been evaluated as medically unstable, ED behaviors
are considered Target 1 (Wisniewski, Safer, & Chen, 2011). An ED behavior is
considered Target 1 if an individual meets criteria for medical conditions such as
bradycardia, arrhythmia, or electrolyte abnormalities.

The second set of behaviors, Target 2 behaviors, includes any behavior (of the
patient or clinician) that interferes with the therapy process. Therapy-interfering
behaviors (TIBs) are considered second in importance only to life-threatening
behaviors, and they include behaviors that interfere with the immediate process of treatment (e.g., not attending sessions and refusing to talk), behaviors that
are related to suicidal acts (e.g., not calling for help before engaging in a suicidal
behavior), and behaviors that mirror problem behaviors in the patient's life (e.g.,
hostile remarks and avoidance of difficult topics). Patients with ED–BPD tend
to have a unique set of TIBs. Eating disorder behaviors may be classified under
Target 2 when they interfere with receiving treatment, such as an inability to
remember what was discussed in session due to malnutrition or purging prior
to session in order to feel numb. Similarly, behaviors that would block progress,
such as lying about food intake or drinking water before being weighed to give the
illusion of weight gain, would be considered therapy-interfering. Box 6.1 contains

Box 6.1

Examples of Therapy-Interfering Behaviors

Behaviors that interfere with receiving therapy

Nonattentive behaviors

Cancel appointment/drop out

Getting admitted to the hospital

Using mind-altering substances prior to a session

Walking out of sessions/groups before they end

Having seizures during session

Dissociating during session

Inadequate intake resulting in inattention during session

Pacing or standing during session

Involuntary vomiting in group

Noncollaborative behaviors

Inability/refusal to work in therapy

Lying

Not talking at all

"I don't know"

Withdrawing emotionally during session

Using water or other weights to make it appear weight has increased

Refusal to work on eating "in vivo"

Lying about intake

Refusing to be weighed

Refusal to allow family members to be involved in treatment when doing so would aid in recovery

Noncompliant behaviors

Not filling out diary cards; partially or incorrectly completing diary cards

Not bringing in diary cards

Not completing or partially completing homework

Refusing to comply with treatment recommendations

Exercising against medical advice

Refusal to agree to higher level of care when necessary

Not bringing in food for therapeutic meal

Hiding food

Behaviors that interfere with other patients

Openly critical, hostile, and judgmental remarks directed at other patients

Critical remarks directed toward treatment program

Wearing revealing clothing to ED treatment

Behaviors that burn out therapists

Behaviors that burn out therapists by pushing the therapists' personal limits (everyone has their own limits that may vary over time and over patients)

Phoning too much

Going to the therapist's house (social media contact?)

Interacting with the therapist's family members

Refusing to engage/accept strategies that the therapist believes are essential to progress

Continuing to lose weight and refusing to collaborate on weight maintenance or gain

Behaviors that burn out therapists by pushing organizational limits

Not waiting for therapist in waiting room

Not paying therapy bill

Openly critical, hostile, judgmental, oppositional remarks toward other staff and therapists

Vomiting in lobby restroom

Statements that burn out therapists by decreasing therapists' motivation

Statements that the therapist is "not a good therapist"

A hostile attitude

Criticism of the therapist's person or personality

Criticism of the therapist's place of work

Demanding refund for therapy

Slow progress

Chronic medical instability due to ED behaviors

Therapy Interfering Behaviors of Therapists

Behaviors creating a therapeutic power imbalance

Imbalance of change versus acceptance

Imbalance of flexibility versus stability: switching strategies in an effort to progress

Rigidly maintaining strategies that produce no progress or extreme distress for patient

Imbalance of nurturing versus change

Doing for the patient versus withholding help

Imbalance of reciprocal versus irreverent communication

Behaviors showing a lack of respect for the patient

Miss or forgets appointment

Frequently cancels or reschedules appointments

Does not return phone calls/messages

Loses papers/files/notes

Is late for appointments

Allows interruptions such as phone calls or messages

Dozes off when with patient

Talks about other patients

Ends sessions prematurely

Therapy-interfering behaviors specific to ED therapists

Not staying current in EDs

Not addressing eating issues as a part of treatment (e.g., weighing patient and food log)

Therapist ED issues interfere with objectivity

Not pushing for family involvement when it would be effective

Failing to recognize or confront persistent lack of progress

---

a comprehensive list of TIBs, with those that are unique to ED patients shown in italics.

Patients with ED–BPD frequently engage in traditional TIBs, such as missing a session or avoiding discussing difficult topics, as well as ED TIBs. Likewise, the professionals who work with these complex diagnoses may find themselves engaging in behaviors with this group that they do not engage in with others (Linehan, 1993). TIBs do not occur in a vacuum. They are generally initiated and maintained via an interaction between the patient and the therapist. Little has been written on the role of behaviors that interfere with treatment of EDs or on how clinicians can effectively address them.

The third set of behaviors, Target 3 behaviors, consists of maladaptive behaviors that interfere with the individual's quality of life. Common Target 3 behaviors include substance abuse, depression, anxiety, and financial issues. Most ED behaviors are actually considered Target 3 behaviors because although they interfere with quality of life, they are unlikely to lead to imminent death.

Patients with BPD can exhibit multiple target behaviors both within and between sessions. It can be particularly challenging for a therapist to determine which behaviors fall into which category and to then structure the agenda in session accordingly. The unique set of behaviors exhibited by patients with BPD and ED can pose an additional challenge for case conceptualization. Another challenge is determining how to prioritize behavioral targets within the same level. For example, it is not uncommon for ED–BPD patients to have ED symptoms that are considered life-threatening (e.g., medical instability due to restriction) alongside suicidal actions and/or self-harm (e.g., recent medication overdose or cutting with razor blades). Similarly, a patient could have multiple TIBs at the same time (e.g., being late to sessions, lying about meal consumption, and failing to complete homework assignments). Therapists must carefully choose which behavior(s) to target based on (1) how recently the behavior occurred and (2) the seriousness of the behavior. The treatment of life-threatening behaviors is discussed elsewhere in this book; thus, the following section is devoted to outlining guidelines for responding to and treating common ED–BPD TIBs, and a case example is presented to illustrate how and when to apply these guidelines with a patient.

GUIDELINES FOR TREATING ED–BPD

Case Example

Sue (an amalgamation of patients designed to obscure identity) is a 26-year-old single woman diagnosed with anorexia nervosa, major depressive disorder, generalized anxiety disorder, and borderline personality disorder. Sue has been treated for her ED on and off since age 16 years, with multiple stays in inpatient, residential, and partial hospital settings. Most recently, she has seen a well-respected cognitive–behavioral therapist who made the referral, hoping that DBT could more effectively address behaviors that had plagued Sue's care, such as frequent (up to monthly) hospitalizations, suicidal ideation and behavior, self-harm, leaving treatment against medical advice, "shutting down," slow change, lying, and significant passivity.

Pretreatment

The pretreatment phase of DBT treatment is of paramount importance in order to orient the patient to the structure of therapy, establish shared goals for therapy, and obtain the patient's commitment to completing the course of therapy. Outlining these guidelines in advance and obtaining commitment to treatment may help strengthen commitment to recovery and prevent dropout. The actual working phase of treatment does not begin until pretreatment is complete. In DBT, potential participants remain in pretreatment until a formal commitment to treatment is made (Linehan, 1993). The therapist agrees to meet with Sue in order to determine if they can formulate the patient's problems and experiences and determine if they can work together.

During the course of three pretreatment sessions, the therapist reviews the theory that ED behaviors, as well as other impulsive, self-destructive behaviors, often represent an attempt to cope with unwanted emotions. Therefore, goals of treatment will include learning to experience, express, and cope with emotions effectively without turning to ED behaviors. Although Sue is ambivalent about recovery and is suspicious about DBT given her past unsuccessful treatment attempts, she reveals a strong desire to finish a semester of college.

Another task during pretreatment is to make patients aware of the treatment targets in DBT and how they will be addressed in and across sessions. As discussed previously, the target hierarchy is a framework with which the therapist and patient are able to consider a behavior's seriousness. The DBT treatment model in general and the target hierarchy in particular have been compared to having a good map that can aid a clinician in navigating difficult terrain (Koerner, 2012). A map may be particularly essential with a patient such as Sue, who has multiple, chronic, serious, and life-threatening problems.

Sue's illness is made more complex by the relationship between her ED and suicidal ideation and behavior. Sue notices that when she eats more adequately, her weight and suicidality increase as well. After the fourth session, Sue makes a commitment to DBT treatment and, as part of this commitment, agrees to stay alive. Sue is willing to address her ED in the service of finishing a semester of school, although she is still quite ambivalent about recovery. The therapist and Sue collaboratively develop a conceptualization of what has prevented Sue from completing a semester of college. After conducting several behavioral chain analyses (BCAs) on her most recent experiences, they hypothesize that Sue's ED symptoms can at times increase to a level that causes medical instability. When this medical instability is paired with a stated and observed unwillingness to change behavior, her providers and family "demand" Sue to leave school and go to treatment midsemester. Sue describes two typical patterns of behavior that generally precede medical instability: (1) increased purging that results in electrolyte imbalance and risk factors for cardiac problems and (2) increased restriction that leads to bradycardia. Although each of these circumstances has resulted in medical hospitalization in the past and Sue is aware that these medical conditions can be lethal, she states that she does not always believe that these medical conditions will actually result in *her* death.

One factor that complicates Sue's clinical picture is that as weight increases, suicidality and self-harm increase as well. Sue notes that four of the past five psychiatric hospital admissions occurred after weight gain. The therapist and Sue agree on the need to focus on life-threatening behaviors and behaviors that lead to medical instability. The therapist and Sue collaborate in order to develop a plan that they hope will succeed in keeping Sue alive and out of the hospital.

Sue is currently restricting 50% of her meal plan and purging twice daily. Sue has identified that in the past, the expectation in treatment that she would completely recover would increase anxiety as well as fears of failure and letting others down. Sue has been able to identify that these fears then contribute to her leaving treatment against medical advice. Given these concerns, Sue and her therapist collaboratively develop a goal that Sue feels motivated to try to achieve: consuming 70% of her recommended meal plan and reducing purging to less than seven times per week. The therapist acknowledges that it may not be adequate to keep Sue out of hospital but believes it is a step in the right direction.

The Treatment: Targeting Life-Threatening Behaviors

All DBT sessions begin with a review of the diary card, and the agenda for the session is set collaboratively according to the target hierarchy. If there are any Target 1 behaviors that have occurred since the previous session, these are addressed first, followed by any Target 2 behaviors and then Target 3 behaviors. Patients are encouraged to either complete a BCA and solution analysis for any Target 1 behaviors prior to session or complete the BCA collaboratively during the appointment (Rizvi & Ritschel, 2014).

Many of Sue's early sessions are spent conducting BCAs on Target 1 episodes of self-harm, urges to quit treatment (Target 2), or the episodes of binge eating, purging, or restriction that exceeded Sue's own goals. Sue remains medically stable during this time, so these ED behaviors are considered Target 3. The collaborative plan to decrease behaviors with the goal of preventing hospitalization is successful during the first 8–12 weeks of treatment. Sue's school attendance is good, and she notices less stress with her family now that she does not need to be hospitalized so often.

As a result of the increased eating and decreased purging, Sue gains approximately 2 pounds, and along with the decrease in ED behaviors, her urges for suicidality increase significantly. Sue is working to use skills to cope with distress rather than resorting to behaviors such as restriction or self-harm. With midterms approaching, Sue is particularly motivated to stay out of the hospital. Thus, she successfully uses the DBT skills of distract and self-soothe to tolerate the distress associated with weight gain, and she has not had any self-harm behaviors during this period despite her high urges.

The Treatment: Targeting Therapy-Interfering Behaviors

Directly naming and addressing TIBs is unique to DBT. Patients who suffer from multiple Axis I and Axis II issues, who often have complicated treatment histories, have the potential to elicit significant emotions in their caregivers. These patients may exhibit problematic behaviors that could result in premature termination, ensuring that they will not receive the treatment they need to recover. Therefore, DBT is organized to address these issues directly and in importance only behind the behaviors that are life-threatening.

For the first 6 months of treatment, Sue makes slow but steady progress: She is not hospitalized and successfully completes a semester of college while continuing to meet her personal goals of 75% meal plan compliance and purging no more than four times per week. The therapist and Sue have been practicing emotion regulation and distress tolerance skills, and despite what is now a 2.5-pound weight gain, she has not self-harmed in the past 4 months. The therapist now begins again to push for change.

The therapist shares with Sue her hypothesis that staying at this level of behavior may eventually result in her becoming medically unstable. The therapist uses a metaphor to convey this to Sue in a way that is memorable without putting her on the defensive. The therapist shares with Sue the following metaphor: "If you are picnicking on a cliff, you don't want to set your blanket up right on the edge. You want get further away, maybe 15 feet or so, to stay safe. Right now, your eating disorder behaviors are keeping you right at the edge of the cliff and I am worried that a strong wind could blow you off!" (L. Hill, personal communication, May 12, 2015).

The therapist's fear is realized when Sue develops the stomach flu and becomes medically unstable briefly. However, Sue is resistant to further decreasing behaviors. After several discussions, the therapist and Sue collaboratively develop a new goal: increase meal plan compliance to 85% and decrease purging to less than four times per week. The therapist is aware of how difficult this change will likely be for Sue and thus extends herself by offering to text Sue an encouraging message or picture every day that she meets her goal.

During the next several weeks and although the therapist is texting Sue when she meets her goals, Sue's weight remains essentially unchanged, and her purging does not decrease. The therapist begins to notice new thoughts and feelings in her work with Sue. She notices having the thought, "Sue is not motivated," and feeling dread before meeting with Sue and anger during sessions. She has noticed frustration coming through in her voice and that she is taking longer to respond to coaching calls. The therapist realizes that she must address the TIBs.

Once a therapist is aware that TIBs may be a part of his or her work with a particular patient, the therapist must decide how to proceed. The first step in addressing behaviors that interfere with treatment is identifying and naming the TIB. Sometimes TIBs are obvious and everyone is aware of their existence (e.g., not doing homework, yelling at the therapist, or not showing up for session). Other times, the behaviors are more subtle, and the therapist may need to use strategies such as talking to the consultation team, conducting BCAs, practicing mindfulness, or a free writing exercise (for a description, see Koerner, 2012). The steps required to address behaviors that interfere with treatment are presented next.

1. *Operationalize the TIB*: It is of primary importance to identify the TIB as accurately as possible because it is difficult to change or address something one cannot describe (Chapman & Rosenthal, 2016). For the TIB to become something that the therapist and patient can effectively address, the behavior must be defined behaviorally and objectively such that it is clearly distinguishable or measurable and ultimately understood in terms of empirical observations.

In Sue's case, the therapist found herself struggling to behaviorally describe the TIBs and instead could identify only the thought, "Sue is unmotivated," leading to feelings of anger. The therapist was aware that it would be ineffective to frame the TIB as Sue being "unmotivated" because the term is often used judgmentally and does not reflect a specific behavior. After conducting several BCAs on her own feelings, the therapist brought the issue to her DBT consultation team. The consultation team helped the therapist to operationalize Sue's TIB as not having made consistent changes in eating and purging since meeting her own initial treatment goals. The team also identified some TIBs on the part of the therapist: not answering calls in a timely manner, talking to Sue with an irritated voice tone, and not balancing the dialectic of change and acceptance.

2. *Apply phenomenological empathy*: After the TIB is identified and opera-tionalized, the therapist must next find a nonjudgmental and compassionate way to *understand* the TIB. In DBT, this is also called the phenomenological empathy (PE) agreement. The PE agreement states that treaters must work to find the most empathic interpretation of a patient's behavior, based on one of the fundamental assumptions of DBT that patients are doing the best they can and want to improve. Developing a phenomenologically empathic understanding of behavior can help to decrease negative affect and judgment.

It is important to note that "any behavior, therapy-interfering or not, is understandable in the context of the patient's (or therapist's) learning his-tory, current contexts and contingencies, and the therapeutic relationship" (Chapman & Rosenthal, 2016, p. 21). The following are questions that may help the therapist develop a phenomenologically empathetic understanding of behavior: Is the behavior filling a need for the patient? Does the patient not have the coping skills needed? Is the patient trying to get a need met with this behavior? Might the patient want to avoid conflict, or has the patient been reinforced for this behavior in the past?

Applying PE in the context of the current case, the therapist was able to con-ceptualize Sue's slow progress as fear of change as well as protection against losing her ED identity. It was also useful for the therapist to use PE in order to understand her own feelings of anger and frustration with Sue. She under-stood that she wanted Sue to have a more full life and that Sue's failure to change quickly challenged her belief that this would be possible. The slow change also made her wonder if she was an effective therapist, which she placed high value on.

3. *Plan and execute the discussion*: Once the TIB has been identified and operationalized as well as understood in a phenomenologically empathic way, the therapist next must consider how and when she will discuss the TIB with her patient. In DBT, the session agenda is determined at the start of the session. TIBs are accorded high priority in the agenda, second only to life-threatening behaviors. The therapist can suggest a particular behavior be put on the agenda as well. The discussion around TIBs will likely be complicated and should occur within the context of a therapy session.

4. *Practice*: Given the power differential between the therapist and the patient, it can be difficult for a therapist to give problematic feedback to any patient. This may be especially true for patients with supreme sensitivity, such as those with BPD. A message must be heard by the patient in order for it to have any impact. Thus, to effectively address TIBs, the therapist could practice prior to the session, either with the consultation team or in her imagination, talking about the TIB in nonjudgmental language. The ther-apist could use a strategy such as writing down what she wants to say using

the DBT interpersonal effectiveness skills. It is important to remember to discuss the interactional nature of the TIB—it is a dance between two people, as opposed to being completely one person's fault. The TIB occurs in the context of this particular relationship, and it may or may not happen in a different context or at a different time in this relationship.

In the current situation, the therapist might say to Sue,

> I have noticed myself taking longer to answer your coaching calls as well as feeling irritated. I haven't felt this way toward you before and I don't like it. So I wanted to understand what is going on. In thinking about these feelings, I also noticed that over the past few months your weight has fluctuated up and down a pound or two each week, without consistent, long-term change. You have also reported that your purging is continuing unchanged as well.

5. *Highlight*: In delivering feedback that may be difficult to receive, it is especially important for the therapist to highlight with the patient why she views the behavior as problematic. In a sense, this allows the therapist to highlight and mindfully observe the patient's actions and her reactions to those behaviors. For example, the therapist may state,

> I am worried that I have let you down as a therapist as I dropped the ball on expecting change and have fallen too far on the side of acceptance. I believe I have been so thrilled by the changes that you have made that have allowed you to complete this semester at college, that I didn't want to "upset the apple cart" so to speak and therefore have not brought this issue up directly. That is not the kind of therapist I want to be! I believe that your wise mind doesn't want that either. As we have discussed over these months, you really want to finish your degree and to get a job.
>
> So continuing to work together without there being a change in ED behaviors is a problem for me: I am in the business of change [in the context of acceptance]. And I am unclear if you are wanting to change more right now. This challenges my belief about what a good therapist does. I am also worried that my focus on change and your not changing will burn me out and make me have less energy for working with you and I really don't want that to happen.
>
> Given our history together and the work we have done, I am wondering if these might be indicators that you have gone as far as you are willing to go right now in your treatment. I sometimes imagine that you think, "I am not having as many behaviors as I used to—I am doing pretty well!" I also wonder if the lack of change here in the face of the fact that you continue to come to sessions weekly might suggest that you are still invested in the therapeutic relationship. Is this correct? [Look for head nod.] If this is the case, you must feel that you are stuck between a rock and a hard place! You have made as many changes as you feel you want right now, and you get

the feeling from me that I am expecting you to change more. Is this correct? [Again, look for head nod.]

6. *Review that the patient heard what you were hoping to say*: The therapist
needs to be open to the notion that the patient might not agree on the assessment of the problem. So be sure to check with the patient whether he or she
understands your point and share your perception of the situation. Increased
emotion dysregulation could result in the patient perceiving the message differently than you have intended. Therefore, the therapist should confirm a
mutual understanding of the problem: "Does this make sense to you? Tell me
back what you are hearing so far."

7. *Ask for collaboration on what to do about it*: Do not assume that the patient
wants to change this TIB. The therapist will need to assess for motivation to
change the behavior. Ask questions such as "Where do you think this leaves
us?" and "How do we resolve this issue?"

8. *Offer solutions, but do not give the solution, if possible*: Once the TIB has
been identified and the patient has expressed willingness to collaborate on
solving the problem, the therapist and patient must work on generating and
choosing solutions. It can be effective for the therapist to help brainstorm
possible solutions and discuss the advantages and disadvantages of these solutions. However, it is best to have the patient choose which solution(s) to try.

Sue's therapist states,

> Some ideas that I have about this are: We can take a break until you are
> ready to work on the ED; we find some ED-related behavior that you are
> willing and ready to work on; we find you a therapist who is OK with your
> not changing. But we cannot continue as is. I am not willing to do therapy
> that is not working, and I don't want our relationship to suffer because we
> aren't pursuing the same goals.

9. *Follow-up*: The first conversation about this topic is not likely to be the
only one. The therapist should make sure that the issue of the TIB is put on
the agenda each week for a while. The therapist should check on the status of
the TIB on behalf of both parties and may focus on reinforcing appropriate
behavior both in session and later. The therapist will be mindful to note and
block problematic behavior if it appears again. If the TIB includes a behavior
that can be practiced (e.g., responding to feedback in a calm voice), doing so
in session can be helpful.

Returning to Sue and her therapist—they agreed to keep Sue's slow change and
the therapist's feelings of burnout on their agenda for Target 2 each week. As in
any relationship of importance that involves patterns of problematic behavior, this

intervention may not have fully resolved the quandary. Sue sometimes changed more slowly than the therapist found acceptable, and the therapist at times had feelings of burnout that showed up in session. However, DBT now afforded the dyad a language with which to discuss as well as an opportunity to continue to work on these concerns.

CONCLUSION

Due to the high rates of comorbidity, practitioners treating patients with eating disorders will almost certainly encounter patients with BPD. These comorbid patients tend to be more complex, with a greater number of target behaviors and therapy-interfering behaviors. Therapy-interfering behaviors, by definition, prevent the therapy from working, and they lead to burnout and frustration in therapists. Thus, it is important that these behaviors be addressed directly and nonjudgmentally. DBT provides a practical framework for approaching these behaviors effectively.

Although there has been extensive research on the full DBT package, as well as research on applications of the model specifically to ED–BPD populations (Ben-Porath et al., 2009; Chen et al., 2008; Federici & Wisniewski, 2013), the authors know of no research supporting the use of DBT's components in the context of other therapeutic approaches. Thus, when working with comorbid ED–BPD, it is recommended that practitioners use an adherent DBT approach, including individual therapy, skills group, phone coaching, and consultation team. Box 6.2

Box 6.2

FURTHER READING AND RESOURCES

Chapman, A., & Rosenthal, M. Z. (2016). *Managing therapy interfering behavior: Strategies from dialectical behavior therapy.* Washington, DC: American Psychological Association.

Linehan, M. M. (1993). *Cognitive–behavioral treatment of borderline personality disorder.* New York, NY: Guilford.

Linehan, M. M. (2015). *DBT skills training manual.* New York, NY: Guilford.

Linehan, M. M. (2015). *DBT skills training handouts and worksheets.* New York, NY: Guilford.

Miller, A. L., Rathus, J. H., Linehan, M. M., & Swenson, C. (2006). *Dialectical behavior therapy with suicidal adolescents.* New York, NY: Guilford.

Safer, D. L., Telch, C. F., Chen, E., & Linehan, M. M. (2009). *DBT for binge eating and bulimia.* New York, NY: Guilford.

The Linehan Institute: behavioraltech.org

---

provides a list of recommended reading and training resources for those who are interested in learning more about applying full-package DBT.

The information provided in this chapter is intended as a brief introduction to working with patients who have comorbid ED–BPD. It is hoped that clinicians can use this chapter as a starting point when treating these patients.

REFERENCES

American Psychiatric Association. (2013). *Diagnostic and statistical manual of mental disorders* (5th ed.). Arlington, VA: American Psychiatric Publishing.

Anderson, L. K., Murray, S. B., Rockwell, R., Le Grange, D., & Kaye, W. H. (2015). Integrating family-based treatment and dialectical behavior therapy for adolescent bulimia nervosa: Conceptual considerations. *Eating Disorders, 23*(4), 325–335.

Arcelus, J., Mitchell, A., Wales, J., & Nielsen, S. (2011). Is there an elevated mortality rate in anorexia nervosa and other eating disorders? A meta-analysis of 36 studies. *Archives of General Psychiatry, 68*, 724–731.

Bateman, A., & Fonagy, P. (2010). Mentalization based treatment for borderline personality disorder. *World Psychiatry, 9*, 11–15.

Ben-Porath, D., Wisniewski, L., & Warren, M. (2009). Differential treatment response for eating disordered patients with and without a comorbid borderline personality diagnosis using a dialectical behavior therapy (DBT)-informed approach. *Eating Disorders, 17*, 225–241.

Cassin, S. E., & von Ranson, K. M. (2005). Personality and eating disorders: A decade in review. *Clinical Psychology Review, 25*(7), 895–916.

Chapman, A., & Rosenthal, M. Z. (2016). *Managing therapy interfering behavior: Strategies from dialectical behavior therapy.* Washington, DC: American Psychological Association.

Chen, E. Y., Matthews, L., Allen, C., Kuo, J. R., & Linehan, M. M. (2008). Dialectical behavior therapy for clients with binge-eating disorder or bulimia nervosa and borderline personality disorder. *International Journal of Eating Disorders, 41*(6), 505–512.

Federici, A., & Wisniewski, L. (2013). An intensive DBT program for patients with multi-diagnostic eating disorder presentations: A case series analysis. *International Journal of Eating Disorders, 46*(4), 322–331.

Haskayne, D., Hirschfeld, R., & Larkin, M. (2014). The outcome of psychodynamic psychotherapies with individuals diagnosed with personality disorders: A systematic review. *Psychoanalytic Psychotherapy, 28*, 115–138.

Johnson, C., Tobin, D. L., & Dennis, A. (1990). Differences in treatment outcome between borderline and nonborderline bulimics at one-year follow-up. *International Journal of Eating Disorders, 9*(6), 617–627.

Kliem, S., Kröger, C., & Kosfelder, J. (2010). Dialectical behavior therapy for borderline personality disorder: A meta-analysis using mixed-effects modeling. *Journal of Consulting and Clinical Psychology, 78*, 936–951.

Koerner, K. (2012). *Doing dialectical behavior therapy: A practical guide.* New York, NY: Guilford.

Lenz, A. S., Taylor, R., Fleming, M., & Serman, N. (2014). Effectiveness of dialectical behavior therapy for treating eating disorders. *Journal of Counseling & Development*, 92, 26–35.

Lieb, K., Völlm, B., Rücker, G., Timmer, A., & Stoffers, J. M. (2010). Pharmacotherapy for borderline personality disorder: Cochrane systematic review of randomised trials. *British Journal of Psychiatry, 196*(1), 4–12.

Linehan, M. M. (1993). *Cognitive–behavioral treatment of borderline personality disorder.* New York, NY: Guilford.

Panos, P. T., Jackson, J. W., Hasan, O., & Panos, A. (2014). Meta-analysis and systematic review assessing the efficacy of dialectical behavior therapy (DBT). *Research on Social Work Practice, 24*(2), 213–223.

Pompili, M., Girardi, P., Ruberto, A., & Tatarelli, R. (2005). Suicide in borderline personality disorder: A meta-analysis. *Nordic Journal of Psychiatry, 59*(5), 319–324.

Preti, A., Rocchi, M. B. L., Sisti, D., Camboni, M. V., & Miotto, P. (2011). A comprehensive meta-analysis of the risk of suicide in eating disorders. *Acta Psychiatrica Scandinavica, 124*(1), 6–17.

Rizvi, S. L., & Ritschel, L. A. (2014). Mastering the art of chain analysis in dialectical behavior therapy. *Cognitive and Behavioral Practice, 21*, 335–349.

Safer, D. L., Robinson, A. H., & Jo, B. (2010). Outcome from a randomized controlled trial of group therapy for binge eating disorder: Comparing dialectical behavior therapy adapted for binge eating to an active comparison group therapy. *Behavior Therapy, 41*(1), 106–120.

Sansone, R. A., Levitt, J. L., & Sansone, L. A. (2005). The prevalence of personality disorders among those with eating disorders. *Eating Disorders, 13*(1), 7–21.

Vitousek, K., & Stumpf, R. E. (2005). Difficulties in the assessment of personality traits and disorders in eating-disordered individuals. *Eating Disorders, 13*, 137–140.

Wisniewski, L., Safer, D., & Chen, E. (2011). Dialectical behavior therapy and eating disorders. In L. A. Dimeff & K. Koerner (Eds.), *Dialectical behavior therapy in clinical practice: Applications across disorders and settings* (pp. 174–221). New York, NY: Guilford.

Woollaston, K., & Hixenbaugh, P. (2008). "Destructive whirlwind": Nurses' perceptions of patients diagnosed with borderline personality disorder. *Journal of Psychiatric and Mental Health Nursing, 15*, 703–709.

Yeomans, F. E., Levy, K. N., & Caligor, E. (2013). Transference-focused psychotherapy. *Psychotherapy, 50*(3), 449–453.

Zanarini, M. C., Frankenburg, F. R., Hennen, J., Reich, D. B., & Silk, K. R. (2004). Axis I comorbidity in patients with borderline personality disorder: 6-Year follow-up and prediction of time to remission. *American Journal of Psychiatry, 161*(11), 2108–2114.

Zanarini, M. C., Reichman, C. A., Frankenburg, F. R., Reich, D. B., & Fitzmaurice, G. (2010). The course of eating disorders in patients with borderline personality disorder: A 10-year follow-up study. *International Journal of Eating Disorders, 43*(3), 226–232.

Zeeck, A., Birindelli, E., Sandholz, A., Joos, A., Herzog, T., & Hartmann, A. (2007). Symptom severity and treatment course of bulimic patients with and without a borderline personality disorder. *European Eating Disorders Review, 15*, 430–438.

7

Body Dysmorphic Disorder and Eating Disorders

DANYALE MCCURDY-MCKINNON AND JAMIE D. FEUSNER ■

INTRODUCTION: BODY DYSMORPHIC DISORDER AND DISORDERED EATING

Prevalence and Background

Body dysmorphic disorder (BDD) is an often-serious psychiatric disorder characterized by clinically significant appearance preoccupations and repetitive behaviors. The classic hallmark of BDD is the preoccupation with perceived flaws in one's appearance that are minor or imperceptible to others (American Psychiatric Association [APA], 2013). BDD affects approximately 2% of the population (Veale, Gledhill, Christodoulou, & Hodsoll, 2016) and is classified as an obsessive–compulsive and related disorder (OCRD). The fifth edition of the *Diagnostic and Statistical Manual of Mental Disorders* (DSM-5) added a criterion that addresses compulsive behaviors, wherein an individual must have, at some point during the course of the disorder, engaged in repetitive behaviors such as mirror checking, grooming, or reassurance seeking (APA, 2013). Clinical significance can be determined by whether the disorder causes undue distress and impairment in social or occupational functioning. In addition, a good marker for what constitutes preoccupation would be an individual spending at least 1 hour per day thinking about his or her perceived defects and engaging in repetitive checking behaviors (APA, 2013). BDD is often very distressing and can be associated with disability, marked functional impairment, social isolation, and depression. Individuals with BDD also often experience suicidal ideation, with approximately one-fourth of those with BDD attempting suicide in their lifetime (Phillips et al., 2005). The morbidity and mortality of BDD highlight the importance of developing a better understanding of this illness. Furthermore, treating this disorder in the context of eating disorders, which are the most lethal of all mental illnesses (Arcelus, Mitchell, Wales, & Nielsen, 2011), is especially important.

The etiology and pathophysiology of BDD and eating disorders are complex. Neurobiological factors, especially those related to visual processing, likely contribute to the maintenance, and possibly the development, of both disordered eating and BDD symptoms. Although neurobiological research in BDD is still in its infancy, recent findings have emerged that may help inform our understanding of BDD's pathophysiology and its relationship to disordered eating.

This chapter explores the research findings regarding visual processing abnormalities and neurobiological overlap in disordered eating and BDD along with treatments for BDD that can be employed in cases in which BDD is comorbid with eating disorders. The chapter discusses effective pharmacological and behavioral treatments for BDD, which can be implemented in patients with comorbid disordered eating and BDD. Finally, it presents a clinically useful decision tree that can be used when treating a patient with comorbid disordered eating and BDD.

Comorbid Presentation

As with BDD, body image disturbance is a primary symptom of eating disorders (Fairburn & Harrison, 2003). Furthermore, BDD and eating disorders share several key common characteristics, including poor insight, early adolescent onset (most commonly), and chronic course. Approximately one-third of individuals with BDD have a comorbid lifetime eating disorder (17.5% eating disorder not otherwise specified, 9.0% anorexia nervosa [AN], and 6.5% bulimia nervosa [BN]), with BDD onset more commonly preceding eating disorder onset (Ruffolo, Phillips, Menard, Fay, & Weisberg, 2006). In addition, almost half of individuals with an eating disorder meet criteria for BDD (Dingemans, van Rood, de Groot, & van Furth, 2012). Thus, the likelihood of encountering a patient with comorbid disordered eating and BDD is high; this emphasizes the importance of understanding the pathophysiological overlap across the disorders.

It is crucial to understand the treatment implications of this overlap due to the seriousness of the combination of these disorders. Patients with an eating disorder and comorbid BDD are more likely to have added dysmorphic appearance concerns, greater anxiety symptoms, and a dissatisfaction with more body parts compared to patients with an eating disorder only (Dingemans et al., 2012). BDD and AN co-occur more often than BDD and BN co-occur, and there is evidence that AN and BDD share a delusional variant marked by poor insight regarding distorted body image beliefs (Konstantakopoulos et al., 2012). Individuals with an eating disorder and comorbid BDD have more severe psychopathology and a potentially greater risk of relapse due to their untreated dysmorphic concerns. Individuals with a primary diagnosis of BDD who meet criteria for a comorbid eating disorder also report more severe symptoms and receive more treatment than individuals with the sole diagnosis of BDD (Ruffolo et al., 2006). Another study indicated that those with eating disorders may have a similar reaction to perceived fatness as those with BDD react to perceived defects in other appearance domains (Mitchison, Crino, & Hay, 2013). Most alarmingly, individuals with AN and comorbid BDD have been found to have triple the suicide rate compared to those with AN alone (Grant, Kim, & Eckert, 2002), highlighting the importance of understanding and effectively treating these comorbid disorders.

VISUAL PROCESSING

Visual Processing in BDD

Individuals with BDD experience distortions of self-perception and appearance, which may contribute to their convictions of disfigurement and ugliness. This, along with impaired performance on tasks pertaining to detailed and global design features, suggests disturbances in visual perception and visuospatial processing. Several studies provide evidence of aberrant global visual processing, and some demonstrate enhanced local processing (Li, Arienzo, & Feusner, 2013; Madsen, Bohon, & Feusner, 2013). Local or detailed processing refers to attending to an image in a piecemeal manner. Global or holistic processing refers to viewing an image as a whole to capture the complete picture—that is, the "forest" rather than the "trees."

A series of studies have used functional neuroimaging to examine the brain correlates of these visual processing abnormalities in BDD. Two utilizing functional magnetic resonance imaging (fMRI) while participants viewed photographs of other (Feusner, Townsend, Bystritsky, & Bookheimer, 2007) and own (Feusner et al., 2010) faces provided evidence of imbalances in global versus local visual processing, specifically diminished configural and holistic processing. Studies testing non-appearance-related stimuli have also found global processing deficiencies, suggesting a more general abnormality (Feusner, Hembacher, Moller, & Moody, 2011). A study examining BDD in relationship to AN using fMRI and electroencephalography (Li, Lai, Bohon, et al., 2015) found similar visual aberrancies, suggesting a common deficiency in holistic processing. Imbalances between global and local processing in BDD, and similarly in AN, could contribute to visual misperception and perceptual distortions for appearance; details may not be adequately integrated and contextualized into a whole, resulting in an inability to determine that most of these "flaws" are minuscule relative to the whole.

Visual Processing in Eating Disorders

Neurobiological findings in eating disorders also point to disrupted visual networks and superior local visuospatial processing at the cost of global integration of stimuli. This is evident in AN and BN and reflects inflexibility and weak central coherence (Lang, Lopez, Stahl, Tchanturia, & Treasure, 2014), also observed in BDD. Several functional and structural imaging studies support these abnormal visual processing findings in eating disorders (Beato-Fernandez et al., 2009; Favaro et al., 2012; Fonville et al., 2013; Li, Lai, Loo, et al., 2015; Mohr et al., 2010; Uher et al., 2005; Vocks et al., 2010; Wagner, Ruf, Braus, & Schmidt, 2003). These studies suggest a similar pattern of atypical visual processing in eating disorders and BDD, manifesting as overly focused on details with less global and "big-picture" integration.

BRAIN STRUCTURE AND CONNECTIVITY

Several structural and connectivity studies in eating disorders also have implications for visuospatial processing and overlap with BDD. Individuals with AN demonstrate structural abnormalities in brain regions relevant to processing body image (Frieling et al., 2012; Suchran et al., 2010). Functional connectivity findings show similar implications in BN (Lavagnino et al., 2014). Thus, there is evidence of aberrant visuospatial processing in eating disorders that may contribute to their disturbed body image, which is similar to that of BDD.

Aberrant white matter network connectivity has been found in BDD, including in tracts that connect visual systems with emotion and memory systems (Arienzo et al., 2013; Buchanan et al., 2013; Feusner et al., 2013). In a white matter connectivity study directly comparing individuals with AN to those with BDD (Zhang et al., 2016), AN demonstrated abnormal modular connectivity patterns in which regions involved in reward were connected with those associated with habit and ritual formation. BDD demonstrated a similar trend. This may reflect the fact that ritualistic behaviors such as calorie counting or compulsive exercise could be experienced as rewarding.

TREATMENT IMPLICATIONS AND OPTIONS

Eating disorders clinicians may tend to attribute body image disturbance to the eating disorder rather than recognizing the disturbance as BDD, or they may be confused as to when both diagnoses should be given. This may be due to a few factors. First, there are some diagnostic issues that convolute the clinical picture. Criterion D for BDD in the DSM-5 states that "the appearance preoccupation is not better explained by concerns with body fat or weight in an individual whose symptoms meet diagnostic criteria for an eating disorder" (APA, 2013, p. 242). However, the manual goes on to state that these disorders can co-occur and both should be diagnosed when criteria for both are met. This diagnostic convolution may perplex even the most astute clinician. The fact that the DSM now includes a compulsion criterion for BDD simultaneously offers more clarity and confusion; clarity is offered because clinicians can now assess for the presence of checking behaviors or rituals in eating disorder patients with dysmorphic concerns, but confusion may arise because most individuals with an eating disorder engage in what could be classified as a repetitive or compulsive behavior (e.g., body checking, compulsive exercise, ritualistic feeding behaviors, compulsive compensatory behaviors, and reassurance seeking).

To detect a comorbid BDD diagnosis, the authors recommend conducting both a diagnostic interview on the specific eating disorder pathology and an assessment of body dysmorphic symptoms independent from the eating disorder symptoms. Distress about body image is typically more pronounced in individuals with both BDD and an eating disorder (Ruffolo et al., 2006), so this severity marker can be a helpful indicator that both disorders are present. In addition to severity, assessing which bodily characteristic(s) an individual focuses on is clinically useful. Patients with disordered eating tend to focus primarily on weight and shape, whereas those with BDD tend to obsess about specific body parts. Despite this, challenging cases can arise in clinical practice. An example is a patient who engages in caloric restriction that results in significantly low body weight and fears gaining weight, but the underlying reason is a perception that his or her face is too wide. Although there is clearly disordered eating, the driving force for this individual might specifically be to achieve a narrower face. In this case, should the person be classified as having an eating disorder or BDD or both? The reality is that it may be quite difficult to discern if an individual's psychopathology in some cases best fits with an eating disorder or BDD or both. As the previously mentioned nascent research comparing BDD and AN suggests, there may be common phenotypes and intermediate phenotypes, and thus a continuum between these disorders likely exists in nature.

Another issue in comorbid cases is that clinicians often miss the BDD symptoms altogether because they may be overshadowed by the "louder" and often life-threatening symptoms of an eating disorder or because body dissatisfaction is a hallmark of disordered eating. For example, when a patient is severely malnourished, abusing laxatives, or vomiting, these symptoms cause more immediate alarm than the often-expected body dysmorphic concerns. In addition, when loved ones notice that a patient is suffering, reach out to them, and help them seek treatment, it is often a response to visually obvious severe emaciation or dangerous purging activity rather than the individual's body image. Thus, the first setting that someone with comorbid BDD and disordered eating would likely enter is a specialized eating disorder clinic rather than a center specializing in BDD or OCRDs. This often leaves the important task of diagnosing co-occurring BDD and eating disorders in the hands of eating disorder specialists. This is especially critical due to the additive severity of comorbid presentation as well as untreated dysmorphic concerns leaving one more vulnerable to relapse. Although the initial focus of treatment should be on stabilizing a patient medically, restoring weight, and disrupting dangerous purging behaviors, attention should also be paid to dysmorphic concerns. If an eating disorder patient additionally meets diagnostic criteria for BDD, it is especially valuable to treat the dysmorphic symptoms with empirically supported treatment approaches for BDD, which are discussed in the following sections.

Pharmacological Treatment of BDD and Implications for Eating Disorders

The first-line pharmacologic treatment for BDD, including delusional variants, is a serotonin reuptake inhibitor (SRI) (Ipser, Sander, & Stein 2009; Phillips, 2002). In both open trials and randomized, placebo-controlled trials, SRIs have been found to be efficacious for BDD. Relatively high doses as well as at least a 12-week trial are recommended for the use of an SRI in BDD (Phillips & Hollander, 2008). Based on the efficacy of SRIs in treating BDD symptoms, it is recommended that all severe cases receive an SRI (Bjornsson, Didie, & Phillips, 2010; National Institute for Health and Care Excellence, 2005). These treatment recommendations differ from those for eating disorders. The only US Food and Drug Administration-approved medication for BN is the SRI fluoxetine, but patients who fail to show significant symptom reduction within 3 weeks are unlikely to benefit from prolonged use (Sysko, Sha, Wang, Duan, & Walsh, 2010). There is also evidence from two small randomized, placebo-controlled trials that topiramate can be effective for binging/purging (Hoopes et al., 2003; Nickel et al., 2005) and other eating disorder symptoms and anxiety (Hedges et al., 2003) in BN. No pharmacological agents have been found to effectively reduce symptoms in AN (Crow, Mitchell, Roerig, & Steffen, 2009). In summary, the use of an SRI in patients with comorbid BDD and eating disorders may improve body dysmorphic-specific symptoms, but there is no evidence that these medications will directly improve eating pathology.

Nonpsychiatric Treatment for BDD and Implications for Eating Disorders

Approximately three-fourths of those suffering from BDD seek nonpsychiatric treatment for their dysmorphic concerns, including dermatologic treatment and cosmetic surgery (Phillips, Grant, Siniscalchi, & Albertini, 2001). Of those who receive medical interventions, only 2.3% report overall BDD symptom severity reduction (Crerand, Menard, & Phillips, 2010). These poor outcomes can have negative consequences for both patients and physicians. Patients are dissatisfied, and physicians have been threatened legally and physically (Sarwer, 2002). Thus, treatments targeting the perceived defects in BDD are extremely ineffective, unlikely to treat BDD symptoms, and risky for physicians.

The effects of cosmetic surgery appear to be very different in nonclinical samples compared with patients who have BDD. Two prospective studies by the same research group examined the effects of cosmetic surgery (abdominoplasty [Saariniemi et al., 2014] and breast augmentation [Saariniemi et al., 2012]) in nonclinical samples on quality of life, psychological distress, and eating disorder symptoms. They found significantly improved body satisfaction and self-esteem, as well as a significantly reduced risk for an eating disorder. It is important to note that in these two studies, generalizability to a clinical sample and inference to long-term outcomes are limited. The population was not a clinical eating disorder sample, and follow-up measures were not taken beyond 6 months. Others have warned of the risk of treating eating disorders with cosmetic surgery and suggest thorough screening and body image treatment prior to proceeding with cosmetic surgery (McIntosh, Britt, & Bulik, 1994). Importantly, in clinical samples, cosmetic surgery has been found to be ineffective in treating disordered eating and may even be a manifestation of the disorder (Willard, McDermott, & Woodhouse, 1996). For treating both BDD and eating disorders, surgical and dermatologic interventions are not recommended.

Behavioral Treatment for BDD and Implications for Eating Disorders

The cognitive–behavioral model of BDD posits that individuals with BDD interpret visual information about their appearance in a biased way, which contributes to negative thoughts and feelings and leads them to engage in behaviors that perpetuate their symptoms (Wilhelm, Phillips, & Steketee, 2013). Although it is common for people in general to occasionally experience negative thoughts about their appearance, individuals with BDD respond in a significantly more biased way and make maladaptive interpretations of these thoughts. The maladaptive interpretations then trigger negative emotions, and the individual subsequently attempts to regulate them with maladaptive behaviors (e.g., mirror checking, grooming, reassurance seeking, and avoidance of social situations). These rituals and avoidance behaviors help maintain the dysfunctional BDD beliefs through negative reinforcement because negative emotions are ameliorated in the short term. Unfortunately, these behaviors serve to maintain the negative beliefs in the long term because the individual does not habituate and discover that everything would be okay if he or she had not engaged in a ritual or avoided. Moreover, the behaviors themselves are time-consuming and typically become onerous and distressing to perform.

Cognitive–behavioral therapy (CBT) has been determined to effectively reduce symptom severity in BDD and is the psychosocial treatment of choice (Rosen, Reiter, & Orosan, 1995; Veale et al., 1996; Wilhelm et al., 2014). The development and validation of CBT specifically designed for BDD (CBT-BDD; Wilhelm et al., 2013) is currently underway. This manualized treatment has already been tested in an open trial (Wilhelm, Phillips, Fama, Greenberg, & Steketee, 2011) and a wait-list controlled trial (Wilhelm et al., 2014), and it is currently being tested in a large randomized treatment comparison trial. The wait-list controlled trial determined CBT-BDD to be an efficacious treatment with a greater than 80% response rate, and post-treatment gains were maintained over an extended follow-up period (Wilhelm et al., 2014). Internet-delivered CBT for BDD has also been demonstrated to be effective in an open trial (Enander et al., 2014) and a single blind randomized control trial (Enander et al., 2016).

CBT-BDD implements standard core components relevant to all BDD patients in addition to optional modules targeting specific symptoms not observed in all patients. The manual *Cognitive–Behavioral Therapy for Body Dysmorphic Disorder* (Wilhelm et al., 2013) is recommended and provides details on this treatment approach. The treatment lasts for an average of 22 sessions, with each session ideally lasting 50–60 minutes. Session frequency is recommended twice weekly for the first 4 sessions and once weekly thereafter, and the final 2 relapse prevention sessions should be spaced 2 weeks apart. The first 3 introductory sessions focus on psychoeducation, case formulation, motivational enhancement, and treatment goals. These are followed by the core treatment components, which consist of cognitive restructuring, exposure and response prevention, and perceptual retraining. Perceptual retraining is tailored specifically to the patient's unique features and usually involves mirror retraining. In addition to core components, optional modules are available for patients with unique symptoms that require tailored interventions. The optional modules include skin picking and hair pulling; weight, shape, and muscularity; cosmetic treatment; and depression. The final 2 sessions of therapy focus on relapse prevention. Booster sessions are also recommended at 1 and 3 months post-treatment.

Other psychological interventions have also been suggested for use in BDD. Interpersonal psychotherapy has been suggested as an alternative to CBT due to frequent interpersonal issues observed in BDD (Bjornsson et al., 2010). A small open pilot trial revealed promising preliminary results (Didie & Phillips, 2009). An affect regulation training program designed for schizophrenic patients (Wolwer et al., 2005) has been suggested to help enhancement of facial affect recognition in individuals with BDD (Rossell, Harrison, & Castle, 2015). Cognitive remediation therapy has also been suggested as an alternative treatment for BDD (Fang & Wilhelm, 2015). This computerized therapy aims to improve neurocognitive functioning, including attention and flexibility, and may help target some of the global processing deficits commonly seen in BDD.

There are no known psychological treatment interventions that have been found to successfully treat AN in adults, but family-based therapy has proven successful for adolescents (Lock et al., 2010). The only empirically supported psychotherapy for BN is CBT adapted for BN (Wilson & Pike, 2001), which targets the maladaptive thoughts and behaviors that maintain binge and purge cycles. Given the paucity of empirically supported treatment for eating disorders, implementation of some of these BDD treatment strategies may prove useful in comorbid BDD and eating disorder.

Treating Comorbid Eating Disorders and BDD

To consolidate and simplify treatment recommendations, the authors designed a decision tree to utilize when an individual presents in the clinician's office with an eating disorder (Figure 7.1).

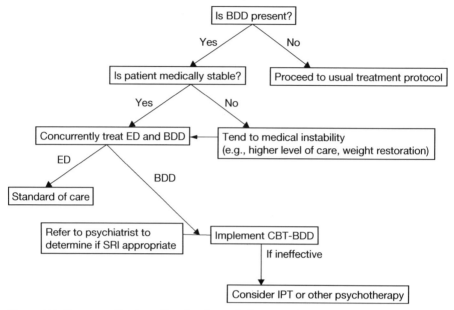

Figure 7.1 Treatment Decision Tree for Comorbid BDD and Eating Disorder.
BDD, body dysmorphic disorder; CBT, cognitive–behavioral therapy; ED, eating disorder;
IPT, interpersonal psychotherapy; SRI, serotonin reuptake inhibitor.

CONCLUSION AND FUTURE DIRECTIONS

The diagnosis and treatment of comorbid BDD and eating disorders can be a complex and challenging endeavor. The neurocognitive and brain imaging data suggest that abnormalities in visual processing systems likely contribute to the pathophysiology of these disorders. Specifically, a focus on details along with deficient holistic visual processing are evident. Aberrant frontostriatal systems may also contribute to the pathophysiology of eating disorders and BDD, and they may contribute to the obsessive and compulsive-like symptoms observed in both. Treatment outcome research is needed for these co-occurring disorders in order to determine which, if any, of the empirically supported treatments for BDD offer positive results for those with a comorbid eating disorder diagnosis. Given the common visuospatial deficits in both disorders, novel perceptual retraining treatments targeting visual processing may be fruitful. Also, taking into account the overlap in obsessive and compulsive symptoms, treatments that involve exposures and response prevention (a validated treatment for obsessive–compulsive disorder and whose techniques are incorporated in CBT-BDD) might also prove helpful.

Timing of treatment focus is an important consideration in comorbid eating disorders and BDD. Although immediately life-threatening starvation states need to be addressed first, the authors nevertheless recommend that clinicians assess and treat the BDD symptoms relatively early in treatment because individuals with comorbid conditions are at a particularly high risk of poor outcome and suicide.

Further research on the treatment of comorbid BDD and eating disorders is sorely needed due to the frequent occurrence and severity of the symptoms associated with this combination. Additional research is also needed to understand the etiological factors contributing to both disorders, and their comorbid presentations, to help with early intervention to prevent or minimize their development.

REFERENCES

American Psychiatric Association. (2013). *Diagnostic and statistical manual of mental disorders* (5th ed.). Arlington, VA: American Psychiatric Publishing.

Arcelus, J., Mitchell, A. J., Wales, J., & Nielsen, S. (2011). Mortality rates in patients with anorexia nervosa and other eating disorders: A meta-analysis of 36 studies. *Archives of General Psychiatry, 68*(7), 724–731.

Arienzo, D., Leow, A., Brown, J. A., Zhan, L., Gadelkarim, J., Hovav, S., & Feusner, J. D. (2013). Abnormal brain network organization in body dysmorphic disorder. *Neuropsychopharmacology, 38*(6), 1130–1139.

Beato-Fernandez, L., Rodriguez-Cano, T., Garcia-Vilches, I., Garcia-Vicente, A., Poblete-Garcia, V., Castrejon, A. S., & Toro, J. (2009). Changes in regional cerebral blood flow after body image exposure in eating disorders. *Psychiatry Research, 171*(2), 129–137.

Bjornsson, A. S., Didie, E. R., & Phillips, K. A. (2010). Body dysmorphic disorder. *Dialogues in Clinical Neuroscience, 12*(2), 221–232.

Buchanan, B. G., Rossell, S. L., Maller, J. J., Toh, W. L., Brennan, S., & Castle, D. J. (2013). Brain connectivity in body dysmorphic disorder compared with controls: A diffusion tensor imaging study. *Psychological Medicine, 43*(12), 2513–2521.

Crerand, C. E., Menard, W., & Phillips, K. A. (2010). Surgical and minimally invasive cosmetic procedures among persons with body dysmorphic disorder. *Annals of Plastic Surgery, 65*(1), 11–16.

Crow, S. J., Mitchell, J. E., Roerig, J. D., & Steffen, K. (2009). What potential role is there for medication treatment in anorexia nervosa? *International Journal of Eating Disorders, 42*(1), 1–8.

Didie, E. R., & Phillips, K. A. (2009, March). *Interpersonal psychotherapy for body dysmorphic disorder: A pilot study*. Paper presented at the annual meeting of the International Society for Interpersonal Psychotherapy, New York, NY.

Dingemans, A. E., van Rood, Y. R., de Groot, I., & van Furth, E. F. (2012). Body dysmorphic disorder in patients with an eating disorder: Prevalence and characteristics. *International Journal of Eating Disorders, 45*(4), 562–569.

Enander, J., Andersson, E., Mataix-Cols, D., Lichtenstein, L., Alstrom, K., Andersson, G., & Ruck, C. (2016). Therapist-guided Internet-based cognitive–behavioural therapy for body dysmorphic disorder: Single blind randomised controlled trial. *British Medical Journal, 352*, i241.

Enander, J., Ivanov, V. Z., Andersson, E., Mataix-Cols, D., Ljotsson, B., & Ruck, C. (2014). Therapist-guided, Internet-based cognitive–behavioural therapy for body dysmorphic disorder (BDD-NET): A feasibility study. *British Medical Journal Open, 4*(9), e005923.

Fairburn, C. G., & Harrison, P. J. (2003). Eating disorders. *Lancet, 361*(9355), 407–416.

Fang, A., & Wilhelm, S. (2015). Clinical features, cognitive biases, and treatment of body dysmorphic disorder. *Annual Review of Clinical Psychology, 11*, 187–212.

Favaro, A., Santonastaso, P., Manara, R., Bosello, R., Bommarito, G., Tenconi, E., & Di Salle, F. (2012). Disruption of visuospatial and somatosensory functional connectivity in anorexia nervosa. *Biological Psychiatry, 72*(10), 864–870.

Feusner, J. D., Arienzo, D., Li, W., Zhan, L., Gadelkarim, J., Thompson, P. M., & Leow, A. D. (2013). White matter microstructure in body dysmorphic disorder and its clinical correlates. *Psychiatry Research, 211*(2), 132–140.

Feusner, J. D., Hembacher, E., Moller, H., & Moody, T. D. (2011). Abnormalities of object visual processing in body dysmorphic disorder. *Psychological Medicine, 41*(11), 2385–2397.

Feusner, J. D., Moody, T., Townsend, J, McKinley, M., Hembacher, E., Moller, H., & Bookheimer, S. (2010). Abnormalities of visual processing and frontostriatal systems in body dysmorphic disorder. *Archives of General Psychiatry, 67*(2), 197–205.

Feusner, J. D., Townsend, J., Bystritsky, A., & Bookheimer, S. (2007). Visual information processing of faces in body dysmorphic disorder. *Archives of General Psychiatry, 64*(12), 1417–1425.

Fonville, L., Lao-Kaim, N. P., Giampietro, V., Van den Eynde, F., Davies, H., Lounes, N., & Tchanturia, K. (2013). Evaluation of enhanced attention to local detail in anorexia nervosa using the embedded figures test: An fMRI study. *PLoS One, 8*(5), e63964.

Frieling, H., Fischer, J., Wilhelm, J., Engelhorn, T., Bleich, S., Hillemacher, T., & Peschel, T. (2012). Microstructural abnormalities of the posterior thalamic radiation and the mediodorsal thalamic nuclei in females with anorexia nervosa—A voxel based diffusion tensor imaging (DTI) study. *Journal of Psychiatric Research, 46*(9), 1237–1242.

Grant, J. E., Kim, S. W., & Eckert, E. D. (2002). Body dysmorphic disorder in patients with anorexia nervosa: Prevalence, clinical features, and delusionality of body image. *International Journal of Eating Disorders, 32*(3), 291–300.

Hedges, D. W., Reimherr, F. W., Hoopes, S. P., Rosenthal, N. R., Kamin, M., Karim, R., & Capece, J. A. (2003). Treatment of bulimia nervosa with topiramate in a randomized, double-blind, placebo-controlled trial: Part 2. Improvement in psychiatric measures. *Journal of Clinical Psychiatry, 64*(12), 1449–1454.

Hoopes, S. P., Reimherr, F. W., Hedges, D. W., Rosenthal, N. R., Kamin, M., Karim, R., & Karvois, D. (2003). Treatment of bulimia nervosa with topiramate in a randomized, double-blind, placebo-controlled trial: Part 1. Improvement in binge and purge measures. *Journal of Clinical Psychiatry, 64*(11), 1335–1341.

Ipser, J., Sander, C., & Stein, D. J. (2009). Pharmacotherapy and psychotherapy for body dysmorphic disorder. *Cochrane Database System Review* (1), CD005332.

Konstantakopoulos, G., Varsou, E., Dikeos, D., Ioannidi, N., Gonidakis, F., Papadimitriou, G., & Oulis, P. (2012). Delusionality of body image beliefs in eating disorders. *Psychiatry Research, 200*(2-3), 482–488.

Lang, K., Lopez, C., Stahl, D., Tchanturia, K., & Treasure, J. (2014). Central coherence in eating disorders: An updated systematic review and meta-analysis. *World Journal of Biological Psychiatry, 15*(8), 586–598.

Lavagnino, L., Amianto, F., D'Agata, F., Huang, Z., Mortara, P., Abbate-Daga, G., & Northoff, G. (2014). Reduced resting-state functional connectivity of the somatosensory cortex predicts psychopathological symptoms in women with bulimia nervosa. *Frontiers in Behavioral Neuroscience, 8*, 270.

Li, W., Arienzo, D., & Feusner, J. D. (2013). Body dysmorphic disorder: Neurobiological features and an updated model. *Zeitschrift für Klinische Psychologie und Psychotherapie (Gottingen), 42*(3), 184–191.

Li, W., Lai, T. M., Bohon, C., Loo, S. K., McCurdy, D., Strober, M., & Feusner, J. (2015). Anorexia nervosa and body dysmorphic disorder are associated with abnormalities in processing visual information. *Psychological Medicine, 45*(10), 2111–2122.

Li, W., Lai, T. M., Loo, S. K., Strober, M., Mohammad-Rezazadeh, I., Khalsa, S., & Feusner, J. (2015). Aberrant early visual neural activity and brain–behavior relationships in anorexia nervosa and body dysmorphic disorder. *Frontiers in Human Neuroscience, 9*, 301.

Lock, J., Le Grange, D., Agras, W. S., Moye, A., Bryson, S. W., & Jo, B. (2010). Randomized clinical trial comparing family-based treatment with adolescent-focused individual therapy for adolescents with anorexia nervosa. *Archives of General Psychiatry, 67*(10), 1025–1032.

Madsen, S. K., Bohon, C., & Feusner, J. D. (2013). Visual processing in anorexia nervosa and body dysmorphic disorder: Similarities, differences, and future research directions. *Journal of Psychiatric Research, 47*(10), 1483–1491.

McIntosh, V. V., Britt, E., & Bulik, C. M. (1994). Cosmetic breast augmentation and eating disorders. *New Zealand Medical Journal, 107*(976), 151–152.

Mitchison, D., Crino, R., & Hay, P. (2013). The presence, predictive utility, and clinical significance of body dysmorphic symptoms in women with eating disorders. *Journal of Eating Disorders, 1*, 20.

Mohr, H. M., Zimmermann, J., Roder, C., Lenz, C., Overbeck, G., & Grabhorn, R. (2010). Separating two components of body image in anorexia nervosa using fMRI. *Psychological Medicine, 40*(9), 1519–1529.

National Institute for Health and Care Excellence. (2005). *Obsessive–compulsive disorder and body dysmorphic disorder: Treatment.* London, England: Author.

Nickel, C., Tritt, K., Muehlbacher, M., Pedrosa Gil, F., Mitterlehner, F. O., Kaplan, P., & Nickel, M. K. (2005). Topiramate treatment in bulimia nervosa patients: A randomized, double-blind, placebo-controlled trial. *International Journal of Eating Disorders, 38*(4), 295–300.

Phillips, K. A. (2002). Pharmacologic treatment of body dysmorphic disorder: Review of the evidence and a recommended treatment approach. *CNS Spectrums, 7*(6), 453–460, 463.

Phillips, K. A., Coles, M. E., Menard, W., Yen, S., Fay, C., & Weisberg, R. B. (2005). Suicidal ideation and suicide attempts in body dysmorphic disorder. *Journal of Clinical Psychiatry, 66*(6), 717–725.

Phillips, K. A., Grant, J., Siniscalchi, J., & Albertini, R. S. (2001). Surgical and nonpsychiatric medical treatment of patients with body dysmorphic disorder. *Psychosomatics, 42*(6), 504–510.

Phillips, K. A., & Hollander, E. (2008). Treating body dysmorphic disorder with medication: Evidence, misconceptions, and a suggested approach. *Body Image, 5*(1), 13–27.

Rosen, J. C., Reiter, J., & Orosan, P. (1995). Cognitive–behavioral body image therapy for body dysmorphic disorder. *Journal of Consulting and Clinical Psychology, 63*(2), 263–269.

Rossell, S. L., Harrison, B. J., & Castle, D. (2015). Can understanding the neurobiology of body dysmorphic disorder (BDD) inform treatment? *Australasian Psychiatry, 23*(4), 361–364.

Ruffolo, J. S., Phillips, K. A., Menard, W., Fay, C., & Weisberg, R. B. (2006). Comorbidity of body dysmorphic disorder and eating disorders: Severity of psychopathology and body image disturbance. *International Journal of Eating Disorders, 39*(1), 11–19.

Saariniemi, K. M., Helle, M. H., Salmi, A. M., Peltoniemi, H. H., Charpentier, P., & Kuokkanen, H. O. (2012). The effects of aesthetic breast augmentation on quality of life, psychological distress, and eating disorder symptoms: A prospective study. *Aesthetic Plastic Surgery, 36*(5), 1090–1095.

Saariniemi, K. M., Salmi, A. M., Peltoniemi, H. H., Helle, M. H., Charpentier, P., & Kuokkanen, H. O. (2014). Abdominoplasty improves quality of life, psychological distress, and eating disorder symptoms: A prospective study. *Plastic Surgery International, 2014*, 197232.

Sarwer, D. B. (2002). Awareness and identification of body dysmorphic disorder by aesthetic surgeons: Results of a survey of American Society for Aesthetic Plastic Surgery members. *Aesthetic Surgery Journal, 22*(6), 531–535.

Suchan, B., Busch, M., Schulte, D., Gronemeyer, D., Herpertz, S., & Vocks, S. (2010). Reduction of gray matter density in the extrastriate body area in women with anorexia nervosa. *Behavioural Brain Research, 206*(1), 63–67.

Sysko, R., Sha, N., Wang, Y., Duan, N., & Walsh, B. T. (2010). Early response to antidepressant treatment in bulimia nervosa. *Psychological Medicine, 40*(6), 999–1005.

Uher, R., Murphy, T., Friederich, H. C., Dalgleish, T., Brammer, M. J., Giampietro, V., & Treasure, J. (2005). Functional neuroanatomy of body shape perception in healthy and eating-disordered women. *Biological Psychiatry, 58*(12), 990–997.

Veale, D., Gledhill, L. J., Christodoulou, P., & Hodsoll, J. (2016). Body dysmorphic disorder in different settings: A systematic review and estimated weighted prevalence. *Body Image, 18*, 168–186.

Veale, D., Gournay, K., Dryden, W., Boocock, A., Shah, F., Willson, R., & Walburn, J. (1996). Body dysmorphic disorder: A cognitive behavioural model and pilot randomised controlled trial. *Behavior Research and Therapy, 34*(9), 717–729.

Vocks, S., Busch, M., Gronemeyer, D., Schulte, D., Herpertz, S., & Suchan, B. (2010). Neural correlates of viewing photographs of one's own body and another woman's body in anorexia and bulimia nervosa: An fMRI study. *Journal of Psychiatry & Neuroscience, 35*(3), 163–176.

Wagner, A., Ruf, M., Braus, D. F., & Schmidt, M. H. (2003). Neuronal activity changes and body image distortion in anorexia nervosa. *Neuroreport, 14*(17), 2193–2197.

Wilhelm, S., Phillips, K. A., Didie, E., Buhlmann, U., Greenberg, J. L., Fama, J. M., & Steketee, G. (2014). Modular cognitive–behavioral therapy for body dysmorphic disorder: A randomized controlled trial. *Behavior Therapy, 45*(3), 314–327.

Wilhelm, S., Phillips, K. A., Fama, J. M., Greenberg, J. L., & Steketee, G. (2011). Modular cognitive–behavioral therapy for body dysmorphic disorder. *Behavior Therapy, 42*(4), 624–633.

Wilhelm, S., Phillips, K. A., & Steketee, G. (2013). *Cognitive–behavioral therapy for body dysmorphic disorder: A treatment manual*. New York, NY: Guilford.

Willard, S. G., McDermott, B. E., & Woodhouse, L. M. (1996). Lipoplasty in the bulimic patient. *Plastic and Reconstructive Surgery, 98*(2), 276–278.

Wilson, G. T., & Pike, K. M. (2001). Eating disorders. In D. A. Barlow (Ed.), *Clinical handbook of psychological disorders* (3rd ed., pp. 332–375). New York, NY: Guilford.

Wolwer, W., Frommann, N., Halfmann, S., Piaszek, A., Streit, M., & Gaebel, W. (2005). Remediation of impairments in facial affect recognition in schizophrenia: Efficacy and specificity of a new training program. *Schizophrenia Research, 80*(2-3), 295–303.

Zhang, A., Leow, A., Zhan, L., Gadelkarim, J., Moody, T., Khalsa, S., & Feusner, J. (2016). Brain connectome modularity in weight-restored anorexia nervosa and body dysmorphic disorder. *Psychological Medicine, 46*(13), 2785–2797.

8

Food Selectivity in Autism Spectrum Disorder

WILLIAM G. SHARP AND VALENTINA POSTORINO ■

Autism spectrum disorder (ASD) is a chronic condition of early childhood onset characterized by impaired social communication, repetitive behavior, and restricted interests affecting 6–14 per 1,000 children (American Psychiatric Association [APA], 2013; Elsabbaugh et al., 2012). The diagnosis occurs four times more often in males than females and is frequently associated with behavioral and medical problems, including a high prevalence of intellectual disability (Yeargin-Allsopp et al., 2003), speech and language deficits (Iverson & Wozniak, 2007), psychiatric disorders (Salazar et al., 2015), toileting issues (Maskey, Warnell, Parr, Couteur, & McConachie, 2013), sleep difficulties (Mazurek & Petroski, 2015), and feeding problems (Sharp, Berry, et al., 2013). Feeding problems among children with ASD include displaying rituals surrounding meals (e.g., requiring certain utensils or presentations) and refusing more foods compared with peers, with food selectivity representing the most commonly cited concern. Food selectivity in ASD increases the risk for nutritional and medical complications, including vitamin and mineral deficiency (Sharp, Berry, et al., 2013) and compromised bone development (Hediger et al., 2008; Neumeyer et al., 2015). In extreme cases, food selectivity may result in severe malnutrition and diet-related diseases not often observed in developed countries, such as scurvy (Ma, Thompson, & Weston, 2016), rickets (Stewart & Latif, 2008), vision loss (McAlbee, Prieto, Kirby, Santilli, & Setty, 2009), and iron-deficiency anemia (Latif, Heinz, & Cook, 2002).

Despite potential for serious health consequences, feeding concerns are often overlooked in relation to other areas of clinical concern, and researchers only recently dedicated resources to examining eating and nutrient intake patterns in ASD. The clinical picture of food selectivity in ASD is distinct from that of other pediatric populations at increased risk for feeding disorders (Ledford & Gast, 2006; Sharp, Berry, et al., 2013). Among children without ASD, pediatric feeding disorders often involve severe restrictions in the volume of food consumed, increasing the risk of growth retardation, malnutrition, and/or invasive medical procedures (e.g., placement of a feeding tube) (Sharp, Jaquess, Morton, & Herzinger, 2010). In such cases, compromised gross anthropometric parameters (i.e., height, weight, and body mass index) represent the most salient symptom of a feeding disorder likely to trigger attention in pediatric settings. Children with ASD, however, most often present with extreme and narrow food preferences leading to deficits in dietary variety—not volume—and, in most cases, children with ASD consume enough food to meet gross energy needs (Sharp, Berry, et al., 2013). This highlights the need to look beyond gross anthropometrics or analysis of overall energy intake to identify and quantify risk for long-term nutritional or medical complications associated with atypical patterns of intake in this population. Unfortunately, the absence of relevant data has prohibited development of evidence-based guidelines to assist parents and clinicians with navigating the unique dietary, medical, and behavioral challenges associated with food selectivity in ASD.

AN ISSUE OF DIETARY DIVERSITY

Food selectivity (e.g., eating only a narrow variety of foods such as starches and snack foods with strong bias against fruits and vegetables) is the most commonly reported and well-researched feeding problem in children with ASD. Ledford and Gast (2006) completed the first summary of the literature on this topic, identifying seven studies (381 total children with ASD) published between 1994 and 2004. All studies reported significant feeding difficulties, most often in the form of food selectivity by type and/or texture. Prevalence estimates of feeding problems in children with ASD ranged from 46% to 89%, suggesting that feeding problems are likely ubiquitous in this population. This wide range of estimates, however, is largely attributed to differences in sample source and assessment methods and makes it difficult to draw definitive conclusions about the magnitude and potential impact of the problem.

Recognizing these limitations, Sharp, Berry, et al. (2013) conducted a meta-analysis focusing exclusively on prospective research involving a comparison group to quantify the magnitude of feeding problems in children (birth to 18 years) with ASD. Findings indicated that children with ASD were five times more likely to experience feeding problems compared to typically developing peers and siblings and three times more likely compared to other children with developmental disabilities (e.g., Down syndrome). Food selectivity was the most frequently documented feeding concern, often in the form of strong preferences for starches and snack foods coinciding with a bias against fruits and vegetables. Disruptive mealtime behavior (e.g., tantrums and crying) and rigidity surrounding eating (e.g., only eating in a specific location and requiring certain utensils) were also prominent concerns. Based on the quality of the extant literature, the review concluded that although evidence supports a high prevalence of food selectivity in ASD, there is a clear need for greater diagnostic clarity and movement toward consensus regarding the definition of food selectivity in ASD.

BEYOND PICKY EATING

Enhanced understanding of feeding concerns in ASD requires differentiating food selectivity from picky eating. Picky eating is a common concern during early childhood, occurring in as many as 50% of children at some point in time (Carruth, Ziegler, Gordon, & Barr, 2004). Characteristics of picky eating include consuming a limited variety of foods, unwillingness to try new foods (food neophobia), and/or displaying strong food preferences (Cano et al., 2015). Vegetables and fruits, particularly items with a bitter taste, tend to be the most frequently rejected foods (Dovey, Staples, Gibson, & Halford, 2008). Although a common problem and source of stress for many caregivers, available evidence also suggests picky eating is a transient behavior, likely to remit over time. Dovey et al. (2008) summarized this trend though a life span model of food neophobia, noting that the reluctance to try new foods increases sharply as a child becomes more mobile, reaching a peak between 2 and 6 years of age, but then decreasing as an individual grows older—reaching a relatively low and stable level in adulthood. The authors also emphasized that most individuals lose bitter taste aversion and eventually learn to enjoy vegetables and fruits without specific programming/treatment.

On the surface, food selectivity and picky eating share many core features, including an unwillingness to try unfamiliar foods, strong preferences for certain food items, and frequent rejection of fruits and vegetables. Food selectivity in ASD, however, is distinct from picky eating in terms of duration and intensity. Evidence suggests that food selectivity represents a chronic concern—persisting into adolescence and adulthood (Kuschner et al., 2015; Suarez, Nelson, & Curtis, 2014). Children with ASD are also more likely to exhibit strong refusal behaviors (e.g., crying, throwing objects, and aggression) when presented with routine feeding demands (Sharp, Jaquess, & Lukens, 2013). These disruptive behaviors may occur in response to the sight or smell of nonpreferred foods. As a result, these children may refuse to sit at the family dinner table and miss opportunities for social engagement, particularly events involving nonpreferred foods (Ausderau & Juarez, 2013).

TOWARD GREATER DIAGNOSTIC CLARITY

A common thread throughout clinical and research activity focusing on food selectivity in ASD is the lack of diagnostic clarity. In past reports, the term *food selectivity* was used to refer to a range of mealtime concerns, including limited food repertoire, reluctance to try new foods, high intake of a single food item, and atypical eating behavior. A rigorous definition of food selectivity must account for both the breadth and the quality of a child's diet. The most recent *Dietary Guidelines for Americans* provides a benchmark for ideal dietary intake, emphasizing the importance of consuming a wide variety of foods across all food groups (US Department of Health and Human Services & US Department of Agriculture, 2015). Consuming a breadth of food groups is essential because each food group provides a unique set of nutrients to promote health and development. In previous research, food selectivity was viewed as a monolithic construct (e.g., total number of items accepted or rejected), without consideration of symptom severity or dietary diversity. Food selectivity in ASD, however, may range from mild to severe. Children with ASD and mild food selectivity may not require intervention or would benefit from low-intensity intervention, such as nutrition education to address gaps in caregiver knowledge (Berry et al., 2015). In contrast, children with moderate or severe food selectivity often require intervention to avoid negative health outcomes (Greer, Gulotta, Masler, & Laud, 2009; Sharp, Jaquess, Morton, & Miles, 2011). Table 8.1 presents a three-tiered framework for differentiating mild, moderate, and severe food selectivity.

Table 8.1 FRAMEWORK FOR DEFINING FOOD SELECTIVITY BY SEVERITY

Category	Criteria[a]	Rationale
Severe food selectivity[b]	Complete rejection of one or more food groups.	Increases the risk of micro- and/or macronutrient deficiency (e.g., scurvy, iron deficiency anemia, and kwashiorkor).
	Accepts five or fewer total food items.	Further narrowing of the diet would eliminate additional food groups.
Moderate food selectivity[b]	Consumes two or fewer items in one or more food groups.	Reflects a diet that may lack diversity of nutrient-dense foods; further restriction increases likelihood of nutrient deficiency.
	Regularly (weekly) accepts at least one item across the five food groups.	Decreases likelihood of being diagnosed with a nutrient deficiency; however, intake may be limited to a handful of preferred items or involve high intake of a single food group.
Mild food selectivity[c]	Diet involves at least three or more items from each good group (15 total foods); more than half of items fall into one food group.	Suggests low probability of nutrient deficiency while recognizing child may show preference for a certain food group (e.g., grains).
	Consistently (daily) accepts foods from all five food groups.	Indicates the child maintains a consistent degree of dietary diversity.

[a] Must meet both criteria within a category.

[b] Both severe and moderate food selectivity also involve disruptive behaviors (e.g., crying, active verbal protest, and tantrums) when presenting with nonpreferred food.

[c] Mild food selectivity also involves reluctance to try new foods and/or difficulty accepting preferred foods across environments.

PSYCHIATRIC CLASSIFICATION

Following the fifth edition of the *Diagnostic and Statistical Manual of Mental Disorders* (DSM-5), food selectivity most closely aligns with the broader psychiatric diagnosis avoidant/restrictive food intake disorder (ARFID), as outlined by the APA (2013). The main diagnostic feature of the disorder involves avoidance or restriction of food intake as reflected by failure to meet nutrition and/or energy needs. The criteria specify that this may manifest as one (or more) of the following clinical indicators: (1) significant weight loss, (2) significant nutritional deficiencies, (3) dependence on enteral feeding or oral nutritional supplementations, and/or (4) marked interference with psychosocial functioning. A notable strength of ARFID is the recognition that not all children with disordered eating will present with weight concerns, which is particularly salient for children with ASD whose primary feeding concern involves poor dietary variety (vs. volume). This definition also recognizes the broader psychosocial impact of feeding disorders, with food selectivity often negatively impacting family routines and overall quality of life, becoming a significant stressor for families.

In clinical practice, it is also important to differentiate ARFID from other eating disorders. For example, ARFID does overlap with anorexia nervosa (AN) in terms of inadequate food intake resulting in a significantly low body weight; however, psychopathology and causes for restrictive eating differ (Uher & Rutter, 2012). Although ARFID may involve restrictive eating and avoiding certain types and textures of food, it is not frequently associated with a disturbance in self-perceived body image. In contrast, body dysmorphia and related behaviors, such as negative body talk, body checking, or frequent weighing, are common with eating disorders. The use of compensatory behaviors, including self-induced vomiting or laxative abuse, is also only found in cases of eating disorders. Body dysmorphia and compensatory behaviors are not frequently associated with food selectivity in ASD. Furthermore, although a connection between feeding disorders in youth and the development of eating disorders later in life has been described (Kotler, Cohen, Davies, Pine, & Walsh, 2001; Micali et al., 2007; Nicholls & Viner, 2009), there is no evidence linking food selectivity in ASD to the development of an eating disorder in adulthood. As emphasized previously, the more likely clinical course involves food selectivity persisting into adolescence and adulthood.

POSSIBLE CONTRIBUTING FACTORS

Gastrointestinal Symptoms

Organic factors leading to difficult or painful eating (e.g., gastroesophageal reflux, gastroenteritis, and food allergies) often precipitate or play a role in the development of chronic feeding concerns in other pediatric populations (Sharp et al., 2010). Estimates suggest as many as 70% of children with chronic medical concerns experience feeding difficulties at some point in time (Lukens & Silverman,

2014). Children with ASD often present with medical conditions affecting multiple organ systems, and dysfunction of the gastrointestinal (GI) tract is among the most frequently cited comorbidities (Kohane et al., 2012). Children with ASD are significantly more likely to use GI medications and experience hospitalizations related to GI disturbance compared to peers (Croen, Nijjar, Ray, Lotspeich, & Bernal, 2006). A meta-analysis indicated that children with ASD were four times more likely to experience general GI complaints, more than three times more prone to experience constipation and diarrhea, and complain twice as frequently about abdominal pain compared to peers (McElhanon, McCracken, Karpen, & Sharp, 2014). Important questions, however, remain regarding the relative contribution of behavioral factors (toileting problems; dietary intake) to increased risk of diarrhea, constipation, and abdominal pain in this population.

Currently, definitive conclusions regarding the relationship between possible pathophysiological process in the GI tract and food selectivity are unavailable. Although there is clear evidence for increased risk of GI symptoms, there is no evidence suggesting a unique GI pathology in ASD (McElhanon et al., 2014). However, high prevalence of food selectivity combined with increased risk of GI symptoms warrants medical involvement in the assessment and treatment process to rule out and/or screen for common organic issues that may cause or exacerbate discomfort or dysfunction along the GI tract (e.g., aspiration, gastroesophageal reflux disease, food allergy, and constipation).

Behavioral Rigidity and Sensory Processing

Core features of ASD, including behavioral rigidity and sensory sensitivity, may contribute to food selectivity. This includes gravitating toward certain types and textures of food—that is, snacks and processed foods that have a more uniform look, taste, and packaging compared to fruits and vegetables. Behavioral rigidity is also likely to carry over into other aspects of eating, such as meal location and/or food presentation. This may include requiring specific utensils or certain food presentations during meals, consuming foods in a repetitive manner, and/or displaying different patterns of food preference depending on the environment (e.g., not eating the same food at day care and at home) (Nadon, Feldman, Dunn, & Gisel, 2011; Provost, Crowe, Osbourn, McClain, & Skippper, 2010; Schreck, Williams, & Smith, 2004).

Sensory processing problems may also underlie preference for certain food items. As emphasized by the DSM-5, hyper- or hyporeactivity to sensory input is common among individuals with ASD, and in some cases, food avoidance or restriction may be related to sensory characteristics of food, such as color, taste, smell, temperature, or appearance (APA, 2013). For example, Nadon et al. (2011) reported that in addition to food texture, children with ASD were more selective with respect to food temperature and type of recipe. Tomchek and Dunn (2007) reported more smell and taste sensitivity in children with ASD compared to a sample of peers without ASD. Bennetto, Kuschner, and Hyman (2007) found that children with ASD had difficulty correctly identifying taste and olfactory sensations, suggesting over- and/or undersensory responsiveness may contribute to the high prevalence of food selectivity in this population. It may also explain the strong emotional response to seemingly benign feeding demands often observed in children with ASD. A clear implication of this line of research is that detailed assessment of food selectivity in ASD should seek to capture environmental and sensory aspects of the meal, including similarities and differences across settings/locations (e.g., home, school, and restaurants), preferences for food presentation (e.g., plates and utensils), and commonalities in food characteristics (e.g., taste, smell, and color).

Parent–Child Interaction

A prominent feature of food selectivity in ASD is persistent, disruptive mealtime behaviors (e.g., intense tantrums and tearful protests) in response to the presentation of nonpreferred foods (Sharp, Jaquess, & Lukens, 2013). Problem behaviors during meals often function as a means to escape aversive feeding experiences (Piazza et al., 2003). In response to these behaviors, caregivers often remove food and end the meal (Piazza, 2008). Consequently, the child escapes the feeding demand, and these behaviors are inadvertently shaped and strengthened over time. The parent also learns that food removal leads to a rapid cessation in the child's challenging behavior, providing escape from unpleasant mealtime interactions. As a result, the caregiver may become more likely to end meals prematurely, and without intervention, a vicious cycle takes hold. Limited exposure to food circumvents key sensory, developmental, physiological, and social processes associated with eating and erodes an already fragile parent–child mealtime relationship. Faced with lack of success introducing new foods, caregivers may cease presenting nonpreferred foods altogether and resort to preparing multiple menus at each meal—one for the child with ASD and one reflecting the more varied diet of the family (Marquenie, Rodger, Mangohig, & Cronin, 2011). The child subsequently has little or no exposure to food outside his or her limited dietary repertoire, which likely contributes to the durability of food selectivity over time.

CONSEQUENCES OF FOOD SELECTIVITY IN AUTISM SPECTRUM DISORDER

Nutritional Status

The primary medical concern regarding food selectivity in ASD is the potential for underlying dietary insufficiencies. Dietary intake in ASD often involves strong preferences for highly processed foods, snacks, and sweets (Schmitt, Heiss, & Campbell, 2008) and a lower intake of fruits and vegetables (Bandini et al., 2010; Lukens & Linscheid, 2008; Martins, Young, & Robson, 2008). Restricted intake or complete rejection of one or more food groups may deprive the body of key nutrients required to function optimally, such as calcium or protein, and increase the risk of diet-related diseases in ASD (Sharp, Berry, et al., 2013). This likely explains evidence suggesting greater deficits in bone development among children with ASD (Hediger et al., 2008; Neumeyer et al., 2015). Case reports have also documented severe health problems, including scurvy, rickets, and permanent vision loss, associated with poor dietary diversity in ASD (Ma et al., 2016; McAbee Prieto, Kirby, Santilli, & Setty, 2009; Stewart & Latif, 2008).Clearly, the potential for such negative health outcomes highlights the importance of nutritional monitoring in children with ASD and food selectivity, including periodic serum testing of vitamin levels in cases involving complete rejection of one or more food groups.

Obesity

Increased risk of dietary insufficiencies in ASD coincides with data suggesting most children with ASD maintain at least minimally adequate anthropometric parameters. As opposed to faltering growth, emerging evidence suggests children with ASD are at increased risk for overweight and obesity compared to children without ASD. This is consistent with evidence indicating that food selectivity in ASD (1) primarily involves preference for calorie-dense foods, such as fats, snacks, and processed foods; and (2) does no coincide with concerns regarding restricted volume. The estimated prevalence of obesity in children with ASD ranges from 10% to 31.8% (Phillips et al., 2014; Whitely, Dodou, Todd, & Shattock, 2004). A large-scale chart review suggests that this risk extends into adulthood and may portend poor health outcomes (Croen, Zerbo, Qian, & Massolo, 2014). Compared to non-ASD peers, adults with ASD experienced a 69% higher incidence of obesity, 42% greater risk of hypertension, and 50% increase in diabetes. This reflects the unfortunate, but not unexpected, long-term health implications of consuming a calorie-dense versus nutrient-dense diet. It also highlights the need to include weight management strategies in efforts to expand dietary variety when obesity co-occurs with food selectivity in ASD.

Family Functioning

Food selectivity and related health concerns increase the challenge of raising a child with ASD and decrease overall quality of life for families. For example, parents of children with food selectivity are significantly more likely to experience high levels of parental stress compared to parents of children with ASD without food selectivity (Postorino et al., 2015). Parents of children with ASD and food selectivity are also more likely to report that their child's behavior at mealtimes negatively impacts their spouse/partner, represents a significant source of stress in the relationship, and influences what other family members consume at meals (Curtin et al., 2015). Many caregivers express deep dissatisfaction with their experience surrounding meals, describing family mealtime as stressful, chaotic, and energy depleting. Caregivers may also be discouraged by unsuccessful attempts to improve mealtime and, due to the persistent nature of their child's feeding concerns, cease conducting family meals altogether to avoid further worry, guilt, and stress (Suarez, Atchison, & Lagerwey, 2014). Thus, meals appear to represent a source of strain for families with ASD as opposed to serving an important role in strengthening the family unit by providing a time to gather, communicate, and develop shared family rituals and routines as is often the case for families uncomplicated by ASD (Fulkerson, Story, Neumark-Sztainer, & Rydell, 2008).

CAREGIVER-MEDIATED DIETARY RESTRICTIONS

Any discussion regarding food selectivity in ASD would be remiss without acknowledging the proliferation of caregiver-mediated dietary restrictions in this population. Compared to peers, children with ASD are significantly more likely to be placed on a restricted diet by caregivers (Kirby & Danner, 2009). Caregiver-mediated diets frequently applied in ASD include the gluten-free, casein-free diet (GFCF; Elder et al., 2006) and the ketogenic diet (Evangeliou et al., 2003). Of concern, these diets restrict or completely eliminate certain food groups, which may further compound risk of macronutrient and micronutrient deficiencies related to food selectivity. For example, the GFCF diet eliminates gluten (found in wheat, barley, and rye) and casein (found in cow's diary milk), placing additional restrictions on a population vulnerable for lower calcium intake. Case in point, evidence suggests use of the GFCF diet may lead to greater deficits in bone development among children with ASD (Hediger et al., 2008; Neumeyer et al., 2015). Furthermore, caregiver-meditated dietary restriction is often used to target core features of ASD (i.e., impairments in social communication, restriction in interests, and repetitive behaviors) rather than underlying medical conditions (e.g., refractory epilepsy in the case of the ketogenic diet). Empirical investigation, however, has not substantiated the use of dietary restriction as an ASD-focused treatment (Elder et al., 2006). Thus, associated risks of these diets appear to outweigh the benefits unless medically indicated. Given the likelihood of encountering this topic in practice, clinicians should be prepared to counsel caregivers on the lack of evidence on the effectiveness of dietary intervention to influence core symptoms of ASD while concurrently emphasizing the importance of promoting a healthy and well-balanced diet in this population (Berry et al., 2015).

RESEARCH ON EATING DISORDERS IN AUTISM SPECTRUM DISORDER

Research on the possible link between ASD and eating disorders, particularly anorexia nervosa (AN), has grown considerably (Westwood et al., 2016). Interest in a possible association between these conditions has been driven by the hypothesis that women with ASD have a higher risk of developing AN. Several studies suggest similarities in cognitive profiles between AN and ASD, including weak central coherence, difficulties in set-shifting, and impaired theory of mind (Baron-Cohen et al., 2013; Rhind et al., 2014; Tchanturia et al., 2013). Rigid thinking, repetitive behavior, and obsessive–compulsive features are also observed in both conditions (Tchanturia et al., 2013). With these similarities in mind, the core features of AN involve intense fear of gaining weight, disturbance in body image, and restriction in energy intake—criteria that stand in stark contrast to the pattern of food selectivity and high rates of obesity documented in ASD. Furthermore, starvation can have profound impacts on brain functioning and may amplify social withdrawal, rigidity, and repetitive behaviors in patients with AN, thus promoting "autistic-like" symptoms. ASD and AN are further distinguished by onset and cognitive profiles. The onset of AN is usually during adolescence, and the lifetime course is highly variable. AN is more common in females (female-to-male ratio [F:M] of 10:1), and a majority of affected individuals have above-average intelligence (Anderluh, Tchanturia, Rabe-Hesketh, Collier, & Treasure, 2009; Lopez, Stahl, & Tchanturia, 2010). In contrast, ASD is a lifelong condition with an early onset (12–24 months of age) that is significantly more prevalent in males (M:F ratio of 4:1); intellectual functioning ranges from well below average to above average (Centers for Disease Control and Prevention, 2014). Finally, prior research in this area primarily involved retrospective investigations focusing on the presence of ASD symptoms among affective individuals with AN (Anckarsäter et al., 2012; Rastam, Gillberg, & Wentz, 2003; Wentz et al., 2005). As such, there remains the need for prospective studies to investigate the emergence and prevalence of AN in ASD.

Separate from the issue of ASD diagnosis is the matter of autistic traits. Several studies have explored the presence of autistic traits in AN samples (Westwood et al., 2016). For example, in a sample of 66 adolescent females with AN, Baron-Cohen et al. (2013) observed elevated autistic traits compared to healthy female adolescents. However, this study omitted key details about diagnosis (e.g., duration of AN), leaving questions about whether autistic traits corresponded with the starvation phase of the illness. A recent meta-analysis also supported increased levels of autistic traits in AN (Westwood et al., 2016), albeit while citing similar limitations to the extant literature. Together, the preponderance of evidence suggests females with AN likely experience cognitive difficulties similar to those observed in ASD—a finding that has guided new models of treatment (e.g., cognitive remediation therapy) focusing on increasing cognitive flexibility, emotion recognition, and switching between mental tasks (set-shifting) in AN (Lock et al., 2013; Tchanturia, Doris, Mountfor, & Fleming, 2015).

INTERVENTIONS FOR FOOD SELECTIVITY

A multidisciplinary approach is recommended in the assessment and treatment of pediatric feeding disorders because cases frequently involve the complex interaction between behavioral, dietary, oral–motor, and medical concerns and thus cross areas of expertise. In practice, this often requires contributions from behavioral psychology, nutrition, speech–language pathology or occupational therapy, and medicine to fully capture the diagnostic complexity of a feeding disorder. Although available data do not support increased risk for organic concerns associated with food selectivity in ASD, the most prudent approach is to follow the same diagnostic and treatment process warranted for any child with a feeding disorder. This ensures important safeguards against possible complications associated with treatment, such as aspiration, severe allergic reactions, and/or anaphylaxis. Prior to intervention, medical evaluation should be completed to detect and address common organic issues that may cause or exacerbate discomfort or dysfunction along the GI tract (e.g., reflux and food allergy). A speech–language pathologist or occupational therapist with expertise in pediatric feeding disorders should also complete an assessment of oral–motor skills and related safety concerns when underlying dysfunction is suspected (e.g., evidence of signs/symptoms of aspiration, recurrent respiratory concerns, and history of aspiration pneumonia). Once medically cleared, the behavioral psychologist can focus on expanding dietary diversity and flexibility with feeding demands, possibly in collaboration with a dietician to identify possible "gaps" in the diet that place a child at risk for micronutrient and macronutrient deficiencies, which is particularly salient for children with severe food selectivity.

Currently, behavioral intervention is the only treatment for severe feeding disorders that has well-documented empirical support (Kerwin, 1999; Lukens & Silverman, 2014; Sharp et al., 2010). Behavioral packages targeting chronic feeding concerns often combine a formalized meal structure with consequence-based procedures (e.g., escape extinction and differential reinforcement of alternative behaviors) and antecedent manipulations (e.g., reduced bite volume or modified food texture) to promote consumption. Evidence suggests ASD-specific adaptations of these techniques can improve feeding behaviors in young children with ASD and selective eating patterns (Ledford & Gast, 2006; Sharp et al., 2011). These adaptations consider the unique cognitive and behavioral profile associated with ASD (e.g., resistance to change and heightened sensory defensiveness) due to the strong emotional response associated with the introduction of novel foods. This includes greater use of antecedent manipulations and shaping to slowly introduce new sensory experiences (taste, texture, and temperature) due to the strong emotional response associated with the introduction of novel foods (Ledford & Gast, 2006). In practice, this involves "persisting with a reasonable feeding demand" during intervention—akin to exposure and response prevention but with a specific emphasis on promoting contact with food while concurrently recognizing that the mere sight or smell of nonpreferred foods may elicit intense refusal behaviors in ASD (Sharp, Berry, et al., 2013).

Antecedent Manipulations

Common antecedent manipulations include modifying the bite volume/portion size, food texture, and variety of foods presented during meals (Sharp et al., 2011).

Reducing the bite volume and portion size of nonpreferred foods may increase a child's willingness to tolerate and/or make contact with new foods. In practice, this may involve presenting a bite volume that approximates the size of a grain of rice or a single green pea. Modifying the texture of nonpreferred foods may also help promote exposure, allowing the child to make contact with certain sensory qualities of the food (e.g., taste and smell) while concurrently reducing the overall response effort (i.e., requirement to chew). In certain cases, this may involve presenting nonpreferred food at a lower texture (e.g., pureed) compared with preferred food. Intervention should also consider the variety of foods presented— limiting the total number of new foods initially introduced during intervention and incorporating preferred foods into meals. For example, Sharp et al. described the use of a ratio approach of low-demand to high-demand bites (i.e., four bites of preferred to one bite of nonpreferred followed by three of preferred to two of nonpreferred, and so on). Initially, the number of bites presented during treatment sessions should be low—such as five bites of a target food—in order to increase the likelihood of the child successfully completing the meal with few concomitant problem behaviors. Each of these antecedent manipulations should be combined with stimulus fading procedures to promote more appropriate feeding behaviors while gradually exposing the child to previously aversive stimuli. Movement through the fading steps should be guided by data, ideally following a decision rule format in which certain target behaviors (e.g., accepting and swallowing target bites and low rates of disruptive behavior, crying, or negative statements) are achieved at stable levels before a shift to the next step in fading.

Consequence-Based Procedures

Escape extinction (EE) is one of the most frequently cited behavioral approaches in the treatment of pediatric feeding disorder (Sharp et al., 2010). In past reports, EE most often involved nonremoval of the spoon (NRS)—a procedure in which a feeder presents a bite of food on a spoon, keeps the bite at the lips, and ignores problem behaviors until acceptance occurs. Although NRS is a well-supported procedure for addressing chronic food refusal (i.e., concerns regarding volume), it can result in high rates of negative behaviors (e.g., crying and disruptions) associated with extinction bursts. In addition, NRS may not be appropriate for older children with well-developed self-feeding skills. At a minimum, use of NRS to address food selectivity in ASD should be approached with caution, relying heavily on antecedent manipulation. With this in mind, EE may also take alternative forms, with the overarching goal of allowing a therapist to persist with a reasonable feeding demand during the meal. For example, Sharp et al. described a version of EE in which children were asked to feed themselves and refusal behaviors were placed on extinction with a less intrusive level of prompting. Termed nonremoval of the "food" or "plate," this approach to EE involves a feeder ignoring disruptive behaviors, redirecting the child back to the table in response to leaving, and continuing the presentation of the food for a set amount of time.

Feeding interventions may also incorporate toys or other preferred activities as a means to enrich the meal or increase certain behaviors. For example, providing noncontingent access to toys during meals has been associated with decreased rates of inappropriate behavior and crying during feeding intervention (Sharp et al., 2010). Differential reinforcement of alternative behaviors is frequently cited as a means to increase acceptance and/or swallowing of target foods (Kerwin, 1999). In most past reports, behavioral packages combined the use of antecedent manipulations and/or rich reinforcement schedules along with EE to balance the need to address the operant function of food refusal (i.e., escape) with maintaining the least restrictive environment and ameliorating possible side effects associated with extinction procedures (Sharp et al., 2010).

SUPPORT FOR BEHAVIORAL INTERVENTION

Most research regarding feeding intervention is derived from intensive intervention at hospital or day treatment programs focusing on children with severe food selectivity, highlighting the need to expand the evidence base to promote greater breadth of treatment options. For example, Sharp et al. (2011) presented outcomes for a sample of 13 children admitted to a day treatment program for severe food selectivity. Upon admission, the children were consuming a median of 3 food items (range, 1–7), with starch representing the primary food accepted during meals. In addition, the presentation of nonpreferred foods was associated with high rates of refusal behaviors (upwards of 75 per minute). At discharge, the group demonstrated a significant improvement in the variety of foods consumed, with an average of 16 foods (from all food groups) introduced into meals. Follow-up data indicated treatment gains persisted more than 1 year following discharge. Laud, Girolami, Boscoe, and Gulott (2009) reported similar levels of improvement for a group of 46 children treated at a multidisciplinary feeding program, with caregivers reporting their children consumed a greater variety of foods while engaging in less refusal behaviors during meals more than 3 years following intervention. Unfortunately, there are few specialized programs available for children with ASD, and they are time and cost intensive. In addition, this level of intervention is not intended for children with mild to moderate food selectivity.

Two recently developed parent training programs hold promise as a means to address moderate food selectivity in ASD. Johnson, Foldes, DeMand, and Brooks (2015) evaluated the feasibility and initial efficacy of a manual-based, behavioral parent-training program. This pilot study involved a nine-session curriculum delivered individually during a 16-week period. The first session reviewed why children with ASD may have more feeding problems, possible functions of these feeding problems, and the antecedent–behavior–consequence model in changing feeding problems. Subsequent sessions focused on prevention strategies and then consequences (reinforcement strategies and compliance procedures). Using a similar model of parent training, but disseminated in a group format, Sharp, Burrell, and Jaquess (2013) evaluated the Autism Managing Eating Aversions and

Limited Variety (MEAL) Plan. The curriculum involved eight, 1-hour-long parent training groups. Topics covered included general behavior management strategies (e.g., routine and consistency and also positive attending) applied during meals, as well as specific interventions for feeding problems associated with ASD (e.g., escape extinction and stimulus fading). Findings from both studies suggest that a structured, behaviorally based parent training curriculum holds potential to fill an important gap in the treatment literature, providing a model of intervention for children with moderate food selectivity whose clinical presentation does not warrant admission to an intensive feeding program.

Finally, there is little research or guidance for addressing mild food selectivity in ASD. With this in mind, the definition of mild food selectivity most closely resembles "pickiness" as often described in young children uncomplicated by ASD. Typically, guidance for caregivers to address concerns regarding picky eating includes offering a wide variety of healthy food choices at meals, maintaining a regular meal schedule/routine, modeling consumption of a wide range of foods, limiting access to snacks and "junk" food between meals, and providing encouragement—without excess pressure—to try new foods (US Department of Agriculture, 2012). Berry and colleagues (2015) developed a guideline for nutritional management of GI concerns in children with ASD, which highlights considerations when adapting existing nutrition practice when working with children with ASD. Although not specifically intended to address mild food selectivity in ASD, the nutrition management algorithm outlined by the authors provides a roadmap for developing and evaluating nutrition management strategies specifically tailored to the unique challenges in this population. Moving forward, there is a clear need to expand resources available to clinicians and caregivers for managing mild food selectivity in ASD.

CONCLUSION

There is now compelling evidence that food selectivity represents a prominent concern in children with ASD. However, important questions remain regarding the cause, impact, and remediation of aberrant feeding patterns in this population. Box 8.1 presents a summary of the current evidence base and recommended next steps to enhance our understanding of food selectivity in ASD. Available evidence suggests poor dietary diversity coinciding with increased risk of macronutrient and micronutrient deficits is the most prominent feeding concern in ASD. Diagnostically, this presentation most closely aligns with ARFID, as reflected by marked interference with psychosocial functioning and significant nutritional deficiency, and should not be confused with other eating disorders (e.g., anorexia nervosa, bulimia nervosa, and binge eating) involving restricted or excessive food intake. Of note, food selectivity in ASD is not frequently associated with compromised growth parameters or restriction of energy intake, but it may coincide with obesity—potentially masking detrimental consequences (e.g., poor bone growth) associated with limited variety in this population. Therefore, movement toward

Box 8.1

SUMMARY OF KEY FINDINGS AND RECOMMENDATIONS
FOR FUTURE RESEARCH ACTIVITIES

What Is Known
1. Food selectivity is primarily an issue of poor dietary diversity; compromised growth is less likely. Associated sequelae may include vitamin and mineral deficiencies, decreased quality of life for families, and increased risk for childhood obesity.
2. Nutritional monitoring, including serum testing of vitamin levels in cases of severe food selectivity, should be included as part of routine health screening to detect possible underlying nutritional insufficiencies.
3. Gastrointestinal symptoms (e.g., constipation and diarrhea) are prevalent in children with ASD; however, the relationship between possible GI dysfunction and food selectivity is unknown.
4. The degree of dietary restriction in ASD ranges from mild to severe. Children with severe food selectivity are at risk for severe malnutrition (e.g., scurvy and rickets), whereas mild food selectivity more closely resembles "pickiness" often observed in young children.
5. Behavioral intervention is the only well-established treatment for food selectivity in ASD, although optimal care should involve contributions from a multidisciplinary team to screen for possible dietary, oral–motor, and/or medical concerns.

Important Next Steps
1. A gold-standard instrument of feeding problems in ASD is required to support increased clinical and research scrutiny in this area.
2. Exportable and cost-effective treatments for children with mild to moderate food selectivity should be developed and tested.
3. The potential interwoven relationship between GI functioning and food selectivity should be further explored, with consideration to factors such as immune abnormalities, mucosal barrier dysfunction, GI motility, and the gut microbiome.
4. The health burden associated with food selectivity in ASD needs to be fully documented, particularly as it pertains to the long-term costs when dietary restriction continues into adolescence and adulthood.

better recognition of underlying dietary risk requires that nutritional monitoring be included as part of routine health care screening. Enhanced detection would also benefit from better measurement (e.g., a frontline screening tool) to support clinical and research activities, including efforts to triage patients to the appropriate level of intervention. In doing so, it is also critical to recognize that food selectivity in ASD can range in severity from mild to severe, and not all children require intensive intervention. To date, research supporting behavioral intervention has focused primarily on severe food selectivity, with treatment delivered in highly structured settings (e.g., inpatient units and day treatment programs) by expert therapists. An important goal moving forward is to develop and evaluate additional treatment options for children who do not warrant this level of intervention. Finally, key questions remain regarding the potential relationship between GI pathology and food selectivity in ASD, as well as the long-term health burden associated with dietary restriction as it persists into adolescence and adulthood.

REFERENCES

American Psychiatric Association. (2013). *Diagnostic and statistical manual of mental disorders* (5th ed.). Arlington, VA: American Psychiatric Publishing.

Anckarsäter, B., Hofvander, E., Billstedt, I. C., Gillberg, C., Gillberg, E., Wentz, M., & Rastam, M. (2012). The sociocommunicative deficit subgroup in anorexia nervosa: Autism spectrum disorders and neurocognition in a community-based, longitudinal study. *Psychological Medicine, 42,* 1957–1967.

Anderluh, M., Tchanturia, K., Rabe-Hesketh, S., Collier, D., & Treasure, J. (2009). Lifetime course of eating disorders: Design and validity testing of a new strategy to define the eating disorders phenotype. *Psychological Medicine, 39,* 105–114.

Ausderau, K., & Juarez, M. (2013). The impact of autism spectrum disorders and eating challenges on family mealtimes. *ICAN: Infant, Child, & Adolescent Nutrition, 5*(5), 315–323.

Bandini, L. G., Anderson, S. E., Curtin, C., Cermak, S., Evans, E. W., Scampini, R., . . . Must, A. (2010). Food selectivity in children with autism spectrum disorders and typically developing children. *Journal of Pediatrics, 157*(2), 259–264.

Baron-Cohen, S., Jaffa, T., Davies, S., Auyeung, B., Allison, C., & Wheelwright, S. (2013). Do girls with anorexia nervosa have elevated autistic traits? *Molecular Autism, 4,* 24.

Bennetto, L., Kuschner, E. S., & Hyman, S. L. (2007). Olfaction and taste processing in autism. *Biological Psychiatry, 62*(9), 1015–1021.

Berry, R. C., Novak, P., Withrow, N., Schmidt, B., Rarback, S., Feucht, S., . . . Sharp, W. G. (2015). Nutrition management of gastrointestinal symptoms in children with autism spectrum disorder: Guideline from an expert panel. *Journal of the Academy of Nutrition and Dietetics, 115*(12), 1919–1927.

Cano, S. C., Tiemeier, H., Van Hoeken, D., Tharner, A., Jaddoe, V. W., Hofman, A., . . . Hoek, H. W. (2015). Trajectories of picky eating during childhood: A general population study. *International Journal of Eating Disorders, 48*(6), 570–579.

Carruth, B. R., Ziegler, P. J., Gordon, A., & Barr, S. I. (2004). Prevalence of picky eaters among infants and toddlers and their caregivers' decisions about offering a new food. *Journal of the American Dietetic Association, 104*(1 Suppl. 1), s57–s64.

Centers for Disease Control and Prevention, Developmental Disabilities Monitoring Network Surveillance Year 2010 Principal Investigators. (2014). Prevalence of autism spectrum disorder among children aged 8 years—Autism and Developmental

Disabilities Monitoring Network, 11 sites, United States, 2010. *Morbidity and Mortality Weekly Report Surveillance Summaries, 63*(2), 1–21.

Croen, L. A., Najjar, D. V., Ray, G. T., Lotspeich, L., & Bernal, P. (2006). A comparison of health care utilization and costs of children with and without autism spectrum disorders in a large group-model health plan. *Pediatrics, 118*(4), e1203–e1211.

Croen, L. A., Zerbo, O., Qian, Y., & Massolo, M. L. (2014). *Psychiatric and medical conditions among adults with ASD.* Paper presented at the 14th Annual Meeting of the International Society for Autism Research (INSAR), Atlanta, GA, May. Abstract retrieved from https://imfar.confex.com/imfar/2014/webprogram/start. html

Curtin, C., Hubbard, K., Anderson, S., Mick, E. Must, A., & Bandini L. G. (2015). Food selectivity, mealtime behavior problems, spousal stress, and family food choices in children with and without autism spectrum disorder. *Journal of Autism Developmental Disorders, 45*(10), 3308–3315.

Dovey, T. M., Staples, P. A., Gibson, E. L., & Halford, J. C. (2008). Food neophobia and "picky/fussy" eating in children: A review. *Appetite, 50*(2-3), 181–193.

Elder, J. H., Shankar, M., Shuster, J., Theriaque, D., Burns, S., & Sherrill, L. (2006). The gluten-free, casein-free diet in autism: Results of a preliminary double blind clinical trial. *Journal of Autism Developmental Disorders, 36*(3), 413–420.

Elsabbaugh, M., Divan, G., Koh, Y. J., Kim, Y. S., Kauchali, S., Marcín, C., . . . Fombonne, E. (2012). Global prevalence of autism and other pervasive developmental disorders. *Autism Research, 5*(3), 160–179.

Evangeliou, A., Vlachonikolis, I., Mihailidou, H., Spilioti, M., Skarpalezou, A., Makaronas, N., . . . Smeitink, J. (2003). Application of a ketogenic diet in children with autistic behavior: Pilot study. *Journal of Child Neurology, 18*, 113–118.

Fulkerson, J. A., Story, M., Neumark-Sztainer, D., & Rydell, S. (2008). Family meals: Perceptions of benefits and challenges among parents of 8- to 10-year-old children. *Journal of the American Dietetic Association, 108*(4), 706–709.

Greer, A. J., Gulotta, C. S., Masler, E. A., & Laud, R. B. (2009). Caregiver stress and outcomes of children with pediatric feeding disorders treated in an intensive interdisciplinary program. *Journal of Pediatric Psychology, 33*, 520–536.

Hediger, M., England, L. G., Molloy, C. A., Yu, K. F., Manning-Courtney, P., & Mills, J. (2008). Reduced bone cortical thickness in boys with autism or autism spectrum disorder. *Journal of Autism Developmental Disorders, 38*, 848–856.

Iverson, J. M., & Wozniak, R. H. (2007). Variation in vocal–motor development in infant siblings of children with autism. *Journal of Autism and Developmental Disorders, 37*(1), 158–170.

Johnson, C. R., Foldes, E., DeMand, A., & Brooks, M. M. (2015). Behavioral parent training to address feeding problems in children with autism spectrum disorder: A pilot trial. *Journal of Developmental & Physical Disabilities, 27*(5), 591–607.

Kerwin, M. E. (1999). Empirically supported treatments in pediatric psychology: Severe feeding problems. *Journal of Pediatric Psychology, 24*, 193–214.

Kirby, M., & Danner, E. (2009). Nutritional deficiencies in children on restricted diets. *Pediatric Clinics of North America, 56*(5), 1085–1103.

Kohane, I. S., McMurry, A., Weber, G., MacFadden, D., Rappaport, L., Kunkel, L., . . . Churchill, S. (2012). The co-morbidity burden of children and young adults with autism spectrum disorders. *PLoS One, 7*(4). e33224.

Kotle, L. A., Cohen, P., Davies, M., Pine, D. S., & Walsh, T. (2001). Longitudinal relationships between childhood, adolescent, and adult eating disorders. *Journal of the
American Academy of Child and Adolescent Psychiatry, 40*, 1434–1440.

Kuschner, E. S., Eisenberg, I. W., Orionzi, B., Simmons, W. K., Kenworthy, L., Martin,
A., & Wallace, G. L. (2015). A preliminary study of self-reported food selectivity in
adolescents and young adults with autism spectrum disorder. *Research in Autism
Spectrum Disorders, 15–16*, 53–59.

Latif, A., Heinz, P., & Cook, R. (2002). Iron deficiency in autism and Asperger syndrome.
Autism, 6(1), 103–114.

Laud, R. B., Girolami, P. A., Boscoe, J. H., & Gulotta, C. S. (2009). Treatment outcomes
for severe feeding problems in children with autism spectrum disorder. *Behavior
Modification, 33*, 520–536.

Ledford, J. R., & Gast, D. L. (2006). Feeding problems in children with autism spectrum disorders: A review. *Focus on Autism and Other Developmental Disabilities, 21*,
153–166.

Lock, J., Agras, W. S., Fitzpatrick, K. K., Bryson, S. W., Jo, B., & Tchanturia, K. (2013). Is
outpatient cognitive remediation therapy feasible to use in randomized clinical trials
for anorexia nervosa? *International Journal of Eating Disorders, 46*(6), 567–575.

Lopez, C., Stahl, D., & Tchanturia, K. (2010). Estimated intelligence quotient in anorexia
nervosa: A systematic review and meta-analysis of the literature. *Annals of General
Psychiatry, 9*, 40.

Lukens, C. T., & Linscheid, T. R. (2008). Development and validation of an inventory
to assess mealtime behavior problems in children with autism. *Journal of Autism and
Developmental Disorders, 38*, 342–352.

Lukens, C. T., & Silverman, A. H. (2014). Systematic review of psychological interventions for pediatric feeding problems. *Journal of Pediatric Psychology, 38*(8),
903–917.

Ma, N. S., Thompson, C., & Weston, S. (2016). Brief report: Scurvy as a manifestation
of food selectivity in children with autism. *Journal of Autism and Developmental
Disorders, 46*, 1464–1470.

Marquenie, K., Rodger, S., Mangohig, K., & Cronin, A. (2011). Dinnertime and bedtime
routines and rituals in families with a young child with an autism spectrum disorder.
Australian Journal of Occupational Therapy, 58(3), 145–154.

Martins, Y., Young, R. L., & Robson, D. C. (2008). Feeding and eating behaviors in
children with autism and typically developing children. *Journal of Autism and
Developmental Disorders, 38*, 1878–1887.

Maskey, M., Warnell, F., Parr, J. R., Couteur, A. L., & McConachie, H. (2013). Emotional
and behavioural problems in children with autism spectrum disorder. *Journal of
Autism and Developmental Disorders, 43*, 851–859.

Mazurek, M. O., & Petroski, G. F. (2015). Sleep problems in children with autism spectrum disorder: Examining the contributions of sensory over-responsivity and anxiety.
Sleep Medicine, 16(2), 270–279.

McAlbee, G. N., Prieto, D. M., Kirby, J., Santilli, A. M., & Setty, R. (2009). Permanent visual loss dye to dietary vitamin A deficiency in an autistic adolescent. *Journal of Child
Neurology, 24*(10), 1288–1289.

McElhanon, B. O., McCracken, C., Karpen, S., & Sharp, W. G. (2014). Gastrointestinal
symptoms in autism spectrum disorders: A meta-analysis. *Pediatrics, 133*(5), 872–883.

Micali, N., Holliday, J., Karwautz, A., Wagner, G., Fernandez-Aranda, F., Badia, A., . . . Treasure, J. L. (2007). Childhood eating and weight in eating disorders: A multi-centre European study of affected women and their unaffected sisters. *Psychotherapy and Psychosomatic, 76,* 234–241.

Nadon, G., Feldman, D. E., Dunn, W., & Gisel, E. (2011). Mealtime problems in children with autism spectrum disorder and their typically developing siblings: A comparison study. *Autism, 15*(1), 98–113.

Neumeyer, A. M., O'Rourke, J. A., Massa, A., Lee, H., Lawson, E. A., McDougle, C. J., & Misra, M. (2015). Brief report: Bone fractures in children and adults with autism spectrum disorders. *Journal of Autism and Developmental Disorders, 45*(3), 881–887.

Nicholls, D. E., & Viner, R. M. (2009). Childhood risk factors for lifetime anorexia nervosa by age 30 years in a national birth cohort. *Journal of the American Academy of Child and Adolescent Psychiatry, 48,* 791–799.

Phillips, K. L., Schieve, L. A., Visser, S., Boulet, S., Sharma, A. J., Kogan, M. D., . . . Yeargin-Allsopp, M. (2014). Prevalence and impact of unhealthy weight in a national sample of US adolescents with autism and other learning and behavioral disabilities. *Maternal and Child Health Journal, 18*(8), 1964–1975.

Piazza, C. C. (2008). Feeding disorders and behavior: What have we learned? *Developmental Disabilities Research Reviews, 14,* 171–181.

Piazza, C. C., Fisher, W. W., Brown, K. A., Shore, B. A., Patel, M. R., Katz, R. M., . . . Blakely-Smith, A. (2003). Functional analysis of inappropriate mealtime behaviors. *Journal of Applied Behavior Analysis, 36,* 187–204.

Postorino, V., Sanges, V., Giovagnoli, G., Fatta, L. M., De Peppo, L., Armondo, M., . . . Mazzone, L. (2015). Clinical differences in children with autism spectrum disorder with and without food selectivity. *Appetite, 92,* 126–132.

Provost, B., Crowe, T. K., Osbourn, P. L., McClain, C., & Skipper, B. J. (2010). Mealtime behaviors of preschool children: Comparison with autism spectrum disorder and children with typical development. *Physical and Occupational Therapy in Pediatrics, 30*(3), 220–233.

Rastam, M., Gillberg, C., & Wentz, E. (2003). Outcome of teenage onset anorexia nervosa in a Swedish community-based sample. *European Child and Adolescent Psychiatry, 12,* 78–90.

Rhind, E., Bonfioli, R., Hibbs, E., Goddard, P., Macdonald, S., Gowers, U., . . . Treasure, J. (2014). An examination of autism spectrum traits in adolescents with anorexia nervosa and their parents. *Molecular Autism, 5,* 56.

Salazar, F., Baird, G., Chandler, S., Tseng, E., O'Sullivan, T., Howlin, P., . . . Simonoff, E. (2015). Co-occurring psychiatric disorders in preschool and elementary school-aged children with autism spectrum disorder. *Journal of Autism and Developmental Disorders, 45,* 2283–2294.

Schmitt, L., Heiss, C. J., & Campbell, E. (2008). A comparison of nutrient intake and eating behaviors of boys with and without autism. *Topics in Clinical Nutrition, 23*(1), 23–31.

Schreck, K. A., Williams, K., & Smith, A. F. (2004). A comparison of eating behavior between children with and without autism. *Journal of Autism and Developmental Disorders, 34,* 433–438.

Sharp, W. G., Berry, R. C., McCracken, C., Nuhu, N. N., Marvel, E., Saulnier, C. A., . . . Jaquess, D. L. (2013). Feeding problems and nutrient intake in children with autism spectrum disorders: A meta-analysis and comprehensive review of the literature. *Journal of Autism and Developmental Disorder, 43*(9), 2159–2173.

Sharp, W. G., Burrell, T. L., & Jaquess, D. L. (2013). The Autism MEAL Plan: A parent-training curriculum to manage eating aversions and low intake among child with autism. *Autism, 18*(6), 712–722.

Sharp, W. G., Jaquess, D. L., & Lukens, C. T. (2013). Multi-method assessment of feeding problems among children with autism spectrum disorders. *Research in Autism Spectrum Disorders, 7*(1), 56–65.

Sharp, W. G., Jaquess, D. L., Morton, J. S., & Herzinger, C. (2010). Pediatric feeding disorders: A quantitative synthesis of treatment outcomes. *Clinical Child and Family Psychology Review, 13*, 348–365.

Sharp, W. G., Jaquess, D. L., Morton, J. F., & Miles, A. G. (2011). A retrospective chart review of dietary diversity and feeding behavior of children with autism spectrum disorder before and after admission to a day treatment program. *Focus on Autism and Other Developmental Disabilities, 26*, 37–48.

Stewart, C., & Latif, A. (2008). Symptomatic nutritional rickets in a teenager with autistic spectrum disorder. *Child: Care, Health and Development, 34*(2), 276–278.

Suarez, M. A., Atchison, B. J., & Lagerwey M. (2014). Phenomenological examination of the mealtime experience for mothers of children with autism and food selectivity. *American Journal of Occupational Therapy, 68*(1), 102–107.

Suarez, M. A., Nelson, N. W., & Curtis, A. B. (2014). Longitudinal follow-up of factors associated with food selectivity in children with autism spectrum disorders. *Autism, 18*(8), 924–932.

Tchanturia, K., Doris, E., Mountfor, V., & Fleming, C. (2015). Cognitive remediation and emotion skills training (CREST) for anorexia nervosa in individual format: Self-reported outcomes. *BMC Psychiatry, 15*, 53.

Tchanturia, K., Smith, E., Weineck, F., Fidanboylu, E., Kern, N., Treasure, J., & Baron Cohen, S. (2013). Exploring autistic traits in anorexia: A clinical study. *Molecular Autism, 4*, 44.

Tomchek, S. D., & Dunn, W. (2007). Sensory processing in children with and without autism: A comparative study using the Short Sensory Profile. *American Journal of Occupational Therapy, 61*, 190–200.

Uher, R., & Rutter, M. (2012). Classification of feeding and eating disorders: Review of evidence and proposals for ICD-11. *World Psychiatry, 11*(2), 80–92.

US Department of Agriculture (2012, May). *Health tips for picky eaters.* Retrieved from https://www.choosemyplate.gov/preschoolers-picky-eating

US Department of Health and Human Services and US Department of Agriculture. (2015, December). *2015–2020 dietary guidelines for Americans* (8th ed.). Retrieved from https://health.gov/dietaryguidelines/2015/guidelines

Wentz, E., Lacey, J. H., Waller, G., Rastam, M., Turk, J., & Gillberg, C. (2005). Childhood onset neuropsychiatric disorders in adults eating disorder patients: A pilot study. *European Child & Adolescent Psychiatry, 14*, 431–437.

Westwood, H., Eisler, I., Mandy, W., Leppanen, J., Treasure, J., & Tchanturia, K. (2016). Using the Autism-Spectrum Quotient to measure autistic traits in anorexia nervosa: A systematic review and meta-analysis. *Journal of Autism and Developmental Disorders, 46*(3), 964–977.

Whitely, P., Dodou, K., Todd, L., & Shattock, P. (2004). Body mass index of children from the United Kingdom diagnosed with developmental disorders. *Pediatrics International, 46*(5), 531–533.

Yeargin-Allsopp, M., Rice, C., Karapurkar, T., Doernberg, N., Boyle, C., & Murphy, C. (2003). Prevalence of autism in a US metropolitan area. *JAMA, 289*(1), 49–55.

PART II

Atypical Symptom Presentations

9

Avoidant/Restrictive Food Intake Disorder

Assessment and Treatment

JESSIE MENZEL ∎

Eating disorders in children have historically been particularly tricky to diagnose, and these problems have been compounded by a flawed diagnostic system. Younger children with more classic eating disorders, such as anorexia or bulimia, were lumped at higher rates into the eating disorder not otherwise specified (EDNOS) category, and the existing childhood eating disorder variant (feeding disorder of infancy and early childhood) was overly narrow and restrictive in its diagnostic criteria (Bryant-Waugh, Markham, Kreipe, & Walsh, 2010; Ornstein et al., 2013). Avoidant/restrictive food intake disorder (ARFID) is a new eating disorder diagnosis in the fifth edition of the *Diagnostic and Statistical Manual of Mental Disorders* (DSM-5; American Psychiatric Association, 2013) that now captures a wide array of long-observed eating difficulties that failed to fit into previously defined categories. Many individuals captured by the ARFID diagnosis are those with "fussy" or "picky" eating who have long been regarded as "normal" or "going through a phase" by parents and pediatricians alike. The ARFID diagnosis validates the challenges and distress faced by these individuals and provides an opportunity for increased awareness and recognition of significant medical and psychological consequences of picky eating. In actuality, ARFID represents a much more heterogeneous category of individuals with restrictive eating patterns. It is a diagnosis that represents not just picky eaters but also individuals who have difficulty meeting their nutritional needs due to other challenges, such as specific food fears or functional gastrointestinal disorders. The broad scope of the diagnosis presents many complexities for the treating eating disorder clinician, and the lack of research on the diagnosis provides little direction.

This chapter describes ARFID and its common presentations to aid in accurate diagnosis and offers preliminary recommendations and guidelines for treatment.

It also summarizes the gaps in our knowledge regarding ARFID and suggests avenues for future research.

DIAGNOSIS

ARFID is defined as the presence of an eating or feeding disturbance that results in the persistent failure to meet one's nutritional or energy needs (American Psychiatric Association, 2013). The eating disturbance must be accompanied by one or more of the following: (1) weight loss or faltering growth (e.g., weight remains stable but a child falls off his or her growth charts with respect to body mass index [BMI]); (2) the presence of a nutritional deficiency, such as anemia; (3) dependence on nutritional supplements, such as Ensure or Carnation Instant Breakfast, or enteral feeding (i.e., tube feeding) to meet nutritional needs; or (4) significant psychosocial distress in conjunction with eating. For many individuals, this distress takes the form of depression or social anxiety (Micali et al., 2011; Zucker et al., 2015). Other common examples of psychosocial impairment include inability to eat outside the home at restaurants, school, or friends' houses; frequent "battles" at mealtimes; a sense of social isolation; and a sense of not feeling "normal." The eating disturbance also cannot be within the context of poor socioeconomic resources (e.g., food insecurity) or religious or cultural observations (e.g., Ramadan). Finally, the eating disturbance cannot be accompanied by a disturbance in body image.

ARFID often reflects a long-standing eating disturbance initially present at birth or in early childhood. Although it has not been systematically studied, in the author's clinical experience, many parents of children or adolescents with ARFID recall feeding difficulties beginning at birth with breast-feeding or with the initial transition to solid foods. Prior to the inclusion of ARFID in the DSM-5, ARFID behaviors were captured by the diagnosis of feeding disorder of infancy or early childhood (FDIC; American Psychiatric Association, 2000). This diagnosis was provided to individuals with the feeding disturbance onset prior to 6 years of age and who failed to eat enough food to gain weight or grow normally over a period of 1 month or longer. Due to the developmental limitations of the diagnosis, older children, adolescents, and adults who presented with eating disturbance unaccompanied by weight or shape concerns were diagnosed with EDNOS or not at all (Kelly, Shank, Bakalar, & Tanofsky-Kraff, 2014). Thus, the category of ARFID was created without an age of onset criterion to better capture the broad spectrum of eating disturbances present across the life span. The scientific literature includes a limited number of case reports concerning picky eating in adulthood, and a significant population of adults identify themselves as picky eaters—as high as 35.5% in one study (Kauer, Pelchat, Rozin, & Zickgraff, 2015; Wildes, Zucker, & Marcus, 2012). Longitudinal studies suggest that when eating problems are detected in childhood, they tend to be relatively stable and persist into adulthood, particularly picky eating (Marchi & Cohen, 1990; Mascola, Bryson, & Agras, 2010). Furthermore, picky eating in adulthood is associated with greater clinical depression compared to that for non-picky eaters (Kauer et al., 2015). These data suggest that a spectrum of eating disturbances are present across the life span and that if eating disturbances are present in childhood, they can continue to cause problems into adulthood if left untreated. With changes in the diagnostic criteria, these individuals can now be recognized for their impairment and thus referred for appropriate treatment.

Differentiating ARFID from other eating disorders, especially anorexia nervosa (AN), can be very challenging. This is especially true in atypical cases of AN in which fear of weight gain or fat phobia are not overtly expressed or in preadolescent patients with AN who have trouble articulating a fear of weight gain (Golden et al., 2003). Many individuals with AN and ARFID present similarly; they may endorse anxiety around eating, be excessively preoccupied with food, skip meals, restrict intake, eat the same foods repeatedly, and present with dangerously low body weight (Fisher et al., 2014; Fitzpatrick, Forsberg, & Colborn, 2015; Nicely, Lane-Loney, Masciulli, Hollenbeak, & Ornstein, 2014). Individuals with ARFID are also more likely to consume predominantly high-carbohydrate or sweet foods that are common staples of binge episodes seen in bulimia nervosa (BN) or binge-eating disorder (BED) (Fitzpatrick et al., 2015). Despite these commonalities, significant differences between ARFID and other eating disorders exist with respect to the experience of body image and course of illness. Individuals with ARFID lack a marked disturbance in their body image and do not endorse undue influence of weight or shape on self-image (American Psychiatric Association, 2013). Individuals with ARFID are more likely to accurately perceive themselves as underweight and often report a desire to gain weight. They may have body preoccupation, but they are more preoccupied with somatic symptoms or complaints (e.g., nausea) rather than size or shape features (Nicely et al., 2014). As opposed to weight loss, restricted intake and food avoidance in ARFID are motivated by lack of interest in food; poor appetite; intolerance of specific tastes or textures; or fears regarding other consequences of eating, such as abdominal pain, choking, vomiting, or allergic reaction. Compensatory behaviors such as the use of laxatives, diuretics, and compulsive exercise are less common in individuals with ARFID (Nicely et al., 2014). Recurrent episodes of vomiting may be present but generally are not self-induced and are not used as a means to achieve weight loss. Based on the author's clinical experience, vomiting may occur instead as the result of anxiety or as a visceral, disgust-triggered response to eating nonpreferred foods.

Data from a British National Surveillance Study provide additional guidance in distinguishing ARFID from AN and BN. An analysis of nine primary eating disorder symptoms in 208 children and adolescents revealed three distinct eating disorder profiles (Nicholls, Lynn, & Viner, 2011). The first profile was characterized by fear of weight gain, excessive exercise, and preoccupation with body weight and shape. The second profile was characterized by low body weight and somatic complaints, lack of binge-eating episodes, and no marked concern for body weight and shape. The final profile was characterized by self-induced vomiting, binge eating, and normal to overweight status. The second profile was most consistent with ARFID, whereas the first and third profiles were consistent with diagnoses of AN and BN, respectively. These data support the idea that individuals with ARFID are not concerned with their body weight or shape, and their persistent food avoidance and restriction is not accompanied by other efforts to manage or lose weight (Nicholls et al., 2011). The presence of any behaviors that are intended to cause weight loss should cause the clinician to consider alternate eating disorder diagnoses.

With respect to course of illness, more "classic" eating disorders such as AN and BN typically onset in mid to late adolescence after a period of relatively normal food intake and development. However, the feeding difficulties that are present in ARFID usually onset early in life and reflect a long-standing pattern of disordered eating behavior (Fitzpatrick et al., 2015). Picky eating in particular is considered to be characteristic of normal childhood development, a possibly adaptive behavior protecting against ingestion of poisonous/harmful foods as a toddler begins to explore his or her environment to a greater extent (Dovey, Staples, Gibson, & Halford, 2008). Carbohydrate-rich foods also help fuel the rapid growth children are undergoing during this age. Approximately 10–35% of children are considered picky eaters, and slightly less than half of these children have picky eating that persists past early childhood (Jacobi, Schmitz, & Agras, 2008; Mascola et al., 2010). In fact, some researchers have referred to picky eating or refusal of new or novel foods as trait-like, emphasizing the stability and relative inflexibility of this eating style (Nicklaus, Boggio, Chabanet, & Issachou, 2005; Skinner, Carruth, Bounds, & Ziegler, 2002). In a minority of cases, however, ARFID may onset following a traumatic incident and thus does not reflect a long-standing aversion to food or historically poor appetite.

Another challenge posed by the ARFID diagnosis is the differential diagnosis of ARFID and other anxiety disorders, such as specific phobia. No data are available comparing the etiology of ARFID and anxiety disorders or even the overlapping characteristics or symptom features of the disorders. ARFID patients tend to have more fears that generalize beyond food, display more obsessive–compulsive symptoms, and are more vigilant and fearful of somatic sensations (e.g., headaches and stomach upset; Fitzpatrick et al., 2015; Wildes et al., 2012). The DSM-5 indicates, however, that the extent of the disturbance of eating should be used as the distinguishing feature between an anxiety disorder and ARFID (American Psychiatric Association, 2013). Thus, if altering or changing eating behaviors will be the primary target of intervention, the diagnosis of ARFID is more appropriate.

PREVALENCE, RISKS, AND CORRELATES

Few data are available in general on the characteristics or correlates of ARFID. The information that is available is based largely on studies within treatment-seeking, eating disorder populations. Historical reviews of patient diagnoses in treatment settings using DSM-5 diagnostic criteria reveal that between 14%

(Fisher et al., 2014) and 22.5% (Nicely et al., 2014) of eating disorder patients meet criteria for ARFID. In a community cohort of Dutch adolescents, the prevalence of ARFID was 6.5%, which is much higher than the rates for AN (1.7%), BN (0.8%), and BED (2.3%) (Smink, van Hoeken, Oldenhinkel, & Hoek, 2014). These data suggest that among children and adolescents, ARFID may be the most common eating disorder, although larger population studies are needed. Patients with ARFID do tend to be younger (average age, 11.1–12.9 years) than patients with AN or BN (average age, 14.0–16.5 years) (Fisher et al., 2014; Nicely et al., 2014). These rates may underestimate the number of young patients with ARFID because many day treatment and intensive outpatient eating disorder treatment settings do not see patients younger than age 10 years. An incidence study of eating disorders in a British population reported that 62% of eating disorder cases in individuals age 12 years or younger were "atypical" in presentation (Nichols et al., 2011). Although the authors of the study did not assess for ARFID, it is notable that children are less likely to be diagnosed with AN or BN, particularly at younger ages (Nichols et al., 2011; Norris et al., 2014). Older estimated ages could also be affected by the fact that patients with ARFID are more likely to have a longer course of illness before presenting for treatment (Fisher et al., 2014). One hypothesis for this longer course of illness is that the tendency of medical providers to reassure parents that picky eating is a normal developmental phase may delay the initiation of treatment (Zucker et al., 2015). Finally, in addition to being younger, a higher proportion of ARFID patients are male (approximately 20–28%) (Fisher et al., 2014; Nicely et al., 2014; Norris et al., 2014).

ARFID is also associated with a number of psychological and medical comorbidities. Although individuals with ARFID present with a higher percentage of expected weight for height compared to those with AN, they present as significantly more weight suppressed than individuals with BN and are more likely to present at an overall lower body weight (Fisher et al., 2014; Norris et al., 2014). In one study, approximately one-fourth of ARFID patients had required hospitalization at some point for medical instability, and few differences existed between patients with ARFID and patients with AN in terms of medical morbidity (Norris et al., 2014). Of note, patients with AN were more likely to suffer from bradycardia, whereas patients with ARFID had significantly worse bone mineral density scores (Norris et al., 2014), reflecting the nutritional rather than caloric deficits characteristic of ARFID. Other findings indicate that patients with ARFID are more likely to be diagnosed with at least one other medical condition and are more likely to present for care to a specialty service, such as a gastrointestinal clinic (Fisher et al., 2014; Nicely et al., 2014; Norris et al., 2014). Compared to people with other eating disorders, individuals with ARFID are more likely to use nutritional supplements, have been diagnosed with a food allergy, have a fear of choking or vomiting, and endorse sensory issues (Nicely et al., 2014). With respect to psychological comorbidities, ARFID patients have a higher rate of comorbid anxiety disorders compared to those with AN and BN, particularly generalized anxiety disorder (GAD); higher rates of autism spectrum disorder (ASD); higher rates of other learning disorders or attention deficit hyperactivity disorder; and lower rates of depression or other mood disorders (Fisher et al., 2014; Nicely et al., 2014). These findings clearly suggest that ARFID is associated with serious medical and psychological risks on par with those seen in other eating disorders.

Although cross-sectional studies fail to find a relationship between picky eating and other eating disorder psychopathology in childhood, data from a limited number of retrospective and adult studies suggest that ARFID may place individuals at risk for the *later* development of another eating disorder (Dellava et al., 2012; Jacobi et al., 2008; Marchi & Cohen, 1990). Longitudinal studies of ARFID do not exist, but some studies have examined the long-term effects of problematic childhood eating behaviors such as picky eating, food avoidance, and high-conflict meals. One epidemiological study followed 800 children and their mothers across three different time points from childhood (ages 1–10 years) through adolescence and early adulthood (ages 11–21 years) (Marchi & Cohen, 1990). Children who exhibited picky eating in childhood or digestive problems, such as diarrhea, vomiting, or stomachaches, were at increased risk for developing symptoms of AN in adolescence. Another retrospective study of 325 women diagnosed with AN found that 11.6% of the women were recalled to be picky eaters as children and 14.5% experienced infant vomiting (Dellava et al., 2012). Picky eating also seems to place children at risk for developing symptoms of BN (Marchi & Cohen, 1990). The latter finding is consistent with data from adults indicating significantly higher rates of BN, BED, and obesity among adult picky eaters (Wildes et al., 2012).

These studies suggest that picky eating behavior in childhood places individuals at greater risk for the development of an eating disorder in the future. It cannot be determined, however, whether the picky eating behavior examined in these studies met DSM-5 criteria for ARFID, and it is unclear if picky eating alone or picky eating that reaches the level of severity of ARFID produces greater risk for the development of later eating pathology. Data from a population cohort of 917 children between the ages of 2 and 6 years did demonstrate that even moderate levels of picky eating were associated concurrently and prospectively with significant psychosocial impairment (Zucker et al., 2015). Moderate and severe levels of picky eating in the study were differentiated by whether or not the limited range of a child's preferred foods made eating with others difficult. The significant psychosocial impairments detected in even moderate levels of picky eating suggest that even this level of picky eating behavior would qualify for the diagnosis of ARFID (Zucker et al., 2015). The growing body of data on problematic eating behaviors in children clearly shows that the risks associated with these behaviors are too great to leave them unaddressed and that conferring the diagnosis of ARFID on these individuals helps ensure that they will receive the intervention they need.

COMMON PRESENTATIONS OF ARFID

The recognition of ARFID in the DSM-5 presents new challenges in terms of treatment. Although ARFID patients will now receive recognition from the medical and mental health community, little evidence is available to guide appropriate treatment for these individuals. To provide clinicians with a clearer path forward, it is helpful to more specifically conceptualize the types of eating disturbances seen in ARFID. The diagnostic criteria for ARFID, although more specific than those for FDIC, are very broad and thus capture a range of heterogeneous eating disturbances. These eating disturbances include picky eating or selective eating, food refusal due to the fear of negative consequences of eating, and food refusal due to poor appetite or stomach upset.

Picky eating is perhaps the most well-known presentation of ARFID, and it comprises approximately 28% of ARFID cases in treatment settings (Fisher et al., 2014). Picky eating is defined as the limitation of foods based on taste, texture, color, brand, and/or smell (Dovey, Staples, Gibson, & Halfod, 2008). Picky eaters also typically exhibit slow pace of eating, micro-biting food, distractability at mealtimes, refusal to come to the table, early satiation, and refusal to try new foods (food neophobia). Conflict surrounding mealtimes is often high; parents report high levels of frustration with preparing meals, negotiating with children to eat, preparing multiple meals at a time, and frequent dinnertime battles. These individuals may also gag when trying new or nonpreferred foods. Dysphagias and other oral motor problems may also be present, particularly in more severe cases of picky eating.

Approximately 17% of ARFID cases appear similar to a specific phobia in which the individual has difficulty eating due to the feared consequences of eating, such as choking, vomiting, or allergic reaction (Fisher et al., 2014). In these individuals, the anxiety appears to be the primary presenting feature of the case. They may avoid only specific foods or whole food groups, such as avoiding all meats because they are difficult to chew or avoiding specific foods with a stringy texture. Decrease in food intake may be sudden or gradual following a traumatic incident. Other anxiety-related symptoms may also be present, particularly somatic complaints such as headaches, tightness in the throat, stomachaches, nausea, and other gastrointestinal upset. In addition, secondary eating disturbances, such as slow pace of eating, prolonged chewing, micro-biting, holding food in mouth, or functional swallowing problems, may be present. Other variants of this presentation may include general fearfulness of negative reactions after eating, such as fear of exacerbating an existing medical condition or triggering other functional gastrointestinal upset.

The final and largest subset of ARFID patients, comprising approximately 40% of cases, represents individuals who generally lack appetite or interest in eating or endorse generalized somatic symptoms secondary to anxiety or another emotional disturbance (Fisher et al., 2014). This latter category of cases is consistent with a syndrome previously described in the literature as food avoidance emotional disorder (FAED; Higgs, Goodyer, & Birch, 1989). FAED has not been systematically studied, but case reports and clinical observations describe these individuals as having a history of medically unexplained physiological symptoms, being troubled by emotions that impair appetite, and having poor eating habits (Higgs et al., 2989). Typically, the presenting concern for these individuals is poor physical health rather than poor mental health. They may have undergone extensive gastrointestinal (GI) workups to discover an organic cause for their symptoms. Often, these individuals are diagnosed with functional GI disorders or have negative workups for other medical conditions. Some clinicians have conceptualized this subcategory of disordered eating as an early precursor of prodromal anorexia (Kreipe & Palomaki, 2012). Because the appetite disturbance in these patients appears to be amotivational or motivated by avoidance of somatic symptoms, a diagnosis of ARFID (as opposed to AN) is conferred.

The diversity of ARFID presentations indicates that there may be unique etiologies for each of the presentations and therefore has implications for treatment. Thus, effective treatment for the ARFID patient will depend on having a clear conceptualization of the type of ARFID present. Other than a limited number of case studies (Bryant-Waugh, 2013; Fischer, Luiselli, & Dove, 2015), no treatment research has been published for ARFID, and our understanding of this disorder is still in its infancy. This diagnosis will likely undergo refinement in the future as we begin to understand the etiologies specific to each presentation. The remainder of this chapter draws on existing research from related fields, such as anxiety, food selectivity, and eating disorders, to provide recommendations for the treatment of ARFID patients.

FAMILY-BASED THERAPY

Given that ARFID appears to onset in younger ages and that families have been involved in the successful treatment of other eating disorders, it is logical that a family-based approach would be recommended for ARFID. Several principles of family-based treatment for anorexia nervosa (FBT; Lock & Le Grange, 2008) are a good match for the treatment of ARFID (Fitzpatrick et al., 2015). First, the primary target of treatment in FBT is restoration of patient weight and/or getting growth back on track. Second, the FBT approach empowers parents to take control of eating with the goal of increasing intake and normalizing eating patterns. This empowerment approach places parents in a position to take charge of and change maladaptive mealtime behaviors and override understimulated appetites that contribute to avoidant/restrictive eating. Third, FBT provides parents with psychoeducation on eating disorders and parent management training to increase parental self-efficacy in shaping mealtime behaviors. Stylistically, FBT takes an atheoretical stance to the development of eating disorders, and clinicians are non-directive in nature and encourage parents to draw upon their own knowledge and skill set to deal with eating problems. Clinicians are considered expert consultants who provide information, but not solutions, on how to restore normal, healthy eating behavior.

Modifications to the traditional FBT approach are necessary, however, to adapt the treatment for use with ARFID. Traditional FBT approaches assume that parents instinctually know the best way to feed their children, given the fact that a child with an eating disorder such as AN or BN likely had a period of relatively normal intake prior to the onset of the eating disorder. Contrary to this assumption, parents of children with ARFID may not know best how to feed their children because the feeding problems in ARFID tend to appear earlier in development and persist longer before treatment. For example, unlike most patients with other eating disorders, a picky or selective eater may never have eaten normally prior to the development of significant impairment resulting from picky eating. Therefore, the therapist treating ARFID with FBT may need to be more directive in his or her approach in guiding the family in establishing more normal eating. Also, given the clear prominence of anxiety in the presentation of several ARFID variants, psychoeducation for the family would likely center around the child's biological predisposition to anxiety and evidence-based approaches to treating the anxiety. Well-established treatments for specific phobias and generalized anxiety (Silverman, Pina, & Viswesvaran, 2008), chronic pain (Palermo, 2012), and obsessive–compulsive disorder (Piacentini, Langley, & Roblek, 2007) can be used to augment the FBT approach to target the treatment of anxiety. Skill instruction can also be provided to parents and patient simultaneously so that parents can assist with skill acquisition at home. Alternatively, FBT sessions can be separated into individual and family components to assist the clinician in delivering another intervention directly to the patient.

FBT consists of three phases of treatment (Lock & Le Grange, 2015). The first phase is a "stabilization" phase in which the parents assume complete control of feeding behaviors to reverse the life-threatening and starvation-related health impacts of the eating disorder on the individual. The second phase is a "transition" phase in which control of eating is gradually transferred back to the child in a developmentally appropriate way. Finally, the third phase of FBT is an "ending" phase in which the focus shifts to address general communication and relationships within the family and other adolescent issues (Lock & Le Grange, 2015). It is also recommended that FBT for ARFID consist of three modified phases (Fitzpatrick et al., 2015). Phase 1 should focus on uniting the family in an effort to correct eating behaviors, educating parents on feeding problems and anxiety, and renourishing the child by either restoring weight or correcting nutritional deficiencies. Phase 2 should transition the intervention focus more fully to (a) targeting anxiety and exposure to feared foods and situations and/or (2) targeting picky eating and the expansion of dietary variety. Phase 3 should be an ending phase in which treatment progress is evaluated, any goals for future treatment are established, and other familial issues are addressed.

As previously noted, FBT should be the foundation of treatment with ARFID. As patients become medically and nutritionally stabilized, treatment may progress toward targeting anxiety or picky eating more directly, depending on the individual's presentation. For patients presenting with the poor appetite variant of ARFID, traditional FBT for anorexia provides a sufficient format for treatment. Overriding low hunger cues, problem solving weight gain and meal completion, and coping with abdominal pain and discomfort are common challenges faced by the FBT practitioner in the treatment of AN. Thus, no additional modifications or interventions may be needed with this presentation of ARFID. However, when anxiety or picky eating are significant contributors to the feeding difficulties, adjunct interventions may be needed. The following two sections describe interventions that can be used to augment FBT to specifically target the common presenting subtypes of anxiety and picky eating.

TREATMENT OF ANXIETY

If the patient presents with the food phobia variant of ARFID, then it is recommended that family-based behavioral and cognitive–behavioral treatments (CBTs) for anxiety disorders be utilized during Phase 2 of FBT for ARFID. These interventions can be used to target specific eating phobias, generalized anxiety, and worry related to exacerbation of chronic GI pain. For parents, these treatments consist of psychoeducation on anxiety and associated parent behavior that influences anxiety (e.g., modeling and accommodation; Rapee, Wignall, Spence, Cobham, & Lyneham, 2008). General psychoeducation about anxiety is focused largely on the role that avoidance and escape play in maintaining anxiety (Piacentini et al., 2007). When a child is presented with an anxiety-producing stimuli, he or she experiences an increase in unpleasant anxiety symptoms and thus engages in either avoidance of or escape from the anxiety-provoking stimuli. The escape or avoidance results in a temporary decrease in anxiety symptoms, and this relief provides negative reinforcement of the escape behavior. Parents are provided with instruction on escape extinction to prevent avoidance of anxious stimuli, active ignoring of safety behaviors (i.e., behaviors that signal safety in the face of an anxiety-provoking stimuli such as seeking reassurance), and reinforcement and shaping of approach behaviors (Freeman & Garcia, 2009; Piacentini et al., 2007). Escape extinction refers to the process of preventing escape or avoidance of anxiety-provoking stimuli, thus decreasing the frequency of this behavior. Active ignoring refers to parents consciously diverting attention away from an unwanted behavior (e.g., reassurance seeking) in order to decrease its frequency. Reinforcement and shaping refer to the gradual rewarding of "brave" behaviors (e.g., trying a feared food) to help a child gradually face his or her fears. These approaches may be particularly useful in managing mealtime behavior for children with ARFID because negotiating, requesting substitutions, and escape from the family table are frequently the result of anxious avoidance. Patients also receive psychoeducation on anxiety, learn relaxation skills, practice cognitive restructuring to cope with worry thoughts, and complete graduated exposure to feared stimuli. CBT delivered in both individual and family-based formats is well supported for the treatment of both specific anxiety disorders and general anxiety (Davis, May, & Whiting, 2011). Several manualized interventions are available to guide practice, such as Kendall and Hedtke's (2006) Coping Cat series.

CBT is also effective in teaching individuals how to cope with chronic pain and the accompanying anxiety and distress related to exacerbating pain (Eccleston et al., 2014). Treatment of chronic pain is relevant to ARFID because many patients are diagnosed with comorbid medical conditions and frequently report anxiety and worry, particularly related to abdominal pain (Fisher et al., 2014;

Nicely et al., 2014). The goal of CBT for chronic pain is to change the emotional and physical response to pain. Training in the use of relaxation skills to respond to pain, including deep breathing, progressive muscle relaxation, hypnosis, guided imagery, and biofeedback, is common to help directly reduce the pain experience through relief of muscle tension and decrease of arousal (Palermo, 2012). Interventions also focus on altering top-down processing of pain experience by addressing cognitive interpretations of pain, worries about future pain or the futility of controlling pain, and beliefs about pain tolerance and coping. Finally, individuals with chronic pain conditions are often isolated and withdrawn from their social supports and normal life. Therefore, treatment also focuses on improving function by helping individuals re-engage in normal activities (e.g., school, extracurricular activities, and hobbies) and resume involvement with peers. Evidence supports that these approaches can be effective in reducing the intensity of the pain experience (Eccleston et al., 2014).

Another anxiety-related treatment that may have efficacy in reducing the anxiety and somatic symptoms of ARFID is the Unified Protocol for the Treatment of Emotional Disorders (UP; Barlow et al., 2011; Ehrenreich, Goldstein, Wright, & Barlow, 2009). The UP can be administered individually to young persons (UP-YP; Ehrenreich et al., 2009), with family involvement, or in an individual or group setting for children (UP-C; Ehrenreich-May & Bilek, 2012). Although still early in its development, the UP shows promise as an efficient and comprehensive treatment model for emotion regulation (Farchione et al., 2012). The UP is delivered in a modular format and consists of (1) psychoeducation about emotions, (2) awareness of emotions, (3) flexible thinking, (4) modification of emotion-driven behaviors using exposure, and (5) relapse prevention. The UP aims to modify emotional experience through teaching broad, emotion regulation skills; this focus on shared, underlying emotion regulation mechanisms allows the UP to be applied to any emotional experience, regardless of its origin or type. Thus, the UP can be used to intervene on somatization, pain, anxiety, or depression (Allen, Tsao, Seidman, Ehrenreich-May, & Zelter, 2012). The applicability of the UP to somatization and pain is especially important for the treatment of ARFID. Patients with ARFID are especially prone and attuned to somatic symptoms of anxiety (Nicely et al., 2014). Treatment studies of CBT for various anxiety disorders have either not reported or failed to find improvement in the physiological experience of anxiety (Davis et al., 2011).

Finally, medication management should also be considered for its effectiveness in managing anxiety in presentations of ARFID. Selective serotonin reuptake inhibitors (SSRIs) are efficacious in reducing anxiety in children, adolescents, and adults. Combination treatments using both psychotherapy and SSRI therapy are superior to unimodal treatment for obsessive–compulsive disorder (OCD), separation anxiety, GAD, and social phobia (Pediatric OCD Treatment Study [POTS] Team, 2004; Walkup et al., 2008). Sertraline is the most well-researched medication for the treatment of child and adolescent anxiety. However, mirtazapine—a tetracyclic antidepressant—may also be an excellent option for the treatment of anxiety in ARFID patients. Mirtazapine has been used to manage somatic symptoms and to stimulate appetite and reduce nausea (Kast & Foley, 2007). In an archival study of 528 patients in a nonpsychiatric inpatient medical setting, mirtazapine was linked to improvement in nausea in 37% of patients and increased appetite in 23.5% of patients (Allen et al., 2016).

TREATMENT OF PICKY EATING

In patients with the picky or selective eating variant of ARFID, expanding dietary variety during Phase 2 of FBT can be particularly challenging. Several considerations should be made in determining how and whether to expand dietary variety as part of the treatment of ARFID.

As reviewed previously, picky eating behavior typically presents early in life and, in many cases, remains stable over time. These characteristics of picky eating indicate that picky eating has a strong genetic and biological basis. Limited food preferences appear relatively early in childhood and are consistent across cultures, indicating that a natural tendency toward sweet and salty foods may be biologically driven (Wardle & Cooke, 2008). For example, children undergo several major growth spurts, and carbohydrate-rich foods provide the fuel for rapid growth. Furthermore, the boost in energy, the flavor, and the sense of satiation that come from eating these calorically dense foods provide a physiological reinforcement (Birch, 1992; Gibson & Wardle, 2003). An avoidance of bitter tastes and pulpy textures—another common aversion—may serve a protective function (from an evolutionary perspective) against food contamination and poisoning (Pliner & Loewen, 1997). Twin studies show high heritability estimates for preference for protein foods and modest heritability for preferences for fruits, vegetables, and desserts (Breen, Plomin, & Wardle, 2006). Sensitivity to specific tastes, such as bitterness, is also highly heritable and is associated with preferences for fruits and vegetables (Dinehart, Hayes, Bartoshuk, Lanier, & Duffy, 2006). Finally, food neophobia—the reluctance to try novel foods—has been associated with temperament traits appearing early in life, such as emotionality and anxiety (Pliner & Loewen, 1997).

The negative impact of picky eating on the physical and emotional health of children is controversial. For example, several studies present conflicting findings on the impact of picky eating on growth and the nutritional adequacy of intake. Multiple studies have found no significant difference between picky eaters and non-picky eaters with respect to weight and BMI (Eckstein, Lanaido, & Glick, 2010; Jacobi et al., 2008; Mascola et al., 2010). Adult studies of picky eating also confirm no overall differences in BMI between groups (Kauer et al., 2015; Wildes et al., 2012). However, Eckstein and colleagues did find that a greater percentage of picky eating children were underweight (20.6%) compared to non-picky eating children (6.6%), and others have confirmed an association between picky eating and lower weight status (Galloway, Fiorito, Lee, & Birch, 2005). Zucker and colleagues (2015) found that reduced growth was the most pronounced impact on physical health in cases of both moderate and high levels of selective eating behavior.

Similar conflicting findings have been found with respect to nutritional adequacy of food intake. One of the major concerns associated with picky eating is often the lack of fruit and vegetable intake and subsequent nutritional deficiencies (Wardle et al., 2003). Parents frequently worry that a poor diet with limited variety will have consequences for their child's overall health and risk for obesity (Wardle et al., 2003). A cross-sectional study of 173 9-year-old, non-Hispanic White girls found that picky eaters consumed significantly less fruits, vegetables, sweets, and fats compared to non-picky eaters (Galloway et al., 2005). Other studies have confirmed that picky eating seems to be associated with avoidance of foods in general as opposed to avoidance of specific food categories (e.g., vegetables; Jacobi et al., 2008). In addition, in Galloway and colleagues' study, picky eating girls consumed less fiber compared to non-picky eating girls. The two groups did not differ significantly, however, with respect to their micronutrient intake. In fact, results indicated that the average intake of all girls, not just picky eaters, fell short of meeting the recommended intake of grains, fruits, vegetables, and meats. Overall energy intake for the two groups was also similar. These results suggest that despite their lower consumption of fruits and vegetables, picky eating girls were not necessarily more nutritionally deprived and they did not eat significantly more sweets and fats compared to their non-picky eating peers. Moreover, picky eating girls were more likely to be underweight and had a lower percentage of body fat compared to non-picky eating girls. These results seem to debunk myths that picky eaters have higher fat diets and consume more sweets compared to non-picky eaters—a diet that would be associated with increased risk for obesity. Data from adults indicate that picky eaters have rates of obesity that are similar to those of the general population and that in picky eaters who are obese, other eating pathology is also likely to be present (e.g., binge eating; Wildes et al., 2012).

However, picky eating does seem to be consistently associated with psychosocial impairment. Picky eating is correlated in cross-sectional studies with negative affect, internalizing and externalizing problems, somatic complaints, social withdrawal, aggressive and delinquent behavior, and higher disgust sensitivity (Jacobi et al., 2008; Micali et al., 2011). Picky eating is also associated with heightened sensory sensitivity and disgust sensation, particularly at the more severe levels (Kauer et al., 2015; Zucker et al., 2015). Picky eating is related to greater psychopathology both cross-sectionally and longitudinally, including behavioral disorders, anxiety, GAD, OCD, depression, and pervasive developmental disorders (Kauer et al., 2015; Micali et al., 2011; Wildes et al., 2012; Zucker et al., 2015). Wildes and colleagues found that picky eating in adults was associated with overall greater eating-related impairment compared to non-picky eaters. Eating-related impairment refers to the extent to which food and food-related habits impact one's life. Individuals with picky eating habits are often limited in their ability to engage in normal social interactions that revolve around food (e.g., going to a restaurant with friends, eating lunch at school or another's house, and attending a birthday party or sleepover) and, thus, are more isolated from their peers. Interestingly, these studies also failed to find any association between picky eating and other disordered eating behaviors, such as dieting, other weight-control behaviors, and binge eating (Jacobi et al., 2008; Kauer et al., 2015).

Taken together, the results of the previously discussed studies suggest that by far the largest associated impairments with picky eating are psychosocial. Because picky eating begins early in life, these children are at greater risk for developing psychological disorders, even at moderate levels of pickiness. More research is needed to determine the mechanisms that tie picky eating to psychopathology. The risk could be the result of social isolation from peers because many of these individuals are aware that their eating habits are not "normal" or different and may feel a great deal of shame or embarrassment about their eating habits. Others suggest that the heightened sensory sensitivity associated with picky eating may reflect an underlying, more generalized sensory sensitivity that makes it difficult to regulate emotion or modulate attention (Zucker et al., 2015). The impact of picky eating on physical health seems to be most prominent for growth as opposed to BMI or overall weight status. Furthermore, it is unclear whether poor growth in picky eaters is the result of overall reduced intake, as suggested by findings indicating a general aversion to and avoidance of foods, or nutritional deficiencies due to inadequate variety. Research seems to offer more support for overall reduced intake of food; consuming less food in general would also increase risk for specific nutritional deficiencies.

CHALLENGES AND RECOMMENDATIONS FOR THE TREATMENT OF PICKY EATING

The picky eating associated with an ARFID diagnosis may result in growth impairment, nutritional deficiencies, or significant psychosocial impairment, as discussed previously. Several challenges arise when attempting to intervene on a child's picky eating. The major challenge is the extent to which the picky eating behavior itself can actually be changed. As the previous review suggests, there is significant evidence that long-standing picky eating behavior may be biologically driven. Furthermore, the persistence of this behavior implies that preference for the same foods and resistance to trying new foods may be trait-like in nature. Conceptualizing picky eating as an eating "personality" or as the extension of an underlying, biological propensity to be hypersensitive to sensation has important implications for treatment. It may be an unrealistic expectation for treatment to achieve a significantly expanded diet or the introduction of foods well outside of one's comfort zone. Moreover, the lack of consensus on the specific health consequences of limited variety suggests that changing "pickiness" may not be essential for reducing impairment. What may be more essential for returning an individual to health may be a focus on improving the volume of intake and reducing associated emotional and physiological arousal.

Another factor to consider is that interventions that focus on expanding dietary variety also have limited efficacy. Literature on the treatment of picky eating is relatively sparse, and published studies consist entirely of single case or small case series designs. Each of these study designs has utilized behavior modification approaches to introduce new foods and expand dietary variety. Essential interventions in these approaches combine escape extinction with various rein-forcement or antecedent procedures, such as differential reinforcement, simul-taneous presentation, stimulus fading, and continuous reinforcement. The goals of behavioral strategies are (1) to prevent avoidance of trying new foods or com-pleting meals and (2) to increase the desirability of new or nonpreferred foods. Detailed explanations of these approaches are readily available (for review, see Bachmeyer, 2009). Introduction of new foods occurs gradually, starting with very small amounts of the new or nonpreferred food, and food chaining (selec-tion of a food based on similarities in taste, appearance, or texture; Fraker, Fishbein, Cox, & Walbert, 2007) is used to guide the selection of new foods. Although these approaches are successful in increasing food variety, their clin-ical significance is marginal. A successfully added new food may be defined as eating one teaspoon full of a new food or sucking in a small amount of liquid through a straw. The approaches are also time intensive and typically conducted within pediatric feeding clinics at children's hospitals. Furthermore, these case studies consist primarily of young (toddler or preschool-aged) children, many with developmental disabilities; thus, these approaches may not generalize to older children or adults. Finally, some data suggest that these procedures may backfire and actually decrease liking of exposed foods (Birch, Marlin, & Rotter, 1984; Newman & Taylor, 1992).

In targeting picky eating in the treatment of ARFID, it may be helpful to care-fully consider the priority of diversifying intake with respect to targeting sensory/emotional sensitivity and regulation more generally. Efforts to add new foods to a patient's diet may have limited success without first addressing the underlying mechanisms that make dietary expansion difficult. At the very least, the addition of new foods should occur in conjunction with interventions that target sensory conditioning and emotion regulation. Treatments described in the section on anx-iety may be helpful in increasing a child's willingness to try new foods. In addi-tion, emotion exposures (in the UP) and relaxation strategies (e.g., biofeedback) may help decrease physiological and somatic arousal and increase an individual's ability to tolerate unpleasant or novel tastes and textures. One published case study using CBT in conjunction with behavioral procedures reported increased consumption of previously avoided foods and a reduction in self-reported anx-iety (Fischer et al., 2015). The authors of this study concluded that the addition of CBT enhanced the effectiveness of behavior modification techniques to add new foods. Prioritizing treatment of anxiety and emotion regulation may have a greater positive impact on the patient compared to a focus on diversification of diet. Improvements in emotion regulation and physiological arousal may help the patient overcome feelings of embarrassment, anxiety, and shame that accompany eating in social situations or in novel settings even without changing diet.

Other factors to take into account in determining whether or not to intervene directly with picky eating behavior are the patient's motivation to change and the severity of the patient's limited palette. To date, no research exists that examines whether or not the severity of picky eating moderates the efficacy of behavioral interventions. However, clinical experience indicates that some patients more readily respond to escape extinction procedures and accept new foods than others. Factors that appear to coincide with more severe levels of picky eating are eating extremely limited numbers of foods (e.g., 5–10 total foods) and dysphagias or other oral–motor dysfunctions. Referrals to speech pathologists and occupational therapists are often necessary in such presentations. Similarly, no studies have taken into account patient motivation on the success of picky eating interventions. However, clinical experience suggests a relationship between a patient's internal motivation to expand diet and success of behavioral interventions. Many young patients with selective eating are not motivated to change their eating behavior due to the high level of aversion to nonpreferred foods. Motivation may be increased by the use of reinforcement procedures; however, patients who are more distressed by their limited palettes are more likely to benefit from treatment. In patients with low motivation, one successful strategy may be to select foods for addition based on their social value. For example, a picky eater may not be generally motivated to change his or her picky eating but may desire to eat French fries or tacos because that is what his or her friends eat.

After stabilizing a patient's weight and correcting any nutritional deficiencies during Phase 1 of treatment, the clinician should balance the treatment of limited diet with the treatment of other factors limiting psychosocial functioning, such as anxiety or sensory sensitivity. In patients with low motivation or severely limited palettes, priority should be given to minimally adding foods to enhance psychosocial functioning and improving sensory and emotion regulation through the use of cognitive–behavioral techniques. In patients with less limited palettes or higher motivation, dietary expansion can be a higher treatment priority that occurs in conjunction with CBT for the management of anxiety or somatic symptoms. To set the stage for success, efforts may need to be made in Phase 1 of treatment to redirect parents' focus and concerns away from diversifying patients' intake by providing psychoeducation on the biological and temperament-based nature of long-standing picky eating.

CONCLUSION

As a new diagnosis in the DSM-5, ARFID is a complex and underresearched psychological disorder. More research is needed to better understand its etiology and refine its diagnostic criteria. The limited data that exist demonstrate both the physiological and the psychosocial impact of ARFID. Its inclusion in the DSM-5 is a victory for parents and adults who have struggled with finding providers to take their concerns seriously and provide intervention. However, the field has a long way to go toward creating a comprehensive and efficacious treatment protocol for ARFID. As reviewed previously, the few treatment studies that exist focused on ASD populations and had small samples and nonrandomized conditions; thus, studies with larger samples and randomized conditions in children, older age groups, and nondisabled populations are needed. In particular, more research is needed to understand the mechanisms that contribute to picky eating that persists past the developmentally normative phase. Current behavioral and cognitive–behavioral treatments seem promising, but their clinical significance and long-term efficacy need further evaluation. The information reviewed in this chapter provides clinicians with a preliminary guidance in helping these individuals while the research continues to evolve.

REFERENCES

Allen, L. B., Tsao, J. C. I., Seidman, L. C., Ehrenreich-May, J., & Zeltzer, L. K. (2012). A unified, transdiagnostic treatment for adolescents with chronic pain and comorbid anxiety and depression. *Cognitive and Behavioral Practice, 19,* 56–67.

American Psychiatric Association. (2000). *Diagnostic and statistical manual of mental disorders* (4th ed., text rev.). Washington, DC: Author.

American Psychiatric Association. (2013). *Diagnostic and Statistical Manual of Mental Disorders* (5th ed.). Arlington, VA: American Psychiatric Publishing.

Bachmeyer, M. (2009). Treatment of selective and inadequate food intake in children: A review and practical guide. *Behavior Analysis and Practice, 2,* 43–50.

Barlow, D. H., Farchione, T. J., Fairholme, C. P., Ellard, K. K., Boisseau, C. L., Allen, L., et al. (2011). *The unified protocol for transdiagnostic treatment of emotional disorders: Therapist guide.* New York, NY: Oxford University Press.

Birch, L. L. (1992). Children's preferences for high-fat foods. *Nutrition Review, 50,* 501–505.

Birch, L. L., Marlin, D. W., & Rotter, J. (1984). Eating as the "means" activity in a contingency: Effects on young children's food preference. *Child Development, 55,* 431–439.

Breen, F. M., Plomin, R., & Wardle, J. (2006). Heritability of food preferences in young children. *Physiological Behavior, 88,* 443–447.

Bryant-Waugh, R. (2013). Avoidant restrictive food intake disorder: An illustrative case example. *International Journal of Eating Disorders, 46,* 420–423.

Bryant-Waugh, R., Markham, L., Kreipe, R. E., & Walsh, B. T. (2010). Feeding and eating disorders in childhood. *International Journal of Eating Disorders, 43,* 98–111.

Davis, T. E., May, A., & Whiting, S. E. (2011). Evidence-based treatment of anxiety and phobia in children and adolescents: Current status and effects on the emotional response. *Clinical Psychology Review, 31,* 592–602.

Dellava, J. E., Trace, S. E., Strober, M., Thornton, L. M., Klump, K. L., Brandt, H., . . . Bulick, C. M. (2012). Retrospective maternal report of early eating behaviours in anorexia nervosa. *European Eating Disorders Review, 20,* 111–115.

Dinehart, M. E., Hayes, J. E., Bartoshuk, L. M., Lanier, S. L., & Duffy, V. B. (2006). Bitter taste markers explain variability in vegetable sweetness, bitterness, and intake. *Physiological Behavior, 87,* 304–313.

Dovey, T. M., Staples, P. A., Gibson, E. L., & Halfod, J. G. (2008). Food neophobia and "picky/fussy" eating in children: A review. *Appetite, 50,* 181–193.

Eccleston, C., Palermo, T., Williams, A. C., Lewandowski, A., Morley, S., Fisher, E., . . . Law, E. (2014, May 5). Psychological therapies for the management of chronic and recurrent pain in children and adolescents. *Cochrane Database of Systematic Reviews, 2014*(5), CD003968.

Eckstein, S., Lanaido, D., & Glick, B. (2010). Does picky eating affect weight-for-length measurements in young children? *Clinical Pediatrics, 49,* 217–220.

Ehrenreich, J. T., Goldstein, C. M., Wright, L. R., & Barlow, D. H. (2009). Development of a unified protocol for the treatment of emotional disorders in youth. *Child and Family Behavior Therapy, 31*, 20–37.

Ehrenreich-May, J. T., & Bilek, E. L. (2011). The development of a transdiagnostic, cognitive behavioral group intervention for childhood anxiety disorders and co-occurring depression symptoms. *Cognitive and Behavioral Practice, 19*, 41–55.

Farchione, T. J., Fairholme, C. P., Ellard, K. K., Boisseau, C. L., Thompson-Hollands, J., Carl, J. R., . . . Barlow, D. H. (2012). Unified protocol for transdiagnostic treatment of emotional disorders: A randomized controlled trial. *Behavior Therapy, 43*, 666–678.

Fischer, A. J., Luiselli, J. K., & Dove, M. B. (2015). Effects of clinic and in-home treatment on consumption and feeding-associated anxiety in an adolescent with avoidant/restrictive food intake disorder. *Clinical Practice in Pediatric Psychology, 3*(2), 154–166.

Fisher, M. M., Rosen, D. S., Ornstein, R. M., Mammel, K. A., Katzman, D. K., Rome, E. S., . . . Walsh, B. T. (2014). Characteristics of avoidant/restrictive food intake disorder in children and adolescents: A "new disorder" in DSM-5. *Journal of Adolescent Health, 55*, 49–52.

Fitzpatrick, K. K., Forsberg, S. E., & Coburn, D. (2015). Family-based therapy for avoidant–restrictive food intake disorder. In K. L. Loeb, D. Le Grange, & J. Lock (Eds.), *Family therapy for adolescent eating and weight disorders* (pp. 256–276). New York, NY: Routledge.

Fraker, C., Fishbein, M., Cox, S., & Walbert, L. (2007). *Food chaining: The proven 6-step plan to stop picky eating, solve feeding problems, and expand your child's diet*. Boston, MA: De Capo Press.

Freeman, J. B., & Garcia, A. M. (2009). *Family-based treatment for young children with OCD*. New York, NY: Oxford University Press.

Golden, N. H., Katzman, D. K., Kreipe, R. E., Stevens, S. L., Sawyer, S. M., Rees, J., . . . Rome, E. S. (2003). Eating disorders in adolescents: Position paper for the Society for Adolescent Medicine. *Journal of Adolescent Health, 33*, 496–503.

Higgs, J. F., Goodyer, I. M., & Birch, J. (1989). Anorexia nervosa and food avoidance emotional disorder. *Archives of Disease in Childhood, 64*, 346–351.

Jacobi, C., Schmitz, G., & Agras, S. W. (2008). Is picky eating an eating disorder? *International Journal of Eating Disorders, 41*, 626–634.

Kast, R. E., & Foley, K. F. (2007). Cancer chemotherapy and cachexia: mirtazapine and olanzapine are 5-HT3 antagonists with good antinausea effects. *European Journal of Cancer Care, 16*, 351–354.

Kauer, J., Pelchat, M. L., Rozin, P., & Zickgraff, H. F. (2015). Adult picky eating: Phenomenology, taste sensitivity, and psychological correlates. *Appetite, 90*, 219–228.

Kelly, N. R., Shanks, L. M., Bakalar, J. L., & Tanofsky-Kraff, M. (2014). Pediatric feeding and eating disorders: Current state of diagnosis and treatment. *Current Psychiatry Reports, 16*, 446–458.

Kendall, P. C., & Hedtke, K. A. (2006). *Cognitive–behavioral therapy for anxious children: Therapist manual* (3rd ed.). Ardmore, PA: Workbook Publishing.

Kreipe, R. E., & Palomaki, A. (2012). Beyond picky eating: Avoidant/restrictive food intake disorder. *Current Psychiatry Reports, 14*, 421–431.

Lock, J., & Le Grange, D. (2015). *Treatment of anorexia nervosa, 2nd edition: A family-based approach*. New York, NY: Guilford.

Marchi, M., & Cohen, P. (1990). Early childhood eating behaviors and adolescent eating disorders. *Journal of the American Academy of Child and Adolescent Psychiatry, 29,* 112–117.

Mascola, A. J., Bryson, S. W., & Agras, W. S. (2010). Picky eating during childhood: A longitudinal study to age 11 years. *Eating Behaviors, 11,* 253–257.

Micali, N., Simonoff, E., Elberling, H., Rask, C. U., Olsen, E. M., & Skovgaard, A. M. (2011). Eating patterns in a population-based sample of children aged 5 to 7 years: Association with psychopathology and parentally perceived impairment. *Journal of Developmental and Behavioral Pediatrics, 32,* 572–580.

Newman, J., & Taylor, A. (1992). Effect of a means-end contingency on young children's food preferences. *Journal of Experimental Child Psychology, 64,* 200–216.

Nicely, T., Lane-Loney, S., Masciulli, E., Hollenbeak, C., & Ornstein, R. (2014). Prevalence and characteristics of avoidant/restrictive food intake disorder in a cohort of young patients in day treatment for eating disorders. *Journal of Eating Disorders, 2*(1), 21.

Nicholls, D. E., Lynn, R., & Viner, R. M. (2011). Childhood eating disorders: British National Surveillance Study. *British Journal of Psychiatry, 198,* 295–301.

Nicklaus, S., Boggio, V., Chabanet, C., & Issanchou, S. (2005). A prospective study of food variety seeking in childhood, adolescence and early adult life. *Appetite, 44,* 289–297.

Norris, M. L., Robinson, A., Obeid, N., Harrison, M., Spettigue, W., & Henderson, K. (2014). Exploring avoidant/restrictive food intake disorder in eating disordered patients: A descriptive study. *International Journal of Eating Disorders, 27,* 495–499.

Ornstein, R. M., Rosen, D. S., Mammel, K. A., Callahan, S. T., Forman, S., Jay, M. S., . . . Walsh, B. T. (2013). Distribution of eating disorders in children and adolescents using the proposed DSM-5 criteria for feeding and eating disorders. *Journal of Adolescent Health, 53,* 303–305.

Palermo, T. M. (2012). *Cognitive–behavioral therapy for chronic pain in children and adolescents.* New York, NY: Oxford University Press.

Pediatric OCD Treatment Study (POTS) Team. (2004). Cognitive–behavior therapy, sertraline, and their combination for children and adolescents with obsessive–compulsive disorder: The pediatric OCD Treatment Study (POTS) randomized controlled trial. *Journal of the American Medical Association, 292,* 1969–1976.

Piacentini, J., Langley, A., & Roblek, T. (2007). *Cognitive behavioral treatment of childhood OCD: It's only a false alarm.* New York, NY: Oxford University Press.

Pliner, P., & Loewen, E. R. (1997). Temperament and food neophobia in children and their mothers. *Appetite, 28,* 239–254.

Rapee, R. M., Wignall, A., Spence, S. H., Cobham, V., & Lyneham, H. (2008). *Helping your anxious child* (2nd ed.). Oakland, CA: New Harbinger.

Silverman, W., Pino, A. A., & Viswesvaran, C. (2008). Evidence-based psychosocial treatments for phobic and anxiety disorders in children and adolescents. *Journal of Clinical Child & Adolescent Psychology, 37,* 105–130.

Skinner, J. D., Carruth, B. R., Bounds, W., & Ziegler, P. J. (2002). Children's food preferences: A longitudinal analysis. *Journal of the American Dietetic Association, 102,* 1638–1647.

Smink, F. R. E., van Hoeken, D., Oldenhinkel, A. J., & Hoek, H. W. (2014). Prevalence and severity of DSM-5 eating disorders in a community cohort of adolescents. *International Journal of Eating Disorders, 47,* 610–619.

Walkup, J. T., Albano, A. M., Piacentini, J., Birmaher, B., Compton, S. N., Sherrill, J. T., . . . Kendall, P. C. (2008). Cognitive behavioral therapy, sertraline, or a combination in childhood anxiety. *New England Journal of Medicine, 359,* 2753–2766.

Wardle, J., & Cooke, L. (2008). Genetic and environmental determinants of childhood food preferences. *British Journal of Nutrition, 99,* S15–S21.

Wardle, J., Cooke, L. J., Gibson, E. L., Sapochnik, M., Sheiham, A., & Lawson, M. (2003). Increasing children's acceptance of vegetables: A randomized trial of parent-led exposure. *Appetite, 40,* 155–162.

Wildes, J. E., Zucker, N. L., & Marcus, M. D. (2012). Picky eating in adults: Results of a Web-based survey. *International Journal of Eating Disorders, 45,* 575–582.

Zucker, N., Copeland, W., Franz, L., Carpenter, K., Keeling, L, Angold, A., . . . Egger, H. (2015). Psychological and psychosocial impairment in preschoolers with selective eating. *Pediatrics, 136,* 1–11.

10

Anorexia Nervosa with a History of Obesity or Overweight

JOCELYN LEBOW AND LESLIE SIM ■

One of the more harmful and erroneous assumptions regarding eating disorders is that individuals with overweight/obesity are unlikely to develop anorexia nervosa (AN). The two conditions, obesity and AN, are frequently perceived as conceptually distinct and are addressed with discrepant, even directly contradictory, approaches. Specifically, AN treatment, which typically falls under the purview of psychiatry/behavioral sciences, generally focuses on reducing weight/shape stigma, broadening food repertoire, decreasing dieting behaviors, and reducing body image dissatisfaction (Irving & Neumark-Sztainer, 2002). Treatment for overweight or obesity, however, tends to be spearheaded by medical professionals, and it often involves opposing interventions to those intended to address eating disorders, including increasing dietary restriction, limiting food choices, identifying "bad" or forbidden foods, and even, in some cases, eliciting or increasing body dissatisfaction in an attempt to motivate behavior change (Irving & Neumark-Sztainer, 2002).

The disparate treatment approaches are contraindicated by data that suggest AN and obesity share many common risk and protective factors (Neumark-Sztainer et al., 2007). Most significantly, dieting behaviors have been identified in longitudinal research as significant predictors of weight gain and obesity, as well as the single most robust risk factor for eating disorders (Irving & Neumark-Sztainer, 2002; Neumark-Sztainer et al., 2007).

Unfortunately, the general lack of awareness of these points of overlap not only leads to significant challenges in identification and treatment of eating disorders but also may place individuals with higher weight status at risk for developing an eating disorder. In particular, due to the misperception that having a history of overweight or obesity precludes one from developing a restrictive eating disorder, symptoms of pathological restriction in higher weight status individuals have the potential to be overlooked, and these individuals may be less likely to be referred for targeted eating disorder screening and treatment. Even more troubling, with the recent public health focus on the "obesity pandemic," practice guidelines mandate that health care providers intervene with higher weight status patients and offer anticipatory guidance that essentially prescribes the symptoms of an eating disorder (dietary restriction, avoidance of foods, etc.) and thus potentially exacerbates these symptoms in those at risk.

PREVALENCE

It is important to note that cases of AN in patients with current or past overweight or obesity are not confined to a small handful of outliers. On the contrary, the consensus in the field is that these cases are not exceptional. In fact, some data suggest that at least a brief period of premorbid overweight is common in most patients who go on to develop AN. For example, a review of longitudinal growth data for 66 adult patients with AN found that in the majority of cases, females had a period during which their weight and height were significantly above expected levels, typically just prior to the onset of AN (Nielsen, 1985). Similarly, after examining the growth charts of 122 adolescent girls with restrictive eating disorders, Swenne (2001) found that despite having normally timed puberty, on average this sample was premorbidly heavier than their peers— either consistently throughout development or via a sudden surge in weight just preceding the eating disorder onset.

In addition, one study reported that 22.6% of adult females with AN who presented for inpatient treatment did so at a weight higher than the criterion for the disorder listed in the fourth edition of the *Diagnostic and Statistical Manual of Mental Disorders* (DSM-IV; American Psychiatric Association [APA], 1994; Watson & Andersen, 2003). Because this sample consisted of patients with AN severe enough to warrant inpatient treatment despite not presenting with established low weight, this is likely an underestimate of the number of patients in the general community with AN and higher weight status. In another study of more than 100 adult patients with AN, the majority of the sample reported a history of premorbid overweight, including 28% who were premorbidly obese (Crisp, Hsu, Harding, & Hartshorn, 1980). A retrospective chart review of 179 adolescents with restrictive eating disorders found that 36.7% had a history of overweight or obesity (Lebow, Sim, & Kransdorf, 2015).

In short, estimates show that approximately one-fourth to well over half of adolescent and adult patients presenting with restrictive eating disorders have a history of overweight or obesity. When presented in the context of population-based statistics—namely that an estimated 33.2% of American adolescents present with either overweight or obesity, and 37.9% of American adults are obese—it is clear that premorbid obesity is at least proportionately represented in patients with AN (Flegal, Carroll, Kit, & Ogden, 2012; Ogden, Carroll, Kit, & Flegal, 2012). These data confirm that these patients represent a sizeable percentage of those presenting for eating disorder treatment.

CHALLENGES WITH DIAGNOSIS

Contributing to the erroneous idea that AN and overweight are mutually exclusive conditions is the fact that AN has not always been diagnosable in higher weight patients based on the DSM. Initially, the third edition of the DSM (DSM-III; APA, 1980) stated that a diagnosis of AN could be made in cases in which the patient had lost greater than 25% of his or her premorbid weight, regardless of the patient's absolute body weight at the time of evaluation. Unfortunately, this criterion was updated in subsequent editions to include an absolute weight requirement. The revision to this edition, the DSM III-R (APA, 1987), added a clause that a patient with AN must be maintaining a body weight at least 15% below "expected." This standard was carried forward into the DSM-IV (APA, 1994) and DSM-IV text revision (APA, 2000), which included the same criterion that individuals must weigh at or below 85% "ideal body weight."

This criterion of ideal body weight is particularly problematic given significant variability in calculating expected or ideal body weight in the literature. Despite the existence of several proposed algorithms—for example, the McLaren method (McLaren & Read, 1972), the Moore method (Moore, Durie, Forstner, & Pencharz, 1985), and the body mass index (BMI) method (Hebebrand, Himmelmann, Heseker, Schafer, & Remschmidt, 1996)—no method is without flaws. Even more concerning, the more commonly used methods involve calculations in which an individual's presenting weight is compared to that which is considered "average" (e.g., the 50th percentile BMI for gender and age) in the population. This means that an individual presenting at a weight greater than the so-called average, regardless of whether he or she has lost a large amount of weight, would be considered to be at, for example, 110% of "ideal body weight" and would not meet criteria for DSM III-R or DSM-IV AN. This has the potential to obscure just how ill a patient might be and to complicate the establishment of treatment goals. Due to the prevalence of thismethod of calculating ideal body weight and the addition of an absolute weight criterion in place of percentage weight loss, many seriously ill patients' eating disorders have potentially gone undetected or have not received a diagnosis of AN, despite meeting all other criteria.

Fortunately, the fifth edition of the DSM (DSM-5; APA, 2013) has transitioned away from the absolute weight criterion. Authors of this revision noted that they believed BMI was not a sufficient statistic for use in determining significantly low body weight and, instead, urged clinicians to use a wide range of historical and present data, in addition to anthropometrics (APA, 2012). Although the elimination of a weight requirement is a positive step, the DSM-5 does still include diagnostic modifiers, classifying a patient as "mild," "moderate," or "severe." These modifiers are based on presenting BMI for adults or BMI percentile for adolescents, meaning that a patient who meets criteria for a very serious case for AN, but whose BMI is still in the average range, might be diagnosed with a "mild" subtype of the disorder.

As another option, the DSM-5 also offers a diagnosis of "atypical anorexia," which falls under the other specified feeding or eating disorders (OSFED) category. This diagnosis includes individuals who have lost a significant amount of weight but have not reached a weight below "normal range" (APA, 2013). The DSM-5 is certainly an improvement over previous diagnostic systems, but it is possible a diagnosis of atypical or mild anorexia might create a false impression that symptoms are less severe or might fail to convey the seriousness of patients' weight loss or symptoms to themselves, to their families, or to other practitioners.

CLINICAL PRESENTATION/COURSE OF ILLNESS

Although the previously discussed DSM-5 diagnostic options represent a substantial improvement, the distinction between "atypical" and full AN has the potential to be misleading. Evidence suggests no significant differences exist in severity or consequences of low weight versus atypical anorexia (Lebow et al., 2015; Sawyer, Whitelaw, Le Grange, Yeo, & Hughes, 2016). In adults, no differences were found between groups for psychological symptoms, including measures of eating disorder severity, depression, or anxiety (Bunnell, Shenker, Nussbaum, Jacobson, & Cooper, 1990; Ricca et al., 2001; Watson & Andersen, 2003). Both groups were also found to be comparable on symptoms of physical distress, including cold intolerance, amenorrhea, bone density, and bradycardia (Watson & Andersen, 2003).

For adolescents, studies have similarly found no difference in measures of eating disorder symptom severity between patients with restrictive eating disorders and a history of premorbid overweight or obesity and patients with restrictive eating disorders and no such history (Lebow et al., 2015; Sawyer et al., 2016). Findings have varied somewhat with regard to medical complications of these patients, although data are conclusive that patients with a history of higher weight status are not at a reduced risk. Sawyer and colleagues found that patients with typical and atypical AN had similar levels of bradycardia and orthostatic instability. In contrast, Peebles, Hardy, Wilson, and Lock (2010) found that another sample of teenagers who had lost greater than 25% of their premorbid weight, but who were greater than 90% of median body weight for their age, were more medically compromised than patients presenting at much lower body weight.

Furthermore, compared to patients with premorbid average weight, adolescents with a history of overweight/obesity have been found to have a significantly larger decrease in BMI before presenting to treatment (Lebow et al., 2015; Sawyer et al., 2016) and take longer to be identified and present to first treatment (almost 20 months compared to 11 months for patients with premorbid average weight) (Lebow et al., 2015). Given that it is well established that early detection is related to better prognosis in eating disorder treatment (Steinhausen, 2009; van Son, van Hoeken, van Furth, Donker, & Hoek, 2010), this substantial discrepancy has important clinical implications, and it suggests that serious eating disorders in patients with a history of overweight are likely to be overlooked until symptoms have progressed and become potentially more intractable.

Weight Suppression

The clinical presentation and treatment progression of eating disorder patients with a history of higher weight has been studied via the model of weight suppression. Weight suppression is defined as the difference between an individual's highest weight and current or lowest weight (Lowe, 1993). Compared to individuals with a typical weight history, patients with restrictive eating disorders with a history of overweight/obesity are likely to be more weight suppressed.

The statistic offers an alternative to absolute BMI as a way of assessing weight change relative to a patient's personal weight history instead of relative to population norms. In studies of patients with bulimia nervosa, higher weight suppression has been found to be correlated with objective binge episodes, longer time until remission, and worse outcomes in cognitive–behavioral therapy, although data for the latter finding are mixed (Butryn, Juarascio, & Lowe, 2011; Butryn, Lowe, Safer, & Agras, 2006; Carter, McIntosh, Joyce, & Bulik, 2008; Lowe, Thomas, Safer, & Butryn, 2007).

In AN, however, research has been more limited, and reliable findings are comparatively sparse. For adults, preliminary data suggest that higher weight suppression is associated with increased eating pathology, distress, and physiological abnormalities, even after controlling for presenting BMI (Berner, Shaw, Witt, & Lowe, 2013). In addition, researchers found that weight restored (defined as at least 90% of ideal body weight, as calculated based on the 50th percentile) women with AN and high weight suppression had lower serum leptin levels and were more likely to be amenorrheic at discharge compared to patients with low weight suppression (Klein et al., 2011). This suggests that weight suppression might be an indicator of illness severity over and above absolute BMI (Klein et al., 2011).

Evidence has also been found that high weight suppression might be related to an increased likelihood of binge/purge behaviors in AN (Berner et al., 2013; Garfinkel, Moldofsky, & Garner, 1980). This is significant because the development of bulimic symptoms in anorexia is associated with a greater severity and longer duration of illness (Peat, Mitchell, Hoek, & Wonderlich, 2009; Steinhausen, 2002). These findings support the need for setting targets in treatment and criteria for discharge that are not based on absolute weights and for considering that patients presenting with high weight suppression might have a more serious illness than their less weight suppressed counterparts, regardless of the BMI at which they present (Berner et al., 2013).

High levels of weight suppression have also been linked to differences in treatment progression compared to that of patients with less weight suppression. Adult patients with high weight suppression and AN have been found to gain more weight in treatment and gain it at a faster rate, regardless of BMI (although the effect was stronger for patients presenting at a lower overall BMI) (Berner et al., 2013; Boden, Jordan, McIntosh, Bulk, & Joyce, 2015; Carter et al., 2015; Wildes & Marcus, 2012). The relationship between the amount and rate of weight gain and treatment outcome is unclear. Although research suggests aggressive refeeding may decrease length of hospitalization and illness, there is also research that suggests that rapid weight gain is associated with a decreased likelihood of achieving target weight, faster weight loss post-treatment, and an increased risk of rehospitalization (Herzog, Zeeck, Hartmann, & Nickel, 2004; Lay, Jennen-Steinmetz, Reinhard, & Schmidt, 2002; Willer, Thuras, & Crow, 2005; but see Lund et al., 2009). This is possibly related to a worsening of the characteristic fear of weight gain and associated efforts to regain control. By itself, weight suppression has not been found to be related to treatment dropout or failure to achieve remission (Wildes & Marcus, 2012). The fact that highly weight suppressed patients with AN gain more weight more quickly suggests that perhaps some of these patients might be able to do well in outpatient treatment as opposed to higher levels of care because they may have the potential to restore large amounts of weight relatively efficiently.

For adolescents with AN, only one small study of weight suppression exists. Researchers found that in a sample of 47 adolescents, high weight suppression was associated with higher BMI at 6- and 10-year follow-ups (Witt et al., 2014). No association between weight suppression and duration of illness was found.

Although additional data are needed to sufficiently parse out the relationship between weight suppression and eating pathology, especially with adolescent samples, mounting evidence suggests that patients with a high percentage of weight lost present with unique and, occasionally, more severe symptomology regardless of absolute presenting BMI (Berner et al., 2013; Garfinkel et al., 1980). Furthermore, these patients potentially can be expected to gain more weight and do so more rapidly than non-weight suppressed patients presenting at the same BMI (Berner et al., 2013; Boden et al., 2015; Carter et al., 2015; Wildes & Marcus, 2012). In other words, it might be more helpful to assess the degree of weight suppression at intake in addition to the lowest or current BMI in order to more accurately establish target weights and predict rate of weight gain in treatment.

IMPLICATIONS FOR PREVENTION, IDENTIFICATION, AND TREATMENT

Prevention

The findings that, at minimum, one-third of adolescents and one-fourth of adults with restrictive eating disorders have a history of overweight or obesity and that, at least in the case of adolescents, these patients do not come to the attention of clinicians until later in the course of their illness have significant implications for providers engaged in the prevention and treatment of eating disorders and obesity. In particular, providers need to examine how their drive to prevent obesity in higher weight status patients may unwittingly promote disordered eating and full syndrome eating disorders. In light of providers' concerns about the health consequences of obesity, many higher weight status patients have likely experienced repeated conversations about their weight with their health care provider.

Unfortunately, these experiences may be a direct catalyst for dieting behavior, a well-established risk factor not only for the development of eating disorders but also for obesity (Neumark-Sztainer, Wall, Story, & Standish, 2012). The same research suggests that experiencing weight-related comments is strongly predictive of increasing weight status even after controlling for baseline weight (Haines, Neumark-Sztainer, Wall, & Story, 2007).

Despite these findings, there continues to be a strong impetus for medical providers to prevent obesity in encounters with their patients by identifying individuals at risk (e.g., tracking at the 85th BMI percentile or higher) and providing weight management counseling interventions (Krebs & Jacobson, 2003). Although these interventions may seem sensible in the context of the increasing prevalence and associated health consequences of obesity, meta-analytic data on primary care-based prevention and intervention programs suggest little or no benefit for children and adolescents (Sim, Lebow, Wang, Koball, & Murad, 2016) or adults (Booth, Prevost, Wright, & Gulliford, 2014). As such, primary care practice guidelines advising BMI screening and counseling need to be revised, and novel models must be considered.

Although there is a concern that higher weight status individuals engage in overeating and sedentary behavior, there unfortunately seems to be less concern about their participation in unhealthy dieting practices and eating-disordered behaviors—behaviors that are highly prevalent, particularly for adolescent patients. Research suggests that greater than 75% of overweight girls have engaged in skipping meals, fasting, restrictive eating, and smoking, and 20% of overweight girls have engaged in vomiting, laxative abuse, or diet pills to control their weight in the past year (Neumark-Sztainer, Hannan, Story, & Perry, 2004). Given the shared risk factors for obesity and eating disorders, one promising avenue for primary care prevention is the development of an integrated approach to preventing both eating disorders and obesity. Such an approach recognizes that overweight individuals are at high risk for disordered eating behaviors that are likely to place them at risk for further weight gain. These programs should not only address balanced eating and physical activity but should also focus on reducing dieting and unhealthy weight control practices. Moreover, patients will need information that dieting promotes binge eating and places one at risk for weight gain. In this context, researchers need to examine whether interventions to support intuitive eating, increase body acceptance, assess weight-related mistreatment, challenge the media-promulgated thin ideal, and other areas of overlap will reduce the risk not only for eating disorders but also for obesity.

Identification/Assessment

In addition to developing interventions that simultaneously address weight gain and unhealthy weight control practices, primary and specialty health care providers are uniquely placed to increase the rate of early identification of unhealthy restriction and weight loss and ensure patients are referred for appropriate follow-up care as efficiently as possible. As such, it is recommended that providers remain aware of three factors when meeting with patients of any BMI.

1. Individuals whose weight falls in the normal, overweight, or even obese range are not exempt from having or developing a restrictive eating disorder.

As described previously, research suggests that serious restrictive eating disorders are possible in individuals presenting at any BMI. This is independent of weight loss method employed or amount or rate of weight loss. To assess unhealthy weight changes, providers are advised to examine the degree of weight suppression as opposed to static weight when assessing symptom severity or determining target weight in adult patients.

For adolescents, a group in which weight suppression has been understudied, it is recommended that providers take into account the patient's full developmental growth curve as opposed to his or her static weight at one point in time. Deviations from an adolescent's typical pattern of growth should be noted with concern, regardless of absolute BMI. In general, given the well-established difficulties even adults have with weight loss (e.g. Bray & Wadden, 2015), any decrease in BMI in a younger patient, even if it results in a weight in the average range, should prompt screening for an eating disorder.

In light of the caution that eating disorder assessment must take into account a full range of physiological, psychological, and behavioral symptoms and signs (APA, 2012), evaluations must be comprehensive. When providers identify weight loss, they should ask the patients what specific behaviors they changed in this effort. A focus on avoidance of specific food categories or meta-nutrients, skipping meals, and/or counting calories should be noted with concern. Even in the absence of low weight, practitioners should remain attuned to the presence of eating-disordered behaviors (e.g., compulsive exercise, binge eating, food avoidance, compensatory behaviors such as purging etc.) or potential physical sequelae of starvation (e.g., cold intolerance, fatigue, amenorrhea, orthostatic symptoms etc.). Evidence of disordered cognitions (e.g., overvaluation of weight and shape, negative and/or skewed body image, rigid dietary rules etc.) and psychological symptoms such as social isolation or moodiness should also prompt physicians to make appropriate referrals for eating disorder screening and possible intervention as immediate as possible.

2. Dieting is a robust risk factor both for eating disorders and obesity.

Providers must avoid discussions or advice that might be interpreted as encouraging dieting. As noted previously, it is well established that dieting behaviors in children and teens are a primary predictor of later eating disorders, as well as obesity (Irving & Neumark-Sztainer, 2002; Neumark-Sztainer et al., 2007). Practitioners must strongly discourage restrictive eating, food avoidance, or other behaviors that promote physical and psychological deprivation. Exercise must also be carefully monitored as researchers have found, in a large population-based sample of adolescent girls, that moderate to vigorous exercise predicted a higher likelihood of disordered eating (Neumark-Sztainer, Wall, Story, & Sherwood, 2009). Feedback and interventions, particularly in a primary care setting, in which follow-up is often only possible on a yearly basis, should focus on realistic goals and specific behaviors. For younger patients, feedback should include caregivers to ensure teens do not unilaterally implement unhealthy or extreme measures to meet unrealistic weight goals. Educating and charging parents/guardians with the task of maintaining regular oversight of adolescents' health behaviors is an important piece in facilitating early detection of eating-disordered behaviors.

3. Weight is not a proxy for health.

Health care practitioners must be cautious of overemphasizing weight as the sole indicator of health. Providers should also avoid language that may have negative connotations and promote or imply weight-based stigma. Research suggests that weight-based stigma has major negative effects on psychological and physical health (Hunger, Major, Blodorn, & Miller, 2015). In particular, for adults, there is evidence that physicians' conversations about weight loss may result in increased weight-related stigma, dieting behaviors, binge eating, and weight gain, as well as an increased risk for eating disorders (Latner, Durso, & Mond, 2013; Puhl & Brownell, 2006; Schvey, Puhl, & Brownell, 2014; Vartanian & Novak, 2011). In addition, weight stigma, including being weighed and given feedback about gaining weight, contributes to adults with higher weight status avoiding or delaying necessary and routine medical appointments (Drury & Louis, 2002).

For younger patients, it has been found that focus on a child's weight by authority figures leads to body dissatisfaction, dieting, low self-esteem, and weight bias (Haines et al., 2007). Moreover, for children, receiving an overweight label predicts weight gain (Hunger & Tomiyama, 2014). In particular, a longitudinal study of a large diverse sample of adolescents found that labeling a child as overweight increased the likelihood of having a BMI in the obese range a decade later, independent of a child's actual BMI (Hunger & Tomiyama, 2014).

Based on research that suggests parents are unable to identify if their child is overweight, there has been an impetus for primary care providers to communicate information to parents about their child's BMI. Unfortunately, no data indicate that sharing this information with parents reduces childhood obesity. Instead, there are strong data suggesting that parents' weight-related comments directed to their children may influence maladaptive weight and shape-related attitudes and behaviors (Smolak, Levine, & Schermer, 1999), as well as disordered eating and weight gain (Hunger & Tomiyama, 2014).

With this in mind, interventions should be designed and implemented thoughtfully, with care taken to assess for and minimize potential adverse events. Interventions should focus on modifiable behaviors that have been proven to positively influence health, even independent of weight. In addition to balanced eating and physical activity, providers should support stress management, body acceptance, and social support. Finally, it is important for providers to appreciate normal variations in weight and that it is unrealistic to expect all individuals to fit into the so-called "normal weight" category. If a patient is above the 85th percentile for weight but is eating a varied balanced diet, physically active, managing stress, and thriving in all other indices of health, this may be a healthy weight for this individual, and this person may not be in need of intervention.

Treatment

The prevalence and severity of AN in patients with premorbid overweight also have implications for treatment planning and outcome assessment. To date, there is no evidence that patients with this history should be treated using different protocols than those used for patients without a history of overweight. Currently, evidence supports the use of Family-Based Treatment (FBT) as a first-line intervention for adolescents with AN (Lock et al., 2010) and also supports full weight restoration as a top priority for all patients with restrictive eating disorders (Baran, Weltzin, & Kaye, 1995; Rigaud, Pennacchio, Bizeul, Reveillard, & Verges, 2011). Special considerations, however, should be made for patients with a history of overweight within evidence-based protocols.

Establishing a target weight is one area in which care should be taken to address the specific psychological and physiological needs of patients with a history of overweight. In particular, clinicians should be aware of the possibility that they and/ or the patient and family may underestimate the target weight necessary for full resolution of symptoms. The fact that studies have shown that weight-suppressed women who were allegedly weight restored at 90% ideal body weight still presented with numerous health concerns (Klein et al., 2011) suggests that our methods for determining "ideal" or "expected" body weight merit scrutiny and revision. Use of one-size-fits-all goal weights for patients has the potential to result in some patients only achieving partial weight restoration before treatment is discontinued. Achieving full weight restoration, as opposed to partially restoring weight, is crucial because the former has been found to be a major predictor of successful outcomes in adolescent-onset AN (Lock & Litt, 2003) and for adult women (Baran et al., 1995; Howard, Evans, Quintero-Howard, Bowers, & Anderson, 1999). In a disorder with as high a rate of relapse as AN (an estimated one-third of patients will relapse; Herzog et al., 1999), undertreating patients or discharging them before weight restoration is fully reached could have significant consequences.

Set point theory may provide guidance in determining successful weight restoration. This theory, which has been widely validated (Brisbois, Farmer, & McCargar, 2012), suggests that individuals have a personalized weight range wherein the body is metabolically driven to return. Once within this range, homeostatic processes will automatically work to maintain weight, and only extreme dietary restriction or extreme calorie consumption can push an individual's weight out of his or her personal range. Evidence suggests that individuals can consume up to as many as 10,000 calories per day and still stay within this biologically determined range (Bouchard et al., 1990; Sims, 1976). In this way, goal weight can potentially be determined simply by charging a patient to eat the high levels of calories needed for weight restoration (Kaye et al., 1986; Weltzin, Fernstrom, Hansen, McConaha, & Kaye, 1991) and determining an endpoint wherever weight levels off despite continued consumption of high levels of calories.

Psychoeducation on set point theory is likely to be helpful in getting patients to understand the need for a higher target weight and can provide a rationale when addressing patient questions. It is not uncommon for patients and families to present with the hope that following full weight restoration, they might be able to lose comparable amounts of weight in the future by "healthy means." It is important to be transparent with regard to data that suggest that individuals must remain in their personal set point range regardless of their preference or risk severe physical and psychological consequences. Being upfront about this biological imperative may cause short-term friction, but it protects against greater patient distress in the long term. Data regarding the body's drive to return to its set point, including through increased binge eating or decreased metabolic rates, are unequivocal (Brisbois et al., 2012) and can provide a sound rationale for the futility of attempting "healthy" weight loss below set point. Citing studies that support dieting behaviors as a predictor of weight *gain* (Irving & Neumark-Sztainer, 2002; Neumark-Sztainer et al., 2007) may also help patients find motivation to eliminate even relatively mild restrictive behaviors from their repertoire. Furthermore, reassurance that the body is physiologically wired to maintain a set point range, even in the face of substantial caloric intake, may help to address patients' commonly held fears that they will "overgain" or that their weight will continue to increase endlessly at an uncontrolled rate.

For adolescents and younger patients, review of their growth charts can provide a helpful visual aid of how weight tends to stay consistently in one range and can also offer providers a rough estimate of where weight may most likely be metabolically inclined to return. When using FBT, it is crucial that parents be made aware of and comfortable with a potential higher weight target. FBT emphasizes parental empowerment and presenting a united front in the face of the eating disorder (Lock & Le Grange, 2013); a therapist–parent split on the subject of goal weight may compromise treatment. Given the wide-ranging publicity on the dangers of obesity, many parents may have concerns about restoring their child to a weight that is higher than that of peers. Parents' concerns may be allayed by providing them information regarding Health at Any Size (HAES; Robison, Putnam, & McKibbin, 2007), an approach that suggests health is not dependent on weight but, rather, on health behaviors and adopting lifestyle habits that support health regardless of size or shape. Similarly, educating parents on research related to relapse and the previously discussed consequences of partial weight restoration is essential to ensure continued commitment to treatment goals.

In addition to differences in target weights, patients with a history of overweight may also experience differences in treatment course. As previously noted, data on weight suppression suggest that weight-suppressed patients might gain weight more quickly than patients without this history. This may allow providers some degree of flexibility in that it is more likely that these patients may be able to be weight restored in an outpatient setting compared to patients without weight suppression.

This is particularly ideal for younger patients, for whom maintaining their daily routine might help them more quickly recoup social and developmental delays secondary to the eating disorder. On the other hand, large increases in weight are certainly bound to be more distressing for the average patient with AN. As such, providers working with highly weight suppressed patients should be prepared to address higher levels of anxiety and distress around weight gain in these patients.

Techniques such as motivational interviewing (Miller & Rollnick, 1991) may be helpful in these cases, although motivational interviewing should be used only as a supplement to established treatments that have been proven to promote weight restoration (e.g., FBT), and it should not be relied on as a sufficient intervention in and of itself (Waller, 2012). Once a patient is largely weight restored, however, using motivational interviewing-based strategies, such as acknowledging the patient-perceived negatives inherent in gaining weight and encouraging the patient to identify both benefits and costs of continued weight restoration, may be helpful. Providing psychoeducation on the physical and psychological costs of weight suppression, as well as emphasizing the relationship between high weight suppression and increased likelihood of binge/purge behaviors, may help patients manage some of their distress. As patients approach their goal weight, having them reflect on some of the positive physical, psychological, and social changes they have noticed as a result of the weight gain may support ongoing acceptance of the need for higher weight. In this effort, providing readings that emphasize the drawbacks of dietary restriction and suppressed weight may be helpful. The Resources section provides a list of helpful readings.

In addition to addressing ineffective cognitive patterns, patients' grief about gaining large amounts of weight and settling at a point that is higher than that of peers should be acknowledged and not minimized. Mindfulness-informed techniques from Dialectical Behavior Therapy, such as radically accepting situations that are not amenable to change, may be helpful (Linehan, 1993). In addition, Acceptance and Commitment Therapy (ACT; Hayes, 2004)—a psychological treatment that focuses on accepting one's thoughts, feelings, and experiences and shifting the focus of attention to pursuits consistent with one's values—may have utility with patients of higher weight status. In this therapy, patients learn that attempts to change one's body and persistent negative body image get in the way of living a life of purpose and meaning. ACT includes specific mindfulness and cognitive defusion strategies that can be helpful to change a person's relationship with thoughts related to the discrepancy between actual and ideal body image and can reduce the suffering associated with the thoughts (Hayes, 2004). Focusing on living a meaningful life not defined by weight and shape may diminish the focus on and gratification associated with maintaining a lower weight. The Anorexia Workbook, by Heffner, Eifert, and Hayes (2004), can be helpful for patients attempting to implement ACT-based strategies.

Finally, fully weight-restored patients who need to maintain a higher weight than average for optimal health may need to complete additional protective work to safeguard against social pressures to conform to the thin ideal. The majority of individuals who use disordered eating behaviors report a history of weight teasing

(Haines, Neumark-Sztainer, Eisenberg, & Hannan, 2006). Patients must be armed with strategies for addressing unhealthy pressure, both from society and from the media in general, as well as well-intended but erroneous implicit and explicit messages from family members, friends, and even health care providers about what their weight "should" be. Dissonance-based interventions, such as those used in The Body Project (Stice, Rohde, & Shaw, 2013), have been shown to reduce an individual's susceptibility to the thin ideal and improve body image. These strategies may be necessary as part of the relapse prevention work that is typically done in the last phase of most eating disorder treatments.

Exercise recommendations should likely not differ for this population compared to patients with AN and no overweight history. As with other patients, care should be taken to prevent exercise that is excessive or driven in nature. The benefits of balanced exercise on mood, anxiety, and body image in addition to health variables are well established (Carraca et al., 2012; Crowley, 2015), and patients should be encouraged to take advantage of this once they are medically cleared and psychologically able to do so. Psychoeducation regarding the limited effect that exercise has on actual weight loss (Church et al., 2009; Fogelholm & Kukkonen-Harjula, 2000) may be provided to reduce the likelihood that patients will use exercise in a compulsive manner or as a way to attempt to change anything other than general metrics of health.

In addition to patient concerns, it is important to note that issues of weight restoration in patients with a history of overweight or obesity have the potential to trigger both anxiety and bias on the part of the clinician. With regard to the former, the increased patient distress caused by insisting on weight restoration to a level that may be higher than that of peers can be difficult for a clinician to tolerate. It has been established that clinicians sometimes avoid using evidence-supported interventions due to their own anxiety or discomfort, for example, weighing patients in therapy or completing other exposure activities (Waller, Stringer, & Meyer, 2012). By extension, it is possible that insisting that a patient weight restore to a weight associated with increased patient distress might trigger substantial clinician anxiety and, thus, avoidance of full weight restoration. Clinicians must remain attuned to any avoidant behaviors in their own practice and check their motivation, either through introspection or consultation, for failing to insist on continued necessary weight gain.

Alternately, the issue of clinician bias and stigma may interfere with a clinician feeling comfortable advising full weight restoration in higher weight patients. Weight stigma has been well validated in the literature (Puhl & Heuer, 2010), with data suggesting that health care providers are as biased against higher weight individuals as the rest of the population (Phelan et al., 2015). Stigma around higher weight individuals may encourage providers to hold back when weight restoring patients or to inadvertently collude with the illness in allowing restrictive behaviors or weight suppression to continue. This potential for bias can be compounded when members of a multidisciplinary team differ on what they believe is a "healthy" weight. Patients potentially may receive discrepant messages about goal weight from medical, psychological, and nutritional providers, which may result in confusion, reduced confidence in treatment, and undermined treatment objectives and may further validate fear of weight gain. In working with these patients, it is important for clinicians to evaluate their own biases regarding obesity and weight and for all members of a team to check in regularly to ensure they are providing consistent messages that are uncompromised by stigma or avoidance.

FUTURE DIRECTIONS

Although we are beginning to recognize that overweight patients are not immune to developing serious restrictive eating disorders, there is much that is still unknown. In particular, the actual prevalence of restrictive eating disorders in patients with a history of overweight is still unclear. Given that research has largely examined treatment-seeking individuals and, at least for adolescents, these patients were found to have a delay in seeking treatment, it is possible that the prevalence found in these studies might actually represent a significant underestimate of a history of overweight or obesity in the general AN population. Research is needed to understand the scope of the problem to support better screening and identification of these individuals.

In addition, more information is needed regarding the course of illness and treatment outcomes of individuals with restrictive eating disorders and a higher weight history. Although weight suppression is currently the topic of much research, studies need to examine whether the influence of weight suppression on treatment progress and symptoms (e.g., the increased likelihood of bulimic symptoms in patients with AN and weight suppression) holds true for all AN patients with premorbid overweight or if weight suppression is a distinct, if heavily overlapping, variable.

In addition to prognosis and treatment course, there is little information to guide clinical decision-making in working with individuals with restrictive eating disorders and a higher weight history. One important clinical question is related to refeeding prescriptions for these individuals. Research suggests that patients with AN are metabolically unique compared to individuals without an eating disorder (Kaye et al., 1986; Weltzin et al., 1991) and therefore need high calorie levels for weight restoration and maintenance post treatment. Given research on weight suppression and faster rates of weight gain, it is unclear whether this is the case for individuals with a higher weight history. It is also unclear how high-calorie diets may influence treatment outcome in these patients. As such, research is needed to examine the caloric prescription and rate of weight gain associated with the best outcome for higher weight status individuals.

In patients with an average weight history, many treatment protocols consider the target for weight restoration as a person's ideal body weight (determined relative to the 50th percentile for age, height, and gender) (Lock et al., 2010). However, as noted previously, many individuals with a higher weight history present to treatment at this "ideal" weight range or higher while still experiencing significant physical symptoms and psychological sequelae of restrictive eating and weight loss (Sim, Lebow, & Billings, 2013). Given that refeeding and weight gain is an established mechanism for resolving many of the physical and psychological sequelae of an eating disorder, weight gain is an appropriate goal for these patients. However, it is unclear what weight percentile may be an appropriate weight target for patients presenting at a higher weight and how this may differ based on weight history. For example, does a person whose weight historically tracked at the 97th percentile have to return to the 97th percentile, or can he or she stabilize at the 85th percentile? Also, the specific markers that help clinicians identify when the patient has reached the best weight to support a full recovery are unclear. If amenorrhea, vital signs, and other markers of starvation resolve at a particular weight but psychological symptoms do not, can this weight be maintained?

Finally, given that patients with a higher weight status are likely to have experienced weight-related mistreatment, weight-based stigma, discrimination, and psychological stress related to these factors, they may experience a legitimate fear of weight gain that may be more impervious to treatment than those without this experience. When this fear is present in conjunction with the faster rate of gain often seen in high weight-suppressed patients, it is understandable that these patients might present with higher than average levels of distress around weight restoration. Research is necessary to examine whether treatment needs to be specifically tailored to address these legitimate concerns.

CONCLUSION

Individuals with a history of overweight or obesity represent a substantial portion of those suffering from restrictive eating disorders. Although these individuals may present with a BMI that is considerably higher than those with a weight history in the normal range, these individuals are equally or more at risk for serious psychological and health consequences, and they may experience a longer duration of illness. Unfortunately, the lack of awareness regarding the incidence of AN in individuals with a higher weight history may contribute to challenges in not only identifying those at risk but also understanding how to tailor treatments to these individuals. In particular, research is needed to address issues with refeeding and weight restoration, as well as on how to address these individuals' fear of weight gain that may be legitimate within a history of stigma and weight-related mistreatment. Finally, understanding unique and shared risk factors for the development of obesity and eating disorders may help support the development of effective preventive interventions.

RESOURCES

Bacon, L. (2010). *Health at every size: The surprising truth about your weight*. Dallas, TX: Bella Books.

Brown, H. (2015). Body of truth: How science, history, and culture drive our obsession with weight—And what we can do about it. Boston, MA: Da Capo Lifelong Books.

Heffner, M., Eifert, G., & Hayes, S. (2004). The anorexia workbook. New York, NY: New Harbinger.

Mann, T. (2015). Secrets from the eating lab: The science of weight loss, the myth of willpower, and why you should never diet again. New York, NY: HarperCollins.

Neumark-Sztainer, D. (2005). "I'm, like, so fat!" Helping your teen make healthy choices about eating and exercise in a weight-obsessed world. New York, NY: Guilford.

REFERENCES

American Psychiatric Association. (1980). *Diagnostic and statistical manual of mental disorders* (3rd ed.). Washington, DC: Author.

American Psychiatric Association. (1987). *Diagnostic and statistical manual of mental disorders* (3rd ed., rev.). Washington, DC: Author.

American Psychiatric Association. (1994). *Diagnostic and statistical manual of mental disorders* (4th ed.). Washington, DC: Author.

American Psychiatric Association. (2000). *Diagnostic and statistical manual of mental disorders* (4th ed., text rev.). Washington, DC: Author.

American Psychiatric Association. (2012). *DSM-5 development: The future of psychiatric development.* Washington, DC: Author.

American Psychiatric Association. (2013). *Diagnostic and statistical manual of mental disorders* (5th ed.). Arlington, VA: American Psychiatric Publishing.

Baran, S., Weltzin, T., & Kaye, W. (1995). Low discharge weight and outcome in anorexia nervosa. *American Journal of Psychiatry, 152*(7), 1070–1072.

Berner, L., Shaw, J., Witt, A., & Lowe, M. (2013). The relation of weight suppression and body mass index to symptomatology and treatment response in anorexia nervosa. *Journal of Abnormal Psychology, 122*(3), 694–708.

Booth, H., Prevost, T., Wright, A., & Gulliford, M. (2014). Effectiveness of behavioural weight loss interventions delivered in a primary care setting: A systematic review and meta-analysis. *Family Practice, 31*(6), 643–653.

Bouchard, C., Tremblay, A., Despres, J., Nadeau, A., Lupien, P., Theriault, G., ... Fournier, G. (1990). The response to long-term overfeeding in identical twins. *New England Journal of Medicine, 322*(21), 1477–1482.

Bray, G., & Wadden, T. (2015). Improving long-term weight loss maintenance: Can we do it? *Obesity, 23,* 2–3.

Brisbois, T., Farmer, A., & McCargar, L. (2012). Early markers of adult obesity: A review. *Obesity Review, 13,* 347–367.

Bunnell, D., Shenker, I., Nussbaum, M., Jacobson, M., & Cooper, P. (1990). Subclinical versus formal eating disorders. *International Journal of Eating Disorders, 9,* 357–362.

Butryn, M., Juarascio, A., & Lowe, M. (2011). The relation of weight suppression and BMI to bulimic symptoms. *International Journal of Eating Disorders, 44,* 612–617.

Butryn, M., Lowe, M., Safer, D., & Agras, W. (2006). Weight suppression is a robust predictor of outcome in the cognitive–behavioral treatment of bulimia nervosa. *Journal of Abnormal Psychology, 115*, 62–67.

Carraca, E., Markland, D., Silva, M., Coutinho, S., Vieira, P., Minderico, C., . . . Teixeira, P. (2012). Physical activity predicts changes in body image during obesity treatment in women. *Medicine and Science in Sports and Exercise, 44*(8), 1604–1612.

Carter, F., Boden, J., Jordan, J., McIntosh, V., Bulik, C., & Joyce, P. (2015). Weight suppression predicts total weight gain and rate of weight gain in outpatients with anorexia nervosa. *International Journal of Eating Disorders, 48*, 912–918.

Carter, F., McIntosh, V., Joyce, P., & Bulik, C. (2008). Weight suppression predicts weight gain over treatment completion or outcome in bulimia nervosa. *Journal of Abnormal Psychology, 117*, 936–940.

Church, T., Martin, C., Thompson, A., Earnest, C., Mikus, C., & Blair, S. (2009). Changers in weight, waist circumference and compensatory responses with different doses of exercise among sedentary, overweight postmenopausal women. *PLoS One, 4*(2), e4515.

Crisp, A., Hsu, K., Harding, B., & Hartshorn, J. (1980). Clinical features of anorexia nervosa: A study of a consecutive series of 102 female patients. *Journal of Psychosomatic Research, 24*, 179–191.

Crowley, S. (2015). Exercise is medicine: The role of exercise in the prevention and treatment of mood and anxiety disorders in children and adults. *Psychoneuroendocrinology, 61*, 18.

Drury, C., & Louis M. (2002). Exploring the association between body weight, stigma of obesity, and health care avoidance. *Journal of the American Academy of Nurse Practitioners, 14*(12), 554–561.

Flegal, K., Carroll, M., Kit, B., & Ogden, C. (2012). Prevalence of obesity and trends in the distribution of body mass index among US adults, 1999–2010. *JAMA, 307*(5), 491–497.

Fogelholm, M., & Kukkonen-Harjula, K. (2000). Does physical activity prevent weight gain? A systematic review. *Obesity Reviews, 1*(2), 95–111.

Garfinkel, P. E., Moldofsky, H., & Garner, D. M. (1980). The heterogeneity of anorexia nervosa: Bulimia as a distinct subgroup. *Archives of General Psychiatry, 37*, 1036–1040.

Haines, J., Neumark-Sztainer, D., Eisenberg, M., & Hannan, P. (2006). Weight teasing and disordered eating behaviors in adolescents: Longitudinal findings from Project EAT (Eating Among Teens). *Pediatrics, 117*(2), e209–e215.

Haines, J., Neumark-Sztainer, D., Wall, M., & Story, M. (2007). Personal, behavioral, and environmental risk and protective factors for adolescent overweight. *Obesity, 15*(11), 2748–2760.

Hayes, S. (2004). Acceptance and commitment therapy, relational frame theory, and the third wave of behavioral and cognitive therapies. *Behavior Therapy, 35*, 639–665.

Hebebrand, J., Himmelmann, G., Heseker, H., Schafer, H., & Remschmidt, H. (1996). Use of percentiles for the body mass index in anorexia nervosa: Diagnostic, epidemiological, and therapeutic considerations. *International Journal of Eating Disorders, 19*(4), 359–369.

Heffner, M., Eifert, G., & Hayes, S. (2004). *The anorexia workbook*. New York, NY: New Harbinger.

Herzog, D., Dorer, D., Keel, P., Selwyn, S., Ekeblad, E., Flores, A., . . . Keller, M. (1999). Recovery and relapse in anorexia and bulimia nervosa: A 7.5-year follow-up study. *Journal of the American Academy of Child & Adolescent Psychiatry, 38*(7), 829–837.

Herzog, T., Zeeck, A., Hartmann, A., & Nickel, T. (2004). Lower targets for weekly weight gain lead to better results in inpatient treatment of anorexia nervosa: a pilot study. *European Eating Disorders Review, 12*, 164–168.

Howard, W., Evans, K., Quintero-Howard, C., Bowers, W., & Andersen, A. (1999). Predictors of success or failure of transition to day hospital treatment for inpatients with anorexia nervosa. *American Journal of Psychiatry, 156*(11), 1697–1702.

Hunger, J., Major, B., Blodorn, A., & Miller, C. (2015). Weighed down by stigma: How weight-based social identity threat contributes to weight gain and poor health. *Social and Personality Psychology Compass, 9*(6), 255–268.

Hunger, J., & Tomiyama, J. (2014). Weight labeling and obesity: A longitudinal study of girls aged 10 to 19 years. *JAMA Pediatrics, 168*(6), 579–580.

Irving, L., & Neumark-Sztainer, D. (2002). Integrating the prevention of eating disorders and obesity: Feasible or futile? *Preventive Medicine, 34*, 299–309.

Kaye, W., Gwirtsman, H., Obarzanek, E., George, T., Jimerson, D., & Ebert, M. (1986). Caloric intake necessary for weight maintenance in anorexia nervosa: Nonbulimics require greater caloric intake than bulimics. *American Journal of Clinical Nutrition, 44*(4), 435–443.

Klein, D., Siegel, M., Grunebaum, Z., Wang, Y., Chen, H., & Walsh, B. (2011). Leptin in anorexia nervosa: Relationship to physical activity and weight suppression. *Appetite, 57*, S23.

Krebs, N., & Jacobson, M. (2003). Prevention of pediatric overweight and obesity. *Pediatrics, 112*(2), 424–430.

Latner, J., Durso, L., & Mond, J. (2013). Health and health-related quality of life among treatment-seeking overweight and obese adults: Associations with internalized weight bias. *Journal of Eating Disorders, 1*(3).

Lay, B., Jennen-Steinmetz, C., Reinhard, I., & Schmidt, M. (2002). Characteristics of inpatient weight gain in adolescent anorexia nervosa: Relation to speed of relapse and re-admission. *European Eating Disorders Review, 10*, 22–40.

Lebow, J., Sim, L., & Kransdorf, L. (2015). Prevalence of a history of overweight and obesity in adolescents with restrictive eating disorders. *Journal of Adolescent Health, 56*, 19–24.

Linehan, M. (1993). *Cognitive behavioral treatment of borderline personality disorder.* New York, NY: Guilford.

Lock, J., & Le Grange, D. (2013). *Treatment manual for anorexia nervosa: A family-based approach* (2nd ed.). New York, NY: Guilford.

Lock, J., Le Grange, D., Agras, W., Moye, A., Bryson, S., & Jo, B. (2010). Randomized clinical trial comparing family-based treatment with adolescent-focused individual therapy for adolescents with anorexia nervosa. *Archives of General Psychiatry, 67*(10), 1025–1032.

Lock, J., & Litt, I. (2003). What predicts maintenance of weight for adolescents medically hospitalized for anorexia nervosa? *Eating Disorders, 11*(1), 1–7.

Lowe, M. (1993). The effects of dieting on eating behaviors: A three-factor model. *Psychological Bulletin, 114*(1), 100–121.

Lowe, M., Thomas, J., Safer, D., & Butryn, M. (2007). The relationship of weight suppression and dietary restraint to binge eating in bulimia nervosa. *International Journal of Eating Disorders, 40*, 640–644.

Lund, B., Hernandez, E., Yates, W., Mitchell, J., McKee, P., & Johnson, C. (2009). Rate of inpatient weight restoration predicts outcome in anorexia nervosa. *International Journal of Eating Disorders, 42*, 301–305.

McLaren, D., & Read, W. (1972). Classification of nutritional status in early childhood. *Lancet, 2*, 146–148.

Miller, W., & Rollnick, S. (1991). *Motivational interviewing: Preparing people to change addictive behaviour*. New York, NY: Guilford.

Moore, D., Durie, P., Forstner, G., & Pencharz, P. (1985). The assessment of nutritional status in children. *Nutrition Research, 5*, 797–799.

Neumark-Sztainer, D., Hannan, P. J., Story, M., & Perry, C. L. (2004). Weight-control behaviors among adolescent girls and boys: Implications for dietary intake. *Journal of the American Dietetic Association, 104*(6), 913–920.

Neumark-Sztainer, D., Wall, M., Haines, J., Story, M., Sherwood, N., & van den Berg, P. (2007). Shared risk and protective factors for overweight and disordered eating in adolescents. *American Journal of Preventive Medicine, 33*(5), 359–369.

Neumark-Sztainer, D., Wall, M., Story, M., & Sherwood, N. (2009). Five-year longitudinal predictive factors for disordered eating in a population-based sample of overweight adolescents: Implications for prevention and treatment. *International Journal of Eating Disorders, 47*(7), 664–672.

Neumark-Sztainer, D., Wall, M., Story, M, & Standish, A. (2012). Dieting and unhealthy weight control behaviors during adolescence: Associations with 10-year changes in body mass index. *Journal of Adolescent Health, 50*, 80–86.

Nielsen, S. (1985). Evaluation of growth in anorexia nervosa from serial measurements. *Journal of Psychiatric Research, 19*(2-3), 227–230.

Ogden, C., Carroll, M., Kit, B., & Flegal, K. (2012). Prevalence of obesity and trends in body mass index among US children and adolescents, 1999–2010. *JAMA, 307*(5), 483–490.

Peat, C., Mitchell, J., Hoek, H., & Wonderlich, S. (2009). Validity and utility of subtyping anorexia nervosa. *International Journal of Eating Disorders, 42*(7), 590–594.

Peebles, R., Hardy, K., Wilson, J., & Lock, J. (2010). Are diagnostic criteria for eating disorders markers of medical severity? *Pediatrics, 125*(5), 1193–1201.

Phelan, S., Burgess, D., Yeazel, M., Hellerstedt, W., Griffen, J., & Ryn, M. (2015). Impact of weight bias and stigma on quality of care and outcomes for patients with obesity. *Obesity Reviews, 16*(4), 319–326.

Puhl, R., & Brownell, K. (2006). Confronting and coping with weight stigma: An investigation of overweight and obese adults. *Obesity, 14*(10), 1802–1815.

Puhl, R., & Heuer, C. (2010). Obesity stigma: Important considerations for public health. *American Journal of Public Health, 100*(6), 1019–1028.

Ricca, V., Mannucci, E., Mezzani, B., Di Bernardo, M., Zucchi, T., Paionni, A., . . . Faravelli, C. (2001). Psychopathological and clinical features of outpatients with an eating disorder not otherwise specified. *Eating and Weight Disorders, 6*(3), 157–165.

Rigaud, D., Pennacchio, H., Bizeul, C., Reveillard, V., & Verges, B. (2011). Outcome in AN adult patients: A 13-year follow-up in 484 patients. *Diabetes and Metabolism, 37*(4), 305–311.

Robison, J., Putnam, K., & McKibben, L. (2007). Health at every size: A compassionate, effective approach for helping individuals with weight-related concerns—Part 1. *AAOHN Journal, 55*(4), 143–150.

Sawyer, S., Whitelaw, M., Le Grange, D., Yeo, M., & Hughes, E. (2016). Physical and psychological morbidity in adolescents with atypical anorexia nervosa. *Pediatrics, 137*(4).

Sim, L., Lebow, J., & Billings, M. (2013). Eating disorders in adolescents with a history of obesity. *Pediatrics, 132*(4), e1026–e1030.

Sim, L., Lebow, J., Wang, Z., Koball, A., & Murad, H. (2016). Brief primary care obesity interventions: A systematic review and meta-analysis. *Pediatrics, 138*(4).

Sims, E. (1976). Experimental obesity, dietary-induced thermogenesis, and their clinical implications. *Clinics in Endocrinology and Metabolism, 5*(2), 377–395.

Smolak, L., Levine, M., & Schermer, F. (1999). Parental input and weight concerns among elementary school children. *International Journal of Eating Disorders, 25*(3), 263–271.

Steinhausen, H. (2002). The outcome of anorexia nervosa in the 20th century. *American Journal of Psychiatry, 159*(8), 1284–1293.

Steinhausen, H. (2009). Outcome of eating disorders. *Child and Adolescent Psychiatric Clinics of North America, 18*(1), 225–242.

Stice, E., Rohde, P., & Shaw, H. (2013). *The body project: A dissonance-based eating disorder prevention intervention, updated edition.* New York, NY: Oxford University Press.

Swenne, I. (2001). Changes in body weight and body mass index (BMI) in teenage girls prior to the onset and diagnosis of an eating disorder. *Acta Paediatrica, 90*, 677–681.

van Son, G., van Hoeken, D., van Furth, E., Donker, G., & Hoek, H. (2010). Course and outcome of eating disorders in a primary care-based cohort. *International Journal of Eating Disorders, 43*(2), 130–138.

Vartanian, L., & Novak, S. (2011). Internalized societal attitudes moderate the impact of weight stigma on avoidance of exercise. *Obesity, 19*(4), 757–762.

Waller, G. (2012). The myths of motivation: Time for a fresh look at some received wisdom in the eating disorders? *International Journal of Eating Disorders, 45*(1), 1–16.

Waller, G., Stringer, H., & Meyer, C. (2012). What cognitive–behavioral techniques do therapists report using when delivering cognitive–behavioral therapy for eating disorders? *Journal of Consulting and Clinical Psychology, 80*, 171–175.

Watson, T., & Andersen, A. (2003). A critical examination of the amenorrhea and weight criteria for diagnosing anorexia nervosa. *Acta Psychiatrica Scandinavica, 108*, 175–182.

Weltzin, T., Fernstrom, M., Hansen, D., McConaha, C., & Kaye, W. (1991). Abnormal caloric requirements for weight maintenance in patients with anorexia nervosa and bulimia nervosa. *American Journal of Psychiatry, 148*, 1675–1682.

Wildes, J., & Marcus, M. (2012). Weight suppression as a predictor of weight gain and response to intensive behavioral treatment in patients with anorexia nervosa. *Behaviour Research and Therapy, 50*, 266–274.

Willer, M., Thuras, P., & Crow, S. (2005). Implications of the changing use of hospitalization to treat anorexia nervosa. *American Journal of Psychiatry, 162*, 2374–2376.

11

Purging Disorder

**PAMELA K. KEEL, K. JEAN FORNEY,
AND GRACE KENNEDY ■**

Although epidemiological data suggest that purging disorder (PD) has existed for some time (Haedt & Keel, 2010), it has gained relatively recent attention in the medical literature as a distinct syndrome (Keel, Haedt, & Edler, 2005), leading to its inclusion as a named and described condition in the other specified feeding or eating disorder (OSFED) category in the fifth edition of the *Diagnostic and Statistical Manual for Mental Disorders* (DSM-5; American Psychiatric Association [APA], 2013). This chapter describes PD and discusses factors related to risk and maintenance of the illness because these may shed light on approaches to help those suffering from PD. Importantly, to date, no randomized controlled treatment trials have been conducted for those with PD. Thus, there are no evidence-based treatments specifically for the disorder. Instead, individuals with PD have been included in a handful of transdiagnostic treatment trials. This chapter discusses the applications of transdiagnostic interventions in PD as well as opportunities for further treatment development. Importantly, all evidence-based treatments begin with the collection of preliminary data in the clinics of those seeking to help patients with eating disorders. It is our hope that this chapter will help clinicians treating patients with PD, and those clinicians will contribute to the development and refinement of improved treatment approaches for PD.

CLINICAL PRESENTATION OF PURGING DISORDER

PD is characterized by recurrent purging behaviors to influence shape or weight in the absence of binge-eating episodes as defined in the DSM-5 (APA, 2013). The most common purging methods are self-induced vomiting, laxative misuse, and diuretic misuse (Ekeroth, Clinton, Norring, & Birgegård, 2013; Forney, Haedt-Matt, & Keel, 2014; Wade, Bergin, Tiggemann, Bulik, & Fairburn, 2006). In addition, more than half of those seeking treatment engage in other compensatory behaviors, including excessive exercise and extreme fasting (Ekeroth et al., 2013). PD typically onsets in late adolescence and early adulthood (Koch, Quadflieg, & Fichter, 2013; Stice, Marti, & Rohde, 2013; Wade, Bergin, et al., 2006) and primarily affects girls and women (Allen, Byrne, & Crosby, 2015; Hammerle, Huss, Ernst, & Bürger, 2016; Hay, Girosi, & Mond, 2015). PD can be present in both normal weight (Hay et al., 2015) and overweight girls and women (Stice et al., 2013; Wade, Bergin, et al., 2006). Because individuals with PD do not have recurrent large binge-eating episodes, they cannot be diagnosed with bulimia nervosa. In addition, PD would not be diagnosed in those who are underweight. Instead, a more appropriate diagnosis would be the binge/purge subtype of anorexia nervosa (APA, 2013). PD can be diagnosed in those whose disordered eating behavior has contributed to significant weight loss as long as that weight loss does not result in the individual being significantly underweight. Thus, PD may be diagnosed in someone who might be considered to have atypical anorexia nervosa. The following two vignettes portray PD in composite patients, representing key features we have encountered across individuals assessed and treated for PD in our clinic.

Case Examples: Jody and Elizabeth

Jody is a 30-year-old mother of two young children who works evenings as a nurse. Although her weight has always been in a healthy range, Jody has tried every diet available. She complains that she has never been able to stop being "chubby." Jody feels incredibly full whenever she eats a "full meal," which to her is a small sandwich from a sub shop. She states that she can "just feel" her stomach stretching out and the fat going to her thighs. When Jody feels she has eaten too much, she gets rid of the food by vomiting. This provides immediate relief from feeling excessively full and alleviates her concerns about becoming fat. As long as she follows her diet at home, she feels comfortable and safe keeping the food down. However, whenever she eats at a restaurant, she feels that she must get rid of the food and will excuse herself to visit the bathroom. Jody often avoids eating with her children because she is worried about them finding out about her vomiting. Instead, she prepares her "safe" meal and eats it before preparing food for her children. She experiences "good" periods and "bad" periods. During her "bad" periods, she will purge nearly daily, sometimes several times per day. Her good periods can last as long as 2 weeks, during which she will not make herself vomit at all.

Elizabeth is an 18-year-old college student who presented for treatment due to feelings of anxiety. She occasionally engages in nonsuicidal self-injury when she has intense feelings of anxiety and distress, but she most often takes laxatives to feel better. Over time, Elizabeth discloses that her anxiety is most frequently precipitated by poking and pinching her body in the mirror. She does this to check her body for fat—a ritual she began when she first started competing in gymnastics. She started taking laxatives after teammates on her high school gymnastics team teased her about her weight. She now takes them daily and finds that she becomes constipated if she tries to take a break from laxatives. She is concerned about her behavior because the laxatives are expensive, and she is finding she needs to take increasingly more to get the empty feeling that calms her fears of being fat.

Central in the clinical presentation of both cases is the recurrent use of purging to influence weight or shape in the absence of binge episodes as they have been defined in the DSM-5. Jody's clinical presentation is very similar to that of a patient who might suffer from bulimia nervosa, with the exception that when Jody perceives herself as having eaten "too much," she has actually consumed a normal amount of food. Although she does not refer to this as a binge and does not endorse a sense of loss of control, there is a clear connection between her eating and purging behavior. Elizabeth, on the other hand, appears to engage in a range of harmful behaviors, including nonsuicidal self-injury and purging with laxatives, in response to anxiety, which is often triggered by body checking behaviors.

By definition, individuals with PD do not experience the DSM-5 binge-eating episodes characterized by a sense of loss of control while eating an unusually large amount of food. However, some individuals with PD experience a sense of loss of control while eating a normal or small amount of food (e.g., two tacos)—referred to as subjective binge episodes. The prevalence of subjective binges varies across study samples, with 30% of adolescents with PD experiencing loss of control eating (Goldschmidt et al., 2016) compared to 76% of adults with PD (Forney et al., 2014). In adults, subjective binge episodes are associated with greater eating disorder severity, more depressive and anxiety symptoms, and greater impulsivity (Brown, Haedt-Matt, & Keel, 2011; Forney et al., 2014). This pattern was not found in an adolescent patient sample (Goldschmidt et al., 2016).

PD is associated with elevated restraint, shape/weight concerns, anxiety, depressive symptoms (Keel et al., 2005; Keel, Wolfe, Gravener, & Jimerson, 2008), and perfectionism (Haedt & Keel, 2010) compared to controls. Thus, it shares many features with anorexia nervosa and bulimia nervosa. In our experience, patients with PD often resemble patients with anorexia nervosa in temperament and interpersonal interactions more than they resemble patients with bulimia nervosa. For example, in a prior study, we experienced greater trepidation among our PD participants during recruitment than seen in our participants with bulimia nervosa. However, once enrolled, PD participants were significantly more likely to follow through with the multivisit protocol compared to bulimia nervosa participants, who were easier to recruit but more difficult to retain (Keel, Wolfe, Liddle, De Young, & Jimerson, 2007). This may reflect greater impulsivity in bulimia nervosa that we observed in our first study comparing these disorders (Keel, Mayer, & Harnden-Fischer, 2001), but we did not replicate this difference in impulsivity in subsequent studies (Keel et al., 2005, 2008).

Similar to Jody's case, individuals with PD frequently report feelings of gastrointestinal distress after eating, and research has shown greater fullness and gastrointestinal distress ratings in PD relative to healthy controls and women with bulimia nervosa (Keel et al., 2007). With regard to underlying biology, women with PD have a significantly greater cholecystokinin (CCK) (Keel et al., 2007) and glucagon-like peptide 1 (GLP-1) (Dossat, Bodell, Williams, Eckel, & Keel, 2015) response to food intake compared to women with bulimia nervosa. This may account for differences in food consumed during binge episodes because both CCK and GLP-1 trigger satiation. However, women with PD did not differ from control participants on either CCK or GLP-1 (Dossat et al., 2015; Keel et al., 2007), leaving unclear the source of their increased fullness compared to controls.

Up to 70% of individuals with PD experience a comorbid mood disorder, up to 43% experience a comorbid anxiety disorder, up to 17% experience a comorbid substance use disorder, and up to 11% experience a comorbid personality disorder (Ekeroth et al., 2013; Keel et al., 2005, 2008; Koch et al., 2013). In addition, somatoform disorders are more common in PD relative to other eating disorders (Koch et al., 2013). Importantly, PD is associated with elevated suicidality (Stice et al., 2013) and risk of deliberate self-harm (Micali et al., 2015). In a community sample, 10% of women with PD endorsed a history of suicide attempts, and they were more likely than women with the restricting subtype of anorexia nervosa to have medically severe suicide attempts requiring medical intervention (Pisetsky, Thornton, Lichtenstein, Pedersen, & Bulik, 2013), highlighting the importance of routine suicide risk assessment in this population. Individuals with PD are at increased risk for later depression, anxiety disorders, drug use, binge drinking, and deliberate self-harm (Field et al., 2012; Micali et al., 2015).

PREVALENCE OF PURGING DISORDER

Lifetime prevalence of PD from epidemiological studies has ranged from 1.1% to 5.3% in adult females depending on sample and diagnostic criteria (Favaro, Ferrara, & Santonastaso, 2003; Keel, 2007; Wade, Crosby, & Martin, 2006). In adolescent females, a lifetime prevalence estimate of 3.4% by the age of 20 years and a point prevalence rate of 0.85% have been reported (Machado, Machado, Gonçalves, & Hoek, 2007; Stice et al., 2013). Point prevalence estimates of 0.5% and 0.6% in adult females have been reported in Australian and Canadian samples, respectively, and estimates of 0.6–0.9% have been reported in US college women (Crowther, Armey, Luce, Dalton, & Leahey, 2008; Gauvin, Steiger, & Brodeur, 2009; Haedt & Keel, 2010; Hay, Mond, Buttner, & Darby, 2008). In a community sample of US women, 2.6% met criteria for PD at the time of the study, which paralleled findings of 2.0% for current or lifetime PD in a sample of female college students (Fink, Smith, Gordon, Holm-Denoma, & Joiner, 2009; Roberto, Grilo, Masheb, & White, 2010). Although less information exists for men with PD, one study reported a point prevalence of 0.1% in US college men compared to 0.9% in women when purging once per week was required (Haedt & Keel, 2010), consistent with the research definition proposed by Keel and Striegel-Moore (2009). Thus, similar to anorexia nervosa and bulimia nervosa, PD is more common in women than in men.

As a proportion of those seeking treatment for an eating disorder, PD is the presenting problem in 5–10% of adult patients and 24–27.7% of adolescent patients (Binford & Le Grange, 2005; Eddy, Doyle, Hoste, Herzog, & Le Grange, 2008;

Mitchell, Pyle, Hatsukami, & Eckert 1986; Rockert, Kaplan, & Olmsted, 2007; Tasca et al., 2012). In a large Swedish sample of female patients receiving care for an eating disorder, 8.2% of patients met criteria for PD (Ekeroth et al., 2013).

TREATMENT OF PURGING DISORDER

As is evident from information presented previously, PD shares much in common with its sister eating disorders. It is characterized by body image concerns, including fear of gaining weight or becoming fat, and undue influence of weight and shape on self-evaluation. In addition, it predominantly affects adolescent and young adult women. Body image concerns may explain why individuals with PD feel compelled to purge after consuming normal or small amounts of food. Another factor specifically relevant to maintenance of self-induced vomiting is increased gastrointestinal distress after food consumption. Importantly, these factors focus on individual differences that have been found to differ between PD and control women—that is, factors that explain why one person develops PD and another does not. Risk factors may be relevant for identifying effective treatments if these risk factors are also maintenance factors. Another approach to identifying maintenance factors is to identify triggers and consequences of purging behavior in individuals who suffer from PD.

Ecological momentary assessment (EMA) is a method specifically designed for collecting information on triggers and consequences of behaviors in real time in the course of people's everyday lives. A recent EMA study in PD identified increases in negative affect preceding purging episodes and decreases in negative affect following purging (Haedt-Matt & Keel, 2015). Similar patterns for bulimic symptoms in bulimia nervosa have been used to support an affect regulation model for binge/purge behaviors, in which these symptoms are efforts to "fix" negative feelings. However, given that affect may change over the course of a day due to other factors (e.g., stresses at work that reduce upon returning home), within-day changes do not provide definitive proof that the changes in affect are specific to the occurrence of purging. To address this limitation, Haedt-Matt and Keel (2015) examined whether the trajectory of negative affect before and after purging on purge days differed from the trajectory of negative affect for a matched time point on non-purge days. These analyses revealed no difference between purge and non-purge days in changes in negative affect prior to purging time. However, a decrease in negative affect after purging time on purge days was significantly greater than observed during that time period on days that purging did not occur. These results suggest that changes in negative affect do not uniquely predict whether a purging episode will occur, but when purging does occur, the behavior contributes to a decrease in negative affect that would not otherwise have occurred. Thus, a decrease in negative affect may negatively reinforce purging and serve to maintain the behavior in PD.

Given that there were no differences in changes in negative affect leading up to purging, Haedt-Matt and Keel (2015) also examined trajectory of positive affect before and after purging on purge days and compared it to trajectory for matched time periods on non-purge days. Compared to the period of time leading up to purging on purge days, there was an increase in positive affect on non-purge days that may have helped to prevent the purging episode on those days. Taken together, these findings suggest that remission from PD may be facilitated by interventions designed to increase positive affect, such as behavioral activation (Dimidjian et al., 2006), as well as those that identify alternative responses to negative affect, such as the mood intolerance and problem-solving components of enhanced cognitive–behavioral therapy (CBT-E) for transdiagnostic treatment of eating disorders (Fairburn et al., 2009). Indirect support for this latter conclusion derives from two randomized controlled trials in which patients with PD have received such interventions (Fairburn et al., 2009; Wonderlich et al., 2014).

Individuals with PD who engaged in self-induced vomiting in response to subjective binge-eating episodes were included in two randomized controlled trials of adults with bulimic symptoms. One was a comparison of two forms of CBT enhanced for transdiagnostic treatment of eating disorders: (1) CBT-E focused on eating disorder psychopathology (CBT-Ef) and (2) CBT-E broadened to address complex presentations marked by clinical perfectionism, emotion dysregulation, and low self-esteem (CBT-Eb) (Fairburn et al., 2009). The second study was a comparison of integrative cognitive–affective therapy (ICAT) with CBT-Ef (Wonderlich et al., 2014). Table 11.1 presents key features of each intervention. Neither study examined whether diagnostic status of PD versus bulimia nervosa moderated treatment response. Although neither study explained this omission, it may be due to the relatively small number of participants who specifically met criteria for PD in each treatment condition. Overall, both studies reported significant improvements across treatment conditions, suggesting that patients with PD may respond to these transdiagnostic interventions. Information on obtaining treatment manuals is provided in the Resources section. A brief summary of findings is also presented to guide expectations for treatment response.

Patients with an eating disorder not otherwise specified (which included PD and binge-eating disorder as well as other subthreshold variants of bulimia nervosa) appeared to be more likely to drop out of CBT-E treatment (27%) compared to patients with bulimia nervosa (14%), but this did not reach statistical significance ($p = .09$) (Fairburn et al., 2009). CBT-E produced symptom remission in 39% of patients in the Fairburn et al. study and 23% of patients in the study by Wonderlich et al. (2014), and ICAT produced symptom remission in 38% of patients (Wonderlich et al., 2014), with no significant difference between CBT-Ef and CBT-Eb (Fairburn et al., 2009) or between CBT-Ef and ICAT (Wonderlich et al., 2014). With regard to having disordered eating scores comparable to community norms, approximately half of patients receiving CBT-E (51.3%) in the Fairburn et al. study, almost half of patients receiving ICAT (47.5%) in the Wonderlich et al. study, and more than one-third of patients receiving CBT-Ef (37.5%) in the Wonderlich et al. study produced healthier scores—again with no differences across treatments. In contrast, patients assigned to waitlist control did

Table 11.1 COMPARISON OF CORE COMPONENTS OF OUTPATIENT TREATMENTS USED IN ADULTS WITH PURGING DISORDER

Component	CBT-Ef	CBT-Eb	ICAT
Number and duration of sessions	90-min intro session + 20 50-min sessions + review session 20 weeks after treatment (Fairburn et al., 2009) 21 50-min sessions (Wonderlich et al., 2014)	90-min intro session + 20 50-min sessions + review session 20 weeks after treatment	21 50-min sessions
Frequency of sessions	19 weeks (Wonderlich et al., 2014) 20 weeks (Fairburn et al., 2009) Twice weekly for first 4 weeks; once weekly thereafter, tapering to once/month	20 weeks Twice weekly for first 4 weeks; once weekly thereafter, tapering to once/month	19 weeks, Twice weekly for first 4 weeks; once weekly thereafter, tapering to once/month

Phases of treatment	1. Psychoeducation, self-monitoring, normalization of eating
	2. Review progress, formulate plan for next phase
	3. Address processes that maintain ED—shape and eating concerns, enhance ability to deal with day-to-day events and moods, address extreme dietary restraint
	4. Maintain progress and minimize relapse
		1. Psychoeducation, self-monitoring, normalization of eating
		2. Review progress, formulate plan
		3. Address processes that maintain ED—shape and eating concerns, enhance ability to deal with day-to-day events and moods, address extreme dietary restraint, and as indicated by individual address
		  a. Mood intolerance
		  b. Clinical perfectionism
		  c. Low self-esteem
		  d. Interpersonal difficulties
		4. Maintain progress and relapse prevention
			1. Motivational enhancement and self-monitoring
			2. Adaptive coping strategies, management of urges to binge/purge, meal planning
			3. Individualized to needs of patient
			  a. Self-directed behavior (control/neglect)
			  b. Interpersonal problems
			  c. Self-discrepancy and evaluative standards
			4. Healthy lifestyle plans, relapse prevention

CBT-Eb, enhanced cognitive–behavioral therapy broadened to address complex presentations marked by clinical perfectionism, emotion dysregulation, and low self-esteem; CBT-Ef, enhanced cognitive–behavioral therapy focused on eating disorder psychopathology; ED, eating disorder; ICAT, integrative cognitive–affective therapy.

not improve during the 8-week delay before commencing treatment (Fairburn et al., 2009).

With regard to adolescents, Le Grange, Crosby, Rathouz, and Leventhal (2007) compared family-based treatment (FBT) to an individual supportive psychotherapy (SPT) and expanded inclusion criteria to those meeting DSM-IV criteria for bulimia nervosa as well as those who "binged or purged at least once per week for 6 months" (p. 1050). Thus, this treatment trial included adolescents with PD and did not require the presence of subjective binge episodes. SPT was designed as a credible control condition with no theoretically based active therapeutic interventions. Table 11.2 presents key features of FBT and SPT from this study.

Table 11.2 Comparison of Core Components of Outpatient Treatments Used in Adolescents with Purging Disorder

Component	FBT	SPT
Number and duration of sessions	20 sessions over 6 months	20 sessions over 6 months
Frequency of sessions	*Weekly for 2 or 3 months during Phase 1, then every other week during Phase 2, then monthly during Phase 3*	*Weekly for 2 or 3 months during Phase 1, then every other week during Phase 2, then monthly during Phase 3*
Phases of treatment	1. Enlist parents as members of treatment team to support a regular pattern of eating in collaboration with the child and to disrupt bulimic symptoms. Increase ego-dystonic aspects of the disorder as external to the child to enhance motivation and collaboration and reduce blame. 2. Shift control over eating to the adolescent so that the child is responsible for maintaining healthy behaviors. 3. Address the impact of the illness on adolescent development. Prepare for termination.	1. Establish therapeutic relationship, explore the development of eating pathology in the personal and family history, and develop patient insight into factors that may have contributed to the eating disorder. 2. Encourage exploration of underlying feelings, expression of those feelings, as well as increased independence in preparation for the third phase. 3. Prepare the patient for termination by reviewing underlying issues and how to address these moving forward.

FBT, family-based treatment; SPT, supportive psychotherapy.
source: Adapted from Le Grange et al. (2007).

Abstinence from bulimic symptoms was achieved by 39% of patients in FBT compared to only 18% of those in SPT, reflecting a significantly greater treatment response to FBT (Le Grange et al., 2007). There was no difference between participants with full versus partial bulimia nervosa on remission rates following treatment. However, again, "partial" bulimia nervosa included those who would meet DSM-5 criteria for bulimia nervosa at the reduced minimum behavioral symptom frequency of once per week, as well as those who would have PD. Thus, results cannot be interpreted as proving equivalent treatment responses between PD and bulimia nervosa. A recent randomized controlled trial for adolescent bulimia nervosa comparing FBT to CBT required that all participants binge *and* purge at least once per week and thus excluded those with PD (Le Grange, Lock, Agras, Bryson, & Jo, 2015). Unfortunately, this has been the rule rather than the exception across randomized controlled treatment trials for eating disorders.

In summary, patients with PD have been included in controlled treatment trials examining the efficacy of two forms of CBT-E, ICAT, and FBT. All studies have supported significant improvements that are attributable to the impact of treatment. Importantly, none have examined whether these improvements are specific to those who do not have objectively large binge episodes but purge on a regular basis. In our experience, the application of CBT-E has been more successful when PD patients purge after subjective binge episodes because the experience of a loss of control over eating is ego-dystonic. Thus, to the extent that Jody, a 30-year-old mother, feels distressed over the times that she cannot eat a normal amount of food without feeling extremely uncomfortable, CBT-E may be a good treatment option.

In contrast, when patients simply purge as a means to control weight or shape, they can be disconcertingly accepting of their own behavior. In such instances, there may be some advantage to ICAT, which includes a motivational enhancement component at the beginning of treatment, or, for adolescents, FBT because it was originally developed for the treatment of anorexia nervosa in which the disorder can be similarly ego-syntonic. Thus, depending on whether Elizabeth, an 18-year-old, is being treated away from home or still lives with her parents while attending college, ICAT and FBT may both be reasonable options to consider. Importantly, all trials indicate that symptom remission occurs in less than half of patients. Thus, clinicians working with a patient with PD may see significant reductions in symptoms without observing complete elimination of the disorder over the course of 4–6 months. This does not mean that treatment has failed or that clinicians are not "doing it right." It means that the field has more to accomplish in developing treatments that help a larger portion of those with the illness.

MEDICAL CONSEQUENCES OF PURGING AND OUTCOME

Self-induced vomiting and severe laxative and diuretic abuse have been associated with electrolyte and fluid imbalances, which can lead to problems in kidney and heart function (Forney, Buchman-Schmitt, Keel, & Frank, 2016). Vomiting expels stomach acid along with food and decreases the concentration of positively charged ions in blood, such as potassium, resulting in hypokalemia. In addition, purging contributes to decreased blood levels of magnesium and calcium. These electrolyte imbalances contribute to fluid retention (edema) when patients attempt to reduce their disordered eating (Forney et al., 2016). Stomach acid in vomit also contributes to significant dental problems through erosion of tooth enamel, leaving teeth vulnerable to plaque and bacteria (Forney et al., 2016). In addition to the direct consequences of vomiting, using instruments or fingers to trigger a gag reflex has produced the rare but serious consequence of tears in the esophagus. Use of fingers to induce vomiting also causes Russell's sign, named after Gerald Russell, who first observed calluses on the back of the hands of his patients who self-induced vomiting. Finally, recurrent vomiting can lead to swelling of the salivary (parotid) glands. Because these glands are near the face, patients sometimes misinterpret this medical consequence as a "fat face," which can exacerbate appearance concerns. A recent review of more than 100 scholarly articles identified self-induced vomiting as causing the majority of medical complications that have been linked to purging (Forney et al., 2016). However, as observed in the case of Elizabeth, misuse of laxatives and diuretics can cause dependence on these substances and withdrawal effects when attempting to discontinue their use. Due to the range and severity of potential medical consequences linked to purging, mental health professionals treating PD should have their patients assessed and followed by a physician to ensure medical stability.

Similar to the post-treatment remission rates reported from controlled trials, the 12-month remission rate for PD was 44% in a treatment-seeking sample (Ekeroth et al., 2013). Much higher spontaneous remission (94%) was reported for a community sample of adolescents with PD (Stice et al., 2013). Importantly, favorable outcomes were reported across diagnostic groups in this school-based sample, with 75% of anorexia nervosa, 100% of bulimia nervosa, 93% of binge-eating disorder, 71% of atypical anorexia nervosa, 100% of subthreshold bulimia nervosa, and 100% of subthreshold binge-eating disorder remitting within 12 months (Stice et al., 2013). Thus, care should be taken in generalizing these very high remission rates to treatment-seeking populations. Most studies of PD show diagnostic stability over time. Only 5–26% develop bulimia nervosa, and 0–5% develop anorexia nervosa (Allen, Byrne, Oddy, & Crosby, 2013; Ekeroth et al., 2013; Keel et al., 2005; Koch et al., 2013; Stice et al., 2013). Problematically, limited data exist on the long-term outcome of PD. A follow-up study of individuals receiving tertiary care found that 41.5% of those with PD were remitted from their eating disorder 6 years later (Koch et al., 2013). Greater depressive symptoms, greater somatization symptoms, and a lower age at intake predicted a worse outcome (Koch et al., 2013).

Overall, 5% of patients receiving tertiary care had died during the 6-year follow-up, representing a significantly increased risk of premature death (standardized mortality ratio = 3.9) in PD (Koch et al., 2013). In a comparison of mortality across eating disorders, Koch et al. found a significantly greater risk of death in PD than in bulimia nervosa and no significant difference between PD and anorexia nervosa. Somatic illness (e.g., epilepsy, cirrhosis, and type 2 diabetes mellitus) was associated with a greater likelihood of death during the follow-up period in PD (Koch, Quadflieg, & Fichter, 2014). Given the severity of illness in this inpatient sample, outcome needs to be examined in community-based and outpatient treatment-seeking samples to increase generalizability. Despite PD's relatively recent recognition as a distinct syndrome (Keel et al., 2005) and its even more recent inclusion in the DSM-5 as a named form of OSFED (APA, 2013), outcome data support its clinical significance in terms of chronicity and mortality.

CONCLUSION AND FUTURE DIRECTIONS

There has been an impressive increase in research on PD in recent years. A PubMed search using the search term "purging disorder" produced 65 articles published since the 2005 article introducing the term to the medical literature (Keel et al., 2005). However, much of this work has focused on the description of PD and comparisons of PD with established eating disorders. Limited work has been completed on course, outcome, and treatment. The dearth of information on how to treat PD is particularly concerning for clinicians who encounter the disorder in up to 1 out of 10 adult eating disorder patients and approximately 1 out of 4 adolescent patients. New transdiagnostic treatments offer rational approaches to the factors that contribute to risk and maintenance of purging behaviors, and results suggest that these treatments are superior to doing nothing and, in the case of FBT, superior to a nondirective supportive psychotherapy for adolescents. However, stronger evidence in support of these interventions requires finer-grained analyses, in which diagnostic status (PD vs. bulimia nervosa) is examined as a potential moderator of treatment response. Moderator analyses require sufficient numbers of patients in both groups to be adequately powered. Thus, an important future direction is the inclusion of larger numbers of patients with PD in controlled trials to permit analyses.

Until evidence-based treatments for PD are identified, clinicians seeking to help their patients can apply evidence-based treatments that have been examined transdiagnostically. Importantly, these treatments have been designed to treat bulimia nervosa, in which purging episodes are preceded by objectively large binge episodes. Thus, they have traditionally focused on factors that contribute to binge-eating behavior under the premise that eliminating binge eating will eliminate purging. This approach may succeed in PD patients who have subjective binge episodes, as required in some prior transdiagnostic trials. However, clinicians do not have the luxury of screening out patients with PD who do not have subjective binge episodes. Thus, crucial to the success of such treatments is tailoring the approach to the individual needs of the client given the heterogeneity present among those suffering from PD.

With regard to how patients with PD may present with different needs than typically encountered in working with bulimia nervosa patients, a key difference is the extent to which PD appears to be more ego-syntonic than bulimia nervosa. In our own research, we attempted to conduct an open trial of selective serotonin reuptake inhibitor treatment in PD with investigators at two other sites. Our recruitment goal was 12–15 patients. Despite having successfully recruited and completed a complex multivisit biological study of gut peptide response in more than 25 participants with PD at our site alone, we were unable to recruit a single individual into the open trial in which participants would receive free treatment. The most common reason provided was that they were afraid that if they discontinued purging, they would gain weight. In this sense, individuals with PD resemble those with anorexia nervosa in their reluctance to engage in a treatment that may cause weight gain. However, a key difference is that patients with PD are not underweight. In this regard, they are more like patients with bulimia nervosa. In CBT for bulimia nervosa, the clinician is guided to educate patients about the role of binge eating in increasing caloric intake and the limited success of purging to rid the body of those excess calories. This psychoeducation is used as a means to encourage patients to engage in a treatment that will help them discontinue binge eating. In our experience, this does not translate easily to PD patients given the absence of objectively large binge episodes. Instead, more work has to be completed to help the patient accept the possible trade-off between ridding herself of her eating disorder and a possible modest weight gain, potentially to her highest weight prior to the onset of her purging.

Another issue that can emerge in the treatment of PD is that patients may experience their vomiting as involuntary. In such instances, it may be useful to review food diaries to get a sense of factors that differentiate times when patients are able to keep food down versus times that they feel unable to do so. It is possible that some patients have food sensitivities or that foods particularly high in fat may contribute to delays in gastric emptying. Physical discomfort combined with fears of the effect of food on weight make it particularly challenging for PD patients to retain a meal. To address this, emphasis should be placed on helping patients establish an eating pattern in which they can retain all food they have eaten early in treatment, which may require delaying introduction of "trigger" foods until later in treatment.

An alternative to adapting transdiagnostic treatments is to develop PD-specific treatments that focus on those aspects of PD that appear to uniquely contribute to the condition. For example, one factor that appears to contribute to purging in PD is gastrointestinal distress after consuming normal or small amounts of food. Akin to treatment of anxiety sensitivity in anxiety disorders, a PD-specific treatment might encourage reinterpretation of somatic symptoms that emerge while eating by having patients engage in exposure exercises. During and after food consumption, patients would be encouraged to reinterpret their physical sensations as a normal part of digestive processes that are neither harmful nor mean the person is "getting fat." As with any exposure exercise, it would be crucial to ensure that the patient did not purge following food consumption to contribute to extinction of that learned behavior. Indeed, it may be useful to frame purging as a behavior that was learned and can be replaced by new learning. To our knowledge, no patient with PD has been purging continuously since birth. Thus, all patients can recall a period of time when they ate without vomiting, and this may be an important source of reassurance that they are capable of returning to healthy eating patterns.

As with the treatment of any eating disorder, a multidisciplinary team-based approach is important to ensure adequate expertise to help patients with nutrition and physical and mental health. In addition, ongoing assessment of symptoms throughout treatment is key to identifying whether expected improvements are occurring. Indeed, assessment is key to identifying factors that contribute to symptom maintenance in the individual patient. Once triggering and maintaining factors have been identified, the clinician can identify interventions with demonstrated efficacy for reducing these factors, whether they are related to somatic experiences, cognitions, affect, or interpersonal conflict. To support such endeavors, we provide a list of resources for further reading. Although none of these resources was developed specifically to address PD, we aim to provide a useful starting point for clinicians working with PD patients. Through the continued efforts of clinicians, we hope that new knowledge will be generated to advance our field's ability to reduce suffering from PD.

RESOURCES

For information on the medical consequences of purging, see

Forney, K. J., Buchman-Schmitt, J. M., Keel, P. K., & Frank, G. K. (2016). The medical complications associated with purging. *International Journal of Eating Disorders, 49,* 249–259.

For information on CBT-E, see

https://www.psych.ox.ac.uk/research/credo
Fairburn, C. G. (2008). *Cognitive behavior therapy and eating disorders.* New York, NY: Guilford.

For information on treating bulimia nervosa with FBT, see

Le Grange, D., & Lock, J. (2007). *Treating bulimia in adolescents: A family-based approach.* New York, NY: Guilford.

For information on ICAT, see

Wonderlich, S. A., Peterson, C. B., & Leone Smith, T. (2015). *Integrative cognitive–affective therapy for bulimia nervosa: A treatment manual.* New York, NY: Guilford.

REFERENCES

Allen, K. L., Byrne, S. M., & Crosby, R. D. (2015). Distinguishing between risk factors for bulimia nervosa, binge eating disorder, and purging disorder. *Journal of Youth and Adolescence,* 44(8), 1580–1589.

Allen, K. L., Byrne, S. M., Oddy, W. H., & Crosby, R. D. (2013). DSM-IV-TR and DSM-5 eating disorders in adolescents: Prevalence, stability, and psychosocial correlates in a population-based sample of male and female adolescents. *Journal of Abnormal Psychology, 122*(3), 720–732.

American Psychiatric Association. (2013). *Diagnostic and statistical manual of mental disorders* (5th ed.). Arlington, VA: American Psychiatric Publishing.

Binford, R. B., & Le Grange, D. (2005). Adolescents with bulimia nervosa and eating disorder not otherwise specified–purging only. *International Journal of Eating Disorders, 38*(2), 157–161.

Brown, T. A., Haedt-Matt, A. A., & Keel, P. K. (2011). Personality pathology in purging disorder and bulimia nervosa. *International Journal of Eating Disorders, 44*(8), 735–740.

Crowther, J. H., Armey, M., Luce, K. H., Dalton, G. R., & Leahey, T. (2008). The point prevalence of bulimic disorders from 1990 to 2004. *International Journal of Eating Disorders, 41*(6), 491–497.

Dimidjian, S., Hollon, S. D., Dobson, K. S., Schmaling, K. B., Kohlenberg, R. J., Addis, M. E., . . . Atkins, D. C. (2006). Randomized trial of behavioral activation, cognitive therapy, and antidepressant medication in the acute treatment of adults with major depression. *Journal of Consulting and Clinical Psychology, 74*(4), 658–670.

Dossat, A. M., Bodell, L. P., Williams, D. L., Eckel, L. A., & Keel, P. K. (2015). Preliminary examination of glucagon-like peptide-1 levels in women with purging disorder and bulimia nervosa. *International Journal of Eating Disorders, 48*(2), 199–205.

Eddy, K. T., Doyle, A. C., Hoste, R. R., Herzog, D. B., & Le Grange, D. (2008). Eating disorder not otherwise specified in adolescents. *Journal of the American Academy of Child & Adolescent Psychiatry, 47*(2), 156–164.

Ekeroth, K., Clinton, D., Norring, C., & Birgegård, A. (2013). Clinical characteristics and distinctiveness of DSM-5 eating disorder diagnoses: Findings from a large naturalistic clinical database. *Journal of Eating Disorders, 1*, 31.

Fairburn, C. G., Cooper, Z., Doll, H. A., O'Connor, M. E., Bohn, K., Hawker, D. M., . . . Palmer, R. L. (2009). Transdiagnostic cognitive–behavioral therapy for patients with eating disorders: A two-site trial with 60-week follow-up. *American Journal of Psychiatry, 166*, 311–319.

Favaro, A., Ferrara, S., & Santonastaso, P. (2003). The spectrum of eating disorders in young women: A prevalence study in a general population sample. *Psychosomatic Medicine, 65*(4), 701–708.

Field, A. E., Sonneville, K. R., Micali, N., Crosby, R. D., Swanson, S. A., Laird, N. M., . . . Horton, N. J. (2012). Prospective association of common eating disorders and adverse outcomes. *Pediatrics, 130*(2), e289–e295.

Fink, E. L., Smith, A. R., Gordon, K. H., Holm-Denoma, J. M., & Joiner, T. E. (2009). Psychological correlates of purging disorder as compared with other eating disorders: An exploratory investigation. *International Journal of Eating Disorders, 42*(1), 31–39.

Forney, K. J., Buchman-Schmitt, J. M., Keel, P. K., & Frank, G. K. W. (2016). The medical complications associated with purging. *International Journal of Eating Disorders, 49*(3), 249–259.

Forney, K. J., Haedt-Matt, A. A., & Keel, P. K. (2014). The role of loss of control eating in purging disorder. *International Journal of Eating Disorders, 47*(3), 244–251.

Gauvin, L., Steiger, H., & Brodeur, J. M. (2009). Eating-disorder symptoms and syndromes in a sample of urban-dwelling Canadian women: Contributions toward a population health perspective. *International Journal of Eating Disorders, 42*(2), 158–165.

Goldschmidt, A. B., Accurso, E. C., O'Brien, S., Fitzpatrick, K., Lock, J. D., & Le Grange, D. (2016). The importance of loss of control while eating in adolescents with purging disorder. *International Journal of Eating Disorders, 49*(8), 801–804.

Haedt, A. A., & Keel, P. K. (2010). Comparing definitions of purging disorder on point prevalence and associations with external validators. *International Journal of Eating Disorders, 43*(5), 433–439.

Haedt-Matt, A. A., & Keel, P. K. (2015). Affect regulation and purging: An ecological momentary assessment study in purging disorder. *Journal of Abnormal Psychology, 124*, 399–411.

Hammerle, F., Huss, M., Ernst, V., & Bürger, A. (2016). Thinking dimensional: Prevalence of DSM-5 early adolescent full syndrome, partial and subthreshold eating disorders in a cross-sectional survey in German schools. *BMJ Open, 6*(5), e010843.

Hay, P., Girosi, F., & Mond, J. (2015). Prevalence and sociodemographic correlates of DSM-5 eating disorders in the Australian population. *Journal of Eating Disorders, 3*, 1–7.

Hay, P. J., Mond, J., Buttner, P., & Darby, A. (2008). Eating disorder behaviors are increasing: Findings from two sequential community surveys in South Australia. *PLoS One, 3*(2), e1541.

Keel, P. K. (2007). Purging disorder: Subthreshold variant or full-threshold eating disorder? *International Journal of Eating Disorders, 40*(Suppl. 3), S89–S94.

Keel, P. K., Haedt, A., & Edler, C. (2005). Purging disorder: An ominous variant of bulimia nervosa? *International Journal of Eating Disorders, 38*(3), 191–199.

Keel, P. K., Mayer, S. A., & Harnden-Fischer, J. H. (2001). Importance of size in defining binge eating episodes in bulimia nervosa. *International Journal of Eating Disorders, 29*(3), 294–301.

Keel, P. K., & Striegel-Moore, R. H. (2009). The validity and clinical utility of purging disorder. *International Journal of Eating Disorders, 42*(8), 706–719.

Keel, P. K., Wolfe, B. E., Gravener, J. A., & Jimerson, D. C. (2008). Co-morbidity and disorder-related distress and impairment in purging disorder. *Psychological Medicine, 38*(10), 1435–1442.

Keel, P. K., Wolfe, B. E., Liddle, R. A., De Young, K. P., & Jimerson, D. C. (2007). Clinical features and physiological response to a test meal in purging disorder and bulimia nervosa. *Archives of General Psychiatry, 64*(9), 1058–1066.

Koch, S., Quadflieg, N., & Fichter, M. (2013). Purging disorder: A comparison to established eating disorders with purging behaviour. *European Eating Disorders Review, 21*(4), 265–275.

Koch, S., Quadflieg, N., & Fichter, M. (2014). Purging disorder: A pathway to death? A review of 11 cases. *Eating and Weight Disorders: Studies on Anorexia, Bulimia and Obesity, 19*(1), 21–29.

Le Grange, D., Crosby, R. D., Rathouz, P. J., & Leventhal, B. L. (2007). A randomized controlled comparison of family-based treatment and supportive psychotherapy for adolescent bulimia nervosa. *Archives of General Psychiatry, 64*, 1049–1056.

Le Grange, D., Lock, J., Agras, W. S., Bryson, S. W., & Jo, B. (2015). Randomized clinical trial of family-based treatment and cognitive–behavioral therapy for adolescent bulimia nervosa. *Journal of the American Academy of Child and Adolescent Psychiatry*, *54*, 886–894.

Machado, P. P., Machado, B. C., Gonçalves, S., & Hoek, H. W. (2007). The prevalence of eating disorders not otherwise specified. *International Journal of Eating Disorders*, *40*(3), 212–217.

Micali, N., Solmi, F., Horton, N. J., Crosby, R. D., Eddy, K. T., Calzo, J. P., . . . Field, A. E. (2015). Adolescent eating disorders predict psychiatric, high-risk behaviors and weight outcomes in young adulthood. *Journal of the American Academy of Child & Adolescent Psychiatry*, *54*(8), 652–659.

Mitchell, J. E., Pyle, R. L., Hatsukami, D., & Eckert, E. D. (1986). What are atypical eating disorders? *Psychosomatics*, *27*(1), 21–28.

Pisetsky, E. M., Thornton, L. M., Lichtenstein, P., Pedersen, N. L., & Bulik, C. M. (2013). Suicide attempts in women with eating disorders. *Journal of Abnormal Psychology*, *122*(4), 1042.

Roberto, C. A., Grilo, C. M., Masheb, R. M., & White, M. A. (2010). Binge eating, purging, or both: Eating disorder psychopathology findings from an Internet community survey. *International Journal of Eating Disorders*, *43*(8), 724–731.

Rockert, W., Kaplan, A. S., & Olmsted, M. P. (2007). Eating disorder not otherwise specified: The view from a tertiary care treatment center. *International Journal of Eating Disorders*, *40*(Suppl. 3), S99–S103.

Stice, E., Marti, C. N., & Rohde, P. (2013). Prevalence, incidence, impairment, and course of the proposed DSM-5 eating disorder diagnoses in an 8-year prospective community study of young women. *Journal of Abnormal Psychology*, *122*(2), 445.

Tasca, G. A., Maxwell, H., Bone, M., Trinneer, A., Balfour, L., & Bissada, H. (2012). Purging disorder: Psychopathology and treatment outcomes. *International Journal of Eating Disorders*, *45*(1), 36–42.

Wade, T. D., Bergin, J. L., Tiggemann, M., Bulik, C. M., & Fairburn, C. G. (2006). Prevalence and long-term course of lifetime eating disorders in an adult Australian twin cohort. *Australian and New Zealand Journal of Psychiatry*, *40*(2), 121–128.

Wade, T. D., Crosby, R. D., & Martin, N. G. (2006). Use of latent profile analysis to identify eating disorder phenotypes in an adult Australian twin cohort. *Archives of General Psychiatry*, *63*(12), 1377–1384.

Wonderlich, S. A., Peterson, C. B., Crosby, R. D., Smith, T. L., Klein, M. H., Mitchell, J. E., & Crow, S. J. (2014). A randomized controlled comparison of integrative cognitive–affective therapy (ICAT) and enhanced cognitive–behavioral therapy (CBT-E) for bulimia nervosa. *Psychological Medicine*, *44*, 543–553.

12

Evidence-Based Treatment Approaches for Night Eating Disorders

KELLY C. ALLISON AND LAURA A. BERNER ■

NIGHT EATING SYNDROME: DEFINITION, DIAGNOSIS, AND PREVALENCE

In the nearly 60 years between the first description of night eating syndrome (NES) in 1955 (Stunkard, Grace, & Wolff, 1955) and the publication of the fifth edition of the *Diagnostic and Statistical Manual of Mental Disorders* (DSM-5; American Psychiatric Association, 2013), the first manual to describe the proposed diagnostic criteria for NES formally, specific diagnostic criteria for the disorder have evolved considerably. These changes and inconsistencies in the assessment measures used in NES research studies (Striegel-Moore, Franko, & Garcia, 2009; Striegel-Moore, Franko, May, et al., 2006) have complicated cross-study comparison and slowed advances in understanding NES. Currently, NES is classified as an otherwise specified feeding or eating disorder (OSFED; American Psychiatric Association, 2013).

Current DSM-5 diagnostic criteria for NES include recurrent episodes of night eating, including nocturnal ingestions characterized by waking from sleep and eating or excessive consumption of food after the evening meal; awareness and recall of night eating; and significant distress or functional impairment associated with the night eating. The night eating cannot be better accounted for by changes in the sleep cycle, cultural norms, binge-eating disorder (BED), another psychiatric disorder, substance abuse or dependence, a general medical disorder, or medication side effects.

Before the DSM-5 criteria were drafted, an international meeting was held in April 2008 to develop a consensus for proposed diagnostic criteria for NES (Allison, Lundgren, O'Reardon, et al., 2010). This description conceptualized NES as a disorder of delayed circadian intake of food and offered additional guidance on criterion requirements; for example, the proposed criteria from the 2008 consensus meeting detail that for "recurrent, excessive evening intake," at least 25% of food intake would have to be consumed after the evening meal, on average, for at least 3 months (Allison, Lundgren, O'Reardon, et al., 2010). In addition, nocturnal ingestions were required to occur at least twice per week for 3 months. Evening hyperphagia and nocturnal ingestions often occur together, but only one of these criteria was required for the concept of delayed circadian rhythm of food intake to be met.

Differential Diagnosis

Although differential diagnosis with other psychiatric disorders should be made carefully, depression and anxiety often co-occur with NES, and their presence does not automatically preclude a diagnosis of NES. In addition, NES can be diagnosed comorbidly with another eating disorder (Allison, Lundgren, O'Reardon, et al., 2010). In fact, among individuals with NES, approximately 7–25% also met criteria for BED as described in the fourth edition, text revision of the DSM (Allison, Grilo, Masheb, & Stunkard, 2005; American Psychiatric Association, 2000; Greeno, Wing, & Marcus, 1995; Stunkard et al., 1996; Tzischinsky & Latzer, 2004). In addition, approximately 40% of individuals with bulimia nervosa (BN) in an inpatient treatment center had night eating symptoms (Lundgren et al., 2011), and roughly 50% of outpatients with BN reported night eating symptoms (Lundgren, Shapiro, & Bulik, 2008). These rates of diagnostic overlap with BED are consistent with those reported in a large Swiss sample of young adults aged 18–26 years (Fischer, Meyer, Hermann, Tuch, & Munsch, 2012); however, this sample included a lower rate (10%) of diagnostic overlap between NES and BN.

The criteria for NES indicate that persons may have just one of the two core criteria—evening hyperphagia or nocturnal ingestions—to receive a diagnosis. Patients often meet both these criteria, but when only evening hyperphagia is present, the differential diagnosis with BED becomes more challenging. Generally, persons with NES graze throughout the evening and feel compelled to eat to relax and fall asleep. This is qualitatively different than eating an objectively large amount of food in a driven way and experiencing a sense of loss of control. Those with NES also generally display a delayed pattern of eating such that they skip breakfast. With BED, binge-eating episodes occur during times of opportunity, and one prime time for these episodes may be at night. Further work is needed to understand the overlap between these phenomena.

When nocturnal ingestions are present, the diagnostic overlap between NES and BED seems less evident. Intake during these episodes can be objectively large but often is the size of a meal or snack. Those with NES typically describe that they feel driven to eat to fall back to sleep and may feel irritable and distressed when prevented from eating. Vinai and colleagues (2014) showed that this belief in the need to eat to fall asleep was the differentiating factor between patients with NES, BED, and insomnia. Persons with NES also seem to diverge from those with other eating disorders in that alexithymia has not been linked to the severity of night eating symptoms as it typically is with BN, BED, and anorexia nervosa (Vinai et al., 2015).

Physicians may aim to treat NES by helping their patients sleep more soundly by prescribing sleep medications; however, with these medications, persons with NES typically still arouse from sleep and seek food but may do so in a somnolent state with little awareness and recall of their actions. This experience is consistent with sleep-related eating disorder. As such, sleeping pills, such as zolpidem, are contraindicated for the treatment of NES (Howell & Schenck, 2009). Sleep-related eating disorder is a parasomnia described in the third edition of the *International Classification of Sleep Disorders* (American Academy of Sleep Medicine, 2014). It consists of periods of involuntary eating during the main sleep period. Persons with this parasomnia may eat nonfood items (e.g., shaving cream), inedible items (e.g., frozen foods), or odd combinations of food items (e.g., salt and sugar sandwich), and they may injure themselves obtaining or preparing food. Sleep-related eating disorder is associated with other primary sleep disorders and may be treated pharmacologically. Psychotherapeutic approaches are not generally effective because there is little or no awareness of the nocturnal eating behavioral while it is happening. Of note, some persons presenting for treatment have nocturnal eating episodes with awareness at times and have them without awareness at other times. Clinically, patients have presented reporting that they were sleepwalking during their eating episodes in the early years of their disorder but gained awareness over time. Clearly, NES and sleep-related eating disorder exist on a continuum, but more work is needed to understand their shared and unique pathophysiology.

Diagnostic Assessment

Accurate diagnosis is critical to the delivery of appropriate care for NES. Multiple validated self-report measures and semistructured interviews have been developed for the assessment of NES symptoms, including the Night Eating Questionnaire (NEQ; Allison et al., 2008), a self-report screening measure; the Night Eating Syndrome History and Inventory (NESHI), a diagnostic interview that was developed as an interview companion to the NEQ (Lundgren, Allison, Vinai, & Gluck, 2012); and the Night Eating Symptom Scale (NESS), a self-report measure based on the NEQ used during treatment to assess symptom change in the previous week (Lundgren, Allison, Vinai, et al., 2012). The Night Eating Diagnostic Scale (NEDS) is another self-report measure designed to be face valid in assessing each NES diagnostic criterion (Lundgren, Allison, Vinai, et al., 2012). In addition, a single item of the Eating Disorder Examination (Fairburn, Cooper, & O'Connor,

2008), a semistructured interview that is considered the "gold standard" in eating disorder assessment, assesses for the presence of nocturnal ingestions.

Prevalence

In light of changing diagnostic criteria and inconsistent assessment techniques, NES prevalence estimates in large community samples range widely. The first estimate was 1.5% in adults (Rand, Macgregor, & Stunkard, 1997). Evening and nighttime food intake data from the Continuing Survey of Food Intakes by Individuals and the National Health and Nutrition Examination Survey–III yielded a wide range of prevalence estimates between 9% and 36% of adults, depending on the time cut points used (Striegel-Moore, Franko, Thompson, Affenito, & Kraemer, 2006). Data from the Swedish Twin Study of Adults: Genes and Environment yielded estimates between 1.7% and 4.6%, depending on the stringency of criteria used (Lundgren, Allison, Stunkard, et al., 2012). Recently, in a large study of college students throughout the United States, NES prevalence was estimated to be 4.2%, and it was estimated to be 2.9% when any binge eating was excluded (Runfola, Allison, Hardy, Lock, & Peebles, 2014). A large study of German adolescents and adults (aged 14–85 years) estimated NES prevalence to be 1.1% (de Zwaan, Müller, Allison, Brähler, & Hilbert, 2014), whereas prevalence of NES in Germany had previously been estimated to be 1.1% in children but 5.8% in mothers and 4.5% in fathers (Lamerz et al., 2005). The point prevalence of NES in psychiatric outpatients was estimated to be between 12.3% and 22.4% (Lundgren et al., 2006; Saraçlı et al., 2015), and in patients with type 2 diabetes it was estimated to be 3.8% (Allison et al., 2007) and 7% (Hood, Reutrakul, & Crowley, 2014). Thus, depending on the population and criteria used, prevalence estimates of NES range widely from 1.1% to 36%.

Clinical Case Example

A recent case treated in the first author's clinic illustrates typical NES symptom presentation. "Bob" was a successful, intelligent business man who seemed to have everything going for him. He presented for treatment saying that he had had many successes in life and had overcome many struggles, but he could not seem to stop his night eating. Bob recounted that he had been abused as a child by his father, who had alcohol use disorder, but he denied any symptoms of posttraumatic stress disorder. Starting at approximately the same time as this abuse, Bob would wake during the night, go to the kitchen, and have a snack. The house was quiet, and it was a time when he could relax and enjoy his eating without other concerns. As he matured, Bob became an athlete and was "known for [his] eating." He could eat large amounts and was very active, so at the time he viewed his ongoing night eating as aiding his attempt to keep his body "fueled for activity." After he stopped playing sports competitively, he started gaining weight and, like his father, developed alcohol use disorder. Bob recounted that he was able to stop his drinking when he realized the impact it was having on him and his family, but despite repeated attempts, he was not able to stop his night eating.

Bob had tried many different approaches, including sleeping in an outbuilding on his property for up to 3 months at a time so he would not have access to food during the night. This intervention was initially successful, but when he would return to sleeping in his bedroom, the night eating resumed. As disciplined as he could be with sports and his business, he could not seem to overcome the urge to eat during the night, and so it continued one to three times every night. Every morning he would wake and exercise before starting his workday, and he tried to eat regularly during the day despite lack of a morning appetite, but the pattern persisted. Although he could abstain completely from alcohol to treat his alcohol use disorder, he could not stop eating altogether or having food in his home, particularly when living with others.

EVIDENCE-BASED TREATMENT APPROACHES FOR NIGHT EATING SYNDROME

Pharmacological Interventions

Several trials have investigated pharmacological treatments for NES symptoms, particularly the use of selective serotonin reuptake inhibitors (SSRIs). One case series of paroxetine or fluvoxamine (Miyaoka et al., 2003), two open-label trials of sertraline (O'Reardon, Stunkard, & Allison, 2004; Stunkard et al., 2006), and one randomized, placebo-controlled trial of sertraline (O'Reardon et al., 2006) indicated that NES can be successfully treated with SSRIs. Dosing of sertraline ranged from 50 to 200 mg, with patients responding at a mode of 150 mg in the randomized controlled trial (O'Reardon et al., 2006). The results of both a 12-week, randomized, placebo-controlled trial of escitalopram (Vander Wal, Gang, Griffing, & Gadde, 2012), another SSRI, and a 12-week open-label trial of escitalopram (Allison et al., 2013) indicated improvements in NES symptoms, but these improvements were not statistically significantly different from those found in the placebo group in the controlled trial (Vander Wal et al., 2012). Finally, case studies suggest that topiramate, an antiepileptic medication that has been used to treat BN and BED in off-label use, also seems promising in the treatment of NES (Winkelman, 2003), but controlled trials are needed in this population.

BEHAVIORAL INTERVENTIONS FOR NIGHT EATING SYNDROME

Early psychotherapeutic approaches for NES symptoms among obese individuals were initially psychodynamically oriented and focused on stress reduction (Stunkard, 1976), followed by behavioral interventions published for two cases with mixed results (Coates, 1978; Williamson, Lawson, Bennett, & Hinz, 1989). Since these initial case studies, two main behavioral treatments have been investigated: progressive muscle relaxation and behavioral weight loss. Only two controlled trials of progressive muscle relaxation for NES have been published. Based on the finding of high levels of stress associated with NES, one study compared a group that received a behavioral stress management intervention—a 1-week, abbreviated progressive muscle relaxation therapy (APMRT; 20 minutes per night)—to a control group that quietly sat for a matched amount of time (Pawlow, O'Neil, & Malcolm, 2003). The APMRT group reported significantly decreased evening appetite and increased morning appetite, in addition to lower levels of stress, fatigue, and anxiety. Decreases in nocturnal ingestion intake and increases in breakfast intake were not statistically significant, but effect sizes for these differences were large. A recent pilot study reported that a brief education session (meant to serve as a control), brief PMR training and practice, and brief PMR training plus exercise instruction all resulted in significant reductions in symptoms of anxiety, depression, stress, and NES (Vander Wal, Maraldo, Vercellone, & Gagne, 2015); however, groups that received PMR interventions showed the greatest reductions in evening hyperphagia. Results from these brief, small trials indicate that further investigation of the efficacy of PMR for NES symptoms is warranted.

Only one study has examined the effects of behavioral weight loss treatment on NES symptoms. Dalle Grave, Calugi, Ruocco, and Marchesini (2011) investigated a 21-day inpatient treatment for obese individuals with or without NES followed by either outpatient treatment with an obesity specialist for 62% of the sample or no treatment for the remaining 38%. Equal proportions of night eaters received ongoing care after discharge. The inpatient program included a low-calorie diet and a regular pattern of eating, daily exercise, and psychoeducational group therapy focusing on behavioral weight loss strategies. This intervention resulted in a reduction in body mass index (BMI) across all individuals: Those with NES ($n = 32$) lost 1.9 kg/m², on average, whereas those without NES ($n = 68$) lost 1.5 kg/m² in the inpatient treatment; however, these reductions in BMI were not statistically significantly different. Similarly, at 6-month follow-up, the percentage of weight loss from baseline weight among those with NES (6.4%) and those without NES (8.2%) did not differ. The authors report that there were no differences in BMI reduction at 6 months for those who continued night eating as opposed to those who had discontinued these behaviors. Although behavioral weight loss did not have a differential impact on weight loss among those with or without NES, only 27.6% of individuals who originally met criteria for NES retained the diagnosis at 6-month follow-up. In addition, 62.1% of those with NES at baseline reported that they had been abstinent from night eating for 3 months. This may have been influenced by lack of availability of food during the inpatient stay, much as Bob's symptoms remitted when he slept outside of his main home for 3 months.

The results of the study by Dalle Grave et al. (2011) suggest that the behavioral weight loss treatment effectively controlled night eating symptoms for a large proportion of those presenting with an NES diagnosis, although these results should be replicated in an outpatient setting, and long-term follow-up of maintenance of the treatment effects should be reported. Behavioral weight loss treatment has also been shown to reduce both binge-eating episode frequency and weight in clients with BED (Munsch, Meyer, & Biedert, 2012), suggesting that the behavior modification approaches contained in structured behavioral weight loss programs impact disordered eating related to overweight and obesity, such as night eating and binge eating.

Although the active ingredients of behavioral weight loss key to reducing night eating symptoms cannot be identified in the investigation of Dalle Grave and colleagues (2011), two elements of the treatment seem likely candidates. First, structured daytime food intake in behavioral weight loss may address the delayed pattern of eating characteristic of NES. Indeed, Boston, Moate, Allison, Lundgren, and Stunkard (2008) showed that individuals with NES do not report scheduled, consistent mealtimes over the 24-hour day as control participants do, and this may drive night eating behaviors. Self-monitoring of food intake is the second likely key element of behavioral weight loss approaches in the treatment of NES. Just as self-monitoring is generally a strong, if not the strongest, predictor of successful weight loss (Wilde & Garvin, 2007), it also may promote increased awareness of the impact of night eating episodes on weight and may help clients re-evaluate their drive to eat and observe patterns in their eating behaviors.

COGNITIVE–BEHAVIORAL THERAPY FOR NIGHT EATING SYNDROME

Theoretical Basis and Treatment Techniques

The success of several behaviorally focused interventions for NES suggests the conflict between the normal boundaries of sleep and the abnormal schedule of food intake characteristic of NES often contributes to the development of faulty cognitions about the function of eating at night or during nocturnal ingestions (Allison, Stunkard, & Thier, 2004). These include a belief that one needs to eat to resume sleep, thoughts about being incapable of avoiding eating at night, and thoughts about needing to eat to alleviate anxiety or agitation in the evening. As mentioned previously, this belief in the need to eat to fall asleep seems to represent an important differential diagnostic indicator between BED and NES (Vinai et al., 2014) and possibly between insomnia and NES.

Cognitive–behavioral therapy (CBT) for NES (Allison, 2012; Allison, Lundgren, Moore, O'Reardon, & Stunkard, 2010) therefore integrates behavioral interventions with cognitive techniques standard in CBT to address these seemingly integral distorted thoughts. This includes the use of dysfunctional thought records, developed by Beck and colleagues (Beck, Rush, Shaw, & Emery, 1979), on which clients record situations, resulting thoughts, emotions, behavioral outcomes, and potential alternative thoughts. This examination of distorted thoughts is complemented in CBT for NES by stimulus control interventions to help clients test the validity of their thoughts (e.g., of the inevitability of their night eating or their inability to resume sleep without eating) via behavioral experimentation. This identification of underlying automatic thoughts and the examination of environmental cues and emotions associated with night eating permit functional analysis of night eating behaviors. Other standard elements of CBT as conceived by Beck et al., including Socratic questioning, the "downward arrow" technique to identify core beliefs, and collaborative empiricism, are employed.

Elements of CBT for insomnia (CBT-I), which has been shown to be highly effective in the treatment of insomnia, also served as a theoretical framework for the development of CBT for NES. Components of CBT-I, such as improving sleep hygiene and standardizing bedtime and morning awakening time (Perlis et al., 2010), represent important elements of CBT for NES.

As is standard in most psychotherapeutic interventions, rapport-building and early investment in the therapeutic alliance are essential to CBT for NES. These more basic aspects of treatment may be particularly critical in this intervention because the workload of this therapy is high, and readiness for such involvement on the part of the client seems crucial for preventing treatment dropout.

Treatment Overview

CBT for NES occurs in three basic stages and consists of 10, 1-hour sessions (Allison, 2012). These sessions initially occur on a weekly basis, and the final 2 sessions are scheduled for every other week.

PRETREATMENT ASSESSMENT

Before beginning treatment, a structured assessment of current NES symptoms is recommended. This may include the use of validated NES measures such as the NEQ (Allison et al., 2008) and the NESHI (Lundgren, Allison, Vinai, et al., 2012). In addition, assessment of potential comorbid disorders that would trump the treatment of NES, including severe depression, suicidal ideation, and anxiety disorders, should be completed before initiation of CBT for NES.

STAGE 1

During the first stage of treatment, the therapist focuses on development of rapport with the client, psychoeducation about night eating, and review of the CBT rationale. Client homework includes self-monitoring of behaviors, completion of thought records, and behavioral experimentation. When night eating episodes occur, behavioral chain analyses are conducted, first collaboratively with the therapist in session and then for homework, to help identify cognitive and behavioral intervention targets. The layout of one's home is explored, and the typical route one takes while night eating is examined. Assignments for decreasing nocturnal ingestions could include placing signs on doors, in the bathroom, and on the refrigerator with statements meaningful to clients that would help them remember their daytime intentions for not eating, thereby disrupting the automation of the typical nighttime eating routine. Other strategies could include placing barriers along the path to the kitchen, removing food or locking cabinets to limit access to preferred night-eating foods, and completing self-monitoring forms to raise awareness and identify intervention targets (Allison, 2012). In addition to reminding patients of their intentions for not wanting to eat at night, these barriers create a pause between waking and eating, giving patients more time to engage in thought restructuring and question whether the effort to obtain the food is consistent with their health behavior goals.

We implemented these strategies in treatment with Bob to break the association between eating upon awakening when he slept in his own bedroom. He placed furniture in front of the kitchen entry, piled up pillows on the chair that he typically sat in to eat during the night, and placed reminder signs along the way to the kitchen from his room. He also kept a bottle of water beside his bed and in the bathroom. All of these cues were present in an effort to help him challenge his assumptions that he could not resist the urge to eat and that he could not fall back to sleep without eating. He also worked with our nutritionist to increase the variety of nutrients he was receiving and to schedule his meals and snacks more regularly throughout the day.

Because similar stimulus control and structured eating pattern interventions are shared by this CBT for NES and by standard behavioral weight loss treatment, weight loss is included in CBT for NES as a goal for those who wish to reduce their weight. For these individuals, caloric monitoring is included with self-monitoring of night eating behaviors and sleep patterns (time of sleep onset, time and duration of nocturnal awakenings, and morning rise time). Bob also tracked his intake with an Internet-based application, which the therapist and nutritionist could review at each session.

STAGE 2

In the second stage of treatment, the therapist and client work collaboratively to identify thematic patterns in self-monitoring that are used to tailor treatment. Cognitive restructuring is taught and practiced, and clients engage in behavioral experiments and stimulus control to challenge automatic thoughts as they are identified. This includes experimentation with how long patients are able to engage in an alternate, quiet task (e.g., in 10-minute increments) while tolerating their drive to eat. The longer they are able to engage in a distracting activity, such as listening to music, deep breathing, or reading in low light, the better able they are to test the assumption that they will not be able to resume sleep without eating. Breakfast is also added to the client's pattern of eating. For clients with comorbid major depression, cognitive distortions beyond the bounds of night eating are also addressed in this second stage of treatment because these automatic thoughts, along with those related to anxiety or stress, may serve as catalysts for night eating (Allison et al., 2004). If appropriate, alternative strategies to night eating, including PMR and deep breathing exercises, are introduced in these Stage 2 sessions. Additional elements of sleep hygiene and physical activity are also addressed in this stage because these are thought to promote sounder sleep and improve weight and stress management.

Bob was already exercising most days when he woke in the morning, but we were able to use PMR and other quiet activities during the night to prevent his going to the kitchen and help him ride out the initial discomfort associated with urges to eat. We also used thought records to address his ongoing stressors, both at work and at home, so that he was not ruminating on these issues during the night when he awoke.

STAGE 3

For the final two sessions, which comprise Stage 3 of CBT for NES, treatment transitions to biweekly. These sessions include summarizing and reflecting on progress and bolstering the client's confidence and sense of self-efficacy to continue on his or her own with successful changes. These final sessions also focus on relapse prevention through prediction of future challenges and anticipatory problem-solving.

Evidence in Support of Cognitive–Behavioral Therapy for Night Eating Syndrome

To date, only one empirical investigation of CBT for NES has been published. This pilot study of the 10-session CBT for NES protocol described previously included 25 individuals with NES (Allison, Lundgren, Moore, et al., 2010). After treatment, the number of nocturnal ingestions decreased significantly, as did calories from nocturnal ingestions (from 8.7 to 2.6 per week). There was a statistically nonsignificant decrease, from 35% to 24.9%, in the proportion of calories consumed after dinner. Total daily intake, number of awakenings, and NESS total scores all decreased significantly. Participants lost a significant amount of weight because this was also a target of treatment for most clients, and depression scores were reduced. The amount of food consumed during nocturnal ingestions was reduced significantly, but the quantity consumed before bedtime was not significantly affected. From the perspective of clinical significance, the percentage of intake consumed after dinner decreased after treatment to a level just below the diagnostic boundary for NES. This effect is largely attributable to the reduction in nocturnal ingestions. Compared to prior investigations, outcome results are similar to those of the aforementioned sertraline trial (O'Reardon, Stunkard, et al., 2004). The results also suggest that the effects of CBT are greater than those of PMR alone (Pawlow et al., 2003).

PHOTOTHERAPY: ANOTHER PROMISING TREATMENT

In addition to the treatments examined previously, phototherapy, or exposure to certain wavelengths of light via a light-emitting device for prescribed amounts of time, has been investigated for the treatment of NES. Traditionally used to treat sleep and mood disorders, phototherapy's effects on melatonin, a key regulator of circadian rhythm, prompted trials of phototherapy as a potential treatment for NES, which has been conceptualized by some as a disorder of delayed circadian rhythm. Phototherapy has demonstrated initial effectiveness for NES in two case studies and an open-label pilot trial. The first case, an obese woman with comorbid nonseasonal major depressive disorder who was also taking paroxetine, remitted from NES after 14 days of daily phototherapy (Friedman, Even, Dardennes, & Guelfi, 2002). This case study followed a "BAB" design in which a no-treatment phase (A phase) followed the initial delivery of treatment (B phase), followed by the reintroduction to treatment (second B phase). The authors report that the client became symptomatic after discontinuation of phototherapy and remitted once more after 12 additional days of phototherapy. The second case, a normal-weight male, remitted from both nonseasonal major depressive disorder and NES following 14 sessions of daily phototherapy (Friedman, Even, Dardennes, & Guelfi, 2004). In an open-label pilot trial of 2 weeks of daily bright light therapy in 15 adults with NES, symptoms of depression, NES, and sleep disturbance all improved from pre- to post-treatment (McCune & Lundgren, 2015). Although these very preliminary findings are promising, they require randomized controlled trials to confirm the efficacy of phototherapy for the treatment of NES.

THE IMPACT OF WEIGHT STATUS ON NIGHT EATING SYMPTOM EXPRESSION AND TREATMENT RESPONSE

In addition to consideration of comorbidities in treatment planning for individuals with NES, research indicates that weight status represents an important variable both in the expression of night eating symptoms and in response to NES treatment. Marshall, Allison, O'Reardon, Birketvedt, and Stunkard (2004) were the first to show that compared to obese individuals with NES, individuals at a normal body weight with NES reported more severe nocturnal eating symptoms, including more awakenings, more cravings when up at night, and more nocturnal ingestions, as measured by the NEQ. Subsequently, Lundgren and colleagues (2008) further characterized normal-weight individuals with NES ($n = 19$), reporting that they consumed 50% of their daily caloric intake after dinner and experienced 13 awakenings (getting out of bed) and 10 nocturnal ingestions per week, on average. These figures are higher than those reported among overweight and obese individuals with NES, who have been reported in one sample ($n = 46$) to consume 35% of their intake after dinner and experience approximately 11 awakenings and 8 nocturnal ingestions per week (O'Reardon, Ringel, et al., 2004).

Findings that normal-weight individuals with NES eat a higher percentage of their intake at night than do overweight and obese persons may seem counterintuitive. One potential explanation may be related to more active daytime intake restriction and exercise in individuals of normal weight with NES to counteract nightly caloric intake. This may result in the first meal of the day occurring much later than that for overweight and obese persons with NES, who report eating more calories generally throughout the day. Increased dietary restriction during the day in the normal-weight group may therefore exert an increased biological pressure to eat, which may in turn trigger more frequent nocturnal ingestions, thereby reinforcing the night eating cycle.

Treatment recommendations for individuals with NES who are normal weight may also differ from those for overweight and obese clients with NES. Because of the more extreme pattern that includes dietary restriction during the day, normal-weight clients with NES may fear weight gain as a result of NES treatment. This may preclude normal-weight clients from adopting a pattern of eating that includes earlier meals for fear that they will be eating all day *and* all night, thus interfering with treatment adherence. The investigation by Allison and colleagues (2010) indicated that this was not the case: Normal-weight participants did not gain weight during this pilot study of CBT. Of note, behavioral weight loss components, including calorie counting, were omitted from the CBT treatment of normal-weight participants. Interventions with normal-weight individuals with NES may require increased focus on weight gain-related fears. Furthermore, normal-weight participants have been found to demonstrate reductions in the percentage of food intake after dinner and their number of nocturnal ingestions per week at a similar rate as overweight and obese participants receiving CBT for NES, but they start and end with higher symptom levels as a result of this baseline difference. Longer term treatment for this normal-weight group may be warranted, given the higher level of symptom severity.

FUTURE DIRECTIONS

Nonstandardized and frequently changing diagnostic definitions of NES have challenged the study of the treatment of the disorder. Initial investigations of SSRIs, phototherapy, and behavioral and cognitive–behavioral interventions for NES have all demonstrated some degree of success in reducing or eliminating night eating. Despite promising evidence from initial trials, further research investigating efficacious treatments for NES is needed. Randomized controlled trials of CBT for NES, alone and in combination with psychotropic medications, are also needed. Furthermore, studies that include larger sample sizes of individuals who are normal weight, overweight, and obese are necessary to parse the relative benefits of CBT for NES across weight classes. In addition to randomized controlled studies comparing CBT with other treatment modalities, dismantling studies to identify the active ingredients in this treatment are warranted. Although extant evidence suggests that 10 sessions of CBT produce promising outcomes, longer durations of treatment should be tested because there have been no long-term studies examining the durability of this treatment generally or the duration of remission in treatment responders. Finally, the effect of psychiatric comorbidities on treatment outcome is unknown, and because of the high rate of overlap between NES and other eating, mood, anxiety, and substance use disorders, structured investigations of the impact of comorbidity on treatment response are needed.

AUTHOR NOTE

1. This chapter represents an update and expansion of our original open-access review article: Berner, L. A., & Allison, K. C. (2013). Behavioral management of night eating disorders. *Psychology Research and Behavior Management, 6*, 1–8. doi:10.2147/prbm.s31929

RESOURCES

The following resources may prove helpful to clinicians treating patients with night eating:

> Allison, K. C. (2012). Cognitive–behavioral therapy manual for night eating syndrome. In J. D. Lundgren, K. C. Allison, & A. J. Stunkard (Eds.), *Night eating syndrome: Research, assessment, and treatment.* New York, NY: Guilford. This is a comprehensive therapist manual for the 10-session CBT protocol described previously, and it includes handouts for the intervention.
>
> Allison, K. C., Stunkard, A. J., & Thier, S. L. (2004). *Overcoming the night eating syndrome: A step-by-step guide to breaking the cycle.* Oakland, CA: New Harbinger. This is a self-help guide for NES.
>
> Lundgren, J. D., Allison, K. C., Vinai, P., & Gluck, M. E. (2012). Assessment instruments for night eating syndrome. In J. D. Lundgren, K. C. Allison, & A. J. Stunkard (Eds.), *Night eating syndrome: Research, assessment, and treatment.* New York, NY: Guilford. This book chapter includes measures that assess NES diagnosis and severity.

REFERENCES

Allison, K. C. (2012). Cognitive–behavioral therapy manual for night eating syndrome. In J. D. Lundgren, K. C. Allison, & A. J. Stunkard (Eds.), *Night eating syndrome: Research, assessment, and treatment.* New York, NY: Guilford.

Allison, K. C., Crow, S. J., Reeves, R. R., West, D. S., Foreyt, J. P., Dilillo, V. G., . . . Stunkard, A. J. (2007). Binge eating disorder and night eating syndrome in adults with type 2 diabetes. *Obesity (Silver Spring), 15*(5), 1287–1293.

Allison, K. C., Grilo, C. M., Masheb, R. M., & Stunkard, A. J. (2005). Binge eating disorder and night eating syndrome: A comparative study of disordered eating. *Journal of Consulting & Clinical Psychology, 73*(6), 1107–1115.

Allison, K. C., Lundgren, J. D., Moore, R. H., O'Reardon, J. P., & Stunkard, A. J. (2010). Cognitive behavior therapy for night eating syndrome: A pilot study. *American Journal of Psychotherapy, 64*(1), 91–106.

Allison, K. C., Lundgren, J. D., O'Reardon, J. P., Geliebter, A., Gluck, M. E., Vinai, P., . . . Stunkard, A. J. (2010). Proposed diagnostic criteria for night eating syndrome. *International Journal of Eating Disorders, 43*, 241–247.

Allison, K. C., Lundgren, J. D., O'Reardon, J. P., Martino, N. S., Sarwer, D. B., Wadden, T. A., . . . Stunkard, A. J. (2008). The Night Eating Questionnaire (NEQ): Psychometric properties of a measure of severity of the night eating syndrome. *Eating Behaviors, 9*(1), 62–72.

Allison, K. C., Studt, S. K., Berkowitz, R. I., Hesson, L. A., Moore, R. H., Dubroff, J. G., . . . Stunkard, A. J. (2013). An open-label efficacy trial of escitalopram for night eating syndrome. *Eating Behaviors, 14*(2), 199–203.

Allison, K. C., Stunkard, A. J., & Thier, S. L. (2004). *Overcoming the night eating syndrome: A step-by-step guide to breaking the cycle.* Oakland, CA: New Harbinger.

American Academy of Sleep Medicine. (2014). *International classification of sleep disorders: Diagnostic and coding manual* (3d ed.). Westchester, IL: Author.

American Psychiatric Association. (2000). *Diagnostic and statistical manual of mental disorders* (4th ed., text rev.). Washington, DC: Author.

American Psychiatric Association. (2013). *Diagnostic and Statistical Manual of Mental Disorders* (5th ed.). Arlington, VA: American Psychiatric Publishing.

Beck, A. T., Rush, A. J., Shaw, B. F., & Emery, G. (1979). *Cognitive therapy of depression.* New York, NY: Guilford.

Boston, R. C., Moate, P. J., Allison, K. C., Lundgren, J. D., & Stunkard, A. J. (2008). Modeling circadian rhythms of food intake by means of parametric deconvolution: Results from studies of the night eating syndrome. *American Journal of Clinical Nutrition, 87*(6), 1672–1677.

Coates, T. J. (1978). Successive self-management strategies towards coping with night eating. *Journal of Behavior Therapy and Experimental Psychiatry, 9,* 181–183.

Dalle Grave, R., Calugi, S., Ruocco, A., & Marchesini, G. (2011). Night eating syndrome and weight loss outcome in obese patients. *International Journal of Eating Disorders, 44*(2), 150–156.

de Zwaan, M., Müller, A., Allison, K. C., Brähler, E., & Hilbert, A. (2014). Prevalence and correlates of night eating in the German general population. *PLoS One, 9*(5), e97667.

Fairburn, C. G., Cooper, Z., & O'Connor, M. (2008). Eating disorder examination (Edition 16.0D). In C. G. Fairburn (Ed.), *Cognitive behavior therapy and eating disorders.* New York, NY: Guilford.

Fischer, S., Meyer, A. H., Hermann, E., Tuch, A., & Munsch, S. (2012). Night eating syndrome in young adults: Delineation from other eating disorders and clinical significance. *Psychiatry Research, 200*(2-3), 494–501.

Friedman, S., Even, C., Dardennes, R., & Guelfi, J. D. (2004). Light therapy, nonseasonal depression, and night eating syndrome. *Canadian Journal of Psychiatry, 49*(11), 790.

Greeno, C. G., Wing, R. R., & Marcus, M. D. (1995). Nocturnal eating in binge eating disorder and matched-weight controls. *International Journal of Eating Disorders, 18,* 343–349.

Hood, M. M., Reutrakul, S., & Crowley, S. J. (2014). Night eating in patients with type 2 diabetes: Associations with glycemic control, eating patterns, sleep, and mood. *Appetite, 79,* 91–96.

Howell, M. J., & Schenck, C. H. (2009). Treatment of nocturnal eating disorders. *Current Treatment Options in Neurology, 11*(5), 333–339.

Lamerz, A., Kuepper-Nybelen, J., Bruning, N., Wehle, C., Trost-Brinkhues, G., Brenner, H., . . . Herpertz-Dahlmann, B. (2005). Prevalence of obesity, binge eating, and night eating in a cross-sectional field survey of 6-year-old children and their parents in a German urban population. *Journal of Child Psychology and Psychiatry, 46*(4), 385–393.

Lundgren, J. D., Allison, K. C., Crow, S., O'Reardon, J. P., Berg, K. C., Galbraith, J., . . . Stunkard, A. J. (2006). Prevalence of the night eating syndrome in a psychiatric population. *American Journal of Psychiatry, 163*(1), 156–158.

Lundgren, J. D., Allison, K. C., O'Reardon, J. P., & Stunkard, A. J. (2008). A descriptive study of non-obese persons with night eating syndrome and a weight-matched comparison group. *Eating Behaviors, 9*(3), 343–351.

Lundgren, J. D., Allison, K. C., Stunkard, A. J., Bulik, C. M., Thornton, L. M., Karin Lindroos, A., & Rasmussen, F. (2012). Lifetime medical and psychiatric comorbidity of night eating behavior in the Swedish Twin Study of Adults: Genes and Environment (STAGE). *Psychiatry Research, 199*(2), 145–149.

Lundgren, J. D., Allison, K. C., Vinai, P., & Gluck, M. E. (2012). Assessment instruments for night eating syndrome. In J. D. Lundgren, K. C. Allison, & A. J. Stunkard (Eds.), *Night eating syndrome: Research, assessment, and treatment*. New York, NY: Guilford.

Lundgren, J. D., McCune, A., Spresser, C., Harkins, P., Zolton, L., & Mandal, K. (2011). Night eating patterns of individuals with eating disorders: Implications for conceptualizing the night eating syndrome. *Psychiatry Research, 186*(1), 103–108.

Lundgren, J. D., Shapiro, J. R., & Bulik, C. M. (2008). Night eating patterns of patients with bulimia nervosa: A preliminary report. *Eating and Weight Disorders, 13*(4), 171–175.

Marshall, H. M., Allison, K. C., O'Reardon, J. P., Birketvedt, G., & Stunkard, A. J. (2004). Night eating syndrome among nonobese persons. *International Journal of Eating Disorders, 35*(2), 217–222.

McCune, A. M., & Lundgren, J. D. (2015). Bright light therapy for the treatment of night eating syndrome: A pilot study. *Psychiatry Research, 229*(1-2), 577–579.

Miyaoka, T., Yasukawa, R., Tsubouchi, K., Miura, S., Shimizu, Y., Sukegawa, T., . . . Horiguchi, J. (2003). Successful treatment of nocturnal eating/drinking syndrome with selective serotonin reuptake inhibitors. *International Clinical Psychopharmacology, 18*(3), 175–177.

Munsch, S., Meyer, A. H., & Biedert, E. (2012). Efficacy and predictors of long-term treatment success for cognitive–behavioral treatment and behavioral weight-loss treatment in overweight individuals with binge eating disorder. *Behaviour Research and Therapy, 50*(12), 775–785.

O'Reardon, J. P., Allison, K. C., Martino, N. S., Lundgren, J. D., Heo, M., & Stunkard, A. J. (2006). A randomized, placebo-controlled trial of sertraline in the treatment of night eating syndrome. *American Journal of Psychiatry, 163*(5), 893–898.

O'Reardon, J. P., Ringel, B. L., Dinges, D. F., Allison, K. C., Rogers, N. S., Martino, N. S., & Stunkard, A. J. (2004). Circadian eating and sleeping patterns in the night eating syndrome. *Obesity Research, 12*, 1789–1796.

O'Reardon, J. P., Stunkard, A. J., & Allison, K. C. (2004). A clinical trial of sertraline in the treatment of night eating syndrome. *International Journal of Eating Disorders, 35*(1), 16–26.

Pawlow, L. A., O'Neil, P. M., & Malcolm, R. J. (2003). Night eating syndrome: Effects of brief relaxation training on stress, mood, hunger, and eating patterns. *International Journal of Obesity and Related Metabolic Disorders, 27*(8), 970–978.

Perlis, M. L., Smith, M. T., Jungquist, C., Nowakowski, S., Orff, H., & Soeffing, J. (2010). Cognitive–behavioral therapy for insomnia. In H. P. Attarian & C. Schuman (Eds.), *Clinical handbook of insomnia* (pp. 281–296). New York, NY: Humana Press.

Rand, C. S. W., Macgregor, A. M. C., & Stunkard, A. J. (1997). The night eating syndrome in the general population and among postoperative obesity surgery patients. *International Journal of Eating Disorders, 22*(1), 65–69.

Runfola, C. D., Allison, K. C., Hardy, K. K., Lock, J., & Peebles, R. (2014). Prevalence and clinical significance of night eating syndrome in university students. *Journal of Adolescent Health, 55*(1), 41–48.

Saraçlı, Ö., Atasoy, N., Akdemir, A., Güriz, O., Konuk, N., Sevinçer, G. M., . . . Atik, L. (2015). The prevalence and clinical features of the night eating syndrome in psychiatric out-patient population. *Comprehensive Psychiatry, 57*, 79–84.

Striegel-Moore, R. H., Franko, D. L., & Garcia, J. (2009). The validity and clinical utility of night eating syndrome. *International Journal of Eating Disorders, 42*(8), 720–738.

Striegel-Moore, R. H., Franko, D. L., May, A., Ach, E., Thompson, D., & Hook, J. M. (2006). Should night eating syndrome be included in the DSM? *International Journal of Eating Disorders, 39*(7), 544–549.

Striegel-Moore, R. H., Franko, D. L., Thompson, D., Affenito, S., & Kraemer, H. C. (2006). Night eating: Prevalence and demographic correlates. *Obesity, 14*(1), 139–147.

Stunkard, A. J. (1976). *The pain of obesity*. Palo Alto, CA: Bull Publishing.

Stunkard, A. J., Allison, K. C., Lundgren, J. D., Martino, N. S., Heo, M., Etemad, B., & O'Reardon, J. P. (2006). A paradigm for facilitating pharmacotherapy at a distance: Sertraline treatment of the night eating syndrome. *Journal of Clinical Psychiatry, 67*(10), 1568–1572.

Stunkard, A. J., Berkowitz, R., Wadden, T., Tanrikut, C., Reiss, E., & Young, L. (1996). Binge eating disorder and the night-eating syndrome. *International Journal of Obesity and Related Metabolic Disorders, 20*, 1–6.

Stunkard, A. J., Grace, W. J., & Wolff, H. G. (1955). The night-eating syndrome: A pattern of food intake among certain obese patients. *American Journal of Medicine, 19*, 78–86.

Tzischinsky, O., & Latzer, Y. (2004). Nocturnal eating prevalence, features and night sleep among binge eating disorders and bulimia nervosa patients in Israel. *European Eating Disorders Review, 12*, 101–109.

Vander Wal, J. S., Gang, C. H., Griffing, G. T., & Gadde, K. M. (2012). Escitalopram for treatment of night eating syndrome: A 12-week, randomized, placebo-controlled trial. *Journal of Clinical Psychopharmacology, 32*(3), 341–345.

Vander Wal, J. S., Maraldo, T. M., Vercellone, A. C., & Gagne, D. A. (2015). Education, progressive muscle relaxation therapy, and exercise for the treatment of night eating syndrome: A pilot study. *Appetite, 89*, 136–144.

Vinai, P., Cardetti, S., Studt, S., Carpegna, G., Ferrato, N., Vallauri, P., . . . Manconi, M. (2014). Clinical validity of the descriptor "presence of a belief that one must eat in order to get to sleep" in diagnosing the night eating syndrome. *Appetite, 75*, 46–48.

Vinai, P., Provini, F., Antelmi, E., Marcatelli, M., Cardetti, S., Vinai, L., . . . Allison, K. C. (2015). Alexithymia is not related to severity of night eating behavior: A useful distinction from other eating disorders. *Eating Behaviors, 17*, 94–98.

Wilde, M. H., & Garvin, S. (2007). A concept analysis of self-monitoring. *Journal of Advanced Nursing, 57*(3), 339–350.

Williamson, D. A., Lawson, O. D., Bennett, S. M., & Hinz, L. (1989). Behavioral treatment of night bingeing and rumination in an adult case of bulimia nervosa. *Journal of Behavior Therapy and Experimental Psychiatry, 20*(1), 73–77.

Winkelman, J. W. (2003). Treatment of nocturnal eating syndrome and sleep-related eating disorder with topiramate. *Sleep Medicine, 4*(3), 243–246.

13

Diabetes and Eating Disorders

LIANA ABASCAL AND ANN GOEBEL-FABBRI ■

Treating a patient with an eating disorder can be challenging and complicated. When comorbidity with diabetes exists, yet another layer of medical and psychological complexity is added. These two diseases can be intricately entwined, and their combined impact on the patient needs to be understood and managed for treatment to be successful. This chapter is aimed at helping the clinician with eating disorder expertise gain more understanding of how diabetes influences an eating disorder presentation and diagnosis and affects the treatment approach for these two conditions.

TYPE 1 AND TYPE 2 DIABETES

Although type 1 and type 2 diabetes are similarly named, they are different chronic diseases with different etiologies and treatment approaches. Type 1 diabetes was previously referred to as "juvenile diabetes" because it is most often diagnosed in childhood; however, it can develop at any age (Haller, 2013). It is an autoimmune condition in which the immune system attacks the insulin-producing cells in the pancreas (beta cells), preventing the production and release of insulin. Insulin is a hormone that allows energy from glucose in the bloodstream to be absorbed by the cells. Without it, the body cannot use the calories from food, glucose levels rise in the blood, and the cells are in a starvation state. Therefore, treatment for type 1 diabetes consists of the administration of insulin through syringe or insulin pump (Haller, 2013). Patients are asked to check their blood glucose levels with a blood glucose meter at least four times a day and either dose appropriately with insulin if their number is higher than targeted or consume some form of glucose (food) if their number is lower than targeted. The target blood glucose range is between 80 and 130 mg/dl for uncomplicated diabetes. Any time a patient consumes a food containing carbohydrates (with a few exceptions), he or she is expected to dose appropriately with insulin—this is because carbohydrates have the greatest influence on blood glucose levels (Haller, 2013). Unfortunately, type 1 diabetes can be an unpredictable and relentless disease. Routinely following current sophisticated care protocols does not guarantee consistent outcomes; patients often feel frustrated with their efforts and results, potentially leading to diabetes distress and burnout (Polonsky, 1999).

Type 2 diabetes was previously referred to as "adult-onset diabetes" because it was once mostly seen in adults. Increasingly, type 2 diabetes is being diagnosed in a younger population (Pinhas-Hamiel & Zeitler, 2005). In type 2 diabetes, the body develops insulin resistance, where it does not use insulin properly. In early stages of the disease, the pancreas makes extra insulin as an attempt to compensate for it. However, over time it is not able to keep up and cannot make enough insulin to keep blood glucose levels in a healthy range. Type 2 diabetes is primarily, but not exclusively, associated with obesity (American Diabetes Association [ADA], n.d.). It is initially treated with lifestyle changes (exercise, healthy diet, and weight loss), oral medications, and eventually insulin (ADA, n.d.).

For both type 1 and type 2 diabetes, the hemoglobin A1C test is typically used to measure and evaluate diabetes management (ADA, n.d.). The A1C is a blood test reflecting the 3-month average of blood glucose levels. The recommended A1C target is less than 7% (ADA, n.d.). This is a challenging goal for those with type 1 diabetes, even with reliable adherence to prescribed treatment protocols; those with type 2 diabetes may be more readily able to reach this goal. Intensive diabetes management is crucial to preventing diabetes complications in both type 1 and type 2 diabetes. Medical complications of diabetes include nerve damage resulting in pain and numbness (neuropathy), eye disease (retinopathy), kidney disease (nephropathy), cardiac disease, stroke, high blood pressure, and difficulty healing, which may result in amputation. The Diabetes Control and Complications Trial (DCCT) and the United Kingdom Prospective Diabetes Study (UKPDS) were instrumental in showing that a reduction in A1C corresponded to a reduction of risk of complications in both type 1 and type 2 diabetes, respectively (DCCT Research Group, 1993; ADA, 1998).

PREVALENCE OF EATING DISORDERS IN THE DIABETES POPULATION

Evidence suggests that women with type 1 diabetes are 2.4 times more at risk for developing an eating disorder and 1.9 times more at risk for developing subthreshold eating disorders compared to women without diabetes (Jones, Lawson, Daneman, Olmsted, & Rodin, 2000). These behaviors have been found to persist, become more common, and increase in severity over time (Colton, Olmsted, Daneman, Rydall, & Rodin, 2004; Peveler et al., 2005). Disordered eating behaviors may include dieting; binge eating; or compensatory behaviors such as self-induced vomiting, laxative or diuretic use, excessive exercise, or insulin restriction (unique to type 1 diabetes; discussed later) (Olmsted, Colton, Daneman, Rydall, & Rodin, 2008). A recent meta-analysis of 13 studies found that both disordered eating and eating disorders were more common in adolescents with type 1 diabetes compared with peers (Young et al., 2013). Another review of prevalence rates found that binge-eating disorder (BED) varied from 1.4% to 10% in adults with type 2 diabetes, was approximately 6% in adolescents with type 2 diabetes, and was 1.7% in adolescents with type 1 diabetes (Pinhas-Hamiel & Levy-Shraga, 2003).

Type 1 diabetes patients may engage in insulin restriction, or omission, as a purging behavior, which results in dangerous and rapid weight loss. The eating disorder involving this behavior is often referred to as "diabulimia." Although no specific diagnostic criteria exist, it can be categorized as bulimia nervosa if binge eating is present because the criteria for compensatory behaviors include "misuse of medications" (American Psychiatric Association [APA], 2013). In the absence of binge eating, diabulimia can classified as other specified feeding or eating disorder (OSFED; APA, 2013). When insulin is omitted, or less is taken than indicated, glucose cannot be processed, driving up blood glucose levels and resulting in glucose being excreted from the body through urine. As many as 57% of young women with type 1 diabetes report intentional insulin restriction, with rates of this behavior peaking in late adolescence and early adulthood (Pinhas-Hamiel & Levy-Shraga, 2003; Polonsky et al., 1994). Although awareness of diabulimia or insulin restriction has increased within the medical community, this sometimes means that eating disorders without insulin restriction can go unrecognized in a diabetes patient. It is important to note that not all patients with disordered eating and type 1 diabetes restrict insulin, but they may still meet the diagnostic criteria for anorexia, bulimia, or BED.

CONSEQUENCES

By far the greatest consequences seen with comorbid diabetes and eating disorders have been studied and reported in patients with type 1 diabetes. There is significant evidence that patients with type 1 diabetes and disordered eating are in poorer glycemic control (with higher A1Cs); have higher rates of hospital and emergency room visits; and are at increased risk for life-threatening diabetic complications, including repeated diabetic ketoacidosis (DKA), kidney failure, retinopathy, neuropathy, cardiovascular disease, stroke, and coma (Bryden et al., 1999; Larrañaga, Docet, & García-Mayor, 2011; Polonsky et al., 1994; Rodin et al., 2002; Rydall, Rodin, Olmsted, Devenyi, & Daneman, 1997; Verrotti, Catino, De Luca, Morgese, & Chiarelli, 1999; Young et al., 2013). The types and severity of complications observed in this population tend to be more advanced than expected for age and duration of diabetes, especially for those endorsing insulin restriction.

Mortality rates are also troubling in this type 1 diabetes population. One study reported mortality rates (per 1000 person-years) as 2.2 in girls with type 1 diabetes (and no eating disorder), 7.3 in girls with eating disorders (and no diabetes), and 34.6 in girls with both type 1 diabetes and an eating disorder (Nielsen, Emborg, & Mølbak, 2002). In a 12-year follow-up of 14 women with type 1 diabetes and anorexia, a mortality rate of 36% was found; the median age of the patients who died was 30 years (range, 25–42 years), with the median duration of diabetes at death of 19 years (range, 14–26 years) (Walker, Young, Little, & Steel, 2002). Merely endorsing insulin restriction alone has been shown to increase mortality risk threefold during an 11-year follow-up period (Goebel-Fabbri et al., 2008).

Within the type 2 diabetes population, there is less research examining the consequences of eating disorder behaviors. Most studies have reported the correlates of binge eating and/or BED comorbid with type 2 diabetes because this is the most frequently observed eating disorder in this population. There are mixed findings regarding the association between A1C and binge eating symptoms (Herbozo, Flynn, Stevens, & Betancourt, 2015). Some studies have found no association between binge eating and/or BED and A1C (Crow, Kendall, Praus, & Thuras, 2001; Gorin et al., 2008; Wing, Marcus, Epstein, Blair, & Burton,1989), whereas others have found positive associations. Kenardy et al. (2001) found that binge eating frequency predicted blood glucose levels after controlling for body mass index (BMI) and exercise level. Mannucci et al. (2002) found a significant positive correlation between severity of eating disorder symptoms and A1C values. There is additional support that type 2 diabetes patients with BED have higher A1Cs, BMIs, triglyceride levels, and rates of hospitalization compared to patients without BED (Meneghini, Spadola, & Florez, 2006; Nicolau et al., 2015).

MODEL OF RISK

The increased prevalence of eating disorders within the diabetes population can potentially be attributed to several factors. Diabetes is strongly associated with a number of the risk factors for eating disorders. For example, people with both type 1 and type 2 diabetes have twice the risk of clinically significant depression compared to those without diabetes (De Groot, Anderson, Freedland, Clouse, & Lustman, 2001). At the time of diagnosis of type 1 diabetes, patients typically have lost a significant amount of weight. Insulin therapy allows for necessary weight regain because the body is again able to utilize calories from food; however, this can sometimes lead to gaining excess weight. Research has found an association between intensive diabetes management and a risk of weight gain (DCCT Research Group, 1988; Domargard et al., 1999). Long-term follow-up with type 1 diabetes patients implies that this weight was difficult to lose (DCCT Research Group, 2001). It may be that the experience of rapid weight loss and regain heightens the risk of an eating disorder among those who may have already been vulnerable prior to their diabetes diagnosis. Fear of this weight gain may create a barrier against appropriate insulin use and to intensive diabetes management. However, these weight gain findings were reported prior to the more sophisticated insulin protocols and technologies available today and therefore may no longer translate to more modern diabetes management. Type 1 and type 2 diabetes treatment involves close attention to food portions and weight, which cannot be avoided but can also be seen as similar to an eating disorder mindset (Goebel-Fabbri, Fikkan,

Connell, Vangsness, & Anderson, 2002). In fact, patients with type 2 diabetes are regularly advised to change their diets and lose weight, which can lead to restriction/binge cycles, priming patients for BED. There is also the risk that binge eating can contribute to weight gain, which can then become a risk factor for developing type 2 diabetes (ADA, n.d.). These weight issues, together with dietary restraints, could further promote and exacerbate the onset of disordered eating (Pinhas-Hamiel & Levy-Shraga, 2003).

TREATMENT RESEARCH

Few studies have examined specific treatment interventions for patients with comorbid diabetes and eating disorders, and they have generally consisted of case studies, nonequivalent control groups, pre–post and other nonexperimental designs, and randomized designs that are psychoeducational in nature.

Type 1 Diabetes and Anorexia Nervosa, Bulimia Nervosa, Binge-Eating Disorder, and Diabulimia

Most research has examined treatment of eating disorders in the type 1 diabetes population, and results have been inconsistent. A small but randomized study of a psychoeducational intervention in a subclinical population found no behavioral or metabolic improvements (Alloway, Toth, & McCargar, 2001). Another randomized psychoeducational intervention study found improvement in reported eating disorder symptoms in a subclinical eating disorder sample but no reduction in insulin omission or improvement in A1C (Olmsted, Daneman, Rydall, Lawson, & Rodin, 2002). Peveler and Fairburn (1989, 1992) conducted a series of case studies of modified cognitive–behavioral therapy with anorexia nervosa and bulimia nervosa patients and were able to show improved A1Cs and eating disorder symptoms. A small study in Japan compared the nonrandomized outcomes of inpatient therapy with outpatient therapy in bulimia nervosa patients and found greater improvements in A1C and eating disorder pathology in the inpatient group; however, average length of inpatient stay was 112 days, limiting the generalizability to the US health care system (Takii et al., 2003). A recent study examined pre–post residential treatment outcomes, and observed significant reductions in blood glucose, eating disorder symptoms, and psychological concerns with a treatment dose response in the psychological symptoms (Dickens, Haynos, Nunnemaker, Platka-Bird, & Dolores, 2015).

Despite some positive results described previously, there is also evidence that patients with comorbid type 1 diabetes do less well in treatment than those without diabetes. Peveler and Fairburn's (1992) case studies suggested that eating disorder symptoms may be more difficult to treat in those with type 1 diabetes than in those without diabetes. Custal et al. (2014) compared outcomes of conventional eating disorder treatment (not customized for diabetes) in patients with type 1 diabetes to those of a matched group without diabetes and found higher dropout rates and poorer treatment outcome in those with diabetes. The authors noted that patients who engaged in insulin omission tended to have lower motivation and gave up easily when frustrated. Colton, Olmsted, Wong, and Rodin (2015) performed a case review of 100 patients with type 1 diabetes who attended a partial hospitalization program for eating disorders, and they found that the patients with diabetes had poorer outcomes and were less likely to achieve full symptom remission than the comparison group without diabetes. They hypothesized that individuals with diabetes may require more sustained or individualized interventions to support behavioral change, given that more complex changes, involving all aspects of diabetes management, are required for stabilization and recovery (Colton et al., 2015).

Treatment Approach

Despite the fact that few treatment outcome studies have been performed, clinical experts do agree on several approaches to care and treatment (Goebel-Fabbri et al., 2009). A multidisciplinary team approach to treatment is considered the standard of care for both eating disorders and diabetes treatment (APA, 2013; Goebel-Fabbri, 2009; Mitchell, Pomeroy, &Adson, 1997). Prior to outpatient treatment, some patients may need a medical or psychiatric hospitalization until they are medically/psychiatrically stable and able to engage in outpatient care. Outpatient teams should include a psychotherapist, a dietician, a psychiatrist, and an endocrinologist, and team members should communicate frequently to maintain congruent treatment goals. Ideally, the therapist should have expertise in both eating disorders and diabetes, but there are few professionals with both of these skill sets. At a minimum, the therapist should be an eating disorder specialist who is interested and willing to learn about the role that type 1 diabetes plays in eating disorders. Laboratory tests, including A1C, and weight should be monitored frequently (Goebel-Fabbri, 2009). The outpatient treatment team must be willing to work collaboratively with the patient to establish small goals that the patient believes are realistic and achievable. This is especially important if a patient has been omitting or restricting insulin.

A critical initial treatment goal involves the patient's ability to maintain medical safety, preventing DKA through routine daily injections of basal insulin (providing 24-hour background coverage). If the patient cannot do this consistently, then he or she may not be safely treated as an outpatient. It is also crucial to improve blood glucose ranges slowly and cautiously. Decreasing A1Cs too quickly is associated with serious risks, creating "treatment-induced complications." Currently, no formal treatment guidelines address how to reduce this risk in a standardized way. However, it is recommended that physicians decrease A1C less than 2 points for every 3-month interval (Gibbons & Freeman, 2014).

It is helpful to discuss and anticipate challenges that might prompt a patient to drop out of treatment. A frequent challenge of this kind is the significant amount of fluid-related weight gain associated with appropriate insulin levels and improved blood sugar. Patients should be educated that this "insulin edema" may trigger body image concerns leading them to feel fat, bloated, and uncomfortable. Edema can be frightening and can trigger relapse, and patients may benefit from frequent reassurance that this fluid retention is temporary. They should be encouraged to drink plenty of water. Some physicians may choose to prescribe a 1-month supply of a low-dose diuretic in order to help the patient tolerate this stage of treatment. Once fluid levels have stabilized, patients' ongoing fears about weight gain unrelated to edema must also be taken seriously. This, too, may decrease the risk of treatment dropout by reinforcing trust in the treatment team.

Type 2 and Binge Eating or Binge-Eating Disorder

No studies have examined treatment of binge eating or BED within a type 2 population. For this reason, what follows are suggestions for how empirically supported treatments for BED may need to be adapted in small ways to address the specific needs of patients with type 2 diabetes. These ideas are rooted in clinical experience and have not been empirically tested.

TREATMENT APPROACH

The treatment literature on binge eating and BED supports the effectiveness of cognitive–behavioral therapy and interpersonal therapy (Mitchell, Devlin, de Zwaan, Crow, & Peterson, 2008). Either approach can be successfully applied to these problems in type 2 diabetes with some modifications that are detailed here (Gagnon, Aimé, Bélanger, & Markowitz, 2012). As is the case for type 1 diabetes, treatment should involve a multidisciplinary team approach—ideally one in which team members are well-versed in issues related to type 2 diabetes (Gagnon et al., 2012; Mitchell et al., 1997).

Treatment often begins with the recommendation to adopt a regular eating pattern in order to try to address the fact that food restriction can trigger binge eating, which then can reinforce the perceived need for food restriction (Fairburn, 2013). Patients are encouraged to keep food records including the time of day, types and amounts of food consumed, context and feelings, and if the eating episode is defined as a binge or not. When integrated into the treatment of bingeing and BED in type 2 diabetes, patients should also record their blood sugar values approximately 2 hours after the meal, snack, or binge. This will help them to learn the impact that their eating patterns have on their diabetes management and can often underscore the need and increase the motivation to change.

Medical providers should understand the struggle and shame involved in binge eating and be able to take a sensitive and nonjudgmental approach, especially because treatment will often involve recommendations to lose weight. The patient may sometimes feel as if the medical and the psychological sides of the team are providing contradictory advice. Patients may interpret their doctor's weight loss recommendations to mean rigid dietary restriction as opposed to the routine eating plan recommended by the eating disorder specialists. This underscores the importance of clear communication between team members in order to emphasize both regular eating and an approach that involves moderate portions for slow and sustainable weight loss.

Binge eating and BED treatments also emphasize identifying negative cognitions and healthier strategies for coping with painful affect (Fairburn, 2013; Mitchell et al., 2008). Eating disorder specialists should be cognizant than some of these thoughts and feelings may be specific to diabetes. For example, patients may blame themselves for developing diabetes, they may perceive diabetes complications as inevitable or even deserved, and they may feel at fault for blood sugar variation. Although these ideas are diabetes specific, they can be readily integrated into cognitive restructuring exercises. Patients are also taught healthier coping skills to help them prevent binge eating during times of distress.

Medications for type 2 diabetes can be classified into two broad categories: those associated with weight gain and those that are either weight neutral or even associated with weight loss. Experts in diabetes treatment recommend avoiding those medicines with the risk of weight gain, if possible, and starting with those that do not have this side effect profile (Hamdy & Carver, 2008). This can help reduce patients' frustration, increase their sense of efficacy, and promote trust in their treaters.

CLINICAL CASE EXAMPLES

Two case examples are presented next to help elucidate the clinical presentation of patients with comorbid eating disorders and diabetes. The first is a "typical" presentation of diabulimia; the second is an example of type 2 and BED.

Example 1: "Diabulimia"

Jenny is a 26-year-old patient with type 1 diabetes since age 13. She had difficulty adjusting to the diagnosis of type 1 diabetes and the burden of self-care that it involves. She lost approximately 10 pounds before being diagnosed and was happy with how her body looked. She received lots of positive feedback from classmates and marveled at how she could lose weight without paying attention to what she was eating. Her parents were concerned by her rapid weight loss and insatiable thirst. Her primary care doctor took a blood glucose reading and sent her and her family to the hospital for confirmation of type 1 diabetes. After a 3-day hospital stay, Jenny's weight was higher than before the weight loss. This was mostly due to replenishment of fluids, but this was not explained to Jenny or her parents. She was started on an insulin regimen in which she would take a long-acting insulin injection at night and take short-acting insulin as needed during the day based on carbohydrate intake or for "corrections" of her blood glucose readings. She and her family met with a Certified Diabetes Educator, from whom they learned the importance of attention to food. Jenny was asked to weigh all her food and keep a log of what she ate, her carbohydrate estimates, her blood glucose numbers, and her insulin doses. This was meant to help her learn how to estimate and count carbohydrates for more accurate insulin dosing.

After several months, Jenny's A1C was down to 7.2%; however, her weight was still higher than it had been before her weight loss and diagnosis. Jenny felt unhappy and self-conscious about her weight and body size. She began reducing the amount of insulin she took in order to lose weight quickly, remembering how her body reacted before being diagnosed and starting insulin. At her next endocrinologist appointment, her A1C had crept up to 8.9%. Jenny denied any knowledge of what could have caused this change. Her diabetes specialist hypothesized that puberty hormones could be affecting her body's insulin sensitivity and making blood glucose management more difficult. This pattern continued and escalated over the course of several years. Jenny would restrict or omit the amount of insulin she took whenever she could. Her A1Cs were generally in the 10–14% range. She was admitted to intensive care treatment multiple times in order treat DKA resulting from dangerously high blood sugars.

Both her parents and her endocrinologist suspected intentional restriction and no longer believed this to be "typical" teenage lackadaisical behavior. Jenny's parents began closely watching what she ate and how much insulin she took. She became more creative in the appearance of reliable diabetes self-care. For example, she would falsify her log, only check her blood glucose when she knew she was in an "OK" range, and mastered how to make it look like she was giving herself an injection but not actually pierce the skin. Sometimes after a hospital scare, she would start taking her insulin as prescribed and being what she called "a good diabetic." However, she would gain weight from "insulin edema," which left her feeling bloated and "like I gained 20 pounds overnight." That feeling would trigger her to relapse into restricting insulin again.

Jenny's parents were very concerned by what they observed. They recognized the fluctuations in Jenny's weight, energy, and mood. Her unexplained high A1Cs values were worrisome, but the repeated DKA episodes were especially frightening. Jenny also seemed to be withdrawing from them, and they felt sure that she was hiding something. They spoke with her about their concern that she had an eating disorder. They urged her to see an eating disorder specialist, but Jenny refused and claimed that she did not have a problem. Without treatment and because of her ongoing medical instability, Jenny's parents would not allow her to go to college away from home. Instead, she attended a local community college and continue to live with them.

By age 22, Jenny began having neuropathy (diabetes-related nerve pain) in her feet, and a routine dilated eye exam found mild retinopathy (the early stage of diabetes-related eye disease). Jenny feared for her health and was also finally able to acknowledge the toll her eating disorder had taken on her life. It affected her family relationship, friendships, got in the way of romantic relationships, kept her living at home, and caused her to live in and out of the hospital. After another episode of DKA and week-long hospitalization, she decided that she had to do something. Jenny agreed to take her long-acting insulin consistently. If she could reliably reach this small goal, she could prevent DKA and likely keep herself out of the hospital. Future goals would involve gradually increasing her short-acting insulin and slowly improving her blood sugars. After years of refusing treatment, Jenny agreed to work with an eating disorder specialist who would collaborate with her diabetes team. Together, they would aim to support her as she faced the likelihood of insulin edema and possible healthy weight restoration, as well as help her to reach small goals for diabetes management. She would also need the help of widely used eating disorder treatments adapted for the unique aspects of type 1 diabetes management through the recommendations of her diabetes team.

Example 2: Binge Eating and Type 2 Diabetes

Lori is a 55-year-old woman who works full-time in customer service, has been married for 25 years, and has two children. Lori has struggled with her weight since high school when she broke her ankle and could no longer play competitive soccer. Her weight increased significantly after the birth of her first child. She has made weight loss attempts, has succeeded in losing the weight, but has repeatedly struggled to maintain the weight loss. During her second pregnancy, she developed gestational diabetes and was required to check her blood glucose and watch her carbohydrate intake. After the birth of her second child, she resumed working full-time and cared for her family. She would often skip meals or have small snacks during her busy workday, share a healthy dinner with her family, and then consume the majority of her calories after her children went to bed. She admits that this felt like a "reward" to her after a difficult day. Five years after the birth of her second child, she was told by her doctor that she had insulin resistance and was "prediabetic." Her doctor encouraged her to lose weight to try to prevent the onset of type 2 diabetes. She started a commercial weight loss plan and lost 55 pounds. Her blood glucose numbers normalized. However, after 8 months, her weight began to creep up and she found herself quickly in the prediabetic range again. She attempted to be more rigid about what she ate, but she noticed how her after-dinner "rewards" grew increasingly larger. Lori felt intense shame as the cycle of daytime restriction and evening binging became out of control. After a year in the prediabetic range, Lori found herself at her highest weight, was diagnosed with type 2 diabetes, and was started on oral diabetes medicine. Her diabetes team explained to Lori that they would attempt to choose diabetes medicines that would either be weight neutral or perhaps even aid in weight loss. She blamed herself for "failing at weight loss" and "causing her diabetes." After each binge, she would wake up with high blood sugar readings feeling bad physically and even worse emotionally.

Despite Lori's embarrassment, she reached out to her diabetes treatment team. Her dietician was kind and approachable—responding with understanding. She told Lori that this was a common struggle and provided her with a referral to a therapy group for binge eaters. Through a collaborative process, Lori would learn the importance of incorporating meals and snacks throughout the day and that food restriction would actually fuel her binge eating. She worked hard to develop a flexible approach to healthy eating. For the first time, she also began to learn strategies to manage stress and other negative emotions without turning to food for comfort. This approach helped her learn how to prevent binges and work to create a healthier approach to eating and weight.

CONCLUSION

Comorbidity of eating disorders and diabetes can be challenging and complicated to treat. Although prevalence numbers are not high, the complications of this comorbidity are devastating. Understanding the combined impact on patient needs as well as adopting a multidisciplinary approach are crucial for treatment success. Research on this population needs to continue, focusing on reducing treatment dropout, which seems to especially plague the type 1 population, and on improving clinical outcomes. Additional resources, collaboration, and education for the eating disorder field will help increase knowledge regarding these two comorbid conditions, ultimately benefiting patients.

RESOURCES

The following resources may prove helpful for eating disorder professionals who want to learn about diabetes and eating disorders:

> "From Research to Practice" special eating disorder section. (2009).
> *Diabetes Spectrum, 22*(3), 135–162.
> Goebel-Fabbri, A. E. (2017). *Prevention and recovery from eating disorders in type 1 diabetes: Injecting hope.* New York, NY: Routledge.

REFERENCES

Alloway, S. C., Toth, E. L., & McCargar, L. J. (2001). Effectiveness of a group psychoeducation program for the treatment of subclinical disordered eating in women with type 1 diabetes. *Canadian Journal of Dietetic Practice and Research, 62*(4), 188–192.

American Diabetes Association. (n.d.). http://www.diabetes.org.

American Diabetes Association. (1998). Implications of the United Kingdom Prospective Diabetes Study. *Diabetes Care, 21*, 2180–2184.

American Psychiatric Association. (2013). *Diagnostic and statistical manual of mental disorders* (5th ed.). Arlington, VA: American Psychiatric Publishing.

Bryden, K. S., Neil, A., Mayou, R. A., Peveler, R. C., Fairburn, C. G., & Dunger, D. B. (1999). Eating habits, body weight, and insulin misuse. A longitudinal study of teenagers and young adults with type 1 diabetes. *Diabetes Care, 22*, 1956–1960.

Colton, P., Olmsted, M., Daneman, D., Rydall, A., & Rodin, G. (2004). Disturbed eating behavior and eating disorders in preteen and early teenage girls with type 1 diabetes: A case–controlled study. *Diabetes Care, 27*, 1654–1659.

Colton, P. A., Olmsted, M. P., Wong, H., & Rodin, G. M. (2015). Eating disorders in individuals with type 1 diabetes: Case series and day hospital treatment outcome. *European Eating Disorders Review, 23,* 312–317.

Crow, S., Kendall, D., Praus, B., & Thuras, P. (2001). Binge eating and other psychopathology in patients with type II diabetes mellitus. *International Journal of Eating Disorders, 30,* 222–226.

Custal, N., Arcelus, J., Agüera, Z., Bove, F. I., Wales, J., Granero, R., . . . Fernandez-Aranda, F. (2014). Treatment outcome of patients with comorbid type 1 diabetes and eating disorders. *BMC Psychiatry, 14,* 140.

De Groot, M., Anderson, R., Freedland, K. E., Clouse, R. E., & Lustman, P. J. (2001). Association of depression and diabetes complications: A meta-analysis. *Psychosomatic Medicine, 63,* 619–630.

The Diabetes Control and Complications Trial Research Group. (1988). Weight gain associated with intensive therapy in the Diabetes Control and Complications Trial. *Diabetes Care, 11,* 567–573.

The Diabetes Control and Complications Trial Research Group. (1993). The effect of intensive treatment of diabetes on the development and progression of long-term complications in insulin-dependent diabetes mellitus. *New England Journal of Medicine, 329,* 977–986.

The Diabetes Control and Complications Trial Research Group. (2001). Influence of intensive diabetes treatment on body weight and composition of adults with type 1 diabetes in the Diabetes Control and Complications Trial. *Diabetes Care, 24,* 1711–1721.

Dickens, Y. L., Haynos, A. F., Nunnemaker, S., Platka-Bird, L., & Dolores, J. (2015). Multidisciplinary residential treatment of type 1 diabetes mellitus and co-occurring eating disorders. *Eating Disorders, 23*(2), 134–143.

Domargard, A., Sarnblad, S., Kroon, M., Karlsson, I., Skeppner, G., & Aman, J. (1999). Increased prevalence of overweight in adolescent girls with type 1 diabetes mellitus. *Acta Paediatrica, 88,* 1223–1228.

Fairburn, C. G. (2013). *Overcoming binge eating* (2nd ed.). New York, NY: Guilford.

Gagnon, C., Aimé, A., Bélanger, C., & Markowitz, J. T. (2012). Comorbid diabetes and eating disorders in adult patients: Assessment and considerations for treatment. *Diabetes Education, 38*(4), 537–542.

Gibbons, C. H., & Freeman, R. (2014). Treatment-induced neuropathy of diabetes: An acute, iatrogenic complication of diabetes. *Brain, 138,* 43–52.

Goebel-Fabbri, A. E. (2009). Disturbed eating behaviors and eating disorders in type 1 diabetes: Clinical significance and treatment recommendations. *Current Diabetes Reports, 9,* 133–139.

Goebel-Fabbri, A. E., Fikkan, J., Connell, A., Vangsness, L., & Anderson, B. J. (2002). Identification and treatment of eating disorders in women with type 1 diabetes mellitus. *Treatments in Endocrinology, 1,* 155–162.

Goebel-Fabbri, A. E., Fikkan, J., Franko, D. L., Pearson, K., Anderson, B. J., & Weinger, K. (2008). Insulin restriction and associated morbidity and mortality in women with type 1 diabetes. *Diabetes Care, 31,* 415–419.

Goebel-Fabbri, A. E., Polonsky, W., Uplinger, N., Gerkin, S., Mangham, D., Moxness, R., . . . Parkin, C. (2009). Outpatient management of eating disorders in type 1 diabetes. *Diabetes Spectrum, 22*(3), 147–152.

Gorin, A., Niemeier, H. M., Hogan, P., Coday, M., Davis, C., DiLillo, V., . . . Yanovski, S. Z; Look AHEAD Research Group. (2008). Binge eating and weight loss outcomes in overweight and obese individuals with type 2 diabetes: Results from the Look AHEAD study. *Archives of General Psychiatry, 65*, 1447–1455.

Haller, M. J. (2013). Type 1 diabetes in the 21st century: A review of the landscape. In A. Peters & L. Laffel (Eds.), *Type 1 diabetes sourcebook* (pp. 1–18). Alexandria, VA: American Diabetes Association.

Hamdy, O., & Carver, C. (2008). The Why WAIT program: Improving clinical outcomes through weight management in type 2 diabetes. *Current Diabetes Reports, 8*(5), 413–420.

Herbozo, S., Flynn, P. M., Stevens, S. D., & Betancourt, H. (2015). Dietary adherence, glycemic control, and psychological factors associated with binge eating among indigenous and non-indigenous Chileans with type 2 diabetes. *International Journal of Behavioral Medicine, 22*, 792–798.

Jones, J. M., Lawson, M. L., Daneman, D., Olmsted, M. P., & Rodin, G. (2000). Eating disorders in adolescent females with and without type 1 diabetes: Cross sectional study. *British Medical Journal, 320*(7249), 1563–1566.

Kenardy, J., Mensch, M., Bowen, K., Green, B., Walton, J., & Dalton, M. (2001). Disordered eating behaviors in women with type 2 diabetes mellitus. *Eating Behaviors, 2*, 183–192.

Larrañaga, A., Docet, M. F., & García-Mayor, R. V. (2011). Disordered eating behaviors in type 1 diabetic patients. *World Journal of Diabetes, 2*(11), 189–195.

Mannucci, E., Tesi, F., Ricca, V., Pierazzuoli, E., Barciulli, E., Moretti, S., . . . Rotella, C. M. (2002). Eating behavior in obese patients with and without type 2 diabetes mellitus. *International Journal of Obesity and Related Metabolic Disorders, 26*(6), 848–853.

Meneghini, L. F., Spadola, J., & Florez, H. (2006). Prevalence and associations of binge eating disorder in a multiethnic population with type 2 diabetes. *Diabetes Care, 29*, 2760.

Mitchell, J., Devlin, M. J., de Zwaan, M., Crow, S. J., & Peterson, C. B. (2008). *Binge-eating disorder: Clinical foundations and treatment.* New York, NY: Guilford.

Mitchell, J., Pomeroy, C., & Adson, D. E. (1997). Managing medical complications. In D. Garner & P. E. Garfinkel (Eds.), *Handbook for treatment of eating disorders* (pp. 383–393). New York, NY: Guilford.

Nicolau, J., Simó, R., Sanchís, P., Ayala, L., Fortuny, R., Zubillaga, I., & Masmiquel, L. (2015). Eating disorders are frequent among type 2 diabetic patients and are associated with worse metabolic and psychological outcomes: Results from a cross-sectional study in primary and secondary care settings. *Acta Diabetologica, 52*(6), 1037–1044.

Nielsen, S., Emborg, C., & Mølbak, A. G. (2002). Mortality in concurrent type 1 diabetes and anorexia nervosa. *Diabetes Care, 25*, 309–312.

Olmsted, M. P., Colton, P. A., Daneman, D., Rydall, A. C., & Rodin, G. M. (2008). Prediction of the onset of disturbed eating behavior in adolescent girls with type 1 diabetes. *Diabetes Care, 31*(10), 1978–1982.

Olmsted, M. P., Daneman, D., Rydall, A. C., Lawson, M. L., & Rodin, G. (2002). The effects of psychoeducation on disturbed eating attitudes and behavior in young women with type 1 diabetes mellitus. *International Journal of Eating Disorders, 32*(2), 230–239.

Peveler, R. C., Bryden, K. S., Neil, H. A., Fairburn, C. G., Mayou, R. A., Dunger, D. B., & Turner, H. M. (2005). The relationship of disordered eating habits and attitudes to clinical outcomes in young adult females with type 1 diabetes. *Diabetes Care, 28*, 84–88.

Peveler, R. C., & Fairburn, C. G. (1989). Anorexia nervosa in association with diabetes mellitus—A cognitive–behavioural approach to treatment. *Behavior Research and Therapy*, *27*, 95–99.

Peveler, R. C., & Fairburn, C. G. (1992). The treatment of bulimia nervosa in patients with diabetes mellitus. *International Journal of Eating Disorders*, *1*, 45–53.

Pinhas-Hamiel, O., & Levy-Shraga, Y. (2003). Eating disorders in adolescents with type 2 and type 1 diabetes. *Current Diabetes Reports*, *13*, 289–297.

Pinhas-Hamiel, O., & Zeitler, P. (2005). The global spread of type 2 diabetes mellitus in children and adolescents. *Journal of Pediatrics*, *46*, 693–700.

Polonsky, W. H. (1999). *Diabetes burnout: What to do when you can't take it anymore.* Alexandria, VA: American Diabetes Association.

Polonsky, W. H., Anderson, B. J., Lohrer, P. A., Aponte, J. E., Jacobson, A. M., & Cole, C. F. (1994). Insulin omission in women with IDDM. *Diabetes Care*, *17*, 1178–1185.

Rodin, G., Olmsted, M. P., Rydall, A. C., Maharaj, S. I., Colton, P. A., Jones, J. M., . . . Daneman, D. (2002). Eating disorders in young women with type 1 diabetes mellitus. *Journal of Psychosomatic Research*, *53*, 943–949.

Rydall, A. C., Rodin, G. M., Olmsted, M. P., Devenyi, R. G., & Daneman, D. (1997). Disordered eating behavior and microvascular complications in young women with insulin-dependent diabetes mellitus. *New England Journal of Medicine*, *336*, 1849–1854.

Takii, M., Uchigata, Y., Komaki, G., Nozaki, T., Kawai, H., Iwamoto, Y., & Kubo, C. (2003). An integrated inpatient therapy for type 1 diabetic females with bulimia nervosa: A 3-year follow-up study. *Journal of Psychosomatic Research*, *55*(4), 349–356.

Verrotti, A., Catino, M., De Luca, F. A., Morgese, G., & Chiarelli, F. (1999). Eating disorders in adolescents with type 1 diabetes mellitus. *Acta Diabetologica*, *36*, 21–25.

Walker, J. D., Young, R. J., Little, J., & Steel, J. M. (2002). Mortality in concurrent type 1 diabetes and anorexia nervosa. *Diabetes Care*, *25*, 1664–1665.

Wing, R. R., Marcus, M. D., Epstein, L. H., Blair, E. H., & Burton, L. R. (1989). Binge eating in obese patients with type II diabetes. *International Journal of Eating Disorders*, *8*, 671–679.

Young, V., Eiser, C., Johnson, B., Brierley, S., Epton, T., Elliott, J., & Heller, S. (2013). Eating problems in adolescents with type 1 diabetes: A systematic review with meta-analysis. *Diabetic Medicine*, *30*, 189–198.

14

Muscle Dysmorphia

Clinical Presentation and Treatment Strategies

SCOTT GRIFFITHS AND STUART B. MURRAY ■

Muscle dysmorphia is relatively new to our clinical lexicon, insofar as the term "muscle dysmorphia" first appeared in 1997 (Pope, Gruber, Choi, Olivardia, & Phillips, 1997). In bodybuilding circles, however, muscle dysmorphia has been noted for considerably longer, with sufferers referred to as having "bigorexia" (Pope, Phillips, & Olivardia, 2000). Muscle dysmorphia has attracted considerable public interest during its relatively short life span. The narrative of larger-than-life, hypermuscular men succumbing to the sorts of body image pressures historically levied toward women has proven a compelling subject for reporters and researchers alike.

The nosology of muscle dysmorphia is unclear and hotly debated. Muscle dysmorphia was officially recognized in the fifth edition of the *Diagnostic and Statistical Manual of Mental Disorders* (DSM-5; American Psychiatric Association, 2013) as a subtype of body dysmorphic disorder. However, muscle dysmorphia will not be recognized in the *International Statistical Classification of Diseases and Related Health Problems—11th Revision* (ICD-11; World Health Organization, in press). The Working Group on the Classification of Obsessive–Compulsive and Related Disorders has not proposed the inclusion of muscle dysmorphia as a subtype of body dysmorphic disorder, citing an absence of evidence supporting its clinical utility (Veale & Matsunaga, 2014). Some researchers have argued that the extant body of research on muscle dysmorphia is insufficient to support its inclusion as a discrete entity in psychiatric diagnostic classification systems (Santos Filho, Tirico, Stefano, Touyz, & Claudino, 2015), whereas others have noted that provisional incorporation of muscle dysmorphia into diagnostic classification schemes is needed to incentivize the critical research that could inform the true nosology of the disorder (Murray, Griffiths, & Mond, 2016).

The extant body of evidence on muscle dysmorphia is small with significant limitations and gaps (Nieuwoudt, Zhou, Coutts, & Booker, 2012; Santos Filho et al., 2015). Very few studies have been conducted using individuals formally diagnosed with muscle dysmorphia, and the preponderance of studies using individuals without clinical diagnoses of muscle dysmorphia are of limited utility and risk conflating muscle dysmorphia and normative muscularity-enhancing pursuits. Various researchers have argued that muscle dysmorphia should be reclassified as an eating disorder (Griffiths, Murray, & Touyz, 2013; Mosley, 2009; Murray, Griffiths, Hazery, et al., 2016). However, differing opinions abound. For example, it has been proposed that muscle dysmorphia and both eating and body dysmorphic disorders ought to be subsumed by a new category labeled "body image disorders" (Phillipou, Blomeley, & Castle, 2016).

Nosology aside, eating disorder professionals may encounter clients with muscle dysmorphia and variants of muscularity-oriented disordered eating, and approaches for treating eating disorders may have some benefit for treating muscle dysmorphia. Although robust epidemiological data for muscle dysmorphia are currently unavailable, anecdotal reports suggest that clinicians are increasingly encountering men with the disorder. The clinical descriptions of muscle dysmorphia provided in this chapter will, as their primary source of evidence, draw upon the few studies that have evaluated samples of individuals clinically diagnosed with muscle dysmorphia rather than the more numerous studies that have examined muscle dysmorphia symptoms in individuals without a clinical diagnosis of the disorder.

The diagnostic criteria for muscle dysmorphia, first proposed by Pope and colleagues (1997), are provided in Box 14.1. To date, only one study has reported the proportion of individuals with muscle dysmorphia who have satisfied each criterion (Hitzeroth, Wessels, Zungu Dirwayi, Oosthuizen, & Stein, 2001). Of 15 men diagnosed with muscle dysmorphia, all subjects, by definition, met criteria A and C, and they frequently also met criteria B(i) (14/15), B(ii) (2/15), B(iii) (13/15), and B(iv) (11/15). The reason why so few men met criterion B(ii) may be because the study sample comprised bodybuilders recruited during an amateur bodybuilding competition. The paucity of data regarding the proportion of individuals with muscle dysmorphia who meet each diagnostic criterion has complicated efforts to answer the question of whether muscle dysmorphia represents a syndrome of frequently co-occurring symptoms (Nieuwoudt et al., 2012), complicating efforts to classify the disorder.

CLINICAL PRESENTATIONS

Demographics

Individuals diagnosed with muscle dysmorphia have tended to be male, aged in their mid-twenties to mid-thirties, White, single, and straight (Cafri, Olivardia, & Thompson, 2008; Hitzeroth et al., 2001; Murray, Rieger, et al., 2012; Olivardia,

Box 14.1

Diagnostic Criteria for Muscle Dysmorphia Proposed by Pope et al. (1997)

A. Preoccupation with the idea that one's body is not sufficiently lean and muscular. Characteristic associated behaviors include long hours of lifting weights and excessive attention to diet.

B. The preoccupation is manifested by at least two of the following four criteria:

    i. The individual frequently gives up important social, occupational, or recreational activities because of a compulsive need to maintain his or her workout and diet schedule.

    ii. The individual avoids situations where his or her body is exposed to others, or endures such situations only with marked distress or intense anxiety.

    iii. The preoccupation about the inadequacy of body size or musculature causes clinically significant distress or impairment in social, occupational, or other important areas of functioning.

    iv. The individual continues to work out, diet, or use ergogenic (performance-enhancing) substances despite knowledge of adverse physical or psychological consequences.

C. The primary focus of the preoccupation and behaviors is on being too small or inadequately muscular, as distinguished from fear of being fat as in anorexia nervosa, or a primary preoccupation only with other aspects of appearance as in other forms of body dysmorphic disorder.

Source: Pope, H. G., Gruber, A., Choi, P., Olivardia, R., & Phillips, K. (1997). Muscle dysmorphia: An underrecognized form of body dysmorphic disorder. *Psychosomatics, 38*(6), 548–557.

Pope, & Hudson, 2000; Pope et al., 2005). We are aware of just one study that recruited women with muscle dysmorphia, wherein 3 of 15 individuals (20%) were female (Hitzeroth et al., 2001). In US studies, the height of men with muscle dysmorphia has been equal to the height of men without muscle dysmorphia (Cafri et al., 2008; Olivardia et al., 2000) and is equal to US population norms for men (Ogden, 2004), controverting the anecdotal stereotype that men who are preoccupied with building muscle are short and suffering from "short man syndrome" or a "Napoleon complex" (Voss, 2001). To date, no study has identified demographic differences between men with muscle dysmorphia and men without muscle dysmorphia, including sexual orientation (Cafri et al., 2008; Hitzeroth et al., 2001; Murray, Rieger, et al., 2012; Olivardia et al., 2000; Pope et al., 2005). In the most comprehensive study of sexuality of men with muscle dysmorphia, men with the disorder were no more likely to be homosexual, and reported a similar history of homosexual experiences, compared with the control men; they further reported similar age of first intercourse and frequency of sexual activity per year (Olivardia et al., 2000).

Age of Onset and Help-Seeking

The average age of onset of muscle dysmorphia is between 19 and 20 years of age (Cafri et al., 2008; Olivardia et al., 2000). Given the average age of men included in studies of muscle dysmorphia, this suggests a chronic course for the disorder. In the only study to inquire about previous help-seeking behavior, only one man, or 7% of the sample, reported a history of psychiatric consultations (Hitzeroth et al., 2001), tentatively suggesting that most sufferers have not come into contact with mental health professionals.

Preoccupation

The defining feature of muscle dysmorphia is an enduring preoccupation that one is insufficiently muscular (Pope et al., 1997). In clinical studies, the average amount of time that men with muscle dysmorphia spent thinking about getting bigger, being too small, or not being big enough ranged from 240 to 330 minutes each day (between 4 and 5.5 hours) compared with just 20–40 minutes each day for gym-using men without muscle dysmorphia (Cafri et al., 2008; Olivardia et al., 2000). Furthermore, men with muscle dysmorphia reported checking mirrors an average of 9–13 times per day compared with 3–5 times per day for gym-using men without muscle dysmorphia (Cafri et al., 2008; Olivardia et al., 2000). Men with muscle dysmorphia weighed themselves four or five times per week compared with just one or two weigh-ins per week for men without muscle dysmorphia (Cafri et al., 2008; Olivardia et al., 2000).

Concealment

Individuals with muscle dysmorphia actively avoid having their bodies exposed in public and, when they must venture outside, may actively conceal or camouflage their bodies, including wearing loose-fitting sweatpants or multiple layers of clothes, even during hot weather. Beaches, swimming pools, and changing rooms may be endured only under intense duress, often despite meticulous preparation (weeks of dieting, body depilation to enhance the visibility of muscularity, etc.). In one study, 21 of 24 men with muscle dysmorphia admitted that they had worn heavy sweatshirts in the summer or refused to take their shirt off in public for fear that someone may think they were too small (Olivardia et al., 2000). In comparison, not one of the 30 healthy controls admitted to doing this (Olivardia et al., 2000). The fear of being exposed without clothes extends even to research settings. In studies of men with muscle dysmorphia, sufferers have reported intense embarrassment and anxiety at needing to remove clothing so that researchers can obtain body fat measurements (Pope et al., 1997). In one study, a participant with muscle dysmorphia remarked that his muscle dysmorphia had kept him housebound for a significant proportion of time since his disorder began (Cafri et al., 2008). A notable exception may be bodybuilding contests, in which a sufferer appears on stage wearing only underwear and performs a choreographed routine of poses aimed at showcasing his physique and muscularity, but only after months of rigorous preparation designed to get him into peak condition. As such, some researchers have questioned whether concealment is central to muscle dysmorphia (Baghurst et al., 2014)—a position consistent with the low proportion of men satisfying diagnostic criterion B(ii) (Hitzeroth et al., 2001). However, given the general paucity of data regarding the proportion of men with muscle dysmorphia meeting each diagnostic criterion (Nieuwoudt et al., 2012), the evidence is far from conclusive.

Body Dissatisfaction

Strong body dissatisfaction is frequently evident in muscle dysmorphia. In one study, 50% of the men with muscle dysmorphia reported being "totally dissatisfied" or "mostly dissatisfied" with their body proportions compared with just 10% of the gym-using men without muscle dysmorphia, with similar patterns observed for the questions, "How fat do you feel?" and "How uncomfortable would you be if you could not exercise for a week?" (Olivardia et al., 2000). Specific areas of greater body dissatisfaction that distinguished men with muscle dysmorphia from men without muscle dysmorphia included the lower torso (the abdominal region), muscle tone, and weight (Choi, Pope, & Olivardia, 2002). Men with muscle dysmorphia and men without muscle dysmorphia reported equal satisfaction with their face, hair, upper torso, mid torso, and height (Choi et al., 2002).

Insight

Individuals with muscle dysmorphia exhibit various levels of insight into their preoccupation. Some have good insight and are able to recognize that despite their need to be bigger, they are already objectively muscular. Others have poor or even no insight, remaining convinced that they are small, puny, or weak despite considerable evidence to the contrary. In one study of 24 men with muscle dysmorphia, 10 (42%) showed excellent or good insight, 12 (50%) showed fair or poor insight, and 2 (8%) had no insight (Olivardia et al., 2000). The 2 men rated as having no insight were completely convinced they were physically small despite repeated demonstrations to the contrary (Olivardia et al., 2000). In another study of 15 men with muscle dysmorphia, 12 (80%) had fair or poor insight, and 3 (20%) had no insight (Cafri et al., 2008). Taken together, it appears that although not all individuals with muscle dysmorphia lack insight, there is a trend toward poor insight into one's preoccupation.

Interpersonal Relationships

Relationship difficulties are common for individuals with muscle dysmorphia. Specific relationships prone to difficulties include sexually intimate relationships, in which appearing naked in front of one's partner may cause embarrassment and anxiety. In one study, men with muscle dysmorphia were more likely to report finding themselves in "awkward sexual situations" compared with control men (54% vs. 13%) (Olivardia et al., 2000). Many sufferers choose to be single, or prefer to live alone, to avoid potential compromises of their training or dieting (Pope et al., 1997). Although family environment and childhood experiences appear to be largely similar between men with and those without muscle dysmorphia, a history of family violence was more common in men with the disorder. Men with muscle dysmorphia were more likely to report that father–mother violence occurred "sometimes" or "often" compared with men without muscle dysmorphia (29% vs. 3%), and they were also more likely to report that mother–child violence occurred "sometimes" or "often" (33% vs. 3%) (Olivardia et al., 2000).

Functional Impairment

The magnitude of impairment in muscle dysmorphia is considerable. In one study, men with muscle dysmorphia reported an average of five instances of being housebound for more than 1 week, and an average of 186 days out of role from work or school, due to their muscle dysmorphia. An additional measure given to the men was an item from the self-report Yale–Brown Obsessive Compulsive Scale Modified for Body Dysmorphic Disorder (BDD-YBOCS; Phillips, Hollander, Rasmussen, & Aronowitz, 1997), which assesses the greatest social and academic/occupational/role interference ever experienced due to muscle dysmorphia. The average score provided by the men with muscle dysmorphia was 6.9 on a scale that ranged from 0 (no interference) to 8 (extreme interference/incapacitating) (Pope et al., 2005). Quality of life scores reported by men with muscle dysmorphia are 1.7–2.6 standard deviations below general population or community norms (Pope et al., 2005; Ware, Snow, Kosinski, & Gandek, 1993). Men with muscle dysmorphia also report more functional impairment specifically associated with their attitudes and behaviors surrounding their size and muscularity relative to men without muscle dysmorphia (Cafri et al., 2008). Furthermore, the size of this difference is large ($d = 2.4$) (Cafri et al., 2008).

Steroids

Steroid use is common in muscle dysmorphia because steroids are extremely effective at building large amounts of muscle in a short amount of time (Bhasin, 2001; Griffiths, Murray, Mitchison, & Mond, 2016). In addition, steroid use helps distinguish men with muscle dysmorphia from men without muscle dysmorphia.

In one study, 12 of the 24 men with muscle dysmorphia reported using steroids compared with just 2 of the 30 men without muscle dysmorphia (Olivardia et al., 2000). In subsequent studies, men with muscle dysmorphia were also more likely than men without muscle dysmorphia to report steroid use (44% vs. 14%, respectively [Cafri et al., 2008], and 40% vs. 13%, respectively [Hitzeroth et al., 2001]), and they were more likely to report steroid abuse or dependence (21.4% vs. 0%, respectively) (Pope et al., 2005). Steroid use is likely underreported in these and other studies of muscle dysmorphia due to the considerable stigma attached to steroid use (Griffiths, Murray, & Mond, 2016) and to illicit drug use more generally (Palamar, Kiang, & Halkitis, 2011). Researchers have noted that some men diagnosed with muscle dysmorphia have denied using steroids despite having a level of muscle mass that is impossible to obtain naturally (Olivardia et al., 2000).

Muscle dysmorphia tends to precede steroid use. In a study that included 11 men with muscle dysmorphia who admitted to using steroids, muscle dysmorphia preceded the steroid use for 8 men (73%), co-occurred for 2 men (18%), and succeeded the steroid use for 1 man (9%) (Olivardia et al., 2000). However, the paucity of data pertaining to the age of onset of muscle dysmorphia and steroid use precludes a definitive answer as to whether steroid use or muscle dysmorphia occurs first (Rohman, 2009).

Eating Disorders

Substantial comorbidity exists between muscle dysmorphia and eating disorders. Men with muscle dysmorphia frequently report a lifetime history of eating disorders. In one study, men with muscle dysmorphia were more likely to report a lifetime history of a comorbid eating disorder, including anorexia nervosa, bulimia nervosa, and binge-eating disorder, than were men without muscle dysmorphia (29% vs. 0%, respectively) (Olivardia et al., 2000). Very high levels of current eating disorder psychopathology were observed, insofar as the average score on the Eating Disorders Inventory (Garner, 1991) for men with muscle dysmorphia was double that of healthy controls (44 vs. 22, respectively) (Olivardia et al., 2000). In another study, 21% of men with muscle dysmorphia reported a lifetime history of an eating disorder, but this was not significantly different from the 8% of men with body dysmorphic disorder unrelated to muscularity who reported an eating disorder (Pope et al., 2005). In a study that considered thinness- and muscularity-oriented eating disorder behaviors separately, men with muscle dysmorphia reported less severe thinness-oriented and equal muscularity-oriented eating disorder behaviors compared to men with anorexia nervosa (Murray, Rieger, et al., 2012). Levels of both forms of disordered eating were considerably higher for men with muscle dysmorphia relative to healthy gym-using men (Murray, Rieger, et al., 2012). Eating disorder behaviors, including binging and purging, may also occur in muscle dysmorphia. For example, in one published case report, missed training sessions frequently led to binge eating: The subject stated, "This is a wasted day now, I feel like I let myself down. I've already blown it so I may as well binge and then go harder tomorrow" (Murray, Maguire, Russell, & Touyz, 2012, p. 71).

Body Dysmorphic Disorder

Substantial comorbidity exists between muscle dysmorphia and body dysmorphic disorder. In one study, men with muscle dysmorphia reported more symptoms of body dysmorphic disorder than did healthy gym-using men, and the size of this difference was large ($d = 3.3$) (Cafri et al., 2008). In another study, of the 15 men with muscle dysmorphia, 12 (86%) had additional body dysmorphic disorder unrelated to their muscle dysmorphia, most often concerning their hair and skin (Pope et al., 2005). In yet another study, 33% of the men with muscle dysmorphia were found to have additional body dysmorphic disorder unrelated to muscularity compared with 0% of the healthy men without muscle dysmorphia (Hitzeroth et al., 2001). Finally, in a study of 193 individuals with body dysmorphic disorder, muscle dysmorphia was found in 18 (9%) (Pope et al., 1997).

Individuals with muscle dysmorphia and individuals with body dysmorphic disorder unrelated to muscularity are distinct in several regards. Excessive weightlifting (71% vs. 12%), excessive exercise (64% vs. 10%), and excessive dieting (71% vs. 13%) distinguish men with muscle dysmorphia from men with body dysmorphic disorder unrelated to muscularity (Pope et al., 2005). Mirror checking, concealing or camouflaging one's body, and comparing one's body to others do not distinguish between the two groups (Pope et al., 2005). Furthermore, men with muscle dysmorphia exhibit greater overall psychopathology compared to men with body dysmorphic disorder unrelated to muscularity. Men with muscle dysmorphia report poorer quality of life, poorer social functioning, and are more likely to report a lifetime history of attempted suicide (Pope et al., 2005).

Compulsive Exercise

Compulsive exercise is common in muscle dysmorphia. In one study, men with muscle dysmorphia reported a greater level of compulsive exercise compared to gym-using controls, and the size of this difference was large ($d = 2.6$) (Murray, Rieger, et al., 2012). Compulsive exercise in muscle dysmorphia is comparable to that reported by men with anorexia nervosa (Murray, Rieger, et al., 2012). Evidence from the study by Murray, Rieger, et al., in addition to case report evidence (Murray, Maguire, et al., 2012), suggests that compulsive exercise may play an affect-regulation role in muscle dysmorphia—helping to both increase positive mood and decrease negative mood. Indeed, in men with anorexia nervosa, it appears that compulsive exercise plays an affect-regulation role more than it does for women with anorexia nervosa (Murray, Griffiths, Rieger, & Touyz, 2013), mirroring a pattern of sex differences in the relationships of emotional functioning with body dissatisfaction and disordered eating (Griffiths, Angus, Murray, & Touyz, 2014).

Time spent in the gym is considerable in muscle dysmorphia. For example, a young man with muscle dysmorphia reported weight training six times per week, at 2 hours per session, for 12 hours of intense weight training per week—purely for body image purposes (Murray, Rieger, et al., 2012). However, it is important to note that the amount of time spent in the gym may not distinguish men with muscle dysmorphia from men without muscle dysmorphia. In one study, men with muscle dysmorphia spent, on average, 12 hours in the gym per week, but this was not significantly different from the 13 hours spent in the gym per week by men without muscle dysmorphia (Hitzeroth et al., 2001). However, the men in this study were all active participants in an amateur bodybuilding contest and were likely training particularly hard in the lead-up to the competition (Hitzeroth et al., 2001). There appear to be instances, however, in which the amount of time spent training appears unequivocally disordered. For example, a man with muscle dysmorphia reported lifting weights 7 days a week, two times per day, for 1 hour and 30 minutes each time—a total of 21 hours spent weight training per week (Cafri et al., 2008). It appears that preoccupation with training and getting bigger, as discussed previously, distinguishes men with muscle dysmorphia from men without muscle dysmorphia, not time spent in the gym per se.

Comorbid Psychiatric Disorders

Comorbidities other than eating disorders and body dysmorphic disorder are frequently present in muscle dysmorphia. In two studies, men with muscle dysmorphia were more likely to report a lifetime history of an anxiety disorder relative to men without muscle dysmorphia (29% vs. 3%, respectively [Cafri et al., 2008], and 43% vs. 7%, respectively [Olivardia et al., 2000]), and they were also more likely to report a lifetime history of depression or bipolar disorder (58% vs. 20%, respectively [Cafri et al., 2008], and 74% vs. 29%, respectively [Olivardia et al., 2000]). In a study comparing men with muscle dysmorphia to men with body dysmorphic disorder unrelated to muscularity, the men with muscle dysmorphia were more likely to report a lifetime history of substance use disorders, including any substance disorder (85% vs. 51%, respectively) and non-alcohol substance use disorders (79% vs. 31%, respectively) (Pope et al., 2005). Men with muscle dysmorphia and men with body dysmorphic disorder unrelated to muscularity are comparable with regard to lifetime history of psychiatric disorders, including mood disorders (85% vs. 82%, respectively) and anxiety disorders (79% vs. 65%, respectively) (Pope et al., 2005).

Suicidality

Alarmingly, in the only study to examine suicidality in muscle dysmorphia, 50% of the 15 men with muscle dysmorphia reported at least one previous suicide attempt compared with just 16% of the men with body dysmorphic disorder unrelated to muscularity (Pope et al., 2005). Given the well-established finding that men are less likely to attempt suicide, but more likely to complete suicide, relative to women (Canetto & Sakinofsky, 1998), the suicide attempt data for individuals with muscle dysmorphia is a cause for concern, small sample size notwithstanding.

Masculinity

Men with muscle dysmorphia typically report significantly stronger adherence to what Western societies consider traditional, "expected" attitudes and behaviors for men living in these societies. Murray, Rieger, Karlov, and Touyz (2013), in a reanalysis of their previously published data (Murray, Rieger, et al., 2012), observed that men with muscle dysmorphia reported more adherence to many traditional domains of masculinity, including the importance of winning, exercising emotional self-control, taking risks, aggressive or violent behavior, exercising power over women, projecting physical and social dominance, being self-reliant and avoiding dependence, disdain for people who are gay, and the importance of pursuing and achieving social status. Only two domains of masculinity were not elevated in men with muscle dysmorphia, namely the importance of building and sustaining one's career and sexual success with women. Men with muscle dysmorphia and healthy gym-using men reported a similar level of adherence to traditional feminine gender norms (i.e., femininity). In summary, men with muscle dysmorphia are more masculine, but not less feminine, than men without muscle dysmorphia.

TREATMENT

Evidence to inform effective treatment approaches for muscle dysmorphia is scant. To date, no randomized controlled clinical trials have been undertaken, forcing reliance on a scattering of treatment case reports (Murray & Griffiths, 2014). Given the nosology of the disorder, treatment approaches that have demonstrated effectiveness for treating eating disorders and body dysmorphic disorder are likely to be successful. Cognitive–behavior therapy and selective serotonin reuptake inhibitors are effective for treating body dysmorphic disorder (Ipser, Sander, & Stein, 2009) and eating disorders (Flament, Bissada, & Spettigue, 2012; Hay, 2013), and they may help individuals with muscle dysmorphia given the links between the three conditions (Morgan, 2008; Tod & Lavallee, 2010).

Family-based treatment (Lock & Le Grange, 2015), which has shown efficacy for treating eating disorders in adolescents, particularly anorexia nervosa (Couturier, Kimber, & Szatmari, 2013), may benefit adolescents with muscle dysmorphia. Murray and Griffiths (2014) published a case report in which an adolescent boy with muscle dysmorphia was treated using eating disorders-focused family-based therapy. At the start of treatment, the patient's full-scale score on the Muscle Dysmorphic Disorder Inventory (MDDI; Hildebrandt, Langenbucher, & Schlundt, 2004) was 59. For reference, the average full-scale MDDI score for men with muscle dysmorphia is 52 (Murray, Rieger, et al., 2012). Consistent with the principles of family-based treatment (Lock & Le Grange, 2015), the patient's parents were enlisted to directly intervene in the maintenance of his muscle dysmorphia symptoms by having them temporally exert full control over his meals at home and at school, including rigorous, noncritical meal supervision, and by having them temporarily disallow exercise. The patient appeared to have recovered after 10 sessions of family-based therapy, and he recorded a full-scale score on the MDDI of 10. For reference, the average full-scale MMDI score for gym-using men without muscle dysmorphia is 25 (Murray, Rieger, et al., 2012).

Although case reports have shown promise, clinicians and researchers must note that the efficacy of family-based treatment, cognitive–behavior therapy, and pharmacotherapy for treating muscle dysmorphia has not yet been established. Further research is needed to establish an empirically supported treatment for muscle dysmorphia. However, there are elements of psychotherapy for muscle dysmorphia that clinicians may wish to focus on, and these are detailed next.

Cognitive Restructuring—Masculinity

Problematic beliefs about what it means to be a man in contemporary Western society may need to be challenged, especially regarding any perceived need to project strength, power, confidence, and control. The theoretical framework linking masculinity and muscle dysmorphia is the "masculinity hypothesis," which posits that adherence to traditional male gender roles may predispose men toward developing muscle dysmorphia (Blashill, 2011; Griffiths, Murray, & Touyz, 2015; Mishkind, Rodin, Silberstein, & Striegel-Moore, 1986). The perception that one's masculinity is threatened, or that one needs to project qualities traditionally thought of as masculine (e.g., physical strength and emotional self-control), may facilitate one to acquire muscle mass as an overt sign of masculinity. Evidence suggests that adherence to traditional male gender norms is elevated among men with muscle dysmorphia (Murray, Rieger, et al., 2013) and men who use steroids (Kanayama, Barry, Hudson, & Pope, 2006), and there is limited evidence that these beliefs may facilitate the development of muscle dysmorphia or muscle dissatisfaction more generally (Blashill, 2011; Griffiths, Murray, et al., 2015). In the aforementioned case report of an adolescent boy with muscle dysmorphia, the patient negatively compared himself with "the more manly boys at school" and described frequent episodes of bullying and "feeling weak" (Murray & Griffiths, 2014).

The masculinity hypothesis is a complement to the well-established "femininity" hypothesis, which posits that adherence to traditional female gender roles may predispose women toward developing anorexia nervosa (Lakkis, Ricciardelli, & Williams, 1999). Evidence suggests that the public perceives men and women with muscle dysmorphia as masculine, and men and women with anorexia nervosa are perceived as feminine (Griffiths, Mond, Murray, & Touyz, 2013). These perceptions are supported by results of studies of men with these conditions: Men with muscle dysmorphia are more masculine, and men with anorexia nervosa more feminine, than healthy controls (Murray, Rieger, et al., 2013).

Clinicians should be aware that strong or strict adherence to traditional masculine norms may translate into derogatory and offensive views, particularly of women and homosexuals, which may complicate building and maintaining a therapeutic alliance. The capacity for offense is particularly salient because mental health professionals, including those who specialize in eating disorders, are more likely to be female (Mathews, Stokes, Crea, & Grenyer, 2010; Waller & Katzman, 1998). Alternatively, men with muscle dysmorphia may be reluctant to disclose these views out of fear of insulting their clinician. Thus, all members involved in the treatment of an individual with muscle dysmorphia should be aware of the potential for sexist and/or homophobic beliefs to be expressed; of the need to detect, explore, and challenge these views in relation to masculinity and muscularity; and of the need to practice self-monitoring in regard to one's own thoughts, feelings, and behaviors in relation to the client.

Cognitive Restructuring—Ego-syntonic Beliefs

Ego-syntonic beliefs, or positive beliefs, about the attitudes and behaviors that constitute muscle dysmorphia are often present in individuals suffering from the condition (Pope et al., 2000). These ego-syntonic beliefs are similar to those expressed by individuals with anorexia nervosa and can be particularly difficult to challenge and change. Muscle dysmorphia beliefs often center around the "health benefits" of dieting or training and specifically about how the health consequences of strict dieting, excessive training, and steroid use are offset by the health benefits of exercise and dieting in general, often with specific reference to unhealthy individuals in the sufferers' lives or more general references to the prevalence of overweight and obesity in society (Pope et al., 2000). There is evidence that endorsement of positive or ego-syntonic beliefs about muscle dysmorphia, including admiration for being able to strictly control one's training and dieting, is tentatively linked with the development of muscle dysmorphia in both young men and women (Griffiths, Mond, Murray, & Touyz, 2015).

Clinicians should be aware that there exists an analogue of pro-anorexia or "thinspiration" social media content that is directed toward men and muscularity, termed "pro-muscularity" (Murray, Griffiths, Hazery, et al., 2016). Exemplar pro-muscularity messages found on the Internet include "Just remember who was by your side when everyone else left" overlaid on a grayscale image of two dumbbells; "Get big. Life is too short to be small" overlaid on an image of a highly muscular man flexing his arms; and "The only person you need to be better than is the person you were yesterday" overlaid on an image of a highly muscular man with his arms extended and palms upturned, presumably in deep contemplation. Basic themes of this content include the importance and primacy of dieting and training. The effects of consuming this material have not yet been studied.

However, given evidence that exposure to "fitspiration" (muscularity-promoting social media content that masquerades as a "healthy" version of thinspiration or pro-anorexia/pro-ana) produces body dissatisfaction, reduced appearance self-esteem, and negative affect among women (Tiggemann & Zaccardo, 2015), it is likely that exposure to pro-muscularity content will have similar effects.

Steroids

Steroids are powerful drugs frequently used by men with muscle dysmorphia to build muscle, and treatment approaches will necessarily involve the cessation of steroid use. Discontinuation of steroid use, however, is fraught with danger, particularly with regard to an increased risk of suicidal ideation and suicide attempts.

The rapid pace with which steroids build muscle (Griffiths, Murray, Mitchison, et al., 2016) is often reflected in the rapid reduction in muscle that occurs when steroid use is discontinued. During the period of cessation, which users refer to as "post-cycle therapy" or "PCT," users frequently take drugs designed to restore the body's natural hormonal balance in an effort to conserve as much muscle as possible. Results vary, however, and some loss of muscle mass typically occurs. Furthermore, during this time, the body must resume natural production of testosterone, which is reduced to zero during the period of steroid use—a status users refer to as "being shutdown." This hormonal instability is linked with emotional instability and irritability, and when combined with overinvestment in body image and muscularity, it can lead to several weeks of intense negative affect, including severe depression and possibly suicidal ideation (Griffiths, McKay, Henshaw, & Dun, in press). The following excerpt from Mosley (2009) of a bodybuilder with muscle dysmorphia is an example of this negative affect:

> When I came off my last [steroid] cycle I got really depressed and even felt suicidal for a few weeks, which really worried me. But I don't want to stop juicing [using steroids] now because I've seen the results and I don't want to lose that edge. (p. 194)

Suicidal ideation arising from repeated episodes of steroid cessation may be one reason why the rate of attempted suicide is so high in muscle dysmorphia. In one study of men with muscle dysmorphia, half reported attempting suicide at least once (Pope et al., 2005).

For most steroid users, this period of emotional instability lasts several weeks. Polypharmacy, the phenomenon wherein steroid users take multiple substances simultaneously (Kanayama & Pope, 2012), further complicates the process of steroid use cessation. No published data are available regarding the treatment of comorbid steroid use and muscle dysmorphia. Physiological dangers notwithstanding, the psychological dangers of discontinuing steroid use make this a critical point during treatment. The support and advice of an endocrinologist are needed, and psychological support should be increased. Endocrinologists with experience working with steroid users, or who have extensive experience working with males and/or with testosterone, are desirable because many steroid users are highly skeptical about health professionals' knowledge of steroids and their effects on the body (Kanayama, Brower, Wood, Hudson, & Pope, 2010). Psychological dependence on steroids is also possible, and it has been formalized into a disorder called anabolic–androgenic steroid dependence (Kanayama, Brower, Wood, Hudson, & Pope, 2009). For more information about treatment for anabolic–androgenic steroid dependence, see the review paper by Kanayama and colleagues (2010).

CONCLUSION

Muscle dysmorphia is a relatively new disorder with little research to characterize it and even less research to inform treatment options. Consequently, clinicians tasked with treating a client with muscle dysmorphia may feel, at times, overwhelmed by the complexity of the disorder and stymied by the paucity of research and clinical advice available to them. Cognitive–behavioral therapy and selective serotonin reuptake inhibitors may be effective for treating muscle dysmorphia, given their demonstrated effectiveness for two closely related disorders, namely body dysmorphic disorder and eating disorders. Family-based therapy, which has demonstrated effectiveness for treating adolescent eating disorders and, in one case report, demonstrated effectiveness for treating adolescent muscle dysmorphia, may be effective for treating adolescents with muscle dysmorphia. Specific strategies worth considering include dismantling toxic and maladaptive beliefs surrounding the relationship between masculinity and muscularity; dismantling pro-muscularity beliefs or ego-syntonic beliefs; and, if steroid use is present, increasing care to greater levels during steroid cessation, preferably with the involvement of an endocrinologist. If steroid dependence is present, as opposed to mere steroid use, a clinician with experience working with individuals with substance use, particularly steroid use, may need to be incorporated into the treatment team.

RESOURCES

The Adonis Complex (Pope et al., 2000) is a book coauthored by Harrison Pope, the "discoverer" of muscle dysmorphia (Pope et al., 1997; Pope, Katz, & Hudson, 1993). The book is aimed at a popular audience and offers an excellent layperson's introduction to muscle dysmorphia and the broader issue of male body dissatisfaction. The book is an excellent resource and can be recommended to clients. Furthermore, the book is relatively well known on Internet forums on which bodybuilders and steroid users congregate and socialize.

The Appearance and Performance Enhancing Drug Use Schedule (APEDUS; Hildebrandt, Langenbucher, Lai, Loeb, & Hollander, 2011) is a semistructured interview designed to assess the core features of appearance- and performance-enhancing drug use—a category inclusive of steroids. This free instrument, available on the lead author's institutional website, is exceptional for introducing laypersons to the terms used to describe patterns of steroid use.

Muscle: Confessions of an Unlikely Bodybuilder (Fussell, 1992) is a first-hand account by Sam Fussell of the eccentric world of bodybuilding. The book details Fussell's punishing workouts, dieting, and steroid use, which ultimately rendered him extremely unhappy. The book is a useful resource for both clinicians and clients.

REFERENCES

American Psychiatric Association. (2013). *Diagnostic and statistical manual of mental disorders* (5th ed.). Arlington, VA: American Psychiatric Publishing.

Baghurst, T., Mwarumba, M., Volberding, J., Brown, T. C., Murray, S. B., Galli, N., . . . Griffiths, S. (2014). Revaluation of physique protection as a characteristic of muscle dysmorphia. *North American Journal of Psychology, 16*, 575–585.

Bhasin, S. (2001). Testosterone dose–response relationships in healthy young men. *American Journal of Physiology: Endocrinology and Metabolism, 281*, 1172–1181.

Blashill, A. J. (2011). Gender roles, eating pathology, and body dissatisfaction in men: A meta-analysis. *Body Image, 8*, 1–11.

Cafri, G., Olivardia, R., & Thompson, J. K. (2008). Symptom characteristics and psychiatric comorbidity among males with muscle dysmorphia. *Comprehensive Psychiatry, 49*(4), 374–379.

Canetto, S. S., & Sakinofsky, I. (1998). The gender paradox in suicide. *Suicide and Life-Threatening Behavior, 28*, 1–23.

Choi, P. Y. L., Pope, H. G., Jr., & Olivardia, R. (2002). Muscle dysmorphia: A new syndrome in weightlifters. *British Journal of Sports Medicine, 36*(5), 375–376.

Couturier, J., Kimber, M., & Szatmari, P. (2013). Efficacy of family-based treatment for adolescents with eating disorders: A systematic review and meta-analysis. *International Journal of Eating Disorders, 46*, 3–11.

Flament, M. F., Bissada, H., & Spettigue, W. (2012). Evidence-based pharmacotherapy of eating disorders. *International Journal of Neuropsychopharmacology, 15*, 189–207.

Fussell, S. W. (1992). *Muscle: Confessions of an unlikely bodybuilder*. New York, NY: William Morrow.

Garner, D. M. (1991). *Eating disorder inventory-2*. Odessa, FL: Psychological Assessment Resources.

Griffiths, S., Angus, D., Murray, S. B., & Touyz, S. (2014). Unique associations between young adult men's emotional functioning and their body dissatisfaction and disordered eating. *Body Image, 11*, 175–178.

Griffiths, S., McKay, F., Henshaw, R., & Dunn, M. (In press). Post-cycle therapy for performance and image enhancing drug users: A qualitative investigation. *Performance Enhancement and Health*.

Griffiths, S., Mond, J. M., Murray, S. B., & Touyz, S. (2013). Young peoples' stigmatizing attitudes and beliefs about anorexia nervosa and muscle dysmorphia. *International Journal of Eating Disorders, 47*, 189–195.

Griffiths, S., Mond, J. M., Murray, S. B., & Touyz, S. (2015). Positive beliefs about anorexia nervosa and muscle dysmorphia are associated with eating disorder symptomatology. *Australian and New Zealand Journal of Psychiatry, 49*, 812–820.

Griffiths, S., Murray, S. B., Mitchison, D., & Mond, J. M. (2016). Anabolic steroids: Lots
of muscle in the short-term, potentially devastating health consequences in the long-
term. *Drug and Alcohol Review, 35*, 375–376.

Griffiths, S., Murray, S. B., & Mond, J. M. (2016). The stigma of anabolic steroid use.
Journal of Drug Issues, 46(4).

Griffiths, S., Murray, S. B., & Touyz, S. (2013). Disordered eating and the muscular ideal.
Journal of Eating Disorders, 1, 15.

Griffiths, S., Murray, S. B., & Touyz, S. (2015). Extending the masculinity hypothesis: An
investigation of gender role conformity, body dissatisfaction, and disordered eating in
young heterosexual men. *Psychology of Men & Masculinity, 16*, 108–114.

Hay, P. (2013). A systematic review of evidence for psychological treatments in eating
disorders: 2005–2012. *International Journal of Eating Disorders, 46*, 462–469.

Hildebrandt, T., Langenbucher, J., & Schlundt, D. G. (2004). Muscularity concerns
among men: Development of attitudinal and perceptual measures. *Body Image, 1*,
169–181.

Hildebrandt, T., Langenbucher, J. W., Lai, J. K., Loeb, K. L., & Hollander, E. (2011).
Development and validation of the appearance and performance enhancing drug use
schedule. *Addictive Behaviors, 36*, 949–958.

Hitzeroth, V., Wessels, C., Zungu Dirwayi, N., Oosthuizen, P., & Stein, D. J. (2001).
Muscle dysmorphia: A South African sample. *Psychiatry and Clinical Neurosciences,
55*, 521–523.

Ipser, J. C., Sander, C., & Stein, D. J. (2009). Pharmacotherapy and psychotherapy for
body dysmorphic disorder. *Cochrane Database of Systematic Reviews, 2009*(1),
CD005332.

Kanayama, G., Barry, S., Hudson, J. I., & Pope, H. G. (2006). Body image and attitudes toward male roles in anabolic–androgenic steroid users. *American Journal of
Psychiatry, 163*, 697–703.

Kanayama, G., Brower, K. J., Wood, R. I., Hudson, J. I., & Pope, H. G., Jr. (2009).
Anabolic–androgenic steroid dependence: An emerging disorder. *Addiction, 104*(12),
1966–1978.

Kanayama, G., Brower, K. J., Wood, R. I., Hudson, J. I., & Pope, H. G., Jr. (2010).
Treatment of anabolic–androgenic steroid dependence: Emerging evidence and its
implications. *Drug and Alcohol Dependence, 109*, 6–13.

Kanayama, G., & Pope, H. G. (2012). Illicit use of androgens and other hormones: Recent
advances. *Current Opinion in Endocrinology, Diabetes, and Obesity, 19*, 211–219.

Lakkis, J., Ricciardelli, L. A., & Williams, R. J. (1999). Role of sexual orientation and
gender-related traits in disordered eating. *Sex Roles, 41*, 1–16.

Lock, J., & Le Grange, D. (2015). *Treatment manual for anorexia nervosa: A family-based
approach* (2nd ed.). New York, NY: Guilford.

Mathews, R., Stokes, D., Crea, K., & Grenyer, B. F. S. (2010). The Australian Psychology
Workforce 1: A national profile of psychologists in practice. *Australian Psychologist,
45*(3), 154–167.

Mishkind, M. E., Rodin, J., Silberstein, L. R., & Striegel-Moore, R. H. (1986). The
embodiment of masculinity: Cultural, psychological, and behavioral dimensions. *The
American Behavioral Scientist, 29*, 545–562.

Morgan, J. F. (2008). *The invisible man: A self-help guide for men with eating disorders, compulsive exercise and bigorexia.* New York, NY: Routledge.

Mosley, P. (2009). Bigorexia: Bodybuilding and muscle dysmorphia. *European Eating Disorders Review, 17,* 191–198.

Murray, S. B., & Griffiths, S. (2014). Adolescent muscle dysmorphia and family-based treatment: A case report. *Clinical Child Psychology and Psychiatry, 20,* 324–330.

Murray, S. B., Griffiths, S., Hazery, L., Shen, T., Wooldridge, T., & Mond, J. M. (2016). Go big or go home: A thematic content analysis of pro-muscularity websites. *Body Image, 16,* 17–20.

Murray, S. B., Griffiths, S., & Mond, J. M. (2016). Evolving eating disorder psychopathology: Conceptualising muscularity-oriented disordered eating. *British Journal of Psychiatry, 208*(5), 414–415.

Murray, S. B., Griffiths, S., Rieger, E., & Touyz, S. (2013). A comparison of compulsive exercise in male and female presentations of anorexia nervosa: What is the difference? *Advances in Eating Disorders: Theory, Research and Practice, 2,* 65–70.

Murray, S. B., Maguire, S., Russell, J., & Touyz, S. W. (2012). The emotional regulatory features of bulimic episodes and compulsive exercise in muscle dysmorphia: A case report. *European Eating Disorders Review, 20*(1), 68–73.

Murray, S. B., Rieger, E., Hildebrandt, T., Karlov, L., Russell, J., Boon, E., . . . Touyz, S. W. (2012). A comparison of eating, exercise, shape, and weight related symptomatology in males with muscle dysmorphia and anorexia nervosa. *Body Image, 9*(2), 193–200.

Murray, S. B., Rieger, E., Karlov, L., & Touyz, S. W. (2013). Masculinity and femininity in the divergence of male body image concerns. *Journal of Eating Disorders, 1*(11), 1–8.

Nieuwoudt, J. E., Zhou, S., Coutts, R. A., & Booker, R. (2012). Muscle dysmorphia: Current research and potential classification as a disorder. *Psychology of Sport and Exercise, 13*(5), 569–577.

Ogden, C. L. (2004). *Mean body weight, height, and body mass index: United States 1960–2002.* Washington, DC: US Department of Health and Human Services, Centers for Disease Control and Prevention, National Center for Health Statistics.

Olivardia, R., Pope, H. G., & Hudson, J. (2000). Muscle dysmorphia in male weightlifters: A case–control study. *American Journal of Psychiatry, 157*(8), 1291–1296.

Palamar, J. J., Kiang, M. V., & Halkitis, P. N. (2011). Development and psychometric evaluation of scales that assess stigma associated with illicit drug users. *Substance Use & Misuse, 46*(12), 1457–1467.

Phillipou, A., Blomeley, D., & Castle, D. J. (2016). Muscling in on body image disorders: What is the nosological status of muscle dysmorphia? *Australian and New Zealand Journal of Psychiatry, 50*(4), 380–381.

Phillips, K. A., Hollander, E., Rasmussen, S., & Aronowitz, B. (1997). A severity rating scale for body dysmorphic disorder: Development, reliability, and validity of a modified version of the Yale–Brown Obsessive Compulsive Scale. *Psychopharmacology Bulletin, 33,* 17–22.

Pope, C., Pope, H. G., Menard, W., Fay, C., Olivardia, R., & Phillips, K. (2005). Clinical features of muscle dysmorphia among males with body dysmorphic disorder. *Body Image, 2,* 395–400.

Pope, H. G., Gruber, A., Choi, P., Olivardia, R., & Phillips, K. (1997). Muscle dysmorphia: An underrecognized form of body dysmorphic disorder. *Psychosomatics, 38*(6), 548–557.

Pope, H. G., Katz, D., & Hudson, J. (1993). Anorexia nervosa and "reverse anorexia" among 108 male bodybuilders. *Comprehensive Psychiatry, 34*(6), 406–409.

Pope, H. G., Phillips, K., & Olivardia, R. (2000). *The Adonis complex: The secret crisis of male body dissatisfaction.* New York, NY: Free Press.

Rohman, L. (2009). The relationship between anabolic androgenic steroids and muscle dysmorphia: A review. *Eating Disorders, 17*(3), 187–199.

Santos Filho, C. A., Tirico, P. P., Stefano, S. C., Touyz, S. W., & Claudino, A. M. (2015). Systematic review of the diagnostic category muscle dysmorphia. *Australian and New Zealand Journal of Psychiatry, 50,* 322–333.

Tiggemann, M., & Zaccardo, M. (2015). "Exercise to be fit, not skinny": The effect of fitspiration imagery on women's body image. *Body Image, 15,* 61–67.

Tod, D., & Lavallee, D. (2010). Towards a conceptual understanding of muscle dysmorphia development and sustainment. *International Review of Sport and Exercise Psychology, 3*(2), 111–131.

Veale, D., & Matsunaga, H. (2014). Body dysmorphic disorder and olfactory reference disorder: Proposals for ICD-11. *Revista Brasileira de Psiquiatria, 36,* 14–20.

Voss, L. D. (2001). Short normal stature and psychosocial disadvantage: A critical review of the evidence. *Journal of Pediatric Endocrinology and Metabolism, 14,* 701–711.

Waller, G., & Katzman, M. A. (1998). Female or male therapists for women with eating disorders? A pilot study of experts' opinions. *International Journal of Eating Disorders, 23*(2), 117–123.

Ware, J. E., Snow, K. K., Kosinski, M., & Gandek, B. (1993). *SF-36 health survey: Manual and interpretation guide.* Boston, MA: The Health Institute, New England Medical Center.

World Health Organization (in press). *International statistical classification of diseases and related health problems—11th revision.* Geneva, Switzerland: Author.

15

Rumination Disorder in Adults

Cognitive–Behavioral Formulation and Treatment

HELEN B. MURRAY AND JENNIFER J. THOMAS ■

CLINICAL PRESENTATION

Formerly classified in the category "feeding and eating disorders of infancy or early childhood" in the fourth edition, text revision, of the *Diagnostic and Statistical Manual of Mental Disorders* (DSM-IV-TR; American Psychiatric Association [APA], 2000), the current edition of the DSM (i.e., DSM-5) categorizes rumination disorder (RD) within the newly unified category "feeding and eating disorders" (APA, 2013). Part of the motivation for moving RD out of the childhood disorders section was the DSM-5 Work Group's recognition that RD can occur across the life span (APA, 2013). RD is also known as "rumination syndrome" by the Rome IV Functional Gastrointestinal Disorders classification system (Drossman et al., 2016). RD occurs in individuals of all ages (e.g., two chart reviews report RD in cases up to 65 years old; O'Brien, Bruce, & Camilleri, 1995; Soykan, Chen, Kendall, & McCallum, 1997). Unfortunately, RD can have a protracted course, with patients often undergoing multiple medical evaluations with frequent misdiagnosis, such as with gastromotility disorders (Chial, Camilleri, Williams, Litzinger, & Perrault, 2003; Kanodia, Kim, & Sturmberg, 2011; Tack, Blondeau, Boecxstaens, & Rommel, 2011). In addition, patients may choose not to disclose symptoms because of the feared negative stigma attached to rumination behavior (Delaney et al., 2015; Parry-Jones, 1994; Tamburrino, Campbell, Franco, & Evans, 1995).

The primary feature of RD is the repeated regurgitation of food during or soon after eating, which typically occurs at least a few times per week, frequently daily (APA, 2013). Regurgitation is followed by rechewing, reswallowing, or spitting out of the regurgitated food. Usually, the volume of the regurgitated material is small, and food will come up recurrently after the eating episode (Tucker, Knowles, Wright, & Fox, 2013). DSM-5 does not specify a time frame after eating during which the food should be regurgitated, but, the Rome IV suggests that regurgitation usually occurs within minutes of eating (Drossman et al., 2016), DSM-5 does not include specifiers for the severity of rumination based on the frequency of episodes; the only specifier for rumination is "in remission" ("after full criteria for RD were previously met, the criteria have not been met for a sustained period of time" [APA, 2013, p. 332]).

Significant psychosocial disturbance can result, including avoidance of work, school, or social situations that involve eating (APA, 2013). In addition, medical complications similar to those of self-induced vomiting can result from rumination behavior, such as malnutrition, dental complications, and electrolyte disturbances (Fredericks, Carr, & Williams, 1998). However, more research on the frequency of complications among individuals with RD is needed.

DIFFERENTIAL DIAGNOSIS

A diagnosis of RD cannot be conferred if the individual has anorexia nervosa, bulimia nervosa, binge-eating disorder, or avoidant/restrictive food intake disorder. Individuals with a gastrointestinal disorder can receive a comorbid diagnosis of RD, but the repeated regurgitation cannot be solely attributable to an associated gastrointestinal condition or other medical explanation (e.g., gastroesophageal reflux; Drossman et al., 2016). For individuals with a comorbid gastrointestinal condition or neurodevelopmental disorder, the rumination symptoms must warrant additional clinical attention in order for an RD diagnosis to be conferred (APA, 2013). Furthermore, some individuals with RD display physical features that may make rumination behavior difficult to identify because these features are shared with gastrointestinal disorders (e.g., delayed gastric emptying that is a result of regurgitation followed by reswallowing or abdominal pain; Chial et al., 2003). In addition, RD may co-occur with other gastrointestinal concerns that are treated with behavioral interventions (e.g., rectal evacuation disorder; Vijayvargiya et al., 2014).

To distinguish rumination behavior from frank vomiting, the regurgitation in RD is effortless, nonretching, and typically without nausea or abdominal pain (APA, 2013; Drossman et al., 2016). Interestingly, some individuals with RD feel they bring up food voluntarily as a purposeful self-soothing strategy, whereas others describe the regurgitation behavior as out of their control. However, it is possible that even those individuals who perceive the regurgitation as involuntarily actually have control over the behavior but may not realize this until treatment is provided, as described by one patient receiving cognitive–behavioral treatment for RD (Thomas & Murray, 2016).

Due to the scant literature on RD, particularly when it is comorbid with another eating disorder, clinicians should exercise caution with regard to a few aspects of the RD diagnostic information in DSM-5. First, DSM-5 does not provide rationale or description of differential characteristics for other eating disorder presentations (e.g., purging disorder). In fact, rumination behavior has been reported as comorbid in eating disorder presentations in a number of publications (Birmingham & Firoz, 2006; Delaney et al., 2015; Eckern, Stevens, & Mitchell, 1999; Fairburn & Cooper, 1984; Larocca & Della-Fera, 1986; Levine, Wingate, Pfeffer, & Butcher, 1983; Tamburrino et al., 1995; Thomas & Murray, 2016; Weakley, Petti, & Karwisch, 1997; Williamson, Lawson, Bennett, & Hinz, 1989). Second, DSM-5's current language suggests that RD is only differential from anorexia nervosa or bulimia nervosa if the individual spits out the regurgitated food. However, reports in the literature describe comorbid presentations in individuals who swallow or rechew the regurgitated food (e.g., Thomas and Murray, 2016). Third, it is unclear whether or not a degree of shape or weight concerns maintaining rumination behavior precludes the diagnosis of RD. It is possible that for some individuals who engage in rumination behavior, shape and weight concerns become later maintainers of the rumination behavior, as was the case for a patient reported by Thomas and Murray (2016).

In summary, rumination behavior may stand alone or present comorbidly with other medical and psychiatric disorders (e.g., another eating disorder). As more research is conducted with RD and transdiagnostic mechanisms, future editions of the DSM may consider rumination behavior as a symptom manifestation of another underlying disorder for some individuals. Regardless of meeting frank diagnostic criteria for RD, once medical causes have been ruled out, clinicians should target rumination behavior keeping an individual's case formulation in mind.

PREVALENCE

DSM-5 explicitly states that prevalence data for RD are "inconclusive" but that reports show it occurs more frequently in certain groups (e.g., individuals with intellectual disabilities) (APA, 2013, p. 333). Although no data on prevalence for isolated RD in adults exist, the adult literature reports co-occurrence of rumination behavior with both developmental disabilities (5–10%; Gravestock, 2000) and eating disorders (e.g., 7.4% of 149 eating disorder patients; Delaney et al., 2015). More attention is needed from clinicians to assess for rumination behavior, particularly those seeing patients with eating disorders. Rumination symptoms may go unnoticed (Delaney et al., 2015; Parry-Jones, 1994; Tamburrino et al., 1995), likely due to the fact that clinicians often do not think to ask about regurgitation behavior.

ASSESSMENT TOOLS

Research on assessment of rumination symptoms is limited, but clinicians can use available self-report and interview-based assessment tools to guide their assessment of the presence, frequency, and maintenance factors of RD. To rule out physiological causes of persistent regurgitation, a medical specialist (e.g., gastroenterologist) should conduct a formal evaluation.

Self-Report Assessment

Historically, the only standard assessment tool for rumination was the Rome III Diagnostic Questionnaire for the Pediatric Functional GI Disorders (Walker et al., 2006), which was used only in children. Recently with the publication of the Rome IV, there is now a group of measures that includes an adult self-report, adolescent (age 10 years and older) self-report and parent report, and child parent report of current rumination symptoms (Drossman et al., 2016; Palsson et al., 2016). The Rome IV measures include 5 to 6 items that are specific to RD out of the larger measure (i.e., the full adult self-report measure has 89 items). However, there are several factors to consider when using the Rome IV measures. First, the way the primary criterion of whether the individual experiences regurgitations may not be specific enough to rumination (e.g., the adolescent parent report asks "In the past month, how often did food come back up into your child's mouth after eating?"; Drossman et al, 2016) and may be confused with vomiting. Second, the criteria for RD across measures is different. For example, the child/adolescent version includes criteria that regurgitations do not occur during sleep and are not accompanied by nausea or vomiting; these criteria do not appear in the adult version and are not part of the Rome IV diagnostic criteria (Drossman et al., 2016). Third, the qualification of criteria is different across measures. For example, for the qualification of the diagnostic criterion of "recurrent" regurgitations, the adult version specifies at least 2-3 days per month, but the child/adolescent version specifies at least several times a week. If clinicians choose to use the Rome IV measures, we suggest that clinicians do not use the RD questions alone to confer diagnosis and rather use the questions as a starting point to inform a broader clinical assessment.

Interview-Based Assessment

A recent clinician-rated measure called the Eating Disorder Assessment-5 (EDA-5) includes three questions regarding RD based on DSM-5 and can be used as a diagnostic assessment for current full-threshold RD (Sysko et al., 2015). The EDA-5 allows clinicians to easily check diagnostic criteria, but it relies heavily on clinical judgment. For example, the EDA-5 has only one question assessing regurgitation: "In the past month, have you rechewed, reswallowed, or spit out your food? How often has this happened?" This question leaves out other characteristics, such as whether or not the regurgitation happens soon after eating and whether or not the individual experiences retching associated with the regurgitation.

A new measure—the Pica, ARFID, and Rumination Disorder Interview (PARDI)—is currently being pilot tested for validity and reliability in an international multisite trial (Bryant-Waugh et al., n.d.). The PARDI is currently the only measure designed in part to assess both the current presence and severity of RD. In addition to conferring a diagnosis by ascertaining each DSM-5 criterion, the PARDI includes items to help the assessor differentiate between RD and related presentations, such as gastroesophageal reflux disease (GERD) and frank vomiting. Moreover, severity items evaluate the interviewee's degree of perceived control over the regurgitation, rumination frequency (both days and episodes), avoidance of social eating, psychosocial impairment, and associated medical complications.

Last, the Longitudinal Interval Follow-up Evaluation, Eating and Feeding Disorders Version (LIFE-EAT 3), has a single item for rumination to assess the frequency of rumination behavior over a pre-specified period of time (e.g., the past month or past year, depending on the study purpose) and includes diagnostic features for the rater to consider (Eddy, Murray, & Thomas, n.d.). As a guide, clinicians can use the assessment questions for rumination symptoms provided in Table 15.1, which are partially drawn from the LIFE-EAT 3 (Eddy et al., n.d.).

Table 15.1 Assessment Questions for Rumination Symptoms

Feature of Interest	Questions
Differentiation from vomiting (rumination does not include retching)	*Has food come back up into your mouth during or after eating in a way that felt different from throwing up or being sick?*
Functional assessment	*Have you rechewed it, reswallowed it, or spit out it out?* • Assess if the regurgitated material has a pleasant or neutral taste. • Assess if spitting out serves the function of getting rid of ingested calories (i.e., motivations related to shape/weight).
Onset and duration (usually onset <1 hour after eating)	*How long after eating does food first come back up into your mouth? How long after eating does the regurgitation last?*
Differentiation from vomiting (typically rumination occurs in waves)	*When food comes back up into your mouth, does it come up all at once or in waves?*
Differentiation from GERD (typically ruminated material contains recognizable food with lower acidic content)	*How much acid is in what comes back up into your mouth? Does it taste sour or acidic? Are there pieces of food in it?*
Presence of pain (can occur, but should not be the mode)	*Does it usually hurt you when the food comes back up into your mouth?*
Presence of nausea (can occur, but should not be the mode)	*Before food comes back up into your mouth, do you ever feel nauseous or have stomach pain?*

MAINTENANCE FACTORS

Although rumination is part of normal digestion in some animals (e.g., cattle), the mechanisms of rumination in humans have not been thoroughly studied. The current understanding of the mechanisms of regurgitation is from a study conducted more than 30 years ago (Shay et al., 1986). According to Shay's theory, when an individual engages in rumination behavior, his or her upper abdominal muscles contract and the esophageal sphincter opens, forcing gastric content up through the esophagus and into the mouth (Chitkara, Van Tilburg, Whitehead, & Talley, 2006; Shay et al., 1986). Some authors describe the behavior as voluntary but unconscious (Chitkara et al., 2006; Soykan et al., 1997; Tucker et al., 2013). Rumination behavior may be habitual in that, over time, it becomes an involuntary process. The etiological mechanisms of rumination are not clear, but initially, hypersensitivity to gastrointestinal symptoms, including stomach pain, may lead to the development of behavioral attempts to ameliorate digestive discomfort by bringing food back up (Tucker et al., 2013).

To our knowledge, no reports to date have formally described a framework to understand processes that maintain rumination behavior, once formed. We propose a functional model of rumination (Figure 15.1) that highlights general maintaining mechanisms common to all cases, as well as individualized maintaining mechanisms that may be superimposed onto this general framework in a subset of cases (indicated by dashed arrows in Figure 15.1). Typically, regurgitations in RD are driven by habit. That is, contraction of the abdominal wall after eating causes a premonitory urge that leads to the opening of the esophageal sphincter, allowing food to come back up into the mouth. This process becomes habitually reinforced (Chitkara et al., 2006). Depending on the patient's presentation, other factors are then superimposed on the model, in that they may negatively reinforce rumination behavior. Internal experiences, such as emotions (e.g., anxiety and disgust) or physical sensations (e.g., oral stimulation), likely negatively reinforce regurgitation for some individuals because the regurgitation serves a soothing purpose. Concerns about shape and weight may also be a maintenance factor for a subset of individuals who engage in rumination behavior (Delaney et al., 2015; Thomas & Murray, 2016). Shape and weight concerns and self-soothing may possibly reinforce subsequent rechewing, spitting out, or reswallowing. In addition, for some individuals, learned associations between rumination and quantities or types of food may maintain behavior, whereas others regurgitate nondiscriminately. That is, regurgitation may be more likely to occur after consuming certain types of food (e.g., because of texture or ease of bringing the food back up) or amounts of food. It is likely that for many individuals, a combination of various processes maintains rumination symptoms. More research is needed to understand the interaction of physiological processes with cognitive and behavioral factors that maintain rumination.

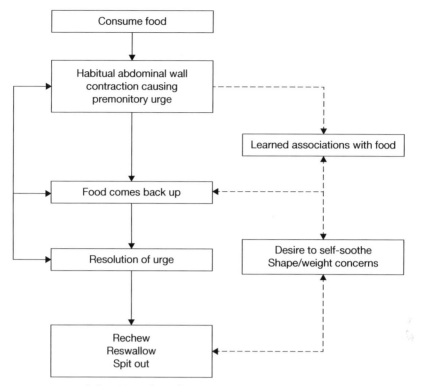

Figure 15.1 Extended CBT-RD formulation.

Case Example

Here, we present an example case (based on a composite of previous cases) to provide a clearer clinical picture of RD.

Theo is a 19-year-old male who recently started college. A gastroenterologist referred Theo for a psychiatric evaluation upon evaluating him for an increased frequency of acid reflux after eating. At age 12 years, Theo was diagnosed with gastroesophogeal reflux. However, during the psychiatric evaluation, he reported that approximately 4 years ago, he started experiencing regurgitation that closely followed eating episodes, and the regurgitated material tasted like food, unlike his prior experience with acid reflux, in which the reflux material was almost completely acidic in content and tasted extremely bitter. Theo's recent gastroenterology evaluation did not identify any motility issues (e.g., gastroparesis), esophageal stenosis, gastric outlet obstruction, achalasia, or other medical rationale for the food regurgitation. His body mass index was in the normal weight range (23.7 kg/m²).

In his initial psychiatric evaluation, Theo endorsed regurgitation consistent with rumination because it was effortless, came in waves, and did not include any retching or gagging. Theo reported that regurgitation typically occurred within 1 hour after eating, and he estimated that food came back up into his mouth approximately 10 times per day. During the past month, he described eating two meals per day—breakfast (at approximately 11:00 a.m.) and dinner (at approximately 7:00 p.m.). Breakfast typically consisted of oatmeal, blueberries, and orange juice. Dinner varied, but it usually comprised a pasta dish with vegetables or a meat and starch. He observed that regurgitation occurred more often when he ate larger amounts of food or denser foods (e.g., mashed potatoes), and it almost always occurred after dinner. Theo estimated that 75% of the time he spat out the regurgitated food (because he found the regurgitation behavior "disgusting") but that he would reswallow it either when he was unable to spit it out or when he liked the taste of the food. However, he reported that when his rumination first started, he enjoyed the taste of the regurgitated material and would often swallow it.

Theo denied any shape and weight concerns. Theo reported that he typically spits out the regurgitated material because he will become nauseous if he reswallows it. In terms of psychosocial impairment, Theo reported that he avoided eating with peers for the past 4 years because he feared that he would ruminate in front of them. Because of this, he reported eating a late breakfast (alone) so that he could skip lunch at the dining hall. Theo reported being motivated to stop his rumination behavior because he felt embarrassed by it. Specifically, he reported concern that he would have trouble developing friendships in college due to his avoidance of social eating, and he also expressed concern that the regurgitated material had been affecting his tooth enamel and leading to bad breath.

TREATMENT APPROACHES

Review of the Case Report Literature

No treatment for RD (neither psychotherapy nor medication) has been rigorously evaluated in a randomized controlled trial. Instead, the treatment literature includes only case reports and chart reviews. In regard to rumination behavior in individuals with developmental disabilities, Lang and colleagues (2011) conducted a systematic review of treatment strategies and found a wide array of strategies ranging from controlling the way food was presented (e.g., withholding certain foods or liquids, forced pacing of food) to manipulation of environmental reinforcers of the rumination behavior (e.g., removing attention from staff members). In regard to individuals without developmental disabilities, the literature is more sparse, but diaphragmatic breathing is a widely used technique (Birmingham & Firoz, 2006; Chial et al., 2003; Cooper, Said, Nunez, Alkhateeb, & McCallum, 2013; Dalton & Czyzewski, 2009; Fernandez, Aspirot, Kerzner, Friedlander, & Di Lorenzo, 2010; Green, Alioto, Mousa, & Di Lorenzo, 2011; Johnson, Corrigan, Crusco, & Jarrell, 1987; Prather, Litzinger, Camilleri, Thumshirn, & Williams,

1997; Thomas & Murray, 2016; Tucker et al., 2013; Vijayvargiya et al., 2014; Wagaman, Williams, & Camilleri, 1998). Diaphragmatic breathing is often delivered simply through a one-session instruction with an occasional follow-up (Tucker et al., 2013; Vijayvargiya et al., 2014). Although the effectiveness of brief outpatient psychoeducation is unclear, diaphragmatic breathing can be incorporated into a broader cognitive–behavioral approach, as was done in two reports (Prather et al., 1997; Thomas & Murray, 2016).

Some case reports have described use of a surgical procedure called Nissen fundoplication (Oelschlager, Chan, Eubanks, Pope, & Pellegrini, 2002). Nissen fundoplication is a laparoscopic procedure used to treat GERD that involves wrapping the upper part of the stomach (gastric fundus) around the lower esophagus to allow the esophageal sphincter to close properly (Oelschlager et al., 2002). However, because there is not adequate evidence for or against less invasive and costly (e.g., behavioral) interventions, Nissen fundoplication should not be the first-line approach to RD. Antidepressants and antianxiety medications have been mentioned as a component of treatment (Khan, Hyman, Cocjin, & Di Lorenzo, 2000); antianxiety medications such as selective serotonin reuptake inhibitors could be a fruitful avenue for future research, particularly if RD is maintained, in part, by anxiety.

Cognitive–Behavioral Therapy for Rumination Disorder

In the absence of evidence-based treatments for RD, we propose a brief cognitive–behavioral therapy for rumination disorder (CBT-RD) informed by published case reports and currently under study in a clinical trial at the Eating Disorders Clinical and Research Program at Massachusetts General Hospital and the Department of Psychology at Drexel University. CBT-RD is designed to last five to eight sessions and involves general CBT techniques that we have tailored specifically for RD. Primary interventions include psychoeducation and self-monitoring to enhance patient awareness of regurgitation timing and triggers (one session), diaphragmatic breathing as a habit-reversal strategy (one session), patient-specific strategies for reducing residual regurgitation episodes (two to five sessions), and relapse prevention (one session). In a preliminary single-case experiment testing the efficacy of CBT-RD, a 27-year-old female patient reduced her rumination frequency from an average of 14 episodes/day to an average of 0 episodes/day, and she maintained this dramatic symptom reduction at 23-week follow-up (Thomas & Murray, 2016). Although clearly more research is needed to determine if CBT-RD should be widely implemented, we present an overview of this treatment as a resource for clinicians who may encounter adults with RD in clinical practice.

PSYCHOEDUCATION
The therapist begins CBT-RD by clearly describing the DSM-5 criteria for RD. Based on the initial clinical evaluation, the therapist explores with the patient

how his or her symptoms appear consistent with DSM-5 criteria. The therapist should also highlight the possible health consequences of rumination (e.g., dehydration, tooth decay, choking, and aspiration)—particularly any that the patient has personally experienced—to enhance motivation for change. The therapist then explains that regurgitation is typically prompted by habitual contraction of the abdominal wall after eating that has become automatic and may be occurring outside the patient's awareness (Chitkara et al., 2006). The therapist should further describe how learned anticipation or hypersensitivity to the sensations of food in the stomach may cause the patient to contract the abdominal wall, open the esophageal sphincter, and allow food to come back up.

In our experience, it is often crucial to help the patient appreciate that his or her persistent regurgitation represents a behavioral pattern that is to some extent within volitional control. Many adults who present de novo for RD treatment have spent years searching for a medical cause and, even upon presentation to a mental health practitioner, continue to hold out the belief that the next round of medical testing may provide the long-awaited solution to their problem. The therapist must therefore emphasize that the patient him- or herself probably plays an active role in promoting the regurgitation—whether consciously or unconsciously—and that a primary goal of treatment is identifying and altering the patient's own behavior. Indeed, the therapist can frame this as welcome news: If the problem is behavioral, then brief CBT could potentially be quite helpful in facilitating symptom resolution.

SELF-MONITORING

Based on prior research indicating that self-monitoring alone can be effective in reducing related behaviors such as purging (Agras, Schneider, Arnow, Raeburn, & Telch, 1989), the next step in CBT-RD is to assign the patient a self-monitoring exercise for homework. Similar to CBT for other eating disorders (Fairburn, 2008; Waller et al., 2007), the therapist may ask the patient to record the timing and contents of every meal or snack throughout the day. However, the most important aspect of monitoring is for the patient to record the number of any regurgitations. Worksheet 15.1 is an example of a self-monitoring record; the therapist should first give the patient a monitoring record with only the first two columns (i.e., time frame and number of regurgitations) because the subsequent columns (i.e., use of diaphragmatic breathing, triggers) will only become relevant in subsequent sessions. After the patient has completed the self-monitoring record, the therapist and patient should review it together in detail to identify patterns, including high-risk times of day for rumination, foods that are more likely than others to be ruminated, and mood states that increase risk for rumination behavior. It is often helpful at this stage to create a rumination timeline, identifying where and when regurgitation typically takes place. For example, some patients avoid ruminating at work or school after lunch but spend hours ruminating in the evening after dinner when home alone. Such a pattern highlights the evening as a high-risk time during which an intervention could be strategically implemented to curtail symptom engagement.

Diaphragmatic Breathing

Diaphragmatic breathing, a form of deep breathing that requires contracting the diaphragm, is a widely used habit-reversal strategy in the treatment of RD because it is incompatible with the abdominal wall contraction required for regurgitation (Birmingham & Firoz, 2006; Tucker et al., 2013; Vijayvargiya et al., 2014). The therapist should demonstrate this technique in session by instructing the patient to place one hand on his or her chest and the other on his or her abdomen and to inhale deeply. The patient is likely to notice that the hand on his or her chest rises, whereas the hand on his or her abdomen remains relatively still. The therapist should then instruct the patient to inhale deeply through the abdomen, trying to keep the hand on his or her chest completely still. The therapist should encourage the patient to breath in and out slowly, allowing at least 3 seconds for each inhale and exhale. The therapist may consider using imagery (e.g., a balloon being inflated and deflated) to help the patient achieve slow, conscious breaths. For patients having difficulty learning the technique while sitting down, practicing diaphragmatic breathing in the supine position can make the rise and fall of the chest and abdomen more salient.

Once the patient has practiced and become confident with diaphragmatic breathing, the therapist should help the patient consult his or her self-monitoring and rumination timeline to identify high-risk times throughout the day when diaphragmatic breathing can be implemented. This is a crucial step in CBT-RD because patients who are familiar with the technique in an abstract sense but do not know when to use it will have difficulty achieving symptom resolution. For example, if the patient ruminates infrequently after breakfast and lunch but does so for a long time after dinner, the therapist can suggest that the patient implement diaphragmatic breathing 1 to 2 minutes after breakfast and lunch but several times during and after dinner (i.e., in between bites while eating, immediately after eating, and also at regularly scheduled intervals after the meal). Early in treatment, it is crucial that the patient follow this schedule every day. The therapist may choose to have the patient record use of diaphragmatic breathing and any additional details in the self-monitoring record (i.e., columns 3 and 4 in the example self-monitoring record shown in Worksheet 15.1).

Similar to the premonitory urge reported by individuals with tic disorders (Reese et al., 2014), some patients also describe a sensory phenomenon immediately preceding rumination episodes (Thomas & Murray, 2016). Going forward in the treatment, in addition to any planned post-meal diaphragmatic breathing sessions, this premonitory urge should always cue the patient to implement diaphragmatic breathing on an ad hoc basis.

Individualized Strategies for Residual Rumination

In our experience, self-monitoring and diaphragmatic breathing are often highly effective in promoting rapid reductions in rumination frequency across the first few sessions of treatment. However, many patients report residual episodes even after they have mastered both self-monitoring and breathing. The maintaining mechanisms for residual regurgitation episodes differ across cases, and those most prominent in the patient's particular case will likely need to be addressed before full symptom resolution can be achieved. Thus, the next task in CBT-RD is for the therapist and the patient to co-create a cognitive–behavioral formulation of the patient's RD presentation based on the patient's insights from the self-monitoring and perceived triggers for residual episodes. Typically, the formulation describes how rumination behavior often occurs habitually, but it may also be negatively reinforcing through subsequent reductions in anxiety or shape and weight concerns. Although the formulation will likely resemble the example presented in Figure 15.1, the therapist should take care to use the patient's own words.

The first possible mechanism is the negatively reinforcing reduction in anxiety that follows rumination behavior. Indeed, many patients perceive rumination behavior as self-soothing. In such cases, the therapist should support the patient in identifying alternative self-soothing activities. For example, some of our patients have found listening to music, reading, talking on the phone, or more diaphragmatic breathing to be effective in this regard. Another possible maintaining mechanism is co-occurring shape and weight concerns. If a patient believes, for example, that spitting out ruminated food is an effective strategy for weight loss or maintenance, this belief can be challenged through behavioral experimentation. For example, the patient could be asked to avoid ruminating entirely, or to reswallow rather than spit out ruminated food, over a period of several weeks to observe the impact, if any, on his or her weight (Thomas & Murray, 2016). A last potential maintaining mechanism is learned associations with specific foods. Some patients report that they are more likely to ruminate after eating particular foods, including those that are soft (e.g., ice cream and pudding) or easily chewable (e.g., bread). In that case, it is often helpful to eliminate these foods from the diet during the early treatment sessions while the patient is focusing on rapid symptom reduction. Once substantial reductions in rumination frequency have been achieved, foods with learned rumination associations can be slowly reintroduced during low-risk mealtimes or snack times (based on the rumination timeline), followed by diaphragmatic breathing. Using this exposure and response prevention strategy, the patient will begin to learn that it is possible to consume any food without ruminating, even those historically associated with regurgitation.

RELAPSE PREVENTION
Toward the end of treatment, the therapist should reduce the patient's reliance on scheduled diaphragmatic breathing and instead encourage the patient to being implementing diaphragmatic breathing only when he or she feels the premonitory urge. This is because, in our experience, after engaging in diaphragmatic breathing regularly for a period of time, the patient is often better able to appreciate his or her role in contracting the abdominal wall prior to rumination. Once the patient has brought these muscle contractions into conscious awareness, he or she is better able to curtail them prior to rumination onset.

In the final session, the therapist should review the patient's progress over the course of treatment. The patient should make a list of CBT-RD strategies that he or she found helpful (e.g., self-monitoring and diaphragmatic breathing), as well as potential triggers for relapse into rumination behavior in the future (e.g., stress at work or school) and how to address these (e.g., resume self-monitoring, implement regular diaphragmatic breathing, and/or return for a booster session of CBT-RD).

Future Research into RD Intervention

Unfortunately, there is a lack of rigorous research on the effectiveness and efficacy of intervention strategies for RD. In addition to the core techniques used in CBT-RD (i.e., self-monitoring and diaphragmatic breathing), other interventions need further research. A few case reports mention the use of biofeedback treatment (Fox, Young, Anggiansah, Anggiansah, & Sanderson, 2006; Khan et al., 2000; Shay et al., 1986), and different forms of biofeedback (e.g., audiovisual feedback to electromyography signals in relation to a meal; Shay et al., 1986) could be further studied. In addition, other strategies, such as progressive muscle relaxation or autogenic training, may serve as a competing response to rumination or be an alternative self-soothing technique.

To test the efficacy of these techniques, randomized control trials are ideal and could use a dismantling design in which the treatment strategy of interest (e.g., diaphragmatic breathing) alone is compared to a treatment involving cognitive–behavioral components (e.g., self-monitoring, behavioral experiments). However, due to the low base rate and the study of RD being in its infancy, case reports are a viable research design for examining the effectiveness of intervention techniques. In fact, we (Murray & Thomas) are currently conducting an open trial of the treatment of RD. With case reports, single-case experimental designs can be easily implemented, particularly when the clinician can introduce, remove, and reintroduce the intervention technique (i.e., ABAB reversal design).

CONCLUSION AND FUTURE DIRECTIONS

Little research exists on RD. The literature currently includes mostly case reports and retrospective chart reviews. More research is needed to better understand the pathophysiology and etiology, prevalence, course, outcome, and maintenance mechanisms of RD. Because RD has a low base rate in the general population, research in this area is challenging. In addition, because rumination symptoms more commonly present in individuals with another eating disorder (Delaney et al., 2015) or developmental disability (Lang et al., 2011), both represent high-risk populations from which participants could be recruited to gain further insight into the maintaining mechanisms and treatment targets. Finally, more research is needed on treatment to determine the most powerful intervention strategies.

Worksheet 15.1

Self-Monitoring Record

Please create an entry for each episode of rumination. Write a hash mark for each time food comes back up and "X" for when you use diaphragmatic breathing according to your schedule you agreed upon with your therapist. In "Triggers" write anything relevant to your triggers for rumination.

Time Frame	Number of Regurgitations	Diaphragmatic Breathing	Triggers

REFERENCES

Agras, W. S., Schneider, J. A., Arnow, B., Raeburn, S. D., & Telch, C. F. (1989). Cognitive–behavioral and response-prevention treatments for bulimia nervosa. *Journal of Consulting and Clinical Psychology, 57*(2), 215.

American Psychiatric Association. (2000). *Diagnostic and statistical manual of mental disorders* (4th ed., text rev.). Washington, DC: American Psychiatric Association.

American Psychiatric Association. (2013). *Diagnostic and statistical manual of mental disorders* (fifth ed.). Arlington, VA: American Psychiatric Publishing.

Birmingham, C., & Firoz, T. (2006). Rumination in eating disorders: Literature review. *Eating and Weight Disorders, 11*(3), e85–e89.

Bryant-Waugh, R., Thomas, J. J., Eddy, K. T., Micali, N., Melhuish, L., Cresswell, L., & Cooke, L. (n.d.). The Pica, ARFID, & Rumination Disorder Interview (PARDI). Manuscript in preparation.

Chial, H. J., Camilleri, M., Williams, D. E., Litzinger, K., & Perrault, J. (2003). Rumination syndrome in children and adolescents: Diagnosis, treatment, and prognosis. *Pediatrics, 111*(1), 158–162.

Chitkara, D. K., Van Tilburg, M., Whitehead, W. E., & Talley, N. J. (2006). Teaching diaphragmatic breathing for rumination syndrome. *American Journal of Gastroenterology, 101*(11), 2449–2452.

Cooper, C. J., Said, S., Nunez, A., Alkhateeb, H., & McCallum, R. W. (2013). Chronic vomiting and diarrhea in a young adult female. *American Journal of Case Reports, 14*, 449–452.

Dalton, W. T., 3rd, & Czyzewski, D. I. (2009). Behavioral treatment of habitual rumination: Case reports. *Digestive Diseases and Sciences, 54*(8), 1804–1807.

Delaney, C. B., Eddy, K. T., Hartmann, A. S., Becker, A. E., Murray, H. B., & Thomas, J. J. (2015). Pica and rumination behavior among individuals seeking treatment for eating disorders or obesity. *International Journal of Eating Disorders, 48*(2), 238–248.

Drossman, D., Chang, L., Chey, W. D., Kellow, J., Tack, J., Whitehead, W. E., & Committees, R. I. (Eds.). (2016). *ROME IV: Functional Gastrointestinal Disorders* (4th ed.). Degnon Associates.

Eckern, M., Stevens, W., & Mitchell, J. (1999). The relationship between rumination and eating disorders. *International Journal of Eating Disorders, 26*(4), 414–419.

Eddy, K. T., Murray, H. B., & Thomas, J. J. (n.d.). Longitudinal Interval Follow-up Evaluation, Eating and Feeding Disorders version.Unpublished measure.

Fairburn, C. G. (2008). *Cognitive behavior therapy and eating disorders*. New York, NY: Guilford.

Fairburn, C. G., & Cooper, P. J. (1984). Rumination in bulimia nervosa. *British Medical Journal, 288*(6420), 826–827.

Fernandez, S., Aspirot, A., Kerzner, B., Friedlander, J., & Di Lorenzo, C. (2010). Do some adolescents with rumination syndrome have "supragastric vomiting"? *Journal of Pediatric Gastroenterology and Nutrition, 50*(1), 103–105.

Fox, M., Young, A., Anggiansah, R., Anggiansah, A., & Sanderson, J. (2006). A 22 year old man with persistent regurgitation and vomiting: Case outcome. *British Medical Journal, 333*(7559), 133.

Fredericks, D. W., Carr, J. E., & Williams, W. L. (1998). Overview of the treatment of rumination disorder for adults in a residential setting. *Journal of Behavior Therapy and Experimental Psychiatry, 29*(1), 31–40.

Gravestock, S. (2000). Eating disorders in adults with intellectual disability. *Journal of Intellectual Disability Research, 44*(6), 625–637.

Green, A. D., Alioto, A., Mousa, H., & Di Lorenzo, C. (2011). Severe pediatric rumination syndrome: Successful interdisciplinary inpatient management. *Journal of Pediatric Gastroenterology and Nutrition, 52*(4), 414–418.

Johnson, W. G., Corrigan, S. A., Crusco, A. H., & Jarrell, M. P. (1987). Behavioral assessment and treatment of postprandial regurgitation. *Journal of Clinical Gastroenterology, 9*(6), 679–684.

Kanodia, A. K., Kim, I., & Sturmberg, J. P. (2011). A personalized systems medicine approach to refractory rumination. *Journal of Evaluation in Clinical Practice, 17*(3), 515–519.

Khan, S., Hyman, P. E., Cocjin, J., & Di Lorenzo, C. (2000). Rumination syndrome in adolescents. *Journal of Pediatrics, 136*(4), 528–531.

Lang, R., Mulloy, A., Giesbers, S., Pfeiffer, B., Delaune, E., Didden, R., . . . O'Reilly, M. (2011). Behavioral interventions for rumination and operant vomiting in individuals with intellectual disabilities: A systematic review. *Research in Developmental Disabilities, 32*(6), 2193–2205.

Larocca, F. E., & Della-Fera, M. A. (1986). Rumination: Its significance in adults with bulimia nervosa. *Psychosomatics, 27*(3), 209–212.

Levine, D., Wingate, D., Pfeffer, J., & Butcher, P. (1983). Habitual rumination: A benign disorder. *British Medical Journal, 287*(6387), 255–256.

O'Brien, M. D., Bruce, B. K., & Camilleri, M. (1995). The rumination syndrome: Clinical features rather than manometric diagnosis. *Gastroenterology, 108*(4), 1024–1029.

Oelschlager, B. K., Chan, M. M., Eubanks, T. R., Pope, C. E., 2nd, & Pellegrini, C. A. (2002). Effective treatment of ruminations with Nissen fundoplication. *Journal of Gastrointestinal Surgery, 6*(4), 638–644.

Parry-Jones, B. (1994). Merycism or rumination disorder. A historical investigation and current assessment. *British Journal of Psychiatry, 165*(3), 303–314.

Prather, C., Litzinger, K. L., Camilleri, M., Thumshirn, M., & Williams, D. E. (1997). An open trial of cognitive behavioral intervention in the treatment of rumination syndrome. *Gastroenterology, 112*, A808.

Reese, H. E., Scahill, L., Peterson, A. L., Crowe, K., Woods, D. W., Piacentini, J., . . . Wilhelm, S. (2014). The premonitory urge to tic: Measurement, characteristics, and correlates in older adolescents and adults. *Behavior Therapy, 45*(2), 177–186.

Shay, S. S., Johnson, L. F., Wong, R. K., Curtis, D. J., Rosenthal, R., Lamott, J. R., & Owensby, L. C. (1986). Rumination, heartburn, and daytime gastroesophageal reflux: A case study with mechanisms denned and successfully treated with biofeedback therapy. *Journal of Clinical Gastroenterology, 8*(2), 115–126.

Soykan, I., Chen, J., Kendall, B. J., & McCallum, R. W. (1997). The rumination syndrome: Clinical and manometric profile, therapy, and long-term outcome. *Digestive Diseases and Sciences, 42*(9), 1866–1872.

Sysko, R., Glasofer, D. R., Hildebrandt, T., Klimek, P., Mitchell, J. E., Berg, K. C., . . . Walsh, B. T. (2015). The eating disorder assessment for DSM-5 (EDA-5): Development and validation of a structured interview for feeding and eating disorders. *International Journal of Eating Disorders, 48*(5), 452–463.

Tack, J., Blondeau, K., Boecxstaens, V., & Rommel, N. (2011). Review article: The pathophysiology, differential diagnosis and management of rumination syndrome. *Alimentary Pharmacology and Therapeutics, 33*(7), 782–788.

Tamburrino, M. B., Campbell, N. B., Franco, K. N., & Evans, C. L. (1995). Rumination in adults: Two case histories. *International Journal of Eating Disorders, 17*(1), 101–104.

Thomas, J. J., & Murray, H. B. (2016). Cognitive–behavioral treatment of adult rumination behavior in the setting of disordered eating: A single case experimental design. *International Journal of Eating Disorders, 49*(10), 967–972.

Tucker, E., Knowles, K., Wright, J., & Fox, M. R. (2013). Rumination variations: Aetiology and classification of abnormal behavioural responses to digestive symptoms based on high-resolution manometry studies. *Alimentary Pharmacology and Therapeutics, 37*(2), 263–274.

Vijayvargiya, P., Iturrino, J., Camilleri, M., Shin, A., Vazquez-Roque, M., Katzka, D. A., . . . Seime, R. J. (2014). Novel association of rectal evacuation disorder and rumination syndrome: Diagnosis, comorbidities, and treatment. *United European Gastroenterology Journal, 2*(1), 38–46.

Wagaman, J. R., Williams, D. E., & Camilleri, M. (1998). Behavioral intervention for the treatment of rumination. *Journal of Pediatric Gastroenterology and Nutrition, 27*(5), 596–598.

Walker, L., Caplan, A., & Rasquin, A. (2006). Rome III diagnostic questionnaire for the pediatric functional GI disorders. In D. A. Drossman et al. (Eds.), *Rome III: The functional gastrointestinal disorders* (3rd ed., pp. 961–990). Degnon Associates.

Waller, G., Cordery, H., Corstorphine, E., Hinrichsen, H., Lawson, R., Mountford, V., & Russell, K. (2007). *Cognitive behavioral therapy for eating disorders: A comprehensive treatment guide.* Cambridge, England: Cambridge University Press.

Weakley, M. M., Petti, T. A., & Karwisch, G. (1997). Case study: Chewing gum treatment of rumination in an adolescent with an eating disorder. *Journal of the American Academy of Child and Adolescent Psychiatry, 36*(8), 1124–1127.

Williamson, D. A., Lawson, O. D., Bennett, S. M., & Hinz, L. (1989). Behavioral treatment of night bingeing and rumination in an adult case of bulimia nervosa. *Journal of Behavior Therapy and Experimental Psychiatry, 20*(1), 73–77.

16

Atypical Eating Disorders and Specific Phobia of Vomiting

Clinical Presentation and Treatment Approaches

ALEXANDRA KEYES AND DAVID VEALE ■

SPECIFIC PHOBIA OF VOMITING: AN OVERVIEW

Specific phobia of vomiting (SPOV), also known as "emetophobia," is categorized as a specific phobia: "other" subtype. SPOV is characterized by an intense and irrational fear of vomiting and avoidance behaviors related to vomiting situations (American Psychiatric Association [APA], 2013). Clinically, SPOV can present in many forms (McNally, 1997). For example, individuals may present with a fear of vomiting themselves, or they may fear being in the presence of other people vomiting. Studies differ in the prevalence of fears reported by people with SPOV. Across studies, 41–75% of participants reported mainly fearing vomiting themselves, 18–45% reported fearing others vomiting, and 8–47% reported fearing both scenarios equally. Fear of others vomiting may be linked to fear of self vomiting, due to perceptions that others are contagious or acting as a trigger for their fear of self vomiting. In addition, 16–62% of people with SPOV report fearing vomiting in a public place (Holler, van Overveld, Jutglar, & Trinka, 2013; Lipsitz, Fyer, Paterniti, & Klein, 2001; van Hout & Bouman, 2012; Veale & Lambrou, 2006). It has been suggested that a fear of seeing others vomiting is associated with lower illness severity, possibly due to less experience of internal sensations and avoidance (Price, Veale, & Brewin, 2012). A survey of individuals with fear of vomit also found fears related to contamination or becoming ill; the sight, smell, and taste of vomit; losing control; the feeling of "gagging"; feelings of helplessness or panic; feeling disgusted of themselves; and others finding them repulsive and not wanting to know them (Holler et al., 2013; van Hout & Bouman, 2012; Veale, Costa, Murphy, & Ellison, 2012; Veale & Lambrou, 2006).

ATYPICAL EATING DISORDERS AND SPOV

Eating disorders (EDs) were formally categorized in the fourth edition of the *Diagnostic and Statistical Manual of Mental Disorders* (DSM-IV; APA, 1994) into three distinct disorders: anorexia nervosa (AN), bulimia nervosa (BN), and eating disorders not otherwise specified (EDNOS). The vast majority of cases fell into this latter residual and atypical category (Machado, Machado, Gonçalves, & Hoek, 2007). This category represents a heterogeneous group of individuals, for which treatment and good outcome may be more challenging. Recent changes to the diagnostic framework of the DSM-5 (APA, 2013) have been made, whereby a broader range of ED profiles are formally recognized, such as binge-eating disorder, pica, and avoidant/restrictive food intake disorder (ARFID). The term other specified feeding or eating disorder (OFSED) has replaced EDNOS as the atypical and residual category of EDs. In the DSM-5, the diagnostic criteria of severity have also been relaxed, further reducing the prevalence of atypical diagnoses (APA, 2013). Research suggests that this reorganization has led to a reduction in OFSED cases in community samples (Machado, Gonçalves, & Hoek, 2013). However, up to 50% of ED cases still fall within the residual OFSED category according to DSM-5 criteria (Keel, Brown, Holm-Denoma, & Bodell, 2011). This suggests that many cases are more diverse in ED psychopathology than is described in the diagnostic spectrum (Murray & Anderson, 2015). It is therefore important to accurately define the motivations for disordered eating in order to facilitate accurate diagnosis and appropriate and timely treatments of specific symptoms profiles (Murray & Anderson, 2015). Furthermore, illness presentations that centrally feature disordered eating pathology but remain outside the formal ED spectrum further complicate this task (Murray & Anderson, 2015).

Research suggests that there may be some crossover between ED and SPOV psychopathology and that it may be possible to have a diagnosis of both. However, comorbidity rates between EDs and SPOV remain unclear. Based on diagnostic interview (Diagnostic Interview for Mental Disorders–Research Version), a lifetime comorbidity rate between all subtypes of specific phobias and EDs was reported as 4% in a German community sample of women (Becker et al., 2007). However, due to very small numbers, no significant association between the two disorders was found (Becker et al., 2007). In a sample of participants using a German Internet forum for emetophobia, 4.29% were diagnosed as also having an ED by a medical professional (Holler et al., 2013). Finally, 7.8% of participants using an emetophobia Internet group reported suffering from AN (Davidson, Boyle, & Lauchlan, 2008). However, this was based on responses to an online questionnaire. Whether this is evidence of a true comorbidity therefore remains unclear due to methodological limitations in studies. It may also be that individuals with SPOV are misdiagnosed with AN due to eating-disordered attitudes and behaviors that are driven by phobic fears as opposed to eating psychopathology (Veale et al., 2012).

The overlap in clinical presentation between atypical ED and SPOV presents a difficult task for the management and treatment of these disorders by professionals. Vandereycken (2011) found that SPOV was unknown among 29.7% of a sample of ED specialists. Due to a lack of research on SPOV, this rate may be even higher, and therefore patients with SPOV often may be overlooked by professionals and commonly misdiagnosed with atypical EDs (Boschen, 2007; Holler et al., 2013; Lipsitz et al., 2001; van Overveld, de Jong, Peters, van Hout, & Bouman, 2008; Veale & Lambrou, 2006). In addition, almost half of ED professionals reported seeing SPOV in their clinics, highlighting the contrast between clinical reality and lack of scientific attention.

Individuals with SPOV may present with similar eating attitudes and behaviors to those typically seen in EDs. Manassis and Kalman (1990) describe case reports of four adolescent girls who had each lost 15% of their body weight and showed significant food avoidance behaviors. However, none of these cases met criteria for AN, and they reported that their refusal to eat was driven by fear of vomiting as opposed to a desire to control weight or shape (Manassis & Kalman, 1990). A portion of patients with SPOV may restrict their food intake in order to eliminate all risk of vomiting (Veale et al., 2012). Restriction may occur in the amount of food eaten, restriction in certain contexts (e.g., food cooked by someone else or restricting the types of food eaten due to a learned association between a type of food and an episode of vomiting) (Holler et al., 2013; Lipsitz et al., 2001; Veale, 2009). Commonly avoided foods appear to be meat and poultry, seafood and shellfish, and foreign foods (Price et al., 2012; Veale & Lambrou, 2006). A systematic study of eating behavior in people with SPOV found that approximately one-third of participants restricted their food and engaged in abnormal eating behavior. Individuals who restricted their food reported significantly higher avoidance of eating in restaurants, salad bars or buffets, food not prepared by themselves, foreign meals, and precooked foods (Veale et al., 2012). Another study found that among a sample of individuals with SPOV, 80% reported abnormal eating behavior due to a fear of vomiting, 61.2% reported food avoidance, and 98% reported avoiding certain foods (Holler et al., 2013).

Food avoidance behavior may be associated with low weight in people with SPOV (Holler et al., 2013). The majority of individuals with SPOV are reported to be of normal weight. In two studies, mean body mass index (BMI) in participants with SPOV was 20.3–22.8 (Holler et al., 2013; Veale et al., 2012). A proportion of SPOV individuals were found to be underweight (3.7% had BMI <17.5, and 8.5% had BMI <18.5) (Veale et al., 2012), and 37.4% had BMI <19 (Holler et al., 2013). The prevalence of underweight in these samples is higher than the estimate of 1.6% underweight adults in the general population (Fryar & Ogden, 2010). Williams, Field, Riegel, and Paul (2011) report a case of SPOV and total food refusal, with BMI of 13.6. Manassis and Kalman (1990) describe four cases with SPOV that had lost 15% of their body weight due to fear of vomiting. Three other case series report loss of weight as a result of restricted eating driven by fear of vomiting, but they do not report BMI (Hunter & Antony, 2009; Kobori, 2011; Whitton, Luiselli, & Donaldson, 2006). Lower weight in SPOV appears to be associated with food restriction (Veale et al., 2012) and avoidance behavior (Holler et al., 2013). Food restriction and underweight may further complicate the differential diagnosis between SPOV and atypical ED (Veale et al., 2012). Interestingly, of the proportion of those found to be underweight in one sample, 16.1% had a diagnosis of an ED, despite more than half (59.2%) perceiving themselves to be too thin. In the underweight group, 91.8% also suffered from symptoms of nausea (Holler et al., 2013). This suggests that the locus of fear differs in SPOV compared to individuals with EDs, in that the eating behaviors in SPOV are driven by reducing the likelihood of vomiting and not due to a desire to lose weight.

Food restriction in SPOV was found to be associated with significant increases in severity of SPOV symptoms, anxiety, and overall impairment (Veale et al., 2012). It was suggested that the relationship between food restriction and weight loss with increased severity of SPOV symptoms is likely to be bidirectional, with one aggravating the other (Veale et al., 2012). For example, food restriction may be associated with increased nausea (Holler et al., 2013), which may be interpreted as evidence of increased risk of vomiting, therefore leading to further restriction. In addition, dietary restriction and weight loss are likely to be positively and negatively reinforcing by feelings of being in control and emotional numbness reducing anxiety, respectively (Veale et al., 2012).

To date, research suggests that SPOV cases may be misdiagnosed as having an atypical ED due to food restriction and, in a small proportion, low weight. It may be possible to present with both atypical ED and SPOV, and in such cases food restriction may be conceptualized as driven by a fear of vomiting. Clinically, it would be important to elicit information regarding the main driver of atypical eating behaviors in making differential diagnoses—for example, fear of weight and shape or losing control versus fear of vomiting. However, a fear of vomiting may also be conceptualized as a contributory factor to an atypical ED. Norris et al. (2014) carried out a retrospective review of adolescent ED patients who qualified for a diagnosis of ARFID compared to a matched sample of AN patients. Participants with ARFID described features of food avoidance, loss of appetite, abdominal pain, and fear of vomiting. A total of 26.5% of patients appeared to be preoccupied with concerns of aversive consequences of eating, such as vomiting, and 17.6% experienced nausea. Interestingly, 12% of the patients with ARFID were later rediagnosed with AN due to the development of body image preoccupations, distortions in weight or shape, and a drive for thinness over the course of treatment (Norris et al., 2014). This suggests that those with ARFID may go on to develop AN and that a fear of vomiting and/or nausea may act as contributory factors. Further research is needed to explore the relationship between fear of vomiting and the development of EDs. This may contribute to existing knowledge of potential triggering factors for atypical EDs, more accurate diagnosis, and better treatment outcomes.

Epidemiology

There is a consistently reported gender bias within SPOV, with studies reporting that samples are between 86% and 97% female (Holler et al., 2013; Lipsitz et al.,

2001; Price et al., 2012; Veale, Hennig, & Gledhill, 2015; Veale & Lambrou, 2006). Women are reported to have a prevalence rate of SPOV that is four times higher than that of men (Becker et al., 2007). This may be due to the fact that women are thought to report more fears than men, although the gender ratio in specific phobias is typically approximately 2 (Ollendick & King, 1991; Stevenson, Batten, & Cherner, 1992). Sex hormones might also interact with conditioning processes to produce such skewed distribution (Merckelbach, de Jong, Muris, & van Den Hout, 1996).

SPOV typically appears to start in childhood, with a mean age of onset reported to be between 7.5 and 15.7 years (Becker et al., 2007; Holler et al., 2013; Lipsitz et al., 2001; McNally, 1997; Price et al., 2012; Veale & Lambrou, 2006; Veale, Murphy, Ellison, Kanakam, & Costa, 2013; Veale et al., 2015). SPOV has a chronic course, with a mean duration of 25.9 years (Lipsitz et al., 2001; Veale & Lambrou, 2006) and a mean duration before presentation to services of 14.25 years (Veale et al., 2015). In a survey of 100 individuals with self-diagnosed SPOV, 52% reported that they had never experienced a remission of their symptoms, 36% reported experiencing partial or brief remissions, and 12% reported periods of full remission lasting 6 months (Veale & Lambrou, 2006).

Prevalence

To date, there has been only one epidemiological study of specific phobias that asked about fear of vomiting (Becker et al., 2007). Data suggest that phobias might be heterogeneous even within DSM-IV categories. A point prevalence rate of 0.1% was found for SPOV. A survey of two self-reported vomit-fearful groups found that fear of vomiting was surprisingly common in the Dutch community, with a point prevalence rate of 8.8% (van Hout & Bouman, 2012). It has been suggested that prevalence rates have so far been underestimated due to an overlap of symptoms with other disorders, such as health anxiety, obsessive–compulsive disorder, and anorexia nervosa (Veale, Murphy, et al., 2013). Therefore, people with SPOV may be likely to be misdiagnosed, thus contributing to an underrecognition and reduction in estimation of prevalence in SPOV (Boschen, 2007; Manassis & Kalman, 1990; Veale, 2009).

Features of SPOV

SPOV is associated with a high degree of anxiety and daily distress (Lipsitz et al., 2001; van Hout & Bouman, 2012; Veale & Lambrou, 2006). In most cases, anxiety is triggered by both external stimuli, such as the sight of food, and internal stimuli, such as sensations in the stomach or nausea (Lipsitz et al., 2001). Fear and avoidance of vomit-related situations are reported as chronic and disabling. SPOV has profound consequences for daily life and personal well-being (Davidson et al., 2008; van Hout & Bouman, 2012; van Overveld et al., 2008). It also impairs work, leisure, social, and home/marital life and romantic relationships (Davidson et al., 2008; Lipsitz et al., 2001; Veale & Lambrou, 2006). Various safety-seeking behaviors are employed by people with SPOV in an attempt to reduce the likelihood of the feared situation occurring (i.e., vomiting). These include looking for escape routes, checking the expiration date on food, avoiding drunk or sick people, carrying antacid medications, avoiding or postponing pregnancy, avoiding travel abroad, and excessive washing and cleaning or reassurance seeking (Lipsitz et al., 2001; Price et al., 2012; van Hout & Bouman, 2012; Veale & Lambrou, 2006; Veale, Murphy, et al., 2013). Other symptoms include gastric complaints when anxious, reported by 100% of a vomit-fearful sample (van Hout & Bouman, 2012), and nausea almost every day (Veale & Lambrou, 2006). Although nausea is not reported to lead to vomiting in the majority of cases, it is associated with high levels of distress and interference with daily routine (Holler et al., 2013).

SPOV is a relatively understudied disorder compared to other specific phobias (van Hout & Bouman, 2012), and it is often misdiagnosed among clinicians. As such, it is important to distinguish the main clinical features of SPOV in order to support accurate diagnoses of SPOV and disorders that feature related symptoms.

NAUSEA

Nausea may be defined as a discomforting and unpleasant sensation that is related to the gastrointestinal system (Holler et al., 2013). It is potentially an important and distinctive feature of SPOV because nausea may be interpreted as a potential precursor of the catastrophic scenario of vomiting (van Hout & Bouman, 2012; Veale & Lambrou, 2006). SPOV may therefore be interpreted as a fear of highly aversive physical cues such as nausea (Holler et al., 2013). The majority of sufferers of nausea present for medical treatment of symptoms, but 13.5% receive no diagnosis. Half of those presenting to clinicians are diagnosed with "psychic causes" for their symptoms (Holler et al., 2013). Sufferers may also be misdiagnosed with irritable bowel syndrome or similar physical disorders instead of SPOV (Holler et al., 2013). A lack of a satisfying outcome following medical consultation may be due to the relative unawareness of SPOV phenomenology by medical professionals (Holler et al., 2013).

The symptom of nausea may also be relevant for the development of SPOV because it may be the predominant symptom perceived by patients. In a sample of 131 participants with SPOV, 80.9% reported suffering from nausea, which was described as permanent in almost one-fourth of cases and at least once a week in the majority (73.6%) (Holler et al., 2013). Another study found that a sample of individuals with SPOV who restricted their food intake reported symptoms of nausea significantly more often than those who did not restrict their food (Veale et al., 2012). The experience of nausea may lead to hypervigilance and selective attention toward internal sensations and therefore increased perception of nausea. This in turn may start a vicious circle whereby fear, hypervigilance, selective attention, and the experience of nausea are self-perpetuating.

INTRUSIVE IMAGERY

Due to the experience of gastrointestinal symptoms in SPOV and the aversive nature of actually vomiting, imagery may play an important part in the experience of physical sensations in SPOV (Price et al., 2012). In a study of 36 participants with SPOV recruited from online support groups and outpatient clinics, 80.6% reported experiencing intrusive imagery about vomiting when they were feeling anxious about their phobia (Price et al., 2012). Of those who experienced intrusive imagery, aversive memories appeared to comprise a significant proportion of imagery: 51.7% experienced imagery related to adult memories of the most recent or striking experience of vomiting, compared to 31% of imagery being related to aversive childhood memories of vomiting. Almost 20% of participants also reported experiencing worse-case scenarios of vomiting or "flashforwards," in which individuals would experience particularly distressing images of potential vomiting experiences. Images were reported to be specifically triggered 87.3% of the time by nausea, internal gastrointestinal sensations, or others looking unwell (Price et al., 2012). In terms of the nature of the imagery, 100% of participants reported visual components to imagery, with 40–48% reporting physical sensations, auditory components, and taste or smell being part of the image. In addition, a significant correlation was found between imagery and phobia severity (Price et al., 2012).

Loss of Control

Another feature associated with SPOV is the tendency of sufferers to have a high desire to retain control over their lives. Davidson et al. (2008) found that participants with SPOV scored significantly higher for internal locus of control compared to phobic and nonphobic control groups. Specifically, the SPOV group was found to score significantly higher than both control groups for internal health locus of control. Similarly, an ED sample was found to have significantly higher scores on external locus of control,–powerful others, negative sense of control, ineffectiveness, and fear of losing self-control compared to a non-ED control group (Froreich, Vartanian, Grisham, & Touyz, 2016). In the same sample, a sense of ineffectiveness and fear of losing self-control were found to be the only significant independent predictors of eating pathology. This suggests that sufferers of SPOV are more likely to regard most aspects of their life, particularly nausea and vomiting, to be within their power or control (Holler et al., 2013). Therefore, the phobia may be related to a fear of vomiting, which is associated with a perceived loss of control. A desire for control may also explain the many behaviors employed by people with SPOV to reduce the likelihood of a physical event that is, by nature, very difficult to control (Davidson et al., 2008; Holler et al., 2013). Arousal may also be greater when patients believe that no control exists and when they are unable to exercise their high desire for maintaining control (Davidson et al., 2008).

Etiology of SPOV

To date, there is little research evidence regarding the factors involved in the etiology of SPOV. In addition to the features described previously, two factors have received empirical attention and are thought to be involved in the development of SPOV: autobiographical memories of vomiting and disgust sensitivity.

AUTOBIOGRAPHICAL MEMORIES OF VOMITING

Aversive experiences of the self and/or other people vomiting at an early age and the associated memories of these events are thought to play an important role in the development of SPOV. McNally (1997) reported that 100% of a sample of individuals with SPOV could recall a triggering incident involving themselves or others vomiting. In a survey of 56 members of an Internet support group for SPOV, 29% of respondents recalled severe or vivid bouts of vomiting, 59% recalled vivid experiences of others vomiting, and 20% recalled distressing experiences of both (Lipsitz et al., 2001). Veale, Murphy, et al. (2013) explored autobiographical memories of self and others vomiting before and after the onset of fear of vomiting in 94 people with SPOV and a control group (n = 90). It was found that a significantly greater number of the SPOV group (100%) could recall at least one memory of themselves vomiting compared to only 93.3% of the control group. Aversive memories of the first episode of vomiting were also recalled at a significantly younger age in the SPOV group than in the control group. The SPOV group also rated these episodes as significantly more distressing and associated vomiting with more aversive social or health consequences.

Interestingly, the SPOV group recalled significantly less lifetime memories of themselves vomiting, yet there were no significant differences in the median number of memories of vomiting before the onset of SPOV compared to control (Veale, Murphy, et al., 2013). This is supported by similar findings that people with SPOV report no significant differences in the number of times they have actually vomited or been ill compared to controls (van Hout & Bouman, 2012; Veale & Lambrou, 2006). This suggests that after the onset of SPOV, sufferers may be successful at slightly reducing the frequency of vomiting episodes due to hypervigilance, avoidance, and safety-seeking behaviors (Veale, Murphy, et al., 2013). Furthermore, vomit-fearful participants reported a longer time since the last episode of vomiting (5–10 years) compared to the control group (van Hout & Bouman, 2012). Data are supportive of an associative learning model for the development of SPOV, in that aversive experiences of vomiting at an early age and associated memories are associated with fear and result in subsequent behavior changes that serve to maintain the SPOV over time.

DISGUST SENSITIVITY

Disgust and fear of contamination have also been proposed as potential factors that may contribute to the development of SPOV. Two concepts of disgust have been proposed by Van Overveld, de Jong, Peters, Cavanagh, and Davey (2006): *Disgust propensity* describes how quickly an individual experiences disgust, and *disgust sensitivity* refers to how negatively the individual evaluates this disgust experience. A group that scored high on fear of vomiting was also likely to report high levels of disgust sensitivity (Veale, Murphy, et al., 2013). In addition, an Internet survey of members of a Dutch website for people with SPOV (n = 172) and a control group (n = 39) found that the SPOV group reported significantly higher levels of both disgust propensity and disgust sensitivity compared to controls. It was also found that disgust sensitivity was the best predictor of SPOV symptom severity (van Overveld et al., 2008). In another study, both disgust sensitivity and disgust propensity showed a strong and positive correlation with SPOV severity in a sample of individuals high in fear of vomiting (Verwoerd, van Hout, & de Jong, 2016). This suggests that individuals with SPOV may be more sensitive to feelings of disgust and may try to avoid the emotion of disgust in an attempt to avoid related feelings of nausea (Boschen, 2007; Lipsitz et al., 2001; Veale & Lambrou, 2006).

Another factor that may implicate the role of disgust in the development of SPOV is emotional reasoning. This involves the use of feelings in order to validate unhelpful thoughts—for example, "If I feel anxious, then this must be dangerous" (Arntz, Rauner, & Van den Hout, 1995). Verwoerd et al. (2016) found that participants high in fear of vomiting generally used emotional response information (anxiety and disgust) to infer danger, risk of contamination and of becoming ill, and that more pronounced emotional reasoning was mainly driven by disgust in this group. This suggests that individuals with a high fear of vomiting show a bias to relate disgust or anxiety to danger or a heightened probability of contamination or disease (Verwoerd et al., 2016). Specifically, this group may tend to overestimate negative or threatening outcomes associated with disgust or anxiety, suggesting that disgust plays a specific role in strengthening illness concerns through emotional reasoning (Verwoerd et al., 2016). This type of disgust-based reasoning may serve as an adaptive function of protecting against illness; however, it is possible that when this bias is very strong, it may become dysfunctional and may serve to develop and maintain a fear of vomiting.

Comorbidity with Other Axis I Diagnoses

Individuals with SPOV are reported to be more likely to be diagnosed with one or more additional Axis I disorders (Sykes, Boschen, & Conlon, 2016; Veale, Murphy, et al., 2013). The most common comorbidities are anxiety disorders such as generalized anxiety disorder, obsessive–compulsive disorder, social phobia, panic disorder, other specific phobias, hypochondriasis, and depression (Becker et al., 2007; Davidson et al., 2008; Lipsitz, Barlow, Mannuzza, Hofmann, & Fyer, 2002; Sykes et al., 2016; Veale, Murphy, et al., 2013). However, it is also important to have a clear differential diagnosis with these disorders.

EVIDENCE-BASED TREATMENT APPROACHES

The evidence base for treatment approaches of SPOV is limited. To date, there is one published randomized controlled trial (RCT) exploring cognitive–behavioral therapy (CBT) for SPOV, and there are various case studies outlining different treatment approaches. The following sections discuss assessment measures, the evidence base for psychological approaches, treatment models, and formulation-based treatment, and a case example is presented.

Assessment Measures

During clinical assessment, it is important to consider the motivation and intention behind food restriction and avoidance when making a diagnosis—for example, food restriction driven by controlling weight and shape or fear of vomiting as a consequence of eating a certain food or amount of food. In some cases, it may be possible to diagnose both, if both intentions are present.

Two validated measures have been developed to assess specific symptomatology related to SPOV:

1. Specific Phobia of Vomiting Inventory (SPOVI)—a 14-item self-report measure of cognitive processes, safety, and avoidance behaviors (Veale, Ellison, et al., 2013)
2. Emetophobia Questionnaire (EmetQ)—a 13-item self-report measure that assesses symptoms of SPOV, including avoidance of feared situations and others who may vomit, and the individual's evaluation of exposure to vomiting (Boschen, Veale, Ellison, & Reddell, 2013)

Evidence Base for Psychological Treatment Approaches

SPOV appears to be difficult to treat due to high rates of drop out, poor response to treatment compared to other specific phobias (Veale & Lambrou, 2006), and high levels of comorbidity (van Hout & Bouman, 2012). van Hout and Bouman reported that 89.5% of participants with fear of vomiting sought help in the past; however, they were more likely to receive treatment for physical complaints compared to a control group. Furthermore, only 56.2% of the SPOV sample reported receiving current therapy (van Hout & Bouman, 2012). An Internet survey found that many individuals with fear of vomiting were treatment avoidant (Lipsitz et al., 2001). Many participants responded that they would not mention their difficulties to clinicians and may refuse medication due to fear of nausea. Despite this, 34% of the sample reported partial benefit from medication, and 11% reported benefit from psychotherapy. Interestingly, more than half of the sample stated that they would not try treatment involving exposure to vomit or related cues (Lipsitz et al., 2001). Research on treatment models is currently limited, with mostly case series reported and no published RCTs to date (van Hout & Bouman, 2012; Veale & Lambrou, 2006).

Behavioral approaches involving graded exposure and cognitive–behavioral approaches including elements of psychoeducation, graded exposure, and cognitive restructuring have received the most research attention to date. Published case reports suggest that SPOV can be successfully treated by CBT (Graziano, Callueng, & Geffken, 2010; Hunter & Antony, 2009; Kahana & Feeny, 2005; Kobori, 2011; Pollard, Tait, Meldrum, Dubinsky, & Gall, 1996; Whitton et al., 2006), behavioral approaches (Faye, Gawande, Tadke, Kirpekar, & Bhave, 2013; Herman, Rozensky, & Mineka, 1993; Lesage & Lamontagne, 1985; Maack, Deacon, & Zhao, 2013;

McFadyen & Wyness, 1983; Philips, 1985; Williams et al., 2011), imaginal coping using competence imagery (Moran & O'Brien, 2005), systemic behavior therapy (O'Connor, 1983), psychotherapy (Manassis & Kalman, 1990), hypnotherapy (McKenzie, 1994; Ritow, 1979), and a combination of behavioral approaches and hypnotherapy (Wijesing, 1974). Further case reports showed CBT plus parent training (Kahana & Feeny, 2005) and group CBT to be effective (Ahlen, Edberg, Di Schiena, & Bergström, 2015). Finally, two case reports support the use of a trauma-focused approach using eye movement desensitization and reprocessing (EMDR) of aversive memories of vomiting in cases in which exposure is not practical or tolerated (De Jongh, 2012; De Jongh, Ten Broeke, & Renssen, 1999). There is one RCT in which 24 participants (23 women and 1 man) were randomly allocated to either 12 sessions of CBT or a wait list (Riddle-Walker et al., 2016). At the end of the treatment, CBT was significantly more efficacious than the wait list, with a large effect size (Cohen's d = 1.53) on the SPOVI between the two groups after 12 sessions. Eight (58.3%) participants who received CBT achieved reliable improvement compared to 2 (16%) participants in the wait-list group.

Treatment of SPOV with Disordered Eating

In all possible cases of SPOV, assessment should routinely include BMI, the degree to which the individual restricts his or her food and the motivation for restriction, as well as other abnormal eating behaviors (Veale et al., 2012). People with SPOV typically restrict their food intake in order to eliminate all risk of vomiting, and they do not wish to be underweight (Murray & Anderson, 2015). Nausea may also be related to food avoidance and therefore an additional complicating factor in the differential diagnosis between SPOV and AN (Holler et al., 2013). It may be helpful to identify the nature of the avoidance; for example, AN may be indicated by avoidance of high-calorie foods, whereas people with SPOV may avoid eating under specific circumstances such as in restaurants or before leaving home (Holler et al., 2013). A correct diagnosis of SPOV in these cases is important because those with a fear of vomiting are unlikely to identify with ED treatments and may feel misunderstood in ED treatment settings (Veale et al., 2012). However, treatment should still center on the restoration of normal eating patterns and, in some cases, weight gain by focusing on the fear of vomiting and early experiences of vomiting (van Hout & Bouman, 2012; Veale, 2009). It should also be noted that in some cases, a SPOV may be a precursor of maintaining factors for AN (Murray & Anderson, 2015); therefore, clinicians should remain aware of this potential risk factor when assessing and treating cases of SPOV with atypical ED features.

In terms of treatment, a family-based model focusing on anxiety and feeding management was shown to be successful in a sample of patients diagnosed with avoidant/restrictive food intake disorder with fear of vomiting (Norris et al., 2014). CBT, graded exposure, and refeeding treatments were also shown to be effective in cases of SPOV with food refusal (Kobori, 2011; Williams et al., 2011). One potential complicating factor regarding treatment that requires consideration is that cognitive flexibility may be affected in cases of severe food restriction and weight loss, which may impact the individual's ability to engage in treatment (Tchanturia et al., 2004).

Cognitive–Behavioral Models of SPOV

Boschen (2007) describes a cognitive and behavioral model for SPOV that involves three phases: (1) a predisposing vulnerability to anxiety and to expressing anxiety through somatic symptoms, especially gastrointestinal symptoms such as nausea (somatization vulnerability); (2) an acute phase whereby individuals interpret interoceptive cues such as nausea as an indication of imminent vomiting and interpret an increase in anxiety and somatization of anxiety as gastrointestinal symptoms; and (3) a phase involving maintenance factors including hypersensitivity and attentional bias to interoceptive cues, concern regarding future vomiting, avoidance of feared situations, and selective confirmation of information that reinforces the idea that nausea leads to vomiting (Boschen, 2007).

Veale (2009) proposes another model whereby aversive memories of vomiting become associated with fear and fused with the present so that they are re-experienced as if they are about to be repeated. Similarly to Boschen's model, it is suggested that once this association is learned, the core cognitive appraisal is that nausea is indicative of impending vomit, and the evaluation of vomiting as one of extreme awfulness leads to further anxiety and nausea (Veale, 2009). Fear of vomiting is then maintained by several processes, including experiential avoidance of thoughts, images, and interoceptive cues related to vomiting and nausea; avoidance of external threats that could lead to vomiting or nausea; hypervigilance for monitoring external threats; self-focused attention for monitoring nausea; worry, self-reassurance, and mental planning of escape routes; an overinflated sense of responsibility and belief in ability to prevent vomiting; and safety-seeking behaviors, including compulsive checking and reassurance seeking (Figure 16.1; Veale, 2009). Such responses have the unintended consequence of increasing thoughts of vomiting and increasing symptoms of nausea, and they prevent the disconfirmation of the threat of vomiting (Veale, 2009).

Formulation-Based Treatment of SPOV

Based on the previously discussed models, CBT of SPOV should include elements directly targeting the described maintenance factors (Boschen, 2007; Veale, 2009). The main aim of therapy is to enable the dropping of safety behaviors and avoidance and also to support individuals to enter situations associated with nausea without self-focused attention and safety behaviors (Veale, 2009). The following sections address each phase of therapy, which targets specific maintenance factors. The use of each phase should be decided based on an idiosyncratic formulation of the client's presenting problem(s).

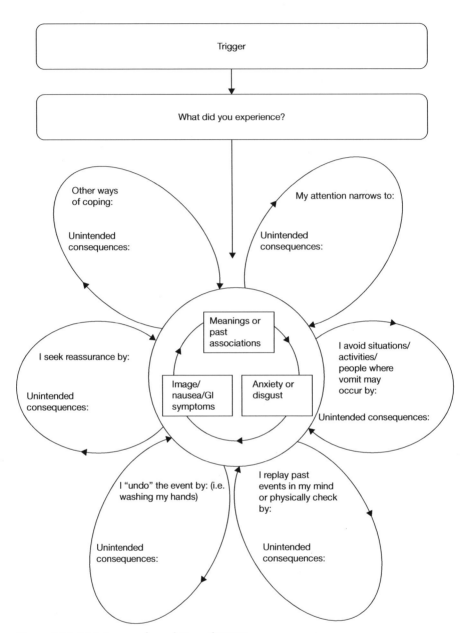

Figure 16.1 Maintenance formulation of SPOV.
SOURCE: Modified from Veale, D. (2009). Cognitive behaviour therapy for a specific phobia of vomiting. *The Cognitive Behaviour Therapist*, *2*(4), 272–288. © British Association for Behavioural and Cognitive Psychotherapies 2009.

Psychoeducation and Engagement

It is helpful to normalize the experience of vomiting as being an adaptive process that increases the chance of survival when ill. Information about the benefit of vomiting in preventing disease by getting rid of toxins can be provided (Veale, 2009).

Graded Exposure

Specific phobias have been found to respond successfully to in vivo exposure (Pull, 2008). A meta-analysis found that exposure-based treatments produced large effect sizes relative to those of alternative active psychotherapeutic approaches for specific phobias (Wolitzky-Taylor, Horowitz, Powers, & Telch, 2008). Treatments involving in vivo contact with the phobic target also outperformed alternative modes of exposure (e.g., imaginal exposure) at post-treatment (Wolitzky-Taylor et al., 2008). A graded hierarchy of feared stimuli should be drawn up based on the formulation (Veale, 2009). This may include exposure to disliked foods, avoided situations or simulated vomit (Boschen, 2007), or audio or video recordings of others vomiting (McFadyen & Wyness, 1983). Both internal (past memories, thoughts, and images) and external cues (avoided situations) should be incorporated into the hierarchy (Veale, 2009). Exposure needs to be done without self-focused attention or use of safety-seeking behaviors, and it must be done continuously in order to tolerate the anxiety (Veale, 2009). For practical reasons, it is not recommended to induce repeated actual vomiting (Boschen, 2007; Veale, 2009). A low BMI and disordered eating are targeted at an early stage within the context of testing one's fears and an alternative understanding of the problem. Food restriction is understandable if one treats it as a vomiting problem. If, however, one is dealing with a fear-of-vomiting problem, then the solution of restriction increases the fear and worry.

Exposure in Imagination and Imagery Rescripting

The cognitive model of SPOV supports the use of imagery rescripting for aversive memories to reprocess memories in context and diffuse them from their associations (Veale, Murphy, et al., 2013). Clients may be asked to describe an aversive memory in different stages—for example, reliving the aversive memory from a child's first-person perspective in the present tense and determining what the child needs. The second phase involves repeating the imagination of the memory from the self-perspective of the client as an adult and encouraging the client to provide what his or her child-self may have needed at that particular moment. It may be important to ask about multimodal imagery—for example, physical, taste, and olfactory aspects of images, in addition to visual aspects (Price et al., 2012). For further details of this procedure, see Arntz and Weertman (1999) and Smucker and Dancu (1999).

Dropping Safety-Seeking Behaviors

These behaviors interfere in exposure treatment and are considered to be the main obstacle to progress (Veale, 2009). Examples include compulsive checking of food expiry dates; reassurance seeking; or excessive cooking of food, washing, or cleaning. An important goal of therapy is therefore to drop responses that are believed to maintain fear, such as worry and attentional biases toward potential risk, and demonstrate that these responses increase worry (Veale, 2009).

Case Example

Sally, aged 30 years, first became aware of a fear of vomiting at approximately age 7 years, and it became a significant problem at approximately age 17 years. She first sought help at age 21 years and had not vomited since she was 12 years old. Her main fear was of herself vomiting, but she had some fears of others vomiting and that she may catch something from them. She had a number of distressing memories of vomiting beginning at age 4 years when she discovered her father vomiting over the side of his bed. He was ill from meningitis and then was in a coma for 7 weeks. She also had other distressing memories from when she was 4 years old of another girl standing in front of her who vomited very suddenly and of the reaction of the teacher, who was very shocked. She can remember various episodes of herself vomiting from stomach infections, beginning at approximately age 9 years; these episodes led her to panic. She had a distressing memory of being at a friend's house when she was 12 years old and vomiting on the floor in front of her friend's parents. When she felt nauseous, she believed she was going to vomit or lose control or act foolishly. She used a number of safety-seeking behaviors when she believed she might vomit, such as looking for an escape route or trying to keep tight control of her vomiting and being very self-focused to monitor her nausea. She took an antiemetic when she felt nauseous and reassured herself that she was not going to vomit. She avoided eating seafood, meat, and eggs. She did not eat at regular times, and some days she did not eat at all if she thought she might vomit. She restricted the amount that she ate so there was less food to vomit. Her BMI was 15.1. She was motivated to gain weight to her previous BMI of 19. She did not want to be at her current weight and had no desire to control her weight or shape. She repeatedly smelled her food, checked the "sell by" date on food items, and overcooked her food. She washed her hands frequently. She would like to have children in the future, but she avoided getting pregnant. She avoided a wide range of people and situations, especially drinking alcohol, drunks, sea travel, flights, certain films that might include vomiting, public toilets, eating in public restaurants, anyone who was ill, or visiting anyone in hospital. The main impairment was at work, where she had reduced the amount of time she spent teaching children and often felt trapped in the classroom. Her social life had become more restricted and contributed to her breakup with her ex-partner. She was spending approximately 4 hours a day worrying about vomiting. She felt depressed and had little interest or pleasure in doing any activities. In addition, her fear of vomiting was interfering with her sleep.

The formulation was of aversive memories of vomiting that had not been emotionally processed and had a sense of "nowness," which created the current sense of threat in the present. When she felt nauseous and panic, she was convinced she was going to vomit. She would respond by various safety-seeking and avoidance behaviors that maintained her fears, including self-focused attention, mental reviewing of the risks, self-reassurance, and checking behaviors. In this case example, ARFID was treated alongside SPOV, in that Sally was encouraged to test fears related to food intake. In her case, food had become the feared object due to the feared consequence of vomiting after eating. Therefore, the main goal of treatment was to reduce her food restriction and increase her weight, but this was treated in the overall context of the fear of vomiting.

CONCLUSION AND FUTURE DIRECTIONS

A small proportion of SPOV cases may be misdiagnosed with AN due to features of disordered eating, such as food refusal and weight loss. Accurate diagnosis is important in such cases because individuals with SPOV are unlikely to respond to standard ED treatments. Assessments should focus on the motivation underlying behaviors such as avoiding cues related to vomiting instead of a desire to lose weight. In cases of SPOV in which weight is low, food refusal and weight gain should still be a primary target of treatment. One RCT provides evidence for CBT that is specific for SPOV. Further research on the nature of SPOV with similar features to EDs, as well as effective treatment approaches, may help to more accurately conceptualize cases with overlapping features. More rigorous research methodology including RCTs with an equally credible treatment and larger sample sizes may help to bridge the gap in our current understanding of SPOV and atypical EDs.

REFERENCES

Ahlen, J., Edberg, E., Di Schiena, M., & Bergström, J. (2015). Cognitive behavioural group therapy for emetophobia: An open study in a psychiatric setting. *Clinical Psychologist, 19*(2), 96–104.

American Psychiatric Association. (1994). *Diagnostic and statistical manual of mental disorders* (4th ed.). Washington, DC: Author.

American Psychiatric Association. (2013). *Diagnostic and statistical manual of mental disorders* (5th ed.). Arlington, VA: American Psychiatric Publishing.

Arntz, A., Rauner, M., & Van den Hout, M. (1995). "If I feel anxious, there must be danger": Ex-consequentia reasoning in inferring danger in anxiety disorders. *Behaviour Research and Therapy, 33*(8), 917–925.

Arntz, A., & Weertman, A. (1999). Treatment of childhood memories: Theory and practice. *Behaviour Research and Therapy, 37*(8), 715–740.

Becker, E. S., Rinck, M., Tuerke, V., Kause, P., Goodwin, R., Neumer, S., & Margraf, J. (2007). Epidemiology of specific phobia subtypes: Findings from the Dresden Mental Health Study. *European Psychiatry, 22*(2), 69–74.

Boschen, M. J. (2007). Reconceptualizing emetophobia: A cognitive–behavioral formulation and research agenda. *Journal of Anxiety Disorders, 21*(3), 407–419.

Boschen, M. J., Veale, D., Ellison, N., & Reddell, T. (2013). The Emetophobia Questionnaire (EmetQ-13): Psychometric validation of a measure of specific phobia of vomiting (emetophobia). *Journal of Anxiety Disorders, 27*(7), 670–677.

Davidson, A. L., Boyle, C., & Lauchlan, F. (2008). Scared to lose control? General and health locus of control in females with a phobia of vomiting. *Journal of Clinical Psychology, 64*(1), 30–39.

De Jongh, A. (2012). Treatment of a woman with emetophobia: A trauma focused approach. *Mental illness, 4*(1), e3.

De Jongh, A., Ten Broeke, E., & Renssen, M. (1999). Treatment of specific phobias with eye movement desensitization and reprocessing (EMDR): Protocol, empirical status, and conceptual issues. *Journal of Anxiety Disorders, 13*(1), 69–85.

Faye, A. D., Gawande, S., Tadke, R., Kirpekar, V. C., & Bhave, S. H. (2013). Emetophobia: A fear of vomiting. *Indian Journal of Psychiatry, 55*(4), 390–392.

Froreich, F. V., Vartanian, L. R., Grisham, J. R., & Touyz, S. W. (2016). Dimensions of control and their relation to disordered eating behaviours and obsessive–compulsive symptoms. *Journal of Eating Disorders, 4*(1), 1.

Fryar, C. D., & Ogden, C. L. (2010). *Prevalence of underweight among adults aged 20 years and over: United States, 2007–2008.* Atlanta, GA: Centers for Disease Control and Prevention, National Center for Health Statistics.

Graziano, P. A., Callueng, C. M., & Geffken, G. R. (2010). Cognitive–behavioral treatment of an 11-year-old male presenting with emetophobia: A case study. *Clinical Case Studies, 9*(6), 411–425.

Herman, D., Rozensky, R., & Mineka, S. (1993). *Cognitive behavioural therapy for panic disorder with a primary fear of vomiting: Conceptual and treatment issues.* Paper presented at the conference proceedings of the Association for Advancement of Behavior Therapy.

Holler, Y., van Overveld, M., Jutglar, H., & Trinka, E. (2013). Nausea in specific phobia of vomiting. *Behavioral Sciences (Basel), 3*(3), 445–458.

Hunter, P. V., & Antony, M. M. (2009). Cognitive–behavioral treatment of emetophobia: The role of interoceptive exposure. *Cognitive and Behavioral Practice, 16*(1), 84–91.

Kahana, S. Y., & Feeny, N. C. (2005). Cognitive behavioral treatment of health-related anxiety in youth: A case example. *Cognitive and Behavioral Practice, 12*(3), 290–300.

Keel, P. K., Brown, T. A., Holm-Denoma, J., & Bodell, L. P. (2011). Comparison of DSM-IV versus proposed DSM-5 diagnostic criteria for eating disorders: Reduction of eating disorder not otherwise specified and validity. *International Journal of Eating Disorders, 44*(6), 553–560.

Kobori, O. (2011). Cognitive therapy for vomit phobia: A case report. *Asia Pacific Journal of Counselling and Psychotherapy, 2*(2), 171–178.

Lesage, A., & Lamontagne, Y. (1985). Paradoxical intention and exposure in vivo in the treatment of psychogenic nausea: Report of two cases. *Behavioural Psychotherapy, 13*(1), 69–75.

Lipsitz, J. D., Barlow, D. H., Mannuzza, S., Hofmann, S. G., & Fyer, A. J. (2002). Clinical features of four DSM-IV-specific phobia subtypes. *Journal of Nervous and Mental Disease, 190*(7), 471–478.

Lipsitz, J. D., Fyer, A. J., Paterniti, A., & Klein, D. F. (2001). Emetophobia: Preliminary results of an internet survey. *Depression and Anxiety, 14*(2), 149–152.

Maack, D. J., Deacon, B. J., & Zhao, M. (2013). Exposure therapy for emetophobia: A case study with three-year follow-up. *Journal of Anxiety Disorders, 27*(5), 527–534.

Machado, P. P., Gonçalves, S., & Hoek, H. W. (2013). DSM-5 reduces the proportion of EDNOS cases: Evidence from community samples. *International Journal of Eating Disorders, 46*(1), 60–65.

Machado, P. P., Machado, B. C., Gonçalves, S., & Hoek, H. W. (2007). The prevalence of eating disorders not otherwise specified. *International Journal of Eating Disorders, 40*(3), 212–217.

Manassis, K., & Kalman, E. (1990). Anorexia resulting from fear of vomiting in four adolescent girls. *Canadian Journal of Psychiatry, 35*(6), 548–550.

McFadyen, M., & Wyness, J. (1983). You don't have to be sick to be a behavior therapist but it can help—Treatment of vomit phobia. *Behavioural Psychotherapy, 11*(2), 173–176.

McKenzie, S. (1994). Hypnotherapy for vomiting phobia in a 40-year-old woman. *Contemporary Hypnosis, 11*, 37–40.

McNally, R. (1997). Atypical phobias. In G. C. Davey (Ed.), *Phobias: A handbook of theory, research and treatment* (pp. 183–200). New York, NY: Wiley.

Merckelbach, H., de Jong, P. J., Muris, P., & van Den Hout, M. A. (1996). The etiology of specific phobias: A review. *Clinical Psychology Review, 16*(4), 337–361.

Moran, D. J., & O'Brien, R. M. (2005). Competence imagery: A case study treating emetophobia. *Psychological Reports, 96*(3), 635–636.

Murray, S. B., & Anderson, L. K. (2015). Deconstructing "atypical" eating disorders: An overview of emerging eating disorder phenotypes. *Current Psychiatry Reports, 17*(11), 1–7.

Norris, M. L., Robinson, A., Obeid, N., Harrison, M., Spettigue, W., & Henderson, K. (2014). Exploring avoidant/restrictive food intake disorder in eating disordered patients: A descriptive study. *International Journal of Eating Disorders, 47*(5), 495–499.

O'Connor, J. (1983). Why can't I get hives: Brief strategic therapy with an obsessional child. *Family Process, 22*(2), 201–209.

Ollendick, T. H., & King, N. J. (1991). Origins of childhood fears: An evaluation of Rachman's theory of fear acquisition. *Behaviour Research and Therapy, 29*(2), 117–123.

Philips, H. C. (1985). Return of fear in the treatment of a fear of vomiting. *Behaviour Research and Therapy, 23*(1), 45–52.

Pollard, C. A., Tait, R. C., Meldrum, D., Dubinsky, I. H., & Gall, J. S. (1996). Agoraphobia without panic: Case illustrations of an overlooked syndrome. *Journal of Nervous and Mental Disease, 184*(1), 61–62.

Price, K., Veale, D., & Brewin, C. R. (2012). Intrusive imagery in people with a specific phobia of vomiting. *Journal of Behavioral Therapy and Experimental Psychiatry, 43*(1), 672–678.

Pull, C. B. (2008). Recent trends in the study of specific phobias. *Current Opinion in Psychiatry, 21*(1), 43–50.

Riddle-Walker, L., Veale, D., Chapman, C., Ogle, F., Rosko, D., Najmi, S., . . . Hicks, T. (2016). Cognitive behaviour therapy for specific phobia of vomiting (emetophobia): A pilot randomized controlled trial. *Journal of Anxiety Disorders,* *43,* 14–22.

Ritow, J. K. (1979). Brief treatment of a vomiting phobia. *American Journal of Clinical Hypnosis, 21*(4), 293–296.

Smucker, M. R., & Dancu, C. V. (1999). *Cognitive–behavioral treatment for adult survivors of childhood trauma: Imagery rescripting and reprocessing.* Lanham, MD: Aronson.

Stevenson, J., Batten, N., & Cherner, M. (1992). Fears and fearfulness in children and adolescents: A genetic analysis of twin data. *Journal of Child Psychology and Psychiatry, 33*(6), 977–985.

Sykes, M., Boschen, M. J., & Conlon, E. G. (2016). Comorbidity in emetophobia (specific phobia of vomiting). *Clinical Psychology & Psychotherapy, 23*(4), 363–367.

Tchanturia, K., Anderluh, M. B., Morris, R. G., Rabe-Hesketh, S., Collier, D. A., Sanchez, P., & Treasure, J. L. (2004). Cognitive flexibility in anorexia nervosa and bulimia nervosa. *Journal of the International Neuropsychological Society, 10*(04), 513–520.

van Hout, W. J. P. J., & Bouman, T. K. (2012). Clinical features, prevalence and psychiatric complaints in subjects with fear of vomiting. *Clinical Psychology & Psychotherapy, 19*(6), 531–539.

van Overveld, M., de Jong, P. J., Peters, M. L., van Hout, W. J., & Bouman, T. K. (2008). An Internet-based study on the relation between disgust sensitivity and emetophobia. *Journal of Anxiety Disorders, 22*(3), 524–531.

van Overveld, W., de Jong, P. J, Peters, M. L., Cavanagh, K., & Davey, G. C. L. (2006). Disgust propensity and disgust sensitivity: Separate constructs that are differentially related to specific fears. *Personality and Individual Differences, 41*(7), 1241–1252.

Vandereycken, W. (2011). Media hype, diagnostic fad or genuine disorder? Professionals' opinions about night eating syndrome, orthorexia, muscle dysmorphia, and emetophobia. *Eating Disorders, 19*(2), 145–155.

Veale, D. (2009). Cognitive behaviour therapy for a specific phobia of vomiting. *The Cognitive Behaviour Therapist, 2*(4), 272–288.

Veale, D., Costa, A., Murphy, P., & Ellison, N. (2012). Abnormal eating behaviour in people with a specific phobia of vomiting (emetophobia). *European Eating Disorders Review, 20*(5), 414–418.

Veale, D., Ellison, N., Boschen, M. J., Costa, A., Whelan, C., Muccio, F., & Henry, K. (2013). Development of an inventory to measure specific phobia of vomiting (emetophobia). *Cognitive Therapy and Research, 37*(3), 595–604.

Veale, D., Hennig, C., & Gledhill, L. (2015). Is a specific phobia of vomiting part of the obsessive compulsive and related disorders? *Journal of Obsessive–Compulsive and Related Disorders, 7,* 1–6.

Veale, D., & Lambrou, C. (2006). The psychopathology of vomit phobia. *Behavioural and Cognitive Psychotherapy, 34*(2), 139–150.

Veale, D., Murphy, P., Ellison, N., Kanakam, N., & Costa, A. (2013). Autobiographical memories of vomiting in people with a specific phobia of vomiting (emetophobia). *Journal of Behavior Therapy and Experimental Psychiatry, 44*(1), 14–20.

Verwoerd, J., van Hout, W. J., & de Jong, P. J. (2016). Disgust- and anxiety-based emotional reasoning in non-clinical fear of vomiting. *Journal of Behavior Therapy and Experimental Psychiatry, 50,* 83–89.

Whitton, S. W., Luiselli, J. K., & Donaldson, D. L. (2006). Cognitive–behavioral treatment of generalized anxiety disorder and vomiting phobia in an elementary-age child. *Clinical Case Studies, 5*(6), 477–487.

Wijesing, B. (1974). Vomiting phobia overcome by one session of flooding with hypnosis. *Journal of Behavior Therapy and Experimental Psychiatry, 5*(2), 169–170.

Williams, K. E., Field, D. G., Riegel, K., & Paul, C. (2011). Brief, intensive behavioral treatment of food refusal secondary to emetophobia. *Clinical Case Studies, 10*(4), 304–311.

Wolitzky-Taylor, K. B., Horowitz, J. D., Powers, M. B., & Telch, M. J. (2008). Psychological approaches in the treatment of specific phobias: A meta-analysis. *Clinical Psychology Review, 28*(6), 1021–1037.

PART III

Atypical Populations

17

Pediatric Eating Disorders

EMILY K. GRAY AND KAMRYN T. EDDY ■

Eating disorders typically appear during childhood or adolescence but can go unrecognized by clinicians or parents, delaying diagnosis and treatment. During childhood and adolescence, there are critical developmental processes occurring that increase vulnerability to malnutrition and medical consequences, which may contribute to more severe or enduring long-term costs. In addition, early disordered feeding and eating patterns in childhood are related to severe symptoms of eating disorders in adolescence and adulthood. However, assessing and treating eating disorders in a pediatric population comprises unique challenges, given the context of the developmental stage and inherent cognitive limitations of the child. For example, a child might be incapable of explaining "why" he or she is unable to eat, which can be frustrating for parents and clinicians and mean that a period of observation may be necessary to formulate a hypothesis. The fifth edition of the *Diagnostic and Statistical Manual of Mental Disorders* (DSM-5; American Psychiatric Association [APA], 2013) defines six feeding and eating disorders in children and adults—pica, rumination disorder (RD), avoidant/restrictive food intake disorder (ARFID), anorexia nervosa (AN), bulimia nervosa (BN), and binge-eating disorder (BED)—with a residual category of other specified feeding or eating disorders (OSFED) that includes atypical AN, BED with low frequency, purging disorder, and night eating syndrome. The diagnosis of unspecified feeding or eating disorders (UFED) is reserved for when criteria for the previously mentioned diagnoses are not ascertained fully, but eating behaviors occur with distress and impaired functioning. The feeding and eating disorders share a common pattern of maladaptive eating behaviors and impaired quality of life, and although the diagnoses have distinct clinical concerns, issues pertaining to assessment and treatment are overlapping. This chapter reviews clinical presentations of feeding and eating disorders, assessment strategies, and treatment approaches with a focus on application to youth aged 7–13 years.

CLINICAL PRESENTATIONS

Like their adolescent and adult counterparts, children can present with the full spectrum of feeding and eating disorders. However, pediatric samples may be even more likely than adolescent or adult cohorts to have symptom presentations that are atypical or that fail to meet diagnostic thresholds (Eddy, Celio Doyle, Hoste, Herzog, & Le Grange, 2008). This is likely due to at least three reasons: (1) Diagnostic criteria and guidelines for assessment are generally based on adolescent or adult patient groups or norms, suggesting that they may not represent or adequately capture child presentations; (2) pediatric patients may have limited insight or difficulty articulating experienced symptoms, rendering ascertainment of diagnostic criteria more difficult; and (3) pediatric patients may be detected earlier in the course of illness (e.g., before full syndrome illnesses are met) because they are under the care and observation of guardians, which may facilitate or increase the likelihood of evaluation or treatment seeking. As mentioned previously, DSM-5 categorizes six diagnoses that may be assigned to children between the ages of 7 and 13 years.

Pica

DSM-5 defines pica as the persistent ingestion of nonnutritive, nonfood substances, inappropriate to the development level of the individual and outside cultural practice, over a period of at least 1 month. If the behavior occurs in the context of another mental disorder (i.e., intellectual developmental disorder or autism spectrum disorder), it must be sufficiently severe to warrant additional clinical attention (APA, 2013). Pica behavior can be a serious and potentially life-threatening behavior that often occurs in children with developmental and intellectual disabilities. Items consumed vary substantially and can include ice, paper, plastic, cloth, dirt, clay, paint, rocks, soap, cigarette butts, hair, and metal artifacts such as coins. Diagnosis is clinical, confirmed by history rather than any single laboratory test, and medical evaluation should be based on the type of pica behavior reported. Iron deficiency can commonly present with unusual cravings and therefore is a necessary rule-out diagnosis because treatment can be curative. Lead levels should be obtained in children ingesting dirt or paint, and mercury levels should be obtained in patients consuming paper. Eating clay or soil can expose the individual to parasitic infections. Serious, potentially fatal, medical complications as a result of pica include intestinal obstruction and perforation, choking, infection, and poisoning (Rose, Porcerelli, & Neale, 2000; Williams & McAdam, 2012). Less dangerous medical issues include nutritional deficiency (e.g., anemia), oral and dental health problems, irritable bowels, enlarged colon, and constipation (Call, Simmons, Mevers, & Alvarez, 2015).

Pica is described as both underreported and underrecognized; therefore, prevalence estimates are difficult to assess. Developmentally typical infants and young children commonly explore their environment with their mouths, and according to some estimates, more than 50% of children aged 18–36 months seek and ingest nonfood items. This behavior decreases as children age, with less than 10% of children older than 12 years engaging in this behavior (Mishori & McHale, 2014). Pica is uncommon in eating disorder clinics (Delaney et al., 2015) and may be a more common comorbidity observed in programs for those with developmental disabilities.

Rumination Disorder

Rumination disorder is defined by recurrent regurgitation of food (it can be rechewed, reswallowed, or spit out) over a period of at least 1 month and is not associated with a medical condition (e.g., gastroesophageal reflux or pyloric stenosis) and occurs outside episodes of other eating disorders (e.g., AN, BN, or purging disorder) (APA, 2013). Individuals often describe episodes as occurring minutes to hours following a meal, feeling involuntary or effortless, and with or without a sensation of increased pressure with the need to belch, increase in nausea, or discomfort or pain prior to the regurgitation (Mousa, Montgomery, & Alioto, 2014). Symptoms of rumination may include halitosis (oral malodor), malnutrition or weight loss, indigestion, and chronically raw or chapped lips, and these may be accompanied by electrolyte imbalances, dehydration, upper respiratory tract distress, dental problems, and aspiration. Although RD was initially thought to be more common in children with intellectual or developmental disabilities, it is now recognized in individuals of all ages with normal cognitive functioning and associated with anxiety, depression, and perfectionistic traits (Green, Alioto, Mousa, & Di Lorenzo, 2011). The diagnosis of rumination is clinical and can be based on history alone, but when there is a question of regurgitation secondary to gastroesophageal reflux disease (GERD) or if an individual or family is reluctant to accept the RD diagnosis, diagnostic confirmation can be made by manometric evaluation with stationary impedance monitoring, which can accurately distinguish between rumination, regurgitation, and belching (Rommel et al., 2010). By evaluating the pressure at various levels in the esophagus to identify a straining episode, as well as measuring for the co-occurrence of retrograde flow, including its contents (e.g., gas vs. liquid), one can discern a pattern that is specific to rumination.

There is a paucity of data on the prevalence of RD in the pediatric population, and most of the existing literature focuses on children with intellectual and developmental disabilities. In a survey of school-aged children in Sri Lanka, the prevalence of RD was found to be 5.1% (5.1% for boys and 5.0% for girls), but the survey did not distinguish if a medical cause (e.g., GERD) was implicated (Rajindrajith, Devanarayana, & Crispus Perera, 2012). Notably, RD cannot be co-diagnosed with other eating disorders, but rumination behavior can occur in individuals with the full spectrum of eating and feeding disorder diagnoses (Delaney et al., 2015).

Avoidant/Restrictive Food Intake Disorder

Avoidant/restrictive food intake disorder is a new diagnosis included in DSM-5 that represents a reformulation of what was formerly called feeding disorder of infancy and early childhood (APA, 2000). ARFID is characterized by a maladaptive eating or feeding pattern, resulting in significant health concerns that may include weight loss or faltering growth, nutritional deficiencies, dependence on enteral feeding or supplements for more than 50% of nutritional intake, and/or psychosocial impairments (APA, 2013). In ARFID, food avoidance or restrictive eating is not motivated by fear of fatness or weight and shape concerns but, rather, is secondary to sensory sensitivities (e.g., tastes or textures), a fear of aversive consequences related to eating (e.g., choking or vomiting), and/or a general lack of interest in eating or low appetite. ARFID presentations are heterogeneous, with variable markers of nutritional insufficiency and rationales for restrictive eating. Whereas some youth will present with failure to thrive and starvation syndrome, others may be overweight or obese. Still others may present as normal weight but with pronounced psychosocial impairment due to selective eating that interferes with social eating, for example.

ARFID often begins in infancy or childhood, but it can onset at any age. Because it is a newly recognized diagnosis, formal prevalence studies are nascent. To date, only one study has investigated ARFID in a population-based sample of children (aged 8–13 years); this study, performed in Switzerland, reported a prevalence of 3% (Kurz, van Dyck, Dremmel, Munsch, & Hilbert, 2015). A small number of studies have investigated ARFID prevalence in clinical samples, finding that between 7% and 17% of youth presenting with feeding or eating disorders to adolescent medicine clinics (Ornstein et al., 2013) and 22.5% among youth in an eating disorder day treatment program (Nicely, Lane-Loney, Masciulli, Hollenbeak, & Ornstein, 2014) had ARFID. By contrast, a retrospective record review of 2,231 consecutive referrals (aged 8–18 years) to pediatric gastrointestinal clinics showed a 1.5% ARFID prevalence (Eddy et al., 2015). ARFID frequently co-occurs with autism spectrum disorders and anxiety disorders (Galloway, Lee, & Birch, 2003; Jacobi, Schmitz, & Agras, 2008). These studies suggest that despite variation in estimates, ARFID is commonly seen clinically.

Anorexia Nervosa

Anorexia nervosa is the restriction of energy intake that leads to low body weight. Delineation of low body weight in growing children can be challenging, and consideration of prior weight gain trajectory using deviations from a prior growth curve can be useful in defining weight loss or low weight. In pediatric populations, low body weight is relative to expected weight, adjusted for age, sex, developmental trajectory, weight history, and physiologic disturbance. Therefore, an individual may not lose weight but, rather, fail to meet weight or height expectations. Also, younger patients may not endorse body image concerns and may be less likely to engage in binge eating or purging behaviors (Peebles, Wilson, & Lock, 2006; Rosen, 2003). For example, a child may not specifically endorse a fear of weight gain but may present eating only fruits and vegetables (avoiding carbohydrates, fats, and sugars) and state, "Cookies make people fat." Historically, many children did not meet full criteria for AN given diagnostic criteria that included amenorrhea, which is not applicable in males or prepubescent females.

The lifetime prevalence of AN is between 0.5% and 2%, with peak age of onset of 13–18 years (Weaver & Liebman, 2011). However, the epidemiology is changing, with recent studies reporting higher rates of eating disorders in younger children, boys, and minority groups (Smink, van Hoeken, & Hoek, 2012; Pinhas, Morris, Crosby, & Katzman, 2011).

Bulimia Nervosa

Bulimia nervosa is characterized by three core features: binge episodes (defined as consumption of an objectively large amount of food accompanied by an experience of loss of control over eating), inappropriate compensatory behaviors, and increased influence of shape or weight on self-evaluation. Bulimia nervosa typically occurs in late adolescence (Allen, Byrne, Oddy, & Crosby, 2013), but there is evidence for an earlier age of onset (Swanson, Crow, Le Grange, Swendsen, & Merikangas, 2011). Using DSM-5 criteria, adolescent BN prevalence rates in population-based samples were 0.7–1.6% in boys and 2.6–8.7% in girls, with 1% of males and 2.5% of females meeting criteria for BN by the age of 14 years (Allen et al., 2013; Stice, Marti, & Rohde, 2013). The prevalence in children is not known, but it is likely low. Many younger patients do not meet criteria for BN given that they are less likely to binge, purge, or use laxatives or diuretics (Fisher, Schneider, Burns, Symons, & Mandel, 2001). However, Peebles and colleagues (2006) found that 19.2% of young (<13 years old) patients with an eating disorder had tried purging to control weight during their lifetime.

Binge-Eating Disorder

Binge-eating disorder includes recurrent binge episodes without compensatory behaviors. However, given that children's nutritional needs vary depending on age, sex, and energy expenditure (Shomaker et al., 2010), determining what constitutes an objectively large amount of food for an individual child is difficult. Therefore, it has been proposed that the sense of loss of control (LOC) is the most clinically relevant feature of a binge episode (Tanofsky-Kraff et al., 2010). Youth with BED are at higher risk of obesity and depression (Field et al., 2012), with more frequent suicide attempts (Swanson et al., 2011) and functional impairment (Stice et al., 2013). Comorbidity is common, with 80% of youth with BED meeting criteria for another psychiatric diagnosis in their lifetime, although they are less likely to seek treatment compared to youth with AN or BN (Swanson et al., 2011).

In two large population-based studies, approximately 1.6% of boys and girls met criteria for BED (Allen et al., 2013; Swanson et al., 2011), with similar prevalence rates across racial/ethnic groups and a median age of onset of 12.6 years (Swanson et al., 2011). Higher prevalence rates are seen in overweight girls and youth seeking weight loss treatment (Eddy et al., 2007; Stice et al., 2013).

ASSESSMENT

Assessment of eating disorders in children typically involves a combination of clinical interview, physical examination, parent or collateral informant report, and, occasionally, self-report questionnaires. Assessment of eating disorder psychopathology in youth can be challenged by cognitive or developmental limitations (e.g., difficulty with abstract reasoning); child difficulty in understanding key terms or concepts (e.g., dieting or lack of control over eating); and discordance between information gathered via child-report, parent-report, and/or interview assessments. Although a number of measurement tools developed for use in adults have been used in child and adolescent populations, Table 17.1 summarizes measures developed specifically for pediatric samples. For a more comprehensive review of pediatric eating disorder assessment tools, see Schvey, Eddy, and Tanofsky-Kraff (2016).

EVIDENCE-BASED TREATMENT APPROACHES

Unfortunately, there are limited data on treatment efficacy for child eating and feeding disorders. The only exception is evidence supporting the use of family-based treatment for adolescent AN. Overarchingly, across the eating and feeding disorders, approaches implemented in practice are frequently behavioral and most often include parents (or other caregivers) to aid in delivery or act as agents of change.

Pica

Treatment approaches are largely based on case reports and focus on individuals with developmental disabilities. Prevention is key for pica, especially in residential facilities, in which the environment can be made safe by training staff to develop procedures to ensure that no dangerous objects are accessible (e.g., proper disposal of rubber gloves) (Williams & McAdam, 2012). Behavioral modification approaches have been proven effective for treating pica, and treatments that combine reinforcement and response prevention have shown good efficacy (Hagopian, Rooker, & Rolider, 2011). Supplementation with iron can decrease or even reverse pica associated with iron deficiency. Use of medication in case-based approaches has been found to be effective, but there are few medications

Table 17.1 ASSESSMENT OF PEDIATRIC EATING AND FEEDING DISORDERS

Measure	Description
Eating Disorder Examination, Child Version (ChEDE; Bryant-Waugh, Cooper, Taylor, & Lask, 1996) Format: Interview (semistructured)	Based on the adult EDE (Fairburn & Cooper, 1993); includes diagnostic, severity, and frequency items; yields Restraint, Eating, Weight, and Shape Concern scales; appropriate for ages 7–14 years.
Questionnaire on Eating and Weight Patterns–Adolescent Version (QEWP-A; Johnson & Grieve, 1999) Format: Self-report; also available in parent-report format	QEWP-A is an adaptation of the original measure (QEWP) that assesses the presence of binge eating and purging and includes information to yield binge-eating disorder diagnosis; appropriate for ages 10–18 years.
Children's Eating Attitudes Test (ChEAT; Maloney, McGuire, & Daniels, 1988) Format: Self-report	ChEAT, adapted from the Eating Attitudes Test (EAT) (Garner & Garfinkle, 1979), is a 26-item scale that assesses dieting, food preoccupation, and concerns about being or becoming overweight; appropriate for ages 8 years or older.
Eating Disorder Inventory-C (EDI-C; Garner, 1991) Format: Self-report	EDI-C is an adaptation of the Eating Disorder Inventory (EDI), a 91-item, nondiagnostic, multiscale assessment of symptoms commonly associated with anorexia and bulimia nervosa. Measure yields three subscales that assess thoughts and behaviors related to eating, shape, and weight and eight subscales that capture psychological features.
Kids Eating Disorder Survey (KEDS; Childress, Brewerton, Hodges, & Jarrell, 1993) Format: Self-report	KEDS is a 14-item self-report nondiagnostic measure of body dissatisfaction, restriction, binge, and compensatory behaviors. Appropriate for ages 9 and 16 years.
Children's Eating Behavior Questionnaire (CEBQ; Wardle, Guthrie, Sanderson, & Rapoport, 2001) Format: Parent-report	CEBQ is a 35-item measure that assesses dimensions of eating style (e.g., satiety responsiveness, fussiness, and emotional overeating); not diagnostic; appropriate for parents of youth aged 2 years or older.
Child Feeding Questionnaire (CFQ; Birch et al., 2001) Format: Parent-report	The CFQ was developed to assess feeding practices, food acceptance, and proneness to obesity in youth aged 2–11 years; not diagnostic.

for use. These include selective serotonin reuptake inhibitors (SSRIs), atypical antipsychotics, and attention deficit hyperactivity disorder (ADHD) medications (Bhatia & Gupta, 2009; Hergüner & Hergüner, 2010; Lerner, 2008).

Case Example

Jessica is a 9-year-old with intellectual disability and anxiety who was brought to the emergency room after ingesting a screw. Jessica lives in a residential treatment facility, and staff have noticed that when a new resident is introduced to the milieu, she becomes highly anxious and ingest objects, which may function to elicit attention and/or gain respite because she is often admitted to the hospital for medical observation. Treatment focused on a behavioral plan to anticipate Jessica's anxiety around transitions, reinforce positive coping mechanisms addressing anxiety, as well as work with the hospital to be "boring" and prevent unintentional reinforcement of the behavior.

Rumination Disorder

Treatment for RD includes a multidisciplinary treatment approach with medical providers and behavioral specialists. Similar to pica treatment, there is a lack of controlled trials, and most evidence consists of case series reports. The mainstay of treatment is an explanation of the condition and the mechanism underlying rumination events, as well as behavioral modification (Tack, Blondeau, Boecxstaens, & Rommel, 2011). Behavioral modification largely employs habit reversal techniques such as diaphragmatic breathing or gum chewing, which compete with the urge to regurgitate (Chitkara, Van Tilburg, Whitehead, & Talley, 2006; Rhine & Tarbox, 2009).

Case Example

Emma is a 10-year-old who is highly anxious and experiences rumination following every meal. After several therapy sessions and discussing diaphragmatic breathing, Emma invented her own "pencil technique" that consists of holding a pencil in her mouth, which functions as both a reminder and a tool to help facilitate diaphragmatic breathing following meals.

Avoidant/Restrictive Food Intake Disorder

Please refer to Chapter 9, which addresses treatment approaches to ARFID in depth.

Anorexia Nervosa

Family-based therapy (FBT) has the most evidence-based support for treatment of AN in adolescents (Lock et al., 2010), and there is growing evidence of the efficacy of FBT in children younger than age 12 years with restrictive eating disorders (Lock, Le Grange, Forsberg, & Hewell, 2006). FBT shifts the focus from etiology and identification of an underlying cause or blame and empowers caregivers to refeed their child back to health. FBT is most often delivered in the outpatient setting, but it has been adapted to the inpatient, residential, and day treatment settings. FBT is divided into three phases of treatment, with high emphasis on externalizing the eating disorder from the child. Phase I tasks caregivers with refeeding, and sessions focus on coaching around weight restoration. Phase II gradually shifts control and responsibility to the child, taking into account what would be developmentally appropriate. Finally, Phase III targets relapse prevention, developmental considerations, and treatment termination. FBT has limitations, including partial remission or no response, as well as the potential for relapse. Other therapy options include individual therapy and cognitive–behavioral therapy (CBT). Evidence for pharmacotherapy is limited given that no randomized controlled studies have been conducted on children with AN. Medication management targets comorbid conditions (e.g., SSRIs for depression and anxiety), as well as eating disorder obsessional thinking (e.g., atypical antipsychotics).

Case Example

Kevin is an 11-year-old, previously healthy, male who presented with low body weight and bradycardia in the context of eating a restricted diet and an increase in exercise. Kevin reports that he started to want to "get in shape" after learning that he was the "heaviest kid in my class" from a class science project in which each student calculated his or her weight on different planets. Kevin used his Fitbit to keep track of his activity level and started to compete with classmates "to burn the most calories." His family noticed that he refused to eat dessert and would come home with his "lunch uneaten." Kevin's weight was restored with FBT, and in the process, Kevin's family returned the Fitbit to the store, planned his meals, and used slow, 10-minute walks to reinforce compliance with meals.

Bulimia Nervosa

Although CBT and interpersonal psychotherapy (IPT) are effective treatments for adults with BN (Kass, Kolko, & Wilfley, 2013; Kelly, Shank, Bakalar, & Tanofsky-Kraff, 2014; Uher & Rutter, 2012), there is no empirical evidence to support these treatments in children. In adolescent populations, FBT has been found to be comparable to CBT and supportive therapy, and it was superior in producing remission at 6- and 12-month follow-ups (Couturier, Kimber, & Szatmari, 2013). Although fluoxetine, an SSRI, has an indication for treatment of BN in adult populations and may be effective in adolescents (Golden & Attia, 2011), no studies have been conducted in the pediatric population.

Case Example

Alexandra is a 12-year-old with ADHD who has a history of weight loss (5 pounds) after the start of stimulant medication for ADHD at age 10 years. She was evaluated by her primary care doctor and found to have gained 20 pounds in the past year, and although she denied any changes in her behaviors, her family was concerned about night-time binge episodes because wrappers of chips and ice cream sandwiches have been found hidden in her room and recently she was found exercising at night. Alexandra was diagnosed with BN, and her family was referred to FBT. During the course of treatment, the family removed Alexandra's bedroom door (in an effort to monitor behaviors) and helped establish regular eating with routine meals and snacks, eliminating both the binge eating and the compensatory exercise.

Binge-Eating Disorder

Although no clinical trials have been performed to evaluate the effectiveness of psychological or pharmacologic treatments for BED in children, two studies have supported the efficacy of IPT and CBT in reducing binge and LOC eating in adolescent girls (Debar et al., 2013; Tanofsky-Kraff et al., 2010). Family-based interventions that focused on enhanced appetite awareness and diminished food cravings led to significant reduction of binge episodes in children (Boutelle et al., 2011).

Case Example

Michael is a 10-year-old who was referred to a weight clinic for obesity. Michael endorsed "never feeling full," secretive eating, as well as a loss of control with food, stating, "I only stop eating when I feel sick because I ate too much." He was diagnosed with BED. He worked with his individual therapist to identify his hunger and satiety cues through exposure therapy and to establish coping mechanisms and alterative activities to deal with boredom as well as stress. His family received psychoeducation regarding meal planning and establishing routine meals and snacks, nutrition guidance regarding appropriate food preparation and selection, and started to limit availability and access to snack foods outside of meal/snack times.

CONSIDERATIONS IN MANAGEMENT
OF PEDIATRIC PATIENTS

Childhood is a period of rapid physical, cognitive, and emotional growth. In children, for whom the expectation is weight gain and growth, any nutritional compromise can have a deleterious effect, and this impact may be felt more rapidly and profoundly than in older patients. For example, any restricting or fasting can have acute effects: A child not eating for a day or two may need to be acutely hospitalized. Furthermore, as nutritional rehabilitation occurs in AN, for example, and weight gains are made, height can also increase, resulting in expected body weight being a moving target. At the same time, an advantage of youth is resiliency.

Children are concrete thinkers. They may take guidelines too seriously (e.g., exercise 1 hour every day) or attempt to implement parent or authority figure rules too literally (e.g., no junk food). In clinical practice, we often encounter youth who onset restrictive eating patterns or fat phobia following exposure to well-intentioned health classes in which messages about what is and is not healthy are presented bluntly without context. For example, the first author treated a 10-year-old who watched the movie *Supersize Me* and concluded that all fast food was "bad" and would lead to weight gain, without the ability to see beyond this dichotomization and appreciate that all types of food can be part of a healthful diet in moderation. Likewise, due to their concrete thinking style and developmentally appropriate difficulty abstracting, children may be more likely than adolescents and adults to misunderstand messages. One example of this is a young child who took the metaphor her therapist offered to her parents in the context of FBT of food as her medicine to mean that her parents were going to begin giving her daily injections. Clinicians need to be sensitive to the possibility that their words will be taken literally and take extra measures to ensure comprehension from child patients by asking follow-up questions ("Does that make sense?") and inviting them to teach their parents what they are learning, whenever possible.

Accompanying their concrete thinking style, children have an ability to think imaginatively, and they are more apt to have magical thinking or unusual beliefs. Clinically, some of the youth in our practices have held magical thinking beliefs that resemble obsessive–compulsive spectrum thought processes (e.g., thought–action fusion). For example, one pediatric patient we worked with who had lost weight from a premorbid overweight by severe restriction began by avoiding all foods he believed to be high in fat but ultimately also began avoiding anything that reminded him of fatness (e.g., a map of China—a country he saw as large) because he believed this would make him fat. Along these lines, we have seen youth who have unusual beliefs about "contracting" fatness—for example, believing that one could gain weight by smelling high-calorie foods.

Children can be both *incredibly difficult* and *amazingly fun* to engage in therapy. Like patients of all ages, some children are more verbal, emotive, and open to talking with someone new, whereas others are quieter. In our experience, it can be very difficult to engage the precocious anti-therapy pre-teen who would rather be anywhere than our office. On the other hand, even some of these more reluctant patients can be engaged with the right hook—identifying things they do wish were different or using child-identified incentives to be worked toward on a behavioral hierarchy. Using rewards for child practices or exposures in more behavior-oriented therapies can be motivating, and educating families about the appropriate use of rewards can be important.

Finally, children come with parents/caregivers, which is an enormous asset (but can sometimes seem like a liability). Parents are on the front line of illness detection, often being the first ones to notice changes in their children. In assessment and treatment, parents are integral reporters offering collateral data to inform diagnosis and help to shape the most appropriate treatment. Parents are typically both present and invested, and they can serve in treatment as key agents of change. Parents often feel undermined or even incapacitated by the child's eating disorder. As clinicians, we view our role as helping set them back on track to find their footing again, offering them language to talk about the eating disorder symptoms directly and helping them develop behavioral strategies to fight the eating disorder head on. Communication is key when working with families and offering guidance while families develop strategies that help every member feel supported and understood. One example is the importance of validation, a skill that is challenging to use when a child or a partner is experiencing difficult feelings (e.g., sadness or anger) because many believe that validating the feeling may convey that one is agreeing with the underlying cognition or accepting/approving a "bad" behavior. Many families intuitively validate and support "good" feelings, and with assistance, they can learn to expand this skill when negative feelings are expressed, tension is high, and conflict seems inevitable. The overall goal is to help the caregivers feel supported, competent, and empowered to address the eating disorder and not feel blamed, judged, or criticized.

CONCLUSION AND FUTURE DIRECTIONS

Diagnosis of eating disorders in children with the DSM-IV was limited, with many individuals failing to meet full criteria for a diagnosis and falling under the category of eating disorder not otherwise specified (EDNOS). However, it was found that individuals under the criteria of EDNOS suffered from similar medical and psychological complications and impairment in functioning, often matching the severity of the full diagnostic categories of AN and BN (Le Grange, Swanson, Crow, & Merikangas, 2012). Accordingly, DSM-5 has broadened eating and feeding disorder diagnoses, including newly specified diagnoses (e.g., avoidant/restrictive food intake disorder) and OSFED types (e.g., atypical AN and subthreshold BN) to capture the majority of youth who even in DSM-5 cannot be diagnosed with full criteria AN or BN. Because subdiagnostic threshold eating disorder pathology can be associated with clinically relevant adverse outcomes (Field et al., 2012; Micali et al., 2015) and more severe eating disorder pathology over time (Tanofsky-Kraff et al., 2011), promotion of early detection in children and adolescents is critical.

REFERENCES

Allen, K. L., Byrne, S. M., Oddy, W. H., & Crosby, R. D. (2013). DSM-IV-TR and DSM-5 eating disorders in adolescents: Prevalence, stability, and psychosocial correlates in a population-based sample of male and female adolescents. *Journal of Abnormal Psychology, 122*(3), 720–732.

American Psychiatric Association. (2000). *Diagnostic and statistical manual of mental disorders* (4th ed., text rev.). Washington, DC: American Psychiatric Association.

American Psychiatric Association. (2013). *Diagnostic and statistical manual of mental disorders* (5th ed.). Arlington, VA: American Psychiatric Publishing.

Bhatia, M. S., & Gupta, R. (2009). Pica responding to SSRI: An OCD spectrum disorder? *World Journal of Biological Psychiatry, 10*(4 Pt. 3), 936–938.

Birch, L. L., Fisher, J. O., Grimm-Thomas, K., Markey, C. N., Sawyer, R., & Johnson, S. L. (2001). Confirmatory factor analysis of the Child Feeding Questionnaire: A measure of parental attitudes, beliefs and practices about child feeding and obesity proneness. *Appetite, 36*(3), 201–210.

Boutelle, K. N., Zucker, N. L., Peterson, C. B., Rydell, S. A., Cafri, G., & Harnack, L. (2011). Two novel treatments to reduce overeating in overweight children: A randomized control trial. *Journal of Consulting and Clinical Psychology, 79*(6), 759–771.

Bryant-Waugh, R. J., Cooper, P. J., Taylor, C. L., & Lask, B. D. (1996). The use of the Eating Disorder Examination with children: A pilot study. *International Journal of Eating Disorders, 19*(4), 391–397.

Call, N. A., Simmons, C. A., Mevers, J. E., & Alvarez, J. P. (2015). Clinical outcomes and behavioral treatments for pica in children with developmental disabilities. *Journal of Autism and Developmental Disorders, 45*(7), 2105–2114.

Childress, A. C., Brewerton, T. D., Hodges, E. L., & Jarrell, M. P. (1993). The Kids' Eating Disorders Survey (KEDS): A study of middle school students. *Journal of the American Academy of Child and Adolescent Psychiatry, 32*(4), 843–850.

Chitkara, D. K., Van Tilburg, M., Whitehead, W. E., & Talley, N. J. (2006). Teaching diaphragmatic breathing for rumination syndrome. *American Journal of Gastroenterology, 101*(11), 2449–2452.

Couturier, J., Kimber, M., & Szatmari, P. (2013). Efficacy of family-based treatment for adolescents with eating disorders: A systemic review and meta-analysis. *International Journal of Eating Disorders, 46*(1), 3–11.

Debar, L. L., Wilson, G. T., Yarborough, B. J., Burns, B., Oyler, B., Hildebrandt. T., . . . Striegel, R. H. (2013). Cognitive behavioral treatment for recurrent binge eating in adolescent girls: A pilot trial. *Cognitive and Behavioral Practice, 20*(2), 147–161.

Delaney, C. B., Eddy, K. T., Hartmann, A. S., Becker, A. E., Murray, H. B., & Thomas, J. J. (2015). Pica and rumination behavior among individuals seeking treatment for eating disorders or obesity. *International Journal of Eating Disorders, 48*(2), 238–248.

Eddy, K. T., Celio Doyle, A., Hoste, R. R., Herzog, D. B., & Le Grange, D. (2008). Eating disorder not otherwise specified in adolescents. *Journal of the American Academy of Child and Adolescent Psychiatry, 47*(2), 156–164.

Eddy, K. T., Tanofsky-Kraff, M., Thompson-Brenner, H., Herzog, D. B., Brown, T. A., & Ludwig, D. S. (2007). Eating disorder pathology among overweight treatment-seeking youth: Clinical correlates and cross-sectional risk modeling. *Behavior Research and Therapy*, *45*(10), 2360–2371.

Eddy, K. T., Thomas, J. J., Hastings, E., Edkins, K., Lamont, E., Nevins, C. M., . . . Becker, A. E. (2015). Prevalence of DSM-5 avoidant/restrictive food intake disorder in a pediatric gastroenterology healthcare network. *International Journal of Eating Disorders*, *48*(5), 464–470.

Fairburn, C. G., & Cooper, Z. (1993). The Eating Disorder Examination (12th edition). In C. G. Fairburn & G. T. Wilson (Eds.), *Binge eating: Nature, assessment and treatment* (pp. 317–360). New York, NY: Guilford.

Field, A. E., Sonneville, K. R., Micali, N., Crosby, R. D., Swanson, S. A., Laird, N. M., . . . Horton, N. J. (2012). Prospective association of common eating disorders and adverse outcomes. *Pediatrics*, *130*(2), 289–295.

Fisher, M., Schneider, M., Burns, J., Symons, H., & Mandel, F. S. (2001). Differences between adolescents and young adults at presentation to an eating disorder program. *Journal of Adolescent Health*, *28*(3), 22–27.

Galloway, A. T., Lee, Y., & Birch, L. L. (2003). Predictors and consequences of food neophobia and pickiness in young girls. *Journal of the American Dietetic Association*, *103*(6), 692–698.

Garner, D. M. (1991). *The Eating Disorder Inventory-C*. Lutz, FL: Psychological Assessment Resources.

Garner, D. M., & Garfinkle, P. E. (1979). The Eating Attitudes Test: An index of the symptoms of anorexia nervosa. *Psychological Medicine*, *9*, 273–279.

Golden, N. H., & Attia, E. (2011). Psychopharmacology of eating disorders in children and adolescents. *Pediatric Clinics of North America*, *58*(1), 121–138.

Green, A. D., Alioto, A., Mousa, H., & Di Lorenzo, C. (2011). Severe pediatric rumination syndrome: Successful interdisciplinary inpatient management. *Journal of Pediatric Gastroenterology and Nutrition*, *52*(4), 414–418.

Hagopian, L. P., Rooker, G. W., & Rolider, N. U. (2011). Identifying empirically supported treatments for pica in individuals with intellectual disabilities. *Research in Developmental Disabilities*, *32*(6), 2114–2120.

Hergüner, S., & Hergüner, A. S. (2010). Pica in a child with attention deficit hyperactivity disorder and successful treatment with methylphenidate. *Progress in Neuro-Psychopharmacology and Biological Psychiatry*, *34*(6), 1155–1156.

Jacobi, C., Schmitz, G., & Agras, W. S. (2008). Is picky eating an eating disorder? *International Journal of Eating Disorders*, *41*(7), 626–634.

Johnson, W. G., & Grieve, F. G. (1999). Measuring binge eating in adolescents: Adolescent and parent versions of the Questionnaire of Eating and Weight Patterns. *International Journal of Eating Disorders*, *26*(3), 301–314.

Kass, A. E., Kolko, R. P., & Wilfley, D. E. (2013). Psychological treatments for eating disorders. *Current Opinion in Psychiatry*, *26*(6), 549–555.

Kelly, N. R., Shank, L. M., Bakalar, J. L., & Tanofsky-Kraff, M. (2014). Pediatric feeding and eating disorders: Current state of diagnosis and treatment. *Current Psychiatry Reports*, *16*(5), 446.

Kurz, S., van Dyck, Z., Dremmel, D., Munsch, S., & Hilbert, A. (2015). Early-onset restrictive eating disturbances in primary school boys and girls. *European Child and Adolescent Psychiatry*, *24*(7), 779–785.

Le Grange, D., Swanson, S. A., Crow, S. J., & Merikangas, K. R. (2012). Eating disorder not otherwise specified presentation in the US population. *International Journal of Eating Disorders, 45*(5), 711–718.

Lerner, A. J. (2008). Treatment of pica behavior with olanzapine. *CNS spectrums, 13*(1), 19.

Lock, J., Le Grange, D., Agras, W. S., Moye, A., Bryson, S. W., & Jo, B. (2010). Randomized clinical trial comparing family-based treatment with adolescent-focused individual therapy for adolescents with anorexia nervosa. *Archives of General Psychiatry, 67*(10), 1025–1032.

Lock, J., Le Grange, D., Forsberg, S., & Hewell, K. (2006). Is family therapy useful for treating children with anorexia nervosa? Results of a case series. *Journal of the American Academy of Child and Adolescent Psychiatry, 45*(11), 1323–1328.

Maloney, M. J., McGuire, J. B., & Daniels, S. R. (1988). Reliability testing of a children's version of the Eating Attitude Test. *Journal of the American Academy of Child & Adolescent Psychiatry, 27*(5), 541–543.

Micali, N., Solmi, F., Horton, N. J., Crosby, R. D., Eddy, K. T., Calzo, J. P., ... Field, A. E. (2015). Adolescent eating disorders predict psychiatric, high-risk behaviors and weight outcomes in young adulthood. *Journal of the American Academy of Child and Adolescent Psychiatry, 54*(8), 652–659.

Mishori, R., & McHale, C. (2014). Pica: An age-old eating disorder that's often missed. *Journal of Family Practice, 63*(7), 1–4.

Mousa, H. M., Montgomery, M., & Alioto, A. (2014). Adolescent rumination syndrome. *Current Gastroenterology Reports, 16*(8), 398.

Nicely, T. A., Lane-Loney, S., Masciulli, E., Hollenbeak, C. S., & Ornstein, R. M. (2014). Prevalence and characteristics of avoidant/restrictive food intake disorder in a cohort of young patients in day treatment for eating disorders. *Journal of Eating Disorders, 2*(1), 21.

Ornstein, R. M., Rosen, D. S., Mammel, K. A., Callahan, S. T., Forman, S., Jay, M. S., ... Walsh, B. T. (2013). Distribution of eating disorders in children and adolescents using the proposed DSM-5 criteria for feeding and eating disorders. *Journal of Adolescent Health, 53*(2), 303–305.

Peebles, R., Wilson, J. L., & Lock, J. D. (2006). How do children with eating disorders differ from adolescents with eating disorders at initial evaluation? *Journal of Adolescent Health, 39*(6), 800–805.

Pinhas, L., Morris, A., Crosby, R. D., & Katzman, D. K. (2011). Incidence and age-specific presentation of restrictive eating disorders in children: A Canadian Paediatric Surveillance Program study. *Archives in Pediatric and Adolescent Medicine, 165*(10), 895–899.

Rajindrajith, S., Devanarayana, N. M., & Crispus Perera, B. J. (2012). Rumination syndrome in children and adolescents: A school survey assessing prevalence and symptomatology. *BMC Gastroenterology, 12*, 163.

Rhine, D., & Tarbox, J. (2009). Chewing gum as a treatment for rumination in a child with autism. *Journal of Applied Behavioral Analysis, 42*(2), 381–385.

Rommel, N., Tack, J., Arts, J., Caenepeel, P., Bisschops, R., & Sifrim, D. (2010). Rumination or belching–regurgitation? Differential diagnosis using oesophageal impedance-manometry. *Neurogastroenterology and Motility, 22*(4), 97–104.

Rose, E. A., Porcerelli, J. H., & Neale, A. V. (2000). Pica: Common but commonly missed. *Journal of the American Board of Family Practice, 13*(5), 353–358.

Rosen, D. S. (2003). Eating disorders in children and young adolescents: Etiology, classification, clinical features, and treatment. *Adolescent Medicine, 14*(1), 49–59.

Shomaker, L. B., Tanofsky-Kraff, M., Savastano, D. M., Kozlosky, M., Columbo, K. M., Wolkoff, L. E., . . . Yanovski, J. A. (2010). Puberty and observed energy intake: Boy can they eat! *American Journal of Clinical Nutrition, 92*(1), 123–129.

Smink, F. R., van Hoeken, D., & Hoek, H. W. (2012). Epidemiology, course, and outcomes of eating disorders. *Current Opinions in Psychiatry, 26*(6), 543–548.

Stice, E., Marti, C. N., & Rohde, P. (2013). Prevalence, incidence, impairment and course of the proposed DSM-5 eating disorder diagnosis in an 8-year prospective community study of young women. *Journal of Abnormal Psychology, 122*(2), 445–457.

Swanson, S. A., Crow, S. J., Le Grange, D., Swendsen, J., & Merikangas, K. S. (2011). Prevalence and correlates of eating disorders in adolescents: Results from the National Comorbidity Survey Replication Adolescent Supplement. *Archives of General Psychiatry, 68*(7), 714–723.

Tack, J., Blondeau, K., Boecxstaens, V., & Rommel, N. (2011). Review article: The pathophysiology, differential diagnosis and management of rumination syndrome. *Alimentary Pharmacology and Therapeutics, 33*(7), 782–788.

Tanofsky-Kraff, M., Shomaker, L. B., Olsen, C., Roza, C. A., Wolkoff, L. E., Columbo, K. M., . . . Yanovski, J. A. (2011). A prospective study of pediatric loss of control eating and psychological outcomes. *Journal of Abnormal Psychology, 120*(1), 108–18.

Tanofsky-Kraff, M., Wilfley, D. E., Young, J. F., Mufson, L., Yanovski, S. Z., Glasofer, D. R., . . . Schvey, N. A. (2010). A pilot study of interpersonal psychotherapy for preventing excess weight gain in adolescent girls at-risk for obesity. *International Journal of Eating Disorders, 43*(8), 701–706.

Uher, R., & Rutter, M. (2012). Classification of feeding and eating disorders: Review of evidence and proposals for ICD-11. *World Psychiatry, 11*(2), 80–92.

Wardle, J., Guthrie, C. A., Sanderson, S., & Rapoport, L. (2001). Development of the Children's Eating Behaviour Questionnaire. *Journal of Child Psychology and Psychiatry and Allied Disciplines, 42*(07), 963–970.

Weaver, L., & Liebman, R. (2011). Assessment of anorexia nervosa in children and adolescents. *Current Psychiatry Reports, 13*(2), 93–98.

Williams, D. E., & McAdam, D. (2012). Assessment, behavioral treatment and prevention of pica: Clinical guidelines and recommendations for practitioners. *Research in Developmental Disabilities, 33*(6), 2050–2057.

18

Eating Disorders in Males

TIFFANY A. BROWN, SCOTT GRIFFITHS,
AND STUART B. MURRAY ■

MALES AND EATING DISORDERS

Eating disorders are frequently and inaccurately perceived as female-centric disorders, with male presentations being perceived as rare and highly atypical. This idea stands in marked contrast to the historical context of eating disorders, in which the very first reported cases depicted male and female eating disorders in equal measure (Morton, 1694). In contrast to these reports, an underrepresentation of males in clinical eating disorder research throughout much of the 20th century led to the notion that eating disorders in males were rare. The development of nosological frameworks throughout this period, predicated on empirical research drawn exclusively from female populations, may have further marginalized males with eating disorders, leading to a female-centric lens to eating disorders (Murray, Griffiths, & Mond, 2016). As a result, males with eating disorders have been uniquely stigmatized. This has led to a large number of males who have likely been misdiagnosed or overlooked regarding having an eating disorder, which has contributed to less research and clinical focus on males, thus maintaining a vicious cycle. However, there has been an increased interest in research and advocacy for males with eating disorders in recent years, which is beginning to shed light on a group of sufferers that has been mischaracterized and misunderstood for many years. This chapter reviews differences in clinical presentation, prevalence, and evidence-based treatment approaches for males with eating disorders to help provide further understanding of males with eating disorders and future directions for improving clinical care.

PREVALENCE

Prevalence estimates vary widely among males, depending on whether samples are community based or treatment seeking. As noted previously, males are underrepresented in treatment-seeking samples, with men constituting approx-imately 10% of those who seek treatment (Sweeting et al., 2015), despite the fact that community-based estimates demonstrate a more equivalent gender ratio. Thus, for clarity, estimates are provided for both community-based and clinical samples to help elucidate these important differences.

Prevalence in Community-Based Samples

In community-based samples of males, lifetime prevalence rates of any eating disorder range from 1.2% to 6.5% (weighted percentage = 3.0%; Hudson, Hiripi, Pope, & Kessler, 2007; Kjelsas, Bjornstrom, & Gotestam, 2004; Smink, van Hoeken, Oldehinkel, & Hoek, 2014; Woodside et al., 2001), whereas the point prevalence within the last year for any eating disorder ranges from 0.5% to 5.0% (weighted percentage = 1.4%; Hay, Loukas, & Philpott, 2005; Hudson et al., 2007; Kjelsas et al., 2004; Smink et al., 2014). Thus, overall, men represent up to 25–36% of individuals with any lifetime eating disorder (Hudson et al., 2007; Kjelsas et al., 2004; Madden, Morris, Zurynski, Kohn, & Elliot, 2009; Woodside et al., 2001). Although some researchers have speculated that there may be an increasing prev-alence of eating disorders among males in recent years, there are inconsistent find-ings regarding any sort of trends in the rates of eating disorder diagnoses in males (Sweeting et al., 2015). However, research has demonstrated that disordered eating practices (e.g., extreme dieting and purging) have increased at a faster rate in males than in females in the past decade (Mitchison, Mond, Slewa-Younan, & Hay, 2013).

Regarding specific eating disorders, more research has been done examining the prevalence of anorexia nervosa (AN), bulimia nervosa (BN), and binge-eating disorder (BED), whereas less is known about the prevalence of avoidant/restric-tive food intake disorder (ARFID) and muscle dysmorphia (MD; see Chapter 14) in community samples. This is due to the fact that ARFID and MD are newer diagnoses and thus there is more limited research. For males, the lifetime preva-lence of AN in community-based samples has ranged from 0.0% to 0.3% (Allen, Byrne, Oddy, & Crosby, 2013; Hudson et al., 2007; Kjelsas et al., 2004; Smink et al., 2014; Woodside et al., 2001), with the gender distribution of AN (female-to-male ratio) as high as 3:1 (Hudson et al., 2007). Estimates of the lifetime prevalence of BN range from 0.1% to 1.6% (Allen et al., 2013; Hudson et al., 2007; Kjelsas et al., 2004; Woodside et al., 2001), with up to a 4:1 female:male ratio (Hudson et al., 2007). For BED, prevalence estimates range from 0.3% to 2.0% (Allen et al., 2013; Hudson et al., 2007; Kjelsas et al., 2004; Smink et al., 2014). Notably, the gender ratio for BED has tended to be more evenly distributed, with one study finding a 1.75:1 female:male ratio (Hudson et al., 2007). Although considerably less research has been conducted on the prevalence of ARFID, research suggests that the prevalence rates are more equivalent. Specifically, in a community-based sample of 8- to 13-year-olds, ARFID was present among 1.3% of boys and 1.9% of girls (Kurz, van Dyck, Dremmel, Munsch, & Hilbert, 2015), representing a 1.5:1 female:male ratio. Epidemiological data for MD are currently unavailable, so it is not possible to determine the population prevalence of the disorder. However, one preliminary study of college students found that up to 6.99% of males were identified as possible cases of MD (Compte, Sepulveda, & Torrente, 2015).

Given the noted differences in the presentation of male eating disorder symptoms (Darcy, 2011), the gender ratio tends to become more equivalent when partial-syndrome eating disorders are examined (Sweeting et al., 2015; Woodside et al., 2001). For example, one study found that the female:male ratio decreased from 4.2:1 for full-syndrome AN to 1.5:1 for partial-syndrome AN. There was an even greater decrease in the female:male ratio from full-syndrome BN (11.4:1) to partial-syndrome BN (1.8:1). Encouragingly, the broadening of many diagnostic criteria in the fifth edition of the *Diagnostic and Statistical Manual of Mental Disorders* (DSM-5; American Psychiatric Association, 2013) has allowed for many presentations that were previously categorized as "not otherwise specified" to be recognized as full-threshold presentations, which may allow for better representation of males among full-threshold syndromes.

Regarding the prevalence of specific eating disorder behaviors in community-based samples, Striegel-Moore et al. (2009) demonstrated that males were generally less likely than females to engage in self-induced vomiting, fasting, and body checking and to endorse loss of control eating; however, men were more likely to engage in objective overeating episodes (women, 18.0%; men, 26.0%). Males and females were found to have equivalent rates of laxative use (women, 3.1%; men, 3.0%) and exercise (women, 6.0%; men, 5.6%). This is generally consistent with results from a sample of undergraduate males, albeit with college-aged males having generally higher levels of symptoms (Lavender, De Young, & Anderson, 2010). Specifically, males had lower rates of self-induced vomiting (women, 8.8%; men, 3.2%) and laxative use compared to sample-matched females (women, 8.3%; men, 2.7%), but they had equivalent rates of objective binge eating (women, 21.3%; men, 25.0%), excessive exercise (women, 30.8%; men, 31.4%), and dietary restraint (women, 25.9%; men, 24.0%).

Prevalence in Treatment-Seeking Samples

Although it is well established that males represent a substantial minority of eating disorder cases in community-based samples, research supports that males are underrepresented based on treatment-seeking samples. In a review, Sweeting and colleagues (2015) estimated that males represent between 5% and 11% of treatment-seeking samples for AN, BN, BED, and eating disorder not otherwise specified (EDNOS). Furthermore, males represent between 21% and 29% of those adolescents seeking treatment for ARFID, suggesting that the underrepresentation of males in treatment-seeking settings extends to both adolescents and adults (Fisher et al., 2014; Nicely, Lane-Loney, Masciulli, Hollenbeak, & Ornstein, 2014; Norris et al., 2014). These findings highlight the importance of continuing to address health disparities for males with eating disorders and for providers to be aware of potential barriers (as described throughout this chapter) in working with males.

Among males who do present for treatment, the distribution of diagnoses typically tends to parallel that for females. Among a male inpatient treatment sample (average age, 14 years), the majority received a diagnosis of AN restricting subtype (AN-R; 56.5%), with 26.1% being diagnosed with AN binge/purge subtype (AN-BP) and 17.3% with EDNOS (Coelho, Kumar, Kilvert, Kunkel, & Lam, 2015). Similar results were found for a residential sample of adolescents and adults, with the exception of a greater percentage of patients with bulimic-type presentations, likely reflecting the (on average) older sample and a later age of onset (Weltzin et al., 2012). Specifically, 37% were diagnosed with AN-R, 23% with AN-BP, 24% with BN, and 23% with EDNOS (5% of whom were diagnosed with BED). Regarding specific symptoms, Coelho and colleagues found that 81.8% of the males overexercised, 42.1% endorsed binge eating, and 35% engaged in self-induced vomiting. Weltzin and colleagues found that 55% had problems with exercise, which they noted may be an underestimate, given the strong connection between exercise and eating disorders for males.

Thus, in clinical practice, a provider at a residential or inpatient level of care might expect to see the majority of males presenting with AN-R (~30–50%), followed by bulimic-type eating disorders (AN-BP and BN; ~20–40%), with BED being more rare (5–17%). Although there are fewer data on prevalence in outpatient practice, outpatient providers will likely see a larger proportion of males with BED, given the more equivalent gender ratio for BED within the community. In addition, although research supports that MD occurs within population-based samples, there are limited data on treatment seeking within this population; thus, this may be a more rare case for clinicians to encounter. Clinicians treating pediatric and adolescent patients are also likely to see male patients with ARFID, given that males represent one-third of treatment-seeking patients with ARFID.

PRESENTATION

Although there are more similarities than differences in the presentation of eating disorders among males and females, it is important to be aware of notable variations in clinical presentation that may contribute to the continued underdetection of male eating disorder cases. One of the most important differences in presentation is that males are less likely to seek treatment for eating disorders (Griffiths, Mond, Li, et al., 2015). There are several hypotheses for why this is the case, including stigma and lack of education and awareness by health care providers, sufferers, their families, and society more broadly. In a qualitative study on males with eating disorders (Raisanen & Hunt, 2014), patients suggested that the perception of eating disorders as a "female" problem contributed to both the individuals and their health providers failing to recognize the patients' behaviors as signs of an eating disorder (Griffiths, Mond, Murray, & Touyz, 2015). Furthermore, males noted the lack of resources and gender-appropriate information for males with eating disorders as a barrier to seeking treatment. Given that eating disorders among males are less researched and less well understood, male sufferers and their family and friends may be less likely to recognize the sufferers' behavior as problematic or harmful (Darcy, 2011). Thus, it is important for providers to be aware of and sensitive to these potential barriers and concerns among males who do present for treatment.

Differences in Clinical Presentation

Regardless of treatment-seeking status, men have been shown to have a later age of onset compared to women (Gueguen et al., 2012; Zerwas et al., 2015). One study found that in females, bulimic symptoms tend to increase from age 14 to 16 years and then decline, whereas for males, bulimic symptoms decline from age 14 to 16 years and then increase in men's twenties (Abebe, Lien, & von Soest, 2012). In one inpatient sample of males with severe AN (Gueguen et al., 2012), the age of onset was 21 years in males compared to 18 years in females. There also tends to be a greater delay between age of onset and age at first treatment in men (Carlat, Camargo, & Herzog, 1997; Muise, Stein, & Arbess, 2003), which is likely explained by the previously noted barriers to males seeking treatment. Carlat and colleagues (1997) found an average of a 6-year delay before men presented for treatment. Importantly, this delay often leads to greater symptom severity for males upon presentation. Indeed, in treatment-seeking samples, men have been found to have higher rates of psychiatric comorbidity compared to women (Carlat et al., 1997), including higher rates of co-occurring alcohol or substance use and psychotic symptoms (Carlat et al., 1997; Striegel-Moore, Garvin, Dohm, & Rosenheck, 1999).

Males also differ from females in relation to weight history and weight presentation. Males are more likely to have a history of being previously overweight and being subjected to weight-related teasing compared to females (Carlat et al., 1997; Gueguen et al., 2012; Strother, Lemberg, Stanford, & Turberville, 2012). They are also more likely to present in treatment with a higher lifetime minimum and maximum body mass index (BMI), higher BMI at admission, and higher desired BMI compared to females (Gueguen et al., 2012; Strother et al., 2012).

Differences in Symptom Presentation

In addition to differences in terms of history and likelihood of seeking treatment, there are also notable differences in the presentation of actual eating disorder symptomatology. First, regarding binge eating, males are equally or more likely to report eating an objectively large amount of food, but they are less likely to report experiencing loss of control eating or distress during these episodes (Lewinsohn, Seeley, Moerk, & Striegel-Moore, 2002; Striegel-Moore et al., 2009). As an illustration, one study found that whereas the rates of objective binge episodes were equivalent among males and females, overall global eating concerns were lower for males than for females (Lavender et al., 2010). This lower distress may contribute to lower rates of treatment seeking among males even though clinical impairment has been found to be equivalent in binge eating among males and females (Striegel, Bedrosian, Wang, & Schwartz, 2012). Thus, it may be helpful to carefully consider impairment over distress for males with binge-eating episodes.

Further differences emerge related to how body dissatisfaction and body image concerns are expressed for males and females. Whereas body dissatisfaction in females tends to focus on thinness, for males it is important to distinguish between both leanness and muscularity concerns (Calzo et al., 2012; Murray et al., 2012). Although sociocultural pressures for women to pursue an unrealistically thin ideal have been well documented, these parallel pressures to pursue an unrealistically low body fat percentage and increased muscle mass exist for men and are equally as damaging. Indeed, pressures to pursue a lean, muscular ideal from family, friends, and the media are all associated with increased dissatisfaction with muscularity and/or body fat either directly or indirectly through the internalization of a lean, muscular body ideal (Tylka, 2011). These dual aspects of body dissatisfaction result in a different presentation of disordered eating and body image concerns in males compared to females. Typically, research has demonstrated that as many males want to lose weight as to gain weight (Drewnowski & Yee, 1987; Middleman, Vazquez, & Durant, 1998), likely reflecting an interest in both being lean and gaining more muscle mass. Indeed, in contrast to females, many males do not perceive their body as being muscular enough and perceive themselves as being too slim. Consistent with this, research has demonstrated that late-maturing males are more likely to experience higher levels of body dissatisfaction (Siegel, Yancey, Aneshensel, & Schuler, 1999). This is likely explained by pubertal development in males being associated with an increase in muscularity, which more closely aligns with the male-specific body ideal. Consequently, disordered eating behaviors often reflect these desires for increased muscle mass and decreased body fat; these behaviors include consuming excessive amounts of protein and protein-based supplements, consuming an increased number of calories and eating beyond the point of feeling full, eating frequently, excessive and/or compulsive exercise, and steroid use (Griffiths, Murray, & Touyz, 2012).

Given that there are well-established differences in the presentation of disordered eating and body image concerns among males, an important aspect to consider when working with this population is that established measures of eating pathology might be inaccurate for males. For example, even adolescent males diagnosed with AN are less likely to endorse the Eating Disorder Examination (EDE) item regarding "desire to have a flat stomach" and instead are more likely to endorse wanting "six-pack" abdominals, which is not traditionally measured on the EDE (Darcy et al., 2012). Furthermore, among treatment-seeking samples, males score lower than females on weight concerns, drive for thinness, and body dissatisfaction (Fernandez-Aranda et al., 2009; Strober et al., 2006). Thus, even at equivalent levels of psychopathology, males score lower on standard measures of eating pathology (Darcy & Lin, 2012). This is likely due to the fact that the measures used to assess eating disorder symptoms in males were designed for and normed on females, which results in these measures not accurately capturing the factors contributing to eating disorders in males (Darcy & Lin, 2012). However, there has been a recent push within the field to develop and evaluate more male-specific measures, some of which are included as resources at the end of this chapter in order to help aid accurate assessment, which is critical for competent clinical care.

Related to these differences in body image concerns among males, MD is the clinical manifestation of excessive muscularity-oriented body image, eating, and training concerns. The chief characteristic of MD is preoccupation with gaining size and muscle mass, and measures to assess the presence and severity of symptoms of the disorder have been developed. The disorder is discussed in detail in Chapter 14.

GROUPS OF MALES AT HIGHER RISK

Sexual Minorities

Research has consistently shown that gay and bisexual men are at increased risk for eating disorders, with as many as 42% of men seeking treatment for an eating disorder self-identifying as gay or bisexual (Carlat et al., 1997; Herzog, Norman, Gordon, & Pepose, 1984; Olivardia, Pope, Mangweth, & Hudson, 1995). Among community-based samples of males, being bisexual or gay has been consistently associated with higher drive for thinness, body dissatisfaction, and higher levels of disordered eating and eating disorders (Beren, Hayden, Wilfley, & Grilo, 1996; Boisvert & Harrell, 2010; Brown & Keel, 2012; Martins, Tiggemann, & Kirkbride, 2007), suggesting that findings in clinical samples are not an artifact of treatment seeking. In contrast, research on women indicates that being bisexual or gay is neither a risk factor nor a protective factor for eating disorders (Morrison, Morrison, & Sager, 2004), suggesting that sexual orientation is a unique risk factor for disordered eating in men. This increased risk among gay males may be in part due to increased pressures from the gay male community, potential partners, peers, and the media to conform to a lean, muscular body ideal (Brown & Keel, 2012, 2015; Tylka & Andorka, 2012). Indeed, single gay men have been shown to have higher levels of eating disorder psychopathology compared to gay men in relationships and all heterosexual men (Brown & Keel, 2012). Other theories, including minority stress theory, note that the stigma and stress that gay males are subjected to likely plays an important role in increasing eating pathology and other negative health outcomes for this population (Ricciardelli & McCabe, 2004).

Athletes

Eating disorder prevalence is generally higher in male athletes compared to nonathletes but lower than that in female athletes (Joy, Kussman, & Nattiv, 2016). Male athletes have also been shown to have higher rates of overall eating pathology compared to non-athletes (Chatterton & Petrie, 2013). Typically, sports emphasizing leanness (e.g., antigravitational sports) and weight class sports (e.g., boxing and wrestling) are more likely to be associated with increased eating pathology and disorders (Bratland-Sanda & Sundgot-Borgen, 2013; Sundgot-Borgen & Torstveit, 2004). Consistent with this, studies have found that the prevalence of eating disorders among males participating in antigravity sports (22%; Sundgot-Borgen & Torstveit, 2004) and weight class sports (17%; Rosendahl, Bormann, Aschenbrenner, Aschenbrenner, & Strauss, 2009) is typically higher than that in endurance sports (9% or 10%; Rosendahl et al., 2009; Sundgot-Borgen & Torstveit, 2004) and ball game sports (5%; Rosendahl et al., 2009). Of note, MD has been explored mostly within the context of bodybuilding and weightlifting (Baghurst & Lirgg, 2009). The use of anabolic steroids and diagnoses of MD are more prevalent in sports in which muscle mass and body strength play an integral role in sport performance (Pope, Gruber, Choi, Olivardia, & Phillips, 1997). It has been suggested that increased rates of eating disorders in male athletes are due to substantial pressures to conform to an often lean and muscular, sport-specific body ideal (Byrne & McLean, 2001). In addition, athletes and individuals with eating disorders share common personality traits, which also may be adaptive in increasing achievement and performance for athletes; these include perfectionism, obsessional tendencies, and overcompliance (Sundgot-Borgen & Torstveit, 2004).

EVIDENCE-BASED TREATMENT APPROACHES

The fact that most treatment studies have focused exclusively on females has led to a significant underrepresentation of males in treatment research studies, resulting in significant challenges for both clinical providers and treatment-seeking males. Despite the dearth of research on eating disorder treatment in males specifically, treatment must begin with sound principles of evidence-based practice and sound case conceptualization (Weltzin et al., 2012). Until further research is conducted, there is no evidence that empirically supported treatments that have demonstrated efficacy for females should not be successful for males (e.g., family-based therapy for children/adolescents with AN and cognitive–behavioral therapy [CBT] for BN).

Consistent with basic standards of care for eating disorders, males benefit from a multidisciplinary treatment team that includes a therapist, psychiatrist, and dietician; they also benefit from early diagnosis/intervention (Andersen, 1990) and the development of a strong therapeutic alliance (Stiles-Shields et al., 2013). General treatment goals for males with eating disorders align with those for females, including: accurate diagnosis, medical assessment and stabilization, psychoeducation for patient and caregivers, nutritional goals that focus on normalizing eating and adequate nourishment, and collaboration with family or caregivers (Ahren et al., 2013; Burns & Crisp, 1984). Special considerations that will help providers improve their competency in working with male patients with eating disorders are discussed next.

Medical Complications in Male Patients with Eating Disorders

One unique medical complication of eating disorders in males is low testosterone, which is often a consequence of weight loss. Assessment of testosterone level may be helpful in providing psychoeducation for males regarding the severity of their disorder and the surrounding medical complications because low testosterone in males with eating disorders is also associated with increased risk of bone loss. Indeed, 36% of males in inpatient treatment for an eating disorder were diagnosed with osteopenia and 26% were diagnosed with osteoporosis (Mehler, Sabel, Watson, & Anderson, 2008). Furthermore, the overall bone mineral density for males was significantly lower than that for females, indicating greater severity of bone loss in males (Mehler et al., 2008). Despite the role that testosterone plays in bone loss in males, there is currently no definitive evidence for the effectiveness of testosterone replacement therapy during weight restoration in significantly increasing bone mineral density. This points to the need for providers to refer underweight male patients to a physician for comprehensive medical assessment.

Treatment Response and Outcomes for Men with Eating Disorders

Although more research is needed to examine treatment response in males and specific predictors of treatment response, current research suggests that males generally have similar course and treatment responses to those of females (Andersen & Holman, 1997; Muise et al., 2003; Woodside & Kaplan, 1994), with some studies finding evidence for better long-term treatment outcomes in males (Strober et al., 2006). One study followed 28 males, on average, for 8 years after admission for inpatient treatment for AN, and it was found that 44% of males met criteria for good outcome, 26% for intermediate outcome, and 30% for poor outcome (Burns & Crisp, 1984). Poor outcome was associated with longer duration of illness, decreased sexual activity, greater previous treatment frequency, and poor relationships with family, suggesting a potential role for family-based therapy for males with eating disorders.

Effects for CBT for AN and BN appear to be equivalent across sexes. One study examining gender differences in response to group CBT for BN found that the treatment was equally as effective for males and females, even though males initially scored lower on measures of eating disorder cognitions and body dissatisfaction (Fernandez-Aranda et al., 2009). Consistent with this, a residential treatment center specializing in the treatment of males, using mostly CBT, found similar rates of recovery for its male and female patients and demonstrated significant effects on weight and eating pathology, as well as comorbid depression, anxiety, and obsessive–compulsive disorder symptoms (Weltzin et al., 2012). Furthermore, the same group demonstrated significant and equivalent increases in quality of life for both males and females after treatment (Weltzin, Bean, Klosterman, Lee, & Welk-Richards, 2015). Of note, although no specific psychopharmacological studies have found a differential treatment response for males and females, males may be more reluctant to take medications that have sexual side effects (Weltzin et al., 2012); thus, psychoeducation about these effects may be helpful at the outset.

More research on gender differences in treatment trials for BED are needed, given the near equivalent gender ratio (Hay, 2013). In this regard, one study found that overall, gender was not a predictor of outcome across various treatment trials for BED (Shingleton, Thompson-Brenner, Thompson, Pratt, & Franko, 2015); however, there was a difference in response for men depending on level of weight and shape concerns. Specially, the authors found that men with lower weight or shape concerns achieved remission in binge eating with a shorter duration of treatment (12 or 16 weeks), whereas men with high shape/weight concerns and women with either high or low shape/weight concerns were more likely to achieve remission with a longer duration of treatment (20 or 24 weeks). Studies such as this are important to help understand the course of treatment for males and possible differences between males based on different symptom presentations.

Addressing Gender Bias in Treatment

Because stigma and gender bias are significant barriers to males seeking treatment, it is important to consider and address these concerns for males in both outpatient and higher levels of care. There are several issues in this regard, including how mixed-gender treatment groups affect men in recovery and how to discuss gender bias in a therapeutic way.

Regarding whether to employ male-only groups, Weltzin and colleagues (2012) emphasized the importance of creating a specialized male treatment track in their residential treatment program to facilitate greater discussion of specific issues related to males, increase treatment engagement, and help restructure eating disorder symptoms as more than "female" problems. Furthermore, they noted that the group dynamic may be helpful for males to identify appropriate emotional expression as a strength rather than a weakness. When feasible, male-only groups can facilitate deeper discussion of various topics related to eating disorders that males may not feel comfortable discussing with females, including, but not limited to, sexual dysfunction; male-specific pressures to pursue a lean, muscular body; and romantic relationships. However, there are situations in which male-only groups are not feasible for various reasons (e.g., clinical resources and the number of males in treatment). Encouragingly, other treatment programs have had no difficulties integrating mixed-gender groups and have demonstrated positive outcomes for both males and females as a result (Woodside & Kaplan, 1994).

Regardless of whether males are separated or included with females in groups, it is important to ensure that males in treatment have some outlet to discuss their experience and comfort level in treatment if they not able to process this with other males. Consistent with this, reducing gender bias is an important aspect of treatment in order to help reduce stigma for males (Bannatyne & Stapleton, 2015). Given that most of the treatment providers in eating disorder centers tend to be female, it is helpful, when possible, to balance the gender ratio in staffing in order to capitalize on the positive effects of peer modeling (Keel, Forney, Brown, & Heatherton, 2013). Regardless of the provider's gender, it may be helpful for providers to assess male patients' attitudes toward treatment and potential concerns during their initial assessment and throughout treatment to ensure a safe space to discuss gender bias. In addition, providing accurate information on the prevalence of eating disorders in males and being well versed in the differences in symptom presentation may help validate that many men suffer from the same problems and increase therapeutic alliance.

CONCLUSION AND FUTURE DIRECTIONS

Males represent a substantial minority of those who suffer from eating disorders, but they are underrepresented in treatment-seeking samples due, in part, to stigma, gender bias, and lack of awareness. Although there are many similarities in eating disorder presentation between men and women, there are also notable differences, including later age of onset in men, differences in weight history and comorbidity, and differences in specific eating disorder symptoms that may reflect different gendered body ideals. Treatment response appears generally equivalent among males and females, but it is essential for eating disorder professionals to be aware of the previously mentioned potential differences and concerns for males in order to be competent and sensitive providers for this population.

Future directions for the field of males and eating disorders include continued refinement of eating disorder and body image assessment measures that accurately capture symptoms in males and spreading advocacy and awareness regarding inaccuracies about males. It is also essential that more males be included in treatment research and randomized controlled trials of both psychological and psychopharmacological interventions to ascertain how gender plays a role in treatment response and outcome. Doing so is important in order to continue to improve males' engagement with treatment and the quality of care for males with eating disorders.

RESOURCES

Measures of Eating Disorder and Related Psychopathology Developed for Males

As discussed previously, many of the eating disorder assessment measures were developed for and normed in female populations. Here, selected measures that were either developed to address specific concerns related to males or have been extensively studied in male populations are presented.

Eating Pathology Symptoms Inventory (for Males and Females)

The Eating Pathology Symptoms Inventory (EPSI; Forbush et al., 2013) consists of 45 items that assess eight constructs related to eating pathology: Body Dissatisfaction, Binge Eating, Cognitive Restraint, Purging, Excessive Exercise, Restricting, Muscle Building, and Negative Attitudes Toward Obesity. The EPSI has demonstrated strong psychometric properties in both women and men, and it is able to differentiate those who do and those who do not have an eating disorder (Forbush, Wildes, & Hunt, 2014).

Eating Disorder Assessment for Men (for Males Only)

The Eating Disorder Assessment for Men (EDAM; Stanford & Lemberg, 2012) consists of 50 items that assess eating disorder symptoms specific to males within five categories: Food Issues, Weight Concerns, Exercise Issues, Body Image/Appearance Concerns, and Disordered Eating Habits. The EDAM has demonstrated strong internal consistency and distinguishes between males who do and males who do not have an eating disorder (Stanford & Lemberg, 2012).

Drive for Muscularity Scale (for Males and Females)

The Drive for Muscularity Scale (DMS; McCreary & Sasse, 2000) is a 15-item measure that assesses desire to be more muscular. The DMS has demonstrated strong internal consistency in both adolescent (McCreary & Sasse, 2000) and adult males (McCreary, Sasse, Saucier, & Dorsch, 2004). The DMS has also demonstrated good construct validity, convergent validity, and discriminant validity in distinguishing between drive for thinness in males (McCreary, & Sasse, 2000).

Male Body Attitudes Scale (for Males Only)

The Male Body Attitudes Scale (MBAS; Tylka, Bergeron, & Schwartz, 2005) consists of 24 items that yield a total score as well as dissatisfaction with body fat, muscularity, and height subscales. Previous research has demonstrated strong internal consistency for both the total score and the specific subscales (Smith, Hawkeswood, Bodell, & Joiner, 2011; Tylka et al., 2005).

Male Body Checking Questionnaire (for Males Only)

The Male Body Checking Questionnaire (MBCQ; Hildebrandt, Walker, Alfano, Delinsky, & Bannon, 2010) is a 19-item measure that assesses the frequency of various body checking behaviors specific to males, with four subscales: Global Muscle Checking, Chest and Shoulder Checking, Other Comparative Checking, and Body Testing. The questionnaire has demonstrated high internal consistency and 2-week test–retest reliability and also divergent validity from a comparable measure in females (Hildebrandt et al., 2010; Walker, Anderson, & Hildebrandt, 2009).

Obligatory Exercise Questionnaire (for Males and Females)

The Obligatory Exercise Questionnaire (OEQ; Thompson & Pasman, 1991) is a 20-item measure that assesses the frequency of exercise-related situations. The

OEQ has demonstrated strong internal consistency and 2-week test–retest reliability (Pasman & Thompson, 1988).

MUSCLE DYSMORPHIC DISORDER INVENTORY (FOR MALES AND FEMALES)
The Muscle Dysmorphic Disorder Inventory (MDDI; Hildebrandt, Langenbucher, & Schlundt, 2004) is a 13-item, self-report questionnaire that measures three core components of MD symptomatology: drive for size, appearance intolerance, and functional impairment. These scales were designed to correspond to proposed diagnostic criteria for MD (Pope et al., 1997). The MDDI has demonstrated strong convergent validity, 1-week test–retest reliability, and internal consistency among college men (Hildebrandt et al., 2004).

Organizations Focusing on Eating Disorders in Males

National Association for Males with Eating Disorders (N.A.M.E.D.; http://namedinc.org)
Men Get Eating Disorders Too (MGEDT; http://mengetedstoo.co.uk)

REFERENCES

Abebe, D. S., Lien, L., & von Soest, T. (2012). The development of bulimic symptoms from adolescence to young adulthood in females and males: A population-based longitudinal cohort study. *International Journal of Eating Disorders, 45*(6), 737–745.

Ahren, J. C., Chiesa, F., Koupil, I., Magnusson, C., Dalman, C., & Goodman, A. (2013). We are family—Parents, siblings, and eating disorders in a prospective total-population study of 250,000 Swedish males and females. *International Journal of Eating Disorders, 46*(7), 693–700.

Allen, K. L., Byrne, S. M., Oddy, W. H., & Crosby, R. D. (2013). DSM-IV-TR and DSM-5 eating disorders in adolescents: Prevalence, stability, and psychosocial correlates in a population-based sample of male and female adolescents. *Journal of Abnormal Psychology, 122*(3), 720–732.

American Psychiatric Association. (2013). *Diagnostic and statistical manual of mental disorders* (5th ed.). Arlington, VA: American Psychiatric Publishing.

Andersen, A. E. (1990). *Males with eating disorders*: New York, NY: Psychology Press.

Andersen, A. E., & Holman, J. E. (1997). Males with eating disorders: Challenges for treatment and research. *Psychopharmacology Bulletin, 33*(3), 391.

Baghurst, T., & Lirgg, C. (2009). Characteristics of muscle dysmorphia in male football, weight training, and competitive natural and non-natural bodybuilding samples. *Body Image, 6*(3), 221–227.

Bannatyne, A., & Stapleton, P. (2015). Educating medical students about anorexia nervosa: A potential method for reducing the volitional stigma associated with the disorder. *Eating Disorders, 23*(2), 115–133.

Beren, S. E., Hayden, H. A., Wilfley, D. E., & Grilo, C. M. (1996). The influence of sexual orientation on body dissatisfaction in adult men and women. *International Journal of Eating Disorders, 20*(2), 135–141.

Boisvert, J. A., & Harrell, W. A. (2010). Homosexuality as a risk factor for eating disorder symptomatology in men. *Journal of Men's Studies, 17*(3), 210–225.

Bratland-Sanda, S., & Sundgot-Borgen, J. (2013). Eating disorders in athletes: Overview of prevalence, risk factors and recommendations for prevention and treatment. *European Journal of Sport Sciences, 13*(5), 499–508.

Brown, T. A., & Keel, P. K. (2012). The impact of relationships on the association between sexual orientation and disordered eating in men. *International Journal of Eating Disorders, 45*(6), 792–799.

Brown, T. A., & Keel, P. K. (2015). Relationship status predicts lower restrictive eating pathology for bisexual and gay men across 10-year follow-up. *International Journal of Eating Disorders, 48*(6), 700–707.

Burns, T., & Crisp, A. H. (1984). Outcome of anorexia nervosa in males. *British Journal of Psychiatry, 145,* 319–325.

Byrne, S., & McLean, N. (2001). Eating disorders in athletes: A review of the literature. *Journal of Science & Medicine in Sport, 4*(2), 145–159.

Calzo, J. P., Sonneville, K. R., Haines, J., Blood, E. A., Field, A. E., & Austin, S. B. (2012). The development of associations among body mass index, body dissatisfaction, and weight and shape concern in adolescent boys and girls. *Journal of Adolescent Health, 51*(5), 517–523.

Carlat, D. J., Camargo, C. A., Jr., & Herzog, D. B. (1997). Eating disorders in males: A report on 135 patients. *American Journal of Psychiatry, 154*(8), 1127–1132.

Chatterton, J. M., & Petrie, T. A. (2013). Prevalence of disordered eating and pathogenic weight control behaviors among male collegiate athletes. *Eating Disorders, 21*(4), 328–341.

Coelho, J. S., Kumar, A., Kilvert, M., Kunkel, L., & Lam, P. Y. (2015). Male youth with eating disorders: Clinical and medical characteristics of a sample of inpatients. *Eating Disorders, 23*(5), 455–461.

Compte, E. J., Sepulveda, A. R., & Torrente, F. (2015). A two-stage epidemiological study of eating disorders and muscle dysmorphia in male university students in Buenos Aires. *International Journal of Eating Disorders, 48*(8), 1092–1101.

Darcy, A. (2011). Eating disorders in adolescent males: A critical examination of five common assumptions. *Adolescent Psychiatry, 1*(4), 307–312.

Darcy, A. M., Doyle, A. C., Lock, J., Peebles, R., Doyle, P., & Le Grange, D. (2012). The Eating Disorders Examination in adolescent males with anorexia nervosa: How does it compare to adolescent females? *International Journal of Eating Disorders, 45*(1), 110–114.

Darcy, A. M., & Lin, I. H. (2012). Are we asking the right questions? A review of assessment of males with eating disorders. *Eating Disorders, 20*(5), 416–426.

Drewnowski, A., & Yee, D. K. (1987). Men and body image: Are males satisfied with their body weight? *Psychosomatic Medicine, 49*(6), 626–634.

Fernandez-Aranda, F., Krug, I., Jimenez-Murcia, S., Granero, R., Nunez, A., Penelo, E., . . . Treasure, J. (2009). Male eating disorders and therapy: A controlled pilot study with one year follow-up. *Journal of Behavior Therapy & Experimental Psychiatry, 40*(3), 479–486.

Fisher, M. M., Rosen, D. S., Ornstein, R. M., Mammel, K. A., Katzman, D. K., Rome, E. S., . . . Walsh, B. T. (2014). Characteristics of avoidant/restrictive food intake disorder in children and adolescents: A "new disorder" in DSM-5. *Journal of Adolescent Health, 55*(1), 49–52.

Forbush, K. T., Wildes, J. E., & Hunt, T. K. (2014). Gender norms, psychometric proper-ties, and validity for the Eating Pathology Symptoms Inventory. *International Journal of Eating Disorders, 47*(1), 85–91.

Forbush, K. T., Wildes, J. E., Pollack, L. O., Dunbar, D., Luo, J., Patterson, K., . . . Bright, A. (2013). Development and validation of the Eating Pathology Symptoms Inventory (EPSI). *Psychological Assessment, 25*(3), 859.

Griffiths, S., Mond, J. M., Li, Z., Gunatilake, S., Murray, S. B., Sheffield, J., & Touyz, S. (2015). Self-stigma of seeking treatment and being male predict an increased like-lihood of having an undiagnosed eating disorder. *International Journal of Eating Disorders, 48*(6), 775–778.

Griffiths, S., Mond, J. M., Murray, S. B., & Touyz, S. (2015). The prevalence and adverse associations of stigmatization in people with eating disorders. *International Journal of Eating Disorders, 48*(6), 767–774.

Griffiths, S., Murray, S. B., & Touyz, S. (2012). Disordered eating and the muscular ideal. *Body Image, 9*, 318–323.

Gueguen, J., Godart, N., Chambry, J., Brun-Eberentz, A., Foulon, C., Divac, S. M., . . . Huas, C. (2012). Severe anorexia nervosa in men: Comparison with severe AN in women and analysis of mortality. *International Journal of Eating Disorders, 45*(4), 537–545.

Hay, P. (2013). A systematic review of evidence for psychological treatments in eating disorders: 2005–2012. *International Journal of Eating Disorders, 46*(5), 462–469.

Hay, P. J., Loukas, A., & Philpott, H. (2005). Prevalence and characteristics of men with eating disorders in primary care: How do they compare to women and what features may aid in identification? *Primary Care & Community Psychiatry, 10*(1), 1–6.

Herzog, D. B., Norman, D. K., Gordon, C., & Pepose, M. (1984). Sexual conflict and eat-ing disorders in 27 males. *American Journal of Psychiatry, 141*(8), 989–990.

Hildebrandt, T., Langenbucher, J., & Schlundt, D. G. (2004). Muscularity concerns among men: Development of attitudinal and perceptual measures. *Body Image, 1*(2), 169–181.

Hildebrandt, T., Walker, D. C., Alfano, L., Delinsky, S., & Bannon, K. (2010). Development and validation of a male specific body checking questionnaire. *International Journal of Eating Disorders, 43*(1), 77–87.

Hudson, J. I., Hiripi, E., Pope, H. G., Jr., & Kessler, R. C. (2007). The prevalence and cor-relates of eating disorders in the National Comorbidity Survey Replication. *Biological Psychiatry, 61*(3), 348–358.

Joy, E., Kussman, A., & Nattiv, A. (2016). 2016 update on eating disorders in ath-letes: A comprehensive narrative review with a focus on clinical assessment and man-agement. *British Journal of Sports Medicine, 50*(3), 154–162.

Keel, P. K., Forney, K. J., Brown, T. A., & Heatherton, T. F. (2013). Influence of col-lege peers on disordered eating in women and men at 10-year follow-up. *Journal of Abnormal Psychology, 122*(1), 105–110.

Kjelsas, E., Bjornstrom, C., & Gotestam, K. G. (2004). Prevalence of eating disorders in female and male adolescents (14–15 years). *Eating Behaviors, 5*(1), 13–25.

Kurz, S., van Dyck, Z., Dremmel, D., Munsch, S., & Hilbert, A. (2015). Early-onset restrictive eating disturbances in primary school boys and girls. *European Child & Adolescent Psychiatry, 24*(7), 779–785.

Lavender, J. M., De Young, K. P., & Anderson, D. A. (2010). Eating Disorder Examination Questionnaire (EDE-Q): Norms for undergraduate men. *Eating Behaviors, 11*(2), 119–121.

Lewinsohn, P. M., Seeley, J. R., Moerk, K. C., & Striegel-Moore, R. H. (2002). Gender differences in eating disorder symptoms in young adults. *International Journal of Eating Disorders, 32*(4), 426–440.

Madden, S., Morris, A., Zurynski, Y. A., Kohn, M., & Elliot, E. J. (2009). Burden of eating disorders in 5–13-year-old children in Australia. *Medical Journal of Australia, 190*(8), 410–414.

Martins, Y., Tiggemann, M., & Kirkbride, A. (2007). Those Speedos become them: The role of self-objectification in gay and heterosexual men's body image. *Personality and Social Psychology Bulletin, 33*(5), 634–647.

McCreary, D. R., & Sasse, D. K. (2000). An exploration of the drive for muscularity in adolescent boys and girls. *Journal of American College Health, 48*(6), 297–304.

McCreary, D. R., Sasse, D. K., Saucier, D. M., & Dorsch, K. D. (2004). Measuring the drive for muscularity: Factorial validity of the Drive for Muscularity Scale in men and women. *Psychology of Men & Masculinity, 5*(1), 49–58.

Mehler, P. S., Sabel, A. L., Watson, T., & Andersen, A. E. (2008). High risk of osteoporosis in male patients with eating disorders. *International Journal of Eating Disorders, 41*(7), 666–672.

Middleman, A. B., Vazquez, I., & Durant, R. H. (1998). Eating patterns, physical activity, and attempts to change weight among adolescents. *Journal of Adolescent Health, 22*(1), 37–42.

Mitchison, D., Mond, J., Slewa-Younan, S., & Hay, P. (2013). Sex differences in health-related quality of life impairment associated with eating disorder features: A general population study. *International Journal of Eating Disorders, 46*(4), 375–380.

Morrison, M. A., Morrison, T. G., & Sager, C.-L. (2004). Does body satisfaction differ between gay men and lesbian women and heterosexual men and women? A meta-analytic review. *Body Image, 1*(2), 127–138.

Morton, R. P. (1694). *Phthisiologia: Or a treatise of consumptions.* London, England: Smith & Walford.

Muise, A. M., Stein, D. G., & Arbess, G. (2003). Eating disorders in adolescent boys: A review of the adolescent and young adult literature. *Journal of Adolescent Health, 33*(6), 427–435.

Murray, S. B., Griffiths, S., & Mond, J. M. (2016). Evolving eating disorder psychopathology: Conceptualising muscularity-oriented disordered eating. *British Journal of Psychiatry, 208*(5), 414–415.

Murray, S. B., Rieger, E., Hildebrandt, T., Karlov, L., Russell, J., Boon, E., ... Touyz, S. W. (2012). A comparison of eating, exercise, shape, and weight related symptomatology in males with muscle dysmorphia and anorexia nervosa. *Body Image, 9*(2), 193–200.

Nicely, T. A., Lane-Loney, S., Masciulli, E., Hollenbeak, C. S., & Ornstein, R. M. (2014). Prevalence and characteristics of avoidant/restrictive food intake disorder in a cohort of young patients in day treatment for eating disorders. *Journal of Eating Disorders, 2*(1), 21.

Norris, M. L., Robinson, A., Obeid, N., Harrison, M., Spettigue, W., & Henderson, K. (2014). Exploring avoidant/restrictive food intake disorder in eating disordered patients: A descriptive study. *International Journal of Eating Disorders, 47*(5), 495–499.

Olivardia, R., Pope, H. G., Jr., Mangweth, B., & Hudson, J. I. (1995). Eating disorders in college men. *American Journal of Psychiatry, 152*(9), 1279–1285.

Pasman, L., & Thompson, J. K. (1988). Body image and eating disturbance in obligatory runners, obligatory weightlifters, and sedentary individuals. *International Journal of Eating Disorders, 7*(6), 759–769.

Pope, H. G., Jr., Gruber, A. J., Choi, P., Olivardia, R., & Phillips, K. A. (1997). Muscle dysmorphia: An underrecognized form of body dysmorphic disorder. *Psychosomatics, 38*(6), 548–557.

Raisanen, U., & Hunt, K. (2014). The role of gendered constructions of eating disorders in delayed help-seeking in men: A qualitative interview study. *British Medical Journal Open, 4*(4), e004342.

Ricciardelli, L. A., & McCabe, M. P. (2004). A biopsychosocial model of disordered eating and the pursuit of muscularity in adolescent boys. *Psychological Bulletin, 130*(2), 179–205.

Rosendahl, J., Bormann, B., Aschenbrenner, K., Aschenbrenner, F., & Strauss, B. (2009). Dieting and disordered eating in German high school athletes and non-athletes. *Scandinavian Journal of Medicine & Science in Sports, 19*(5), 731–739.

Shingleton, R. M., Thompson-Brenner, H., Thompson, D. R., Pratt, E. M., & Franko, D. L. (2015). Gender differences in clinical trials of binge eating disorder: An analysis of aggregated data. *Journal of Consulting & Clinical Psychology, 83*(2), 382–386.

Siegel, J. M., Yancey, A. K., Aneshensel, C. S., & Schuler, R. (1999). Body image, perceived pubertal timing, and adolescent mental health. *Journal of Adolescent Health, 25*(2), 155–165.

Smink, F. R., van Hoeken, D., Oldehinkel, A. J., & Hoek, H. W. (2014). Prevalence and severity of DSM-5 eating disorders in a community cohort of adolescents. *International Journal of Eating Disorders, 47*(6), 610–619.

Smith, A. R., Hawkeswood, S. E., Bodell, L. P., & Joiner, T. E. (2011). Muscularity versus leanness: An examination of body ideals and predictors of disordered eating in heterosexual and gay college students. *Body Image, 8*(3), 232–236.

Stanford, S. C., & Lemberg, R. (2012). Measuring eating disorders in men: Development of the Eating Disorder Assessment for Men (EDAM). *Eating Disorders, 20*(5), 427–436.

Stiles-Shields, C., Touyz, S., Hay, P., Lacey, H., Crosby, R. D., Rieger, E., . . . Grange, D. (2013). Therapeutic alliance in two treatments for adults with severe and enduring anorexia nervosa. *International Journal of Eating Disorders, 46*(8), 783–789.

Striegel, R. H., Bedrosian, R., Wang, C., & Schwartz, S. (2012). Why men should be included in research on binge eating: Results from a comparison of psychosocial impairment in men and women. *International Journal of Eating Disorders, 45*(2), 233–240.

Striegel-Moore, R. H., Garvin, V., Dohm, F. A., & Rosenheck, R. A. (1999). Psychiatric comorbidity of eating disorders in men: A national study of hospitalized veterans. *International Journal of Eating Disorders, 25*(4), 399–404.

Striegel-Moore, R. H., Rosselli, F., Perrin, N., DeBar, L., Wilson, G. T., May, A., & Kraemer, H. C. (2009). Gender difference in the prevalence of eating disorder symptoms. *International Journal of Eating Disorders, 42*(5), 471–474.

Strober, M., Freeman, R., Lampert, C., Diamond, J., Teplinsky, C., & DeAntonio, M. (2006). Are there gender differences in core symptoms, temperament, and short-term prospective outcome in anorexia nervosa? *International Journal of Eating Disorders, 39*(7), 570–575.

Strother, E., Lemberg, R., Stanford, S. C., & Turberville, D. (2012). Eating disorders in men: Underdiagnosed, undertreated, and misunderstood. *Eating Disorders, 20*(5), 346–355.

Sundgot-Borgen, J., & Torstveit, M. K. (2004). Prevalence of eating disorders in elite athletes is higher than in the general population. *Clinical Journal of Sports Medicine, 14*(1), 25–32.

Sweeting, H., Walker, L., MacLean, A., Patterson, C., Raisanen, U., & Hunt, K. (2015). Prevalence of eating disorders in males: A review of rates reported in academic research and UK mass media. *International Journal of Men's Health, 14*(2).

Thompson, J. K., & Pasman, L. (1991). The obligatory exercise questionnaire. *The Behavior Therapist, 14,* 137.

Tylka, T. L. (2011). Refinement of the tripartite influence model for men: Dual body image pathways to body change behaviors. *Body Image, 8*(3), 199–207.

Tylka, T. L., & Andorka, M. J. (2012). Support for an expanded tripartite influence model with gay men. *Body Image, 9*(1), 57–67.

Tylka, T. L., Bergeron, D., & Schwartz, J. P. (2005). Development and psychometric evaluation of the Male Body Attitudes Scale (MBAS). *Body Image, 2*(2), 161–175.

Walker, D. C., Anderson, D. A., & Hildebrandt, T. (2009). Body checking behaviors in men. *Body Image, 6*(3), 164–170.

Weltzin, T., Bean, P., Klosterman, E., Lee, H. J., & Welk-Richards, R. (2015). Sex differences in the effects of residential treatment on the quality of life of eating disorder patients. *Eating & Weight Disorders, 20*(3), 301–310.

Weltzin, T. E., Cornella-Carlson, T., Fitzpatrick, M. E., Kennington, B., Bean, P., & Jefferies, C. (2012). Treatment issues and outcomes for males with eating disorders. *Eating Disorders, 20*(5), 444–459.

Woodside, D. B., Garfinkel, P. E., Lin, E., Goering, P., Kaplan, A. S., Goldbloom, D. S., & Kennedy, S. H. (2001). Comparisons of men with full or partial eating disorders, men without eating disorders, and women with eating disorders in the community. *American Journal of Psychiatry, 158*(4), 570–574.

Woodside, D. B., & Kaplan, A. S. (1994). Day hospital treatment in males with eating disorders—Response and comparison to females. *Journal of Psychosomatic Research, 38*(5), 471–475.

Zerwas, S., Larsen, J. T., Petersen, L., Thornton, L. M., Mortensen, P. B., & Bulik, C. M. (2015). The incidence of eating disorders in a Danish register study: Associations with suicide risk and mortality. *Journal of Psychiatric Research, 65,* 16–22.

19

Eating Disorders and Disordered Eating in the LGBTQ Population

JON ARCELUS, FERNANDO FERNÁNDEZ-ARANDA, AND WALTER PIERRE BOUMAN ■

Many epidemiological studies investigating prevalence rates of eating disorders and disordered eating psychopathology in sexual minorities have used the term *LGBT* to define the population studied. The term LGBT stands for lesbian, gay, bisexual, and transgender people (Canaday, 2014). This term, used since the 1990s, has been adopted by the majority of sexuality and gender identity-based communities and by the media of most English-speaking countries.

The terms *lesbian, gay,* and *bisexual* are used to refer to people (men and women) with a sexual attraction to members of their own sex (or to both, as is the case for people who identify as bisexual). The term *transgender*, or *trans*, is used to describe a diverse population of people who do not present and/or identify as the gender they were assigned at birth, either some or all of the time (Richards & Barker, 2013). Transgender identities include transgender women and men, respectively, who feminize or masculinize their bodies with cross-sex hormone treatment and/or gender-confirming surgery, and other gender-variant individuals, who may identify and/or present in a way that is outside the gender dichotomy of man/woman. This can include nonbinary people (not part of the binary gender), genderqueer (neither entirely male nor entirely female), bigender (encompasses both binary genders), pangender (infinite number of genders), genderfluid (gender identity varies over time), or agender (no gender), among others (Richards, Bouman, & Barker, 2017). Lately the letter "Q" has been added to the LGBT term in order to clarify that people who identify as queer (or nonbinary) or those questioning their gender identity are also included under this term. The term "cisgender" is used to describe people whose assigned gender at birth matches their gender identity (Richards et al., 2016). LGBTQ is therefore used to refer to anyone who identifies as nonheterosexual and/or non-cisgender.

Although the term LGBTQ is intended to emphasize a diversity of sexuality and gender identity-based culture, it remains unclear, and sometimes confusing, why people with a diverse sexual orientation are grouped together with people with a diverse gender identity. Although the fight for equal rights and civil liberties has brought sexual and gender identity minorities together as part of the same group (Knauer, 2009), scientifically it may not be as helpful because research findings from sexual minority studies are not necessarily generalizable to gender identity minorities.

The grouping of transgender people with gay, lesbian, and bisexual people in scientific literature is likely due to the low prevalence rates of transgender people in society. A recent study investigating meta-analytical prevalence rates of transgender people accessing transgender health services found 4.6 transgender people per every 100,000 individuals; it was 6.8 for transgender women and 2.6 for transgender men, with time analysis finding an increase in reported prevalence rates during the past 50 years (Arcelus et al., 2015). However, this study includes only a very specific population of transgender people, namely those fulfilling a rather narrow clinical diagnosis of being transgender as well as those accessing transgender health services. Because not every transgender person requires gender-confirming medical intervention (Beek, Kreukels, & Cohen-Kettenis, 2015; Bockting, Coleman, & De Cuypere, 2011), and therefore access to transgender services, the meta-analytical prevalence rates found in the study by Arcelus et al. likely underestimate the true prevalence of transgender people in the community (Makadon, 2011). Recent population surveys, with much wider inclusion criteria, have found prevalence rates of gender incongruity between 1.1% and 4.6% among people assigned male at birth and 0.8% and 3.2% among people assigned female at birth (Kuyper & Wijsen, 2014; Van Caenegem et al., 2015).

The high prevalence rates of people reporting gender incongruity in population studies may explain the significant increase in the number of people referred to transgender health services in Europe and North America (Aitken et al., 2015; de Vries, Kreukels, T'Sjoen, Ålgars, & Mattila, 2015). This increased prevalence is likely due to a number of interrelated factors, including an increase in the visibility of transgender people in the media, the wide availability of information on the Internet, and the increased availability of gender-confirming medical treatments and transgender health services in certain countries (Coleman et al., 2012; Wylie et al., 2014).

Gay, lesbian, and bisexual people, as well as transgender people, are a very diverse group. This is important to understand because generalizing findings from a group of people who identify as gay or lesbian to all people who identify as gay or lesbian is not always valid. The gay world is often represented as some sort of monolithic whole that shares the same culture. This is not true. For example, within the male gay culture, several groups have been socially constructed that are primarily based on femininity, masculinity, and body shape. Among these groups is the "bear" group, which is composed of usually large, hairy, and masculine-looking gay men (Gough & Flanders, 2009; Moskowitz, Turrubiates, Lozano, & Hajek, 2013). However, not every gay man belongs to a specific group, and a large number of gay men do not view themselves as belonging to any group. Studies that have investigated eating disorders among the gay population have frequently selected a subgroup of gay men who are single and young. For example, a study by Meyer, Blissett, and Oldfield (2001) showed that the relation between homosexuality in men and women and dieting behavior (or subclinical restrictive eating) is linked to levels of femininity and not to sexual orientation. Meyer et al. hypothesized that femininity might be viewed as a specific risk factor for the restrictive type of eating disorders, whereas masculinity is likely to be a protective factor. However, this study focuses on only restrictive eating and not on current diagnosis of eating disorder. When other potential confounding variables (namely self-esteem) were considered, both high femininity and high masculinity were found to be associated with eating problems (Heep, Spindler, & Milos, 2005). Accordingly, more recent studies (Griffiths, Murray & Touyz, 2015) have identified that masculinity can also be a risk factor for specific eating disorders, which are linked to muscularity (Murray, Rieger, Karlov, & Touyz, 2013).

PREVALENCE OF EATING DISORDERS AND DISORDERED EATING IN THE LGBTQ POPULATION

Prevalence Rates in Transgender People

Epidemiological studies in the field of eating disorders have identified different prevalence rates in females compared to males. Although it has been traditionally assumed that 1 in 10 eating disorder cases are men (Fernández-Aranda & Jiménez-Murcia, 2014; Hoek & Van Hoeken, 2003), recent community samples report a ratio of 4:1 (Hudson, Hiripi, Pope, & Kessler, 2007; Mitchison, Hay, Slewa-Younan, & Mond, 2014). These results are based on the binary assumption of gender (male and female) as per assigned gender at birth.

If gender is not considered binary but, rather, is regarded as part of a spectrum (as sexuality is), providing prevalence rates of eating disorders according to gender becomes more complicated. The very few studies describing eating disorders among transgender people are case reports (Fernández-Aranda et al., 2000; Hepp & Milos, 2002; Hepp, Milos, & Braun-Scharm, 2004; Winston, Acharya, Chaudhuri, & Fellowes, 2004); therefore, conclusions about prevalence rates of eating disorders among this population are not possible.

The studies that have aimed to investigate prevalence rates of eating disorders in transgender people have focused on eating disorder psychopathology rather than clinically diagnosed eating disorders. In addition, these studies rarely include a control group. They also exclusively involve transgender people who are in contact with transgender health services, which limits the generalizability to the larger transgender population. Three studies have explored the relationship between eating disorder psychopathology and transgender people. More than 25 years ago, Silverstein, Carpman, Perlick, and Perdue (1990) distributed questionnaires to 188 women at a US university with the aim to explore the presence of a conflict in their gender identity. The study found that women who reported gender identity conflict were more likely to also report purging or frequent binging in comparison to women not reporting a conflicted gender identity. It is important to note that this study did not describe people who identified as transgender, so it is difficult to generalize the results to the overall transgender population. Despite this, the results are of interest because they suggest a relationship between unhappiness with one's gender identity and binging/purging.

A relatively recent UK study further investigated degrees of eating disorder psychopathology in transgender people (Khoosal, Langham, Palmer, Terry, & Minajagi, 2009). The authors explored how eating disorder psychopathology changed during the course of gender-confirming medical treatment in a sample of 112 transgender women accessing a transgender health service. The study found that transgender women on cross-sex hormone treatment reported lower levels of eating disorder psychopathology and body image dissatisfaction in comparison to transgender people not on treatment. The study was limited by the lack of control for known risk factors for eating disorder psychopathology, such as age or personality factors. In an attempt to address some of the limitations of the aforementioned study, Witcomb et al. (2015) compared a large group of transgender people ($n = 200$) to a large group of people with a diagnosis of eating disorders ($n = 200$) and cisgender people ($n = 200$). The three groups were all matched by age and gender. The authors found that both transgender males and transgender females showed similar scores for drive for thinness, which were comparable to those of cisgender females and higher than those of cisgender males. The authors suggested that a female identity, by birth or by experienced gender, may be a risk factor for the development of eating disorders. The authors hypothesized that transgender females and males may internalize the same ideals that natal females do with regard to the ideal female body (Witcomb, Arcelus, & Chen, 2013). The strength of this study was that it included a large group of transgender people and compared this transgender sample with a matched control group. However, a limitation of the study is that the sample consists of only treatment-seeking transgender individuals, and the results do not necessarily translate to all transgender people.

The lack of studies focusing on an adequate number of transgender people makes it difficult to reach firm conclusions as to whether or not being transgender increases the risk of developing an eating disorder. Hence, clinical experience may also be taken into account. Two authors of this chapter (JA and WPB) work at a national service for transgender health care in the United Kingdom. This is one of the larger centers of its kind in Europe, with more than 1,000 new referrals per year. The clinical experience of the authors is that very few people who, at the time of assessment, present with a clinically diagnosable eating disorder. However, eating problems and eating disorder psychopathology may be underreported to clinical professionals by the transgender community. Some transgender people waiting to be assessed at a transgender health service may worry about reporting their eating disorder symptoms out of fear of not being accepted for gender-confirming medical treatment (Bouman & Arcelus, 2016). The term *transnorexia* has been adopted by certain transgender women (at least in the UK) to describe episodes of food restriction (Bouman & Arcelus, 2016). This is an underresearched area, and it appears to describe subthreshold levels of eating disorders. This particular group may be most at risk for developing severe psychopathology and, potentially, clinically significant eating disorders, suggesting the need for future studies targeting this group (Jones, Haycraft, Murjan, & Arcelus, 2016). As the number of transgender people in society increases, the number of people with a transgender identity who may present with an eating disorder may also increase.

Prevalence Rates in LGB People

Epidemiological studies have shown that there is a disproportionate number of gay men among the group of men with eating disorders. For example, Strong, Williamson, Netemeyer, and Geer (2000) found that eating disorder symptoms were 10 times more frequent among gay and bisexual men than among heterosexual men (10% and 1%, respectively). Among lesbian women, the data are less unequivocal. Whereas some studies found that lesbian and bisexual women had fewer symptoms of eating disorders compared to heterosexual women (Lakkis, Ricciardelli, & Williams, 1999; Strong et al., 2000), others found no differences (Feldman & Meyer, 2007). Some studies have reported female homosexuality to be a protective factor (Schneider, O'Leary, & Jenkins, 1995), whereas others have reported sexual orientation to be a risk factor (Heffernan, 1996). One explanation for these conflicting findings is the lack of any attempt to distinguish between the different groups of homosexual women, thus grouping them all into one category.

TREATMENT OF EATING DISORDERS IN THE LGBTQ POPULATION

In view of the higher prevalence of eating disorders among the LGBTQ population, particularly gay men, attempts have been made to develop preventative interventions. One study showed positive results when using a dissonance-based eating disorders program to prevent eating disorder psychopathology among the gay population (Brown & Keel, 2015). After randomizing 87 gay males to either a cognitive dissonance-based intervention (two sessions) or wait-list control condition, the authors found improvement in body dissatisfaction after 4 weeks of follow-up. Regarding treatment for eating disorders in the LGBTQ population, no studies have been published. Although there have been modifications of treatments for eating disorders, such as cognitive–behavioral therapy (CBT) and interpersonal psychotherapy (IPT), for males, they have not been specifically adapted for the LGBTQ people (Greenberg & Schoen, 2008). In addition, although some of the characteristics and themes inherent to being grouped as an LGBTQ population may be specific and particular to this group only, there is no clinical indication that the development of different types of treatment for the LGBTQ population with eating disorders is required. Treatments such as CBT and IPT have been found to be as useful, or not, for an LGBTQ person with an eating disorder as for anyone else (Fernández-Aranda et al., 2009). Based on our clinical experience, some of the issues that need to be considered when working with the LGBTQ population are described next.

Establishing Rapport

Before addressing the eating disorder, it is important to establish a positive rapport with the patient. This may be even more important with LGBTQ people due to possible experiences of discrimination and abuse. Establishing trust toward the professional may take longer than with other patients, but it is vital for a positive outcome.

It is important to ask how the person wants to be addressed; including the name and the pronoun the person prefers (and do not assume anything). For example, many people who identify as nonbinary prefer the pronoun "they" to be used (Richards et al., 2016). The professional may also want to ask how the person identifies (as male, female, transgender, nonbinary, etc.). Unfortunately, many LGBTQ people have encountered and continue to encounter abuse and discrimination (Clements-Nolle, Marx, & Katz, 2006; Yang, Manning, Van den Berg, & Operario, 2015). This occurs not only in their social and family life and at work but also within the health service (McNeil, Bailey, Ellis, Morton, & Regan, 2012; Whittle, Turner, & Al-Alami, 2007). Consequently, the person may feel anxious and cautious when talking to others, and the person may appear defensive in the first instance. The professional may want to spend some time putting the patient at ease and establishing a rapport.

Legally, it is important to understand that transgender people are protected by law in many countries. Information regarding previous names and identity may be accessible only with the permission of the patient or, in some cases, not at all. Such information may not be necessary or relevant, but some professionals may require access to previous treatment and historical information from the medical history. It is vital to remember that the transgender person needs to give consent. If inpatient treatment is offered, professionals also need to be aware of the law regarding the use of certain facilities, such as toilets (Eliason, Dibble, & Robertson, 2011). Transgender people must be able to use the toilet and changing room and, in case of single sex wards, be placed according to their expressed gender identity.

Once rapport has been established, a treatment plan can be developed. Some of the aims of treatment, particularly when targeting maintaining factors of the eating disorder, are described next and summarized in Table 19.1.

Table 19.1 SUMMARY OF THE AIMS OF THERAPY WHEN WORKING WITH THE LGBTQ
POPULATION WITH EATING DISORDERS

Aim	Treatment
Understanding the role of the eating disorder	If stopping the development of their adult body is the goal, consider a referral to transgender health services.Addressing self-acceptance, fears of coming out, fears of non-acceptance by others, or having to be part of the LGBTQ community
Addressing body dissatisfaction	Adapting body image treatments for this specific population aiming at challenging ideal bodiesWorking with expectations regarding gender-confirming medical treatment
	Challenging thoughts regarding ideal male and female bodies
Targeting concurrent mental health problems and low self-esteem	Assessing the need for concurrent treatment for mental health problems, such as antidepressantsUsing interventions to address self-esteem and its roots, keeping the minority stress theory in mind
Increasing support	Working with families or the coupleProviding space for psychoeducation and negotiation
	Discussing grief, guilt, or fears about the future
Reducing interpersonal problems and increasing interpersonal skills	Use of interpersonal psychotherapy (IPT) to address eating disorders and concurrent mental health problems by targeting interpersonal skills and relationships. IPT will examine the gains and losses of the new role using "role transition" as the main focus of treatment.

Understanding the Role of the Eating Disorder

Understanding the role of the eating disorder in the life of the LGBTQ person may be the first aim of the assessment, in preparation for treatment. Ålgars, Alanko, Santtila, and Sandnabba (2012) found that the majority of transgender individuals reported current or past disordered eating in an attempt to suppress features of their biological gender or to accentuate features of their gender identity. This makes sense theoretically; however, only the small qualitative study by Ålgars et al. has reported these findings.

For many LGBTQ people, the eating disorder may function to block painful and distressing feelings about their gender or their sexuality, including the "coming out" process (Bekker & Boselie, 2002; Lampard, Byrne, McLean, & Fursland,

2011). In these cases, therapy may allow LGBTQ people to disentangle their feelings from their eating. This may take a significant amount of time. Self-acceptance and addressing internalized trans- and/or homophobia will be required first, and therapy could offer a space for this (Bockting & Coleman, 2016). The LGBTQ person may also discuss fears of not being accepted by others, worries about establishing relationships in the future, and the pressures of having to fit into specific communities, among other themes. For example, previous qualitative studies have described the worries that some gay men have about peer group influences and how these can affect their body image (Fernández-Aranda & Jiménez-Murcia, 2014; Morgan & Arcelus, 2009). They express concerns that gay bars and clubs are unhealthy environments due to the huge level of competition between men. Morgan and Arcelus discuss how young gay men may be extremely susceptible when coming out, due to media and peer group influences, as they seek to identify with role models and a new range of social norms.

Addressing Body Dissatisfaction

A commonly cited explanation for the increase in eating disorder psychopathology, such as a drive for thinness, among the LGBTQ population (male and female) may be linked to their body dissatisfaction, which has been widely reported (Cash, Winstead, & Janda, 1986). This is particularly important because the literature suggests that body dissatisfaction plays a key role in the development of eating disorders and disordered eating in the general population (Ålgars et al., 2012; Jones et al., 2016; Silverstein et al., 1990).

Studies investigating body image in transgender people have found higher levels of body dissatisfaction among this population compared to cisgender people (Ålgars, Santtila, & Sandnabba, 2010; Vocks, Stahn, Loenser, & Legenbauer, 2009). However, many of these studies have measured levels of body dissatisfaction using tools not specifically designed for the transgender population, which may limit their results. It is not surprising that people who believe that their body does not match their gender identity will be dissatisfied with any part of their body that reminds them of the gender assigned at birth. This will include not only their primary and secondary sexual characteristics but also their height, legs, hands, neck, hips, or shoulders, among other parts (Becker et al., 2016; Fernández-Aranda et al., 2000). Several studies have investigated body image in the transgender population. For example, Fisher et al. (2013) found that transgender females dislike more body parts than do transgender males. These findings are consistent with clinical findings suggesting that a past history of disordered eating is more common among transgender females than males.

The stage of transition of a transgender person, which may include being on cross-sex hormones and having undergone gender-confirming surgery, may also affect the level of body dissatisfaction among this population. Two studies found that body dysphoria and dissatisfaction decrease only after cross-hormone treatment has been commenced (de Vries, Steensma, Doreleijers, &

Cohen-Kettenis, 2011). This was also confirmed in a study by Bandini and colleagues (2013), which found that transgender individuals without gender-confirming surgery had levels of body dissatisfaction (measured as body uneasiness) higher than those of controls and comparable to those of individuals with eating disorders. However, after gender-confirming surgery, transgender people reported lower levels of body dissatisfaction compared to those without surgery, but not as low as those of cisgender controls (Bandini et al., 2013). This study supports the view that body dissatisfaction in transgender people, although it can be reduced via gender-confirming medical interventions, is still higher than in cisgender people. Exploring the roots of this body dissatisfaction in more depth, Witcomb et al. (2015) found that although the body parts that caused the most dissatisfaction were those associated with gender assigned at birth, they also included those related to body shape, such as stomach, waist, hips, and bottom. Because these aspects of the body can be changed by dietary restriction, the authors suggest that this may put this population at higher risk of developing disordered eating.

Studies of eating disorders/body image and sexual orientation are complicated by rapidly changing cultural pressures on men and women and also the fluidity of definitions of sexual orientation and gender diversity. Male body image objectification seems to be increasing among men in general, and younger straight men are increasingly confronted with the same impossible body image ideals that have challenged women and gay men throughout the years (Cash et al., 1986; Morgan & Arcelus, 2009; Núñez-Navarro et al., 2012). This may also explain the increased rate of body dissatisfaction and eating disorders symptomatology among straight men (Allen, Byrne, Oddy, & Crosby, 2013; Raevuori, Keski-Rahkonen, & Hoek, 2014; Striegel-Moore et al., 2009). Although body dissatisfaction appears to be high among gay men (Cash et al., 1986; Greenberg & Schoen, 2008), research has shown that lesbian and bisexual women have lower levels of body dissatisfaction compared to heterosexual women (Herzog, Newman, Yeh, & Warshaw, 1992).

Addressing body dissatisfaction as a preventative measurement or as part of the eating disorders treatment for the LGBTQ population may require adapting some of the body image treatments currently available (Morgan, Lazarova, Schelhase, & Saeidi, 2014).

Targeting Concurrent Mental Health Problems and Low Self-Esteem

The prevalence of Axis I mental health problems, such as depression and anxiety, among LGBTQ people has been found to be higher than in the general heterosexual, cisgender population, even when risk factors such as age and gender are taken into account (Dhejne, Van Vlerken, Heylens, & Arcelus, 2016). This is not surprising because non-acceptance and stigmatization by others can force people into isolation, affecting their self-esteem and confidence (Núñez-Navarro et al., 2012). As a consequence, depressive and anxiety symptoms may develop. Depression has also been found to be comorbid with and predicts the development of certain eating disorders, such as bulimia nervosa (Fernández-Aranda et al., 2007). In addition, depression may act as a maintaining factor for an eating disorder. If that is the case, the treatment of the eating disorder may also require the management of concurrent mental health disorders. The minority stress model described by Meyer (1995) explains that the stress which particular minority groups can experience is due to the relationship between minority and dominant values that results in conflicts with their social environment. This model suggests that stress in specific minority groups, which include LGBTQ people, can be explained predominantly by stressors induced by a hostile, trans- or homophobic culture, which often results in a lifetime of harassment, abuse, victimization, and discrimination. Although difficult, addressing and increasing self-esteem should be part of any intervention aimed at reducing eating disorder symptoms.

Increasing Support and Understanding

Studies examining levels of social support among the LGBTQ population have found lower levels of reported social support among this group, particularly among transgender women, compared to controls (Davey, Bouman, Arcelus, & Meyer, 2014). Lack of social support has also been found to predict mental health problems among this population (Brown & Keel, 2013). Within gay culture, studies investigating eating disorders in this group found that being married or in a relationship protects the person from developing an eating disorder (Brown & Keel, 2013), as is the case in the straight population. Social support, particularly among gay men, can be a double-edged sword. On the one hand, having a close and supportive group of gay friends will increase support and self-esteem; on the other hand, social life may be limited mainly to gay bars and clubs, which may portray an unhealthy image of what it is like to be gay (Morgan & Arcelus, 2009).

Because lack of social support may be a risk factor for the development of eating disorders (Sharpe, Schober, Treasure, & Schmidt, 2014), it can be an important focus for treatment. Family and/or couples therapy can be useful interventions to increase social support for the LGBTQ person with eating disorders. Themes that may need to be addressed when working with this population and their families include feelings of grief (e.g., the loss of the son or daughter who is transitioning to a different gender), fears about the future (e.g., about abuse and discrimination), worries about making a mistake (e.g., "What if this is only a phase?"), guilt (e.g., false beliefs about the etiology of LGBTQ and different modes of parenting), and how to disclose to the rest of the family (including children). Therapy sessions can be a useful source for psychoeducation and negotiations about the future. Improving social and family support may provide a sense of acceptance and improve the person's mental health, including the person's eating disorder. As suggested in previous studies, CBT group therapy (in small groups) might offer an effective therapy option for addressing some of these topics (Fernández-Aranda & Jiménez-Murcia, 2014).

Reducing Interpersonal Problems

The term *interpersonal* relates not only to the interaction between the individual and significant others but also to the process by which these interactions are internalized and form part of the self-image (Sullivan, 1968). Good interpersonal skills are considered crucial to good mental health and aid the development of meaningful relationships (Klinger, 1977). Being involved in secure and fulfilling relationships is perceived by most individuals as critical to well-being and happiness (Berscheid & Peplau, 1983). It is therefore not surprising that interpersonal difficulties are strongly associated with many mental health problems, including eating disorders (Arcelus, Haslam, Farrow, & Meyer, 2013).

Regarding transgender people, a recent study found more interpersonal problems in this population than in a matched cisgender control group (Davey, Bouman, Meyer, & Arcelus, 2015). The authors found that among the transgender group studies, there were greater difficulties with being sociable and assertive. These findings suggest that trusting people may be more difficult for some transgender people, which may be a reflection of years of victimization and nonacceptance by society (Clements-Nolle et al., 2006; Yang et al., 2015). The role of interpersonal difficulties and their association with mental health problems in young transgender people has also been highlighted in a recent study (Arcelus, Claes, Witcomb, Marshall, & Bouman, 2016). This study identified interpersonal problems as the main predictors of mental health problems among the population studied. Lack of interpersonal skills throughout the transitional process may make the individual more vulnerable to the development of mental health problems, such as depression and eating disorders (Arcelus et al., 2013).

Interpersonal psychotherapy is regarded as a useful treatment for eating disorders (Arcelus, Whight, & Haslam, 2011; Klerman, Weissman, Rounsaville, & Chevron, 1984), and it may be an appropriate treatment to consider when working with a member of the LGBTQ population with an eating disorder. This is not only due to the interpersonal problems found in the transgender population (Davey et al., 2015) but also because IPT has been found to reduce eating disorder symptoms and depression while at the same time focusing on the transitioning process. One of the problem areas that can be addressed in IPT is "transitional role" (transitioning from one gender to another or from a straight life to a gay one). Therapists can help patients assess their life before and after transitioning and how their interpersonal life has change for good or bad (Whight et al., 2011). The focus of IPT could be to explore transition and acknowledge the losses and gains from the transitional process.

CONCLUSION

Studies have demonstrated an overall increase in eating disorder psychopathology among the LGBTQ population. Regarding transgender people, possibly due to the low reported prevalence rate of transgender people in society, very few studies have reached a clear conclusion as to whether being transgender increases the risk of developing an eating disorder. Studies investigating eating disorders among the LGB population have reached more firm conclusions, with more eating disorders among gay men compared to straight men but not compared to lesbian women. Femininity has been hypothesized as a possible risk factor for the development of eating disorders, more so than sexual orientation, with masculinity as a protective factor; however, this requires further study. The rapid increase in the number of transgender people attending transgender health services may affect the number of these people who develop an eating disorder and attend eating disorder services for treatment. For transgender people, pressure to conform to a gender, which is incongruous with their body, could precipitate body dissatisfaction for both genders and an eating disorder as a consequence. For gay men, trying to conform to specific roles, and the effect of the media, may also affect body dissatisfaction. In addition, concurrent mental health problems, such as depression, low self-esteem, and interpersonal difficulties, in the LGBTQ population may make these individuals more vulnerable to developing eating disorders. As part of an evidence-based treatment for their eating disorders, the following could be helpful: addressing the maintaining factors of the eating disorder through therapy; considering specific themes for this population, such as coming out, fears of rejection, and personal and society acceptance; and improving interpersonal skills.

REFERENCES

Aitken, M., Steensma, T. D., Blanchard, R., VanderLaan, D. P., Wood, H., Fuentes, A., . . . Zucker, K. J. (2015). Evidence for an altered sex ratio in clinic-referred adolescents with gender dysphoria. *Journal of Sexual Medicine, 12,* 756–763.

Ålgars, M., Alanko, K., Santtila, P., & Sandnabba, N. K. (2012). Disordered eating and gender identity disorder: A qualitative study. *Eating Disorders, 20*(4), 300–311.

Ålgars, M., Santtila, P., & Sandnabba, N. K. (2010). Conflicted gender identity, body dissatisfaction, and disordered eating in adult men and women. *Sex Roles, 63,* 118–125.

Allen, K. L., Byrne, S. M., Oddy, W. H., & Crosby, R. D. (2013). DSM-IV-TR and DSM-5 eating disorders in adolescents: Prevalence, stability, and psychosocial correlates in a population-based sample of male and female adolescents. *Journal of Abnormal Psychology, 122,* 720–732.

Arcelus, J., Bouman, W. P., Van De Noortgate, W., Claes, L., Witcomb, G. L., & Fernández-Aranda, F. (2015). Systematic review and meta-analysis of prevalence studies in transsexualism. *European Psychiatry, 30*(6), 807–815.

Arcelus, J., Claes, L., Witcomb, G. L., Marshall, E., & Bouman, W. P. (2016). Risk factors for nonsuicidal self injury among trans youth. *Journal of Sexual Medicine, 13*(3), 402–412.

Arcelus, J., Haslam, M., Farrow, C., & Meyer, C. (2013). The role of interpersonal functioning in the maintenance of eating psychopathology: A systematic review and testable model. *Clinical Psychology Review, 33,* 156–167.

Arcelus, J., Whight, D., & Haslam, M. (2011). Interpersonal problems in people with bulimia nervosa and the role of interpersonal psychotherapy. In P. Hay (Ed.), *New insights into the prevention and treatment of bulimia nervosa* (pp. 3–12). Rijeka, Croatia: InTech.

Bandini, E., Fisher, A. D., Castellini, G., Lo Sauro, C., Lelli, L., Meriggiola, M. C., . . . Ricca, V. (2013). Gender identity disorder and eating disorders: Similarities and differences in terms of body uneasiness. *Journal of Sexual Medicine, 10*, 1012–1023.

Becker, I., Nieder, T. O., Cerwenka, S., Briken, P., Kreukels, B. P. C., Cohen-Kettenis, P. T., . . . Richter-Appelt, H. (2016). Body image in young gender dysphoric adults: A European multi-center study. *Archives of Sexual Behavior, 45*(3), 559–574.

Beek, T., Kreukels, B. P. C., & Cohen-Kettenis, P. T. (2015). Partial gender request and underlying motives of applicants for gender affirming interventions. *Journal of Sexual Medicine, 12*, 2201–2205.

Bekker, M. H. J., & Boselie, K. A. H. M. (2002). Gender and stress: Is gender role stress? A re-examination of the relationship between feminine gender role stress and eating disorders. *Stress and Health, 18*(3), 141–149.

Berscheid, E., & Peplau, L. A. (1983). The emerging science of relationships. In H. H. Kelley, E. Berscheid, A. Christensen, J. H. Harvey, T. L. Huston, G. Levinger, . . . D. R. Peterson (Eds.), *Close relationships* (pp. 1–19). New York, NY: Freeman.

Bockting, W., & Coleman, E. (2016). Developmental stages of the transgender coming out process: Toward an integrated identity. In R. Ettner, S, Monstrey, & E. Coleman (Eds.), *Principles of transgender medicine and surgery* (pp. 185–209). New York, NY: Routledge.

Bockting, W., Coleman, E., & De Cuypere, G. (2011). Care of transsexual persons. *New England Journal of Medicine, 364*, 2259–2560.

Bouman, W. P., & Arcelus, J. (2016). Body dissatisfaction and maladaptive eating behaviors among people with gender dysphoria. *National Eating Disorder Information Centre Bulletin, 31*, 1–4.

Brown, T. A., & Keel, P. A. (2013). The impact of relationships, friendships, and work on the association between sexual orientation and disordered eating in men. *Eating Disorders, 21*(4), 342–359.

Brown, T. A., & Keel, P. A. (2015). A randomised controlled trial of a peer co-led dissonance-based eating disorders prevention program for gay men. *Behavioural Research Therapy, 74*, 1–10.

Canaday, M. (2014). LGBT history. *Frontiers, 35*(1), 11–19.

Cash, T. F., Winstead, B. W., & Janda, L. H. (1986). The great American shape-up: Body image survey report. *Psychology Today, 20*(4), 30–37.

Clements-Nolle, K., Marx, R., & Katz, M. (2006). Attempted suicide among transgender persons: The influence of gender-based discrimination and victimization. *Journal of Homosexuality, 51*(3), 53–69.

Coleman, E., Bockting, W., Botzer, M., Cohen-Kettenis, P., DeCuypere, G., Feldman, J., . . . Zucker, K. (2012). Standards of care for the health of transsexual, transgender, and gender-nonconforming people, version 7. *International Journal of Transgenderism, 13*, 165–232.

Davey, A., Bouman, W. P., Arcelus, J., & Meyer, C. (2014). Social support and psychological well-being in gender dysphoria: A comparison of patients with gender dysphoria and matched controls. *Journal of Sexual Medicine, 11*(12), 2976–2985.

Davey, A., Bouman. W. P., Meyer, C., & Arcelus, J. (2015). Interpersonal functioning among individuals with gender dysphoria. *Journal of Clinical Psychology, 71*(12), 1173–1185 de Vries, A. L. C., Kreukels, B. P. C., T'Sjoen, G., Ålgars, M., & Mattila, A. (2015). Increase of referrals to gender identity clinics: A European trend? In *Transgender healthcare in Europe*. Ghent, Belgium: European Professional Association of Transgender Health.

de Vries, A. L. C., Steensma, T. D., Doreleijers, T. H., & Cohen-Kettenis, P. T. (2011). Puberty suppression in adolescents with gender identity disorder: A prospective follow-up study. *Journal of Sexual Medicine, 8*, 2276–2283.

Dhejne, C., Van Vlerken, R., Heylens, G., & Arcelus, J. (2016). Mental health and gender dysphoria: A review of the literature. *International Review of Psychiatry, 28*(1), 44–57.

Eliason, M. J., Dibble, S. L., & Robertson, P. A. (2011). Lesbian, gay, bisexual, and transgender (LGBT) physicians' experiences in the workplace. *Journal of Homosexuality, 58*(10), 1355–1371.

Feldman, M. B., & Meyer, I. H. (2007). Eating disorders in diverse lesbian, gay and bisexual populations. *International Journal of Eating Disorders, 40*(3), 218–226.

Fernández-Aranda, F., & Jiménez-Murcia, S. (2014). Evidence-guided treatment for males with eating disorders. In I. Dancyger & V. Fornari (Eds.), *Evidence based treatments for eating disorders: Children, adolescents and adults* (2nd ed., pp. 203–218). New York, NY: Nova.

Fernández-Aranda, F., Krug, I., Solano, R., Núñez, A., Jiménez-Murcia, S., . . . Treasure, J. (2009). Male eating disorders and therapy: A pilot study. *Behaviour Therapy and Experimental Psychiatry, 40*, 479–486.

Fernández-Aranda, F., Peri, J. M., Badía-Casanovas, A., Navarro, V., Turón-Gil, V., & Vallejo- Ruiloba, J. (2000). Transsexualism in anorexia nervosa: A case report. *Eating Disorders: Treatment and Prevention, 8*, 63–66.

Fernández-Aranda, F., Poyastro Pinheiro, A., Tozzi, F., Thornton, L. M., Fichter, M. M., . . . Bulik, C. M. (2007). Symptom profile of major depressive disorder in females with eating disorders. *Australian and New Zealand Journal of Psychiatry, 41*, 24–31.

Fisher, A. D., Castellini, G., Bandini, E., Casale, H., Fanni, E., Ferruccio, N., . . . Rellini, A. H. (2013). Cross-sex hormonal treatment and body uneasiness in individuals with gender dysphoria. *Journal of Sexual Medicine, 11*(3), 709–719.

Gough, B., & Flanders, G. (2009). Celebrating "obese" bodies: Gay "bears" talk about weight, body image and health. *International Journal of Men's Health, 8*(3), 235–253.

Greenberg, S. T., & Schoen, E. G. (2008). Males and eating disorders: Gender-based therapy for eating disorder recovery. *Professional Psychology: Research and Practice, 39*(4), 464–471.

Griffiths, S., Murray, S. B., & Touyz, S. (2015). Extending the masculinity hypothesis: An investigation of gender role conformity, body dissatisfaction, and disordered eating in young heterosexual men. *Psychology of Men & Masculinity, 16*(1), 108–114.

Heffernan, K. (1996). Eating disorders and weight concern among lesbians. *International Journal of Eating Disorders, 19*, 127–138.

Hepp, U., & Milos, G. (2002). Gender identity disorder and eating disorders. *International Journal of Eating Disorders, 32*(4), 473–478.

Hepp, U., Milos, G., & Braun-Scharm, H. (2004). Gender identity disorder and anorexia nervosa in male monozygotic twins. *International Journal of Eating Disorders Review, 35*(2), 239–243.

Hepp, U., Spindler, A., & Milos, G. (2005). Eating Disorder Symptomatology and Gender Role Orientation. *International Journal of Eating Disorders, 37*(3), 227–233.

Herzog, D. B., Newman, K. L., Yeh, C. J., & Warshaw, M. (1992). Body image satisfaction in homosexual and heterosexual women. *International Journal of Eating Disorders, 11*, 391–396.

Hoek, H. W., & Van Hoeken, D. (2003). Review of the prevalence and incidence of eating disorders. *International Journal of Eating Disorders, 34*(4), 383–396.

Hudson, J. I., Hiripi, E., Pope, H. G., & Kessler, R. C. (2007). The prevalence and correlates of eating disorders in the National Comorbidity Survey Replication. *Biological Psychiatry, 61*(3), 348–358.

Jones, B., Haycraft, E., Murjan, S., & Arcelus, J. (2016). Body image and disordered eating in the trans population: A systematic review of the literature. *International Review of Psychiatry, 28*(1), 81–94.

Khoosal, D., Langham, C., Palmer, B., Terry, T., & Minajagi, M. (2009). Features of eating disorder among male-to-female transsexuals. *Sexual and Relationship Therapy, 24*, 217–229.

Klerman, G. L., Weissman, M. M., Rounsaville, B., & Chevron, E. (1984). *Interpersonal psychotherapy for depression.* New York, NY: Basic Books.

Klinger, E. (1977). *Meaning and void: Inner experience and the incentives in people's lives.* Minneapolis, MN: University of Minnesota Press.

Knauer, N. J. (2009). LGBT elder law: Toward equity in aging. *Harvard Journal of Law & Gender, 32*(1), 1–73.

Kuyper, L., & Wijsen, C. (2014). Gender identities and gender dysphoria in the Netherlands. *Archives of Sexual Behavior, 43*, 377–385.

Lakkis, J., Ricciardelli, L. A., & Williams, R. J. (1999). Role of sexual orientation and gender-related traits in disordered eating. *Sex Roles, 41*, 1–16.

Lampard, A. M., Byrne, S. M., McLean, N., & Fursland, A. (2011). Avoidance of affect in the eating disorders. *Eating Behaviors, 12*(1), 90–93.

Makadon, H. J. (2011). Ending LGBT invisibility in health care: The first step in ensuring equitable care. *Cleveland Clinic Journal of Medicine, 78*(4), 220–224.

McNeil, J., Bailey, L., Ellis, S., Morton, J., & Regan, M. (2012). *Trans mental health and emotional well-being study.* Edinburgh, Scotland: Scottish Transgender Alliance.

Meyer, C., Blissett, J., & Oldfield, C. (2001). Sexual orientation and eating psychopathology: The role of masculinity and femininity. *International Journal of Eating Disorders, 29*(3), 314–318.

Meyer, I. H. (1995). Minority stress and mental health in gay men. *Journal of Health and Social Behavior, 36*, 38–56.

Mitchison, D., Hay, P., Slewa-Younan, S., & Mond, J. (2014). The changing demographic profile of eating disorder behaviors in the community. *BMC Public Health, 14*(1), 943.

Morgan, J. F., & Arcelus, J. (2009). Body image in gay and straight men: A qualitative study. *European Eating Disorders Review, 17*, 435–444.

Morgan, J. F., Lazarova, S., Schelhase, M., & Saeidi, S. (2014). Ten sessions body image therapy: Efficacy of a manualised body image therapy. *European Eating Disorders Review, 22*(1), 66–71.

Moskowitz, D. A., Turrubiates, J., Lozano, H., & Hajek, C. (2013). Physical, behavioral, and psychological traits of gay men identifying as bears. *Archives of Sexual Behavior, 42*, 775–784.

Murray, S. B., Rieger, E., Karlov, L., & Touyz, S. W. (2013). An investigation of the transdiagnostic model of eating disorders in the context of muscle dysmorphia. *European Eating Disorders Review, 21*(2), 160–164.

Núñez-Navarro, A., Agüera-Imbernón, Z. P., Krug, I., Araguz, N., Saldaña, S., Gorwood, P., . . . Fernández-Aranda, F. (2012). Do men with eating disorders differ from women in clinics, psychopathology and personality? *European Eating Disorders Review*, *20*(1), 23–31.

Raevuori, A., Keski-Rahkonen, A., & Hoek, H. W. (2014). A review of eating disorders in males. *Current Opinion in Psychiatry*, *27*, 426–430.

Richards, C., & Barker, M. (2013). *Sexuality and gender for mental health professionals: A practical guide*. London, England: Sage.

Richards, C., Bouman, W. P., & Barker, M. (Eds.). (2017). *Genderqueer and non-binary gender*. London, England: Palgrave Macmillan.

Richards, C., Bouman, W. P., Seal, L., Barker, M. J., Nieder, T. O., & T'Sjoen, G. (2016). Non-binary or genderqueer genders. *International Review of Psychiatry*, *28*, 95–102.

Schneider, J. A., O'Leary, A., & Jenkins, S. R. (1995). Gender, sexual orientation, and disordered eating. *Psychological Health*, *10*, 113–128.

Sharpe, H., Schober, I., Treasure, J., & Schmidt, U. (2014). The role of high-quality friendships in female adolescents' eating pathology and body dissatisfaction. *Eating and Weight Disorders*, *19*(2), 159–168.

Silverstein, B., Carpman, S., Perlick, D., & Perdue, L. (1990). Nontraditional sex role aspirations, gender identity conflict, and disordered eating among college women. *Sex Roles*, *23*(11-12), 687–695.

Striegel-Moore, R. H., Rosselli, F., Perrin, N., DeBar, L., Wilson, G. T., May, A., & Kraemer, H. C. (2009). Gender difference in the prevalence of eating disorder symptoms. *International Journal of Eating Disorders*, *42*, 471–474.

Strong, S. M., Williamson, D. A., Netemeyer, R. G., & Geer, J. H. (2000). Eating disorder symptoms and concerns about body differ as a function of gender and sexual orientation. *Journal of Social & Clinical Psychology*, *19*, 240–255.

Sullivan, H. (1968). *The interpersonal theory of psychiatry*. New York, NY: Norton.

Van Caenegem, E., Wierckx, K., Elaut, E., Buysse, A., Dewaele, A., Van Nieuwerburgh, F., . . . T'Soe, G. (2015). Prevalence of gender nonconformity in Flanders, Belgium. *Archives of Sexual Behavior*, *15*, 1281–1287.

Vocks, S., Stahn, C., Loenser, K., & Legenbauer, T. (2009). Eating and body image disturbances in male-to-female and female-to-male transsexuals. *Archives of Sexual Behavior*, *38*, 364–377.

Whight, D., McGrain, L., Baggott, J., Meadows, L., Langham, C., & Arcelus, J. (2011). *Interpersonal psychotherapy for bulimia nervosa* (IPT BNm). London, England: Troubador.

Whittle, S., Turner, L., & Al-Alami, M. (2007). *Engendered penalties: Transgender and transsexual people's experiences of inequality and discrimination*. Wetherby, England: Communities and Local Government Publications.

Winston, A. P., Acharya, S., Chaudhuri, S., & Fellowes, L. (2004). Anorexia nervosa and gender identity disorder in biologic males: A report of two cases. *International Journal of Eating Disorders*, *36*(1), 109–113.

Witcomb, G., Arcelus, J., & Chen, J. (2013). Can cognitive dissonance methods developed in the West for combatting the "thin ideal" help slow the rapidly increasing prevalence of eating disorders in non-Western cultures? *Shanghai Archives of Psychiatry*, *25*(6), 332–341.

Witcomb, G. L., Bouman, W. P., Brewin, N., Richards, C., Fernández-Aranda, F., & Arcelus, J. (2015). Body image dissatisfaction and eating-related psychopathology in trans individuals: A matched control study. *European Eating Disorders Review, 23*(4), 287–293.

Wylie, K. R., Barrett, J., Besser, M., Bouman, W. P., Bridgeman, M., Clayton, A., ... Ward, D. (2014). Good practice guidelines for the assessment and treatment of adults with gender dysphoria. *Sexual and Relationship Therapy, 29*, 154–214.

Yang, M.-F., Manning, D., Van den Berg, J. J., & Operario, D. (2015). Stigmatization and mental health in a diverse sample of transgender women. *LGBT Health, 2*(4), 26–29.

20

Considerations in the Treatment of Eating Disorders Among Ethnic Minorities

ANA L. RAMIREZ, EVA TRUJILLO-CHIVACUÁN, AND MARISOL PEREZ ■

INTRODUCTION

Eating disorders (EDs) and eating pathology are well-recognized entities known to affect all racial and ethnic groups. However, evidence-based treatments (EBTs) for EDs have been developed and tested in largely Caucasian populations (Reyes-Rodríguez & Bulik, 2010). As a result, regarding the treatment of ethnic minority individuals suffering from EDs, clinicians face a conundrum: How to provide culturally sensitive treatments while adhering to evidence-based protocols.

In addition, cross-cultural research on EDs is still in its infancy. Thus, when deciding on a treatment for an ethnic minority client, the clinician has three options with regard to research-supported treatments: adopt it, adapt it, or abandon it (Morales & Norcross, 2010). Morales and Norcross discuss the strengths and limitations of each decision to guide a clinician in the process. For example, the clinician should choose to adopt a research-supported treatment when that treatment has been tested on the target problem and found to be effective *and* the clinician feels confident in using the research-supported treatment. The weakness in this approach is that the target problem may be influenced by culturally relevant issues that the treatment is not designed to address. The authors also highlight that clinicians should consider adapting a research-supported treatment when they believe that the treatment has utility but is not entirely adequate for the particular patient, problem, or context. Adaptations can entail modifying or supplementing the treatment due to the patient's particular problems, culture, or context (Morales & Norcross, 2010). These adaptations assume the clinician is competent in the cultural/linguistic characteristics of the client and has experience integrating all these variables in a culturally competent manner (Morales & Norcross, 2010). The weakness in this approach is that it is unknown what impact the changes will have on efficacy, with the potential of losing/reducing the essential elements of the treatment as it was intended. Clinicians should consider abandoning a research-supported treatment when the treatment fails to yield similar results or when the clinician believes the treatment will not generalize to the patient or the cultural context. Thus, the decision-making process of adopting, adapting, or abandoning falls on the clinician's shoulders, and unfortunately there is limited research on the outcome of these approaches.

To relieve some of the burden that clinicians face when deciding to use or adapt an EBT and to assist them in engaging in culturally sensitive evidence-based practice, this chapter provides an overview of the treatment literature across three major ethnic minority groups. The clinical presentation and prevalence rates of EDs for Latinos/Hispanics, Blacks/African Americans, and Asian Americans are first discussed. A discussion of the research on evidence-supported treatments for each ethnic group follows, highlighting if and how the treatments have been culturally adapted.

Important Considerations When Reading This Chapter

There are several important points to keep in mind when reading this chapter. The first is that race and ethnicity are socially constructed variables. Often, race and ethnicity are treated as static and stable traits both in research and in people's social lives, when in fact they are constantly evolving at a group and individual level (Perez & Plasencia, 2016). For example, there are individuals who immigrate to the United States who, upon entering the country, become "Black" by the country's definition, even though these individuals were not previously labeled as such and do not identify culturally with American Black culture. The same applies to the overgeneralization of "Asian" or "Asian American" terms and "Hispanic" or "Latino" because these tend to group together a diverse group of individuals from vastly different nations and cultural backgrounds. It is also important to consider that the number of individuals residing within the United States who describe their race as "mixed" is increasing significantly (Perez & Plasencia, 2016; US Census, 2012). Even among those who do identify with one particular race or culture, it is important to also consider that the degree of ethnic self-identification can fluctuate across time and context within individuals (Kiang & Fuligni, 2009; Saylor & Aries, 1999). Finally, there is vast heterogeneity across each racial and ethnic group and the degree to which culturally relevant variables influence eating disorder behaviors, symptoms, and subjective distress (Franko, Becker, Thomas, & Herzog, 2007; Perez & Plasencia, 2016). This is problematic because these factors can make ED criteria inadequate for ethnic minorities to begin with, given that a different presentation of the disorder may not fit the criteria for diagnosis as is currently accepted amongst ED professionals (Cummins, Simmons, & Zane,

2005; Wonderlich, Joiner, Williamson, & Crosby, 2007). For example, a Latina woman may engage in restrictive behaviors motivated by a desire to achieve a "curvy ideal" rather than a fear of fat/weight gain.

PREVALENCE AND CLINICAL PRESENTATION

Until recently, there had been a major debate in the literature regarding whether the prevalence of EDs in non-Western patients differs in comparison to EDs in patients of Western nations. However, it is now known that EDs are diagnosed in all ethnic and socioeconomic groups and that some ethnic minority groups may be especially vulnerable (Marques et al., 2011). Note that the diagnostic framework and clinical measurements are developed and validated with Caucasian samples and thus may reflect a Caucasian-centric focus. This section reviews the clinical presentation of EDs among Latinos/Hispanics, Black/African Americans, and Asian Americans.

Latinos/Hispanics

One group at particular risk to develop EDs is Latina women (Gordon et al., 2010). Continuous growth in the number of cases of EDs and risky eating behaviors has been observed in the past two decades, thus increasing the interest in this ethnic group among clinicians and researchers in both Latin countries and within the United States. When discussing prevalence rates of EDs among Latinos living in the United States, it is important to consider different factors, such as immigration status and level of acculturation (e.g., modification of habits, language, lifestyle, and values due to the closed contact to a new culture and society), social context, and transculturation (Gómez Peresmitré et al., 2000; Perez, Ohrt, & Hoek, 2016).

A few studies of EDs in Latinos suggest prevalence rates are similar to those of Caucasians in the United States. Lifetime prevalence rates of EDs among Latinos within the United States are 0.08% for anorexia nervosa (AN), 1.61% for bulimia nervosa (BN), 1.92% for binge-eating disorder (BED), and 5.61% for any binge eating behaviors (Alegria et al., 2007). The lifetime prevalence of AN is lower than that of non-Hispanic White samples in the United States, whereas the prevalence rates of BN and BED in Latinos are comparable to those in non-Hispanic White groups in the United States; however, a recent review of epidemiological studies found higher lifetime prevalence rates of BED in Latin America compared to Western countries (Perez, Ohrt, & Hoek, 2016). Among Hispanics/Latinos, BED is the most common ED, with comparable rates across the ethnic groups in the United States (Lydecker & Grilo, 2016; Perez et al., 2016). It is important to consider that most current epidemiological research is still based on studies using criteria from the fourth edition of the *Diagnostic and Statistical Manual of Mental Disorders* (DSM-IV; American Psychiatric Association, 1994). Prevalence rates may increase among Latinos in the coming years because the DSM-5 (American Psychiatric Association, 2013) diagnostic criteria for EDs were changed in an effort to increase cultural sensitivity and allow ED diagnoses to capture these disorders across cultures (Perez et al., 2016).

The clinical presentation of EDs among Latinos has some unique aspects. Studies have identified that the conflicts experienced when women are asked to juggle two cultural worlds—the world of their ethnic culture and the world of the popular mainstream culture—can result in the development of eating pathology through media exposure associated with changing aesthetic ideals (to the mainstream thin-ideal) and body dissatisfaction (Katzman & Lee, 1997). A significant number of Latina women in the United States are at risk for body dissatisfaction, disordered eating behaviors, and EDs (Franko, Jenkins, & Rodgers, 2012). Exposure to Western cultures is not irrefutably associated with eating disturbances nor with body image issues (Soh, Touyz, & Surgenor, 2006). However, in trying to understand the development of EDs among Latinos, it can be helpful for clinicians to think of them as problems of disconnection (using eating as a coping method when living between two cultures), transition (attempting to move between two worlds), and oppression (efforts to adapt to a new popular culture resulting in an attempt to perfect the physical self as a method of coping with prejudices and isolation) rather than exclusively disorders of dieting, weight, and fear of fat (Katzman, 1993). Eating disorders may present differently in patients with a non-Western background due to factors such as differing cultural values, family structure, and body composition (Soh et al., 2006). For example, among mid-adolescent Latinas, there was an overwhelming consensus that a slender but curvy figure was the ideal body in Latino culture and that European Americans valued the unrealistically thin beauty ideal more (Romo, Mireles-Rios, & Hurtado, 2016). Furthermore, eating is considered a family affair and a bonding experience in many Latin cultures; therefore, individuals struggling with EDs may experience additional shame and guilt in regard to their symptoms.

It is clear that food is central in the Latino culture and community. Family ties, cultural identity, and comfort are some of the roles that food plays in the Latino culture (Reyes-Rodríguez et al., 2016; Weller & Turkon, 2015). The eating patterns of Latinos are influenced by cultural norms and the experience of immigration (Reyes-Rodríguez et al., 2016). Food is a primary symbol used to maintain group solidarity and personal identity. By acting as the bridge between immigrants and their homeland, food also functions as a reservoir that immigrants draw on to resist incorporation and to pass their cultural identity on to their children (Ferrero, 2002; Weller & Turkon, 2015). Food is thought of as an act of nostalgia—a physical manifestation of memory that connects immigrants to geographically and chronologically distant family members, experiences, and communities (Weller & Turkon, 2015). Food preparation and consumption are physical and symbolic acts that are often used to communicate individuality or membership within a larger group (Wilk, 1999). Immigration is almost always associated with the incorporation of new food and the loss of traditional ones (Vallianatos & Raine, 2008).

Level of acculturation, immigration status, lack of health insurance, and stigma are other factors that play an important role in the development and presentation of EDs in Latinos (Perez et al., 2016). A study found that many patients preferred to seek support from informal sources because of stigma associated with receiving professional help for these issues (Shea et al., 2012). Latinos also tend to have a lesser understanding of EDs (especially if they are less acculturated or from older generations), making it difficult for sufferers to receive support from family members (Higgins & Bulik, 2015; Shea et al., 2012). Latina women who receive messages from their family to celebrate a curvy figure and eat traditional foods in abundance, but who are also attuned to the popular cultural media messages that thin is desirable, may struggle with issues of eating, weight, and shape concerns in an attempt to both please their family and respond to idealized beauty standards of the mainstream culture (Edwards, George, & Franko, 2010).

Within a social context, several factors have been found to affect the development of EDs in Latinos. In a significant percentage of people with EDs, the exposure to a traumatic event plays an important role in the development of their disorder (Ackard & Brewerton, 2010; Brewerton, 2007; Holman, 2012). Sociopolitical violence and armed conflict have been proposed as potential risk factors for mental illnesses (Londoño, Romero, & Casas, 2012). This is an important consideration for US clinicians who are treating immigrants from countries in which these situations are a common occurrence. For example, Colombia has been in armed conflict for the past 50 years (Wilches, 2009), and the "National Survey on Mental Health 2015" by the Ministry of Health in Colombia reported a statistically significant association between the increase of eating pathology and exposure to traumatic events and history of armed conflict and violence.

In reviewing the previously discussed clinical presentation of EDs among Latinos, it is important to keep in mind that those who self-identify as Latinos are not part of a homogeneous group. Rather, they are individuals who view themselves as possessing multiple social identities as they negotiate life as part of a minority group in the United States (Calderon, 1992; Weller & Turkon, 2015).

Black/African Americans

Epidemiological research has found that African Americans report fewer and often no cases of AN compared to Caucasian samples (Striegel-Moore et al., 2003; Taylor, Caldwell, Baser, Faison, & Jackson, 2007). The lifetime prevalence rate among Black/African American samples was 0.17% for AN and the 12-month prevalence was 0.05%, with illness duration ranging from 1 to 7 years (Taylor et al., 2007). Whereas the average age of onset of AN for Caucasian individuals tends to be approximately age 15.4 years (Striegel-Moore et al., 2003), the average age of onset among African American individuals is younger at age 14 years (Taylor et al., 2007). The findings on BN are mixed, with some studies indicating similar rates to those of Caucasian women (Taylor et al., 2007), some indicating higher rates (Marques et al., 2011), and some indicating lower rates (Striegel-Moore et al., 2003). Lifetime prevalence rates are 1.49% for BN, 1.66% for BED, and 5.08% for any binge eating (Taylor et al., 2007). Age of onset for BN ranges from 14 to 21 years (Taylor et al., 2007). BED is the most common ED reported in this population (Marques et al., 2011; Striegel-Moore et al., 2003; Taylor et al., 2003).

Regarding the clinical presentation of EDs among this population, our knowledge is limited to only 13 published case studies on EDs in Black/African American female adolescents, in which common themes among all cases were overall similar to the common themes among adolescents with AN in general (Maresh & Willard, 1996; Pumariega, Edwards, & Mitchell, 1984). For Black/African American individuals suffering from BN, the literature highlights a few differences. For example, in a study on BN and substance use, history of sexual or physical abuse, and self-harm, Black/African American women had higher rates of sexual abuse but were less likely to report use of at least one substance, substance problems, or self-harm compared to Caucasian women (Dohm et al., 2002). Black/African American individuals with BN have shorter episode durations compared to Caucasian individuals (8.3 years) as well as binge-eating episodes, with the persistence of BN ranging from 1 to 7 years (Hudson, Hiripi, Pope, & Kessler, 2007; Taylor et al., 2007). Among treatment-seeking samples, Black/African American individuals tended to have higher body mass index (BMI) and higher rates of depression compared to Caucasian individuals with BN (Chui, Safer, Bryson, Agras, & Wilson, 2007). In summary, Black/African American individuals suffering from BN present with numerous similarities to Caucasian individuals, including ED psychopathology, severity, and functioning.

Overall, there are more similarities than differences between Black/African American individuals and Caucasian individuals with BED. Similarities include mental, physical, and psychosocial functioning; comorbidity; disordered eating attitudes; frequency of binge-eating episodes; and rates of metabolic syndromes (Elliot, Tanofsky-Kraff, & Mirza, 2013; Franko, Thompson-Brenner, et al., 2012; Gayle, Fitzgibbon, & Martinovich, 2004; Udo et al., 2015). Differences emerge in events that precede onset of the ED, with Black/African American women reporting significantly higher rates of pregnancy than White women 12 months prior to the onset of the ED (Pike et al., 2006). Black/African American women also report significantly higher stress from school/work and significantly more critical comments about weight, shape, or eating from others as major life events that precede BED onset (Pike et al., 2006). Similar to BN, past research has found a shorter duration of BED and binge eating compared to those of other ethnic groups (Taylor et al., 2007). Black/African American women are more likely to develop any binge eating with an age of onset in early adulthood (Taylor et al., 2003). Given the later age of onset, researchers have proposed that binge eating may be a coping mechanism against environmental stressors rather than due to weight and shape concerns as seen in the majority of individuals with AN and BN (Taylor et al., 2007). Finally, Black/African American samples seeking treatment tend to have higher BMI, higher self-esteem, less depression, higher levels of stress, and higher levels of dietary restraint compared to Caucasian samples (Azarbad, Corsica, Hall, & Hood, 2010; Franko, Thompson-Brenner, et al., 2012; Mazzeo, Saunders, & Mitchell, 2005).

Asian Americans

An epidemiological study conducted using the National Latino and Asian American Study sample reported a lifetime prevalence rate of 0.10% for AN among Asian American groups, which is not significantly different from the prevalence rate among Whites (Marques et al., 2011). The lifetime prevalence for BN among Asian Americans is 1.50%, which is also similar to that for Whites (Marques et al., 2011). Finally, the lifetime prevalence for BED among Asian American individuals is 1.24% and not significantly different from the rate in Whites, although there was a significant difference between Asian Americans (4.74%) and Whites (2.53%) in the lifetime prevalence of any binge eating (Marques et al., 2011). Another epidemiological study found that there was no correlation between level of acculturation and lifetime prevalence of EDs (Nicdao, Hong, & Takeuchi, 2007), challenging the idea that being part of an Asian American group serves as a protective factor. Some smaller studies have found lower levels of disordered eating in Asian samples in comparison to other groups (Regan & Cachelin, 2006; Tsai & Gray, 2000), whereas other studies have found similar levels (Franko et al., 2007; Shaw, Ramirez, Trost, Randall, & Stice, 2004). A literature review concluded that the degree of risk for Asian American women is approximately equal to that for Caucasian women (Wildes, Emery, & Simons, 2001).

In presenting the available information on the prevalence of EDs among Asian Americans, it is important to highlight that individuals who are part of this ethnic group generally underutilize mental health services (Leong, Chang, & Lee, 2007; Miranda et al., 2005). In addition, it is important to keep in mind that assessment measures are not always designed to adapt to the differences in clinical presentation among Asian Americans (Tsong & Smart, 2014). Reliability and validity data for assessment of EDs in Asian American samples are not available, possibly complicating accurate diagnostic processes and impacting the reported prevalence rates. As stated previously, the rates of diagnosed EDs are subject to the limitations of the diagnostic criteria, and clinicians are encouraged to consider cultural factors in assessing for the presence of an ED among Asian Americans.

The existing literature on EDs among Asian Americans has been inconclusive in terms of identifying different presentation of symptoms. For example, a meta-analysis by Wildes and colleagues (2001) concluded that Asian samples often show greater levels of disordered eating and body dissatisfaction compared to White samples. However, the level of disordered eating among Asian American women tends to be overshadowed in cross-cultural studies due to the fact that Asian American women are often grouped with African American women, who tend to exhibit lower levels of disordered eating (Wildes et al., 2001). Furthermore, some studies have shown that Asian Americans are more satisfied with their bodies (Akan & Grilo, 1995), whereas other studies, including a meta-analysis (Grabe & Hyde, 2006), have shown that they are equally dissatisfied with their bodies compared to European American women (Kennedy, Templeton, Gandhi, & Gorzalka, 2004; Koff, Benavage, & Wong, 2001). Nonetheless, a number of studies point toward some unique factors that are important to consider within this ethnic minority group.

A common previous misconception in the field about Asian American women was that they have a cultural "protection" against EDs (Wonderlich et al., 2007). This assumption has been found to be inaccurate, and the opposite can be true in that native cultural factors may make Asian Americans more vulnerable to EDs (Jackson, Keel, & Lee, 2006), but these can present differently than they typically do in Western cultures. For example, the virtue of fasting to the point of emaciation is included in the Daoist text *Sandong Zhunang* (Rieger, Touyz, Swain, & Beumont, 2001), which would meet criteria for a diagnosis of atypical AN or other specified feeding or eating disorder (OSFED). In addition, EDs among Asian women have been hypothesized to be a way for them to express distress without risking the family's loss of face (Yokoyama, 2007) or violating the norm of emotional restraint that is typical in many Asian cultures (Jackson et al., 2006), which is a different conceptualization from what is typically described in White individuals.

Further support for these differences was provided in a qualitative study by Smart, Tsong, Mejia, Hayashino, and Braaten (2011). Clinicians interviewed in this study reported that Asian American clients often presented with a mix of subclinical features and often the eating disorder was not the presenting issue (Smart et al., 2011), which is an important consideration for clinicians treating EDs. In addition, a study of college students found that Asian Americans presenting with EDs may be more concerned with shape or specific body parts than with weight (Mintz & Kashubeck, 1999).

Although limited research is available to pinpoint specific differences, it appears that Asian Americans with EDs present with slightly more preoccupation with specific body parts versus overall fear of fatness, and their ED behaviors may be considered subclinical per the general diagnostic criteria. Furthermore, the ED can be viewed as a way to cope with other stressors in order to preserve familial values. Despite these differences, EDs among Asian Americans appear to be just as severe as those in White individuals.

EVIDENCE-BASED TREATMENT APPROACHES AND CULTURAL ADAPTATIONS

Despite the common misconception that minority groups do not develop EDs, in the past few decades, the prevalence of EDs in ethnic minorities has been extensively documented (Alegria et al., 2007; Kolar, Mebarak Chams, & Mejia Rodríguez, 2016). As previously noted, EBTs for EDs have been developed mainly for mainstream White populations; therefore, their validity in ethnic minorities is uncertain (Smolak & Stiegel-Moore, 2001). This results in the conundrum described previously: whether to adopt, adapt, or abandon EBTs for the treatment of EDs with ethnic minority individuals. Mental health providers in the community often express resistance to implementing EBTs because they are not trained in the delivery of these treatments, they do not believe that EBTs sufficiently address common comorbidities, or they believe manualized treatments are overly rigid and do not seem adequate for their clients' unique needs (Mussell et al., 2000; Simmons, Milnes, & Anderson, 2008). The current EBTs for EDs include family-based treatment (AN and BN), cognitive–behavioral therapy (BN and BED), interpersonal psychotherapy (BN and BED), and dialectical behavioral therapy (AN, BN, and BED) (Fairburn, 1997; Le Grange & Lock, 2007; Lock & Le Grange, 2012; Kass, Kolko, & Wilfley, 2013). This section discusses the available data from trials for each of the three ethnic minority groups discussed in this chapter, and it presents considerations to keep in mind when adapting these treatments.

Latinos/Hispanics

As previously stated, Latinos have elevated rates of any binge eating and BED but low prevalence of AN and BN (Alegria et al., 2007; Kolar et al., 2016). Although there are no available EBTs for AN that are specific to the Latino population, the central cultural role that family plays within these populations lends itself to the core tenets of family-based treatment interventions.

Despite the fact that prevalence rates of BN and BED among Latinos are comparable to those of the general population, few interventions and treatment trials have focused on this group (Shea, Cachelin, Gutierrez, Wang, & Phimphasone, 2016). Cognitive–behavioral therapy (CBT) for BN was recently adapted for Hispanics/Latinas (Shea et al., 2012). Nevertheless, cultural adaptation of EBTs is an important step for promoting treatment accessibility and engagement among underserved groups to reverse public health disparities. Three themes emerged from this treatment adaptation of CBT for EDs: (1) increased family, partner, and peer involvement; (2) the adjustment of meal plans to culturally important and affordable food options and the family dynamics around the food; and (3) the maintaining of cultural and body image values and problem solving of acculturative stress within the family, family meals, and the patient (Perez et al., 2016).

There are no EBT studies that have integrated the family in a culturally sensitive treatment for Latinos with EDs. Latino families tend to have traditional values and children who are dependent on parents (even adult children). For example, it is expected that females remain in the family house until marriage, thus staying in the home of origin longer than is typical for White women (Altabe & O'Garo, 2002). As a result, there is the potential for increased influence by family values. Within the Latino community, families are profoundly involved in treatment, and as with other mental illnesses, their warmth and support can play a very important role in treatment and medication adherence and relapse prevention (López & Kopelowicz, 2003; Ramírez-García, Chang, Young, López, & Jenkins, 2006; Reyes-Rodríguez & Bulik, 2010). Both the direct family and the extended family are typically involved with the patients, so their inclusion must be considered as a support network in the treatment of EDs in this population (Guadalupe-Rodríguez, Reyes-Rodríguez, & Bulik, 2011). Bernal and Sáez-Santiago (2005) stated that the perception of emotional involvement and acceptance from family members appears to be extremely important for Latinos. Involvement of the family in the early stages of detection and treatment may assist with motivation for treatment and help the family deal with the process of supporting their loved one while simultaneously providing practical guidance for such behaviors and managing medical complications (Guadalupe-Rodríguez et al., 2011).

In a study on cultural adaptation of a CBT-guided self-help program for Mexican American women with BED, Shea and colleagues (2012) found that some participants reported a strong identification with their family, whereas others described their family as overbearing and intrusive and wished to keep their treatment decision private. It is likely that different acculturation levels within the family contribute to the gap in understanding and a sense of disconnection between some Mexican American women and their families. Therefore, despite knowing that one of the core values that must be approached in a culturally sensitive treatment for Latinos is the role of the family and its dynamic around food and body image, this finding highlights that it is important not to overgeneralize and perpetuate group stereotypes (e.g., "All Latino patients are family oriented").

Providing EBTs in the Latino population in the United States can be challenging. Many factors can play out as disadvantages, such as low education, language barriers, difficulty entering treatment, illegal status, early treatment dropout, and lack of health insurance. Among Latinas and racially/ethnically diverse samples, the fear of stigmatization and lack of knowledge about EDs have been found to prevent treatment seeking (Cachelin, Rebeck, Veisel, & Striegel-Moore, 2001; Reyes-Rodríguez, Ramírez, Davis, Patrice, & Bulik, 2013). Reyes Rodríguez and Bulik (2010) proposed a model of intervention for Latinos with EDs in the United States in which relevant cultural issues are incorporated, such as mental health community services; bilingual treatment (English/Spanish); and cultural dynamics around food, family, and body image.

Given that family tends to be a major source of support, our efforts should focus on translating the needs of Latino patients and family members into finding culturally appropriate ways to incorporate family into treatment by (1) promoting psychoeducational and supportive interventions of EDs for family members and patients to reduce stigma and increase support, (2) increasing our understanding that the level of acculturation may impact the presentation and treatment of ED, and (3) exploring the role that the adoption of American beauty ideals and the stress of balancing two different cultures can play in treatment.

Black/African Americans

There have been only a few case studies on the treatment of AN among Black/African American individuals, and because most did not focus specifically on treatment, little guidance has been provided (Maresh & Willard, 1996; Pumariega et al., 1984). Borrowing from other literatures, motivational interviewing can be a useful tool for therapists who encounter treatment ambivalence and treatment compliance issues that often present in AN patients. Motivational interviewing has been shown to be effective with Black/African American individuals in increasing the modification of dietary behavior (Resnicow et al., 2001) and treatment adherence for medications (Arkowitz, Miller, & Rollnick, 2015).

Regarding the treatment of BN for Black/African American individuals, there is one randomized controlled trial that compared CBT and interpersonal psychotherapy (IPT) (Chui et al., 2007). The CBT treatment yielded higher rates of abstinence from binge eating and purging compared to the IPT treatment (60% vs. 30%, respectively), but IPT yielded a greater reduction in objective binge-eating episodes compared to CBT. The authors of the study suggest that because CBT yielded better overall treatment outcome across eating disorder symptoms, this should be the preferred treatment for Black/African American patients with BN. However, if CBT were to not be effective, IPT did yield some symptom resolution, and in some studies IPT has been found to be more effective than CBT for the treatment of depression among Black/African American individuals (Markowitz, Spielman, Sullivan, & Fishman, 2000). A second study examined efficacy results for family-based treatment in Black/African American adolescents with BN and found significant reductions in ED behavior and depressive symptoms and a significant increase in self-esteem (Doyle et al., 2009). It is important to note that patients received these treatments without any cultural adaptations.

There are a few more studies available on the treatment of BED for this population. A lifestyle study designed to increase physical activity and improve dietary habits for African American women found that women with moderate scores on the Binge Eating Scale reduced their binge-eating symptoms post-intervention, but women with severe scores on the scale did not (Mama et al., 2015). Another study combined the data of 11 trials of a diverse array of psychosocial treatments for BED, resulting in a sample of 79 Black/African Americans (Thompson-Brenner et al., 2013). Compared to Caucasian individuals, Black/African Americans were twice as likely to drop out of treatment, but those who stayed in treatment had lower ED symptoms. Black/African Americans were similar to Caucasian individuals across all other variables. Of note, all trials reviewed utilized manualized treatments and included discussions of antecedents of binge eating, identification of psychological triggers for binge eating, and strategies to avoid binge eating.

Asian Americans

To date, no studies or randomized control trials have been conducted specifically with Asian American samples. A few studies have examined the effectiveness of CBT with adult Asians, Latinos, and Africans combined, and none were for ED treatment (Horrell, 2008). Only one study has included a small number of Asian participants in clinical trials comparing CBT and IPT for EDs (Chui, Safer, Bryson, Agras, & Wilson, 2007). In reviewing the treatment literature for Asian Americans, one case example of cultural adaptations to enhanced CBT (Fairburn, 2008) was found for Asian American women with EDs (Smart, 2010). Cultural considerations recommended in this case example included a time-limited nature and solution-focused structure of treatment; inclusion of significant others (in the case example, the patient brought her sister to a session to target issues of stigma, shame, and hierarchy in the family system); an empathic but authoritative approach to the therapeutic relationship; a personalized formulation of what maintains the ED (with a focus on awareness of how culture and gender might influence these maintaining mechanisms); an examination of the overevaluation of shape and weight (which is likely to require attention to gender, culture, and possibly internalized racism); and use of the expanded form of the treatment to allow for more work with the cultural influences on perfectionism, self-esteem, and interpersonal relationships (Smart, 2010).

When assessing and planning treatments for eating disorders with Asian American individuals, additional contextual factors must be taken into consideration. For example, clinicians must consider the age, place of residence, experiences with discrimination, and adherence of traditional Asian or family cultural values or practices (Tsong & Smart, 2014). Although the role of acculturation in the risk of developing an ED in Asian Americans is inconclusive (Cummins et al., 2005), there is some research to support that ethnic minority women who have endured racist and oppressive aggression can experience lower self-esteem, helplessness, and a loss of sense of control (Fernando, 1984). Family factors, such as parental control and overprotection, have also been found to be associated with EDs in Asian American women (Ahmad, Waller, & Verduyn, 1994).

Furthermore, it is important that clinicians practice flexibility and cultural sensitivity when utilizing the DSM criteria for EDs, given that some of the central criteria, such as intense fear of fatness, may not be very useful in assessing and treating Asian American individuals. Other cultural factors to consider when adapting EBTs specifically for Asian American clients include the role of acculturation in identity, self-construal, collectivism, and communication style (Leong & Lee, 2006). For example, the self-construal factor of loss of face concerns can negatively impact an individual's willingness to engage in therapies requiring self-disclosure (Hall & Eap, 2007). In addition, differences in communication styles among Asian American individuals, such as the value of nonverbal/nonexplicit language, can have important implications in therapy because any form of confrontation or verbal assertiveness may be considered rude (Leong & Lee, 2006). These are reflective of the general collectivistic values that are common among Asian American individuals. At the same time, clinicians should remain aware of the vast differences that may exist between and within Asian groups (Smart, 2010).

CONCLUSION AND FUTURE DIRECTIONS

Returning to the clinical dilemma faced by clinicians in determining whether to adopt, adapt, or abandon EBTs in the treatment of ethnic minority individuals with EDs, the data thus far suggest to first adopt. It is very apparent that there is a need for more research on treatment of EDs among Latino/Hispanic, Black/African American, and Asian American individuals. Although the current literature suggests adopting EBTs for ethnic minorities with BN and BED, there are significant limitations. Manualized treatments are the equivalent of GPS navigation systems that provide road maps and driving directions to get the clinician to the final destination (i.e., symptom reduction). However, manualized treatments do not provide instructions on the dialogue, content, or in-the-moment decision-making that therapists are required to do in session (i.e., the quality of the driving). In the few studies of cultural adaptations to research-supported treatments for ED, it is unknown if and how the content, in-the-moment decision-making, and experience of therapists differed from those when working with White individuals. This is a critical and important piece of information for other providers seeking to apply research-supported interventions with minority groups and to achieve comparable results. More research and well-documented case studies by independent practitioners working with the current EBT models and adapting them to achieve cultural sensitivity are needed.

To clinicians working with ethnic minority populations, we offer the following suggestions based on our literature review of treatment for EDs: (1) Consider involving the family in treatment, even for adults; (2) include a clinician or member of the treatment team from the country of origin or someone who is familiar with the core cultural values specific to the individual being treated; (3) practice flexibility in assessing the symptomatology of EDs among culturally diverse individuals because the presentation of symptoms may deviate from the current diagnostic criteria included in the DSM-5 (e.g., absence of fear of fatness, higher weight/BMI, and differing body ideals); and (4) seek support for the practice of EBTs and appropriate cultural adaptations from professional organizations such as the Academy for Eating Disorders and the published guidelines created for other countries that have mandatory supervision and regulations of practice.

Consistent with the conclusions outlined previously, in adapting EBTs to the treatment of ethnic minorities, readers are encouraged to follow the American Psychological Association's (2003) guidelines on multiculturalism, which include self-awareness, awareness of other people's culture, and appropriate strategies for intervention. In addition, clinician attitudes and beliefs, knowledge, and skills about specific cultures of the individuals they are treating are imperative in adapting EBTs for ethnically diverse individuals (Whaley & Davis, 2007). Cultural accommodations proposed by Leong and Lee (2006) require clinicians to recognize specific cultural features as fundamentally important in understanding clients' behavior and are to be added to EBTs to improve their relevance. Finally, multicultural competency calls for clinician's self-awareness, knowledge, and skills across a range of cultural issues, including recognition of biases within the therapist and within the treatment modalities used (Sue, Arredondo, & McDavis, 1992). Therefore, these biases must be openly explored because the identification of these can inform ED treatments with ethnic minority groups and aid clinicians in adapting EBTs to the individual and his or her culture.

RESOURCES

American Psychological Association guidelines on multiculturalism: http://www.apa.org/pi/oema/resources/policy/multicultural-guidelines.aspx
Academy for Eating Disorders research practice guidelines in Spanish: http://www.aedweb.org/index.php/19-education/129-research-practice-guidelines-spanish
National Eating Disorders Association resources in Spanish: https://www.nationaleatingdisorders.org/neda-espanol
Dialectical behavior therapy skills training manual for treating borderline personality disorder in Spanish: Linehan, M. (2003). *Manual de tratamiento de los trastornos de personalidad limite* (R. Santandreu, Trans.). Barcelona, Spain: Ediciones Paidos Iberica.

REFERENCES

Ackard, D. M., & Brewerton, T. D. (2010). Comorbid trauma and eating disorders. In M. Maine, B. Hartman McGilley, & D. W. Bunnell (Eds.), *Treatment of eating disorders: Bridging the research–practice gap* (pp. 251–267). San Diego, CA: Academic Press.

Ahmad, S., Waller, G., & Verduyn, C. (1994). Eating attitudes among Asian schoolgirls: The role of perceived parental control. *International Journal of Eating Disorders, 15*(1), 91–97.

Akan, G. E., & Grilo, C. M. (1995). Sociocultural influences on eating attitudes and behaviors, body image, and psychological functioning: A comparison of African-American, Asian-American, and Caucasian college women. *International Journal of Eating Disorders, 18*, 181–187.

Alegria, M., Woo, M., Cao, Z., Torres, M., Meng, X., & Striegel-Moore, R. (2007). Prevalence and correlates of eating disorders in Latinos in the US. *International Journal of Eating Disorders, 40*(Suppl.), S15–S21.

Altabe, M., & O'Garo, K. (2002). Hispanic body images. In T. Cash & T. Pruzinsky (Eds.), *Body image: A handbook of theory, research, and clinical practice* (pp. 251–256). New York, NY: Guilford.

American Psychiatric Association. (1994). *Diagnostic and statistical manual of mental disorders* (4th ed.). Washington, DC: Author.

American Psychiatric Association. (2013). *Diagnostic and statistical manual of mental disorders* (5th ed.). Arlington, VA: American Psychiatric Publishing.

American Psychological Association. (2003). Guidelines on multicultural education, training, research, practice, and organizational change for psychologists. *American Psychologist, 58*, 377–402.

Arkowitz, H., Miller, W. R., & Rollnick, S. (2015). *Motivation interviewing in the treatment of psychological problems* (2nd ed.). New York, NY: Guilford.

Azarbad, L., Corsica, J., Hall, B., & Hood, M. (2010). Psychosocial correlates of binge eating in Hispanic, African American, and Caucasian women presenting for bariatric surgery. *Eating Behaviors, 11*, 79–84.

Bernal, G., & Sáez-Santiago, E. (2005). Toward culturally centered and evidenced based treatments for depressed adolescents. In W. M. Pinsof & A. J. Lebow (Eds.), *Family psychology: The art of the science* (pp. 471–489). New York, NY: Oxford University Press.

Brewerton, T. (2007). Eating disorders, trauma and comorbidity: Focus on PTSD. *Eating Disorders, 15*, 285–304.

Cachelin, F. M., Rebeck, R., Veisel, C., & Striegel-Moore, R. H. (2001). Barriers to treatment for eating disorders among ethnically diverse women. *International Journal of Eating Disorders, 30*, 269–278.

Chui, W., Safer, D. L., Bryson, S. W., Agras, W. S., & Wilson, G. T. (2007). A comparison of ethnic groups in the treatment of bulimia nervosa. *Eating Behaviors, 8*, 485–491.

Cummins, L. H., Simmons, A. M., & Zane, N. W. S. (2005). Eating disorders in Asian populations: A critique of current approaches to the study of culture, ethnicity, and eating disorders. *American Journal of Orthopsychiatry, 75*, 553–574.

Dohm, F. A., Striegel-Moore, R. H., Wilfley, D. E., Pike, K. M., Hook, J., & Fairburn, C. G. (2002). Self-harm and substance use in a community sample of Black and White women with binge eating disorder or bulimia nervosa. *International Journal of Eating Disorders, 32*, 389–400.

Elliott, C. A., Tanofsky-Kraff, M., & Mirza, N. M. (2013). Parent report of binge eating in Hispanic, African American, and Caucasian youth. *Eating Behaviors, 14*, 1–6.

Fairburn, C. G. (1997). Interpersonal psychotherapy for bulimia nervosa. In D. M. Garner & P. E. Garfinkel (Eds.), *Handbook of treatment for eating disorders* (pp. 278–294). New York, NY: Guilford.

Fairburn, C. G. (2008). *Cognitive behavior therapy and eating disorders*. New York, NY: Guilford.

Fernando, S. (1984). Racism as a cause of depression. *International Journal of Social Psychiatry, 30*(1-2), 41–49.

Ferrero, S. (2002). "Comida sin Par": Consumption of Mexican food in Los Angeles: Foodscapes in a transnational consumer society. In W. Belasco & P. Scranton (Eds.), *Food nations: Selling taste in consumer societies* (pp. 194–219). New York, NY: Routledge.

Franko, D. L., Becker, A. E., Thomas, J. J., & Herzog, D. B. (2007). Cross-ethnic differences in eating disorder symptoms and related stress. *International Journal of Eating Disorders, 40*, 156–164.

Franko, D. L., Coen, E. J., Roehrig, J. P., Rodgers, R. F., Jenkins, A., Lovering, M. E., & Dela Cruz, S. (2012). Considering J. Lo and Ugly Betty: A qualitative examination of risk factors and prevention targets for body dissatisfaction, eating disorders, and obesity in young Latina women. *Body Image, 9*(3), 381–387.

Franko, D. L., Jenkins, A., & Rodgers, R. F. (2012). Toward reducing risk for eating disorders and obesity in Latina college women. *Journal of Counseling & Development, 90*, 298–307.

Franko, D. L., Thompson-Brenner, H., Thompson, D. R., Boisseau, C. L., Davis, A., Forbush, K. T., . . . Wilson, G. T. (2012). Racial/ethnic differences in adults in randomized clinical trials of binge eating disorder. *Journal of Consulting and Clinical Psychology, 80*(2), 186–195.

Gayle, J. L., Fitzgibbon, M. L., & Martinovich, Z. (2004). A preliminary analysis of binge episodes: Comparison of a treatment-seeking sample of Black and White women. *Eating Behaviors, 5*, 303–313.

Guadalupe-Rodríguez, E., Reyes-Rodríguez, M. L., & Bulik, C. M. (2011). Exploratory study of the role of family in the treatment of eating disorders among Puerto Ricans. *Revista Puertorriqueña de Psicología, 22*, 7–26.

Hall, G. C. N., & Eap, S. (2007). Empirically supported therapies for Asian Americans. In F. T. L. Leong, A. G., Inman, A. Ebrero, L. H. Yang, L. Kinoshita, & M. Fu (Eds.), *Handbook of Asian American psychology* (2nd ed., pp. 449–467). Thousand Oaks, CA: Sage.

Holman, C. (2012). Trauma and eating disorders. In J. R. Fox & K. P. Goss (Eds.), *Eating and its disorders* (pp. 139–153). Chichester, England: Wiley.

Horrell, S. C. V. (2008). Effectiveness of cognitive–behavioral therapy with adult ethnic minority clients: A review. *Professional Psychology: Research and Practice, 39*, 160–168.

Hudson, J. I., Hiripi, E., Pope, H. G., & Kessler, R. C. (2007). The prevalence and correlates of eating disorders in the National Comorbidity Survey Replication. *Biological Psychiatry, 61*, 348–358.

Jackson, S. C., Keel, P. K., & Lee, Y. H. (2006). Trans-cultural comparison of disordered eating in Korean women. *International Journal of Eating Disorders, 39*, 498–502.

Kass, A. E., Kolko, R. P., & Wilfley, D. E. (2013). Psychological treatments for eating disorders. *Current Opinions in Psychiatry, 26*(6), 549–555.

Katzman, M. A. (1993). *Women in groups: Experiments in taking up space.* Plenary address presented at the National Association of Anorexia Nervosa and Associate Disease National Eating Disorders Conference, Chicago, IL, April 19–21.

Katzman, M. A., & Lee, S. (1997). Beyond body image: The integration of feminist and transcultural theories in the understanding of self starvation. *International Journal of Eating Disorder, 22*, 385–394.

Kennedy, M. A., Templeton, L., Gandhi, A., & Gorzalka, B. B. (2004). Asian body image satisfaction: Ethnic and gender differences across Chinese, Indo-Asian, and European-descent students. *Eating Disorders, 12*, 321–336.

Kiang, L., & Fuligni, A. J. (2009). Ethnic identity in context: Variations in ethnic exploration and belonging within parent, same-ethnic peer, and different-ethnic peer relationships. *Journal of Youth and Adolescence, 38*(5), 732–743.

Koff, E., Benavage, A., & Wong, B. (2001). Body image attitudes and psychosocial functioning in Euro-American and Asian-American college women. *Psychological Reports, 88*, 917–928.

Kolar, D. R., Mebarak Chams, M., & Mejia Rodríguez, D. (2016). *Prevalence of eating disorders in Latin America: A systematic review.* Poster session presented at ICED 2015, Boston, United States.

Le Grange, D., & Lock, J. (2007). *Treating bulimia in adolescents: A family-based approach.* New York, NY: Guilford.

Leong, F. T. L., Chang, D. F., & Lee, S. (2007). Counseling and psychotherapy with Asian Americans: Process and outcomes. In F. T. L. Leong, A. G. Inaman, A. Ebreo, L. H. Yang, L. Kinoshita, & M. Fu (Eds.), *Handbook of Asian American psychology* (2nd ed., pp. 429–448). Thousand Oaks, CA: Sage.

Leong, F. T. L., & Lee, S. (2006). A cultural accommodation model for cross-cultural psychotherapy: Illustrated with the case of Asian Americans. *Psychotherapy Theory, Research, Practice, and Training, 43*, 410–423.

Lock, J., & Le Grange, D. (2012). *Treatment manual for anorexia nervosa: A family-based approach*. New York, NY: Guilford.

Londoño, A., Romero, P., & Casas, G. (2012). The association between armed conflict, violence and mental health: A cross sectional study comparing two populations in Cundinamarca department, Colombia. *Conflict and Health, 6*, 12.

López, S. R., & Kopelowicz, A. (2003). Family interventions for serious mental illness: Translating research to practice. *World Psychiatry, 2*, 34–35.

Lydecker, J. A., & Grilo, C. M. (2016). Different yet similar: Examining race and ethnicity in treatment seeking adults with binge eating disorder. *Journal of Consulting and Clinical Psychology, 84*(1), 88–94.

Mama, S. K., Schembre, S. M., O'Connor, D. P., Kaplan, C., Bode, S., & Lee, R. (2015). Effectiveness of lifestyle interventions to reduce binge eating symptoms in African American and Hispanic women. *Appetite, 95*, 269–274.

Maresh, R. D., & Willard, S. G. (1996). Anorexia nervosa in an African-American female of a lower socioeconomic background. *European Eating Disorders Review, 4*(2), 95–99.

Marques, L., Alegria, M., Becker, A. E., Chen, C., Fang, A., Chosak, A., & Belo Diniz, J. (2011). Comparative prevalence, correlates of impairment, and service utilization for eating disorders across US ethnic groups: Implications for reducing ethnic disparities in health care access for eating disorders. *International Journal of Eating Disorders, 44*, 412–420.

Mazzeo, S. E., Saunders, R., & Mitchell, K. S. (2005). Binge eating among African American and Caucasian bariatric surgery candidates. *Eating Behaviors, 6*, 189–196.

Mintz, L. B., & Kashubeck, S. (1999). Body image and disordered eating among Asian American and Caucasian college students: An examination of race and gender differences. *Psychology of Women Quarterly, 23*, 781–796.

Miranda, J., Bernal, G., Lau, A., Kohn, L., Hwang, W., & LaFramboise, T. (2005). State of the science on psychological interventions for ethnic minorities. *Annual Review of Clinical Psychology, 1*, 113–142.

Morales, E., & Norcross, J. C. (2010). Evidence-based practices with ethnic minorities: Strange bedfellows no more. *Journal of Clinical Psychology: In Session, 66*, 821–829.

Mussell, M. P., Crosby, R. D., Crow, S. J., Knopke, A. J., Peterson, C. B., Wonderlich, S. A., & Mitchell, J. E. (2000). Utilization of empirically supported psychotherapy treatments for individuals with eating disorders: A survey of psychologists. *International Journal of Eating Disorders, 27*, 230–237.

Nicdao, E. G., Hong, S., & Takeuchi, D. T. (2007). Prevalence and correlates of eating disorders among Asian Americans: Results from the National Latino and Asian American Study. *International Journal of Eating Disorders, 40*(Suppl.), S22–S26.

Perez, M., Ohrt, T. K., & Hoek, H. W. (2016). Prevalence and treatment of eating disorders among Hispanics/Latino Americans in the United States. *Current Opinions in Psychiatry, 29*(6), 378–382.

Perez, M., & Plasencia, M. (2016). Psychological perspectives on ethnic minority eating behavior and obesity. In A. Blume (Ed.), *Social issues in living color: Challenges and solutions from the perspective of ethnic minority psychology*. New York, NY: Praeger.

Pike, K. M., Wilfley, D., Hilbert, A., Fairburn, C. G., Dohm, F. A., & Striegel-Moore, R. H. (2006). Antecedent life events of binge-eating disorder. *Psychiatry Research, 142*, 19–29.

Pumariega, A. J., Edwards, P., & Mitchell, C. B. (1984). Anorexia nervosa in Black adolescents. *Journal of the American Academy of Child Psychiatry, 23*(1): 111–114.

Ramírez-García, J., Chang, C. L., Young, J. S., López, S. R., & Jenkins, J. H. (2006). Family support predicts psychiatric medication usage among Mexican American individuals with schizophrenia. *Social Psychiatry and Psychiatric Epidemiology, 41*(8), 624–631.

Resnicow, K., Jackson, A., Wang, T., De, A. K., McCarty, F., Dudley, W. N., & Baranowski, T. (2001). A motivational interviewing intervention to increase fruit and vegetable intake through Black churches: Results of the Eat for Life trial. *American Journal of Public Health, 91*(10), 1686–1693.

Reyes-Rodríguez, M. L., & Bulik, C. M. (2010). Hacia una adaptación cultural para el tratamiento de trastornos alimentarios en latinos en Estados Unidos. *Revista Mexicana de Trastornos Alimentarios, 1*(1), 27–35.

Reyes-Rodríguez, M. L., Ramírez, J., Davis, K., Patrice, K., & Bulik, C. M. (2013). Exploring barriers and facilitators in eating disorders treatment among Latinas in the United States. *Journal of Latina/o Psychology, 1*(2), 112–131.

Rieger, E., Touyz, S. W., Swain, T., & Beumont, P. J. (2001). Cross-cultural research on anorexia nervosa: Assumptions regarding the role of body weight. *International Journal of Eating Disorders, 29,* 205–215.

Romo, L. F., Mireles-Rios, R., & Hurtado, A. (2016). Cultural, media, and peer influences on body beauty perceptions on Mexican American adolescent girls. *Journal of Adolescent Research, 31*(4), 474–501.

Saylor, E. S., & Aries, E. (1999). Ethnic identity and change in social context. *Journal of Social Psychology, 139*(5), 549–566.

Shea, M., Cachelin, F., Gutierrez, G., Wang, S., & Phimphasone, P. (2016). Mexican American women's perspectives on a culturally adapted cognitive–behavioral therapy guided self-help program for binge eating. *Psychological Services, 13*(1), 31–41.

Shea, M., Cachelin, F., Uribe, L., Striegel, R. H., Thompson, D., & Wilson, G. T. (2012). Cultural adaptation of a cognitive behavior therapy guided self-help program for Mexican American women with binge eating disorders. *Journal of Counseling and Development, 90,* 308–318.

Simmons, A. M., Milnes, S. M., & Anderson, D. A. (2008). Factors influencing the utilization of empirically supported treatments for eating disorders. *Eating Disorders, 16,* 342–354.

Smart, R. (2010). Treating Asian American women with eating disorders: Multicultural competency and empirically supported treatment. *Eating Disorders, 18,* 58–73.

Smart, R., Tsong, Y., Mejia, O. L., Hayashino, D., & Braaten, M. E. T. (2011). Therapists' experiences treating Asian American women with eating disorders. *Professional Psychology: Research and Practice, 42*(4), 308–315.

Soh, N., Touyz, S. W., & Surgenor, L. J. (2006). Eating and body image disturbances across cultures: A review. *European Eating Disorders Review, 14,* 54–65.

Striegel-Moore, R. H., Dohm, F. A., Kraemer, H. C., Taylor, C. B., Daniels, S., Crawford, P. B., & Schreiber, G. B. (2003). Eating disorders in White and Black women. *American Journal of Psychiatry, 160,* 1326–1331.

Sue, D. W., Arredondo, P., & McDavis, R. J. (1992). Multicultural counseling competencies and standards: A call to the profession. *Journal of Counseling and Development, 70,* 477–486.

Taylor, J. Y., Caldwell, C. H., Baser, R. E., Faison, N., & Jackson, J. S. (2007). Prevalence of eating disorders among Blacks in the National Survey of American Life. *International Journal of Eating Disorders, 40*(Suppl.), S10–S14.

Thompson-Brenner, H., Franko, D. L., Thompson, D. R., Grilo, C. M., Boisseau, C. L., Roehrig, J. P., . . . Wilson, G. T. (2013). Race/ethnicity, education, and treatment parameters as moderators and predictors of outcome in binge eating disorder. *Journal of Consulting and Clinical Psychology, 81*(4), 710–721.

Tsong, Y., & Smart, R. (2014). Assessing eating pathology in Asian Americans. In L. T. Benuto (Ed.), *Guide to psychological assessments with Asians* (pp. 243–260). New York, NY: Springer.

Udo, T., White, M. A., Lydecker, J. L., Barnes, R. D., Genao, I., Garcia, R., . . . Grilo, C. M. (2015). Biopsychosocial correlates of binge eating disorder in Caucasian and African American women with obesity in primary care settings. *European Eating Disorders Review, 24*, 181–186.

US Census. (2012, September 27). *2010 Census shows multiple-race population grew faster than single-race population*. Census news release. Retrieved from https://www. census.gov/newsroom/releases/archives/race/cb12-182.html

Vallianatos, H., & Raine, K. (2008). Consuming food and constructing identities among Arabic and South Asian immigrant women. *Food, Culture and Society, 11*(3), 355–373.

Weller, D. L., & Turkon, D. (2015). Contextualizing the immigrant experience: The role of food and foodways in identity, maintenance and formation for first- and second-generation Latinos in Ithaca, New York. *Ecology of Food and Nutrition, 54*(1), 57–73.

Whaley, A. L., & Davis, K. E. (2007). Cultural competence and evidence-based practice in mental health services: A complementary perspective. *American Psychologist, 62*, 563–574.

Wildes, J. E., Emery, R. E., & Simons, A. D. (2001). The roles of ethnicity and culture in the development of eating disturbance and body dissatisfaction: A meta-analytic review. *Clinical Psychology Review, 21*, 521–551.

Wilk, R. R. (1999). Real Belizean food: Building local identity in the transnational Caribbean. *American Anthropologist, 101*(2), 244–255.

Wonderlich, S. A., Joiner, T. E., Williamson, D. A., & Crosby, R. D. (2007). Eating disorder diagnoses: Empirical approaches to classification. *American Psychologist, 62*, 167–180.

Yokoyama, K. (2007). The double binds of our bodies: Multiculturally-informed feminist therapy considerations for body image and eating disorders among Asian American women. *Women and Therapy, 30*, 177–192.

21

Midlife-Onset Eating Disorders

CRISTIN D. RUNFOLA, JESSICA H. BAKER,
AND CYNTHIA M. BULIK ■

The fifth edition of the *Diagnostic and Statistical Manual of Mental Disorders* (DSM-5; American Psychiatric Association [APA], 2013) includes four main eating disorder diagnoses, all of which can be diagnosed in men or women during midlife (arbitrarily defined as onset at approximately age 40 years): anorexia nervosa (AN), bulimia nervosa (BN), binge-eating disorder (BED), and other specified feeding and eating disorder (OSFED; previously eating disorder not otherwise specified [EDNOS]). Regardless of diagnosis, midlife eating disorders present in one of three ways:

- *Early onset chronic disorder*: An eating disorder onset early in life—adolescence or young adulthood—that persists throughout adulthood
- *Early onset relapsed disorder*: Relapse of a remitted disorder that occurred earlier in life
- *Late-onset disorder*: An eating disorder onset at age 40 years or later

Although the early onset chronic disorder and the early onset relapsed disorder may be the most common presentations of midlife eating disorders, late-onset disorder presentations do exist. The available data suggest that approximately 30–70% of midlife eating disorder cases may represent a true late-onset disorder (Keel, Gravener, Joiner, & Haedt, 2010; Lapid et al., 2010). This chapter provides a concise review of the prevalence, incidence, and clinical presentation of midlife eating disorders, and it also discusses evidence-based treatments for midlife individuals with these disorders.

PREVALENCE OF MIDLIFE EATING DISORDERS AND DISORDERED EATING

Few epidemiological studies exist that examine the prevalence and incidence of eating disorders at midlife. Data from six European countries across different age cohorts indicate that although eating disorders do decrease with increasing age, they do not disappear (Preti et al., 2009). Using DSM-IV-TR diagnostic criteria (APA, 2000), Preti and colleagues reported a lifetime risk of 0.17% for AN, 0.21% for BN, and 0.61% for BED. In a community-based study of 715 Australian women aged 40–60 years (Mangweth-Matzek et al., 2014), the point prevalence for DSM-IV eating disorders was estimated to be approximately 4.6%, with 1.4% meeting criteria for BN, 1.5% for BED, and 1.7% for EDNOS.

Similar to other age groups, eating disorder symptoms are more common in midlife women than threshold diagnoses (Gagne et al., 2012; Mangweth-Matzek et al., 2014; Marcus, Bromberger, Wei, Brown, & Kravitz, 2007). A cross-sectional study (Hilbert, de Zwaan, & Braehler, 2012) suggests that midlife may be a risk period for eating disorder symptoms because a peak in symptom prevalence in a 45- to 54-year-old age group and lower symptom prevalence thereafter were observed. In the Gender and Body Image (GABI) study of 1,849 women older than age 50 years in the United States, Gagne et al. (2012) found that 13.3% of women reported at least one current core eating disorder symptom.

It appears that binge eating, food restriction, and body dissatisfaction are the most prevalent eating disorder symptoms observed in this age group. In the GABI study (Gagne et al., 2012), the most prevalent current symptoms were purging in the absence of binge eating in the past 5 years (7.8%) and binge eating only (3.5%). In a younger (aged 42–55 years) multiethnic sample of 589 women in the United States (Marcus et al., 2007), 11% of women reported recurrent binge eating (at least two or three times per month), 13.4% reported extreme restriction or fasting (eating little or nothing for at least a day) to control weight and shape, and 9.2% reported marked fear of weight gain. In a study of women aged 40–66 years in Switzerland, Drobnjak, Atsiz, Ditzen, Tuschen-Caffier, and Ehlert (2014) found that 10.8–13.3% of participants endorsed regular binge-eating symptoms and 15.7% reported restrained eating. Body dissatisfaction is also pervasive into midlife, with approximately 89% of women exhibiting body size dissatisfaction (Runfola et al., 2013).

Males

To our knowledge, only one epidemiological study of eating disorder symptoms in middle-aged or older men exists. In a community-based study of 470 Austrian men aged 40–75 years (Mangweth-Matzek et al., 2016), 6.8% reported eating disorder symptoms. Specifically, 0.8% had a body mass index (BMI) <18.5, 2.3% endorsed binge eating, 1.5% reported binge eating and purging, and 2.1% reported purging without binge eating. Only 9% of the men with an identified current core eating disorder symptom had scores on the Eating Disorder Examination Questionnaire (EDE-Q) exceeding the threshold for eating disturbance. Thus, the EDE-Q significantly underestimated the number of men with disordered eating in the sample. The authors suggested that conventional instruments may fail to capture eating disorder symptoms in men, contributing to potential underdiagnosis and failure to provide adequate treatment. Because there is such limited information on eating disorders in midlife males, we focus our continued discussion on women.

Presentation for Treatment

Of women older than age 40 years who present for outpatient treatment, the majority are diagnosed with OSFED (33.2%), followed by BN (29.9%), BED (24.7%), and AN (12.1%) (Elran-Barak et al., 2015). Individuals with BED often first present to treatment in their forties (Grilo, 2002; Striegel-Moore et al., 2004). Indeed, midlife women seeking outpatient treatment are significantly more likely to have BED and OSFED and significantly less likely to have BN compared to young adults (Ackard, Richter, Frisch, Mangham, & Cronemeyer, 2013; Kally & Cumella, 2008). The percentage of outpatients diagnosed with AN may not differ by age group. Overall, the case mix of clinicians treating older adults may differ somewhat from that of those who treat younger groups.

ETIOLOGY

Whether the etiological factors underlying eating disorders at midlife differ meaningfully from those of eating disorders at other ages is unknown. It is presumed that genetic, biological, and psychosocial factors play a role in eating disorder onset regardless of age (for a review, see Culbert, Racine, & Klump, 2015). Here, we discuss research specifically addressing the etiology of eating disorders at midlife.

Although no study to date has examined the genetic influences on eating disorder symptoms after age 41 years, population-based twin studies indicate that additive genetic factors account for approximately 40–60% of the liability to eating disorders (Trace, Baker, Penas-Lledo, & Bulik, 2013). In girls, the genetic effects on eating disorder symptoms change with age (Klump, 2013), such that genetic effects are nonexistent in preadolescence, significantly increase between early and mid-adolescence, and then remain constant up to the early forties (the end of the study period). Twin studies strongly suggest that puberty, not chronological age, accounts for this change (Klump, 2013). Thus, the influence of genetic factors on eating disorder risk may also vary across older ages, specifically during additional periods of reproductive change.

Hormonal and weight factors may also play a role. Risk for eating disorders and related symptoms increases during times of reproductive hormone and physical change, including pregnancy (Coker, Mitchell-Wong, & Abraham, 2013) and the menopause transition (i.e., perimenopause—the period of time when menstrual cycles begin to become irregular; Mangweth-Matzek et al., 2013). For example, in a community-based sample of Austrian women aged 40–60 years, Mangweth-Matzek et al. found that the prevalence of any eating disorder diagnosis was significantly higher in perimenopausal than in premenopausal women. Compelling evidence that robust hormonal processes, specifically changing estrogen levels, influence risk for eating disorders in girls at puberty (Klump, 2013) suggests estrogen may play a role in eating disorder risk at the other periods of reproductive hormone change later in life, namely perimenopause (Baker & Runfola, 2016).

Age-related weight gain and abdominal fat increase (Sheehan, DuBrava, DeChello, & Fang, 2003; Pascot et al., 1999) also appear to increase risk for the onset of eating disorders, at least indirectly (Slevec & Tiggemann, 2011). A number of studies support an association between elevated BMI (and obesity, BMI > 30) and disordered eating in middle-aged women and also between body dissatisfaction, aging anxiety, and disordered eating (Slevec & Tiggemann, 2011). A qualitative study revealed that women older than 50 years of age feel blindsided and distressed by the physical changes that happen at this age (Hofmeier et al., 2017). Such distress may culminate in unhealthy attempts to control weight/shape.

Psychosocial stressors that are characteristic of midlife also play a role in etiology. In older age groups, grief and loss appear to be among the most common stressors (Forman & Davis, 2005; Lapid et al., 2010; McCormack, Lewis, & Wells, 2014). Specific precipitating stressful events identified in a study of women with eating disorders who were older than age 50 years (Lapid et al., 2010) included widowhood and bereavement (42%), medical illness (surgery and pneumonia; 23%), partner-related difficulties (19%), parenting-related role transitions or challenges (15%), residential moves (8%), retirement (4%), and immigration (4%). Other studies have added divorce and trauma history, specifically weight-related teasing and sexual or physical abuse, to this list (Slevec & Tiggemann, 2011). Furthermore, intra- and interpersonal challenges may play a role in symptom maintenance or relapse in adult eating disorders (Arcelus, Haslam, Farrow, & Meyer, 2013).

Negative emotions, such as anxiety, stress, feelings of inadequacy, or depression, and low self-esteem have been cited as exacerbating or triggering eating disorders at mid- or late life (Slevec & Tiggemann, 2011). Although perhaps an unconscious decision, some women describe controlling their food intake as a way to feel more in control of their life or to cope with the negative emotional states. For example, binge eating can be an effective (albeit harmful) way to "numb" painful emotions temporarily.

Clinical case reports of late-onset AN cases (Gonidakis, Georgantopoulos, Konstantakopoulos, & Varsou, 2014; Lapid et al., 2010) have also cited patients as using eating disorder behaviors as a way to communicate or to create change within a family system. Specifically, these case studies found that some patients perceived positive changes within their family system, including feeling more heard, better cared for, and more respected by spouses and other family members, as a result of the AN symptomatology. In one case report (Gonidakis et al., 2014), two late-onset AN patients had purportedly described AN as a way to communicate nonverbally their feelings to loved ones; both were in relationships described as cold and distant.

Additional sociocultural factors may play a role. Pressure from the media, family, and peers to maintain a youthful, slender appearance has been found to predict body dissatisfaction and disordered eating in midlife and older women (Slevec & Tiggemann, 2011). Thin ideal internalization and importance of appearance also predict disordered eating at this age. There are few authentic, nonaltered aging women in the media (Wasylkiw, Emms, Meuse, & Poirier, 2009), and research suggests this fact does not go unnoticed by women (Hofmeier et al., 2017).

Thus, the combination of age-specific psychosocial stressors together with genetic and biological factors, including chaotic hormonal fluctuations and aging-related body change, may contribute to eating disorder etiology in women at midlife or later.

CLINICAL PRESENTATION

Midlife eating disorders occur across socioeconomic strata, race/ethnicity, and educational attainment. In general, research suggests that eating disorder symptoms present similarly at midlife compared with adolescence and young adulthood.

Behavioral

Core behavioral symptoms may include dietary restriction, binge eating, self-induced vomiting, laxative abuse, diet pill abuse, steroid or supplement abuse, and compulsive exercise. One study examining differences in behavioral symptoms across diagnosis and age in a treatment-seeking sample found very few differences in AN and BN across age groups (Elran-Barak et al., 2015). However, midlife women with BED and OSFED showed significantly less severe eating disorder behavioral symptoms compared with the younger comparison groups. Specifically, in the month before assessment, there were significantly fewer episodes of binge eating among the midlife BED group, laxative use among the midlife OSFED group, and compulsive exercise among the midlife BN, BED, and OSFED groups compared with their younger counterparts. In contrast, another study (Cumella & Kally, 2008) observed greater eating disorder severity in midlife eating disorder patients receiving treatment on an inpatient unit compared with a younger group of eating disorder patients. Taken together, these findings suggest that behaviors may present in midlife populations with less severity in treatment-seeking samples and with greater severity in inpatient samples than in younger cohorts.

Psychological

An important psychological feature of a majority of midlife eating disorders is body image disturbance (Peat, Peyerl, & Muehlenkamp, 2008), and body image may be more complex with age. Community-based studies of women older than age 50 years suggest that, similar to youth, women at midlife grapple with overall body size/shape dissatisfaction as well as dissatisfaction with certain body parts, such as the stomach, hips, and thighs (Gagne et al., 2012; Runfola et al., 2013). However, in contrast to younger presentations, this research found that individuals at midlife also contend with aging-related changes, such as sagging skin and loss of muscle mass. Similarly, "fat talk" (speech that reinforces or endorses the thin-ideal standard of female beauty; e.g., "I am disgustingly fat") remains common and consistent across age (except beyond 60 years), whereas "old talk" (speech that reinforces or endorses the young-ideal standard of beauty; e.g., "Ugh, I'm getting wrinkles") grows more common with increasing age (Becker, Diedrichs, Jankowski, & Werchan, 2013). Thus, in addition to body size/shape, aging may affect body dissatisfaction in midlife women.

Physical

Weight is often the most salient physical symptom of eating disorders, given that weight is part of the diagnostic criteria for AN. Similar to young adults, midlife patients with AN typically present as significantly underweight, whereas individuals with BN and OSFED typically present as normal weight or overweight and those with BED as overweight or obese (Elran-Barak et al., 2015). Despite the somewhat similar presentation of weight across the eating disorders in younger and older cohorts, there are important changes in weight and body fat distribution with age that must be acknowledged.

In the general population, total body weight and fat distribution changes over time. Weight tends to increase until middle age, stabilize, and then begin to decrease at approximately age 60 years (Sheehan et al., 2003). Furthermore, midlife women have elevated levels of total abdominal and visceral adipose tissue and greater body fat mass and waist circumference compared to younger women (Pascot et al., 1999). In the eating disorder population, similar trends are observed across age for BN, BED, and OSFED. Comparing midlife and younger age groups, Elran-Barak and colleagues (2015) observed a significantly higher BMI in the BED and OSFED midlife groups, as well as a higher BMI approaching significance in the BN midlife group. Interestingly, the BMI of midlife AN patients did not differ from that of younger AN patients, suggesting that individuals at midlife with AN may be engaging in a degree of dietary restriction and compensatory behaviors that combat typical weight trajectories or reflect underlying genetically mediated metabolic components of AN (Bulik-Sullivan et al., 2015; L. Duncan, personal communication, September 2, 2016). This may partially explain the greater eating disorder severity observed in midlife AN inpatients.

Psychiatric Comorbidity

Similar to younger cohorts, psychiatric comorbidity is common in individuals with eating disorders at midlife. Depression and anxiety are often co-occurring, and a lifetime history of one of these disorders seems to be the norm (Andersen &

Ryan, 2009; Scholtz, Hill, & Lacey, 2010). One study conducted in the United Kingdom found that 46% of women aged older than 50 years with eating disorders (mainly AN) had depression at the time of referral to an eating disorder service and that all these individuals had recurrent episodes of depression within the 10-year period following presentation (Scholtz et al., 2010). Other common diagnoses on presentation included anxiety disorders (31%), alcohol dependence (19%), and personality disorders (19%). Currently, it is unclear whether the risk for a comorbid disorder is the same during young adulthood as at midlife.

Medical Comorbidity

Regardless of age, eating disorders can affect cardiac, neurological, pulmonary, gastric, hematological, and dermatological systems. However, midlife women (40+ years) appear to have significantly more medical complications compared to young adult women (18–25 years; Elran-Barak et al., 2015). Specifically, one or more medical comorbidities was reported by 60% of midlife women with AN compared with 10% of young adults, 46% of midlife women with BN compared with 15% of young adults, 83% of midlife women with BED compared with 40% of young adults, and 75.7% of midlife women with OSFED compared with 35.3% of young adults. Thus, it appears that midlife women may be up to six times more likely to experience medical comorbidities compared to their young adult counterparts. Other research confirms a worse medical profile in midlife patients with eating disorders than in youth with these disorders (Forman & Davis, 2005; Scholtz et al., 2010).

Regarding specific medical comorbidities, a clinical record case review and follow-up interview (Scholtz et al., 2010) found that the most common physical comorbidity among women aged 50 years or older with eating disorders was osteoporosis at 38%. This increased to 73% within the decade following presentation to an eating disorder clinic. Other common diagnoses include fertility problems (21%), gastrointestinal problems (17%), infections (17%), iron deficiency anemia (13%), and thyroid illness (13%). Midlife eating disorders may also pose a serious risk for cardiovascular disease, kidney disease, and brain damage (Cohen, 2002).

The medical complications that arise from eating disorder symptoms could be intensified at midlife due to the body's diminished ability to resist and rebound from physical insult in older age or cumulative effects due to chronicity of illness (Fairburn & Harrison, 2003). Alternatively, eating disorder symptoms may further complicate medical conditions that are more common at midlife, such as obesity, cardiac disease, and osteoporosis. Additional research is needed to identify the various factors contributing to a poorer medical profile.

Mortality

Individuals with eating disorders are at increased risk of death secondary to eating disorder complications and suicide (Hewitt, Coren, & Steel, 2001). Older age is associated with an increased mortality rate (Arcelus, Mitchell, Wales, & Nielsen, 2011). A review of published midlife (age >50 years) eating disorder cases found a mortality rate of 21% (Lapid et al., 2010) compared with a mortality rate of 6% in samples with a more traditional age of onset (Chesney, Goodwin, & Fazel, 2014).

Role of Chronology and Course

The presentation of midlife eating disorders appears to vary somewhat as a function of chronology and course. In general, individuals with an early onset chronic disorder present with more entrenched symptoms and impairment in functioning than other presentations (Podfigurna-Stopaa et al., 2015).

EVIDENCE-BASED TREATMENT APPROACHES

Unfortunately, to date, there have been no clinical research trials examining the effectiveness of evidence-based treatment approaches that were developed primarily for younger populations with eating disorders delivered specifically for individuals in midlife. Furthermore, no adult treatment studies have broken their results down by age. However, one randomized controlled trial (McLean, Paxton, & Wertheim, 2011) investigated the efficacy of a facilitated group cognitive–behavior therapy (CBT) program tailored to address body dissatisfaction and disordered eating at midlife in individuals with BMI ≥18.0 by comparing it with a delayed treatment control condition and found the intervention to show promise. The intervention was developed to address importance of appearance, internalization of appearance ideal, self-care, age-specific changes to appearance, body avoidance (e.g., avoiding looking at one's body in the mirror), body comparison behaviors, and acceptance of bodily changes in eight group sessions, each 2 hours in duration (see original article for a detailed session-by-session list of treatment components). Results showed that intervention group participants had significant reductions in body dissatisfaction, weight and shape concerns, body avoidance, appearance comparison, internalization of thin ideal, appearance importance, external eating, and emotional eating while having significant improvements in cognitive reappraisal and self-care (physical and attitudinal) from pre- to post-treatment, with improvements maintained at 6-month follow-up. Significant differences between groups (intervention vs. delayed treatment control group) at post-treatment and follow-up were observed, with the intervention group exhibiting significantly better scores on all measures compared with the control group. These data suggest that transdiagnostic eating disorder treatment approaches may be feasible and effective in reducing eating disorder symptoms at midlife, at least for individuals with a BMI ≥18.0. It is unclear how underweight patients would respond to such interventions because very few were included in the previously described design. Furthermore, the intervention did not appear to reduce levels of dietary restraint.

Despite the lack of evidence for specific treatments in midlife, the presentation and course of eating disorders at midlife for the most part parallel those of eating disorders in young adulthood. Thus, there is strong reason to believe that multi-disciplinary treatments developed in younger populations would be effective in older populations, and we have observed this to be true in various eating disorder clinics. However, it is possible that certain types of treatment may be more effective for a midlife population than for a young adult population. Specific evidence-based treatments for each disorder are reviewed briefly in the following sections. Of note, it has been postulated that the duration and intensity of therapy may need to be doubled in older patients with AN because treatment outcome may be worse in adults with this disorder (Treasure, 2005). Furthermore, the National Institute for Clinical Excellence (NICE) eating disorder practice guidelines recommend the active involvement of families in treatment for adults (NICE, 2004).

Anorexia Nervosa

No specific approach to the treatment of adult AN has demonstrated unequivocal superiority (Galsworthy-Francis & Allan, 2014; Watson & Bulik, 2013). Evidence supports the effectiveness of enhanced cognitive behavior therapy (CBT-E) in the treatment of adult AN (Dalle Grave, El Ghoch, Sartirana, & Calugi, 2016). However, a systematic review of CBT for AN reported that although improvements were observed in outcomes such as eating disorder symptoms, BMI, and general psychopathology, CBT was not reliably superior to other treatments, including specialist supportive clinical management (SSCM; previously termed nonspecific supportive clinical management), interpersonal psychotherapy (IPT), behavioral family therapy, and dietary counseling (Galsworthy-Francis & Allan, 2014). Moreover, outcome was poorer than desired and treatment dropout rate was high at approximately 25% (Berkman et al., 2006), suggesting that few AN patients are accepting of existing individually based treatments.

A case series of the Maudsley Model for treatment of Adults with Anorexia Nervosa (MANTRA; Wade, Treasure, & Schmidt, 2011)—a more novel treatment based on the cognitive–interpersonal maintenance model (Schmidt & Treasure, 2006) that places a primary emphasis on motivational interviewing, normalization of eating, and weight gain—yielded more positive results, but this model has not yet been compared in a randomized controlled trial against other existing treatment modalities. In this study conducted in an Australian sample of AN outpatients, 30% of patients had a "good outcome," defined as obtaining a BMI ≥ 18.5 and a global EDE score ≤ 1 standard deviation from Australian community norms, with 26% remaining in this category at 3- and 12-month follow-up. During the course of treatment, patients experienced a mean BMI gain of 1.8 kg/m^2 and significant reductions in anxiety (but not depression). Dropout was 17.9%, with retention poorer for patients with binge and/or purge symptomatology.

A couple-based intervention, Uniting Couples in the treatment of Anorexia Nervosa (UCAN; Bulik, Baucom, & Kirby, 2012; Bulik, Baucom, Kirby, & Pisetsky,

2011), which was designed as an augmentation to individual therapy, nutritional counseling, and medication management, has shown preliminary promise for improving outcome (Bulik & Baucom, 2012; Baucom et al., 2016). In this treatment, clinicians work with couples to reach joint decisions regarding how to work together toward recovery from AN, with treatment incorporating principles of CBT for AN and cognitive–behavioral couple therapy. Results from an open trial (Baucom et al., 2016) revealed a lower dropout rate of 10% compared to previous clinical trials, suggesting that including partners in treatment may help keep patients in treatment. Furthermore, the open trial reported a substantially greater weight gain (mean BMI increase of 2.9) and higher recovery rate (of 25%) by the end of treatment compared to those of other clinical trials (Berkman et al., 2006; McIntosh et al., 2005; Zipfel et al., 2014). Partners benefited from treatment as well, experiencing reductions in depression and anxiety symptoms during the course of treatment. Furthermore, relationship adjustment improved from pre- to post-treatment. A case report of strategic couple therapy augmenting individual therapy for an adult with AN who previously failed individual treatment only was also encouraging (Murray, 2014). These preliminary data suggest that adding a couple-based component to existing individual-based interventions may improve adult AN treatment outcome.

Given the state of the current literature, a combination of renourishment and psychotherapy such as SSCM, enhanced CBT, or IPT with adjunctive couple or family therapy is likely the best practice approach to treating this pernicious disorder in women at midlife.

Bulimia Nervosa

In contrast to AN, there are empirically supported treatments for BN, including, but not limited to, CBT and IPT. However, compared with other psychological treatments, CBT is generally found to be superior (Hay, Bacaltchuk, Stefano, & Kashyap, 2009; Wilson, Fairburn, Agras, Walsh, & Kraemer, 2002). In a review of the psychological treatments for BN, patients receiving CBT were significantly more likely to be in remission at the end of treatment compared to patients who received any other psychotherapy treatment. CBT for BN in adults is effective in reducing core symptoms, such that it reduces or eliminates binge eating and purging in approximately two-thirds of patients (Hay et al., 2009). IPT may show similar gains in the long term, but CBT generates these gains more rapidly. Similar to AN, clinical trials of BN treatment are plagued by high dropout rates, averaging approximately 24% across treatment modalities (Hay et al., 2009).

The effectiveness of family-based treatments for adolescents with BN (Le Grange, Lock, Agras, Bryson, & Jo, 2015) suggests that incorporating family into the treatment of adult BN may show benefits similar to those observed when the family (i.e., partner) in treatment for AN. One case report of couple-based therapy (as an adjunct to individual CBT) for an adult with BN suggested this approach is feasible (Reyes-Rodriguez, Baucom, & Bulik, 2014). However, no larger studies examining efficacy exist.

Based on the empirical evidence of effective treatments for BN, CBT should likely be the first line of treatment for midlife women with BN (Agras, Walsh, Fairburn, Wilson, & Kraemer, 2000; Hay et al., 2009; Shapiro et al., 2007), and adjunctive family therapy may be considered.

Binge-Eating Disorder

An Agency for Healthcare Quality and Research evidence-based review of the efficacy of BED treatment identified 23 psychological and behavioral studies involving CBT, dialectical behavior therapy (DBT), IPT, psychodynamic interpersonal therapy, behavioral weight loss, and inpatient treatment (Berkman et al., 2015). Of these treatments, investigators only found strong evidence for the efficacy of therapist-led CBT for BED, whereas insufficient data existed to draw definitive conclusions about the efficacy of other CBT variations (e.g., partially therapist led and guided self-help) or other treatment modalities. However, IPT and DBT were described as "promising" treatments. Dropout from BED treatment is less problematic than that from AN or BN treatment, but it may still pose an issue. Across BED trials, dropout rates range from 16% (IPT) to 34% (CBT).

Growing evidence for the efficacy of guided self-help for BED approaches exists, and these approaches offer the potential to reduce dropout rates (Berkman et al., 2015). NICE (2004) guidelines for the treatment of BED recommend that clinicians encourage patients to undergo an evidence-based guided self-help program as a possible first step in treatment. Given that these approaches are less time intensive for both patients and providers, they may better fit the scheduling needs of midlife adults, who often already struggle with balancing their various life demands and role obligations—for example, from work, parenting, partnership, and caring for aging parents. However, whether these treatments can be delivered in "real-world" settings is not yet known; for example, lack of insurance coverage for phone sessions may pose a treatment barrier.

Evidence from a pilot study of a couple-based intervention for BED (including weekly couple therapy and nonspecific individual therapy) suggests this treatment may add value (Runfola, Kirby, Baucom, Baucom, & Bulik, 2016). In a pilot study of nine couples, the therapy program, called UNiting couples In the Treatment of Eating disorders (UNITE)–BED edition, was found to significantly reduce binge-eating episodes and related symptoms to the extent that patient mean scores on an eating disorder assessment were in line with community norms (Mond, Hay, Rodgers, Owen, & Beumont, 2004) by the end of treatment. Specifically, 78% of participants were binge abstinent, defined as having no binge-eating episodes in the 28 days prior to testing, and 67% were in binge remission, defined as no binge-eating episodes in the 3 months prior to testing. In contrast to other behavioral treatments, including CBT (Berkman et al., 2015), patients also experienced a significant reduction in depression symptoms and improvement in their emotion regulation. Partners benefited from the treatment as well, showing significant improvements in their emotion regulation abilities. Importantly, the relationship did not deteriorate, with relationship satisfaction maintained throughout the treatment program. Similar to the UCAN trial, dropout was 10%. Thus, a couple component in treatment may help reduce dropout.

Because the previously discussed study was a pilot, it is not yet clear whether the couple component adds additional benefit to individual therapy. Gorin, Le Grange, and Stone (2003) compared group CBT with group CBT plus spousal involvement and found no statistically significant differences between the two groups, suggesting that spousal involvement in a group setting may not provide additional benefit over and above standard group CBT in the short term. The study did not investigate whether differences existed between groups in the longer term, leaving unanswered the question of whether partner support in treatment reduces relapse. Furthermore, the type of spousal involvement studied in the group program was different from that of the UNITE study, which was not group based and focused more on communication skill building and helping couples become their own therapists over time. Thus, differences in outcomes may exist, especially in the long term, depending on the format of partner support.

Taken together, current evidence points to CBT as a first-line treatment for BED, with guided self-help CBT a potential first step in treatment. IPT and DBT are reasonable alternative treatments, and we await additional evidence regarding whether involving the partner in treatment with UNITE may provide added benefit for reducing dropout and preventing relapse.

Other Special Considerations

Special considerations exist when working with the midlife eating disorder client in treatment. First, clinicians interested in working with midlife patients may find that their caseload differs from that of clinicians working with younger populations. Clinicians who treat adults with eating disorders can expect a higher frequency of BED or OSFED cases in outpatient settings and AN cases in inpatient settings. This diagnostic mix differs from what is experienced in child and adolescent clinics, in which more AN cases present (Ackard et al., 2013; Kally & Cumella, 2008). Presentation for treatment often occurs long after onset in adulthood (Ackard et al., 2013), and research suggests that middle-aged women (aged ≥40 years) have a longer duration of eating disorder illness when presenting for treatment compared to younger women (aged 18–39 years; Ackard et al., 2013). In general, women older than age 50 years often report not feeling heard or having their needs taken seriously by their health care providers (Hofmeier et al., 2017), suggesting previously missed opportunities for prevention and intervention. False-negative findings from eating disorder screening measures developed for youth but used with midlife patients may have sent women home with the belief that "they are just fine" or that their eating disorder is not serious enough to warrant clinical attention. Therapists may need to work with patients to correct these inaccurate thoughts using psychoeducation and cognitive techniques. They can do so by having frank conversations about the seriousness of the disorders and exploring the various personal consequences of living with the disorder. As part of this conversation, patients in midlife should be informed that they are, in fact, more at risk than youth for medical complications and death secondary to the disorder. Furthermore, it is not uncommon to encounter midlife patients with extreme feelings of hurt, anger, or frustration related to such previous interactions with providers for errors in misdiagnosis and subsequent treatment planning. Addressing these feelings early on in treatment may assist with rapport building, corrective therapeutic experiences, and opportunities for patients to practice effective emotion-regulation strategies—for example, by engaging in emotional expressiveness in the room or writing a letter to their previous provider.

On the other hand, midlife patients may present later for treatment due to difficulty with help seeking. They may have been hesitant to disclose eating disorder symptoms due to embarrassment, shame, or fear of judgment resulting from the belief that older individuals do not suffer from these disorders or "should have it all together at this age." They may fear judgment from providers. Therapists can correct such misconceptions early in treatment while providing data on the genetic, biological, and developmental aspects of the disorders to reduce stigma and feelings of shame. Open conversations, countering previous avoidance behavior, will assist patients in working through anxiety related to discussing the disorder with others. Doing so in the room with a therapist may then open up discussions related to expanding the midlife patient's support system by exploring options for discussing symptoms with loved ones who may be well positioned to aid in recovery. Research suggests that adults who have recovered from eating disorders view supportive relationships as one of the main factors in their recovery (Tozzi, Sullivan, Fear, McKenzie, & Bulik, 2003). Thus, it is imperative to help midlife patients foster these relationships with others.

Second, the biological and physical changes that are unique to midlife must be addressed as part of treatment. For example, midlife is when women experience perimenopause and menopause. The average age of menopause in women is 51 years old, with perimenopause occurring during the few years prior to menopause. During perimenopause, estrogen levels decline in an erratic manner, whereas during menopause estrogen levels remain quite low and stable. It has been empirically established that estrogen plays a role in normal food intake and that there is an association between decreasing estrogen and eating disorder symptoms (Baker, Girdler, & Bulik, 2012). Thus, it stands to reason that eating behaviors may become more chaotic during perimenopause, which may play a role in the exacerbation of symptomatology. The clinician working with the midlife population needs to have an understanding of the empirical associations observed between changing estrogen and eating disorder symptoms. In treatment, the clinician should provide psychoeducation to the patient about the association between changing hormone levels and eating disorder symptoms. The clinician should also teach coping skills and relapse prevention strategies for managing the possible triggering effect of changing hormones. Referral to a gerontologist, who is specialized in the field of aging (including the social, psychological, cognitive, and biological aspects of aging), for consultation should be considered.

In collaboration with other multidisciplinary team members, gerontologists may assist with setting weight gain goals for older patients with AN and realistic weight expectations for those with BN, BED, and OSFED. As mentioned previously, most women experience an increase in BMI and weight distribution changes over the life span. These typical developmental physical changes likely account for the fact that midlife women with eating disorders (other than AN) present with higher BMIs compared to young adults. The higher BMIs may also be due to long-standing eating disorder symptoms, namely chaotic dieting and binge-eating-related behavior that lead to weight gain over time (Goldschmidt et al., 2011; Masheb, Grilo, & White, 2011). Clinicians treating eating disorders across the life span are challenged to adapt weight goals and interventions to deal appropriately with the evolving clinical presentations in weight.

Clinicians also need to be attuned to the fact that an increased deviation of the body from what culture and society emphasize as "ideal" may further increase body dissatisfaction and place added pressure to engage in unhealthy behaviors to conform to this ideal for midlife women. Relatedly, midlife women also experience aging-related physical changes, such as sagging skin, loss of muscle mass, and an increase in wrinkles, that may contribute to body dissatisfaction. It is important for the clinician to address these unique age-related concerns in treatment. A specific treatment addressing cultural thin-ideal internalization and age-related concerns for midlife populations was developed by McLean et al. (2011), as discussed previously. In general, clinicians can manage these factors in the same manner as they would for younger cohorts. This can include providing psychoeducation about the typical weight trajectory and physical changes that occur with age, discussion of the sociocultural factors influencing body image, teaching skills to challenge negative thoughts around these changes, and working with the patient to accept the changes that occur with age.

To ensure a comforting and inviting environment conducive to open, honest discussion about any challenges related to body image or aging, clinicians treating midlife eating disorders may also benefit from attending to their clinic environment and resources. Women report being discouraged by the lack of products and services tailored for older women (Hofmeier et al., 2017; Liechty, 2012; Yarnal, Son, & Liechty, 2011); thus, clinicians may consider tailoring resources to midlife patients. For example, visible brochures, pictures, and magazines featuring "real-life" (nondoctored) older women with observable signs of aging (i.e., wrinkles and aging skin) may help patients recognize that they are not alone with this disease and may normalize aspects of aging experienced as distressing in these older women. Furthermore, messages that focus on health, not appearance, may subtly help promote thinking patterns and behavior associated with body satisfaction in women at midlife (Runfola et al., 2013).

However, most midlife adults with BED and comorbid obesity have a strong desire to lose weight at presentation to treatment. Explicit discussion regarding typical weight outcomes is important when first discussing treatment options with midlife adults. Prospective patients can be informed that CBT, IPT, and DBT have been found to effectively reduce binge eating but not weight, whereas behavioral weight loss approaches have been found to effectively reduce weight but not binge eating (Berkman et al., 2015; Grilo, Masheb, Wilson, Geueorguieva, & White, 2011). Individuals should be made aware of the likelihood of long-term weight regain following behavioral weight loss intervention (McElroy, Guerdjikova, Mori, Munoz, & Keck, 2015) and that they would ideally benefit from control over symptoms prior to undergoing specific weight management attempts (e.g., bariatric surgery).

Third, the midlife population experiences unique psychosocial stressors that may serve to trigger, worsen, or maintain an eating disorder, and these must be addressed in treatment. As discussed previously, many of these life events relate to grief, loss, medical events, and interpersonal stressors. We have also seen in our clinic apparent associations between the stereotypical "midlife crisis" and the questioning of the meaning, purpose, and value of life. First and foremost, the clinician must conduct a thorough assessment to evaluate for the presence of these associated psychosocial stressors and modify treatment accordingly. For example, we have seen benefit of acceptance and commitment therapy, with a focus on values and living in accordance with one's values, in reducing eating disorder symptoms for clients reporting an existential crisis. Also, although CBT generally shows the most evidence of treatment effectiveness for the eating disorders, IPT, or its core concepts, may prove more effective for midlife women who have experienced grief, loss, or a disruption in relationships. Similarly, for individuals in committed relationships, adjunctive couple-based treatment has seemed to help midlife clients in their recovery. As previously described, we have observed value in incorporating partners into treatment with a focus on enhancing understanding of the disorder via psychoeducation, reducing secrecy and shame while building back trust in the relationship by talking openly about each partner's experience of its symptoms and co-occurring features, and targeting unhelpful communication patterns (e.g., mutual avoidance and pursuer–withdrawer patterns) or behaviors (e.g., partner food policing behavior) while collaboratively building effective ways for the couple to work together as a team in recovery.

Fourth, dropout is an issue in eating disorders treatment, and research suggests this may be especially a problem with midlife populations. According to a longitudinal retrospective study examining patterns in eating disorder outpatient mental health treatment by age in 5,445 patients who were treated for an eating disorder covered by Cigna health care insurance provider (Ballard & Crane, 2015), individuals aged 55 years or older had the highest dropout rate (28.0%) of any age group and the lowest return to care rate (19.5%). Preliminary data suggest couple-based interventions may reduce dropout from treatment while also boosting remission rates. It is yet to be determined whether some benefit might also result from incorporating partners into treatment in a more restricted manner (e.g., brief psychoeducational sessions) or whether involving other loved ones (e.g., parents, siblings, or children) in treatment may assist with improving outcome as well. In the absence of data, clinicians should use their clinical judgment when considering inclusion of family members.

Finally, because of the physical and medical changes that occur during mid-life, a referral to a physician for medical evaluation and monitoring and to a psychiatrist to discuss potential medication options and whether these would be appropriate for patients in this age group is warranted. Ideally, these providers would have expertise in geriatrics. Note that although some medications have been proven effective in the treatment of adult eating disorders, no studies have focused specifically on the midlife population.

CONCLUSION AND FUTURE DIRECTIONS

Midlife eating disorders are real. Research is woefully inadequate to document the frequency with which they occur and how they differ from presentations earlier in life. Eating disorders in men in midlife have been practically ignored. Epidemiological evidence is required to document the prevalence of these illnesses across age, sex, sexual orientation, and sexual identities. We cannot assume automatic generalizability from research on younger populations to older populations. Research on mid- and late-life eating disorders must consider the eating disturbances within the developmental context of the individuals under study. Similarly, treatment must address the impact of mid- and late-life eating disorders on the individual and his or her family because responsibilities (e.g., those involving work, children, and aging parents) may serve as very different triggering and maintaining factors than those seen in youth. Most important, preconceived and erroneous notions of eating disorders being constrained to youth need to be dispelled to support individuals who are suffering from eating disorders later in life and also to reduce stigma and barriers to seeking appropriate care.

RESOURCES

The following are recommended reading for providers, patients, and family members:

Bulik, C. (2013). *Midlife eating disorders: Your journey to recovery.*
    New York, NY: Walker.
Maine, M., & Kelly, J. (2016). *Pursuing perfection: Eating disorders, body
    myths and women at midlife and beyond.* New York, NY: Routledge.

Professional organizations that have blogged about midlife eating disorders include the following:

Eating Disorder Hope: https://www.eatingdisorderhope.com
National Eating Disorders Association: https://www.nationaleatingdisorders.org
Psychology Today: https://www.psychologytoday.com/blog/
    midlife-eating-disorders

Various Twitter chats hosted by the Academy for Eating Disorders (AED) on topics pertinent to midlife eating disorders are freely downloadable on the Internet from the AED website as well (http://www.aedweb.org/index.php/education/education-chats). Providers may wish to inform their patients of these existing resources for additional information and support.

REFERENCES

Ackard, D. M., Richter, S., Frisch, M. J., Mangham, D., & Cronemeyer, C. L. (2013). Eating disorder treatment among women forty and older: Increases in prevalence over time and comparisons to young adult patients. *Journal of Psychosomatic Research, 74,* 175–178.

Agras, W. S., Walsh, T., Fairburn, C. G., Wilson, G. T., & Kraemer, H. C. (2000). A multicenter comparison of cognitive–behavioral therapy and interpersonal psychotherapy for bulimia nervosa. *Archives of General Psychiatry, 57,* 459–466.

American Psychiatric Association. (2000). *Diagnostic and statistical manual of mental disorders* (4th ed., text rev.). Washington, DC: Author.

American Psychiatric Association. (2013). *Diagnostic and statistical manual of mental disorders* (5th ed.). Arlington, VA: American Psychiatric Publishing.

Andersen, A. E., & Ryan, G. L. (2009). Eating disorders in the obstetric and gynecologic patient population. *Obstetrics & Gynecology, 114,* 1353–1367.

Arcelus, J., Haslam, M., Farrow, C., & Meyer, C. (2013). The role of interpersonal functioning in the maintenance of eating psychopathology: A systematic review and testable model. *Clinical Psychology Review, 33,* 156–167.

Arcelus, J., Mitchell, A. J., Wales, J., & Nielsen, S. (2011). Mortality rates in patients with anorexia nervosa and other eating disorders. *Archives of General Psychiatry, 68,* 724–731.

Baker, J. H., Girdler, S. S., & Bulik, C. M. (2012). The role of reproductive hormones in the development and maintenance of eating disorders. *Expert Review Obstetrics & Gynecology, 7,* 573–583.

Baker, J. H., & Runfola, C. D. (2016). Eating disorders in midlife women: A perimenopausal eating disorder? *Maturitas, 85,* 112–116.

Ballard, J., & Crane, D. R. (2015). Eating disorders treatment patterns by age. *Eating Disorders, 23,* 262–274.

Baucom, D. H., Kirby, J. S., Fischer, M. S., Baucom, B., Hamer, R. M., & Bulik, C. M. (2017). Findings from a couple-based open trial for adult anorexia nervosa. *Journal of Family Psychology,* Epub ahead of print.

Becker, C. B., Diedrichs, P. C., Jankowski, G., & Werchan, C. (2013). I'm not just fat, I'm old: Has the study of body image overlooked "old talk"? *Journal of Eating Disorders, 1,* 6.

Berkman, N. D., Brownley, K. A., Peat, C. M., Lohr, K. N., Cullen, K. E., Morgan, L. C., . . . Bulik, C. M. (2015). AHRQ comparative effectiveness reviews. In *Management and outcomes of binge-eating disorder.* Rockville, MD: Agency for Healthcare Research and Quality.

Berkman, N. D., Bulik, C. M., Brownley, K. A., Lohr, K. N., Sedway, J. A., Rooks, A., & Gartiehner, G. (2006). *Management of eating disorders.* Evidence Report/Technology

Assessment No. 135. Prepared by the RTI International–University of North Carolina Evidence-Based Practice Center under Contract No. 290-02-0016. Rockville, MD: Agency for Research and Quality.

Bulik, C. M., & Baucom, D. H. (2012). *Uniting Couples (in the treatment of) Anorexia Nervosa (UCAN).* Workshop presentation, International Conference on Eating Disorders, Austin, TX, May 3–5.

Bulik, C. M., Baucom, D. H., & Kirby, J. S. (2012). Treating anorexia nervosa in the couple context. *Journal of Cognitive Psychotherapy, 26,* 19–33.

Bulik, C. M., Baucom, D. H., Kirby, J. S., & Pisetsky, E. (2011). Uniting Couples (in the treatment of) Anorexia Nervosa (UCAN). *International Journal of Eating Disorders, 44,* 19–28.

Bulik-Sullivan, B., Finucane, H. K., Anttila, V., Gusev, A., Day, F. R., Loh, P. R., . . . Neale, B. M. (2015). An atlas of genetic correlations across human diseases and traits. *Nature Genetics, 47,* 1236–1241.

Chesney, E., Goodwin, G. M., & Fazel, S. (2014). Risks of all-cause and suicide mortality in mental disorders: A meta-review. *World Psychiatry, 13,* 153–160.

Cohen, D. (2002). The challenges of eating disorders in later life. *Journal of Mental Health and Aging, 8,* 91–94.

Coker, E. L., Mitchell-Wong, L. A., & Abraham, S. F. (2013). Is pregnancy a trigger for recovery from an eating disorder? *Acta Obstetricia Gynecologica Scandinavica, 92,* 1407–1413.

Culbert, K. M., Racine, S. E., & Klump, K. L. (2015). Research review: What we have learned about the causes of eating disorders—A synthesis of sociocultural, psychological, and biological research. *Journal of Child Psychology and Psychiatry, 56,* 1141–1164.

Cumella, E. J., & Kally, Z. (2008). Comparison of middle-age and young women inpatients with eating disorders. *Eating and Weight Disorders, 13,* 183–190.

Dalle Grave, R., El Ghoch, M., Sartirana, M., & Calugi, S. (2016). Cognitive behavioral therapy for anorexia nervosa: An update. *Current Psychiatry Reports, 18,* 2.

Drobnjak, S., Atsiz, S., Ditzen, B., Tuschen-Caffier, B., & Ehlert, U. (2014). Restrained eating and self-esteem in premenopausal and postmenopausal women. *Journal of Eating Disorders, 2,* 23.

Elran-Barak, R., Fitzsimmons-Craft, E. E., Benyamini, Y., Crow, S. J., Peterson, C. B., Hill, L. L., . . . Le Grange, D. (2015). Anorexia nervosa, bulimia nervosa, and binge eating disorder in midlife and beyond. *Journal of Nervous and Mental Disease, 203,* 583–590.

Fairburn, C. G., & Harrison, P. J. (2003). Eating disorders. *Lancet, 361,* 407–416.

Forman, M., & Davis, W. N. (2005). Characteristics of middle-aged women in inpatient treatment for eating disorders. *Eating Disorders, 13,* 231–243.

Gagne, D. A., Von Holle, A., Brownley, K. A., Runfola, C. D., Hofmeier, S. M., Branch, K. E., & Bulik, C. M. (2012). Eating disorder symptoms and weight and shape concerns in a large web-based convenience sample of women ages 50 and above: Results of the Gender and Body Image (GABI) study. *International Journal of Eating Disorders, 45,* 832–844.

Galsworthy-Francis, L., & Allan, S. (2014). Cognitive behavioural therapy for anorexia nervosa: A systematic review. *Clinical Psychology Review, 34,* 54–72.

Goldschmidt, A. B., Le Grange, D., Powers, P., Crow, S. J., Hill, L. L., Peterson, C. B., . . . Mitchell, J. E. (2011). Eating disorder symptomatology in normal-weight vs. obese individuals with binge eating disorder. *Obesity (Silver Spring), 19,* 1515–1518.

Gonidakis, F., Georgantopoulos, G., Konstantakopoulos, G., & Varsou, E. (2014). Late onset anorexia nervosa and the role of parental family: Presentation of two cases. *Eating and Weight Disorders, 19,* 409–412.

Gorin, A. A., Le Grange, D., & Stone, A. A. (2003). Effectiveness of spouse involvement in cognitive behavioral therapy for binge eating disorder. *International Journal of Eating Disorders, 33,* 421–433.

Grilo, C. M. (2002). Binge eating disorder. In C. G. Fairburn & K. D. Brownell (Eds.), *Eating disorders and obesity: A comprehensive handbook* (2nd ed., pp. 178–182). New York, NY: Guilford.

Grilo, C. M., Masheb, R., Wilson, G., Geueorguieva, R., & White, M. (2011). Cognitive–behavioral therapy, behavioral weight loss, and sequential treatment for obese patients with binge-eating disorder: A randomized controlled trial. *Journal of Consulting and Clinical Psychology, 79,* 675–685.

Hay, P. P., Bacaltchuk, J., Stefano, S., & Kashyap, P. (2009). Psychological treatments for bulimia nervosa and binging. *Cochrane Database of Systematic Reviews, 2009*(4), CD000562.

Hewitt, P. L., Coren, S., & Steel, G. D. (2001). Death from anorexia nervosa: Age span and sex differences. *Aging and Mental Health, 5,* 246–248.

Hilbert, A., de Zwaan, M., & Braehler, E. (2012). How frequent are eating disturbances in the population? Norms of the eating disorder examination-questionnaire. *PLoS One, 7,* e29125.

Hofmeier, S. M., Runfola, C. D., Sala, M., Gagne, D. A., Brownley, K. A., & Bulik, C. M. (2017). Body image, aging, and identity in women over 50: The Gender and Body Image (GABI) study. *Journal of Women and Aging, 29,* 3–14.

Kally, Z., & Cumella, E. J. (2008). 100 midlife women with eating disorders: A phenomenological analysis of etiology. *Journal of General Psychology, 135,* 359–377.

Keel, P. K., Gravener, J. A., Joiner, T. E. J., & Haedt, A. A. (2010). Twenty-year follow-up of bulimia nervosa and related eating disorders not otherwise specified. *International Journal of Eating Disorders, 43,* 492–497.

Klump, K. L. (2013). Puberty as a critical risk period for eating disorders: A review of human and animal studies. *Hormones and Behavior, 64,* 399–410.

Lapid, M. I., Prom, M. C., Burton, M. C., McAlpine, D. E., Sutor, B., & Rumans, T. A. (2010). Eating disorders in the elderly. *International Psychogeriatrics, 22,* 523–536.

Le Grange, D., Lock, J., Agras, W. S., Bryson, S. W., & Jo, B. (2015). Randomized clinical trial of family-based treatment and cognitive–behavioral therapy for adolescent bulimia nervosa. *Journal of the American Academy of Child and Adolescent Psychiatry, 54,* 886–894.

Liechty, T. (2012). "Yes, I worry about my weight . . . but for the most part I'm content with my body": Older women's body dissatisfaction alongside contentment. *Journal of Women & Aging, 24,* 70–88.

Mangweth-Matzek, B., Hoek, H. W., Rupp, C. I., Kemmler, G., Pope, H. G., Jr., & Kinzl, J. (2013). The menopausal transition—A possible window of vulnerability for eating pathology. *International Journal of Eating Disorders, 46,* 609–616.

Mangweth-Matzek, B., Hoek, H. W., Rupp, C. I., Lackner-Sifert, K., Frey, N., Whitworth, A. B., . . . Kinzl, J. (2014). Prevalence of eating disorders in middle-aged women. *International Journal of Eating Disorders, 47,* 320–324.

Mangweth-Matzek, B., Hoek, H. W., Rupp, C. I., Lackner-Sifert, K., Frey, N., Whitworth, A. B., . . . Kinzl, J. (2016). Eating disorder symptoms in middle-aged and older men. *International Journal of Eating Disorders, 49*(10), 953–957.

Marcus, M. D., Bromberger, J. T., Wei, H. L., Brown, C., & Kravitz, H. M. (2007). Prevalence and selected correlates of eating disorder symptoms among a multiethnic community sample of midlife women. *Annals of Behavioral Medicine, 33*(3), 269–277.

Masheb, R. M., Grilo, C. M., & White, M. A. (2011). An examination of eating patterns in community women with bulimia nervosa and binge eating disorder. *International Journal of Eating Disorders, 44*(7), 618–624.

McCormack, L., Lewis, V., & Wells, J. R. (2014). Early life loss and trauma: Eating disorder onset in a middle-aged male—A case study. *American Journal of Men's Health, 8*, 121–136.

McElroy, S. L., Guerdjikova, A. I., Mori, N., Munoz, M. R., & Keck, P. E. (2015). Overview of the treatment of binge eating disorder. *CNS Spectrums, 20*, 546–556.

McIntosh, V. V., Jordan, J., Carter, F. A., Luty, S. E., McKenzie, J. M., Bulik, C. M., . . . Joyce, P. R. (2005). Three psychotherapies for anorexia nervosa: A randomized, controlled trial. *American Journal of Psychiatry, 162*, 741–747.

McLean, S. A., Paxton, S. J., & Wertheim, E. H. (2011). A body image and disordered eating intervention for women in midlife: A randomized controlled trial. *Journal of Consulting and Clinical Psychology, 79*, 751–758.

Mond, J. M., Hay, P. J., Rodgers, B., Owen, C., & Beumont, P. J. (2004). Validity of the Eating Disorder Examination Questionnaire (EDE-Q) in screening for eating disorders in community samples. *Behaviour Research and Therapy, 42*, 551–567.

Murray, S. B. (2014). A case of strategic couples therapy in adult anorexia nervosa: The importance of systems in context. *Contemporary Family Therapy, 36*, 392–397.

National Institute for Clinical Excellence. (2004). *National clinical practice guideline: Eating disorders—Core interventions in the treatment and management of anorexia nervosa, bulimia nervosa, and related eating disorders.* London, England: Author.

Pascot, A., Lemieux, S., Lemieux, I., Prud'homme, D., Tremblay, A., Bouchard, C., . . . Despres, J. P. (1999). Age-related increase in visceral adipose tissue and body fat and the metabolic risk profile of premenopausal women. *Diabetes Care, 22*, 1471–1478.

Peat, C. M., Peyerl, N. L., & Muehlenkamp, J. J. (2008). Body image and eating disorders in older adults: A review. *Journal of General Psychology, 135*(4), 343–358.

Podfigurna-Stopaa, A., Czyzyka, A., Katulskia, K., Smolarczykb, R., Grymowiczb, M., Maciejewska-Jeskea, M., & Meczekalskia, B. (2015). Eating disorders in older women. *Maturitas, 82*, 146–152.

Preti, A., de Girolamo, G., Vilagut, G., Alonso, J., de Graaf, R., Bruffaerts, R., . . . Morosini, P.; ESEMeD-WMH Investigators. (2009). The epidemiology of eating disorders in six European countries: Results of the ESEMeD-WMH project. *Journal of Psychiatric Research, 43*, 1125–1132.

Reyes-Rodriguez, M. L., Baucom, D. H., & Bulik, C. M. (2014). Culturally sensitive intervention for Latina women with eating disorders: A case study. *Revista Mexicana de Trastornos Alimentarios, 5*, 136–146.

Runfola, C. D., Kirby, J. S., Baucom, B. R., Baucom, B., & Bulik, C. M. (2016). *Pilot study of a novel couple-based intervention for binge-eating disorder: UNITE.* Paper presented at the International Conference on Eating Disorders, San Francisco, CA, May 5–7.

Runfola, C. D., Von Holle, A., Peat, C. M., Gagne, D. A., Brownley, K. A., Hofmeier, S. M., & Bulik, C. M. (2013). Characteristics of women with body size satisfaction at midlife: Results of the Gender and Body Image (GABI) study. *Journal of Women and Aging, 25*(4), 287–304.

Runfola, C. D., Von Holle, A., Trace, S. E., Brownley, K. A., Hofmeier, S. M., Gagne, D. A., & Bulik, C. M. (2013). Body dissatisfaction in women across the lifespan: Results of the UNC-SELF and Gender and Body Image (GABI) studies. *European Eating Disorders Review, 21,* 52–59.

Schmidt, U., & Treasure, J. (2006). Anorexia nervosa: Valued and visible—A cognitive–interpersonal maintenance model and its implications for research and practice. *British Journal of Clinical Psychology, 45*(Pt. 3), 343–366.

Scholtz, S., Hill, L. S., & Lacey, H. (2010). Eating disorders in older women: Does late onset anorexia nervosa exist? *International Journal of Eating Disorders, 43,* 393–397.

Shapiro, J. R., Berkman, N. D., Brownley, K. A., Sedway, J. A., Lohr, K. N., & Bulik, C. M. (2007). Bulimia nervosa treatment: A systematic review of randomized controlled trials. *International Journal of Eating Disorders, 45*(Pt. 3), 343–366.

Sheehan, T. J., DuBrava, S., DeChello, L. M., & Fang, Z. (2003). Rates of weight change for Black and White Americans over a twenty year period. *International Journal of Obesity, 27,* 498–504.

Slevec, J. H., & Tiggemann, M. (2011). Predictors of body dissatisfaction and disordered eating in middle-aged women. *Clinical Psychology Review, 31,* 515–524.

Striegel-Moore, R. H., Dohm, F. A., Wilfley, D. E., Pike, K. M., Bray, N. L., Kraemer, H. C., & Fairburn, C. G. (2004). Toward an understanding of health services use in women with binge eating disorder. *Obesity Research, 12*(5), 799–806.

Tozzi, F., Sullivan, P. F., Fear, J. L., McKenzie, J., & Bulik, C. M. (2003). Causes and recovery in anorexia nervosa: The patient's perspective. *International Journal of Eating Disorders, 33,* 143–154.

Trace, S. E., Baker, J. H., Penas-Lledo, E., & Bulik, C. M. (2013). The genetics of eating disorders. *Annual Review of Clinical Psychology, 9,* 589–620.

Treasure, J. (2005). Treatment of anorexia nervosa in adults. *Psychiatry, 4,* 10–13.

Wade, T. D., Treasure, J., & Schmidt, U. (2011). A case series evaluation of the Maudsley model for treatment of adults with anorexia nervosa. *European Eating Disorders Review, 19,* 382–389.

Wasylkiw, L., Emms, A. A., Meuse, R., & Poirier, K. F. (2009). Are all models created equal? A content analysis of women in advertisements of fitness versus fashion magazines. *Body Image, 6,* 137–140.

Watson, H. J., & Bulik, C. M. (2013). Update on the treatment of anorexia nervosa: Review of clinical trials, practice guidelines and emerging interventions. *Psychological Medicine, 43,* 2477–2500.

Wilson, G. T., Fairburn, C. C., Agras, W. S., Walsh, B. T., & Kraemer, H. (2002). Cognitive–behavioral therapy for bulimia nervosa: Time course and mechanisms of change. *Journal of Consulting and Clinical Psychology, 70,* 267–274.

Yarnal, C., Son, J., & Liechty, T. (2011). "She was buried in her purple dress and her red hat and all of our members wore full 'Red Hat Regalia' to celebrate her life": Dress, embodiment and older women's leisure: Reconfiguring the ageing process. *Journal of Aging Studies, 25,* 52–61.

Zipfel, S., Wild, B., Gross, G., Friederich, H. C., Teufel, M., Schellberg, D., . . . Herzog, W. (2014). Focal psychodynamic therapy, cognitive behaviour therapy, and optimised treatment as usual in outpatients with anorexia nervosa (ANTOP study): Randomised controlled trial. *Lancet, 383*(9912), 127–137.

22

Eating Disorders in Athletes

Detection, Diagnosis, and Treatment

CAROLYN R. PLATEAU AND JON ARCELUS ■

Sportsmen/women and dancers possess a distinct combination of physical and psychological attributes that can contribute toward their success within their sporting and dance context. This includes qualities such as physical and psychological resilience, an unyielding commitment to exercise, the continuous pursuit of excellence, and the ability to withstand intense physical exertion. However, because close attention to diet and weight control is very important in some sports and dance modalities, athletes are also at a significantly increased risk of developing an eating disorder. This chapter presents an overview of the current evidence on the presentation, prevalence, risk factors, and treatment strategies for eating disorders among athletes.

PRESENTATION OF EATING DISORDERS AMONG ATHLETES

The fifth edition of the *Diagnostic and Statistical Manual of Mental Disorders* (DSM-5; American Psychiatric Association [APA], 2013) classification system for diagnosing eating disorders is applicable and widely utilized with the athletic population. However, differentiating between normal eating behaviors and disordered eating practices among athletes and dancers does present some challenges. Athletic eating behavior is often characterized by close attention to diet and weight, which may involve restrictions on some food groups and the quantity of food consumed, in view of attaining optimal sporting performance (Currie & Morse, 2005). Concerns may therefore emerge when these behaviors are no longer performance directed, self-evaluation becomes centered on weight and shape, and intake fails to normalize outside of the sporting context.

In recognition of the unique nature of the athletic population, researchers have proposed a variety of alternative terms and classifications in order to identify athletes at risk of a potential eating disorder, including *anorexia athletica*, the *female athlete triad*, and *relative energy deficiency in sport*. These athlete-specific eating disorders and related conditions are not recognized within either the DSM-5 or the *International Statistical Classification of Diseases and Related Health Problems—10th Revision* (ICD-10; World Health Organization, 2010) criteria for eating and feeding disorders. However, these terms are commonly referred to within the sport literature to describe the key presenting features of eating disorders among athlete groups.

Anorexia Athletica

The features of anorexia athletica (AA) are broadly similar to those of anorexia nervosa (AN), with an extreme fear of weight gain and distorted perceptions of body weight and shape central to the condition. Weight loss in AA is usually accomplished through excessive amounts of physical activity in addition to a normal training regime. The criteria for AA also proposes that athletes who weigh just 5% less than expected could be at an increased risk of an eating disorder, due to increase muscle mass and decreased fat mass. However, the definition of AA has become largely redundant in recent years due to the removal of the weight status criterion from the diagnostic classification for AN in the DSM-5 (APA, 2013) and an increased understanding and recognition of the causal and maintenance role for exercise within the eating disorders (Meyer, Taranis, & Touyz, 2008; Mond, Hay, Rodgers, & Owen, 2006; Shroff et al., 2006).

The Female Athlete Triad

The female athlete triad (FAT) refers to the interrelationship between bone mineral density, menstrual function, and energy availability among exercising females (Nattiv et al., 2007). Low energy availability can result in changes to menstrual function and reduced bone mineral density. Insufficient energy availability can be a result of a clinical or subclinical eating disorder, but it may also occur in individuals with inadvertent low energy intake and without distorted perceptions of their body image. Prevalence estimates of FAT range from 1.2% to 16% of female athletes who display all three elements of the triad; however, cross-sectional studies lack validity due to the temporal delay between the etiological factor of low energy availability with menstrual dysfunction and lowered bone density, and few prospective studies have been conducted (Nattiv et al., 2007). In addition, objectively measuring energy availability is challenging; hence, proxy measures of disordered eating attitudes and behaviors are often utilized as a substitute, which may underestimate the prevalence of the triad (Loucks, Kiens, & Wright, 2011). However, symptoms of menstrual dysfunction and a history of bone injuries, such as stress fractures in female athletes, may suggest the existence of FAT and may require further investigation into the eating attitudes and behaviors of these athletes.

Relative Energy Deficiency in Sport

The International Olympic Committee has recently revised the terminology around the female athlete triad to address the wider implications of energy deficiency on athlete psychological and physical health and also to incorporate some of the recent evidence concerning male athletes (Mountjoy et al., 2014). The term *relative energy deficiency in sport* (RED-S) has been proposed to recognize individual differences in energy availability thresholds and the impact of low energy availability on bodily functions, including immune function, psychological well-being, and cardiovascular and gastrointestinal function. However, the broad and sometimes subtle nature of RED-S means that screening and diagnosis is challenging, and a high index of suspicion is needed. The guidelines promote utilizing screening tools for eating disorders as one method of identifying athletes at potential risk of RED-S (Mountjoy et al., 2014). Importantly, there is evidence that low energy availability and specifically eating disorders are associated with reduced athletic performance (El Ghoch, Soave, Calugi, & Dalle Grave, 2013). Therefore, athletes presenting with reduced responsiveness to training (e.g., decreases in endurance and decreased muscle strength), regular incidences of illness and injuries, poor concentration and coordination, and/or negative affect may require further investigation with regard to a potential eating disorder.

Compulsive Exercise

The link between exercise attitudes and behaviors and eating psychopathology has been the focus of much recent research. Activity levels often increase prior to onset and during the acute phase of an eating disorder, highlighting a potential etiological and maintenance role for exercise. Among eating disorder patients, exercise is associated with increased likelihood of relapse and longer treatment times, potentially indicating a more severe eating disorder. Initial conceptualizations of exercise in the eating disorders posited it purely as a mechanism for weight control and calorie wasting. However, the evidence now suggests that the role of exercise in the development and maintenance of eating disorders is more complex. A relatively recently developed cognitive–behavioral model of compulsive exercise identifies the causal and maintenance role of exercise within the eating disorders (Meyer, Taranis, Goodwin, & Haycraft, 2011). As well as exercising for weight control, the model recognizes additional cognitive–behavioral elements that may also serve to maintain eating psychopathology, including compulsivity (feelings of guilt when unable to exercise and exercising despite illness or injury) and rigid exercise behaviors. The model also encapsulates the mood-regulatory function of exercise, particularly with regard to the avoidance of negative emotions of low mood or anxiety.

This model has recently been explored among the athletic population (Plateau et al., 2014), highlighting that exercise motivations to avoid negative mood and for weight control were strongly associated with athlete eating psychopathology. Longitudinal studies exploring exercise attitudes in athletes are yet to emerge. Athletes who display features of compulsive exercise may require further investigation into their eating attitudes and behaviors. New screening tools have been developed specifically for this population (Plateau et al., 2014; Appendix 22.1) in order to assess the compulsivity of exercise in athletes, including its relationship with eating behaviors.

Comorbid Conditions

Limited data currently exist regarding the prevalence of comorbid mental health and other medical conditions among athletes with eating disorders. Competitors in aesthetic sports (e.g., gymnastics) have been found to present with the highest incidence of mental health issues, including eating disorders and anxiety disorders (Schaal et al., 2011). A study involving British athletes indicated that those who displayed eating disorder symptoms at baseline were more likely to also present with depression at a follow-up 6 months later (Shanmugam, Jowett, & Meyer, 2014). Cardiac complications are also common among patients with eating disorders, and participation in vigorous sporting activity may intensify the likelihood of these occurring. Similarly, there are suggestions that athletes with eating disorders may be more at risk of developing orthopedic problems, although this has yet to be fully explored.

Clinicians should therefore consider and assess athletes and dancers for other potential comorbid physical and mental health issues, which may maintain their eating disorders. Further research is needed to explore the co-occurrence of other medical conditions among athletes with eating disorders, such as type 1 diabetes and gastrointestinal conditions including celiac disease, lactose intolerance, and delayed gastric emptying (Joy, Kussman, & Nattiv, 2016).

PREVALENCE OF EATING DISORDERS AMONG ATHLETES

A considerable volume of research has attempted to (1) establish whether an increased prevalence of eating disorders exists among athletes and dancers and (2) identify the groups of athletes who are at the most risk of developing an eating disorder.

Prevalence Statistics

To address the first issue, it is noted that the prevalence estimates of eating disorders in athletes vary considerably, ranging from 1% to 46%. Two meta-analysis studies of sports conducted 10 years apart (Coelho, Soares, & Ribeiro, 2010; Smolak, Murnen, & Ruble, 2000) both concluded that due to the heterogeneity of studies and lack of longitudinal evidence, definitive conclusions regarding the prevalence of eating disorders in athletes could not yet be drawn. The studies tentatively suggest a small overall increased risk for athletes compared to non-athletes for eating disorders and disordered eating, although sports participation can be protective in some scenarios, particularly among participants in non-elite, non-lean sports. A recent meta-analysis that specifically examined dancers found that the overall meta-analytical prevalence of eating disorders among dancers was 12.0% (16.4% for ballet dancers); it was 2.0% (4% for ballet dancers) for anorexia, 4.4% (2% for ballet dancers) for bulimia, and 9.5% (14.9% for ballet dancers) for other eating disorders not otherwise specified (EDNOS) (Arcelus, Witcomb, & Mitchell, 2014).

The main limitation of the majority of studies aiming to identify prevalence rates of eating disorders is the use of self-report questionnaires. It is acknowledged that studies that use a clinical interview to determine the prevalence of eating disorders in athletes are likely to be the most reliable with regard to assessing the prevalence of eating disorders in athletes. The most stringent study to date exploring the prevalence of eating disorders in athletes was conducted with the Norwegian elite athlete population (Sundgot-Borgen & Torstveit, 2004). This study revealed that 20% of female elite athletes (compared to 9% of female control participants) and 8% of male elite athletes (compared to 0.5% of male controls) fulfilled diagnostic criteria for a clinical eating disorder, pointing to a significantly increased prevalence of eating disorders among the athlete population. In line with the general population, female athletes seem to be more vulnerable than male athletes. There have been few studies beyond those conducted by Sundgot-Borgen and Torstveit that have adopted a similarly rigorous exploration of prevalence rates among athletes, which makes it difficult to generalize their findings to other countries. In addition, it is noted that the focus in the literature has been on point prevalence studies, with longitudinal studies still rare within the field. Longitudinal investigations would be arguably more useful for both researchers and clinicians in identifying athlete groups in which the risk for eating disorders is consistently elevated.

Lean Versus Non-Lean Athletes

The most commonly used method of grouping athletes when investigating prevalence rates from different sports is to differentiate between *lean* and *non-lean* sports. Lean sports are defined as those that place a competitive or aesthetic value on leanness, such as endurance events, aesthetic sports such as gymnastics and dance, antigravitation sports such as high jump, and weight-dependent sports such as lightweight rowing. On the contrary, non-lean sports are those in which leanness is not necessarily considered advantageous for performance. Examples include ball sports such as football and hockey, technical sports such as golf, and power sports such as shot putt and javelin throw. This method of classifying athletes according to sport type has been used consistently within the field when investigating heterogeneous athlete groups. As a consequence, some studies have managed to include very large but somewhat heterogeneous samples of athletes from a variety of sports, whereas studies with more homogeneous groups tend to have substantially smaller samples, from which it is difficult to infer population prevalence rates of eating disorders.

The evidence from this body of work has pointed toward an increase in eating disorder incidence among athletes competing in lean sports as opposed to non-lean sports (Sundgot-Borgen & Torstveit, 2004; Torstveit, Rosenvinge, & Sundgot-Borgen, 2008). Specifically, the evidence suggests that participants in lean sports (in which a thin body size and shape is emphasized) may be at an increased risk for anorexia nervosa. It has been suggested that participation in such sports could potentially precipitate anorexic symptoms; equally, individuals who are predisposed to develop anorexia nervosa could be drawn to engaging in such sports (Thompson & Sherman, 2010). In contrast, it has been suggested that bulimic symptoms are more common among athletes in weight category sports, in which quick weight loss techniques are often employed and endorsed in the run-up to competition to gain a competitive advantage. There is a small body of evidence indicating that competitors in weight-class sports are at an increased risk of disordered eating behaviors, particularly binging and purging. In recent years, the evidence has also indicated that athletes in non-lean (and specifically power) sports may be at a high risk of muscularity-oriented disordered eating behaviors. For example, a study of collegiate male athletes indicated that those competing in non-lean sports were more likely to endorse a muscularity-oriented body image and muscularity behaviors (Galli, Petrie, Reel, Greenleaf, & Carter, 2015), which have been previously linked to disordered eating practices in non-athlete samples (Bratland-Sanda & Sundgot-Borgen, 2012; Murray et al., 2012). This is without doubt an important area for future investigation, with a particular focus on sports that have not traditionally been thought to pose a high risk for disordered eating.

Subclinical Eating Disorders

Disordered eating behaviors and subclinical eating disorders are also common among athletes, with an estimated 20–45% of female athletes reporting disordered eating symptoms and pathological methods of weight control. There is also evidence indicating that male athletes demonstrate higher levels of disordered eating compared to their non-athletic counterparts. Overall, however, there are few studies investigating the prevalence of disordered eating in athletes that have included a comparison control group. Where a control group has been included, the findings vary considerably, and wide variations in prevalence estimates are reported. There is also a distinct lack of consensus across the literature as to whether the definition of disordered eating is also valid for athletes. Only longitudinal studies can demonstrate whether disordered eating symptoms in athletes should be taken seriously by establishing the subsequent risk of developing a clinical eating disorder and associated physical complications or by identifying that disordered eating symptoms are part of the sport and resolved without any consequences for the athlete.

Summary: Prevalence of Eating Disorders in Athletes

A large body of literature has explored the prevalence of eating psychopathology across a wide variety of athlete groups and points toward an increased rate of these disorders among specific athletes groups, particularly those in lean sports and dance. However, the field is still some way from conclusively determining the specific characteristics in athletes that place them at particular risk for the development of eating psychopathology. It is difficult to draw conclusions from, or make comparisons across, point prevalence studies conducted with heterogeneous athlete groups. Moving forward, the focus should be on conducting high-quality longitudinal research that assesses a wide range of risk factors (including the role of disordered eating) that may contribute to the development of eating disorders in athletes. The findings of such research could then help to inform the development of future treatment and preventative programs specifically for athletes.

THE ROLE OF COACHES AND SPORTS PERSONNEL

It is has been widely acknowledged that the potential physical and psychological benefits of participating in sport considerably outweigh the potential risks (Thompson & Sherman, 2010). However, there are elements of the sporting context that have been identified as potential risk factors for the development of eating psychopathology among athletes. For example, the requirement to wear revealing clothing can heighten body surveillance, comparison with other athletes, and promote body dissatisfaction (Greenleaf, 2004). Research has also focused on the attitudes and behaviors of coaches and sports professionals, with evidence indicating that critical comments about weight and weight monitoring practices can elicit or exacerbate disordered eating practices in some athletes (Kerr, Berman, & De Souza, 2006; McMahon & Dinan-Thompson, 2011).

The coach–athlete relationship is arguably one of the most important and influential relationships that an athlete will experience. Athletes spend a significant amount of time with their coaches, and the influence of coaches often extends beyond that of athletes' physical training, encompassing factors such as education, social interests, and their dietary practices. In many cases, coach behavior can have a highly positive impact on athletes in terms of their perception of their level of competence, their autonomy, and their levels of motivation (Mageau & Vallerand, 2003). In the context of eating disorders in sports, the literature has tended to focus on the negative role of coaches and the potential of their attitudes and behaviors to elicit disordered eating practices among athletes. However, it is also important to acknowledge that coaches and other sports professionals can have an important positive impact, particularly in terms of promoting early identification and management of eating problems among athletes (Selby & Reel, 2011). Encouraging and supporting coaches to take on this role through providing appropriate training opportunities is important.

SCREENING FOR EATING DISORDERS IN ATHLETES

A large number of different tools have been proposed to screen for eating disorders among athletes. In the United States, athletes in high school and at collegiate level often undergo a preparticipation physical examination (PPE), the guidance to which has been collaboratively produced by several sports medicine professional organizations (including the American Medical Society for Sports Medicine and the American College of Sports Medicine; Bernhardt & Roberts, 2010). The PPE includes several questions that are designed to identify potential disordered eating behaviors (see Box 22.1).

A wide variety of additional questionnaire-based screening measures have been used within the literature to detect eating psychopathology among athletes, including the traditional measures that are often used within the clinical context, such as the SCOFF (Morgan, Reid, & Lacey, 1999), the Eating Disorders Examination Questionnaire (EDE-Q; Fairburn & Beglin, 2008), and the Questionnaire for Eating Disorder Diagnoses (Q-EDD; Mintz, O'Halloran, Mulholland, & Schneider, 1997). The validity of using these measures with athlete populations has yet to be explored in great depth (Pope, Gao, Bolter, & Pritchard, 2015).

Box 22.1

PREPARTICIPATION PHYSICAL EXAMINATION (PPE): DISORDERED EATING QUESTIONS

1. Do you worry about your weight?
2. Are you trying to or has anyone recommended that you gain or lose weight?
3. Are you on a special diet or do you avoid certain types of food?
4. Have you ever had an eating disorder?
5. Have you ever taken any supplements to help you gain or lose weight or improve your performance?

SOURCE: Adapted from Bernhardt, D. T., & Roberts, W. O.; American Academy of Family Physicians and American Academy of Pediatrics (2010). *PPE: Preparticipation physical evaluation* (4th ed.). Elk Grove Village, IL: American Academy of Pediatrics.

One of the most commonly used questionnaires in primary care is the SCOFF, which asks the following five questions (Morgan et al., 1999):

1. Do you make yourself sick because you feel uncomfortably full?
2. Do you worry that you have lost control over how much you eat?
3. Have you recently lost more than one stone in a 3-month period?
4. Do you believe yourself to be fat when others say you are too thin?
5. Would you say that food dominates your life?

The authors recommend scoring 1 point for every "yes" answer, and a total score of 2 or more indicates a likely case of anorexia nervosa or bulimia.

Researchers have also developed a number of athlete-specific screening measures to assess eating psychopathology, including scales such as the Weight Pressures in Sport Scale (for females: Reel, Petrie, SooHoo, & Anderson, 2013; for males: Galli, Reel, Petrie, Greenleaf, & Carter, 2011), the Female Athlete Screening Tool (FAST; McNulty et al., 2001), and the Brief Eating Disorders in Athletes Questionnaire (BEDA-Q; Martinsen, Holme, Pensgaard, Torstveit, & Sundgot-Borgen, 2014). The BEDA-Q has shown promising results for distinguishing between female athletes with and without eating disorders, but it has yet to be validated in male athletes.

However, athletes may underreport disordered eating behaviors, perhaps due to fear of being stopped from training and competing or losing their sponsorship, funding, or place on a team (Sundgot-Borgen, 1993; Yates, Edman, Crago, & Crowell, 2001). Utilizing an exercise-based screening measure (e.g., the Compulsive Exercise Test; see Appendix 22.1) may be a suitable alternative because although it may lack the specificity of an eating measure, athletes may be less likely to distort their responses due to the lower face validity. Identifying unhealthy exercise behaviors and attitudes may facilitate the subsequent prevention of clinical eating disorders in athletes.

EATING DISORDERS AMONG MALE ATHLETES

Much of the literature on eating disorders has focused on female athletes. However, as evidenced by the move toward RED-S and the increasing preponderance of male athlete-specific screening measures, our understanding of eating disorders among male athletes is improving. It is important to note potential differences in the presentation and risk factors for eating disorders among male athletes.

Drive for Muscularity

The majority of eating disorder assessment tools focus on a drive for thinness, which is characteristic of the female presentation of eating disorders. However, a drive for muscularity has been suggested to be a more important feature when considering eating disorders among males. The link between the drive for muscularity and eating psychopathology in male athletes has yet to be fully explored. Currently, muscle dysmorphia appears as a subtype of body dysmorphic disorder in the DSM-5 rather than within the eating disorders diagnostic classification (APA, 2013). The observed similarities between muscle dysmorphia and AN have provided support for inclusion of muscle dysmorphia within the eating disorder spectrum, as opposed to the somatoform disorder spectrum (Murray, Rieger, Touyz, & De la Garza Garcia, 2010). The obsessive–compulsive features of the disorder in relation to rigid training schedules and dietary manipulation bear close similarities to the behavioral rigidity and cognitive disturbances observed in AN, particularly in those with high levels of compulsive exercise. Reconceptualizing muscle dysmorphia within the eating disorder spectrum may offer greater clinical utility in recognizing the "male experience" of eating psychopathology because currently a high proportion of men with eating disorders are classified within the residual category (Murray et al., 2010).

A related issue to the drive for muscularity observed among males is the increasing use of sports supplements, many of which are protein based and marketed to improve muscle recovery and promote muscle growth. Athletes may utilize such products to improve their recovery and promote strength gains, although those at a high level will exercise caution in the use of unregulated substances due to the risk of violating World Anti-Doping Agency rules. However, these products are not just marketed at the relatively small population of elite athletes but also capitalize on the body image concerns of recreational exercisers, with up to one in five college students reporting taking a protein-based supplement (Lieberman et al., 2015). In addition, recent studies have reported that the use of such substances is linked closely to body dissatisfaction and restricted eating behavior; up to 22% of users reported replacing meals with dietary supplements such as protein shakes (Achiro & Theodore, 2015). In recognition of this emerging evidence base, clinicians may need to explore underlying patient motivations for the intake of supplements.

The Male Athlete Triad

The introduction of RED-S was partially in response to emerging evidence that male athletes experience some of the same hormonal and bone mineral density consequences from low energy availability as female athletes (Mountjoy et al., 2014). Although the evidence in this area is growing, it is still limited, and additional studies are needed to explore the consequences of low energy availability in male athletes in more depth.

EVIDENCE-BASED TREATMENT APPROACHES

Exercise and Treatment

To date, there have been no randomized controlled studies exploring the relative efficacy of different forms of therapy for athletes with eating disorders. However, there is evidence that patients for whom exercise is a feature of their eating disorder are more likely to relapse and take longer to recover than those who do not exercise, and compulsive exercise may be a significant feature for athletes with eating disorders (Plateau et al., 2014). A treatment program that incorporates sessions on coping with and reducing features of compulsive exercise may be of particular relevance for athletes.

However, prohibiting exercise among eating disorder patients is an area of some contention, particularly with regard to athletes. Where features of compulsive exercise are present, it is likely that exercise and sport participation may be contributing to the psychopathology of the eating disorder while at the same time representing a vital part of the athlete's self-esteem and self-value. Indeed, the usual protocol for significantly underweight patients (BMI <16 kg/m^2) and patients with moderate to severe bulimia nervosa (purging four or more times per week) is to cease all exercise participation, particularly during the weight restoration or normalization phase of treatment. However, one athlete-specific eating disorder program currently being trialled in the United States (*The Victory Program*; McCallum Place, 2016) is exploring the introduction of low-level, exercise-based activities among athletes meeting weight targets to support athletes' gradual reintroduction into training and exercise. There is emerging evidence from broader clinical populations that low-level exercise can be beneficial in eating disorder recovery (Carei, Fyfe-Johnson, Breuner, & Brown, 2010), but the efficacy and acceptability of this approach with athletes has yet to be explored. In addition, there are no known statistics concerning the proportion of athletes who are able to make a successful return to sport following treatment for an eating disorder or, indeed, the proportion of athletes who relapse. This is an important area for research to establish so as to ensure treatment can be tailored effectively to the needs of this group.

Pharmacotherapy

Pharmacological medications to treat comorbid conditions such as depression and anxiety are often prescribed for non-athlete eating disorder patients. However, these have not been rigorously explored in terms of their impact on athletic performance. In addition, potential interactions between medications and sports performance need to be considered, such as the impact of sedating medications. Clinicians should also be aware of the substances that are on the World Anti-Doping Agency's prohibited list for high-level athletes.

Multidisciplinary Team

Despite the lack of clinical trials with regard to treatment efficacy, a number of guidelines have been developed by sporting organizations to support clinicians and sports professionals in the identification and management of athletes with eating disorders. The majority of these promote a multidisciplinary approach that involves a physician, dietician, mental health professional, and the athlete but may also include the parents, coach, or athletic trainer. Involving the coach in the treatment process can be a positive experience for both the athlete and the coach. It can help coaches to understand the treatment process, as well as the necessity and value of the treatment. Similarly, for athletes, it may offer a continued validation of their athletic identity, despite reduced engagement with their sport. In particular, guidelines regarding the return to training and competition for athletes with eating disorders have been developed because this can be a challenging decision to make when working with athletes (Thompson & Sherman, 2010).

It is not unusual for sports professionals to look to the eating disorders specialist for answers regarding when it is appropriate for the eating disorder sufferer to return to sport activities and competition. As yet, there are no clear answers. Sporting organizations seeking to develop guidance for sports personnel are often eager to impose clear-cut guidelines related to BMI or weight status to guide a safe return to sport, but there is not yet sufficient scientific evidence for this. Instead, a case-by-case approach must be employed. Use of a multidisciplinary approach involving the coach, the family, the sufferer, and the eating disorder professional is a necessity. The role of the sport in the life of the sufferer needs to be understood. Is the sport environment a healthy environment for the athlete because it promotes his or her self-esteem? It is possible that for some athletes, preventing them from engaging with their sport and exercise may hinder their progress in treatment due to the removal of their identity and an important source of self-esteem. Alternatively, the sporting context may be a negative environment that emphasizes their competitive nature and reinforces their desires to exercise in a compulsive way. For these athletes, exercising and involvement in competitive sport will always be a risk factor for the development of an eating disorder and thus returning to sporting activities may not be appropriate. In these cases, the role of the therapist will be to help the sufferers to understand this and to work through the process of withdrawing from competitive sport. For others, returning to their sport activities may be healthy, and the professional will work together with the coach, the sufferer, and the family to develop a plan (which may include a treatment contract; see Appendix 22.2) for the athlete to initially return to sporting activities and eventually competition.

Return to Play

The International Olympic Committee (IOC) has developed a return-to-play model in relation to RED-S. A traffic light system is used to determine sports participation status. The guidelines are presented in Table 22.1. Athletes in the

Table 22.1 RISK ASSESSMENT MODEL: RELATIVE ENERGY DEFICIENCY IN SPORT

Risk Status Indicators

High Risk	**Recommendation for sport participation**
Clinical eating disorder or other serious conditions linked to low energy availability and/or extreme weight loss.	Engagement in competition should be suspended
	Training permitted once medically cleared. Training may need to be adapted and supervised.
	Governing bodies, colleges or schools may wish to use a written contract to outline expectations around therapy adherence for continued participation in sport.

Moderate Risk	**Recommendation for sport participation**
Weight related concerns e.g., considerable weight loss, slowed growth (young athletes), sustained low body fat percentage.	Training and competition permitted once medically cleared.
Altered hormonal function; e.g., change in menstrual function or delayed onset of menarche in females.	Continued participation contingent on engagement with therapy and adherence to written contract
History of bone injury and/or indicators of reduced bone density	
Lack of therapy adherence and/or disordered eating negatively affecting teammates.	

Low risk	**Recommendation for sport participation**
Normal eating habits with no indicators of low energy availability. Hormonal and bone mineral density profile is normal.	Participants can continue to train and compete as normal.

NOTE: Adapted from Mountjoy et al., (2014). The IOC consensus statement: beyond the Female Athlete Triad—Relative Energy Deficiency in Sport (RED-S). *BJSM, 48,* 491–497.

"high-risk" or red category should be prevented from engaging with training and competition due to the potentially severe impact of their condition on their health. Athletes in the "moderate risk" or yellow category may be able to participate in training and competition, subject to suitable supervision and engagement with appropriate treatment protocols. The IOC return-to-play model recommends regular reevaluations of athletes to ensure escalations in severity are quickly identified and appropriate actions can be put in place. Similarly, athletes who make good progress can be recategorized to a lower risk level. In addition, further guidelines suggest developing a written contract between the athlete and members of the multidisciplinary team to promote engagement with therapy (Bonci et al., 2008; De Souza et al., 2014). Athletes who fail to meet the terms of the contract may be removed from the team and prevented from training and competing. Such contracts are likely to include details about the required treatment frequency and type; expectations with regard to body weight; and the intensity, duration, and frequency of training (and competition, where applicable) permitted. Consequences of breaches to the contract should also be made explicit. A sample contract is provided in Appendix 22.2.

PREVENTION

The prevention of eating disorders in athletes requires action and support across a wide variety of stakeholders, including (but not limited to) coaches, athletes, athletic trainers, parents, athletic administrators, and sports governing bodies. Coaches admit to a lack of knowledge and confidence in identifying and managing potential eating disorders among their athletes, highlighting the need for comprehensive coach education and resources to be made widely available (Plateau, Arcelus, McDermott, & Meyer, 2015). A study conducted in Norway demonstrated that educational interventions for coaches can be effective at improving their knowledge and confidence in recognizing the signs and symptoms of eating disorders (Martinsen, Sherman, Thompson, & Sundgot-Borgen, 2015). Some sports governing bodies, such as the National Collegiate Athletic Association (NCAA), have developed a range of educational materials for coaches, athletes, and sports professionals, including tips for preventing and spotting potential signs of disordered eating among athletes (Kroshus, 2015).

A number of different primary prevention programs exist for athletes; however, few have been formally evaluated. Two examples of athlete-specific prevention programs that have been demonstrated to be effective include a cognitive dissonance prevention program for college athletes titled the Female Athlete Body Project (Becker, McDaniel, Bull, Powell, & McIntyre, 2012) and a school-based educational intervention that has been trialled in Norway (Martinsen, Bahr, et al., 2014). The results of both projects pointed toward a reduction in eating disorder symptoms and risk factors among female athletes post intervention, although these differences were not sustained at 1-year follow-up. Further studies and investigations are needed to develop prevention programs that are suitable for male athletes and that are effective over longer time periods.

CONCLUSION AND FUTURE DIRECTIONS

Much of the current literature exploring eating psychopathology among athletes has adopted a self-report and cross-sectional approach. Further longitudinal studies that utilize a clinical interview to assess eating psychopathology would provide greater insight and methodological rigor when assessing the risk and trigger factors for eating disorders in this population. Further research is needed to improve our understanding of the causes, presentation, and consequences of male athlete eating disorders. Prevention and educational efforts can be effective at reducing the risk of eating disorders in athletes and promoting early identification. However, further efforts are needed to identify programs with long-term efficacy and that are suitable for both male and female athletes. Treatment for athletes with eating disorders should incorporate a multidisciplinary team, which may also involve the athlete's coach or trainer. Recent return-to-play guidelines are a welcome addition for clinicians working with athletes because they provide a useful framework within which to consider continued exercise and sporting participation.

APPENDIX 22.1

COMPULSIVE EXERCISE TEST FOR ATHLETES

Instructions

Listed below are a series of statements regarding exercise. Please read each statement carefully and circle the number that best indicates how true each statement is of you. Please answer all the questions as honestly as you can.

Never true	Rarely true	Sometimes true	Often true	Usually true		Always true			
0	1	2	3	4		5			

1.	I feel happier and/or more positive after I exercise	0	1	2	3	4	5
2.	I exercise to improve my appearance	0	1	2	3	4	5
3.	I feel less anxious after I exercise	0	1	2	3	4	5
4.	If I feel I have eaten too much, I will do more exercise	0	1	2	3	4	5
5.	If I cannot exercise, I feel low or depressed	0	1	2	3	4	5
6.	I feel extremely guilty when I miss an exercise session	0	1	2	3	4	5
7.	I feel less stressed and/or tense after I exercise	0	1	2	3	4	5
8.	I exercise to burn calories and to lose weight	0	1	2	3	4	5
9.	If I cannot exercise, I feel agitated and/or irritable	0	1	2	3	4	5
10.	Exercise improves my mood	0	1	2	3	4	5
11.	If I cannot exercise, I worry that I will gain weight	0	1	2	3	4	5
12.	If I cannot exercise, I feel angry and/or frustrated	0	1	2	3	4	5
13.	I feel like I've let myself down if I miss an exercise session	0	1	2	3	4	5
14.	If I cannot exercise, I feel anxious	0	1	2	3	4	5
15.	I feel less depressed or low after I exercise	0	1	2	3	4	5

SOURCE: Modified from Plateau, C. R., Shanmugam, V., Duckham, R. L., Goodwin, H., Jowett, S., Brooke-Wavell, K. S., . . . & Meyer, C. (2014). Use of the Compulsive Exercise Test with Athletes: Norms and links with eating psychopathology. *Journal of Applied Sport Psychology,* 26(3), 287–301.

Example Eating Disorder Treatment and Participation Contract

Athlete name: _____ Sport: _____ Date: _____

I understand that the following are a list of requirements which must all be met in order for me to continue to have medical clearance to participate in training and competition.

1. Receive individual psychotherapy from _____ once a week.

2. Meet with the team physician, Dr. _____ for medical evaluation of my health status at least once a month, including lab tests if necessary.

3. Participate in nutritional counseling sessions according to a schedule recommended by the (name of organization) registered dietician,

_____.

4. Maintain my body weight over _____ kg with progress towards a goal of _____ kg (if applicable). Anticipate weekly monitoring of my weight if it falls below this level.

5. Sign and leave on file a release of information permitting (name of organization) health care professionals to communicate openly and freely with each other, members of the coaching staff, and my parents and caregivers at home.

6. Check-in routinely with my certified physiotherapist or athletic trainer,

_____.

7. Participate in a maximum of _____ hours of training each week, to be supervised by _____ (coach's name). Training can include the following activities:

_____

(detail relevant sessions and activities that are permitted).

I understand the above requirements are in place to help me to manage my current health concerns. I understand that noncompliance with any of the above requirements may result in removal from athletic participation at any time.

I understand that I am expected to comply with all necessary medical and personal advice to facilitate my recovery.

Athlete's signature _____ Date _____

Team physician's signature _____ Date _____

Psychologist's signature _____ Date _____

Sport dietician's signature _____ Date _____

Coach's signature _____ Date _____

SOURCE: Modified from Bonci, C. M., Bonci, L. J., Granger, L. R., Johnson, C. L., Malina, R. M., Milne, L. W., . . . Vanderbunt, E.M (2008). National Athletic Trainers' Association position statement: Preventing, detecting and managing disordered eating in athletes. *Journal of Athletic Training, 43*(1), 80–108.

REFERENCES

Achiro, R., & Theodore, P. (2015). *Excessive workout supplement use: An emerging eating disorder in men.* Paper presented at the APA annual convention, Toronto, Canada, August 2015.

American Psychiatric Association. (2013). *Diagnostic and statistical manual of mental disorders* (5th ed.). Arlington, VA: American Psychiatric Publishing.

Arcelus, J., Witcomb, G. L., & Mitchell, A. (2014). Prevalence of eating disorders amongst dancers: A systemic review and meta-analysis. *European Eating Disorders Review, 22*(2), 92–101.

Becker, C. B., McDaniel, L., Bull, S., Powell, M., & McIntyre, K. (2012). Can we reduce eating disorder risk factors in female college athletes? A randomised exploratory investigation of two peer-led interventions. *Body Image, 9*(1), 31–42.

Bernhardt, D. T., & Roberts, W. O.; American Academy of Family Physicians and American Academy of Pediatrics (2010). *PPE: Preparticipation physical evaluation* (4th ed.). Elk Grove Village, IL: American Academy of Pediatrics.

Bonci, C. M., Bonci, L. J., Granger, L. R., Johnson, C. L., Malina, R. M., Milne, L. W., . . . Vanderbunt, E. M. (2008). National Athletic Trainers' Association position statement: Preventing, detecting and managing disordered eating in athletes. *Journal of Athletic Training, 43*(1), 80–108.

Bratland-Sanda, S., & Sundgot-Borgen, J. (2012). Symptoms of eating disorders, drive for muscularity and physical activity among Norwegian adolescents. *European Eating Disorders Review, 20,* 287–293.

Carei, T. R., Fyfe-Johnson, A. L., Breuner, C. C., & Brown, M. A. (2010). Randomized controlled clinical trial of yoga in the treatment of eating disorders. *Journal of Adolescent Health, 46*(4), 346–351.

Coelho, G. M., Soares, E. A., & Ribeiro, B. G. (2010). Are female athletes at increased risk for disordered eating and its complications? *Appetite, 55*(3), 379–387.

Currie, A., & Morse, E. D. (2005). Eating disorders in athletes: Managing the risks. *Clinics in Sports Medicine, 24*(4), 871–883.

De Souza, M. J., Nattiv, A., Joy, E., Misra, M., Williams, N. I., Mallinson, R. J., . . . Matheson, G. (2014). 2014 Female Athlete Triad Coalition consensus statement on treatment and return to play of the female athlete triad. *British Journal of Sports Medicine, 48,* 289.

El Ghoch, M., Soave, F., Calugi, S., & Dalle Grave, R. (2013). Eating disorders, physical fitness and sport performance: A systematic review. *Nutrients, 5*(12), 5140–5160.

Fairburn, C. G., & Beglin, S. (2008). Eating Disorder Examination Questionnaire (EDE-Q 6.0). In C. G. Fairburn (Ed.), *Cognitive behavior therapy and eating disorders* (pp. 309–314). New York, NY: Guildford.

Galli, N., Petrie, T., Reel, J. J., Greenleaf, C., & Carter, J. E. (2015). Psychosocial predictors of drive for muscularity in male collegiate athletes. *Body Image, 14,* 62–66.

Galli, N., Reel, J. J., Petrie, T., Greenleaf, C., & Carter, J. (2011). Preliminary development of the Weight Pressures in Sport scale for males. *Journal of Sport Behavior, 34*(1), 47–68.

Greenleaf, C. (2004). Weight pressures and social physique anxiety among collegiate synchronised skaters. *Journal of Sport Behavior, 27*(3), 260–276.

Joy, E., Kussman, A., & Nattiv, A. (2016). 2016 update on eating disorders in athletes: A comprehensive narrative review with a focus on clinical assessment and management. *British Journal of Sports Medicine, 50,* 154–162.

Kerr, G., Berman, E., & De Souza, M. J. (2006). Disordered eating in women's gymnastics: Perspectives of athletes, coaches, parents and judges. *Journal of Applied Sport Psychology, 18*(1), 28–43.

Kroshus, E. (2015). 10 eating disorder awareness tips for coaches and athletics professionals. Retrieved from http://www.ncaa.org/health-and-safety/sport-science-institute/10-eating-disorders-awareness-tips-coaches-and-athletics-professionals

Lieberman, H. R., Marriott, B. P., Williams, C., Judelson, D. A., Glickman, E. L., Geiselman, P. J., . . . Mahoney, C. R. (2015). Patterns of dietary supplement use among college students. *Clinical Nutrition, 34*(5), 976–985.

Loucks, A. B., Kiens, B., & Wright, H. H. (2011). Energy availability in athletes. *Journal of Sports Sciences, 29*(Suppl. 1), S7–S15.

Mageau, G. A., & Vallerand, R. (2003). The coach–athlete relationship: A motivational model. *Journal of Sport Sciences, 21*(11), 883–904.

Martinsen, M., Bahr, R., Borresen, R., Holme, I., Pensgaard, A. M., & Sundgot-Borgen, J. (2014). Preventing eating disorders among young elite athletes: A randomised controlled trial. *Medicine and Science in Sports and Exercise, 46*(3), 435–447.

Martinsen, M., Holme, I., Pensgaard, A. M., Torstveit, M. K., & Sundgot-Borgen, J. (2014). The development of the Brief Eating Disorder in Athletes Questionnaire (BEDA-Q). *Medicine and Science in Sports and Exercise, 46*(8), 1666–1675.

Martinsen, M., Sherman, R. T., Thompson, R., & Sundgot-Borgen, J. (2015). Coaches' knowledge and management of eating disorders: A randomised controlled trial. *Medicine and Science in Sports and Exercise, 47*(5), 1070–1078.

McCallum Place. (2016). *The Victory Program.* Retrieved fromhttps://www.mccallumplace.com/the-victory-program.html

McMahon, J. A., & Dinan-Thompson, M. (2011). Body work- regulation of a swimmer body: An autoethnography from an Australian elite swimmer. *Sport, Education and Society, 16,* 35–50.

McNulty, K. Y., Adams, C. H., Anderson, J. M., & Affenito, S. G. (2001). Development and validation of a screening tool to identify eating disorders in female athletes. *Journal of the American Dietetic Association, 101*(8), 886–892.

Meyer, C., Taranis, L., Goodwin, H., & Haycraft, E. (2011). Compulsive exercise and eating disorders. *European Eating Disorders Review, 19,* 174–189.

Meyer, C., Taranis, L., & Touyz, S. (2008). Excessive exercise in the eating disorders: A need for less activity from patients and more from researchers. *European Eating Disorders Review, 16*(2), 81–83.

Mintz, L. B., O'Halloran, M. S., Mulholland, A. M., & Schneider, P. A. (1997). Questionnaire for Eating Disorder Diagnoses: Reliability and validity of operationalising DSM-IV criteria into a self-report format. *Journal of Counseling Psychology, 44*(1), 63–79.

Mond, J. M., Hay, P., Rodgers, B., & Owen, C. (2006). An update on the definition of "excessive exercise" in eating disorder research. *International Journal of Eating Disorders, 39*(2), 147–153.

Morgan, J. F., Reid, F., & Lacey, J. H. (1999). The SCOFF questionnaire: Assessment of a new screening tool for eating disorders. *British Medical Journal, 319,* 1467–1468.

Mountjoy, M., Sundgot-Borgen, J., Burke, L., Carter, S., Constantini, N., Lebrun, C., . . . Ljungqvist, A. (2014). The IOC consensus statement: Beyond the female athlete triad—Relative Energy Deficiency in Sport (RED-S). *British Journal of Sports Medicine*, 48, 491–497.

Murray, S. B., Rieger, E., Hildebrandt, T., Karlov, L., Russell, J., Boon, E., . . . Touyz, S. W. (2012). A comparison of eating, exercise, shape and weight related symptomatology in males with muscle dysmorphia and anorexia nervosa. *Body Image*, 9(2), 193–200.

Murray, S. B., Rieger, E., Touyz, S. W., & De la Garza Garcia, Y. (2010). Muscle dysmorphia and the DSM-5 conundrum: Where does it belong? A review paper. *International Journal of Eating Disorders*, 43(6), 483–491.

Nattiv, A., Loucks, A. B., Manore, M. M., Sanborn, C. F., Sundgot-Borgen, J., & Warren, M. P. (2007). American College of Sports Medicine position stand: The female athlete triad. *Medicine and Science in Sports and Exercise*, 39(10), 1867–1882.

Plateau, C. R., Arcelus, J., McDermott, H. J., & Meyer. C. (2015). Responses of track and field coaches to athletes with eating problems. *Scandinavian Journal of Medicine and Science in Sports*, 25(2), e240–e250.

Plateau, C. R., Shanmugam, V., Duckham, R. L., Goodwin, H., Jowett, S., Brooke-Wavell, K. S., . . . & Meyer, C. (2014). Use of the Compulsive Exercise Test with Athletes: Norms and links with eating psychopathology. *Journal of Applied Sport Psychology*, 26(3), 287–301.

Pope, Z., Gao, Y., Bolter, N., & Pritchard, M. (2015). Validity and reliability of eating disorder assessments used with athletes: A review. *Journal of Sport and Health Sciences*, 4, 211–221.

Reel, J. J., Petrie, T. A., SooHoo, S., & Anderson, C. M. (2013). Weight pressures in sport: Examining the factor structure and incremental validity of the weight pressures in sport—Females. *Eating Behaviors*, 14(2), 137–144.

Schaal, K., Tafflet, M., Nassif, H., Thibault, V., Pichard, C., Alcotte, M., . . . Toussaint, J. F. (2011). Psychological balance in high level athletes: Gender-based differences and sport-specific patterns. *PLoS One*, 6(5), e19007.

Selby, C., & Reel, J. J. (2011). A coach's guide to identifying and helping athletes with eating disorders. *Journal of Sport Psychology in Action*, 2(2), 100–112.

Shanmugam, V., Jowett, S., & Meyer, C. (2014). Eating psychopathology as a risk factor for depressive symptoms in a sample of British athletes. *Journal of Sports Sciences*, 32, 1587–1595.

Shroff, H., Reba, L., Thornton, L. M., Tozzi, F., Klump, K. L., Berrettini, W. H., . . . Bulik, C. M. (2006). Features associated with excessive exercise in women with eating disorders. *International Journal of Eating Disorders*, 39(6), 454–461.

Smolak, L., Murnen, S. K., & Ruble, A. E. (2000). Female athletes and eating problems: A meta-analysis. *International Journal of Eating Disorders*, 27(4), 371–380.

Sundgot-Borgen, J. (1993). Prevalence of eating disorders in female elite athletes. *International Journal of Sports Nutrition*, 3, 29–140.

Sundgot-Borgen, J., & Torstveit, M. K. (2004). Prevalence of eating disorders in elite athletes is higher than in the general population. *Clinical Journal of Sports Medicine*, 14(1), 25–32.

Thompson, R. A., & Sherman, R. T. (2010). *Eating disorders in sport.* New York, NY: Routledge.

Torstveit, M. K., Rosenvinge, J. H., & Sundgot-Borgen, J. (2008). Prevalence of eating disorders and the predictive power of risk models in female elite athletes: A controlled study. *Scandinavian Journal of Medicine and Science in Sports, 18*(1), 108–118.

World Health Organization (2010). *International statistical classification of diseases and related health problems—10th revision.* Geneva, Switzerland: Author.

Yates, A., Edman, J. D., Crago, M., & Crowell, D. (2001). Using an exercise-based instrument to detect signs of an eating disorder. *Psychiatry Research, 105,* 231–241.

Printed in Great Britain
by Amazon